W9-CHO-045

SCHOOL OF
ORIENTAL AND AFRICAN STUDIES

ŚIVA

THE EROTIC ASCETIC

ŚIVA

THE EROTIC ASCETIC

Wendy Doniger O'Flaherty

OXFORD UNIVERSITY PRESS
Oxford New York Toronto Melbourne

First published by Oxford University Press,
London and New York,
for the School of Oriental and African Studies, 1973,
under the title
Asceticism and Eroticism in the Mythology of Śiva
First issued as an Oxford University Press paperback, 1981,
under the title *Śiva: The Erotic Ascetic*

Library of Congress Cataloging in Publication Data

O'Flaherty, Wendy Doniger.
Śiva, the erotic ascetic.

Reprint of the ed. published by
Oxford University Press, London and New York,
under title:
Asceticism and eroticism in the mythology of Śiva.
Bibliography: p.
Includes indexes.
1. Siva (Hindu deity) 2. Mythology, Hindu. I. Title.
BL1218.034 1981 294.5'211 81-127
ISBN 0-19-520250-3 (pbk.) AACR2

Printing: 987654321

Printed in the United States of America

FOR

RITA AND LESTER

ACKNOWLEDGEMENTS

THIS book took shape over a period of many years, in many countries, with the help of many friends. I cannot thank them all, and I can only hope that they will accept this book itself as their *gurudakṣinā*, their payment from pupil to teacher. Special thanks are due, however, to my five 'editors'—the Honourable Lady Betjeman (Penelope Chetwode), Julie Galant, Dr. Richard Gombrich, Lester L. Doniger, and Dennis M. O'Flaherty—for useful and encouraging comments on early drafts. It is a pleasure to have this opportunity to thank the cheerful, helpful staff of the Indian Institute, Oxford, and particularly Mr. Alderman and Mrs. de Goris, for patient and painstaking help on many occasions. I owe much to my colleagues at the Institut Vostokovedeniia in Moscow and Leningrad, and at Shantiniketan, Bengal, for their helpful criticisms. Professor Mircea Eliade offered lengthy and perceptive comments on the first draft, for which I am most grateful. And I am deeply indebted to my adviser and guru, Professor Daniel H. H. Ingalls of Harvard University, for bibliographies, warnings, suggestions, corrections, help in the selection and treatment of this topic, and invaluable remarks on the first draft.

I am grateful to the *Journal of the Royal Asiatic Society*, *History of Religions*, and *Purāṇa*, who published early versions of parts of this work, and to the Archaeological Survey of India, the International Institute for Comparative Music Studies and Documentation (Berlin), the Victoria and Albert Museum, the India Office Library, the Indian National Museum (New Delhi), the Government Museum and Art Gallery (Chandigarh), Dover Publications, the Hamlyn Publishing Group, Jeffery Gorbeck, and Penelope Chetwode, for illustrations.

A grant from the American Institute of Indian Studies enabled me to travel for a year in India, and the International Research and Exchanges Board made it possible for me to spend a year in Moscow completing the final draft. The last but most important financial aid came from the Publications Committee of the School of Oriental and African Studies, University of London, without whose generous support the publication of this work would have been virtually impossible.

Moscow, 14 February 1971

CONTENTS

LIST OF ILLUSTRATIONS

GUIDE TO PRONUNCIATION

Sanskrit vowels are pronounced very much like Italian vowels, with the exception of the short *a* which is pronounced like the *u* in the English word 'but'; long *ā* is pronounced like the *a* in 'father'. As for the consonants, a reasonable approximation will be obtained by pronouncing *c* as in 'church', *j* as in 'jungle', *ṣ* as in 'shun', *s* as in 'sun', and *ś* as something half-way between the other two *s*'s. The aspirated consonants should be pronounced distinctly: *th* as in goat-herd, *ph* as in top-hat, *gh* as in dog-house, *dh* as in mad-house, *bh* as in cab-horse.

ṛ is a vowel, pronounced mid-way between 'ri' as in 'rivet' and 'er' as in 'father'.

1

THE INTERPRETATION OF HINDU MYTHOLOGY

A. THE CHALLENGE OF HINDU MYTHOLOGY

'THAT which cannot be found here exists nowhere'[1]—this was the boast of the author of the great Hindu epic, the *Mahābhārata*, and it is an excellent description of the Purāṇas, encyclopedic compendia of hundreds of thousands of Sanskrit verses dealing with every subject under the Indian sun. Here are found dynastic histories of obscure kings, detailed recipes for ritual offerings, hair-splitting philosophical arguments, tedious discussions of caste law, and, imbedded in the midst of all of this ('like a lotus in the mud', as the Hindus say), countless sublimely beautiful myths.

It is a time-consuming task to sift through the Purāṇas in search of the myths, but none of it is wasted labour, for the mud is as valuable as the lotus which it nourishes: the myths come alive only in the context of history, ritual, philosophy, and social law. Hidden somewhere in this maze is the key to the Hindu world view, vivid, startling, fascinating, and complex. The mythology of Śiva forms only a small part of the material of the Purāṇas, but it is an ideal model which reveals a pattern which pertains to the material as a whole. Śiva is not only an extremely important Hindu god; he is in many ways the most uniquely Indian god of them all, and the principles which emerge from an intensive study of his mythology lie at the very heart of Hinduism.

Can the mythology of Śiva be used to reveal a still more general, perhaps universal, truth? Questions of this sort have long tempted the student of mythology. It is an old maxim that we often find our home truths in foreign lands. The great Indologist, Heinrich Zimmer, once tried to explain his love for Indian myths by citing the Hassidic tale of the old Jew who travelled from Cracow to Prague only to learn from a young Christian soldier (who did not believe or understand the words that he spoke in jest and mockery) that a treasure of gold was buried under the stove in the old man's home, back in Cracow. As Zimmer remarks,

> Now the real treasure, to end our misery and trials, is never far away. . . .

But there is the odd and persistent fact that it is only after a faithful journey to a distant region, a foreign country, a strange land, that the meaning of the inner voice that is to guide our quest can be revealed to us.[2]

Yet the more reasonable goal—and the more rewarding—is simply to understand the myths *in situ*, to use methods which reveal the meanings that the Hindus saw in them, to enjoy them as the exotic and delightful creations that they are.

To extract these meanings without *reducing* the myths in any way is no simple task. The dilemma is at first complicated, but ultimately resolved, by the fact that there are many 'meanings' in a Hindu myth: 'Hindu mythology is much like a plum pudding. If you do not like the plums in the slice you have, or have been deprived of a favour, you may always cut another one.'[3] The first plum is the story itself, usually a rather good story, occasionally of the shaggy-dog variety but frequently with an immediately recognizable point on at least one level, which might be termed the narrative level. Closely related is the divine level, which concerns mythology as it used to be understood by scholars of the classics: the metaphorical struggles of divine powers and personalities. Above this is the cosmic level of the myth, the expression of universal laws and processes, of metaphysical principles and symbolic truths. And below it, shading off into folklore, is the human level, the search for meaning in human life, the problems of human society.

No one meaning can be labelled the deepest or the truest. . . . The best words are ambiguous, and the more richly ambiguous the more suitable for the poet's or the myth-maker's job. Hence there is no end to the number of meanings which can be read into a good myth.[4]

The various levels are simultaneous rather than alternative:

Each level always refers to some other level, whichever way the myth is read. . . . We can only choose between various degrees of enlargement: each one reveals a level of organization which has no more than a relative truth and, while it lasts, excludes the perception of other levels.[5]

In my analyses, I have certainly not exhausted all the meanings of each myth; I have not even mentioned all the meanings that I personally see in them. I have only discussed those themes in each myth which play a part in the basic schema of the corpus. This may seem a Procrustean method—to select one theme and then to maintain that it is uniquely important—but it is justified by the materials: I have selected that one theme because it *is* central. As one reads through the enormous mass of Purāṇic mythology, certain recurrent elements clearly emerge; myths which at first appeared obscure suddenly become obvious; one senses what the myths are about. No single myth contains the key, which is given only by the totality of variations. The pattern which they form involves a finite number of elements but will be seen to apply equally well to other (theoretically infinite) groups of myths, for the pattern is basic to Hindu thought. The completed model reveals that the apparent contradictions in individual variants are merely incomplete views of the whole, like the varying opinions of the blind men grasping the different parts of an elephant ('It is a rope', 'It is a wall', 'It is a snake'): it is, in fact, unmistakably an elephant. Although the themes in terms of which I have chosen to analyse the Śaiva cycle are not the only themes present in the myths, they are certainly extremely significant. This is evident from the impressive frequency with which their patterns recur, the ease and simplicity with which they account for otherwise puzzling idiosyncrasies in the texts, and the convincing number of explicit discussions (within the myths and in other Indian materials) of the problems which they represent.

A further note of caution must be voiced here on the subject of arbitrary selection. Not only are the myths and themes themselves selected, but the very episodes and words of the myths are necessarily slanted as well. The Sanskrit Purāṇas are extremely garrulous and digressive, and in order to include as wide a selection of myths as possible I have summarized rather than translated, omitting large bodies of material superfluous to the present study, such as hymns of praise, ritual instructions, detailed descriptions, and philosophical discourses. This extraneous material is not only unwieldy but would have tended to obscure the patterns which emerge from a more selective treatment. I have also omitted those portions of the text which seem hopelessly corrupt, and in some instances where the meaning seems quite clear in spite of the garbled text I have given the best sense I could make of it. I have not (knowingly) added anything that is not in the text, but I may have omitted in one version certain details that occur in another, thus inadvertently disguising an actual correspondence in the text. In other circumstances I may translate in similar words two sentences which differ in the wording of the originals, thus suggesting a correspondence which does not in fact exist. I have omitted non-recurring proper names and I have standardized epithets throughout my translations. (Secondary sources have been quoted literally unless enclosed in brackets to indicate my own summary.) A general indication of the degree to which any particular citation has been compressed may be obtained by comparing the length of the English version with the length of the Sanskrit text as indicated in the bibliographic note. In taking these liberties I hope I have not distorted the meanings of the myth, and in so doing I take heart from the words of Claude Lévi-Strauss, who has said that while poetry may be what is lost in translation, 'the mythical value of myths remains preserved through the worst translations'.[6]

These measures, which are particularly necessary in a method of analysis which relies upon numerous different versions of a myth, have been defended by Lévi-Strauss:

> To avoid making the demonstration too unwieldy, I had to decide which myths to use, to opt for certain versions, and in some measure to simplify the variants. Some people will accuse me of having adapted the subject matter of my inquiry to suit my own purposes.[7]

He answers these objections by arguing that, although the selection is to some extent arbitrary, further incidents would only be variants of those selected:[8]

> A certain stage of the undertaking having been reached, it becomes clear that its ideal object has acquired sufficient consistency and shape for some of its latent properties, and especially its existence as an object, to be definitely placed beyond all doubt.[9]

That the selected themes are mutually reinforcing and fully integrated is taken as evidence of their significance. These criteria are necessary but not sufficient. The recurrence of the isolated themes in other myths, as well as in other texts, iconography, and ritual, is further proof of their importance.

B. THE CENTRAL PARADOX OF ŚAIVA MYTHOLOGY

The wide applicability of the recurrent supplementary themes from the Purāṇic corpus is evident from the role that they play in one of the enduring problems of Hindu mythology, the paradox of Śiva the erotic ascetic. This problem has often been noted and by now is sometimes accepted as a matter of fact: the great ascetic is the god of the phallus (the *liṅga*). The *meaning* of this paradox, however, has never been properly explored.

The character of Śiva has always been an enigma to Western scholars. Only a small portion of the corpus of ancient Śaiva mythology has been translated from the Sanskrit; with this inadequate representation, it is not surprising that the mythology of Śiva was considered contradictory and paradoxical by scholars who saw only the two ends of the spectrum. Śiva the Creator and Destroyer, Life and Death, the *coincidentia oppositorum*—this much was accepted as consistent with Indian metaphysical thought, and the apparent sexual ambiguity of the god was regarded as simply one more aspect of a basically ambiguous character or a result of the chance historical assimilation of two opposing strains, a process well known in Indian religion. In the absence of critical editions of the Śaiva Purāṇas (medieval Sanskrit texts containing numerous myths), the problem was never properly considered, and the very fact of its paradoxical nature was taken as an accepted quality of Śaiva thought, a property upon which further speculation could be based.

At the beginning of the nineteenth century, the Abbé J. A. Dubois described with shocked disbelief the seemingly contradictory concept of sexuality exemplified by the forest-dwelling ascetics:

> By one of those contradictions which abound in Hindu books, side by side with the account of the punishments inflicted on a hermit for his inability to conquer his sensual passions, we find, related with expressions of enthusiasm and admiration, the feats of debauchery ascribed to some of their *munis*
> [ascetic sages]—feats that lasted without interruption for thousands of years; 24ea*
> and (burlesque idea!) it is to their pious asceticism that they are said to owe this unquenchable virility.[10]

This very 'burlesque idea' is the core of the nature of Śiva, who is the god of ascetics, but out of its mythological context it could have no significance. Nor has contemporary scholarship found a satisfactory solution to the enduring enigma of Śiva: 'Permanently ithyphallic, yet
perpetually chaste: how is one to explain such a phenomenon?'[11] 26ea

The problem was intensified by uncertainties regarding Śiva's place in the historical development of Hinduism. Failure to connect him with the Vedic gods Indra, Prajāpati, and Agni led to the assumption that the sexual elements of his cult were 'non-Āryan' or at least non-Vedic,[12] and obvious correspondences between Śaiva myths and Tantric cult led some scholars to seek the origins of Śiva's sexual ambiguity in this comparatively late development.[13] Yet what is striking about the problem is that it extends from the period of the Vedas (*c.* 1200 B.C.) and even earlier, from the prehistoric civilization of the Indus Valley (*c.* 2000 B.C.), through the development of Tantrism, to the religion of present-day India.

The ancient Hindus themselves attempted to explain the Śaiva

* The significance of these marginal numbers will be explained below (pp. 20 ff.).

phenomenon. A Sanskrit poem dating from perhaps A.D. 900 muses upon Śiva:

28ea If he is naked what need then has he of the bow?
6cd If armed with bow then why the holy ashes?
22ea If smeared with ashes what needs he with a woman?
43a Or if with her, then how can he hate Love?[14]

In the Purāṇas, the nature of Śiva is often a source of worry for gods and mortals who become involved with him. When Himālaya learns that his daughter is to marry Śiva, he says, 'It is said that Śiva lives
22ea without any attachments and that he performs asceticism all alone. How then can he interrupt his trance to marry?'[15] Explicit reasons for Śiva's behaviour are given in the course of the myths, but the metaphysical arguments are both secondary and subsequent to the story. If philosophy could express the problem, there would be no need for the myth to mediate between the two opposed facets; the myth takes over where philosophy proves inadequate. Śiva himself is said to be troubled by the ambivalence in his character, for when Kāma, the god of desire, wounds him, shattering his trance and stirring his desire, Śiva muses, 'I dwell ever in asceticism. How is it then that I am enchanted by Pārvatī?'[16] Only involvement in the eternal cycle of the myth can reveal—even to the god himself—the answer to this question.

B. 1. *The Resolution within the Texts*

The solution is not an arbitrary construction of armchair scholarship, meaningless to the creators and preservers of the myths. Throughout Hindu mythology, even from the time of the Vedas, the so-called opposing strands of Śiva's nature have been resolved and accepted as aspects of one nature. They *may* be separated in certain contexts, and are frequently confused and misunderstood even by the tellers of the tales, but in every age there have been notable examples of satisfactory resolution. The Śiva of Brahmin philosophy is predominantly ascetic; the Śiva of Tantric cult is predominantly sexual. But even in each of these, elements of the contrasting nature are present, and in the myths—which form a bridge between rational philosophy and irrational cult—Śiva appears far more often in his dual aspect than in either one or the other.

As early as the Atharva Veda hymn to the *brahmacārin* (a young student who has undertaken a vow of chastity), there is a detailed description of a sage who has been identified with Śiva himself, the
26ea great *brahmacārin* but also the great *liṅga*-bearer, who spills his seed

upon the earth.[17] The first explicit reference to Śiva's ambiguous 21e
sexuality appears in the *Mahābhārata* (*c.* 300 B.C.), in a hymn in praise
of Śiva:

> Whose semen was offered as an oblation into the mouth of Agni, and whose 10c 44a
> semen was made into a golden mountain? Who else can be said to be a naked 21e 9cd
> *brahmacārin* with his vital seed drawn up? Who else shares half his body with 28ea
> his wife and has been able to subjugate Kāma?[18] 21a 32e 43a

The seed spilt creatively and contained in chastity, the ultimate act of desire and the conquest of desire—the essence of Śaiva mythology is in this passage.

Statements of resolution persist throughout the Purāṇas. Śiva says 27ea
that if he marries, his wife must be a *yoginī* (female ascetic) when he
does yoga, and a lustful mistress (*kāminī*) when he is full of desire.[19]
The sage Nārada describes Śiva:

> On Kailāsa mountain, Śiva lives as a naked yogi. His wife Pārvatī is the 28ea
> most beautiful woman in the universe, capable of bewitching even the best of 22ea
> yogis. Though Śiva is the enemy of Kāma and is without passion, he is her 43a
> slave when he makes love to her.[20] 36e

And constantly, in less explicit ways, the two aspects of the god are
equated or interchanged. It is said that Śiva is a great yogi, but in his
meditation he fixes his mind upon his wife.[21] Devī (the Goddess, who 25ea[2]
becomes incarnate as Satī and Pārvatī) says:

> Ever since I killed myself, Śiva has thought of me constantly, unable to 6d
> bear his separation from me. He wanders naked, and has become a yogi, 28ea
> abandoning his palace, wearing unconventional clothing. Miserable because 28a
> of me, he has abandoned the highest pleasure that is born of desire. He is 42a
> tortured by longing and can find no peace as he wanders everywhere, weeping 43ea
> and behaving like a lover in distress.[22]

In this passage, the two roles are enacted simultaneously: Śiva wears
the garb of a yogi, but his behaviour is that of a lover in separation. In
fact, he is a yogi *because* he is a lover. This may be read as a contradiction
but psychologically it is entirely logical. So completely are the roles of
ascetic and lover combined that the myth-makers themselves often confuse them. The Seven Sages say to Pārvatī, 'How can you enjoy the 29ea
pleasures of the body with an ascetic [*yati*] like him, so terrifying and 19ea
disgusting?'[23] But in another version of the same text they say, 'How 29ea
can you enjoy the pleasures of the body with a husband [*pati*] like him, 19ea
so terrifying and disgusting?'[24] The sense remains the same in both
readings, for the two roles are being compared and in fact interchanged.

The Pine Forest sages say, 'If we have served Śiva from our birth 34a

24ea[1] with *tapas* [asceticism], then let the *liṅga* of this libertine [Śiva in dis-
32a guise] fall to the earth.'[25] Thus they swear by Śiva the ascetic in order
to destroy Śiva the erotic, not realizing that the two are one. This
dualism is implicit in other versions of the Pine Forest myth as well,
for the sages use the *tapas* of Śiva (their fiery curse) against the lust of
Śiva (his *liṅga*), and they must be taught the unity of the two powers.
The contrasting aspects of Śiva are artfully combined in a late poem of
7cd[1] praise which invokes him first as the three-eyed god (ascetic, the third
31e eye having burnt Kāma), then as the clever dancer (erotic), then as the
24ea[2] wandering beggar (ambiguous, as in the Pine Forest), then as the rider
45e[2] on the bull (erotic), the poison-eater (ascetic), and finally as the god
5c[2] 9d whose *liṅga* is worshipped by yoga (ambiguous).[26]

For the yogi himself, using Śiva as his model, the god might appear in either aspect according to the worshipper's need: 'The yogi who thinks of Śiva as devoid of passion himself enjoys freedom from passion. The yogi who meditates upon Śiva as full of passion himself will certainly enjoy passion.'[27] Nor was this choice limited to the initiated;
a popular hymn to Śiva in Orissa says, 'He is the much beloved husband
19ea of Gaurī [Pārvatī] and the only object of adoration by the ascetic.'[28]
This dualism is taken for granted even in a modern English novel based
upon the Śiva myth:

> Śiva . . . had two simultaneous identities. There was Śiva austere on the Himalaya, rambling down granite causeways . . . and yet at the same time a young buck around town, boyish, eager, with a shock of black hair over his eyes, and a girl on either arm. For it is possible 'to comprehend flowering and fading simultaneously . . . '.[29]

Thus it would seem that this ambiguity has been comprehended and accepted by men of various ages and beliefs, notwithstanding its apparent logical contradiction and the difficulties which arise when its implications are literally applied to an actual or mythological social situation.

B. 2. *The Iconic Resolution of the Paradox: The Ithyphallic Yogi*

In many texts, Śiva is said to be ithyphallic (with an erect phallus),
an image which would certainly seem to be unambiguous sexually but
for its particularly Hindu connotations, which tie it to the world of
asceticism as strongly as it is naturally related to the realm of eroticism.
Of all the characteristics of Śiva, this is perhaps the most basically
iconic; images and paintings of Śiva frequently incorporate aspects
26ea described in the myths, but the image of the erect phallus preceded the

myths related about it.[30] The study of the ambiguity of the image, therefore, begins with the study of its earliest iconic form.

Sir John Marshall noted in the prehistoric Indus Valley civilization
a seal on which was depicted a male god whom he identified as a prototype of Śiva; the god, seated in a position of yoga, has an exposed, erect 26ea
phallus[31] [Plate 1]. More recently, Sir Mortimer Wheeler has suggested
that another Indus Valley figure, the dancing torso from Harappā, also
apparently ithyphallic, may be a prototype of Śiva Nāṭarājā ('Lord of 26ea
the Dance').[32] So specific an identification of cult cannot be made with 31e 31a
certainty, but there is evidence in the Indus Valley of yogic practices[33]
as well as of the phallic worship mentioned by the Ṛg Veda itself as
characteristic of the enemies of the Āryans.[34] Thus even at this early
time there is a connection between the postures of yoga and of sexuality.
The interrelation of asceticism and desire in the medieval Purāṇas, then,
cannot be explained by any historical synthesis, but must be accepted
as a unified concept which has been central to Indian thought from pre-
historic times.

Ithyphallic images are as early as any Śiva images,[35] and the Gūḍi- 26ea
mallam *liṅga*, an erect phallus on which an image of Śiva is carved,
has been called the earliest known Hindu sculpture[36] [Plate 2]. Many
images of ithyphallic yogis represent Lakulīśa ('The Lord of the Club'), 26ea
an incarnation of Śiva.[37] Śiva mounted upon his bull should be ithy- 33ea[5]
phallic, according to one textbook of aesthetics, and 'the end of the 45e[2]
phallus must reach the limit of the navel'.[38] Similarly, Śiva is ithyphallic 26ea
as Nāṭarājā, as the androgyne, and frequently when sitting in a yogic 31e 31a
posture beside Pārvatī, whose hand sometimes touches his erect 32e
phallus.[39] Even Gaṇeśa, the son of Śiva, has the *ūrdhvaliṅga* (erect 36e 26ea
phallus) when he dances the dance of death (*tāṇḍava*) in imitation of his 31a
father.[40] It has been suggested that several of the bearded figures portrayed on the Śaiva temples at Khajuraho are yogis participating in ritual orgies, and that some of their more convoluted poses represent 'sexo-yogic' attitudes or esoteric yogic *āsanas* (postures).[41] If this interpretation is accepted, the domain of the ithyphallic yogi is widely extended, even within purely Śaiva limits.

The ambiguity of ithyphallicism is possible because, although the
erect phallus is of course a sign of priapism, in Indian culture it is
a symbol of chastity as well. Śiva is described as ithyphallic,[42] particularly 26ea
in the Pine Forest,[43] and this condition is often equated with a state
of chastity:[44] 'He is called *ūrdhvaliṅga* because the lowered *liṅga* sheds 21e
its seed, but not the raised *liṅga*.'[45] The basic Sanskrit expression for 21a

the practice of chastity is the drawing up of the seed (*ūrdhvaretas*), but,
21a by synecdoche, the seed is often confused with the *liṅga* itself, which is
'raised' in chastity. The raised seed is a natural image of chastity; only
21e Pārvatī can transform Śiva from one whose seed is drawn up into one
21a whose seed has fallen.[46] His seed 'falls' when he begets Skanda, yet he
44a is described as *ūrdhvaretas* even at the moment when he gives Agni his
seed.[47] The commentator glosses this term as *ūrdhvagāmivīryaḥ*, 'with
his seed moving upwards', which may describe either the drawing up
21a of the seed in chastity or the motion of the seed shed in the absence of
26ea chastity. Thus Śiva is both the god whose seed is raised up and the god
whose *liṅga* is raised up.[48] Even without this confusion, the image of
the erect phallus is in itself accepted as representative of chastity. When
26a the seed is drawn up, Śiva is a pillar (*sthāṇu*) of chastity,[49] yet the pillar
is also the form of the erect *liṅga*: 'It is in this form of the Lord of
5cd 26a Yogins that he becomes Sthāṇu or of *liṅga* form.'[50] Since, in the context of the Hindu attitude toward sexual powers, Śiva's chastity is his
power of eroticism, the erect phallus can represent both phases:

> 26ea In many of his icons he [Śiva] is ithyphallic; often he appears with his
> 36e consort. At the same time he is the patron deity of yogis. . . . This is not
> 34a inconsistent with his sexual vitality. For the source of the yogi's power is his
> 24ea^2 own divine sexuality, conserved and concentrated by asceticism.[51]

26ea The ithyphallic condition has been attributed by some not to pria-
21a pism but to the Tantric ritual of seminal retention.[52] To a certain extent,
this technique may be considered a manifestation of yogic chastity, but
Śiva's raised *liṅga* is symbolic of the power to spill the seed as well as
to retain it.

> Shiva, the god of eroticism, is also the master of the method by which the
> virile force may be sublimated and transformed into a mental force, an
> intellectual power. This method is called Yoga, and Shiva is the great yogi,
> 26ea the founder of Yoga. We see him represented as an ithyphallic yogi. . . .
> 8c Assuming the various postures of Yoga, Shiva creates the different varieties
> of beings. . . . Then in the posture of realisation (*siddhāsana*) he reintegrates
> 8d into himself all the universe which he has created. It is in this posture that
> he is most often represented. His erect phallus is swollen with all the poten-
> tialities of future creations.[53]

The yogi here gathers up his creative powers, retaining the promise of procreation in the form of the erect phallus, the embodiment of creative *tapas*. The raised *liṅga* is the plastic expression of the belief that love and death, ecstasy and asceticism, are basically related.[54]

For the image retains its primary, more natural significance; it may

symbolize actual, as well as potential or sublimated eroticism. This is 26ea
clear from the statues of the ithyphallic Śiva embraced by Pārvatī.[55] 36e
The wives of the Pine Forest sages touch Śiva's erect phallus,[56] which 26ea
is adorned with red chalk and bright white charcoal[57] or with many
bracelets,[58] the latter a characteristic to which Dakṣa particularly ob- 28e
jects.[59] In a tribal myth it is said that a woman found an amputated 5c[2]
phallus, and, 'thinking it to be Mahadeo's [Śiva's] *liṅga*, took it home
and worshipped it. At night she used to take it to bed with her and use 5c[2]
it for her pleasure.'[60] In a similar manner, a female figure carved on the
temple at Konārak is obviously using a stone Śiva-*liṅga* as a dildo,[61] 35ea
an act which seems to be explicitly prohibited in the lawbooks.[62] In
a variant of the episode in which Śiva tempts Pārvatī to abandon her
tapas, he sends a flood to wash away the sand *liṅga* which she is worshipping, and she protects the *liṅga* by embracing it and smothering it 5c[2]
with her breasts.[63] Here *liṅga* worship replaces the usual episode of 25ea[1, 2]
tapas with an image of unmistakable eroticism. In this way, the image 4
of the ithyphallic yogi, simultaneously representative of chastity and sexuality, retains its ambiguities in myth, icon, and cult.

C. PROBLEMS AND METHODS

The paradox thus clearly represented in Indian art and explicitly discussed in philosophical texts also underlies the great corpus of Śaiva mythology, which combines the image and the idea. When this central pivot is selected, it is possible to balance the subsidiary themes around it in such a way that they become mutually illuminating. At this point we must reconsider the problem of mythological analysis.

C. 1. *Various Methods of Mythological Analysis*

Just as there are many meanings in a myth, many themes that may be extracted, so there are many theories of interpretation that have been or might be applied to Hindu myths: There is the nature interpretation of the nineteenth-century German school (Rudra is the storm; Brahmā's daughter is the dawn), and, in reaction to this oversimplification, the school which 'tried to reduce the meaning of myths to a moralizing comment on the situation of mankind'[64] (Rudra is death, Kāma is love). There is the metaphysical interpretation of the Hindu theologians (Indra is the soul; the gods are the objects of the senses) and the ritual interpretation of the Hindu priests (Dakṣa is the sacrificial goat) and of certain anthropologists (Dakṣa's goat-head is the totemistic symbol of the clan). There is the Euhemerist or historical theory, often favoured by Hindus as it lends a 'scientific' air to tales once scoffed at by Europeans (the battle between Indra and the serpent Vṛtra represents the Āryan conquest of Nāga tribes in 1500 B.C.), and the related Marxist view (the battle represents the supplanting of an agrarian economy by a martial proletariat). There is the etiological method (the myth explains why the eclipse of the moon takes place); the psychological interpretations of Freud, Jung, and Rank; the comparative mythology of Sir James Frazer; Stith Thompson's attempt to index the entire spectrum of world-wide mythological and folk motifs; the structural methods of Vladimir Propp and Lévi-Strauss; and the text-historical method, which 'explains' a myth by finding its earliest known sources.

The text-historical method is the one which has been most frequently applied to Indian mythology. Scholars attempted to discount apparently incongruous elements of a myth by tracing them back to originally unrelated '*Ur*-texts'; the persistence of such elements in an inappropriate context in the later myth was thus attributed to an accidental historical conflation of several myths. If, on the other hand, these elements could not be found in any *Ur*-text, they were ignored as modern accretions, irrelevant to the analysis of the 'essential' myth. This technique is generally unrewarding when applied to the Sanskrit sources, which are extremely difficult to date with any accuracy, and Madeleine Biardeau has commented on the unsuitability of the text-historical approach to Purāṇa material of this nature: 'The approach of historical philology will never be suitable for an oral tradition, which has no essential reference to its historical origin.'[65] Moreover, the historical method is misleading even when it succeeds; for the question to ask is not where the disparate elements originated, but why they were put together, and why kept together. It is when the combination seems most contradictory and arbitrary that it is most rewarding to analyse it as a combination—for only a strong emotional bond can bridge a wide logical gap. Lévi-Strauss uses the image of the *bricoleur*, the handyman who uses whatever tools and scraps are at hand, to describe the method of the myth-maker who uses pre-constrained images and actions.[66] The interesting question is not where the tools came from but why the *bricoleur* persists in combining certain tools in certain ways once he has them. One of the first Europeans to study Indian mythology complained, 'Hindu mythology is . . . very confused and contradictory, and almost any two things may be mythologically assimilated',[67] but this is not true. Only those things are persistently assimilated which have some basic relationship in the Hindu view.

For these reasons, among others, the structuralists have rejected the text-historical emphasis on chronology, and Lévi-Strauss treats all versions of a myth, including what are usually called interpretations, as equally relevant or authentic.[68] I have used 'versions' of the Śiva myths written by modern Hindu authors (R. K. Narayan, Nirad Chaudhuri), eighteenth-century European scholars, and even one contemporary Western novelist (David Stacton). As Mary Douglas has remarked of this technique, 'This challenging idea is not merely for the fun of shocking the bourgeois mythologist out of his search for original versions.'[69] The Hindu myths are part of an oral tradition extending through thousands of years. No one teller of a myth would include all the details that he might have known, and so a later version may express an idea which has been current in the tradition for a long time. Sometimes quite late versions make explicit what is present in an obscure form in a very early version: 'These later sequences are organized in schemata which are at the same time homologous to those which have been described and more explicit than them.'[70] Even when later versions seem to contradict earlier ones, the pattern of the earlier myth will often persist. In many cases the explicit meaning of the myth will contradict the pattern which comparison with other versions will reveal in it; in such instances, the pattern is usually more basic to the myth than the superficial meaning. Similarly, the explicit intention of a character may contradict his actual behaviour, and comparison with other versions usually reveals the action to be older than the intention. In this way the new wine of later versions will often reveal the shape of the old bottles, and *all* variants may be considered on an equal basis.

Thus the text-historical method is of limited value in determining the pattern of the myth as a whole. It is, however, extremely useful in illuminating the individual elements of that pattern, the themes and motifs. For example, no Vedic '*Ur*-text' exists to clarify the episode in
which Agni interrupts Śiva's love-play in order to take away Śiva's 44ea
seed. However, once having *isolated* the significant motifs by means of 44a
a number of modern variants, having established that Agni usually
assumes the form of a bird to steal the seed, we may then come to 30e
understand the motif better in the light of the history of the Vedic symbolism of the bird and the seed.

I have followed a modified text-historical method in tracing the historical backgrounds of the Śiva myths in the Vedas and Epics

(Chapters II to IV) and the subsequent development of the motifs within the Purāṇa myths (Chapters V to VII). The reader may trace the history of each motif through the citations in the index of motifs (Appendix F), bearing in mind the fact that, although it is impossible to 'date' any particular Purāṇic text, it is reasonable to postulate several broad areas of Indian mythology: Ṛg Veda (*c.* 1200 B.C.), Brāhmaṇas and Atharva Veda (900 B.C.), Upaniṣads (700 B.C.), *Mahābhārata* (300 B.C.–A.D. 300), *Rāmāyaṇa* (200 B.C.–A.D. 200), early Purāṇas (*Brahmāṇḍa*, *Mārkaṇḍeya*, *Matsya*, *Vāyu*, and *Viṣṇu*, 300 B.C.–A.D. 500), middle Purāṇas (*Kūrma*, *Liṅga*, *Vāmana*, *Varāha*, *Agni*, *Bhāgavata*, *Saura*, and *Devī*, A.D. 500–1000), late Purāṇas (*Brahmavaivarta*, *Skanda*, and all others, A.D. 1000–1500), and modern Hindu texts. In analysing the meaning of the myths as a whole, however (Chapters V to X), I have ignored chronology.

Almost every one of the traditional methods is applicable to some portion of some myth, though none can explain them all:

> There is some truth in almost all theories—as that myth is primitive philosophy or science, that its inner meaning is sexual, agricultural or astrological, that it is a projection of unconscious psychic events, and that it is a consciously constructed system of allegories and parables. No one of these theories accounts for all myths, and yet I do not doubt that each accounts for some.[71]

The mythologist, like the myth-maker himself, cannot be too proud to accept diverse scraps from dubious sources. It is interesting to take note of Freudian overtones in analysing certain parts of the Hindu cycle, such as the castration myths; Lévi-Strauss himself, though objecting to the widespread Jungian interpretation of mythological functions in absolute terms,[72] nevertheless (according to Edmund Leach) assumes that a myth is a kind of collective dream expressing unconscious wishes.[73] Similarly, one need not stubbornly refuse the assistance of the ritualists in analysing other myths (such as the destruction of Dakṣa's sacrifice). Each has its place.

It may seem perverse to ignore the work of Frazer when analysing myths with obvious parallels in other cultures (such as the myth of primeval incest, or the androgyne), yet I have done so almost without exception. There seems little point in drawing attention to the parallels in primitive or Greek myths; readers who are familiar with those materials may draw their own parallels, while to others such comparisons would be cumbersome and meaningless. Only in a few particularly striking and obscure cases have I indicated the correlations, where these might help to elucidate the *Hindu* meaning of the myth. I had originally planned to key my entire analysis to Stith Thompson's index of world folklore motifs, in order to enable folklorists to identify motifs of other cultures, but I soon abandoned this plan when I discovered that, even on a superficial level, well over a thousand motifs of his index occurred in my material. A more serious objection, however, lay in the misleading nature of this use of the index, for a great many of these motifs were in fact cited by Thompson as known only from Indian folklore; thus a list of motifs from my corpus which appeared in the Thompson index would often suggest, wrongly, that a motif of purely Indian occurrence was a 'world-wide' motif. The final objection, however, was one of basic method and philosophy: such a random and minute identification of motifs added nothing to one's understanding of the myths. As Lévi-Strauss has often pointed out, the motifs mean nothing in any abstract sense until they are placed in the context of the myth, in a structural relationship with other motifs.

The prevalence of certain of the Śaiva motifs—such as fire and water—in non-Indian cultures obviates the possibility of explaining them *only* in terms of Indian beliefs. But patterns within the Indian context reveal a particular meaning that the motifs do not have in any other cultures and may even serve to clarify some meanings in those cultures. In general, it seems to me that the universal elements of the myth are precisely the *least* important elements, that the point of the myth is to be sought in those areas in which the Hindu myth diverges from the general pattern. Betty Heimann has expressed this opinion:

> India can only be explained through its own nature. . . . Seemingly corresponding details that invite comparison are essentially unrelated as they sprang from different sources, and their seeming similarity is actually incidental, a common basis being lacking.[74]

Even Lévi-Strauss has granted that a myth can be properly analysed only in the context of the culture of the listeners and tellers:

> I claim the right to make use of any manifestation of the mental or social activities of the communities under consideration which seem likely to allow me, as the analysis proceeds, to complete or explain the myth. . . . You cannot make mythology understood by somebody of a different culture without teaching him the rules and particular traditions of that culture.[75]

Indeed, purely structural, Lévi-Strauss-inspired analyses of Indian tribal mythology have yielded interesting results;[76] the authors have tried to relate these myths to the Hindu ritual materials at their disposal, but had they been able to make use of the full range of Sanskrit myths upon which the tribal stories are based, their conclusions might have been more subtle, if not necessarily more sound.

The validity of the method of analysis utilizing non-mythological materials for background is further supported by the manner in which characters within the myths actually cite Hindu lawbooks and philosophical works; the student of the myth seems justified in emulating their example. Once the Hindu myths have been set forth and analysed in their own right, it is possible to use them as the basis of more universal theories of myth, proceeding from the particular to the general, just as the general theories serve to illuminate the particular myths.

Yet the myth cannot be explained by ethnography alone, for if this were so, the myth could not add anything to the knowledge available in the ethnography. Moreover, the ambiguous relationship between myth and reality (the fact that the myth sometimes expresses a real situation by describing the reversal of actual conditions) produces yet another logical circle, for 'ethnographic observation must decide whether this image [of a myth] corresponds to the facts'.[77] For these reasons, ethnographic commentary, though necessary, is not sufficient, nor is it able to compensate for certain shortcomings of the structural approach: 'We soon find that the ethnographic commentary merely underlines even more sharply those aspects of the myth which cannot be further interpreted by this "semantic procedure".'[78]

C. 2. *Variants and Multiforms*

The main source of explanatory material for any myth is not in ethnography but in other related myths: 'A myth derives its significance not from contemporary or archaic institutions of which it is a reflection, but from its relation to other myths within a transformation group.'[79] A myth must be analysed in terms of its relationship to the 'total myth structure' of the culture:[80] 'Each myth taken separately exists as the limited application of a pattern, which is gradually revealed by the relation of reciprocal intelligibility discerned between several myths.'[81] This theory is particularly well adapted to the variants of Hindu myths:

> The orthodox Hindu consciousness has always found it . . . easy to accept wide variations in the texts. Any scientific study should first of all preserve these variations and determine the kind of socio-religious idea they conveyed to people.[82]

The latent structure of the myths can only be grasped by working through a large corpus of myths which express in many different ways certain similarities of structure, the repetition itself emphasizing the form behind the slight variations.[83] 'The ultimate conclusion of the analysis is not that "all the myths say the same thing" but that "collectively the sum of what all the myths say is not expressly said by any of them".'[84] Thus each myth within the cycle is a variant of every other myth.

The very delimitations of the episodes and symbols can only be identified by the comparison of several versions: integral units are those which appear in one version but not in another, on the principle of minimal pairs. As in algebra, the more terms (characters, episodes, symbols) involved in a myth, the more 'equations' (variant myths) required to isolate the terms:

> Divergence of sequences and themes is a fundamental characteristic of mythological thought, which manifests itself as an irradiation; by measuring the directions and angles of the rays, we are led to postulate their common origin, as an ideal point on which those deflected by the structure of the myth would have converged had they not started, precisely, from some other point and remained parallel throughout their entire course.[85]

The Śaiva myths involve many terms, and many permutations of each, so that literally hundreds of myths, all interrelated through their mutual characters and episodes, are required to elucidate even a relatively short sequence.

Moreover, one version may explain a particular element that is unclear in another:

> If one aspect of a particular myth seems unintelligible, it can be legitimately dealt with, in the preliminary stage and on the hypothetical level, as a transformation of the homologous aspect of another myth, which has been linked with the same group for the sake of argument, and which lends itself more readily to interpretation.[86]

Biardeau has applied this method to Hindu mythology, with considerable success:

> As our text sheds very little light on this point, we may look for some similar stories where the symbolic meaning would be made more explicit. What appears to many people as an unmanageable overgrowth of myths in epics and *puranas* is actually an invaluable source of information for a better understanding of each of them. . . . The regional variants are all authentic as long as the overall significance of the epic remains. . . . The major variations in the text are likely each to have its own significance fitting into the whole.[87]

This technique employed by the mythologist is justified by the theory that it is simply the mirror image of the technique employed by the myth-maker in the first place. Leach compares a myth with a message transmitted over a great distance (in time and space) and therefore repeated several times, with different wordings, so that when the different versions are reunited 'the mutual consistencies and inconsistencies will make it quite clear what is "really" being said'.[88] The mythologist is merely reassembling what the culture as a whole has fragmented.

Repetition enables the mythologist not only to separate the discrete units but to distinguish the more important elements from the trivial. The essential themes in a myth, impossible to identify from a simple reading of one version, emerge upon consideration of a number of other versions of that myth in which, despite various changes and reversals, certain elements persist. What is important is what is repeated, reworked to fit different circumstances, transformed even to the point of apparent meaninglessness, but always retained. In this way an element which occupies a relatively small part of a particular myth may be shown, in the context of the mythology as a whole, to be at the heart of that myth.

Multiple variants have a special importance in the analysis of myths which, like the Śaiva cycle, deal with contradictions. Myths which contain an insoluble problem are particularly prone to proliferate into many versions, each striving toward an infinitely distant solution, no one version able to confess its failure outright.[89] The perplexing point, the crux, is constantly reworked in a vain attempt to find an emotional or logical resolution. This is apparent on the simple linguistic level as well, where false readings, alternative phrases, and blatantly corrupt or incorrect Sanskrit terms betray a point which the myth-maker did not himself understand but was unwilling to omit altogether, knowing it to be somehow essential.

For all of the foregoing reasons, it should be clear why it was necessary to include what may at first glance appear to be an overwhelming number of almost identical versions of certain myths. In the first place, they are *not* identical, and it is the seemingly insignificant minor variation that holds the key to the isolation of a motif, which in turn contributes to the final reconstruction of the total symbolism of the cycle. Every version adds an essential detail, the significance of which only becomes apparent when the entire cycle has been analysed.

The use of multiple variants, and the analogy of an imperfectly transmitted message, are supported by the irrefutable evidence that the ancient Hindu myth-makers were in fact well aware of the existence of these variants. Although it is possible that no one person knew all the versions of a particular myth (a theoretically infinite amount of material), it is likely that each author was acquainted with at least more than one version, and consciousness of these variants is demonstrated explicitly from time to time in the Purāṇas. Many myths are cited by characters within other myths or by the Paurāṇika (the bard reciting the Purāṇa) as apt examples or parallel situations.[90] A frequent device used to accommodate multiple versions of a myth is the reference to multiple aeons of cosmic development. The seven variants of the birth of the Maruts describe how in seven former eras the Maruts were born, each time in a different way; a similar series of different versions of the birth of Rudra, in different eras, is narrated in another text.[91] One passage refers explicitly to this technique: 'Because of the distinction between eras, the birth of Gaṇeśa is described in different ways.'[92] Another text reveals an even more overt awareness of the use of this technique: the bard recites a myth in which a sage forgives his enemies; the audience then interrupts, saying, 'We heard it told differently. Let us tell you: the sage cursed them in anger. Explain this.' The bard then replies, 'That is true, but it happened in a different era. I will tell you.' And he narrates the second version of the myth.[93] Similar references are often made to incidents occurring in a series of incarnations.

In addition to these, there are frequent variations of a different sort within a single myth, where an entire episode is told and then retold in a slightly different form as an expansion of the original theme, producing a series of multiforms similar to the multiforms of episodes in different myths. Leach has pointed out the redundancies of this type in the Bible:

> It is common to all mythological systems that all important stories recur in several different versions. Man is created in Genesis (chapter I, verse 27) and then he is created all over again (II, 7). And, as if two first men were not enough, we also have Noah in chapter VIII. Likewise in the New Testament, why must there be four gospels each telling 'the same' story yet sometimes flatly contradictory on details of fact? . . . As a result of redundancy, the believer can feel that, even when the details vary, each alternative version of a myth confirms his understanding and reinforces the essential meaning of all the others.[94]

This is a common artifice used in the composition of oral poetry, and it is appropriate to the rather florid style of the Purāṇas, which tend constantly to incorporate additional details and incidental material. In this way, for example, one Paurāṇika was forced to invent an elaborate episode to act as a bridge in order to include two different versions of the

way in which Pārvatī accumulated her ascetic power (*tapas*): after
narrating the first version, the Purāṇa states that Śiva then appeared in
33ea^{3,4} 17c the form of a water demon and threatened to devour a small child unless
8cd Pārvatī transferred her *tapas* to him; Pārvatī agreed and then had to
start all over again to accumulate her *tapas*; (there then follows the
second version, which the Paurāṇika was loath to omit).[95] A similar
example of multiforms within the myth may be seen in a version of the
Pine Forest story which distributes three different variants of the visit
1 of Śiva to the forest in three different visits, each incorporating certain
new details.[96] One Purāṇa gives two multiforms of the birth of Skanda
1 from Śiva's seed, one following immediately after the other but transferred from Skanda to Gaṇeśa, Śiva's other son; another Purāṇa gives
1 two different versions of the story of Jalandhara, one clearly conscious
of the other.[97]

By comparing these variants and multiforms it is possible to isolate the basic themes and motifs out of which further versions, when and if they might be found or created, would be built as well, for the number of possibilities is infinite. The so-called repetitions are never *exactly* the same; beneath the apparent symmetry of structure is a fluctuation of detail, like the variations in a Persian carpet. We never reach a point when 'all the variants' have been considered, yet we may establish a reasonably complete basic vocabulary:

> There is no real end to mythological analysis, no hidden unity to be grasped once the breaking-down process has been completed. Themes can be split up *ad infinitum*. Just when you think you have disentangled and separated them, you realize that they are knitting together again in response to the operation of unexpected affinities.[98]

This resistance against logical fragmentation leads the mythologist from one variant to another. 'Myths are translations of one another, and the only way you can understand a myth is to show how a translation of it is offered by a different myth.'[99] The final 'reconstruction' of the myth, once it has been dissected into some of its components, is simply a re-reading of the corpus in terms of these basic units. Thus I have constructed a chart of the basic motifs (see below, pp. 22–3), arranged according to the levels on which they occur (motifs of structure, symbolic motifs, ascetic/erotic motifs, and motifs of the interrelationships of Śiva with other characters), and reintroduced these motifs (designated by number) in the margins of all the myths I have cited. Moreover, after treating the component motifs as they occur in the principle myths of the Śiva cycle, I have discussed more general themes of function and structure which apply to the mythology on a broader scale (Chapters VIII to X).

There are many myths dealing with each theme, and many themes within each myth. There is no way to begin with any 'basic' myth or any 'basic' theme, for the entire corpus interlocks and feeds back so that the total fabric resembles a piece of chain-mail rather than the brachiated, family-tree structure sought by the text-historical analysts and some structuralists. I have, therefore, selected certain myths best suited to illustrate certain motifs, while indicating in the margin other motifs which also occur therein. At some point the reader will have to re-read myths cited before their component motifs have been discussed; the chicken must precede the egg, and vice versa.

The final 'explanation' of the myth cycle is thus the cycle itself, re-read with a richer awareness of at least some of the resonances and harmonies behind the flickering images. It is to be hoped that the reader will not be disappointed with this 'explanation', but rather, as Lévi-Strauss suggests,

> will find himself carried toward that music which is to be found in myth and which, in the complete versions, is preserved not only with its harmony and rhythm but also with that hidden significance that I have sought so laboriously to bring to light, at the risk of depriving it of the power and majesty that cause such a violent emotional response when it is experienced in its original state, hidden away in the depths of a forest of images and signs and still fresh with a bewitching enchantment, since in that form at least nobody can claim to understand it.[100]

The present analysis has been patched up and amended and revised in successive incarnations until it became obvious that, unchecked, it would continue to generate new variants, like a myth itself, 'until the final deluge', as the Hindus say. Paul Valéry once wrote that a poem is never finished; it is merely abandoned. Perhaps this is also true of any work of research in the arts; certainly it is true of any analysis of a body of mythology. For my part, I have had to force myself to abandon this opus for the moment; but it is of course unfinished.

D. MOTIFS OF HINDU MYTHOLOGY

1. Chart of Motifs
2. Explanation of Motifs
3. Interconnections between Motifs
4. The Śaiva Cycle Analysed by Motifs
5. The Value of Motifs and Variants

D. 1. *Chart of Motifs*

A. MOTIFS OF STRUCTURE

1. Conscious multiforms
2. Homoeopathic curses
3. Heteropathic curses
4. Reversed roles or episodes

B. MOTIFS OF SYMBOLISM

	creative	*creative/destructive*	*destructive*
	5. 1. sexual creation	flame *liṅga*	doomsday fire/darkness
	2. *liṅga*-worship		
FIRE	3. sun		
	6. rebirth from pyre	ashes	funeral pyre
	7. erotic fire	1. third eye	excess *tejas*
		2. eyes	
	8. creative *tapas*	transfer *tejas*	destructive *tapas*
	9. fiery seed in water	liquid gold	poison
FIRE	10. oblation in fire	death and sex	*tapas* in water
AND	11. sweat	tears	water destroys fire
WATER	12. ashes in water	fire/water balance	fire destroys water
	13. passion submerged	1. submarine mare	anger quenched
		2. taming	
		3. fire in mouth	
	14. 1. cosmic waters	ocean	doomsday flood
	2. Soma		
	3. moon		
WATER	15. rain as seed	blood	drought
	16. drink seed	food and sex	drugs/liquor
	17. woman bathing	*yoni*	*vagina dentata*

C. MOTIFS OF EROTICISM AND ASCETICISM

erotic	*erotic/ascetic*	*ascetic*
18. sons for immortality	two paths	*tapas* for immortality/youth
19. need/love children	married ascetic	dangerous son of ascetic
20. curse of rebirth	unnatural birth	release from rebirth
21. spill seed	*apsaras* seduces ascetic	retain seed
22. impregnation period	wife seduces ascetic	wife reviles ascetic
23. 1. marriage	adulterous ascetic	ascetic *v.* in-laws
2. house		
24. sex cures lust	1. false ascetic	ascetic reviled
	2. erotic ascetic	
25. sex destroys *tapas*	1. *tapas* for *kāma*	*tapas* restores/expiates sex
	2. *tapas* for spouse	
	3. *tapas* for child	
26. 1. bamboo reed	ithyphallic ascetic	Sthāṇu (ascetic pillar)
2. tree of Kāma		
27. incest	erotic *yoginī*	regard woman as mother
28. erotic clothes	nakedness	ascetic clothes
29. eroticism/fertility	erotic/horrible	barrenness
30. birds	wind	snakes
31. erotic dance/motion	1. erotic inaction	*tāṇḍava* dance/ascetic motion
	2. ascetic inaction	
32. androgyne	change sex	castration
33.	masquerade:	
	1. as opposite sex	
	2. as spouse	

3. spouse as non-spouse
4. as animal
5. god as mortal
6. false accusation
7. *līlā*/play-acting/games

D. MOTIFS OF ŚIVA'S RELATIONSHIPS

(Ś = Śiva; B = Brahmā; P = Pārvatī; K = Kāma; A = Agni; D = Dakṣa)

	erotic Śiva	*erotic/ascetic Śiva*	*ascetic Śiva*
34.	Ś *v.* ascetic	Ś for married ascetic	Ś for ascetic
35.	Ś for ascetic's wife	Ś tempts/seduces ascetic's wife	Ś *v.* ascetic's wife
36.	Ś marries/embraces P	P seduces Ś 1. by *tapas* 2. by *kāma*	Ś reviles/leaves P
37.	Ś competes with B	Ś and B combine to create	B curses Ś
38.	Ś revives B/D	Ś assists B	1. Ś beheads/curses B/D 2. skull
39.	B (= Ś) commits incest	B performs *tapas* for Ś	Ś punishes incest
40.	B (= Ś) *v.* ascetic sons	sons use both paths	B *v.* ascetic sons (= Ś)
41.	B (= Ś) creates Kāma/Rati	B (= Ś) burnt by Kāma	B (= Ś) curses Kāma
42.	Ś = K/Ś increases K	Ś competes with K	Ś ignores/diminishes K
43.	Ś/P revives K	K burns Ś	Ś burns K
44.	A (= Ś) puts seed in Ganges	A interrupts couple	Ś burns A with seed/curse
45.	Ś (= Indra) 1. phallic god 2. bull	Indra performs *tapas* for Ś	Indra *v.* ascetic (= Ś)

D. 2. *Explanation of Motifs*

The chart presents the most important motifs of the Śaiva cycle; Appendix F is an index to the major occurrences of these motifs in the present work. If some of the arrangements seem arbitrary or illogical, the reader may come to see the point of my designation after retracing the motif through its contexts. Since the chart merely represents in a schematic form the ideas which form the subject of this entire work, it will only become fully comprehensible in the course of the book, but as the reader will wish to refer to it throughout, a preliminary introduction is necessary here.

The first category (A: Motifs of Structure, 1–4) notes the most frequent *significant* devices used by the myth-maker, those which contribute to the content as well as to the form of the myth. Motifs of Symbolism (B, 5–17) are arranged by two intersecting factors: each motif represents an aspect of fire, water, or a mediating or combined element, and each is manifest in a creative (c), destructive (d), or ambiguous form (cd). Thus the flame *liṅga* (5cd) is an aspect of fire which is creative and/or destructive. Sweat (11c) is a combination of fire and water which is creative. The mediating categories, which are the most important and the most frequent, may function in any of four ways: they may be ambiguous, both categories existing simultaneously (such as 9cd, liquid gold, simultaneously fire and water); or they may represent a transition from one stage to another (such as 6cd, ashes, the result of destruction and the source of creation); or they may represent a permanent combination (such as 12cd, the balance of water and fire); or the mediating agent may be a substance which sometimes represents one aspect, sometimes another (such as 5cd, the flame *liṅga*, sometimes a source of creative seed, sometimes a destructive fire).

Motifs of Eroticism and Asceticism (C, 18–33) are arranged on a single scale, the erotic motifs corresponding to the creative motifs of category B, the ascetic to the destructive. This category encompasses the general, human level of the myths. The final category (D, 34–45) represents Śiva's relationships with the major characters of the myths. The erotic and ascetic aspects of Śiva correspond to the creative/destructive, erotic/ascetic aspects of categories B and C.

In all categories, those motifs which appear with significant variations are subdivided.

Some of the categories should be fairly obvious, and others will be explained by the material presented in the course of this book, but it may be useful to elucidate at the start the more obscure motifs and those which may have been abbreviated beyond the point of obvious reference:

1. Conscious multiforms include a few obvious repetitions of episodes within a myth but more often indicate explicit references within one myth to another myth considered to be a close parallel.
2. Homoeopathic curses are those in which a character is cursed to experience an exaggeration of that aspect of his nature which prompted the curse.
3. Heteropathic curses bring a reversal of aspect and/or experience.
4. Reversed roles occur in passages in which a character plays a role directly opposed to his usual nature, or in which two characters exchange roles; reversed episodes are those which appear out of their usual sequence in the myth, often in place of episodes of a similar structure or symbolism. Only a few of the more important of these are indicated, as the entire Śaiva cycle is constructed out of such reversals of roles (one god replacing his 'opposite') and episodes (*tapas* replacing *kāma*).

5–17. Separate motifs of fire or of water are frequently transitional, for fire alone or water alone, as well as their combination, may serve as a medium of transformation, as in the 'sea-change' or rebirth from fire.

5. Cosmically creative or destructive fire; the *liṅga* partakes of both aspects. The doomsday fire functions as its own inverse (darkness). [Plates 2 and 3]

6. The funeral fire. [Plates 10 and 14]

7. Fire within the human body.

8. *Tapas* as fire. 8d includes non-creative as well as destructive *tapas*. 8cd: *tejas* is fiery energy, potentially destructive unless transferred or controlled.

9. The fiery seed, in itself ambiguous, sometimes acts like fire, and is placed in water, but at other times is in itself a form of water (usually a lake) considered to be liquid fire. [Plate 11]

10. Thematically, this is a form of water in fire, the inverse of 9c. Butter, Soma, seed, and the human body are used as oblations. [Plates 4 and 9]

11. c and cd are multiforms of the seed, fiery liquids in the body.

13. The control of emotions, passion (c) or anger (d). This control is expressed by the image of the mare who must be tamed. [Plate 3]

14. This is the liquid counterpart of 5. Soma is stored in the moon.

16. Ingestion of liquids. [Plate 9]

17. Woman, symbolically equivalent to water. The bathing motif is connected with erotic attraction and impregnation; *vagina dentata* represents the dangerous, destructive aspect of women, important in the misogynist tradition of asceticism, and the *yoni* (the female sexual organ) is ambivalent. [Plate 3]

19. This includes in its erotic category both the need for children yet unborn and the love for one's existing children; the dangerous son may also be unborn, or dangerous merely by virtue of his embarrassing existence. [Plates 10 and 16]

21ea. The *apsaras* is the celestial prostitute who tempts the sage. [Plate 5]

22. This category represents the ascetic's relationship with his wife. The 'impregnation period' refers to the *ṛtugamana*, the husband's duty to impregnate his wife during her fertile period.

23. The ascetic's relationship with conventional society, or with his in-laws.

24. The Tantric ascetic and society. 24e represents the philosophy of Tantrism as it appears to the non-Tantric; 24ea represents the true

erotic ascetic (2) and the Tantric ascetic as he appears to his enemies, or may in fact behave (1).

24ea is ambiguous: the erotically attractive but chaste as well as the actively lustful ascetic.

25. The stages of the major fluctuating cycles of *tapas* and *kāma*.

26. Trees and pillars as phallic symbols. The reed, which contains the seed, is a metaphor for the phallus, as are the tree of Kāma and the related Indra-pole. The contrasting aspect is the Sthāṇu pillar of chastity. The mediating factor is the ithyphallic ascetic himself. [Plates 1, 4, and 16]

27. Another manifestation of the ascetic's attitude to women, in this case taboo women. Incest represents the violation of the taboo; 27a represents ascetic chastity, the inverse of incest; and the erotic *yoginī* (female ascetic) mediates as a woman who is taboo but all the more desirable by virtue of that taboo.

29. The separation of eroticism and fertility includes both love-play that fails to produce children and impregnation devoid of lust, the former closely related to barrenness (29a), the latter the inverse of barrenness. The combination of the erotic and the horrible mediates between apparently barren and apparently erotic motifs. [Plates 4 and 10]

30. Birds and snakes are opposed in many ways. Birds represent heaven, life, eggs, and are associated with the seed which they carry in their beaks. Snakes represent death and the underworld, but also rebirth (for they slough their skins and are 'reborn'). They are also connected with the yogic aspect of Śiva and with his phallic emblem. In spite of this ambiguity in the symbolism of snakes, birds and snakes as natural enemies symbolize opposition in Indian thought. Both animals are used as disguises in the interruption episodes, as is their mediating form, wind, which plays a creative role in the cosmogony and a destructive role at doomsday, where it further mediates between the conflagration and the flood. [Plates 8, 10, and 15]

31. The *tāṇḍava* is Śiva's dance of death. The Nāṭarājā includes both aspects of Śiva's dance. [Plate 7]

32. The androgyne indicates the presence of both sets of sexual organs; castration the presence of none; and 'change of sex' the presence of first one and then the other. [Plate 8]

33ea. All masquerades are forms of mediation between the real and the imagined. 'God as mortal' includes too many episodes to be listed in the index; the most important episode is Śiva's appearance as a beggar. 'Masquerade as animal' appears in a double mediation in those motifs in which the masquerade affects only the head (monkey, elephant, bull, goat, or horse), so that the character is half animal, half human. '*Līlā*/play-acting/games' is also widely applicable, but limited here to explicit statements and to the game of dice.

35. The mediating motif is erotic when Śiva actually seduces the ascetic's wife and ascetic when he merely tempts her in order to demonstrate her evil nature. [Plate 12]

36. The mediating motif is transitional in either aspect, but obviously belongs more to the erotic category when it is Pārvatī's beauty that seduces Śiva and more to the ascetic category when it is her *tapas* that succeeds. [Plates 7, 8, 10, 15]

38. The ascetic aspect is represented not only by references to the beheading but also to its result—the skull that the Kāpālika carries. [Plates 10 and 12]

40. The conflict between Brahmā and his ascetic sons appears in two aspects, depending upon whether Śiva is identified with the Prajāpati or with the sons.

41. Śiva may be associated with either aspect of Brahmā, as Śiva eventually participates in a clear multiform of the Brahmā/Kāma myth.

45. Śiva's bull ($45e^2$) is a link with Indra, a motif inherited from him. [Plates 7, 8, and 10]

D. 3. *Interconnections between Motifs*

It will be apparent that some of the motifs are merely specific examples of more general themes which appear as other motifs. It is difficult to strike the perfect balance here in selecting the motifs. If the categories are too broad, one risks the sometimes pointless abstractions and reductions of certain structuralists, with everything reduced to a conflict between male and female or sacred and profane; on the other hand, if too many details are included, one falls into the opposite trap of the encyclopedic folk-index, with 'dog seduces mother-in-law' and 'rabbit seduces mother-in-law' placed in totally unrelated categories; here the pattern never emerges at all. I have attempted to produce a mediation between these two opposed extremes without losing the benefits of either one, but in so doing a number of partially overlapping motifs have been incorporated in the chart. These repetitions are by no means simply evidence of the flaws in the present analysis, for such interlocking relationships (and in fact the whole problem of several simultaneous levels of magnification and subdivision) are intrinsic in the nature of myth itself.

Because of this network of interactions, many motifs act as pivots in several lines, or form categories in addition to those indicated by the scheme I have chosen. Most of these overlapping motifs occur within the same basic aspect (creative/erotic, destructive/ascetic, or mediating); some include mediating categories with unilateral categories, and a few are linked oppositionally with motifs in opposing categories. Many overlaps occur between motifs in B or C and the plot motifs of D, the latter expressing a particular instance of a general motif. On the other hand, some plot motifs encompass more general situations: thus 44ea (Agni's interruption of Śiva and Pārvatī) is used to apply to related motifs of interruption, and many motifs of fire (5–8) apply not only to Agni but to other plot motifs, for many of the interrelationships are expressed in terms of characters burning one another.

Some of the more significant interactions are indicated below:

2 (homoeopathic curses) is a general category to which 24e (sex cures lust), 20e (curse of rebirth), and several specific curses (37a, 38a, 41a, 44a) belong.

3 (heteropathic curses) includes 25e and 25a, which function in this way.

$5c^1$ (sexual creation) is a broad category related to 19e, 22e, 24e, 25e, 27e, 29e, 31e, and 36e—all involving sexual intercourse. $5c^1$ is also to be contrasted with 8c (creative *tapas*), as they represent the two contrasting (though not opposed) methods of human creation, both expressed as metaphors of fire.

$5c^2$ and $14c^2$ are the two forms of ritual creation and worship, one involving fire (the *liṅga*) and the other water (Soma).

$5c^2$ is further linked to 5cd, 26, 32, 45e, and 17cd by the image of the phallus.

$5c^3$ and $14c^3$ are the planetary forms of fire and water.

6c, which concerns revival, is thus linked to 20e, 18a, 38e, and 43e.

6cd and 12c are linked by the motif of ashes.

6d (funeral pyre) is often contrasted with $23e^2$ (house).

7d (excess *tejas*) is a general category including other destructive forces such as 5d, 8d, 31e, and 31a. It is still more directly and frequently connected with 8cd, the cure for the problem presented by 7d.

7cd is related to 11cd, as tears flow from the eye.

8c is a general category which includes various aspects of productive *tapas*: 13d, 18a, and 25a.

9c is related to other motifs of the seed, in which the fiery or watery aspects predominate: in 15c and 16c the seed is water; in 21e and 21a it is ambiguous; in 44e and 44a it is fire.

9d is related by the theme of ingestion to 14c², 16d, 16cd, 16c; and by reverse ingestion, it is related to 13cd³.

9d is related to 30a, as snakes contain poison.

10c and 14c² are linked, as Soma is often used as the oblation.

10cd, based upon the belief that sex is dangerous, is thus related to 17cd, 17d, 25e, 32a; and it is an aspect of 29ea. 10cd is also related to 25e through the many myths in which a sexual episode is used to destroy the *tapas* of an enemy so that he may then be killed.

13cd is a combination of 11d and 12d. It is also related to 33ea⁴ through the animal factor.

13cd³ and 44a (and 16c) all describe fire being swallowed.

16c is one process of unnatural birth and impregnation (20ea).

17c (woman bathing) is often combined with 28ea (nakedness), when the point of the bathing is that the woman is naked. It is also related to 21ea, not only because seduction usually results from the sight of the woman, but because the *apsaras* is a water nymph (the word *apsaras* meaning literally, 'One who moves in the water').

18e is related by the theme of children to 19e, 19a, 25ea³, and (inversely) 29a.

18ea is a general theme applied to Śiva and Brahmā (37ea) and to the sons of Brahmā (40ea).

19ea is a general theme which includes 34 and 35 as well as 36 (Śiva and his wife); yet 19ea is itself a variant of the more general 22, 23, and 24ea.

20e is equivalent to 33ea⁵.

21ea is linked to a number of themes which concern seduction (22ea, 23ea, 24ea, and 36ea), all of which are manifestations of 25e. 45a is a particular method of this seduction, and 35ea is a reversal of 21ea (in which the man takes the active role). 43ea is related to these.

21ea and the related seduction motifs are transitional motifs, moving from *tapas* to *kāma*. They are thus the inverse of the transitional motif of interruption (44ea), moving from *kāma* to *tapas*, with its particular agents—birds, snakes, and wind (30). The other transitional motif is the moment of erotic or ascetic inaction (31ea) poised between two phases. 25ea is also transitional.

21e is a general motif which includes particular manifestations of the shed seed (39e and 44a), as well as the other motifs of the seed and of unnatural birth (20ea).

21a is a metaphor for asceticism, as are 26a, 34a, and (more loosely) 27a.

22a is a variant of 24a, and 36a is a specific example.

24ea^2 is another aspect of 26ea, and its female manifestation is 27ea.

24ea^1 has an inverse in 33ea^6; in the former, a lustful man pretends to be chaste, while in the latter a chaste man appears to be lustful.

25ea^2 is the general theme of which 27ea and 36ea^1 are examples.

27e is the general theme of which 39e is an example.

29a is the female condition corresponding to 32a.

30e and 30a, together with 45e^2, are particular animals whose appearances are subsumed under 33ea^4.

32a is related to 38a both through the natural association of physical mutilation and the particular contexts of the myths.

32ea is the actual process of which 33ea^1 is an imitation.

38a is the particular manner in which 39a is manifest.

D. 4. *The Śaiva Cycle analysed by Motifs*

To demonstrate the manner in which this chart of motifs may be used to elucidate the myths of the Śaiva cycle, I have summarized that cycle below and noted the motifs in the outer margins. The myths involving Śiva's erotic/ascetic ambivalence may be viewed as one myth containing several episodes, each of which may appear as a separate myth. Although I know of no text which actually relates all of the episodes in an uninterrupted sequence, each episode is connected to its sequel in at least one text (see Appendix A), and references are frequently made within one episode to another in the cycle. Through this series of overlaps, the myth as a whole may be reconstructed in general terms as follows:

8c 8d When Brahmā's *tapas* failed to create, he made Kāma, who wounded him.
41e 41ea Brahmā desired his daughter, who fled from him, taking the form of a deer.
39e 33ea^4 He pursued her in the form of a stag, and his seed fell upon the ground and
21e was offered as an oblation into the fire, where it created various sages and
10c 39a 38a^1 animals. Rudra pursued Brahmā and beheaded him, and Brahmā cursed
2 41a Kāma, who had inspired this incestuous passion in him, to be destroyed by
37a Śiva, and Śiva, who had mocked him, to be excited by Kāma.
19ea Dakṣa, a son of Brahmā, gave his daughter Satī in marriage to Śiva, but
23a he did not invite Śiva to his sacrifice. Satī, in anger, burnt herself to death.
10cd 6d Śiva destroyed Dakṣa's sacrifice and beheaded Dakṣa, but when the gods
38e 33ea^4 38a^1 praised Śiva he restored the sacrifice and gave Dakṣa the head of a goat.

When Śiva learned that Satī had killed herself, he took up her body and 10cd
danced in grief, troubling the world with his dance and his tears until the 31e 11cd 31a
gods cut the corpse into pieces. Where the *yoni* fell, Śiva took the form of 17cd
a *liṅga*, and peace was re-established in the universe. 13c 5cd 13d

The demon Tāraka usurped the throne of Indra, for Brahmā had promised 19e 45a
Tāraka that he could only be killed by a son born of Śiva, who was deeply 31ea[2] 26a
absorbed in asceticism. Satī was then born again as Pārvatī, the daughter of 6c 23a
the mountain Himālaya and his wife Menā. When Nārada told them that 24ea[2]
their daughter was to marry Śiva, they were at first displeased, for they did 30ea 43ea 25a
not consider Śiva to be a suitable husband, but Pārvatī wished to marry him. 36ea 43a
Indra sent Kāma (in the form of a breeze) to inspire Śiva with desire for 7cd[1]
Pārvatī, but Śiva burnt Kāma to ashes with the fire of his third eye [Plate 36ea
13]. Pārvatī then performed *tapas* to obtain Śiva for her husband, and Śiva 33ea[3, 5]
appeared before her disguised as a *brahmacārin* and tested her by describing 35ea 6cd
all those qualities of Śiva which made him an unlikely suitor—his ashes, three 7cd[1]
eyes, nakedness, and antipathy to Kāma, his snakes and his garland of skulls 28ea 43a
and his home in the burning-grounds. When Pārvatī remained steadfast in 30a
her devotion to Śiva, the god revealed himself and asked her to marry him. 38a[2] 23e[1] 6d
He then sent the Seven Sages to Himālaya to ask for Pārvatī on his behalf. 36e

When Śiva had burnt Kāma, the combined blaze of their fires had threatened 43a
to destroy the universe. The gods begged Śiva for protection, and his fire 44e 5d
was given to a river to carry to the ocean, where it assumed the form of a mare 13cd[1, 3]
with flames issuing forth from her mouth, devouring the ocean waters while 14cd
waiting for doomsday and the final flood. 12d 14d

Meanwhile, the wedding preparations took place, and Śiva's ascetic gar- 28a
ments served in place of the conventional ornaments of a bridegroom. At the 28e
wedding, Brahmā himself acted as the priest, but he was excited by the sight 39e
of Pārvatī and shed his seed upon the ground. Śiva threatened to kill him and 21e 10c
to replace Brahmā as the creator, but Viṣṇu placated Śiva and demonstrated 37e
to him the necessity of fulfilling his own role as destroyer. The seed of 37ea
Brahmā was made into the clouds of doomsday in the sky. 15c 14d

After the wedding, Rati, the wife of Kāma, came to Śiva and begged him 43e
to revive Kāma [Plate 14]. Pārvatī interceded on Kāma's behalf, and Śiva 36e
revived him. Śiva began to make love to Pārvatī, but one day he teased her 36a
for having a dark skin, and as her pride was hurt she departed in order to 25ea[1] 33ea[4]
perform *tapas* to obtain a golden skin. While she was gone, the demon Āḍi 44ea 30a
came there in order to kill Śiva. Taking the form of a snake in order to elude
the doorkeeper, he then assumed the form of Pārvatī, having placed ada- 32ea
mantine teeth within his *yoni*. Śiva made love to the false Pārvatī, but when 33ea[1, 2]
he realised the deception he killed the demon with his own *liṅga*. 10cd 17d 5cd

When Pārvatī returned, having obtained great *tapas* and a golden skin, 36e
Śiva again began to make love to her, but his own powers began to diminish 25e
after he had indulged in sexual pleasures for so many years, and for this reason 25a
he was challenged by the demon Andhaka. Śiva went away to the Pine Forest 33ea[2]
to perform a vow of *tapas*, and while he was gone Andhaka came to Pārvatī 7cd[1]
in the form of Śiva in order to seduce her. Andhaka had been born one day 11c
when Pārvatī covered the three eyes of Śiva and a drop of sweat had fallen 10c 20ea 19a

27e 42ea into the third eye; Pārvatī was thus his mother, but he was overcome with
27a lust for her. Pārvatī recognized that he was not Śiva, and she disappeared.
7cd[1] Śiva then returned and impaled Andhaka upon his trident, burning him with
7cd[1] 43a 43e the fire of his third eye and purifying him of his sins. Andhaka then became
19e the son of Śiva and Pārvatī [Plate 6].

7d While Śiva had been away performing his vow of *tapas*, the earth had begun
8d to shake and the gods begged Śiva to discontinue his *tapas*. Śiva complied,
34e but when the earth continued to tremble he went to seek the cause and dis-
31e 31a 15cd covered the sage Maṅkanaka, who was dancing in joy because of a miracle:
26e[2] when he had cut his thumb on a blade of grass, vegetable sap flowed from the
6cd wound instead of blood. Śiva then pierced his own thumb, and ashes white as
34a snow flowed from the wound, and Maṅkanaka stopped dancing.

33ea[5] Śiva then wandered into the Pine Forest, and the wives of the sages there
35ea fell in love with him and followed him everywhere. Śiva was naked, ithyphallic,
28ea 26ea dancing, and begging with a skull in his hand [Plate 12]. The sages became
31e 3 38a[2] furious and cursed his *liṅga* to fall to the ground. The *liṅga* fell but began to
32a cause a terrible conflagration; Brahmā and Viṣṇu tried in vain to find the top
5cd 5d and bottom of it, and peace was only restored when the sages agreed to wor-
5c[2] 34ea ship the *liṅga*, together with their wives.

33ea[1] When Śiva had entered the Pine Forest, Viṣṇu had assumed the form of
34e 34a Mohinī in order to seduce the sages while Śiva seduced their wives. When
35e 35a Śiva saw the beauty of Mohinī, he embraced her and a child was born from
21e 23ea 20ea his seed. (Mohinī was the form that Viṣṇu had assumed in order to seduce the
21ea demons, when, at the time of the churning of the ocean, they had stolen the
14c[2] 9d Soma; at this time, Śiva had saved the gods by drinking the blazing poison
16c 5d that had emerged from the ocean, threatening the universe.)

36e When Śiva returned to Pārvatī and began to make love to her again, the
31e gods were frightened of the friction generated by their great love-play and
19e they worried that it would fail to produce the son they needed, or that the
19a 30e son produced in this way would be a danger to the universe. Indra sent Agni
44ea (in the form of a bird) to their bedroom [Plate 15], and when Agni inter-
2 29a rupted them Pārvatī cursed the gods' wives to become barren as she was.
16c 44a Agni drank the seed of Śiva, and all the gods became pregnant with the seed
32ea 44e [Plate 9]. When they could bear it no longer, the seed was placed in the river
26e[1] Ganges [Plate 11], who threw it into a clump of reeds. There it was taken up
17c by the six Kṛttikās who bathed there, and from them Skanda was born
20ea [Plate 16].

D. 5. *The Value of Motifs and Variants*

The numbers in the margin are the key to an analysis which would
occupy many pages if translated into verbal form. To indicate how this
30e key may be used, I will expand only one motif, that of birds/wind/
30ea 30a snakes (30).

The motif first appears in its mediating form, that of a breeze, when
Kāma attacks Śiva, interrupting his *tapas*; here it clearly assumes an

erotic force. When Śiva reverts to his asceticism, his snakes reappear, and then the demon Āḍi becomes a snake to interrupt that asceticism. Finally, Agni takes the form of a bird to interrupt the love-play, an apparently anti-erotic act which in fact results in an erotic episode (the giving of Śiva's seed). In this way, one thread of the complex pattern may be traced, but the significance of the thread is revealed only by numerous details which have been omitted from this bare framework and which only become apparent when individual versions are compared. For example, snakes play an important role in some versions of the Pine Forest story; in one variant, Kāma appears as a bird in place of Agni; sometimes Kāma does not transform himself into a breeze. Moreover, the symbolism of birds and snakes is shown by a number of other myths more loosely connected with the Śaiva cycle, as will be evident from the index of motifs (Appendix F), and by non-mythological material cited in the course of the book. Variant myths are particularly necessary to establish the interrelationship of aspects of the motif, the manner in which birds, snakes, and the wind replace one another in different contexts and serve as links to introduce sub-episodes which bring out the submerged meanings of the central episodes.

Within each myth, the connection between motifs whose relationship is not obvious without the chart becomes clear from a glance at the marginal numbers. These numbers reveal the structural pattern of the myth, the repetition of themes and variations, the balance between different aspects of a single motif, the tension between episodes of eroticism and asceticism, the constant re-emergence of transitional motifs. This establishes the dialectic flux of the problem, the continual process of conflict, resolution, and new conflict.

E. THE NATURE OF MYTHOLOGICAL CONTRADICTION

E. I. *The Equivalence of Opposites*

In analysing the myth on its various levels, in seeking patterns and in seeking meanings within these patterns, it is necessary to rely upon a basic principle of equivalences: once a meaning has been found for a certain term (from explicit statements in a myth or within the background of Hinduism), that meaning can be applied to another term which is equivalent in function, or, conversely, if two identical or equivalent terms appear in apparently different contexts, a similarity in function may be sought. For example, the Vedic god Agni may be considered 'equivalent' to the aspect of Śiva as he appears in a modern

Hindu play, if it can be shown that they have identical functions in the two myths; or, if Agni appears in two apparently different myths, their 'equivalence' may be established through the uniformity of his behaviour. Even insignificant details may establish important correspondences in this way; the combination of ethnographic material and overlapping myths establishes, through minimal pairs and distinctive features, the pattern of variants and multiforms.

But 'equivalent' is a term that must be taken here in a rather special sense. The Sanskrit word '*vai*' which frequently connects two terms as a kind of emphatic copula cannot be read as an equals sign. 'Indro *vai* Rudraḥ', 'Rudro *vai* Agniḥ', 'Agnir *vai* Indraḥ'—if the terms are taken as literally equal, the algebraic formula cancels out everything and one is left with simple pantheism. '*Vai*' implies an affirmation of relationship, and it can include various relations: 'Kāmo *vai* Śivaḥ', 'sun *vai* fire', 'man *vai* wife'. As the latter implies, it can frequently signify an essential relationship of opposites, for these are, in the Hindu view, as closely correlated as the so-called identities; the statement 'fire is water' must be taken in this sense. But this opposition does not prevent the myth-maker from transferring qualities—and whole myths—from one god to another. In short, Hindu mythology treats correlative opposites as well as correlated identities as essential relationships, and this is the basis of the underlying pattern of the myths of Śiva. When the myth says, 'The eye is the sun', it does not mean 'for "eye" read "sun"'; the eye and the sun simply share certain essential qualities. In this way, each god shares several qualities with other gods and will replace them in certain situations. In the nature of these situations lies the key to the particular qualities symbolized by the god, and the character of the god as known from other myths will illuminate a particular situation in which he appears.

In this way, Śiva plays many roles, assuming the character of Brahmā or Agni or Indra or Kāma, yet he can only replace a god in a context in which his own nature belongs, assuming a characteristic which he already has. He does not change, but different aspects of his eternal nature are manifest from time to time, producing or receiving the forces which are the true dramatis personae of Hindu mythology. Thus Śiva may be the cause of lust, the enemy of lust, the death of lust, or all of these at once. His character is in *some* way connected with this force, and it is neither a contradiction nor a paradox to say that he is both the creator of Kāma and his enemy: 'Śivo *vai* Kāmaḥ'—there is something between them.

E. 2. *The Resolution of Mythological Contradictions*

Although the apparently contradictory strains of Śiva's nature may well have originated at different times and places, they have resulted in a composite deity who is unquestionably whole to his devotees. This is why the Hindus accept and glorify what an outsider might consider a meaningless patchwork, a crazy-quilt of metaphysics. Yet the paradoxes are occasionally as confusing to the Hindu as to the outsider, and this perplexity is often directly expressed by characters within the myths, as well as being indirectly evidenced by the myth-maker's frequent confusion of several myth components whose relationships are unclear to him.

In spite of this, one must avoid seeing a contradiction or paradox where the Hindu merely sees an opposition in the Indian sense—correlative opposites that act as interchangeable identities in essential relationships. The contrast between the erotic and the ascetic tradition in the character and mythology of Śiva is not the kind of 'conjunction of opposites' with which it has so often been confused. *Tapas* (asceticism) and *kāma* (desire) are not diametrically opposed like black and white, or heat and cold, where the complete presence of one automatically implies the absence of the other. They are in fact two forms of heat, *tapas* being the potentially destructive or creative fire that the ascetic generates within himself, *kāma* the heat of desire. Thus they are closely related in human terms, opposed in the sense that love and hate are opposed, but not mutually exclusive. Nevertheless, their apparent opposition on certain levels is often taken as the starting-point for a series of mediations within the myths, and as such *tapas* and *kāma* are dynamically opposed, acting against one another in spite of (or rather because of) their innate similarities.

Lévi-Strauss has said, 'It is the nature of myth to provide a logical model capable of overcoming a contradiction.' According to his analysis,

> The structure of myth is a dialectic structure in which opposed logical positions are stated, the oppositions mediated by a restatement, which again, when its internal structure becomes clear, gives rise to another kind of opposition, which in its turn is mediated or resolved, and so on.[101]

Thus one might postulate the thesis (Śiva is a yogi) and the antithesis 34a
(Śiva is the lover of Pārvatī). The synthesis, however, is more complex 36e
than appears to be the case with the cultures studied by Lévi-Strauss, for it involves the actual tempering of each of the first terms—that is, the realization of elements of *kāma* in *tapas* and of *tapas* in *kāma*—as

well as an interaction between them in so far as they *are* opposed. One statement of the synthesis of this particular opposition would be: Śiva's
27ea wife is a *yoginī* (the erotic *yoginī* being a mediating figure). This synthesis
8c then gives rise in turn to new oppositions: (her *tapas* is necessary in
19e 8d order for her to be able to bear his son/ her *tapas* is so great that it is
19a too dangerous for her to bear his son). Almost always, the different poles may be somehow incorporated in one another even before they are mediated. In this way, a great many of the Śaiva myths may be analysed in terms of Lévi-Strauss's oppositions and resolutions.

The mediating principle that tends to resolve the oppositions is in most cases Śiva himself. Among ascetics he is a libertine and among libertines an ascetic; conflicts which they cannot resolve, or can attempt to resolve only by compromise, he simply absorbs into himself and expresses in terms of other conflicts. Where there is excess, he opposes and controls it; where there is no action, he himself becomes excessively active. He emphasizes that aspect of himself which is unexpected, inappropriate, shattering any attempt to achieve a superficial reconciliation of the conflict through mere logical compromise. Mediating characters of this type are essential to all mythologies which deal in contradictions:

> 'Mediation' (in this sense) is always achieved by introducing a third category which is 'abnormal' or 'anomalous' in terms of ordinary 'rational' categories. Thus myths are full of fabulous monsters, incarnate gods, virgin mothers. This middle ground is abnormal, non-natural, holy.[102]

The erotic ascetic is precisely such an 'abnormal' and 'anomalous' figure. Śiva is particularly able to mediate in this way because of his protean character; he is all things to all men. He merely brings to a head the extreme and therefore least reconcilable aspects of the oppositions which, although they may be resolved in various ways on the divine level, are almost never reconciled on the human level.

E. 3. *The Failure to Resolve Mythological Contradictions*

It is the essential nature of the ambivalent mythological image to represent a reconciliation of oppositions which, 'in the factual and practical world, would seem impossible or immoral'.[103] This is the very *raison d'être* of the myth: 'The extreme positions are only *imagined* in order to show that they are *untenable*.'[104] In this way, the image of the married ascetic functions as a negative truth about one possible way of resolving the paradox at hand, and the image of Śiva, by expressing the extreme and therefore untenable position, illustrates the contradiction inherent in the social facts, the difficulty in human terms of reconciling conflicting moral injunctions.

The expression of contradiction is significant in itself, even without the possibility of resolution, for the problems are difficult to understand and to face, and the myth brings them to a level at which they can be confronted. Like the individual subconscious, myth expresses unconscious wishes which, being in some way inconsistent with conscious experience, cannot be expressed directly:

> All the paradoxes conceived by the native mind, on the most diverse planes: geographic, economic, sociological, and even cosmological, are, when all is said and done, assimilated [in Tsimshian mythology] to that less obvious yet so real paradox which marriage with the matrilateral cousin attempts but fails to resolve. But the failure is *admitted* in our myths, and there precisely lies their function.[105]

The psychological value of myth in neutralizing oppositions in behaviour has been analysed by A. M. Piatigorskii.[106] These considerations are particularly pertinent to the study of the Śaiva cycle, where, as will be pointed out below, compromise is consistently avoided and contradiction usually stressed and exaggerated. This tendency to increase rather than to minimize the distance between conflicting ideas is basic to Indian thought. In applying the structural method to the mythology of the Ṛg Veda, B. L. Ogibenin has pointed out the clearly emphasized oppositions in the structural concept of the cosmos, the recurrent statement that the contrasting cosmic elements should and must be kept separate.[107]

This world-view makes all the more acceptable the mythological statement of contradictions. Moreover, the tacit admission of failure is made possible by the facility which mythology has in disguising unpleasant facts. Emil Durkheim has spoken of myths which 'no doubt explain nothing and merely shift the difficulty elsewhere, but at least, in so doing, appear to attenuate its crying illogicality'.[108] The particular characteristic of mythology which carries out this masquerade is the very element of repetition which constitutes the basis of our analysis: 'The repetitions and prevarications of mythology so fog the issue that irresolvable logical inconsistencies are lost sight of even when they are openly expressed.'[109] Not only is repetition in one sense the cause of the smoke-screen, but it is in a more important sense itself caused by the necessity to produce such a screen. The collective 'message' of the myth is only split up into numerous incomplete fragments (variants and multiforms) in the first place because their collective statement is 'a necessary poetic truth which is an unwelcome contradiction'.[110] That is, many versions are necessary because no one version is willing to state the full paradox.

The inevitable failure to resolve the contradiction leads to an infinite series of quixotic attempts:

> Since the purpose of myth is to provide a logical model capable of overcoming a contradiction (an impossible achievement if, as it happens, the contradiction is real), a theoretically infinite number of slates [isolated interrelated themes] will be generated, each one slightly different from the others. Thus, myth grows spiral-wise until the intellectual impulse which has produced it is exhausted. . . . Mythical thought for its part is imprisoned in the events and experiences which it never tires of ordering and re-ordering in its search to find them a meaning.[111]

The myths make the Hindu aware of the struggle and of its futility. They show him that his society demands of him two roles which he cannot possibly satisfy fully—that he become a householder and beget sons, and that he renounce life and seek union with god. The myth shows the untenable answer arrived at by compromise—the forest-dweller with his wife—and suggests a solution finally in the re-examination of the nature of the two roles, of the presence of each in the other, so that a balance may be sought without any of the unsatisfactory accommodations necessary in real life. The myth makes it possible to admit that the ideal is not attainable.[112]

E. 4. *The Irrational Solution*: Bhakti

The ideas of the myth have parallels in philosophy and cult, the former expressing the ideas on an intellectual level, the latter on an emotional level. By combining the two, the myths infuse life simultaneously into concept and image, lending character to the processes and action to the images, thus strengthening the warp and woof of the drama: actors (cult images) and plot (philosophy). Certain contradictions which can otherwise only be resolved in the ultimate abstraction of philosophy are brought to the emotional and popular level by the myth, and for those problems which cannot be solved rationally at all, the myth utilizes the solution of irrational cult, allowing emotion to achieve what intellect cannot.

One irrational answer to the insoluble problem occurs in an explicit form at many points in the myths where reason is trapped: the excuse of *bhakti*, of devotion of the worshipper toward the god and of the god toward the worshipper, a compelling love which overcomes all rational barriers. Although this is a fairly late solution, it merely makes explicit a tendency which is implicit in the earlier versions as well: the tendency to appeal to the emotions to transcend a rational impasse.

Thus *bhakti* is used to justify the castration of Śiva in the Pine Forest:
'Hearing the curse of the sages, in order to show consideration for his
devotees, Śiva by his own wish caused his phallus to fall to the ground, 32a
and he pretended to be a little angry.'[113] *Bhakti* explains the transfor- 33ea[7]
mation of Śiva's ascetic ornaments into conventional ones: 'Showing his
pity for Menā [the mother of Pārvatī], and out of affection for his 23a
devotees, Śiva assumed a handsome form.'[114] *Bhakti* justifies both sides 28e
of Śiva's nature: in spite of the fact that love for a woman is ostensibly
incompatible with the goals of asceticism, Śiva is said to perform *tapas* 25ea[2]
in order to win the love of Pārvatī,[115] in order to keep the universe alive,
for the sake of his devotees, or simply as part of his (irrational) divine 33ea[7]
sport, *līlā*. Similarly, Śiva's sexual activity is rationalized in spite of his
ascetic commitments. After arguing against marriage for a yogi, Śiva
concedes to the gods: 'Nevertheless, I will do what you ask, for the
benefit of the world. Though the practice of marriage is not suitable for 19ea
me, as I delight only in *tapas*, nevertheless I will marry for the sake of
my devotees.'[116] Pārvatī herself says to Śiva, 'You are the best among
yogis, but out of pity you have become intent upon love-making.'[117] 19ea
It is pity alone that can transcend the austere logical purity of Śiva and
introduce a merciful sentimentality. Only the emotional involvement,
the pity of the gods, causes them to forget that they are above it all—
as metaphysics demands—and reduces them to the human level—as
mythology demands.

Even when logic can reconcile *tapas* and *kāma*, ascetic and householder, the desire to have it *both* ways remains. Śiva proves to Pārvatī
that there is no logical reason for him to have a son, as a mortal man must
have; she replies, 'What you say is true, but nevertheless I wish to have 19a
a child. I long for the kiss of a son's mouth.'[118] That 'nevertheless' is 19e
the mythopoetic and philosophical nexus of the cycle of countless
versions of myths, told and retold in an eternal search for the impossible
solution. The myth expresses the need that can never be fulfilled, that is
always just out of reach on one side or the other, even in the world of
the gods.

II

ASCETICISM AND EROTICISM IN EARLY INDIAN MYTHOLOGY

Śiva—or one of his prototypes, Rudra—is associated with asceticism in a late Ṛg Vedic hymn which describes an ecstatic figure clearly dissociated from the sacrificial cult, a forerunner of the later yogis:[1]

8c 9d The long-haired one sustains fire, poison, and the two worlds. . . . The
28ea 28a wind-clad [naked] sages wear yellow and soiled [clothes]. . . . Frenzied by
30ea asceticism we pursued the winds. You, O mortals, behold our bodies. The
13cd[1] 30ea sage . . . flies through the air. The horse of the storm, the only friend of the
14cd wind, the sage is impelled by the gods. He rules over both oceans, the Eastern
21ea and the Western. Moving in the path of the *apsarases* and *gandharvas* [celestial
13cd[2] nymphs and musicians], the path of the wild animals, the long-haired one is
9d aware of our call. The long-haired one drank a vessel of poison with Rudra.[2]

In addition to the actual use of Rudra's name, there are several clearly Śaiva elements in this hymn—fire, long hair (later to become the matted locks of the yogi), nakedness, the ochre robe and soiled garments, *apsarases*, wild animals (particularly horses), and, above all, the frenzy, so clearly antithetical to the ritual of conventional Vedic religion and so essential to later Śaivism.[3]

A. THE IMPORTANCE OF CHASTITY AND CREATIVE *TAPAS*

Chastity was characteristic of Indian asceticism from the very start.[4]
20a The Upaniṣads say that one may realize the Self by practising *tapas* in
18a the forest, free from passion.[5] A Purāṇa passage states: 'The 88,000
20e 18e sages who desired offspring went South and obtained graves, but the
18a 88,000 who did not desire offspring went North and obtained immor-
20a tality.'[6] Sexual excitement represented a threat against which the ascetic
must constantly be on guard. When Brahmā desired his daughter, he
25e lost all the *tapas* which he had amassed in order to create,[7] and a nymph
fell from heaven when she destroyed her *tapas* by falling in love with
25e a mortal man.[8] In a late version of the story of Viṣṇu's avatar as a boar,

Śiva appears in a characteristic role, that of the ascetic who rescues a man from the troubles arising from marital involvements:

Once long ago, when the Earth was in danger of drowning in the cosmic 14d
floods, Viṣṇu took the form of a boar and saved her. Śiva then said to him, 33ea[4]
'Now that you have accomplished the task for which you assumed the form
of a boar, you must abandon that form. The Earth cannot bear you and is 7d
becoming exhausted. She is full of passion and she has become heated in the 13c 12d
water. She has received from you a terrible embryo, who will be born as 19a
a demon harmful to the gods. You must abandon this erotic boar form.'
Viṣṇu agreed with Śiva, but he kept the form of a boar and continued to make
love to the Earth, who had taken the form of a female boar. Many years
passed, and the Earth brought forth three sons. When Viṣṇu was surrounded
by his sons and his wife he forgot all about his promise to abandon his body. 19e
The sons played together and shattered all the worlds, but still Viṣṇu did not 19a
stop them, for he loved them, and his passion for his wife grew greater and 19e
greater. Finally he remembered his promise and begged Śiva to kill him. Śiva 22ea
took the form of the marvellous *śarabha* beast and killed Viṣṇu and his three 33ea[4]
sons, and the essence of Viṣṇu was freed from the boar form.[9] 20a

Deluded by involvement with a woman and children, Viṣṇu finds himself unable to do what he knows to be right, and although he wishes to be free of his body—as the mortal sage wishes to escape from rebirth—he needs the help of Śiva, the great ascetic, to enlighten him.

Although in human terms asceticism is opposed to sexuality and fertility, in mythological terms *tapas* is itself a powerful creative force, a generative power of ascetic heat. In a late Ṛg Vedic creation hymn,
it is from *tapas* that the One is born, and the Atharva Veda *brahmacārin* 8c
creates by performing *tapas* in the ocean.[10] In the Brāhmaṇas, Prajāpati,
the Creator, assumes the *brahmacārin*'s role: 10d

Prajāpati was alone here in the beginning. He wished, 'May I exist, may 8c
I reproduce myself.' He exerted himself and performed *tapas*, and when he
was exhausted and heated the waters were created from him, for waters are 10d
born from the heated man. The waters said, 'What is to become of us?' He 11c
said, 'You shall be heated.' They were heated and created foam. . . .[11] 12d

The creative power of ascetic heat, particularly when placed in water, is the starting-point in all of these cosmogonic myths. From *tapas*,
Prajāpati proceeds to create fire, light, air, sun, moon, dawn, etc.[12] 8c

Another form of creation resulting from *tapas* and chastity is the production of rain. This theme developed from the Ṛg Vedic identification of rain with the sweat produced by ritual activity (the waters born from
'the heated man') and from the simple analogy of the shedding of seed 11c
and the shedding of rain, also found in the Ṛg Veda.[13] Indra, leader of 15c

the Rudras and a fertility-god in his own right, is said to derive his
15c cosmic forces from rain, which is stored in the sperm of living beings.[14]
6c Upon cremation, some people enter the smoke of the pyre; they first
15c become clouds, then rain, then vegetables, and, if eaten, are at last
16cd emitted as sperm.[15] Agni, the Rudras, the Aśvins, and Indra are all
closely connected with heat, as well as with the rain which it is their
12cd primary function to produce, because heat is needed to generate rain.[16]
This belief is naturally very compelling in a land where the monsoon so
dramatically shatters the intolerable heat of summer.

The motif of the seed as rain appears in an incident during the wedding of Śiva and Satī:

> 39e 36ea[2] Brahmā looked at Satī's face and was filled with lust. As he became excited
> 21e 43ea his seed fell upon the earth and turned into thundering clouds which covered
> 15c 38a[1] the sky, releasing their water. Śiva was looking at Satī and was fiercely
> 39a excited by Kāma, but nevertheless he raised his trident to kill Brahmā.[17]

A longer version of this story elaborates upon the nature of the clouds:

> 39e Brahmā lifted the veil from Satī's face and was overcome with desire. He
> 21e spilled four drops of his seed upon the ground like a mound of snow. Fearing
> 15c [Śiva's] *tapas*, Brahmā concealed the drops of seed with his feet, but Śiva
> 7cd[1] saw everything with his divine eye, and he said in anger, 'Evil one, you have
> 37e done a reprehensible thing, to gaze with passion upon the face of my bride
> 38a at my wedding. Did you think to deceive me?' At first he raised his trident to
> 39a kill Brahmā, but then, calmed by Viṣṇu, he instructed Brahmā to wander on
> 2 13d earth in human form, as expiation. Then Śiva said, 'These four drops of seed
> 20e 33ea[5] 25a will become the clouds of doomsday in the sky.' Immediately the seed became
> 15c the four doomsday clouds, roaring and releasing water, covering the sky.
> 14d Then Śiva was satisfied.[18]

B. THE SEDUCTION OF THE ASCETIC BY THE PROSTITUTE: ṚṢYAŚṚṄGA

It is the shedding of Brahmā's seed, rather than its retention in chastity,
that causes the rain, and indeed the simple physical analogy seems to
45a function best in this way. But in the philosophy of Hindu asceticism, it
15c is the chastity itself which generates the power to produce rain; the sage
Agastya uses his unspent *tapas* to cause Indra to send rain.[19] The ascetic
must remain chaste to generate *tapas*: this belief underlies the famous
myth of Ṛṣyaśṛṅga, which appears in several significantly different
versions in Indian literature.

Perhaps the oldest version of the story appears in two Buddhist Jātaka texts, the first of which entirely omits the rain motif and tells a fairly straightforward seduction myth:

> A Brahmin ascetic lived in the forest. A doe drank water mixed with his 16c
> semen, fell in love with him, and gave birth to a male child named Isisinga 20ea
> [Ṛṣyaśṛṅga, 'Antelope-horn']. When the boy came of age, his father warned 19a
> him against the wiles of women, initiated him into the practice of asceticism, 33ea^{4}
> and died. Isisinga practised such fierce asceticism that Indra, fearing that the 17d
> sage would depose him, sent the *apsaras* Alambusā to seduce him. When 45a
> Isisinga saw her, he immediately desired her and pursued her; she embraced 21ea
> him and his chastity was destroyed. For three years he made love to her, but 25e
> then he came to his senses and realized that he had neglected his duties. He
> gave up the path of desire, and he forgave and blessed the *apsaras*. When she 25a
> returned to heaven, Indra offered to grant her any wish, and she chose never
> to be made to tempt another sage.[20]

The seduction here is entirely unequivocal, as is the ultimate return to chastity, which in this version alone is made to include the *apsaras* as well as the sage. This is the classical pattern of the myth of the ascetic seduced by a prostitute, an important theme in Indian literature[21] 21ea
[Plate 5]. Indra appears as the enemy of the ascetic and causes his seduction; the sage returns to his meditation; the phases of chastity and sexuality alternate.

The second Jātaka text introduces the theme of drought and the secondary motif, common to most versions of this story, of the ascetic so innocent that he mistakes a woman for a man:

> Indra feared that the powers of a certain great sage posed a threat to him, 45a
> and so he sent an *apsaras* to seduce the sage, who shed his seed at the sight 21ea
> of her. A gazelle ate some grass and water mixed with the sage's seed and 21e
> became pregnant. She brought forth a son named Isisinga, who was raised 16c
> by the sage in seclusion in the forest. 19a
>
> Isisinga performed such great *tapas* that Indra was shaken and determined 45a
> to break down his virtue. For three years Indra sent no rain, advising the 15d
> king, 'Send your daughter Naḷinikā to break the virtue of Isisinga and it will 21ea 21a
> rain, for his fierce *tapas* has caused the rain to stop.' She went to him and 8d
> enticed him, and he thought her to be some marvellous ascetic. His virtue 33ea^{1}
> was overcome, his meditation broken off, and he made love to her. Then she 25e 27ea
> ran away from him, and Indra sent rain that day. Isisinga longed for Naḷinikā, 15c
> still thinking that she had been an ascetic, until his father realized from
> Isisinga's tale that a woman had broken his virtue. He told his son, 'This was 17d
> a female demon. You must always avoid them.' Then Isisinga returned to his 21a
> meditation.[22] 25a

The simple seduction by the *apsaras* is here transferred from the son to the father, while the episode of Isisinga has become a more complicated multiform, involving a princess. Yet the rain motif operates as a straightforward analogy; the ascetic's chastity is a *threat* to rain and fertility, not a source of it.

Other versions of the myth differ on several of these essential points. The *Mahābhārata* tells the story in a yet more elaborate form:

> 20e An *apsaras* was cursed to become a female deer and to remain in this form
> 33ea[4] until she bore a son to a sage. One day the sage Vibhāṇḍaka, the son of
> 19e 21ea 20a Kaśyapa, caught sight of another *apsaras* and shed his seed. The female deer
> 21e 20ea 16c 33ea[4] drank his seed and bore Ṛṣyaśṛṅga, who had a horn on his head.
> 15d Years later, a certain king transgressed against a Brahmin, and so Indra
> 21a sent no rain in his land. The king's ministers advised him to bring to the palace
> 15c the sage Ṛṣyaśṛṅga, who had lived in complete chastity in the forest all his
> 21ea 33ea[1] life and had never seen a woman. They said, 'If Ṛṣyaśṛṅga may be enticed and
> 27ea 45a lured into your kingdom, Indra will send rain immediately.' The king sent
> 16d a prostitute to the forest, and Ṛṣyaśṛṅga, thinking her to be a new, delightful
> 28e 28a sort of ascetic, invited her to perform *tapas* with him. She served him and plied him with garlands, drinks, and embraces, until he was overpowered with love for her, emotionally aroused, and maddened with passion. When he described to his father the qualities of this 'ascetic', 'his' beautiful 'rosaries' (garlands) and 'matted locks' (long hair perfumed and bound with gold), his
> 17d father warned him against such demons. Nevertheless, the young sage took advantage of his father's temporary absence and followed the prostitute to
> 15c the women's quarters of the palace, and the rain fell. The king gave his
> 19ea daughter, Śāntā, to Ṛṣyaśṛṅga in marriage.
> 8d When Vibhāṇḍaka returned and saw that his son had gone, he became
> 23a furious and went to the palace to burn the king with his *tapas*. The king, how-
> 13d ever, having foreseen the wrath of Vibhāṇḍaka, had given much land and
> 19e cattle to Ṛṣyaśṛṅga, and when Vibhāṇḍaka saw his son's wealth he was paci-
> 19ea fied. He said to Ṛṣyaśṛṅga, 'When a son is born, let the two of you come to
> 27ea the forest.' Ṛṣyaśṛṅga agreed, and later he returned to the woods, with his wife Śāntā, to become a forest-dweller.[23]

In this version, Ṛṣyaśṛṅga is responsible not for the drought but for the rain, which he produces by his steadfast chastity rather than by allowing himself to be seduced. (Another cause of the drought must then be postulated, the king's vague 'transgression against a Brahmin'.) The Epic states that Ṛṣyaśṛṅga's purity and chastity gave him the power
15c to bring the rain,[24] and although the prostitute embraces him, she does not actually seduce him. Even when he is overcome by her charms, he mistakes her for an ascetic. (Similarly, in a closely related version of the
33ea[1, 4] tale, Ṛṣyaśṛṅga remarks that the 'ascetic' has two lovely horns on 'his'
27ea chest, round and very pleasant to touch,[25] thus mistaking the prostitute not only for a yogi, but for a beast/ascetic like himself.) This is the ascetic viewpoint reduced to the absurd.

Other versions support this latter attitude, that Ṛṣyaśṛṅga remains chaste and that his mere presence causes the rain. A king to whom the tale is told asks, 'Tell me why Indra, out of fear of that wise child 15c 15d 45a
[Ṛṣyaśṛṅga], sent rain when there had been a drought.'[26] Another text remarks, 'When Ṛṣyaśṛṅga came to the city, Indra, out of fear of him, sent much rain'; and a later tradition maintains that, when Ṛṣyaśṛṅga was twelve years old, Śiva and Pārvatī bestowed upon him the ability 45a
to destroy drought within 144 miles of his abode.[27] In these stories, Ṛṣyaśṛṅga either explicitly remains chaste or is seduced in such vague 15c 15d
and euphemistic terms as to leave the question unresolved.

On the other hand, there is much to suggest that Ṛṣyaśṛṅga is in fact seduced, and that it is his fall from chastity, rather than his unbroken chastity, that brings the rain. Even in the *Mahābhārata* he must be 'enticed' rather than summoned by royal command in order for the rain to fall, and he is so overpowered with love for the prostitute that he in no way resists her enticements but follows her to the palace. The myth may be the reworking of a generation rite in which sexual union actually took place, the union itself causing the rain.[28] This pattern works on the principle of sympathetic magic, and it is substantiated by several other versions of the story in which, as in the second Jātaka tale, it is Ṛṣyaśṛṅga's *tapas* that causes the drought, and his seduction that ends it:

> [One day when Ṛṣyaśṛṅga was carrying a pitcher of water, rain fell in such 14d
> torrents that the pitcher broke. In anger, Ṛṣyaśṛṅga cursed the gods to send 3
> no rain for twelve years. Famine arose, and the priests told the king, 'This 15d
> drought is due to the anger of a sage. If his *tapas* is destroyed, Indra will send 8d
> rain.' The king sent his daughter, Śāntā, to Ṛṣyaśṛṅga, who gave himself up 45a
> to pleasure with the woman, and his magic power vanished. Rain fell. Śāntā, 21ea
> having conquered the sage with love, brought him to the king, who gave her 25e
> to him as his wife.][29] 15c 19ea

Not only is the seduction absolutely clear, but its effect is unmistakable: Ṛṣyaśṛṅga loses his magic powers to produce *drought*. A Chinese Buddhist version of the myth emphasizes these aspects:

> [The sage Ekaśṛṅga [Ṛṣyaśṛṅga] had obtained the five supernatural faculties 8c
> [*abhijñās*]. One day when the rain had made the ground slippery on the 14d
> mountain where he lived, the sage slipped and fell; and, since he had the
> feet of a deer and was clumsy, he injured one of his feet. Irritated, he used 33ea[4]
> a magic formula to prevent the Nāgas from sending rain for twelve years. 8d
> A great famine arose, and the king of Benares proclaimed, 'If anyone can 15d
> make this hermit fall from his five supernatural faculties and become an 25e
> ordinary subject, I will give him half of my kingdom.' . . . Śāntā, a courtesan,
> took 500 of her women to the forest, where they plied the sage with wine and

16d 'pills of joy'. They all bathed together, and when the women touched him,
17c Ekaśṛṅga conceived sensual desires in his heart. He lost all of his supernatural
25e 21ea faculties, and rain fell from the sky for seven days and seven nights.][30]
15c

The king realizes that the drought will cease when the sage can be made to become 'an ordinary subject', and so it does.

The antiquity and authenticity of this version has been challenged on the grounds that it is 'strange' that the sage *prevents* the rain, since then it would suffice (for the king's purposes) to have him seduced, and it would not be necessary to lead him back to the city.[31] (At the end of the Chinese version cited above, the king states explicitly that, as the drought is over, the sage need no longer dwell in the city, thus admitting the superfluity of the motif of leading the sage to the city in that particular version.) In fact, although it is sometimes stated that Ṛṣyaśṛṅga must be brought to the city,[32] more often this is *not* required: the rain falls after he is seduced, before he enters the city, and in the Jātaka tale (where the seduction is most clear) the rain falls when Naḷinikā enters the city alone.[33]

Moreover, in the majority of texts, the sage is obviously seduced.
21ea Even the *Mahābhārata* remarks, 'Tell me how Śāntā filled the deer-
born one with lust',[34] and other texts revel in the details of the seduction: 'She kissed him and pressed her breasts against him, and the foolish Ṛṣyaśṛṅga reached the summit of passion. . . . Several lovely women of equivocal character gradually initiated the unsophisticated young Rishi in the pleasures of the world.'[35] The Chinese pilgrim Hsüan Tsang told the story, as he heard it in Northern India in the seventh century A.D., in brief but unambiguous terms:

21ea [Ekaśringa Rishi . . . being deceived by a pleasure-woman, lost his spiritual
25e 22a faculties. The woman, mounting his shoulders, returned to the city.][36]

Another Chinese text retains this proof of the woman's power over the sage and implies that he becomes addicted to aphrodisiac drugs as well:

[Śāntā gave Ekaśṛṅga pills of joy composed of a multitude of medicinal
16d plants, and he thought that they were fruits. . . . When it had rained for seven days and nights, there were no pills left, and when the sage began to eat ordinary fruits again he did not enjoy their taste and he longed for the other 'fruits'. Śāntā told him that he could have more of the pills if he went with her to a place near by; he agreed, and she led him to the city. On the way, she said that she was too tired to go on, and he said, 'If you wish, you may ride
22a astride on my neck.'][37]

Even in those versions which hesitate to describe the actual fall of Ṛṣyaśṛṅga, the seduction of his misogynist father is narrated:

[A certain sage was urinating into his ablution bowl when he caught sight
of a pair of deer coupling. Sensual thoughts arose in him and his seed fell 44ea
into the bowl. A female deer drank the seed and became pregnant, giving 21e
birth to a human child with the horn and feet of a deer.][38] 16c 33ea[4] 20ea

Merely the sight of coupling deer excites the sage in this text, but other versions introduce more traditional motifs which provide a clear multiform of the seduction of the son:

[The sage Vibhāṇḍaka performed *tapas* for 3,000 years, until flames [arising 8d
from his *tapas*] penetrated Indra's heaven and seriously disturbed the gods. 45a
Indra sent Urvaśī ('the head of celestial frail beauties') to the sage, who was 21ea
'deeply smitten with the celestial nymph' when he went to bathe in the river. 17c
A doe unknowingly drank the water, became pregnant, and gave birth to 16c
a human male child with two horns.][39] 33ea[4] 20ea

In this version, which later actually describes Ṛṣyaśṛṅga's seduction, that of his father is told in unusually euphemistic terms. The two episodes thus seem to vary inversely, one appearing in stronger terms as the other is weakened. That they are variants on a single theme is apparent from the identical cause of both seductions: the excess of the sage's *tapas* threatens Indra.

Other facets of the father's behaviour fit remarkably well with certain characteristics that the pattern of the myth would lead one to expect in the son:

When the drought came and the king wished to have his courtesans bring 15d
Ṛṣyaśṛṅga to the court, they feared to do so, lest Vibhāṇḍaka become furious 8d
and burn all of them with the flame from his eye. The king promised to 7cd[1]
propitiate Vibhāṇḍaka. . . . When Ṛṣyaśṛṅga had come, the king gave his 19ea 23a
daughter, Śāntā, to him, fearing the arrival of Vibhāṇḍaka. Vibhāṇḍaka
arrived, furious, to burn the king with the fire of his anger, which blazed
forth from his two eyes and his mouth. But as he began to burn everything 13cd[3]
up, the king sent Ṛṣyaśṛṅga and his wife to him, and they persuaded him to 13d
become calm.[40] 13c

The father here displays the classical behaviour of the ascetic who falls in love with a princess, is rejected by her father, and threatens to burn the king with his *tapas* unless he is given the princess in marriage. The destructive *tapas* which causes drought here becomes a more directly destructive fire. The usual cause of the ascetic's fiery anger is reversed on the explicit level (he burns the king because the princess *has* been married to his son), but the pattern reveals the implicit cause: he is calmed when he sees that the princess has been married. Since in this context the son functions as a multiform of the father, the father's behaviour follows the course that one would expect if it were he to whom the princess had been given. This method of calming the angry sage is far more significant than the method described by the *Mahābhārata*, in which the sage is forestalled when he sees all the wealth that the king has given his son.[41] The multiform of the father also suggests a cause of the ambiguous identity of the seductress in various texts: originally, it would seem, she was the king's daughter (Śāntā or Naḷinikā) but later she appears as a courtesan, who seduces Ṛṣyaśṛṅga and then brings him back to marry the princess. The duplication of the seductress, together with the duplication of the sage/father, has arisen from the combination of two closely related but inverted themes: (1) The sage (the active son) falls in love with the princess and uses his *tapas* to obtain her, and (2) The sage (the passive father) is seduced by a prostitute and thereby loses his *tapas*. These two themes are constantly combined and confused throughout the mythology of Śiva, where they account for many apparent ambivalences in his relationship with Pārvatī.

A further complication is introduced when Vibhāṇḍaka is sometimes
pacified not by his son's marriage but rather by what at first appears to
19e be the reverse: by Ṛṣyaśṛṅga's promise that he will return to the forest
after he has begotten a son.[42] This condition provides a resolution of
the two aspects of Ṛṣyaśṛṅga's chastity—his ability to remain chaste/
cause drought and his ability to induce fertility/cause rain. The importance of this latter quality is evident from the *Rāmāyaṇa* version
25ea3 of the myth, which introduces the episode with the statement that
19e Ṛṣyaśṛṅga was summoned in order to perform a sacrifice for King
Daśaratha to obtain a son,[43] an indication of the sage's procreative
powers. In fact, one Buddhist version states that Ekaśṛṅgī was sent for
not in order to prevent a drought but simply in order that he might
19e marry Nalinī (*sic*) and preserve the lineage of the king.[44]

In those versions which emphasize the drought, however, no such marriage need take place:

25e 21ea [After the courtesan Śāntā had brought him to the city, the king ordered
him to remain there, treating him with respect, satisfying all his desires, and
making him one of his ministers. But after some time, Ekaśṛṅga began to pine
away; he dreamed of the contemplative calm of forest life and was tired of the
24e desires of the world. He said to the king, 'Though I have satisfied my five
desires, I dream always of the forest life.' The king said, 'My primary aim
was to end the calamity of drought; why should I do violence to a man by
removing him from that which he wishes to have?' Ekaśṛṅga returned to
25a his mountain, perfected himself, and recovered his five supernatural faculties.][45]

Having first caused the drought and then removed it, the sage returns to his asceticism; the incident with the courtesan is a mere episode. In most of the texts, the ascetic nature of the sage prevails, and he abandons his wife and returns to his *tapas*.[46] According to the *Rāmāyaṇa* and *Padma Purāṇa*, however, he remains with Śāntā and does not return to the forest, while the *Mahābhārata* suggests a compromise of considerable significance in the context of the Indian ascetic paradox: 19ea
Ṛṣyaśṛṅga returns to the forest, but with his wife.[47] (It will be noted 27ea
that even when the father demands that Ṛṣyaśṛṅga return to the forest, he does not specify that he should leave his wife behind.) In this way, Ṛṣyaśṛṅga reconciles the conflicting aspects of his nature by taking refuge in the forest-dweller stage of life, a compromise between asceticism and marriage. One Buddhist text adds yet another cycle: after
abandoning his asceticism to marry the princess, Ekaśṛṅga goes with 21ea 19ea
her to the palace; later he takes her with him to the woods, but he then 23e[2]
returns with her to the palace, and finally, after begetting many sons 27ea 23e[2]
and grandsons, he goes alone to the forest.[48] Sometimes the paradox is 18e 18a
exaggerated, Ṛṣyaśṛṅga's sexuality eventually rebounding and causing him to leave his wife:

> [After Śāntā had seduced Ṛṣyaśṛṅga, his magic powers vanished, the rain 21ea
> fell, and there was a good harvest. Śāntā brought Ṛṣyaśṛṅga to the palace and 25e
> they were married. Then Ṛṣyaśṛṅga began to make love to other women, and 15c 19ea
> Śāntā, jealous, hit him on the head with a shoe. Ṛṣyaśṛṅga thought, 'Why 23ea
> should I, who would not brook the thunder of the clouds, allow a woman to 22a
> make naught of me?' And he returned to his *tapas*.][49] 36a

The ambiguity in Ṛṣyaśṛṅga's attitude to his wife may be viewed in the light of the two overlapping patterns: as the sage enamoured of the princess, he stays with her; as the ascetic seduced by the prostitute, he abandons her.

Certain of the conflicts in Ṛṣyaśṛṅga may be illuminated by his mediating character as beast and man, a quality which may also connect him more closely with Śiva. That Ṛṣyaśṛṅga is part deer is stressed in every text; it is in fact his only invariable characteristic. Sometimes he has only one horn, sometimes two, sometimes the feet of a deer, as
well as the horn,[50] and he mistakes the breasts of the prostitute for two 33ea[4]
horns.[51] In iconography, he is often represented as having not only the horns but the entire head of a gazelle.[52] The sage's beast nature has important bearings upon his relationship with the prostitute/princess. Much of the Ṛṣyaśṛṅga story resembles the tale of Enkidu in the Gilgamesh Epic: Enkidu, whose mother was a gazelle, had lived in chastity

13cd[2] among the animals in the wilderness until a harlot was sent to tame him
so that he could become human and gentle enough to befriend Gilgamesh.[53] There may be a historical link between the myths of Enkidu
and Ṛṣyaśṛṅga, shedding considerable light upon the beast nature of
the sage, the element of sympathetic magic, the bringing of fertility and
rain, and the implication that the sage is performing asceticism due to
25a some former lapse from his vow.[54] The Hindu ascetic, like Enkidu, must
13cd[2] be 'tamed'.

The single horn of Ṛṣyaśṛṅga suggests a connection with the myth of
33ea[4] the unicorn, who can only be captured by a maiden.[55] It is interesting
to note in this context that the unicorn is an important motif on the
Indus Valley seals, while the two horns of the sage may be connected
with Śiva's aspect of Paśupati ('Lord of Beasts') as he appears on an
Indus Valley seal: horned, ithyphallic, and surrounded by animals.[56]
26ea Here again the Gilgamesh material is pertinent, for ties have been established between the Indus Valley and Babylonian civilizations. More generally, the horns of the beast-ascetic are indicative of his sexual powers:
horned animals (bulls, rams, he-goats, and deer) are noted for their
21a sexual vitality, and the horns on the ascetic's head symbolize the pro-
tuberance of the seed that he has drawn up through his spinal column.
14e[3] Śiva's horns are retained in later iconography in the form of the crescent
or 'horned' moon on his head and in his high-piled matted locks.

In addition to these iconographical hints, there are strong philosophical and structural ties between the myths of Ṛṣyaśṛṅga and Śiva.
45a In the tale of Ṛṣyaśṛṅga, as in the temptation of Śiva by Pārvatī (who is
36ea[2] sent by Indra),[57] there seems to be a very real ambiguity about the
success or failure of the seduction. The two myths are explicitly compared by Kāma, who has no doubts about either seduction:

> 43ea My command is never disobeyed even by people like Ṛṣyaśṛṅga, who had
> 1 never known sexual pleasure and didn't even know the difference between men
> 33ea[1] and women; yet Śāntā, whom he thought to be an ascetic, led the foolish boy
> to her father's house. How much more effective, then, will my powers be over
> 36e Śiva, who has tasted an excess of the pleasure of sexual satiation![58]

In fact, it is the combination of the two—the sage's original steadfastness
and his eventual surrender—that produces the desired result, but
different versions emphasize one aspect or the other to produce an
apparent paradox.

In several myths of ascetics and prostitutes, the ultimate purpose of
the encounter is to strengthen the ascetic's chastity. In one late myth,
a multiform of the primeval incest myth, the seductress is Mohinī

('The Enchantress'), the most famous of the celestial prostitutes who serve Indra:

> The *apsaras* Mohinī fell in love with Brahmā. After performing *tapas* and
> gaining the assistance of Kāma, she went to Brahmā and danced before him, 25ea[1]
> revealing her body to him in order to entice him, but Brahmā remained with- 31e
> out passion. Then Kāma struck Brahmā with an arrow, and Brahmā wavered 21ea 42a
> and felt desire, but after a moment he gained control. Then, recognizing 41ea
> the work of Kāma, he cursed him, even though Kāma was his son, saying, 41e 41a
> 'Because of this insult to your parent, your pride will be broken.' Kāma went 3
> away in fear, and Brahmā said to Mohinī, 'Go away, Mother; your efforts are 27a
> wasted here. I know your intention, and I am not suitable for your work. The
> scripture says, "Ascetics must avoid all women, especially prostitutes." I am 25e
> incapable of doing anything that the Vedas consider despicable. You are
> a sophisticated woman; look for a sophisticated young man, suitable for your
> work, and there will be virtue in your union. But I am an old man, an ascetic
> Brahmin; what pleasure can I find in a prostitute?' Mohinī laughed and said
> to him, 'A man who refuses to make love to a woman who is tortured by 22e
> desire—he is a eunuch. Whether a man be a householder or ascetic or lover, 29e 32a
> he must not spurn a woman who approaches him, or he will go to Hell. Come
> now and make love to me in some private place', and as she said this she
> pulled at Brahmā's garment. Then the sages bowed and said to Brahmā, 40e
> 'How is it that Mohinī, the best of the celestial prostitutes, is in your pres-
> ence?' Brahmā said, to conceal his shame, 'She danced and sang for a long
> time and then when she was tired she came here like a young girl to her father.' 27e 27a
> But the sages laughed, for they knew the whole secret, and Brahmā laughed 39e
> too. Then Mohinī became angry and she said, 'Brahmā, you are the creator
> of the Vedas, but you desired your own daughter. How then can you laugh 1
> at a dancing-girl? I am a celestial prostitute, created by Śiva. Since you have 37e
> laughed at me out of pride, Viṣṇu himself will soon break your pride.' Then 3
> Mohinī went quickly to the palace of Kāma, and there she made love with
> Kāma and was freed of the fever of her passion. When she had regained her 24e
> senses, she wept with remorse, and Brahmā sought refuge with Viṣṇu, who
> enlightened him and broke his pride.[59]

Ignoring, for the moment, the many themes taken from the major Śiva myths, one may say that the purpose of this seduction—after the most immediate purpose, to satisfy the desire of Mohinī—is simply to teach Brahmā a lesson, to break his pride and remind him of his carnal nature. This is frequently the explicit purpose of such incidents, especially when Śiva is involved, as he is here and (also accompanied by Mohinī, in some versions) in the Pine Forest.[60] The ascetic must acknowledge his weakness. Thus, after the ancient Mahāvrata ritual of the prostitute and the *brahmacārin*, the prostitute must say to her partner, 'You who have misbehaved! You who have violated your vow of continence!' adding insult to injury.[61]

Except in the more ribald versions, and sometimes even there, the ascetic learns something of value from his contact with the woman of the world. The necessity for a prostitute as the partner of the ascetic is not merely the result of the metaphysics of the conjunction of opposites, but is in part a consequence of the simple logistics of the necessary plot. After his experiences with the woman, the ascetic must be free to return to his yoga, in order to avoid the problems attendant upon the combination of asceticism and marriage. The one woman who can allow him to do this is the prostitute, who is sexually free just as he is, moving below the morals of conventional Hinduism just as he moves above them. It is she who reminds the ascetic of the need to participate in the world of the flesh as well as the world of the spirit.

C. CHASTITY AND THE LOSS OF CHASTITY: AGASTYA

In the attempt to combine and give full value to the experiences of the two worlds, the myth of Ṛṣyaśṛṅga comes to terms with a problem central to Hindu mythology: both chastity and the loss of chastity are necessary for fertility. The earliest expression of this conflict appears in a hymn of the Ṛg Veda, a dialogue between the sage Agastya and his wife Lopāmudrā:[62]

1. [*Spoken by Lopāmudrā*]: 'For many years I have exhausted myself and
22e now I have become old. Age wears away the beauty of bodies. Men should
27ea go to their wives.' [Sāyaṇa, the commentator, notes that the wives also
practise *tapas*.]
2. [*Spoken by Lopāmudrā*]: 'The pious sages of ancient times, who conversed
about sacred truths with the gods, ceased [from the performance of *tapas*]
for they did not find the End. [*Commentator*: Without achieving success in
8d *brahmacarya*, they died.] Women should go with their husbands.'
18e 3. [*Spoken by Agastya*]: 'Not in vain is all this [ascetic] toil, which the gods
22ea encourage. We two must undertake all struggles. By this we will win the
race that is won by a hundred artifices, when we unite together as a pair.'
25ea[3] [*Commentator*: 'We will win the battle of sexual intercourse when we procreate in the proper way'—in this way he accedes to the sexual union that
she spoke of.]

[Ritual intercourse may have taken place here.][63]

4. [Here there are two significantly different possible interpretations]:
45e[2] (*a*) [*Spoken by Lopāmudrā*]: 'Desire for the bull who roars and is held back
24ea[2] [*Commentator*: He holds back his seed as he practises chastity] has over-
21a come me, coming upon me from all sides.' OR:
26e[1] (*b*) [*Spoken by Agastya*]: 'The desire of my swelling reed [i.e. phallus],
26ea which is held back, overwhelms me, coming upon me from all sides.'[64]

[*Spoken by* (*a*) *the poet or* (*b*) *Agastya*]: 'Lopāmudrā entices the man; the
foolish woman sucks dry the wise man.' 25e
5. [*Agastya*]: 'By this Soma which I have drunk, in my innermost heart $14c^2$
I say: Let him forgive us if we have sinned, for a mortal is full of many 25a
desires.'
6. [*The poet*]: Agastya, digging with spades, wishing for progeny, children,
and strength, nourished both paths [*Commentator*: *kāma* and *tapas*], for he 18ea
was a powerful sage. Among the gods, he found fulfilment of his desires.

In this complex and intriguing hymn, Agastya's position is unclear and yet crucial. Lopāmudrā (whose name, significantly, means 'Breaker of the Seal'), seduces him eventually, but it is not clear whether he merely yields to her desire (as indicated by the first interpretation of the fourth verse), or actively desires her (as suggested by the second interpretation). A traditional Indian exposition favours the second interpretation:

> The sage began, from desire of secret union, to talk to his wife, the illus- 17c
> trious Lopāmudrā, when she had bathed after her period. With the two 22e
> stanzas she expressed what she wished to do. Then Agastya, desiring to make 22ea
> love to her, satisfied her with the two following stanzas.[65] $24ea^2$

The statement that Agastya himself desires the union seems to be based upon the third and fourth verses; Lopāmudrā merely convinces Agastya to abandon his chastity sooner than he had intended. Yet the verse of expiation seems to indicate that Agastya experiences a certain remorse at having been persuaded to violate his vow, and it may be noted in this
context that the *brahmacārin* who spills his seed expiates this sin with $14c^2$
Soma juice (a multiform of the spilt seed), just as Agastya does.[66] The 25a
poet speaks with disdain of the foolish woman who sucks the wise man dry, an instance of the traditional misogyny of the Indian ascetic tradition, but he also notes that Agastya found strength and power by nourishing both paths, chastity and sexuality. Agastya speaks several
times of the need for progeny, while Lopāmudrā's wishes are purely 29e
sensuous;[67] here, as often in Indian mythology, sexuality and fertility are combined, even confused, but either or both may be unambiguously contrasted with asceticism, the second path. The hymn speaks of sin and expiation, but it speaks too of the winning of the race and the fulfilment of desire among the gods.

In the *Mahābhārata* version of the myth of Agastya, the sage desires to break his vow of chastity and in fact has difficulty in persuading Lopamudrā (*sic*) to break *her* vow:

> The chaste sage Agastya was asked by his ancestors to marry and produce 18e

19e offspring to perform the death rites for them in perpetuity. Agastya created
8c a beautiful woman whom he caused to be born as the daughter of the king of
Vidarbha, named Lopamudrā. When Agastya asked the king for her, the
23a king was unwilling to give her to him, but then Agastya threatened to burn
8d everything with the power of his *tapas*, and Lopamudrā herself asked to be
24ea[2] 28a given to Agastya. He then asked her to discard her ornaments and to dress
27ea herself in rags, bark clothes, and deer-skins; then they practised *tapas* to-
4 gether. When he saw her shining with her *tapas*, the sage asked her to make
28a love with him, but she said, ashamed, 'I will not approach you dressed in the
28e rags of asceticism, for this ochre robe must not be made impure in any way.
25e But dress me and yourself in heavenly ornaments, and I will come to you.'
He argued that if he used his powers of *tapas* to obtain riches it would destroy
his ascetic powers, but she was adamant. After various adventures, Agastya
19e succeeded in fulfilling the conditions, and Lopamudrā bore him a great son.[68]

Elements of the Ṛṣyaśṛṅga tale may be seen here: the princess comes to the ascetic at the command of her father, to avoid a curse (here the threat of *tapas* replaces the drought of the Ṛṣyaśṛṅga tale); she performs asceticism with him. The force of the Vedic hymn of Agastya is retained, although the roles are somewhat reversed.

The pattern of the myth of Agastya is essential to an understanding of the myth of Śiva and Pārvatī. The continuity of the tradition is demonstrated by such stories as the tale of Diti and Kaśyapa, composed two millennia after the Vedic hymn of Agastya but preserving elements of that hymn as well as other harmonious Śaiva themes:

Diti, the daughter of Dakṣa [and therefore a sister of Satī], married the
sage Kaśyapa [one of the Seven Sages, like Agastya]. Once when she was full
22e of desire she asked him to make love to her, for she wished for children, but
19e he was performing the sunset worship of Śiva and he asked her to wait until
35a he had completed his devotions. Her senses were whirled about with desire,
21ea and she grabbed at his clothing like a prostitute. When he realized that she
was set upon this evil action, he made love to her; afterwards he touched water
22ea 25a and muttered a prayer [of expiation]. Then Diti was ashamed of her sin, and
she begged Kaśyapa to make sure that Śiva, in anger at her offence [inter-
35a rupting his worship by the impure act of intercourse], would not destroy the
36a unborn child. Kaśyapa, whose sunset worship had been interrupted now for
3 the second time, cursed her in his impatience, promising her two wicked sons.
2 19a She begged him to relent, and he modified his curse by promising her a vir-
19e tuous grandson, and she was satisfied.[69]

Imposed upon the traditional elements of seduction, expiation, and tentative resolution (here in the form of ambiguous offspring—first evil, then good), there appears the character of Śiva in his ascetic aspect, both as the god whose worship is in conflict with the begetting of the child, and—through the medium of the common father-in-law, Dakṣa—as the ascetic himself, seduced by his wife. The myth expresses in various ways the conflict between the two paths, chastity and procreation.

D. THE EROTIC POWERS OF THE ASCETIC

In the *Mahābhārata* reworking of the Agastya hymn, Lopamudrā stirs her husband's passion when she becomes a female ascetic (a role which, according to Sāyaṇa, she plays in the Vedic hymn). In the earlier version, Agastya excites her when he practises asceticism: 'She desires the bull who is held back.' In either case, the force is clear and psychologically valid: the ascetic, whose chastity generates powers of fertility, becomes an object of desire, in part merely because he is taboo:

> A Brahmin woman, widowed in her childhood, took a vow of chastity and 27ea
> performed great *tapas*. A demon named Mūḍha ['The Fool'] came there and
> saw the beautiful young woman, and he was overcome by the arrows of Kāma.
> He displayed his lust and wished to make love to her, but she was intent on
> meditation upon Śiva and as she delighted only in *tapas* she did not shed
> a lustful glance upon him. Thus disdained, he threatened her, and in terror
> she cried out to Śiva to protect her virtue. To protect and delight her, Śiva
> appeared there and reduced the lovesick demon to ashes. Then he granted 43a
> her the boon of eternal devotion.[70]

Here again Śiva appears in his anti-erotic form to defend the *tapasvinī* against the seducing demon. But, in another context, he is himself the one who tries to turn the *tapasvinī* (Pārvatī) from *tapas* to marriage, sometimes even employing the argument antithetical to the concept of the erotic *yoginī*—the statement that *tapas* will make her charm disappear and her body waste away,[71] as Lopāmudrā also complains.

In spite of the element of 'forbidden fruit' which characterizes this
motif, the appeal of the ascetic is best understood in terms of powers
rather than of morals. 'The yogin becomes as strong and beautiful as
a god, and women desire him, but he must persevere in chastity; on 24ea^2
account of the retention of semen there will be generated an agreeable 21a
smell in the body of the yogin.'[72] By 'drawing up his seed', the yogi
preserves all his powers, particularly, of course, those that he is explicitly
restraining. Even in the *Kāmasūtra*, the textbook of erotic science and
hence ostensibly opposed to the ascetic establishment, this concept, so
basic to *all* Hindu thought, emerges: the successful lover is one who
has conquered his senses and is not excessively passionate; he obtains
his powers by *brahmacarya* and great meditation.[73] The chaste ascetic 24ea^2
is not only sexually attractive; he is sexually active. The Atharva Veda

26ea *brahmacārin* carries a great phallus along the earth and pours seed
21e upon the surface of the earth,[74] and ascetics appear throughout Hindu
mythology in creative and erotic roles.[75] The women of the Pine Forest
use their *tapas* as an erotic power, for when they are overcome with
passion for Śiva they say, 'You must consent to our desires, for we are
27ea female ascetics and we do what we wish, whether we are naked or
28ea clothed.'[76] In the Hindu lawbooks, a *brahmacārin* or *tapasvin*, in the
sense of one who has *completed* a vow of chastity, is said to be a par-
24ea[2] ticularly suitable bridegroom.[77] With this in mind, Nārada predicts
a husband for a princess whom he desires to marry: 'Your daughter,
O king, is greatly endowed; her husband will certainly be an uncon-
43a quered hero, like Śiva, the conqueror of Kāma.'[78] Though Nārada
clearly has himself in mind, he mentions characteristics considered ideal
in a husband. Since one of the most important requirements of a bridegroom is his virility (the purpose of marriage being to beget children),
24ea[2] the man of chastity is a good choice by virtue of the sexual powers
amassed by his continence.[79]

Tapas may be used not only to build up the ascetic's sexual powers but also to restore these and other powers after he has spent them in sexual activities. As a kind of expiation, therefore, his *tapas* promises future powers even while implying the possibility that he has already proved himself capable of employing those powers. The sage Kāpota makes explicit reference to this ability when he attempts to seduce Tārāvatī:

> 25e Tārāvatī said to Kāpota, 'You should not speak to me like this, for such
> an act would destroy your *tapas*.' Kāpota said, 'Whether or not the destruc-
> tion of my *tapas* or some other evil may befall me, I could not bear not to
> 24e make love to you. You must save me from Kāma or he will burn me, and then
> 43ea I will burn you with a curse.' And Kāpota thought to himself, 'After I have
> made love to her, I will release her from her marital sin by the power of my
> 25a *tapas*.'[80]

Kāpota's threat is a motif taken from the false ascetic who uses *tapas* as a pretext to gain sexual favours. The fire of *kāma* is fed by the fire of *tapas*, revealing the mutual destruction and restoration of the two powers.

A similar interchange takes place when Śiva demands from a king the
privilege of spending the night with the king's wife. When the king
25e protests, 'The evil amassed by an adulterer cannot be washed away by
25a a hundred expiations', Śiva replies, 'I can scatter with my *tapas* the sin
25a of brahminicide, so what is adultery to me? Give me your wife.'[81] For

this reason, the wanderings of Śiva as a Kāpālika, particularly in the 35ea
Pine Forest,[82] may be considered expiations for his well-known lust- 38a2
fulness as well as for the acts of violence which are their ostensible cause,
and his violation of the sages' wives is a re-enactment of the original
sin which forced him to undertake the expiation in the forest.[83] The
tradition of *tapas* as expiation thus contributes to the image of the erotic
ascetic by bearing witness to his erotic vulnerability. One text states
that Śiva must wander as a Kāpālika with a skull in his right hand to 38a2
replenish the powers lost by making love to Pārvatī.[84] Any *brahmacārin* 25e 25a
who has shed his seed in violation of his vow of chastity must put on the 21e
skin of an ass and go to seven houses, begging and proclaiming his mis- 25a
deed,[85] and a Brahmin who invites to his bed a woman other than his 23ea
wife must wander over the earth as a beggar.[86] The *brahmacārin* who 25a
seduces his guru's wife must spend a year wearing bark garments and 23ea
performing *tapas* in a lonely forest;[87] a similar expiation is prescribed 25a
for one who has accidentally committed incest or had relations with his 27e
stepmother.[88] A man should perform *tapas* if he feels lust,[89] a clear 25a
suggestion of the sexual nature of the ascetic; and if an ascetic makes
love to a woman because of lust, he must torture himself with yogic
breathing exercises, while another kind of breathing exercise, together 25a
with a fast, is prescribed for the ascetic who spills his seed by looking 21e
at a woman.[90] By the time of the later texts, purification is automatic: 16d
'One who drinks wine or makes love to the wife of another man or kills 23ea
a Brahmin or seduces his guru's wife is released from all sins by *tapas*.'[91] 25a
This is precisely the boast of Śiva to the king.

The paradox only arises when sexual powers are actually used by a man who is supposedly practising chastity *at that time*. Various solutions are offered on various levels: Hindu society divided the life-span into separate ages with a type of sexual activity appropriate to each; Śaiva mythology substitutes for this the principle of cycles alternating in a manner roughly parallel to the different 'ages'; another solution, applied in the mythology to common yogis as well as to Śiva himself, is to allow the ascetic to make use of his powers in various ways other than by the technical breaking of his vow. These solutions, none of them entirely satisfactory, will be discussed at length below.

E. THE REJUVENATION OF THE ASCETIC: CYAVĀNA

Just as the chaste *brahmacārin* may progress to the next stage, in which he marries and becomes sexually active, so the mythology depicts many

ascetics who move backwards in the life-cycle: the old ascetic, supposedly at the end of the four stages, past (or never having known) the
active period, is made virile again by virtue of his *tapas*. The Ṛg Veda
24ea[2] 18a hints at such a story: 'You Aśvins took away the mortal sheath from the
aged Cyavāna as if it had been a cloth. You extended the life of him
who had been cast off and you made him the husband of young women.
[The Aśvins] made the aged Cyavāna young again, and he fulfilled the
desire of his wife.' Other Vedic texts imply that the Aśvins or Agni
18a 10d rejuvenated the sage by means of his own *tapas* and by immersion in
32ea water.[92] (Similarly, the sage Āsaṅga, having been cursed by the gods
26ea 25a to turn into a woman, used his *tapas* to turn back into a man and to
stiffen his previously 'boneless' phallus, a transformation which greatly
pleased his wife.)[93] The hints of Cyavāna's rejuvenation are supported
by his Vedic epithet 'Seven Times Impotent' ('Saptávadhri').[94] Sāyaṇa's
explanation, however, implies that the sage was quite virile, and was
merely prevented from joining his wife:

23a The enemies of the sage had placed him in a box at night to keep him from
his wife. The sage was unhappy, and the Aśvins rescued him. He sported
22e with his wife, but then at dawn, afraid, he returned to the box and conceived
25a the hymn to the Aśvins.[95]

This ambiguous attitude to Cyavāna's potency persists in the Brāhmaṇas, which introduce a secondary motif central to the mythology of Śiva: the mocking of the ascetic:

When the race of Bhṛgus had reached heaven, one of them, Cyavāna, was
abandoned, having attained a senile form. One day the children of Śaryāta,
24a a king of the race of Manu, saw the senile body and, considering it worthless,
8d pelted it with clods of earth. Cyavāna was furious, and he created discord
23a among them. Disturbed, Śaryāta discovered the cause of this misfortune and
21ea took his daughter, Sukanyā ['The Fair Maiden'] to Cyavāna. He offered
19ea 13d her to him, Cyavāna was appeased, and the tribe became reconciled and at
peace.

27ea One day the Aśvins approached Sukanyā and wished to seduce her. They
35ea said, 'Why do you sleep with this senile body? Come with us.' She refused
24ea[2] to leave the man to whom her father had given her, and when Cyavāna
learned from her what had happened he told her how to get the Aśvins to
18a make him young again. She did this, and they told her to take her husband
10d into a certain pond; when he emerged, he was of the age that he desired.[96]

Another Brāhmaṇa tells the same basic story, but adds further details: Cyavāna had the divine knowledge of Rudra (Vāstupa); Cyavāna said, 'I will become young again, and I will find a young wife.' . . . the sons of Śaryāta smeared Cyavāna with dirt and dung; Cyavāna asked

Śaryāta for his daughter Sukanyā; the king, though unwilling, was per- 23a
suaded to give her to him; her brothers told her to run away from the 22a
old man; she was about to do so, but was prevented by the snake who 30a
dwelt in the pool; she remained there with Cyavāna until the Aśvins
came there; . . . the Aśvins entered the lake with Cyavāna and all of 18a
them emerged looking exactly alike, but Cyavāna told Sukanyā how to 33ea^2
recognize him.[97] This version explicitly connects Cyavāna with Rudra–Śiva, as well as with Śiva's phallic snakes, whose sloughed skins symbolize ascetic rejuvenation. In elaborating upon the earlier versions of the myth, this text emphasizes both Cyavāna's old age (for the girl's brothers, as well as the Aśvins, try to persuade her to abandon the 'old man') and his youth (for he determines to become young, and marry a young wife, even before he meets Sukanyā). She remains with him not out of filial devotion or wifely duty towards an old man, but because she realizes the erotic aspects of his asceticism (the snake in the pool).

The final motif—the identical appearance of Cyavāna and the Aśvins—appears in the *Mahābhārata* version:

> Cyavana [*sic*], the son of the great sage Bhṛgu, practised *tapas* by the side 10d
> of a lake. After many years he was entirely covered by an anthill. One day
> king Śaryāti [*sic*] came to the lake with his 4,000 wives and his daughter
> Sukanyā. When Cyavana saw her he rejoiced and was overcome with desire, 21ea
> although his powers of *tapas* were great. He spoke to her, but she did not hear
> him, and when she saw his two red eyes glowing through the anthill she 7cd^2
> was curious, and, saying, 'What is this?' she pierced his eyes with a thorn. 22a
> Cyavana, furious, put a curse on the soldiers of Śaryāti, to make them unable 8d
> to urinate or defecate. Upset, Śaryāti sought the cause of this affliction, and 23a
> Sukanyā told him what she had done. Śaryāti took her to Cyavana, who agreed 21ea
> to remove the curse if the king would give Sukanyā to him. The king gave his 13d
> daughter to the sage. 19ea
>
> After some time, the Aśvins saw Sukanyā when she had bathed, and when 17c
> she told them that she was the wife of Cyavana they laughed and said, 'How 24a
> could your father give a lovely girl like you to an old man far past the pleasures
> of desire? Leave that ascetic and choose one of us. Don't waste your youth.' 35ea
> But she replied, 'I am well satisfied by Cyavana.' Then they said to her, 'We 18a
> will make your husband young and handsome, and then you can choose
> between him and us.' She told her husband of this, and he agreed. The
> Aśvins told him to enter the water, and they entered with him; all three 10d
> emerged young and handsome, but she recognized Cyavana and chose him. 33ea^2
> Cyavana and Sukanyā made love together like two gods.[98] 36e

In these last two versions, the ascetic is first abused physically by the king's child and then reviled by the Aśvins; he curses the king first with mere strife and then with the more imaginative affliction invented by the

Epic bard. In later versions of this theme, the abuse, curse, and marriage are causally joined: it is the father of the girl (Dakṣa, for example) who reviles the sage and is cursed, and it is because of the sage's desire for the girl that he is abused. In the *Mahābhārata* text, it is significant that even before he is rejuvenated, Cyavana is (though senile) considered lustful and a satisfactory husband.

A later Purāṇa, however, reverses this premiss and emphasizes
Cyavana's asceticism, viewing him (as the Aśvins do in all versions) as
a totally unsatisfactory husband. The text follows that of the *Mahā-*
bhārata in essence, but it elaborates on certain significant points: Cyavana
27a does not desire the girl when he first sees her, but says, 'Go away, wide-
eyed one. I am an ascetic', and he denies that he cursed the king's army
because she had annoyed him and pierced his eyes. But then he continues:

7cd[2] 'Though I did not curse you, your unhappiness has arisen from the evil
that befell me when I was not at fault. Now I am blind and alone. How can
I perform *tapas*, and who will serve me? If you give me your daughter as
23a a servant, my welfare will result, and hence your troubles will cease.' Śaryāti
thought, 'How can I give my daughter to a blind, old, deformed man? If she
marries Cyavana and she is tortured by the arrows of Kāma, how will she
45a pass the time? When Ahalyā, who had youth and beauty, married the ascetic
1 Gautama she was quickly seduced by Indra and she was cursed by her husband for this transgression. Therefore I will not give my daughter to him.'
But Sukanyā herself offered to give herself to the sage, saying, 'I will serve
28e 28a the old ascetic. I have no desire for sensual enjoyments.' The king gave her
to Cyavana, the army was relieved, and all was well. The princess gave away
her royal garments and ornaments and put on bark garments and animal skins,
27ea in order to perform *tapas*. She said, 'Do not worry about having given me,
1 a young woman, to an old man. Just as Arundhatī serves Vasiṣṭha and Anasūyā
23a serves Atri, so I will be a faithful wife to Cyavana.' The king wept to see her
in bark garments, and he went home feeling very depressed.
27ea Sukanyā served Cyavana, performing *tapas* with him, and resisted the
24a advances of the Aśvins. They then offered to make her husband young and
10d handsome, and to restore his eyes. All three entered the water together and
emerged with equal beauty, but Sukanyā chose Cyavana. Then Cyavana,
7cd[2] having obtained beauty, youth, his eyes, and his wife, said to the Aśvins,
'You have done me a great favour. When I obtained this lovely wife I was
very unhappy, for I was blind, very old, and devoid of sensual enjoyments.
18a But you have given me youth, beauty, and sight.'[99]

Here it is made explicit that Cyavana is blinded by Sukanyā, and he uses the excuse of his eyesight to marry the girl, just as in other contexts the ascetic uses the fire from his eye as a more direct threat. The Aśvins, the physicians of the gods, cure his blindness as they restore his youth, and it is clearly stated that they grant him powers of 'sensual enjoyment' which he did not have before. Cyavana's impotence is further emphasized by the king's fear that the sage will not be able to satisfy Sukanyā sexually, an objection worded in terms very similar to Dakṣa's misgivings about Śiva. The ambiguity of the sage's actual nature remains in the Śiva myth: the apparently impotent ascetic usually has secret erotic powers of which only his wife is aware, but if he is in fact impotent, the faithfulness of his wife transforms him into a young lover. This is an enduring motif, and Cyavana and Sukanyā reappear in later Hindu mythology as Atri and Anasūyā (to whom Sukanyā refers), the epitome of the apparently senile ascetic and his faithful wife.[100]

A Tamil Śaiva text contains a myth which is striking in its parallels to the Vedic story of Cyavāna's rejuvenation:

[A certain potter once violated his marriage vows by making love to a 23ea
dancing-girl. His wife made him swear by the name of Śiva that he would 21ea
never touch any woman, not even her. Many years passed, and Śiva came to 27a
their house disguised as a Śaiva yogi in order to reveal to everyone how holy a 25a
person the potter was. The yogi demanded that the potter take hold of his wife 33ea[5]
and bathe in the sacred tank of the temple. The potter explained his sin and 35ea
subsequent vow, but as the yogi was adamant the potter satisfied him by 10d
taking hold of one end of a bamboo stalk while his wife held the other end. 26e[1]
They entered the tank together and arose from the water young. Śiva then 18a
revealed himself and made the potter a saint.][101]

It is interesting to note that it is a prostitute (dancing-girl) who initiates the process of rejuvenation, and also that a bamboo reed forms the life-line, as it does in so many of the Skanda birth stories.

Śiva participates in a different way in another version of the myth of the virtuous potter. Here Śiva himself is the husband, instead of the god, and is 'saved' from the water by the virtuous wife (Pārvatī), who thinks that she is violating her vow in order to save him, just as the potter technically violates his vow that he will not touch his wife:

When Śiva had burnt Kāma, Pārvatī performed *tapas* to obtain Śiva for 43a
her husband. After a while a *brahmacārin* came to the lake near her hermitage, 25ea[2]
and, in order to see her, he fell into the lake and cried out for help. As all of 33ea[5]
Pārvatī's friends rushed to save him, he said, 'Do not touch me. I would rather 10d
die than touch a woman who has not been purified by *tapas*.' Pārvatī had just 27ea
finished her vow of *tapas*, and she came there and offered him her left hand, 17c
which he rejected as impure. Pārvatī then said, 'I cannot give you my right
hand, for only Śiva may take it [in the marriage ceremony]. I swear this by
all my *tapas*.' Then the *brahmacārin* said, 'What haughtiness! You should 35ea
honour a Brahmin who is in mortal danger.' Pārvatī gave him her right hand

and drew him out of the lake. Śiva revealed his own form and grasped her
36ea[1] garment, saying, 'I am your slave, bought by your *tapas*. Command me.'[102]

This episode elaborates upon the theme of the temptation of the devotee's wife (Sukanyā/Pārvatī) by a god (Aśvins/Śiva). The holding of the hand, as in marriage, is a euphemism for a sexual encounter,[103] but the motif of immersion in water is a direct link with the theme of rejuvenation. Rejuvenation in water is more closely associated with the theme of rejuvenation through *tapas* in another brief myth:

10d A sage performed great *tapas* lying in the water, and the gods feared his
8d terrible powers. Agni sent five *apsarases* to the sage, who was overcome by
44ea 21ea lust and made them his wives. From then on, he lived happily with them,
17c 18a having obtained youth through his *tapas*.[104]

Although the sage is impeded in his asceticism, he offers no resistance and gives no curses, but simply turns his *tapas* to erotic uses.

1 One text offers as a specific parallel to the myth of Śiva and Pārvatī
the story of Pippalāda and Padmā, who are considered to be incarnations
of the god and his wife.[105] Pippalāda was born when a pregnant woman
6c mounted her husband's funeral pyre; another version states that he was
20ea born when a woman wearing the loincloth of her brother, stained with
17c his seed, bathed and became pregnant, whereupon, in fear of her hus-
33ea[6] band, she deposited the child at the foot of a fig tree (*pippala*), whence
26e[2] his name.[106] Both birth stories contain a number of motifs from the
Skanda myth, and Pippalāda is further assimilated to Śiva through
13cd[1] the motif of the submarine mare.[107] But the particular relevance of the
Pippalāda story is clearly illustrated by the manner in which it is cited
in order to convince Himālaya to give his daughter to Śiva:

Vasiṣṭha and the Seven Sages urged Himālaya to give his daughter to
23a Śiva, concluding, 'If you do not give her willingly, the wedding will take place
8d anyway, for Śiva promised to marry her, and his word can never be reversed.
You should give your daughter to Śiva in order to protect all your friends and
1 family, just as King Anaraṇya did.' Himālaya asked who this king was and
how he had averted disaster, and Vasiṣṭha told him this story:

27e 'Anaraṇya was a great king who loved his daughter, Padmā, more than his
hundred sons. When she was of marriage age, a great sage named Pippalāda
44ea happened to come across a *gandharva* making love with great skill to a woman
21ea in the middle of Pippalāda's hermitage. Seeing this, the sage was full of lust
17c and thought no longer of *tapas*. One day he went to bathe in the river and saw
24ea[1] Padmā there. Overcome by lust, he went to the palace and begged for Padmā
23a as alms. When the king hesitated, Pippalāda threatened to burn everything
8d to ashes. The king, grief-stricken, gave his daughter to the sage, handed his
19ea kingdom over to his sons, and went to the forest to do *tapas*. After a short time,
he and his queen died of sorrow.

'Then the aged Pippalāda took Padmā to his hermitage, where he lived
happily, doing *tapas*, without great lust, and Padmā served him devotedly.
One day Dharma saw her bathing, and he assumed the form of a magnificent 17c
young man, the very image of Kāma, adorned with precious ornaments, and 28e 35ea
he said to Padmā, in order to test the emotion of her heart, "You lovely, 33ea[5]
desirable, enchanting creature, you do not really shine properly in the pres- 24a
ence of that senile Pippalāda who takes pleasure only in *tapas* and looks
forward to old age, devoid of ardour. I am a master of the *Kāmasūtra*, the
lover of a thousand beautiful women, troubled only by the force of my desire.
Take me as your lover and leave your old husband." He dismounted from
his chariot and tried to take her, but she was faithful to her husband, and she
said, "Go away, you evil man. If you look upon me with lust, you will be
destroyed. How could I leave Pippalāda, whose form has been purified by 25e
tapas, to make love with you, a womanizer and a libertine? You will be 2
destroyed by the lust which causes you to speak to me in this way instead
of regarding me as a mother." Then Dharma was frightened, and, revealing 27a
his true form, he said, "Mother, I am Dharma, who considers every man's
wife to be his own mother. I have come to test you, not to mislead you."
Then she said, "Dharma, you are the witness of everyone's behaviour, so
how can you deceive me in order to know my mind?" Then Dharma said,
"You are a worthy and faithful woman, and I will therefore give you a boon
for your husband. Let him become a young man, a master of sexual pleasure, 18a
handsome, youthful for ever. Joined in marital bliss, you will both remain 24ea[2]
eternally young, and you will be the mother of ten great sons." Thus he 19e
blessed her, and thenceforth she knew constant pleasure in making love with
her young husband, and they experienced every joy.'[108]

The essential motifs are retained in a second version of this myth which begins in the same way but then introduces several modifications made necessary by the fact that in this version Pippalāda is explicitly an incarnation of Śiva, so that nothing to his discredit must be allowed. Thus he marries Padmā because of his love for her rather than his lust; King Anaraṇya does not go off to die in the forest; and when Pippalāda takes Padmā home the entire Dharma episode is omitted and the story merely concludes, 'There, though he was decrepit with old age, he lived with his wife, doing *tapas*, without great lust, and Padmā served him devotedly. Thus he sported with his young wife, becoming young through his power of illusion, and ten great sons, of great *tapas*, were born to them. Thus Śiva became incarnate to aid the world.'[109] By remaining steadfast in her chastity, despite the temptation of a god, the faithful wife transforms her ascetic husband into the very lover that she resisted, all the more virile by virtue of his asceticism.

E. W. Hopkins has remarked wisely upon the apparent paradox of this myth's persistence in India, where

to Brahman and Buddhist alike, the aim of man has not been rejuvenation but cessation from physical activity. But, on the other hand, it may be because of this very teaching that the tale was so well liked and preserved among the people, who had, perhaps, more human nature than either Brahman priest or Buddhist monk could eradicate.[110]

It is precisely this element of 'human nature' that asserts itself so strongly throughout Purāṇic mythology, even in the myths of priests and monks.

F. SEXUAL PLEASURES AS THE REWARD FOR ASCETICISM

THE FALSE ASCETIC

The rejuvenation motif is merely a variation of the basic Hindu division
into temporal cycles. Just as the old ascetic changes into a young lover,
so in general the yogi's chastity ultimately affords him not only sexual
powers but the right to use them. Agastya wins Lopamudrā by means
25ea[1] of the threat of his *tapas*, a force which he also uses to satisfy the conditions under which she will allow him to enjoy her. Śiva says to
Pārvatī, 'By *tapas* one wins *kāma*', and this concept appears often in
passages encouraging the practice of *tapas*, as well as in occasional
passages in praise of *kāma*: 'It is for the sake of sensual pleasures that
25ea[1] one performs *tapas*.'[111] So basic is this belief that a speech challenging
it is put in the mouth of a libidinous and heretical Śaiva ascetic, who
maintains that since effects resemble causes, *tapas* in this life cannot
bring bliss in the next.[112] The belief that beautiful women await one in
6c 6d heaven is old: a funeral hymn beseeches the funeral fire not to burn up
32a the phallus of the dead man[113] for this reason. The *apsarases* are the
particular reward of the ascetic, just as their earthly counterparts are
his frequent temptation in mortal life. One *apsaras* says, 'All the men
21ea of Puru's race that come here delight us through their ascetic merit, and
they do not transgress by this.'[114]

Women as well as men may obtain sensual rewards for their asceticism. Mohinī performed *tapas* in order to seduce Brahmā, and even
25ea[2] Indra, the traditional enemy of ascetics, is won as a husband by the
tapas of several different women.[115] This motif is central to the story
of Sandhyā:

> 39e Brahmā had displayed desire for his daughter, Sandhyā ['Twilight'] as
> 41a soon as she was born, and she had desired him. As a result of this, Brahmā
> 43a cursed Kāma [who had caused the trouble] to be burnt by Śiva. When every-
> 3 one had departed, Sandhyā resolved to purify herself and to establish for all
> 25a time a moral law: that new-born creatures would be free of desire. To do
> 10c 6d this, she prepared to offer herself as an oblation in the fire.

Knowing of her intention, Brahmā sent the sage Vasiṣṭha to instruct her 35ea
in the proper manner of performing *tapas*. Vasiṣṭha disguised himself as
a *brahmacārin* with matted locks and taught her how to meditate upon Śiva. 33ea[5]
Śiva then appeared to her and offered her a boon. She said, 'Let all new-born 35ea
creatures be free of desire, and let me be reborn as the wife of a man to whom 25ea[2]
I can just be a close friend. And if anyone but my husband gazes upon me 3
with desire, let his virility be destroyed and let him become an impotent 3
eunuch.' Śiva said, 'Your sin has been burnt to ashes, purified by your *tapas*. 32a
I grant what you ask: henceforth, creatures will only become subject to 25a
desire when they reach adolescence, and any man but your husband who
looks upon you with desire will become impotent.' Then Sandhyā, meditating
upon the chaste Brahmin for her husband, entered the sacrificial fire. Her 6d
body became the oblation, and she arose from the fire as an infant girl, named 10c
Arundhatī. She grew up in a sage's hermitage and married Vasiṣṭha.[116] 6c
19ea

In this myth, the explicit intention seems at variance with the implicit achievement. Ostensibly, Sandhyā enters the fire to die—but she is reborn from it, like Satī; her act is creative rather than destructive because she offers herself as an oblation in place of the seed of Brahmā that is usually offered as an oblation at this point in the myth. She performs *tapas* for the sake of chastity—general chastity (in the form of a moral law) and her own future chastity (in the form of a curse on any potential adulterer)—but she obtains a promise of general sexuality (at the proper stage of life) and a husband. She is guilty of the supreme sexual sin (incest, although committed only in thought) and as a result she is reborn as the most famous chaste wife in the whole of Hindu mythology, Arundhatī. Her *tapas* is an angry reaction against her relationship with Brahmā, but it is he who sends Vasiṣṭha to help her (or, in terms of the *pattern* of the myth, to turn her from her *tapas* to sexuality—i.e. to seduce her, just as Śiva appears to Pārvatī, disguised, like Vasiṣṭha, as a *brahmacārin*). The fact that Vasiṣṭha appears to her in disguise, although at that time she has no reason to know who he is, let alone to wish to marry him, shows that the myth follows the seduction pattern, though its overt purpose is the opposite—to extol the power of chastity. The forces of *tapas* and *kāma* are by this time so thoroughly intertwined as to be confused in the story-teller's mind.

The placing of the ascetic's reward in another life or in heaven would seem to resolve the paradox by a temporal division akin to that dividing the stages of life on earth: first *tapas*, then sensual pleasures. But this is an artificial distinction. Though it is said that the yogi will enjoy with tenfold intensity in heaven all the pleasures he has renounced on earth,
it is also said that, even on earth, the yogi is attended by heavenly 25ea[1]

women.[117] The erotic and ascetic experiences are, as usual in India, considered simultaneously.

The structure of Sanskrit and the conventions of Sanskrit verse are such that large elements of a poem, and indeed whole poems, may be construed in either of two entirely different ways. One such punning verse may be read in either the ascetic or the erotic mode:

Ascetic: Do *tapas* somewhere on the sandy back of the Narmadā river,
O you whose heart is peaceful, confident one, firm one.
What other action is there that brings a blessing in this world,
20a Than to unite with the highest Self?
Erotic: In summer, when my heart is stirred and emboldened,
I pursue a play-mate and enjoy the lust of love.
What other action is there that brings pleasure in this world,
23ea Than to unite with another man's wife?[118]

The spirit of this verse is hardly devotional, which raises the question of the intention behind the myths of the seduced ascetic. The poet Bhartrhari, like the Śaiva heretic cited above, casts aspersions on the concept of *apsarases* won by asceticism:

24ea[1] You cheat yourself and others with your lies,
Philosopher, so foolish-wise,
In that you state
A celibate
25ea[1] Has greater grace to win the prize.
21ea Are there not heavenly nymphs beyond the skies?[119]

It should be evident that there is a serious and ancient tradition for ascetic practices to culminate in erotic rewards, but there are also many myths in which the aroused ascetic is simply a dirty old man.[120] When the ascetic himself is the active party in the seduction, as in the *Mahābhārata* tale of Agastya, the myth often shades off into a closely related folk theme: the false ascetic who uses his *tapas* as a pretext with which to obtain lustful rewards.

A Hindu jurist remarked, 'The billy-goat and a Brahmin learned in
24ea[1] the Vedas are the two lewdest of all beings.'[121] This opinion was shared
by Buddhists and Europeans and prevails to the present day in India.[122]
Śaiva ascetics in particular are depicted as 'foolish, illiterate, voracious,
24ea[1] lecherous, and scoundrelly'.[123] The philosophical basis for the sexuality
of yogis does not automatically justify every breach of the vow of
chastity; true ascetics objected to the charlatans who gave them all
24ea[1] a bad name.[124] Śiva, the true ascetic, exposes the weaknesses of the Pine
Forest sages who pretend to imitate him but who are not truly free of

lust, yet Śiva himself is often depicted as a false ascetic.[125] The god may 24ea[1]
use his real asceticism as a false pretext—even to achieve a goal to which his asceticism legitimately entitles him (sensual pleasures).

This confusion was due in part to the ambivalent attitude toward asceticism in Hindu society. Although from the time of the Upaniṣads much lip service was paid to the ascetic, conventional Hinduism always maintained a very real hostility toward renunciation. The Śaiva ascetic was considered a despiser of Vedic rites and religious institutions, and his mere existence was a slur upon the conventional society which he rejected.[126] The non-Vedic Vrātya ascetic was classed with the dregs of society, such as incendiaries, poisoners, pimps, spies, adulterers, abortionists, atheists, and drunkards.[127] Fringe members of society could find a comparatively respectable status among the Śaiva sects, and this led to a general decline in the moral reputation of Śaivas, while Śiva himself was eventually condemned as the author of their rites.

Particularly open to satire and censure was the Śaiva ascetic's reputed ability to procreate asexually. Common sense objected to the mythology of supernatural fertility:

> A boy boasted that his father had maintained an unbroken vow of chastity all his life. When people asked how the boy came to be born, he replied 'I was mind-born', and they all laughed at his foolishness.[128]

The confidence placed by many Hindus in the power of certain yogis to impregnate barren women is ridiculed by the Abbé Dubois, who remarks upon the belief that a woman who spent a night with the god Veṅkaṭeśvara (a form of Śiva) in the temple of his priest would conceive by him:

> I must draw a curtain over the sequel of this deceitful suggestion. The 24ea[1]
> reader already guesses at it. . . . Fully convinced that the god has deigned
> to have intercourse with them, the poor [women] return home enchanted, 33ea[3]
> flattering themselves that they will soon procure for their husbands the 35ea
> honour of paternity.[129] 19e

The Abbé's low opinion of the Śaiva priest may not have been justified, but it was shared by a great many conventional Hindus. And in later times, at least—even up to the present day—the behaviour of some yogis seems to substantiate the myths of the false ascetic. The persistence of certain classical motifs in this behaviour is evident from this claim made by the disciple of a Śaiva yogi in Benares recently:

> He says they have another puja [ritual] called Kumari Puja—Virgin Puja.
> Avadhut [the yogi] lies on his back and girl is standing over him. Then she
> pours wine over head and it runs down her body and into the mouth of 16d

16c Avadhut. After this he has intercourse with her but without orgasm—thus
21a she is still virgin. It is difficult to find girls in India for this puja and now they
25a are only doing it in Assam. He says he has not yet performed this puja but
29a he has special kiss between legs for barren women. He is wanting to give this
24a kiss to a lady at the hotel who is barren, but husband is not allowing it.[130]

Stripped of his true philosophical mantle, the erotic yogi may easily be viewed as a false ascetic.

G. THE IMPORTANCE OF PROCREATION

The most frequent and compelling objection to asceticism, however, is based not upon its occasional bawdy misuses but, quite the contrary, upon its conflict with the deep-seated Hindu belief in the importance of descendants, a belief central to Indian thought from the time of the Vedas to the present day. Although from one standpoint the erotic ascetic could be said to make the best of both worlds (to gain the powers and honours of chastity and the pleasures of sexuality), from another
standpoint he could have neither. *Brahmacārins* were said to undertake
24a their vows for forty-eight years in order to conceal their lack of virility.[131]
25a A similar idea (or perhaps simply its mirror image, the accusation of
lustful hypocrisy) may underlie the stanza in which the poet Bhartṛhari
24a mocked various ascetics (including Jains, Buddhists, and Kāpālikas) for
25a abandoning women and being driven mercilessly by Kāma to undertake
25e 24ea[1] their fruitless vows.[132] The Vedas certainly did not revere celibacy;
Lopāmudrā summed up Vedic opinion when she said, 'Men should go
to their wives.' This injunction was elaborated by the time of the Epic
as the formal duty of a man to make love to his wife during her fertile
period: 'By ignoring the fertile period, a man commits a sin which leads
22e him to hell.'[133] The ancestors' request for descendants causes Agastya
to seek the hand of Lopamudrā.

This is in part a sexual, rather than strictly procreative, phenomenon.
22e Thus Mohinī says to Brahmā, 'Whether a man be a householder or
29e ascetic or lover, he must not abandon a woman who comes to him or
33ea[2] he will go to hell.' (Similarly, a demon disguised as Śiva tries to seduce
Pārvatī, saying, 'Women who deny sexual intercourse to a man racked
with pain are certain to fall into hell.')[134] But the basic reason for the
18e injunction is to ensure progeny, particularly sons. To this day, it is
believed in India that a man who dies childless will become a ghost,[135]
for a son is responsible for the ceremonies upon which the peace of his
dead ancestors depends.

One Purāṇa text says, 'The man without a son has an empty house, 19e 8d
and his *tapas* is cut off',[136] thus denying to the ascetic both the pleasures which he has voluntarily abandoned and the very goal for which he has sacrificed them. The logic of this double curse is evident from several myths:

The sage Mandapāla followed the path of the sages who have drawn up
their seed in chastity. He practised *tapas*, conquered his senses, and finally 21a
abandoned his body and went to the world of his ancestors. But there he did 18a
not receive the fruits of his *tapas*, and he saw many people without rewards,
though they had mastered asceticism. He asked the reason for this and was
told, 'If a man has mastered *tapas* and performed the rituals, but has no 18e
children, he does not obtain the reward. Beget children and you will enjoy the 18ea
eternal fruits.' Upon hearing this, Mandapāla immediately begat four sons 19ea
upon a bird-woman, for he knew the fecundity of birds. Then he abandoned 30e 20ea
them and took another wife, upon whom he begat many sons. In time he 21e 19a
returned to his first wife, and although both wives were jealous he lived with 36a
them and with his many sons.[137] 19ea

In this myth, chastity is not in itself considered bad, but merely insufficient. The ascetic takes pains to remedy the deficiency and reaps the promised reward in the end, though he experiences some of the problems typical of the attempt to combine the ascetic life with marriage—quarrels with his wife and the loss of his sons. The latter motif is so strongly associated with this myth cycle that it is introduced here even when it merely forces the sage to embark upon another episode of procreation. Similar stories are told of other sages:

A primeval ascetic creator (*prajāpati*) named Ruci was begged by his 19e
ancestors to marry, but he preferred detachment and retirement from worldly 21a
actions. Persuaded at length, he did *tapas*, married an *apsaras*, and begat 25ea²
a son upon her.[138] 21ea

Even though Ruci agrees to marry, he obtains his wife by the very method that endangered his ancestors—by *tapas*—and his wife is the traditional partner of those ascetics who for any reason break their vow of chastity: she is an *apsaras*. Thus Ruci manages to satisfy both traditions somewhat, to beget a son and to remain an ascetic.

A similar story is told about Vetāla and Bhairava, sons born to Tārāvatī (an incarnation of Pārvatī) when she has been raped by Śiva. As they are immortals, the sons do not need to produce offspring in order to secure their own immortality, but this does not excuse them (as Śiva uses his divinity to excuse himself) from procreating; they are merely made to seek immortal mothers for their sons:

Vetāla and Bhairava wandered about performing *tapas*, and they did not 21a

$45e^2$ marry. One day Nandin [the bull of Śiva, and often personified as his gate-
keeper] took them aside and said, 'You have no sons, and this is not right.
20a Not by *tapas* does Śiva cause a man to find Release, but only by the birth of
19e a son. You must beget sons upon goddesses, for you were given immortality
18e by Devī when she suckled you, and you must beget sons immortal like your-
21ea selves. Then you will be dear to Śiva and Devī.' Bhairava made love to an
$45e^2$ *apsaras*, who bore him a son and then left him. Vetāla begat a bull in the
20ea marvellous Wishing Cow.[139]

Again the *apsaras* appears as the proper partner of the ascetic, who must be free to return to his yoga after the birth of his son.

A short but complex example of the attempt to resolve *tapas* and marriage for the sake of progeny is the story of Gālavi:

8c A great sage did *tapas* and mentally produced a beautiful daughter.
19ea Though she was promised to a husband, the blameless girl did not wish to
marry, for she saw no husband suitable for her. She performed *tapas* until,
18a considering her life fulfilled, she wished to go to the other world. But the sage
18e Nārada came and told her that she could not go to the other world, for she
8cd had not yet mastered the ordinary goals of this world. She promised to give
27ea half of her accumulated *tapas* to any man who would marry her. The sage
19ea Gālavi agreed to marry her on condition that she would spend a night with
22a him. She married him, spent the night with him, and then left him. She
abandoned her body and went to heaven, and the sage missed her so much
$25ea^2$ that he used the *tapas* she had given him to perfect himself, and he followed
her to heaven.[140]

Though the pattern of the myth is that of the Mandapāla story, there is no actual reference to sons, but merely to the 'ordinary goals of this world', marriage and sexual experience. As in many Hindu myths, sexuality and fertility are confused. Several conflicting themes merge in this story: the *tapasvinī* herself is produced by *tapas* rather than by sexual intercourse, but for her this practice of *tapas* is insufficient. She marries a sage, whose sexual demands are a breach of his chastity, but this very emotional involvement on his part leads him to follow the path of asceticism—to rejoin his wife.

H. THE PRAJĀPATI AND HIS ASCETIC SONS

A similar attempt to balance the roles of creative *tapas* and normal sexuality permeates two of the basic Hindu creation cycles: the myth of Brahmā and his sons and the myth of Dakṣa and his sons, which differ in certain details but may be considered basically two variants of the same myth. Even in this cycle of myths, which rejects *tapas* as a complete creative method, the one who makes creation ultimately possible is Śiva, the lord of ascetics. Yet Śiva appears in his anti-ascetic, androgynous form, though his appearance is a reward for Prajāpati's *tapas*. Thus each of the reversals is in turn reversed:

> Brahmā created many creatures, but they failed to increase. Brahmā began 8c 8d
> to worry, and a voice said, 'You must create by means of sexual intercourse',
> but as Śiva had not yet created the race of women, this was hardly possible. $5c^{1}$
> Then Brahmā performed *tapas* and Śiva came to him in his androgynous 39ea
> form. The woman became separate and gave Brahmā a female creative power. 32e
> She herself re-entered Śiva's body and disappeared. Brahmā rejoiced, and 38ea
> creation proceeded by intercourse.[141] $5c^{1}$

Several texts combine this myth with a related motif: the unwillingness of the sons of Brahmā to create. This transfers the onus of impotence from the god himself to his descendants:

> Brahmā produced mind-born sons by means of meditation, but they did 8c 8d
> not increase. He became angry, and from his anger Rudra was created. Still
> his sons did not increase, for they were wise and devoid of passion and hatred,
> without any ambition or any desire for progeny. Then Brahmā became very 21a
> angry, and from his brow an androgyne appeared. Brahmā said to the andro- 32e
> gyne, 'Divide yourself', and then he disappeared. The male half was Śiva, 40e
> who divided himself into the eleven Rudras and told them to busy themselves
> tirelessly with the activities of people. The female half, full of *tapas*, was
> instructed by Brahmā to divide herself in half, and from her many women 27ea
> were produced, and creation proceeded.[142] $5c^{1}$

In another version of this myth, the woman is considered to be Brahmā's daughter, with whom he commits incest, and the man is not Śiva but Kāma. The pattern of the myth allows for the assistance of either the great yogi (who appears here in his sexual aspect) or the great god of desire (to assist Brahmā, who in this case is himself considered the great yogi), in order to strike the balance of creative forces:

> Once when Brahmā wished to create he brought forth sons mentally. He 8c
> told them to perform creation, but they disregarded their father's commands 19a
> and went to do *tapas*. Then in anger Brahmā, the great yogi, created the eleven 21a
> Rudras and more sons, and then he created a son, Kāma, and a beautiful 40a
> daughter. Brahmā said to Kāma, 'I have made you for the sake of the pleasure 41e
> of a man and a woman. Invade the hearts of all creatures by means of yoga, $5c^{1}$
> and you will delude and madden them always.' Having given magic arrows to
> Kāma, Brahmā looked at his daughter to give her a boon, but at this moment
> Kāma decided to test his weapons, and he pierced the great yogi [Brahmā] 41ea
> with his arrows. Brahmā pursued his daughter, determined to possess her, 39e
> but her brothers, the ascetics, spoke angrily to their father, saying, 'What is 40a
> this disgusting act that you are bent upon, to wish to enjoy your own daughter?'
> Then Brahmā was so ashamed that he abandoned his body by means of yoga, 10cd
> and the girl, seeing her father dead, wept and killed herself as he had. But

38e Viṣṇu then appeared and revived them both, giving the girl in marriage to
23e[1] 4 Kāma, to become Rati, goddess of sexual pleasure.[143]
41e

In this version, the 'Rati' which was merely an activity in the earlier version is personified as a goddess, the wife of Kāma, just as Kāma himself appears in place of generalized sexual intercourse. The daughter of Brahmā, in other versions reborn as Arundhatī (the incarnation of chastity) is here reborn as the incarnation of sexuality. Śiva is represented both by 'the great yogi' (Brahmā) who is shot by Kāma (as Śiva is shot later in the myth) and by the ascetic sons (Rudras) who revile Brahmā for his act of incest as Śiva usually does.

In another version of this creation myth which incorporates the first story, Śiva appears more explicitly in a double capacity of yogi and erotic god:

8c 8d Brahmā began creation by meditation, but darkness and delusion overcame
21a him. His mind-born sons, all passionless yogis devoted to Śiva, did not want
40a to create, so Brahmā performed *tapas* in order to create, but he did not suc-
38ea ceed. He begged Śiva to help him in the work of creation and Śiva agreed,
18a but the creatures that Śiva made were immortals like himself, and they filled
19a 10cd the universe. Brahmā said, 'Do not create this sort of creatures, but make
8d them subject to death.' Śiva said, 'I will not do that; create such mortals
21a yourself, if you wish.' Then Śiva turned away from creation and remained
26a with his seed drawn up in chastity from that day forth.
5c[1] Brahmā then wished to create by means of sexual intercourse. He did *tapas*
39ea for Śiva, who appeared in his androgynous form and gave Brahmā his female
32e 27ea creative power. Brahmā then began the process of creation by intercourse.
25ea[2] He divided himself into a man and a woman. The woman did *tapas* and
5c[1] obtained the man for her husband. Together they begat the race of mortals.[144]

Most of the creative themes are here: the yogi Śiva appears as the object of the *tapas* of the sages and of Brahmā and as the god who refuses to create, maintaining his chastity. But as the erotic god, Śiva neglects to reward the ascetic sons, and he himself appears as the androgyne and produces creatures who fill the universe. Creative methods alternate similarly, intercourse replacing *tapas* and being replaced in turn. The final creation is by a combination of the methods: the woman uses *tapas* to obtain her husband and then procreates sexually.

In another series of variations on this theme, the ascetic sons of
Brahmā are caused to partake in normal birth and rebirth as the result
of a curse pronounced by Brahmā: 'Since you disregard my instructions
3 to beget children, and you have become passionless, despising your life,
20e longing for immortality, you will be reborn seven times as fools. And
2 in your seventh birth you will obtain perfection.'[145] In this way, Brahmā

restores the balance that his sons destroyed in their desire for complete perfection: because they sought knowledge he makes them fools, and because they practise chastity they are cursed to become involved in rebirth. In yet another group of variations, the curse is more specifically sexual in nature, and is applied not to all the sons, but only to Nārada:

> Brahmā created many five-year-old sons by meditation, and he told them 8c 40a
> to perform creation, but they refused and went to do *tapas*. Brahmā became 21a
> angry; flames shot forth from him, and the eleven Rudras appeared from his 19a
> forehead. Then Brahmā created more sons, including Nārada, and he told 7cd[1] 8c 21a
> them to create, but Nārada refused. Brahmā cursed Nārada, saying, 'Your 24ea[1]
> knowledge will be destroyed, and you will become lascivious, lusting for 20e
> women, the husband of fifty lusty women. You will be master of all the erotic 3
> textbooks and a glutton for orgies, a clever lover, handsome, a secret seducer
> of women.' Though Brahmā modified this curse, saying, 'At the end of 100,000
> celestial years you will be born again as my son, endowed with true knowledge', 2
> Nārada retaliated and cursed Brahmā to be no longer worshipped.[146]

A later text adds a stronger retaliation: Brahmā cursed Nārada to be
young for ever, to make love in deserted forests, and to beget children 3
in a Śūdra woman (of the fourth, lowest class). Nārada then cursed
Brahmā to be without worship and to desire a woman who should not 3
be desired. Because of this, Brahmā lusted for his own daughter and was
ashamed.[147] In this way, the cycle is completed: the final curse produces 39e
the primeval incest from which the central episode originally arose. The curse is both a way of moving from one phase to another and a reinforcement of the natural development of the myth: excessive desire for *tapas* ultimately results in excess lust.

In another version of this myth, however, a resolution is reached without the necessity for a curse, by a division into periods:

> Brahmā told Nārada to marry, and he extolled at length the virtues of the 19e
> householder. Nārada, however, argued that all contact with women was 23e[1, 2]
> dangerous and evil. Brahmā then complained that half of his sons had dis- 25e 17d
> obeyed him and become ascetics, and he begged Nārada to marry first, and 40a 19a
> later to become an ascetic if he wished. Nārada agreed to marry only after 18ea
> he had performed *tapas*, and he went to Śiva, who taught him the vow of 25ea[2]
> chastity.[148] 40ea 34a

But the more usual conclusion to the story is a curse, and this is true of the series of stories, variants of the above myth, in which Nārada acts as an ascetic opposed to the creative behaviour of the sons of Dakṣa, who represent sexual creation.

I. NĀRADA AND THE SONS OF DAKṢA

Dakṣa, a son of Brahmā, is the most famous of the *prajāpatis*, and he is
5c[1] the one particularly responsible for the idea of sexual intercourse as
a method of procreation[149] (an invention elsewhere attributed to Śiva).
When Brahmā instructs Dakṣa in this new creative method, Nārada as
usual opposes it:

> 8c 8d Dakṣa produced many creatures mentally, but they failed to increase.
> 19e Brahmā told him to marry and engender sons by intercourse, but when he
> 5c[1] 19a commanded these sons to create they went to do *tapas* in order to increase
> 8c 40a progeny. When Nārada learned of this he sent Dakṣa's sons on the road of no
> 8d return, and they were destroyed. Dakṣa begat more sons, but Nārada sent
> 5c[1] 8d them after their brothers. Then Dakṣa, in anger, said to Nārada, 'Why did
> 24a you teach my little boys to be beggars? The man who disregards the three
> 20a debts and leaves his home and parents, desiring Release, commits a sin.
> 20e 2 I curse you to wander for ever over the earth, never remaining at rest.'[150]

Dakṣa plays the anti-ascetic role in this myth, while Nārada is the
ascetic son. This enmity stems from the time of the Epic,[151] and although
the teachings of Nārada are not explicitly hostile to Dakṣa, they are
clearly contrary to Dakṣa's intention. Whereas Brahmā cursed Nārada
to be sexual, Dakṣa here curses him to be chaste (homeless), a harmon-
izing rather than contrasting curse, which becomes more explicit in
2 another version in which Dakṣa says to Nārada, 'Therefore, you will
21a wander for ever without children.'[152] The character of a wanderer is
particularly appropriate to Nārada, a notorious meddler and gossip, who
frequently acts as a mediating agent in these myths, catalysing the
transition from one phase to the next by inspiring anger, jealousy, or
lust in characters formerly uninvolved in the myth or temporarily
inactive. The Seven Sages tell Pārvatī the story of Nārada and Dakṣa's
1 sons in order to discredit Nārada, who has meddled on Śiva's behalf,
and they remark:

> 23e[2] Who ever listened to Nārada's instructions and had a home to live in? He
> 24a gave advice to Dakṣa's sons and they never saw their home again. . . . Any
> 1 man or woman who listens to Nārada's advice is sure to leave home and
> become a beggar.[153]

The enmity between Nārada and Dakṣa is resolved in another version by the mediation of Śiva, who has sympathies with both roles:

> 8c 8d Dakṣa practised *tapas* to create, but his creatures did not increase, for they
> 34e 19a were cursed by Śiva. Then he produced sons by intercourse with a great
> 40e *tapasvinī*, but Nārada said to Dakṣa's sons, 'You must not create children to

people the surface of the earth when you do not know the measure of the
earth. You would create too much or too little in your ignorance, and that 40a
would be a sin.' Dakṣa's sons, thinking, 'When we have learned the measure
of the earth, then we will create happily', went forth on the path of the wind, 30ea
and they (and their brothers, whom Nārada sent after them) have never yet 8d
returned, like men who have been shipwrecked at sea. Then Dakṣa was angry 14d
and he said, 'Let Nārada be destroyed and become an embryo.' Dakṣa then 3
begat sixty daughters and gave them as wives to Śiva and the other great 20e
sages. But Nārada was frightened by Dakṣa's curse and sought help from 36e 19ea
Brahmā, who made an agreement with Dakṣa that Nārada would be reborn 20e
as a son of Śiva, begotten upon a daughter of Dakṣa.[154] 19e

Here the contrasting curse re-emerges: Nārada's anti-erotic activities bring upon him the curse of rebirth and marriage, involvement in life. The exact nature of the 'path of the wind' or the 'road of no return' is clear from other texts which describe this teaching as Sāṅkhya yoga or state that Nārada cursed Dakṣa's sons to become ascetic beggars before they had experienced life or discharged their three debts.[155]

The South Indian tradition tells a similar story, but reverses the values:

[Dakṣa told his sons to perform *tapas* in order to obtain the power to create. 8c
Nārada came and taught them that only the three-eyed god (Śiva) had the 7cd[1]
function of creating and destroying, and that their efforts would be in vain. 8d
(Moreover, he explained, the power to create beings would give them nothing 19a 40a
but boredom and anguish. The sons of Dakṣa changed their intention and 20a
aspired to Salvation.)[156] Dakṣa created other children, and they too worshipped 5c[1]
the *liṅga* and obtained beatitude. Then Dakṣa became furious and cursed 5c[2] 40a
Nārada to remain celibate, never to marry or have children. Nārada in turn 20a
cursed Dakṣa to be chastised by Śiva, the god with an eye in his forehead. 2 21a
And so, years later, Dakṣa's sacrifice was destroyed by Śiva.][157] 2 38a[1] 7cd[1]

Although from the context and the pattern of the myth it is clear that the sons remain celibate, they are said to worship the *liṅga* of Śiva rather than his ascetic aspect. Moreover, in this later, more devout Śaiva context, the failure to create is rewarded with enlightenment instead of with the curse of rebirth and ignorance. Here again Nārada is cursed by Dakṣa to be celibate rather than sexual, and it is evident that the South Indian poet does not condemn this celibacy. For Dakṣa, the sexual creator, is also cursed, and his punishment comes from Śiva, to whom the story is devoted—Śiva this time in his ascetic aspect, the patron of Nārada and the enemy of Brahmā and Dakṣa. The story has been given a complete change of significance while retaining the traditional pattern and motifs.

Another popular version of the story reveals the same pro-ascetic outlook:

8c [Brahmā, wishing to create, produced four youths who meditated until
34a Śiva appeared to them and told them that the world was only illusion and that,
40a 20a if they wished to be free, they must refuse to become the fathers of the human
21a race. The youths, seeing the truth of this, refused to create. Brahmā then
18e created the eight *prajāpatis*, including Dakṣa, to people the universe, but
19a Dakṣa's sons, in their turn, refused to create offspring. Dakṣa then changed
40a himself into a woman and had many daughters, from whom creation then
32ea 5c^{1} proceeded.][158]

Here the two stories are combined: Brahmā's sons and Dakṣa's sons appear together in the role that they play in separate myths. And Śiva's aspects are divided: he himself retains his ascetic aspect, turning the sons of Brahmā from the world, while Dakṣa assumes Śiva's androgynous form and is responsible for creation by intercourse. In both of these popular myths, asceticism is a preferred alternative to conventional methods of creation for Dakṣa's sons, yet that alternative is only acceptable on the assumption that sexual creation will in fact be performed by someone else.

J. THE TWO FORMS OF IMMORTALITY

Throughout the mythology, whether or not *tapas* is accepted as a valid means of creation, it is practised for another goal: immortality, freedom from rebirth. In the Vedas, *tapas* is able to accomplish the chief desideratum, fertility; in the Upaniṣads, *tapas* is the means to the new goal, Release. Both are forms of immortality, both promising continuation of the soul without the body—Release giving complete freedom of the soul (or absorption into the Godhead), progeny giving a continuation of the soul's life in the bodies of one's children. Thus from the earliest times there was a choice set before the worshipper. The poet of the Agastya hymn speaks of the goal which is won by both paths, and the Purāṇic myths may be read as an attempt to reap the rewards of both worlds in this way.

One passage in a Hindu lawbook praises chastity as the way to
18a immortality,[159] but another states, 'You create progeny and that's your
18e immortality, O mortal.'[160] If one cannot have it both ways, one can at least succeed by the path particularly suited to the individual. The poet Bhartṛhari expressed this view:

In this vain fleeting universe, a man
18ea Of wisdom has two courses: first he can

Direct his time to pray, to save his soul, 18a
And wallow in religion's nectar bowl. 14c^{2}
But, if he cannot, it is surely best
To touch and hold a lovely woman's breast,
And to caress her warm round hips, and thighs,
And to possess that which between them lies.[161] 17cd

Hindus were thus faced with what almost amounted to an existential choice between the life of the spirit and the life of the body; scripture could be cited to support either preference. Bhartṛhari himself experienced this dilemma:

Even the state of tranquillity, so arduously won, is threatened by sensuous beauty. Bhartrihari does not simply vacillate between worldly indulgence and asceticism; his confusion is more profound. He currently experiences delight in the fullness of the world, anxiety over its cruel transience, and the feeling that this tension is inescapable . . . that none of life's possibilities are what they seem to be.[162]

The Seven Sages, trying to dissuade Pārvatī from her desire for Śiva,
maintain that he is able to offer neither the gratification of the body nor 18ea
peace of mind,[163] implying that Pārvatī might choose either one. Such
a decision must have been all the more perplexing in a society in which
every other important choice in life was dictated for the individual by
society in the form of caste law. Even in this case, the choice was limited
by natural propensities as well as by *svadharma*, the individual's particular place in Hindu society. The god Indra was once enlightened by 45ea
Śiva and left his wife in order to devote himself to *tapas*; his wife at 22ea
length persuaded him to return to her and to rule his kingdom, in order
to fulfil his own role, his *svadharma* as king of the gods.[164] In discussing
this myth, Zimmer wrote of 'the re-establishment of a balance. . . . We
are also taught to esteem the transient sphere of the duties and pleasures
of individual existence, which is as real and vital to the living man as
a dream to the sleeping soul.'[165] It is the function of Indra, and of Śiva,
to maintain this balance, to defend the fullness of life against the negation
threatened by metaphysical emptiness. The resolution of the two paths
and the two goals, the yogic fire and the elixir of love, is expressed in
this metaphor: 'He who burns his body with the fire of Śiva and floods 8c
it with the elixir of his consort by the path of yoga—he gains immor- 10d
tality.'[166] 14c^{2} 18ea

K. THE ATTEMPT TO RECONCILE THE HOUSEHOLDER AND ASCETIC IN SOCIETY

The tension which is manifested in metaphysical terms as the conflict between the two paths to immortality, between Release and the dharma of conventional society (in particular, the dharma of marriage and procreation),[167] appears in social terms as the tension between the different stages of Hindu life. These four stages provide a superficial solution in temporal terms: first one should be a *brahmacārin* (chaste student), then *gṛhastha* (married householder), then *vānaprastha* (the man who dwells in the forest with or without his wife), and finally the *sannyāsin* (the ascetic who has renounced everything). There is little disagreement about the value of the first stage, for it does not preclude any of the others. The third stage poses special problems which will be discussed at greater length below. The basic conflict remains between the second and fourth stages, the householder and the ascetic, who represent the two basic paths.

In praising the ascetic life, the Upaniṣads condemn the values of
the householder: 'One must overcome the desire for sons and live as
19a a mendicant.'[168] Some Purāṇas, too, maintain that the man who fears
18a rebirth does not even marry: 'How can a man who is a householder find
20a Release?'[169] This is the ascetic 'party line', a direct contradiction of the
conventional religious view represented by such stories as the *Mahā-*
bhārata tale of Sudarśana, who became a householder thinking, 'As
18e a householder, I will conquer death.'[170] According to the law books,
a man has three debts to pay: he owes sacrifice to the gods, children to
18ea his ancestors, and the study of the Vedas to the holy sages. If he does not
20a pay these debts but seeks Release instead, he is condemned to Hell.[171]
These are the debts to which Dakṣa refers in his arguments with
Nārada.

The main stream of Hinduism attempted to reassure the members of
each group that by fulfilling the dharma of that group—necessary for
the survival of the system as a whole—they would still be able to reap
the rewards of other groups as well. The jurists incorporated the ascetic
'heresy' and added its goals to those of the conventional life. The Epics
state that a married man may comply perfectly with the laws of chastity
22e by abstaining from intercourse with his wife except during her fertile
period; by this he gains the merit of a true *brahmacārin*.[172] A similar
19e equation appears in another lawbook: 'The begetting of a son by the
18ea husband is [equivalent to] the experience of the forest-dweller stage.'[173]

In this way, the values of asceticism were absorbed into conventional society.

At the other end of the spectrum, the yogi could extend his worldly involvement almost limitlessly without renouncing any aspect of the ascetic life. Yogis engaged in extensive commercial enterprises, became rich, and even formed trade unions.[174] The self-controlled yogi may even be a householder and still attain Release if he remains unattached to household affairs;[175] the intention is all-important in this context. Thus Brahmā says to the Pine Forest sages, 'You live in a hermitage but you
are overcome by anger and lust. Yet the true hermitage of a wise man 23e[2]
is his home, while for the man who is not a true yogi even the hermitage is merely a house.'[176] And this is the philosophy behind much of the Tantric sexuality of the later Purāṇas: one may perform the *act* of sexual intercourse without losing one's purity, as long as the *mind* remains uninvolved.

Thus the two realms may meet on either side of the line—the householder may embrace the philosophy and even the chastity of the ascetic,
or the ascetic may go so far as to take a wife and become a house- 18ea
holder.[177] The same text which teaches a man that he must overcome the desire for sons and become a sage goes on to say that before attaining final Release he must also overcome the desire to be a sage.[178] Similarly, one must absorb the wisdom of both desires. The ideal for Hinduism in
general was a fully integrated life in which all aspects of human nature 18ea
could be of value.[179]

L. THE FOREST-DWELLER: AN INADEQUATE COMPROMISE

The third stage, that of the forest-dweller, is the most complex, for it is here that the two traditions meet in the married ascetic. The forest-dweller did not emerge historically as a compromise between the householder and the ascetic, for the original triad was chaste student/householder/forest-dweller, to which the fourth stage, asceticism, was only subsequently added, ultimately replacing the forest-dweller stage in function. The latter was maintained as an archaism in the theory, however, precisely in order to function as a compromise between the second and fourth stages. The main factor distinguishing the forest-dweller from the *sannyāsin* was that the former was allowed to have a wife. To compensate for this indulgence, the forest-dwellers were said to practise a more violent kind of *tapas*.[180] Yet even here there is some confusion, for some law books grant the forest-dweller the alternative

of leaving his wife to the care of his sons.[181] The textbooks are unanimous, however, in their belief that it was *better* to go into the forest without a wife.[182] Even if the sage does take his wife with him, he is advised to avoid her as much as possible, or, in the words of the Abbé
19ea Dubois, 'to use the privileges of marriage with the greatest modera-
tion'.[183] Several law books state that the forest-dweller should live in
21a complete continence, with his seed drawn up;[184] if his desire causes
22ea 25e him to have intercourse with his wife, his vow is ruined and he must
perform expiation.[185] One jurist allowed the forest-dweller to go to his
25a 22e wife during her fertile period,[186] a dispensation similar to that granted
to the householder.

This is a delicate compromise, and one which the mythology never accepted. In one version of the Pine Forest story, the sages insist that they are jealous of Śiva's handsomeness, and irked by his seduction of their wives, not because of their lust for their wives but only because of the women's ritual value:

> 10c When our wives are here, our oblation reaches the world of heaven, but
> when they are gone the oblation is destroyed and our sins are upon the family.
> But what can we do? We cannot marry again. . . . We are not as handsome as
> [Śiva] is. Then how can these women feel desire for our bodies rather than for
> him? . . . [Śiva] has turned against us these women who are our assistants
> 35ea in the sacrifice.[187]

This is the traditional Vedic role of women in religion, and it is a partial justification for the presence of wives among the forest-dwellers. But the point of the Pine Forest story is, above all, to illustrate the conflicts and difficulties of married ascetic life.

One tribal myth contains several elements of the Pine Forest myth and illustrates the dangers of the life of the forest-dweller:

> 19ea 36a [A sage lived in the forest with his wife. For some reason he was cross with
> 22a her and did not go to her. The woman thought, 'If only some other man
> 27ea would come here, I would enjoy myself with him.' A man came to her begging
> 7c 21ea for fire, and she seduced him. The sage caught them and poured water on
> 13c 2 17d them, cursing her to be hard to satisfy thenceforth.][188]

Here, as in many myths of this pattern, the curse is merely an exaggeration of the fault which caused the original transgression: she is cursed to be insatiable because her insatiable nature offended her husband in the first place. The ascetic tradition, based as it is upon a profound misogyny, is quick to challenge the chastity of any woman, and is therefore suspicious of the wife of the forest-dweller.

1. Ithyphallic yogi, horned, surrounded by animals. Steatite seal from the Indus Valley. *c.* 2000 B.C. MOTIF: 26ea.

2. Gūḍimallam *liṅga*. First century B.C. Five feet high. MOTIF: 5c², 5cd, 26a.

3. Atomic Reactor, Trombay, as depicted on the ten-rupee stamp. *Liṅga* in the *yoni*. MOTIF: $5c^2$, 5cd, 5d, 12cd, 13cd, 17cd.

4. Ithyphallic skeleton gate-keeper. Mahākūṭeśvara temple, Mysore. MOTIF: 10cd, 26ea, 29ea, 44ea.

Physical chastity can be regulated, but in this realm it is the elusive chastity of the mind that is put to the test. A famous and typical story illustrating this problem is the tale of Jamadagni:

> The ascetic Jamadagni performed *tapas* for many years. Then, at the gods' 8d
> command, he went to the king and asked for the hand of the princess Reṇukā 21ea
> in marriage. Having obtained her, he went back to his hermitage with her 8c
> and they performed *tapas* together for many years, during which five sons 27ea 25ea^{3}
> were born to them. One day when the sons were out gathering fruit, Reṇukā 19e
> went to bathe, and in the river she saw a king with his wife. Then Reṇukā was 17c
> overcome with desire for him, and because of that transgression she fainted. 44ea
> She recovered and returned to the hermitage, but as soon as her husband
> saw her, devoid of her holy lustre, he knew that she had lost her virtue. He 25e
> was furious, and when he had reviled her he asked each of his sons in turn 36a
> to kill her. The first four refused, but the youngest took an axe and killed his 27e 27a
> mother, for which his father praised him highly, offering him a boon. The son 19a
> asked that his mother be revived, and this was granted.[189] 6c

The sin, committed in mind alone, is so slight in proportion to the punishment that, setting aside the possibility that this may be a somewhat Bowdlerized account of Reṇukā's transgression (an unlikely possibility in the light of the Epic's general disinclination to mince words), it seems necessary to seek the true fault in the situation itself, not only in the troublesome presence of the wife, but in the sons as well, whose birth to ascetics is a constant problem in the mythology. The virtue of the wife is often the crucial point in the forest-dweller's dilemma.

E. M. Forster noted the Hindu tendency to social extremes but wrongly interpreted it in terms of compromise:

> As a boy, [the Maharajah] had thought of retiring from the world, and it was an ideal which he cherished throughout his life, and which, at the end, he would have done well to practise. Yet he would condemn asceticism, 18ea declare that salvation could not be reached through it, that it might be Vedantic but it was not Vedic, and matter and spirit must both be given their due. Nothing too much! In such a mood he seemed Greek.[190]

The Maharajah is anything but Greek. He simultaneously reveres and accepts asceticism and (as Forster hints) sensuality. 'Everything too much' would better express his mood.

The yogi in myth is very closely bound up with normal existence,[191] but at the same time entirely divorced from it. This made sense to the ancient Hindu in a way that the forest-dweller compromise never did. As a metaphorical mediation, the third stage remained valuable, and so it is the focal point of most of the yogi-householder stories, but as a way of life it was rejected,[192] even forbidden.[193] The situation of the

married ascetic is one of compromise, but compromise is never the Hindu way of resolution, which proceeds by a series of oppositions rather than by one entity which combines the two by sacrificing the essence of each. There are, in fact, scattered Sanskrit epigrams closely akin to the Greek *meden agan* that Forster thought he saw in the Maharajah: 'Excess must be avoided in all things.'[194] But this is not the prevalent Hindu attitude, nor is it the attitude underlying the mytho-
12cd 31e logical texts, which by their very nature tend to exaggerate all polarities,
31a including potentially dangerous excesses.

Hinduism has no 'golden mean'; it seeks the exhaustion of two golden extremes. It was perhaps as a reaction against this extremism that the Buddha called his teaching 'the Middle Path', explicitly rejecting both the voluptuous life which he had known as a prince and the violent asceticism which he had mastered at the start of his spiritual quest. Although the Buddhists also stated the problem explicitly in positive
18ea terms, recognizing the merit of both goals, the final choice was a negative
one: there are two pleasures, the pleasure of the householder and the pleasure of asceticism, but the latter is pre-eminent.[195] For the Buddha taught *nirvāṇa*—literally, the extinguishing of the flame—while Śiva embodied the flame and danced within it. Hinduism has no use for Middle Paths; this is a religion of fire and ice.

III

THE VEDIC ANTECEDENTS OF ŚIVA

MANY of the characteristics which contribute to the apparently paradoxical nature of the Purāṇic Śiva may be traced back to individual characteristics of gods of the Vedic pantheon. Both Śiva and Brahmā derive their creative attributes from the Vedic figure of Prajāpati (see Chapter IV), but other Vedic gods supply more anthropomorphic qualities. From Indra, Śiva inherits his phallic and adulterous character, from Agni the heat of asceticism and passion, and from Rudra he takes a very common epithet (Rudra), as well as certain dark features.

A. RUDRA, GOD OF DESTRUCTION

Although an over-emphasis on the identity of Rudra and Śiva has led
to certain misleading generalizations, there is nevertheless a significant
relationship between them. Śiva's paradoxical nature in the Purāṇas
may be traced back to the superficially ambiguous nature of Rudra as
creator and destroyer, the god with a shining exterior and a dark
interior,[1] god of the storm and of healing herbs. Primarily, however, 30ea
it is the destructive aspect of Rudra which he bequeathed to Śiva. In the
Ṛg Veda, Rudra is invoked as a god of death: 'Do not slaughter our 10cd
father or our mother.'[2] In later metaphysical developments, death
becomes less personal, and Śiva destroys the universe by fire at the end 5d
of each era, purifying it by sprinkling it with ashes.[3] This cosmic role 6cd
appears in the later mythology as a kind of necrophilia attributed to
Śiva, who frequents funeral grounds and is smeared with the ashes of
corpses,[4] even becoming incarnate in a corpse.[5] Although there are sometimes erotic overtones to this aspect of Śiva, as in the myths describing
his passionate dance with the corpse of Satī, it is his ascetic nature which
is most closely tied to the shadowy Rudra, for celibacy is often associated 10cd
with gods of death.[6] This significant characteristic of Śiva, together with the name of Rudra which is given to Śiva throughout the Purāṇas, is derived almost entirely from the Vedic Rudra, to whom the name of Śiva ('The Auspicious One') was later given as a euphemism.

B. INDRA

But the other aspect of Śiva, the phallic god, the giver of seed, is not merely an arbitrary philosophical reversal of his destructive role. Certain facets of his sexuality may be derived from his ancient connection with the ascetic cults and their sexual manifestations, but many of the myths of fertility and much of the phallic religion are due to Śiva's close con-
45e nection with Indra, the Vedic king of the gods.[7]

One strong tie between Indra and Śiva is formed by the group of the
30ea Maruts or Rudras, storm-gods. In the Ṛg Veda, the Maruts at first
belong to Rudra, but they and their acts are so Indra-like that they come to be regarded as the brothers or companions of Indra.[8] Thus, historically, Indra may be said to have 'adopted' the Maruts. In the mythology, however, the situation is seen in reverse, and Śiva is said to have adopted them after Indra attempted to kill them:

> 25ea[3] Diti, the mother of the demons, once performed great *tapas* and obtained
> 45a from her husband, Kaśyapa, an embryo destined to slay Indra [who had slain
> 45e[1] all her other sons]. Indra, learning of this, entered her womb in a minute form
> and divided the embryo into forty-nine parts, cutting them with his thunder-
> 11cd bolt. They all came forth from the womb and wept. Śiva and Pārvatī, who
> 19e happened to be passing by, saw the Maruts, and Pārvatī said to Śiva, 'If you
> love me, let all these bits of flesh become my sons.' Śiva gave them to her as sons, and therefore they are called the sons of Rudra, and he is called the father of the Maruts.[9]

In addition to their association with the Maruts, the two gods share many characteristics. Both are said to have three eyes[10] or a thousand eyes,[11] and for the same reason:

> 21ea Once the *apsaras* Tilottamā was sent to seduce two demons from their
> 31e *tapas*. While she danced before them, Śiva and Indra wanted to see more of
> 7cd 21ea her, and for this purpose Śiva became four-faced and Indra thousand-eyed.[12]

7cd The epithet 'thousand-eyed' is also applied to Soma in the Ṛg Veda[13]
and may originally have been an attribute of celestial and ruling gods: Varuṇa, god of the waters, has a thousand eyes, as has Agni, the god of fire.[14] In Iran, Mithra has 10,000 eyes or 10,000 spies.[15] Whatever its original source, the motif of the extra eyes when applied to Indra and Śiva takes on erotic connotations. The appearance of supplementary eyes or faces to see a beautiful woman is a popular theme: Skanda is said to have sprouted his six heads in order to see the beautiful goddesses around him, Brahmā to have made five heads in order to see his

own daughter.[16] (Brahmā is also said to have lusted for Tilottamā,[17] as 39e
Indra and Śiva do.)

B. 1. *Indra as Phallic God of Fertility*

The cause and use of the extra eyes is a sexual one, and both Indra
and Śiva here play the part of the seduced ascetic. Both are fertility
gods. Śiva's mount is the bull and he himself is called a bull, as are $45e^2$
Indra and Rudra in the Vedas,[18] the bull being a symbol of sexual power.
Indra in the *Mahābhārata* is the god of the seed, who dissuades a king $45e^1$ 45a
from his *tapas* and teaches him to erect 'Indra-poles',[19] phallic emblems $26e^2$
analogous to the Śiva-*liṅga*. In the Ṛg Veda, Indra is said to bestow
wives and to receive the offerings as a loving husband embraces his
loving wives.[20] Women who are hated by their husbands vow to unite
with Indra, and by his favour pregnant women are allowed sexual intercourse, otherwise forbidden them.[21] Indra is said to have chosen his
wife for her sensuousness; he ravished her and slew her father to escape
his curse,[22] just as Śiva beheaded his father-in-law, Dakṣa. Since Śacī, $38a^1$
the wife of Indra, is sometimes said to be a daughter of Dakṣa,[23] the
father-in-law slain by Indra may even be the very person slain by Śiva.
Moreover, Indra is said to have beheaded the sacrifice, or, in a peculiar
reversal, to have beheaded Rudra when Rudra was excluded from the 4
sacrifice,[24] just as Rudra–Śiva, excluded from Dakṣa's sacrifice, beheads
Dakṣa. Indra's wife is described as the most lascivious of women, who 22ea
boasts of her husband's sexual prowess, rejoices in the dimensions of
his sexual organ, and tries to get him drunk.[25] 16d

All of these myths and characteristics are appropriate to a fertility god, and all of them are inherited by Śiva from Indra.

With these qualities goes a series of myths that are told about both
gods. Like Śiva, Indra is a notorious adulterer, famed for the seduction 23ea
of Ahalyā, the wife of Gautama. This is a very old story, for one Brāhmaṇa refers to Indra as 'the lover of Ahalyā'.[26] The *Mahābhārata* relates
the reaction of Gautama, who curses Indra to wear a green beard, or, in
another version, to bear the marks of a thousand *yonis* (female sexual 17cd
organs).[27] Other texts, however, state that Gautama caused Indra to 3
be castrated,[28] a theme of great importance to the mythology of Śiva. 32a
Both of these punishments—the castration and the branding with the mark of the *yoni*—are apparently reversals of Indra's manhood, but each in fact ultimately contributes to it, the castration by giving to Indra the testicles of a ram and the branding by being assimilated to the motif

of the erotic eye: the curse is modified and the marks are changed to
7cd[2] eyes, so that Indra is called Sahasrākṣa ('Having a Thousand Eyes')
17cd or Netrayoni ('Having Eyes for Female Organs').[29] The Ahalyā story
seems to be thus somewhat muddled with the myth of Tilottamā, and
one text states that Indra was cursed to have a thousand *yonis* upon him
until, when he beheld Tilottamā, they turned into a thousand eyes.[30]
The tie thus formed between Indra and Śiva may be traced to the Ṛg
45e[1] Veda tradition that gives both Indra and Agni the epithet Sahasramuṣka
('Having a Thousand Testicles').[31] Moreover, Indra is said to have
created a male organ on every limb of the Brahmin Sumitra so that the
45e[1] Brahmin could marry a demoness who had a female organ on every
limb and who refused to marry him until he could match her.[32] The
punishment of Indra also reflects the tradition of Hindu law which
ordained that a man who had violated his guru's bed must be branded
17cd with the *yoni*.[33] (This motif is further assimilated to Śiva by the tribal
myth in which Lingal, an aspect of Śiva, is born with '*ling*' on his hands,
feet, throat, and head.)[34]

Closely related to the castration motif is the motif of changing from
man to woman, with which Indra is also associated. Indra fell in love
with a demon woman and went to live among the demons, as a man
32ea among men and a woman among women.[35] An Indian folk-tale expands
this motif and relates it to Śiva and Pārvatī:

> 24a [Indra asked Pārvatī how she could bear a husband who always wore the
> 3 32ea garb of an anchorite. She cursed him to bear a woman's name and to be
> 17cd turned to water. Indra propitiated Śiva, who persuaded Pārvatī to modify
> 45ea her curse so that a river with a woman's name (Indrāṇī) sprang from Indra's
> 14c[1] body.][36]

Other forms of transformation are also associated with Indra. He is
33ea[2] said to have taken the form of a Brahmin guest or of Gautama himself[37]
33ea[5] in order to seduce Ahalyā. This particular masquerade is an essential
motif of the Śaiva mythology of the false ascetic: Śiva assumes the role
of the Brahmin guest when he seduces the wives of the Pine Forest
sages. The link between this myth and the tale of Ahalyā is made
1 explicit in one version of the Pine Forest tale which refers to the castra-
32a tion of Indra when describing the same fate as it befalls Śiva.[38] Both
gods are associated with anti-Brahmanical, heterodox acts, and each
loses his right to a share of the sacrifice.[39] Indra once killed a Brahmin
whose head pursued him until he was purified of his sin,[40] just as Śiva,
38a[1, 2] having beheaded Brahmā, was plagued by Brahmā's skull.

The story of Indra and Srucāvatī is in many ways a model for the episode of the *tapas* performed by Pārvatī to win Śiva:

A beautiful young girl named Srucāvatī was determined to win Indra for
her husband, and she began to perform terrible *tapas*. Indra came to her 25ea[2]
hermitage disguised as Vasiṣṭha, a sage of great *tapas*, and when she received 33ea[5]
him with the honour due to a guest she said, 'I will give you whatever you
wish—anything but my hand, which I am saving for Indra alone.' Indra
smiled and praised her for her *tapas*, and then he asked her to cook some 35ea
jujubes for him. As she cooked she began to run out of fuel for the fire, and 16cd
so she began to burn her own body. Then Indra revealed his true identity 6d
and took her to dwell with him as his wife in heaven.[41] 6c

The appearance of the desired husband in disguise, the refusal to give
her hand, and the attempted self-immolation are all elements of the
story of Śiva and Pārvatī. Moreover, in this very episode Indra narrates
to Srucāvatī the episode in which Arundhatī (the wife of Vasiṣṭha) 1
cooked jujubes for Śiva[42]—an explicit multiform.

B. 2. *Indra versus the Ascetic*

In one series of myths, variants of the theme of the ascetic and the
prostitute, Indra comes into conflict with ascetics in a manner which
forms an important motif of later Śaiva mythology. As a phallic god,
Indra opposes various ascetics in order both to maintain the balance of
power in the universe and to maintain his own supremacy in heaven.
For, weakened as he is by his own profligacy, Indra's throne is actually
heated by the *tapas* amassed by ascetics on earth, so that he becomes
physically uncomfortable and must find a way to disperse the ascetic
heat. Indra's vow of truth is this: 'If a Brahmin on earth be not afraid
of me from birth, by his chastity and *tapas* he will cause me to fall from 45a
heaven. By this truth I swear.'[43] As one king comments on the seduction
of a great sage by an *apsaras*, 'The gods do have this fear of other 21ea
people's ascetic powers.'[44] 45a

Occasionally Indra uses fairly subtle methods to turn ascetics from their *tapas*:

Yavakrīt performed great *tapas* until he generated heat in Indra. Indra 7d
asked the cause of his *tapas*, and the ascetic replied that he wished to become 45a
omniscient. Indra said, 'This is not a proper path. Go and study with a guru.
You have undertaken an impossible goal, and you will never win enlightenment this way, which is forbidden by the Vedas.' When Yavakrīt still per-
sisted, Indra took the form of a Brahmin ascetic many centuries old, weak and 33ea[5]
feeble, trying to build a bridge of sand across the Ganges. When Yavakrīt

8d pointed out the futility of this task, Indra said, 'It is equally futile to try to
win the Vedas by *tapas*.'[45]

Although the particular goal of Yavakrīt's *tapas*—omniscience—is considered impossible (as it was for the sons of Dakṣa), Indra's objection to
30e 9cd asceticism is more broadly based. He appears as a golden bird before
45a a group of forest-dwellers and explains to them the inferiority of
asceticism compared to the normal life of a householder.[46] He success-
45a fully tempts another sage by assuming the form of a mercenary soldier
33ea[5] and enchanting him with the appeal of glittering arms.[47] Frequently the
45a encounter is more violent; Indra is said to have fed a group of yogis to
jackals.[48]

45a Usually, however, Indra plots, 'How can he be made addicted to
21ea sensual enjoyments so that he will cease his *tapas*?'[49] Indra sends an
21ea *apsaras* to the sage, who abandons his chastity and usually sheds his
21e seed.[50] Indra sends *apsarases* to disturb a number of famous sages,[51]
21ea and he sends Kāma himself to interfere with Nārada's *tapas* when he
fears that Nārada wants to usurp his kingdom.[52] He sends a nymph to
tempt the son of the sage Gautama, who sheds his seed in the familiar
26e[1] clump of reeds,[53] and when he sends Kāma to seduce the sage Viśvā-
30e mitra, Indra himself assumes the form of a cuckoo,[54] just as Agni and
21ea Kāma appear as birds in similar situations. Indra uses his own wife,
Śacī, to overpower a demon by playing upon the demon's desire for
her,[55] just as Śiva later uses his wife to seduce various demons. In one
version of this myth, it is Indra's daughter who helps to trick the
threatening demon:

> During a great battle between the gods and the demons, Śukra, the pre-
> 34a ceptor of the demons, performed a great vow of *tapas* in order to obtain
> a boon from Śiva to aid the demons. While he was performing this vow, Indra
> 45a sent his daughter Jayantī, who first served Śukra in his *tapas* and then induced
> 27ea him to make love to her for many years. While Śukra was thus engaged, Indra
> 21ea tricked the demons into distrusting Śukra and spurning the boon that he had
> obtained for them.[56]

In this myth, Indra is the enemy of Śukra and of his benefactor (the
ascetic Śiva), not only as the king of the gods opposed to demons (whom
Śiva often assists), but as the phallic god opposed to ascetics, as is
evident from the technique which he uses. In another variant of this
34e myth, Śiva aids the gods against Śukra, whom he causes to be seduced
45a by a horrible female demon.[57] As usual, the gods change sides but the
4 pattern persists.

On those extremely rare occasions when the sage failed to respond to the *apsaras*, Indra often succeeded anyway by annoying the sage until he used up his *tapas* in cursing the would-be seductress. The law books state unequivocally that an ascetic must never insult or curse anyone, even when he is himself insulted or cursed.[58] A Purāṇa tale in praise of a great sage relates that, although capable of reducing to ashes the demon who was annoying him, the sage wished to preserve his *tapas* and therefore merely gazed up at the sky and sighed a long, hot sigh.[59] Pārvatī 13d
does not curse the demon Andhaka, though he has tried to seduce her, for she wishes to guard her *tapas*, and an ascetic whose wife Indra has attempted to seduce pities Indra and does not burn him with a curse.[60]
Indra justifies his adultery with Ahalyā by saying that, for the welfare 13d
of the gods, he seduced her in order to anger her husband and thus causan obstacle to his *tapas*.[61] Similarly, though Viśvāmitra resists the temptae tions of Kāma he nevertheless falls prey to anger towards Indra, which destroys his *tapas* just as effectively.[62]

Thus, although Indra and Śiva share their fertility aspects, and Śiva uses the very methods of Indra to seduce the Pine Forest sages (causing them to succumb to anger as well as to lust), nevertheless Śiva often opposes this aspect of Indra, who uses these methods against Śiva. In this way, Indra is responsible for Kāma's seduction of Śiva and Śiva's outburst of *tapas*-dispelling anger. This ambiguity in the later mythology stems not from any true ambiguity in the character of Indra but rather from the fact that Śiva on different occasions assumes the part of the protagonist or the antagonist in the traditional Indra myth of the seduced ascetic.

The two gods occasionally impersonate one another. Indra takes the 45ea
repulsive form of a Śaiva heretic and even performs *tapas* for Śiva, in 45e 25ea[3]
order to obtain a son, while Śiva assumes the handsome form of Indra himself.[63] Thus each god increases that quality—*tapas* or *kāma*—which already exists within him in subordination to the complementary force. The commentator on the Epic remarks that Śiva may assume the epithet of Indra because there is no difference between them, and Indra, trying to dissuade a householder from performing *tapas* for Śiva, says, 'Śiva is no different from me.'[64] In this context, in this role, there *is* no dif- 45a
ference. Indra and Śiva were not identified with each other because they happened to amass similar characteristics; rather, from the time of the late Vedas, Rudra and Indra were *given* similar attributes because they served an identical function.

C. AGNI, THE EROTIC FIRE

The ascetic Śiva of the Purāṇas frequently uses his *tapas* as a weapon
against his enemies, particularly against Kāma. In the Ṛg Veda, most
of the verses in which *tapas* is used as heat against enemies are hymns
to Agni, the god of fire,[65] who blasts with his *tapas* those who are
impious and who perform the ritual with an evil purpose,[66] just as
8d Śiva burns the impious Pine Forest sages. The fiery power of *tapas*
serves as a natural bridge between Agni and Śiva, and it is said, 'All the
various forms of fire are ascetics, all takers of vows, and all are known
to be parts of Rudra himself.'[67]

But Agni is often personified not as the heat of *tapas* but as the opposite force, the heat of sexual desire, and many Śaiva myths are based upon a combination of the two. Springing from the natural physiological analogy, the tie between Agni and Kāma was supported by the Vedic symbolism of the two fire-sticks, the upper one male and the lower one female, whose friction is described in anthropomorphic terms.[68] This symbolism was maintained in Hindu thinking by the identification of ritual heat, *tapas*, with sexual heat, *kāma*, and Agni was called Kāma.[69]

7c A hymn invokes Agni to madden a man with love;[70] another text
states, 'Agni is the cause of sexual union. . . . When a man and woman
7c become heated, the seed flows, and birth takes place.'[71] When Kāma
pursues Śiva, he wounds him with the arrow called Saṃtāpa ('The
7c Heater'), and, thus wounded, Śiva heats the whole universe.[72] According
to one tribe, fire originated from the intercourse of two dirty people.[73]
A similar tale is told among another tribe:

> 7c Agnisur Dano [the demon god of fire] lived in a cave in the depth of the
> 24ea forest. A Baiga woman fell in love with him, for he was beautiful and light
> 16c came from all parts of his body. [She slept with him, and then she wanted
> 17c to take fire from his mouth. When she bathed, he opened his mouth and fire
> 13cd^3 issued forth from it. Thenceforth there was fire in the world.][74]

An interesting example of fire imagery in modern Hindu mythology is Nirad Chaudhuri's perhaps unconscious adaptation of the image in a quasi-historical analysis of sex in India:

> I have my images for the sexual life of the Hindus and its successive phases.
> 7c Down to the epic age from the Vedic, we see an honest wood-fire. . . . But in
> the age which followed, that of classical Hindu attitudes, a benevolent but
> erratic daimon threw a handful of magnesium into that yellow fire, to change
> 8d the flames into a dazzling, blinding, and cascading mass of white light. Then
> 6d it went out, and what was left behind were beds of dirty red cinders, smoulder-

ing and hissing, and there clung to them an obstinate odour of burnt flesh and
hair which always lingers in the atmosphere of our burning ghats and crema- 5d
toriums. . . . It was a world of death, in which fire itself was death. An
adventure which had started as an act of generation was ending as an act of 10cd
dying.[75]

What Chaudhuri describes as 'my images' are merely a set of motifs from Śaiva mythology: the fire of Kāma in conflict with the fire of *tapas*, the fire of death which is a part of the fire of lust. This is the myth of Kāma and Śiva. The Pine Forest myth affords yet another example of fire against fire, one which has also been analysed as a variant of 'the classical model of Hindu mythology: the burning up of Kāma—a form of Agni—by [Śiva]'. In this myth, Śiva represents the demoniacal, earthly form of the fire god, and the sages of the forest are the
procreators and masters of fire in all its forms, especially of the *liṅga* 5cd
fire that radiates from the god.[76]

As a personified deity, Agni is an unscrupulous seducer of women and
an adulterer, qualities which cause him to be identified with Śiva.[77] 23ea
Even in the Ṛg Veda, Agni is the lover of maidens and the husband of wives, and it is he who instigates the act of divine incest.[78] When Śiva destroys the triple city of the demons his weapon is fire, one of his eight elemental forms, and the burning of the demon women (by means of an arrow, which is Kāma's weapon) is described in erotic terms:

> When Śiva burnt the triple city with his fiery arrow, the women were burnt 42e
> as they made love with their lovers in close embraces. One woman left her 43ea
> lover but could go nowhere else, and she died in front of him. One lotus-eyed 7c
> woman, weeping, cried, 'Agni, I am another man's wife. You, who witness 10cd
> the virtue of the triple world, should not touch me. Go away, leaving this 23ea
> house and my husband who lies with me.' . . . Some women were burnt as
> they ran from their husbands' embraces. Others, asleep and intoxicated,
> exhausted after love-making, were half burnt before they awoke and wandered 43ea
> about, stunned. . . . The five arrows of Kāma, which had formerly been shot 43a
> into Śiva and were repelled by him, now became the sweating limbs of the 11c
> demon women with their demon lovers.[79] 43e

Erotic death by fire is frequently associated with the motif of self-immolation, the original 'suttee' having been Satī, who entered the fire when Śiva was dishonoured. When Satī, reborn as Pārvatī, was about to marry Śiva again, the women of Himālaya's city spurned their lovers and praised Śiva, saying, 'What use have we for our lovers and our nights
of love-making? We will not continue on the wheel of life, but we will 10cd
enter the fire, and Śiva will be our husband.'[80] 6c

Agni in his anthropomorphic form is usually depicted as the lascivious Brahmin priest, in the tradition of the ascetic and the prostitute:

Once when Agni saw Sudarśanā, the beautiful daughter of a king and the
21ea holy river Narmadā (personified as a woman), he was overcome by desire for
33ea[5] her. He assumed the form of a Brahmin and said to the king, 'I am a Brahmin
of low descent and great poverty, and I am disgusted with chastity, lonely,
and tortured with desire. I want to marry your daughter.' The king said,
23a 'I will not give her to a man without possessions, a man not her equal. Go
24a away.' Then Agni vanished from the king's sacrifice [i.e. his elemental form,
8d the sacrificial fire, vanished]. When his Brahmin priests told him that this
catastrophe had been caused because Agni had come to seek his daughter,
19ea the king rejoiced and consented to the marriage, and Agni promised to remain
with the king always.[81]

In this myth, Agni plays the role of the erotic ascetic, and is reviled. The
curse which Agni gives in retaliation is merely the absence of his essence
(fire) and the consequent destruction of the sacrifice. The same curses
are given by Śiva to the sages of the Pine Forest and to Dakṣa when they
oppose his sexual demands. When the sages have cursed and reviled
5cd[3] Śiva, the sun gives no warmth, fire no light, and all is plunged into dark-
5d ness; the fiery energy of Śiva's *liṅga* is withdrawn from the world.[82] The
5d other curse of the Pine Forest is simply the inverse of this: the fiery *liṅga*
5cd[2] begins to burn up all the universe,[83] just as Śiva burns up Dakṣa's
23a sacrifice and as Ṛṣyaśṛṅga's father threatens to burn the palace until the
princess is given in marriage. The spurned ascetic often threatens to
8d burn the king with his *tapas*, for fire is the weapon both of asceticism and
of thwarted lust.

Several interesting manifestations of the sexual symbolism of fire may be seen among the Agaria tribe, whose religion centres around fire.[84] Verrier Elwin notes the natural analogy between the action of the fire-stick and fire-drill and the sexual act, an analogy which is supported by Vedic ritual symbolism. Two Agaria myths illustrate this symbolic link:

8c [A sage performed asceticism for twelve years without food and water,
meditating upon fire although he had no fire and had never seen any fire but
7c the fires in the sky. At last fire in the form of a virgin stood before him and
said, 'I am very cold. Make a fire for me.' She showed him how and he made
a fire, but when he saw the fire the sage's nature changed, and he gave up his
26e[1] asceticism and went to the nearest village. . . . The dry bamboos there rubbed
30ea against one another in the wind and caught fire, and so fire began in the
world.]

The culture-hero is superimposed upon the motif of the ascetic seduced and led from the wilderness to civilization ('the nearest village'). The bamboo reed, associated with the seed of fire in Śaiva mythology, plays a new role here as the source rather than the receptacle of the blazing seed. Another Agaria myth bears a more striking resemblance to the episode of Agni and Sudarśanā:

[The Sun sought the beautiful daughter of a king, but the king put out one $5c^3$ 23a
of the Sun's eyes. The Sun then took his full fiery shape and destroyed the 21ea
kingdom. The princess, pregnant, ran away and jumped into a pot of butter- 7cd
milk; later she gave birth to a son called Jwala Mukhi ('Fire-Mouth'). When $13cd^3$ 7d 14cd 8d
he grew up and the other boys teased him for having no father, his mother 13c 30ea
told him the story of his birth. He sought the Sun across the ocean, and cap- 3
tured him, causing darkness in the world. The people sent the Wind to find 3 19a
him, and Jwala Mukhi cursed the Sun to go to his wife (the Moon) only 6cd
during her (fertile) period. The Sun then cursed Jwala Mukhi that his wealth 5d
would disappear like ashes. When the Sun saw an Agaria with his wife, he $14c^3$ 22e 44ea
kicked them and knocked them over. The Agaria cursed the Sun: if you ever 3
go to your wife, you will die.] 10cd

Several Śaiva motifs occur here in curious transformation. The Sun has one eye too few rather than too many, but he burns his unwilling father-in-law with the ascetic blaze of thwarted lust usually associated with the third eye. The pregnant woman enters liquid instead of the usual funeral pyre but gives birth to a child whose mouth contains fire. The Sun, captured, causes darkness, which is the inverse of the blaze which he originally causes and is also the usual effect of the 'capturing' or blinding of Śiva's eyes (which are the Sun and Moon). The motif of the Wind sent to find the Sun corresponds to the episode of Kāma (in the form of a wind) or Agni sent to interrupt Śiva and Pārvatī in their love-play and results in the two curses usually associated with that interruption: first relative and then absolute barrenness. The first curse in itself amounts to an interruption, for the Sun is separated from his wife, and yet another episode of interruption follows immediately, but with the Sun acting as the cause rather than the recipient of the act. These motifs are all associated with Śiva (through his connection with fire and the Sun) and with the Agaria sun god for the same reason: the sexual symbolism of fire in Indian tradition.

C. 1. *Agni and the Pine Forest Sages*

Śiva is more explicitly related to the erotic, destructive fire in the myth of the Pine Forest, which can be traced directly to the story of Agni and the wives of the Seven Sages, a text which is the source of much of the Skanda myth as well.[85] In the Vedas, Agni is associated with illicit sexuality; in one text, he himself sheds his fiery seed at the sight of Uṣas 44e

39e 4 (Dawn), just as Prajāpati does.[86] Another Vedic text says, 'The waters
13c 21e were the wives of Varuṇa [god of the waters]. Agni desired them and
26e united with them. His seed fell and became the earth, the sky, and the
8cd plants that are eaten by fire.'[87] This statement foreshadows the role of
44e fire and water in the Skanda story (in which the seed of Śiva is placed
first in Agni and then in the Ganges). Another version concludes,
9cd 'Agni's seed fell and became gold',[88] and the seed of Śiva is gold.

All later versions describe the seduced women not as the wives of Varuṇa but as the wives of the Seven Sages:

> Originally, the Kṛttikās [the Pleiades] were the wives of the Bears [or
> Stars, the constellation Ursa Major], for the Seven Sages were in former times
> called the Bears. They were, however, prevented from intercourse [with their
> 44ea husbands], for the Seven Sages rise in the North, and they [the Kṛttikās] in
> 35ea the East. Now, it is a misfortune for one to be prevented from intercourse
> 44e [with his wife]. . . . But in fact Agni is their mate, and it is with Agni that they
> have intercourse.[89]

No causal relation seems to be suggested here between the Kṛttikās'
separation from their husbands and their connection with Agni. In many
33ea[6] of the later versions, however, it is stated that they were abandoned by
their husbands because of their impregnation by Agni (or Śiva), and in one version they are cursed to become constellations as a result of this abandonment.[90] Yet in the earliest full version of the myth, in the *Mahābhārata*, they are given the *reward* of becoming constellations and dwelling for ever in heaven as compensation for having been abandoned by their husbands:

> 35ea Once when Agni saw the beautiful wives of the great sages sleeping in their
> 21ea hermitage, he was overcome by desire for them. But he reflected, 'It is not
> proper for me to be full of lust for the chaste wives of the Brahmins, who are
> 7c not in love with me.' Then he entered the household fire so that he could
> touch them, as it were, with his flames, but after a long time his desire became
> 10cd still greater, and he went into the forest, resolved to abandon his corporeal
> 10c form. Then Svāhā [the oblation], the daughter of Dakṣa, fell in love with him
> and watched him for a long time, seeking some weak point, but in vain. When
> she knew that he had gone into the forest full of desire, the amorous goddess
> 33ea[3] decided to take the forms of the wives of the Seven Sages and to seduce Agni;
> 22ea thus both of them would obtain their desire. Assuming the form of each of
> 23ea the wives in turn, she made love with Agni, but she could not take the form
> 21e of Arundhatī, wife of Vasiṣṭha, because Arundhatī had such great powers of
> chastity. Taking Agni's seed in her hand each time, she reflected, 'Anyone
> 33ea[6] who chances to see me in this form in the forest will falsely accuse the sages'
> wives of committing adultery with Agni', and so to avoid this she took the
> 30e form of the Gāruḍī bird and left the forest. She threw the seed into a golden

lake on the peak of the white mountain guarded by Rudra's hosts. The seed 9c 9cd
generated a son, Skanda, and some time later the six sages' wives came to 20ea
Skanda and told him that their husbands, thinking that Skanda had been born 33ea[6]
of them, had abandoned them. They begged Skanda to let them dwell for
ever in heaven, and by his grace they became the constellation of the Kṛttikās,
considered the mothers of Skanda. Then Svāhā married Agni.[91] 19ea

Two conflicting aspects of a single theme are at play here: the chaste ascetic seduced by the prostitute (Svāhā) and the lustful ascetic who seduces chaste women (the sages' wives). This leads to ambiguities about the intentions of both the sage and the women in later versions which combine both episodes in a single encounter, ambiguities which are foreshadowed here in the sages' mistaken accusation of their wives (who are, nevertheless, not entirely innocent, for they are contrasted with Arundhatī, whose chastity protects her). The elemental Agni, as well as the anthropomorphic, is very much in evidence here. He comes to the sages' wives in the form of the household fire, and, when spurned, he withdraws his elemental form. His wife, Svāhā, is merely the personification of the oblation, the natural partner of the sacrificial fire; she is a daughter of Dakṣa, like Satī who makes herself an oblation (a suttee).

Svāhā's role is almost entirely excluded in one strangely garbled version of the myth:

Agni saw the wives of the Seven Sages, and he lost his control and went to 7c
the forest. But the women in that forest were protected by a curse [so that 23ea
they could not be seduced]. Therefore, making images of them, desiring them 35ea
more and more, Agni placed his seed in a golden pot, and, assuming the form 33ea[7, 4]
of a Garuḍa bird, he brought it to the peak of the white mountain, where 9cd 30e
a child was born from it, Kārtikeya [Skanda, son of the Kṛttikās]. He could 20ea
not make the form of Arundhatī, however, because of her fidelity to Vasiṣṭha.
Kārtikeya became the son of Pārvatī.

It was because Agni did not enjoy making love to Svāhā that he made the 36a
imitation Kṛttikās and seduced other women.[92]

As a result of Svāhā's exclusion from the main part of this version, Agni himself 'makes' the forms of the sages' wives (whose forms Svāhā 'takes' in the earlier version) and becomes a male Garuḍa to replace the female Gāruḍī bird. Yet the basic structure of the myth has been preserved with the essential elements: Agni's desire for the sages' wives and the birth of the child Skanda from Agni's seed on the mountain. (The mountain persists later in the form of Pārvatī, daughter of Himālaya.)

A late text combines the stories of Agni and of Śiva in an explicit way, reintroducing Svāhā. There are two sets of parents and two sets of children, though the redundant children are merely anthropomorphs of the gold which is an essential theme of the myth:

19ea Agni married Svāhā, the daughter of Dakṣa. She performed *tapas* to obtain
25ea[3] a son, until her husband said, 'You will have children. Cease from this *tapas*',
and she obeyed him. Śiva married Pārvatī and began to make love to her, and
30e after some time Agni took the form of a parrot and stood at the window of
44ea Śiva's house, averting his face. Śiva saw him and laughed and said, 'Look at
the parrot, Pārvatī. It is Agni, sent by the gods.' Then she was ashamed and
she said to Śiva, 'Enough, my lord', and Śiva summoned the bird and said,
16c 'You have been recognized, Agni. Open your mouth and receive this', and
32ea he threw his seed into Agni's mouth. Pregnant with the seed, Agni went to
44e 8cd the bank of the Ganges, exhausted. There he threw the seed to the Kṛttikās,
20ea and what was left of the seed of Śiva in his body he gave to his wife, in two
9cd pieces, because she desired a son. In time, twins were born to Svāhā, named
19a Suvarṇa and Suvarṇā ['Gold'], a boy and a girl. He seduced the wives of the
7c gods and she seduced the gods, and for this they were cursed. But Agni
sought refuge with Śiva, who promised that all wealth would dwell in the
twins for ever.[93]

The Ganges is not needed here to fulfil the role of mother (which is doubly filled, by Svāhā and the Kṛttikās) and so she appears merely as the place *at* which the birth takes place, rather than the element *in* which it takes place. The sages' wives assume only an implied function, the birth of Skanda not being actually narrated in this story but inevitably resulting from the seed given to them. The innovation is that Agni does not leave Svāhā for the sages' wives, but gives her children. This is a feedback from the later story of Śiva and Pārvatī, as is the manner in which Svāhā gets the boon of children, by doing *tapas* from which she must be dissuaded. The golden twins are multiforms of their original parents: the son seduces the wives of the gods as Agni–Śiva seduces the wives of the sages, and the daughter seduces the gods as Svāhā seduces Agni.

Svāhā appears in a larger role in a version of the birth of Skanda which relates her story in the middle of the derivative myth:

25ea[3] When Pārvatī had completed her vow of *tapas*, Śiva said, 'Now you are
36e worthy, and I will give you a son who will make you famous.' He made love
44ea to her for a thousand years, and the gods, worried, sent Agni to find out what
30e Śiva was doing. Agni took the form of a turtle-dove and entered Śiva's
presence. Then Śiva said to him, 'It was not proper for you to shake my seed
44a from its place. Now you must take it or I will burn you in anger.' Terrified,
32ea Agni accepted the seed, and, since he was the mouth of all the gods, it entered
9c all of their stomachs, split them open, and poured out to form a lake. But the
44e seed that remained in Agni tortured him until he spilt it into the Ganges, and
8cd she, in turn, threw it up upon her waves, and it became a white mountain.

5. Ascetic sages with *apsaras*. Aihole, Bījāpur District. Sixth century (?). MOTIF: 21ea, 25ea.

6. Śiva impaling Andhaka on his trident. Virūpākṣa temple, Pattadakal. Eighth century. MOTIF: 31a, 39a.

7. Śiva dancing with Pārvatī and Nandin. Pāpanātha temple, Pattadakal, Mysore. Eighth century. MOTIF: 31e, 36e, 45e².

8. Śiva, the androgyne, wearing snakes, with Pārvatī, Nandin, and a skeleton. Cave one, Bādāmī, Mysore. Sixth century. MOTIF: 30a, 32e, 36e, 45e².

> When Agni had cast Śiva's seed into the Ganges, Himālaya summoned him
> to participate in a fire oblation that the Seven Sages were performing. There 10c
> Agni saw the wives of the sages, and he was overcome by desire for them. 21ea
> [Here it continues just like the *Mahābhārata* story of Agni and Svāhā, with 35ea
> minor changes: the Gāruḍī bird throws the seed into a golden pot in a clump 30e 9cd
> of reeds, rather than into a golden lake.] 26e[1]
> When Agni had thrown Śiva's seed into the Ganges, the six wives of the 44e
> sages bathed there and the seed entered them. Troubled by that seed, and in 17c
> fear of their husbands, they hid on the banks of the Ganges until Svāhā, the 33ea[6]
> wife of Agni, entered their bodies and took the seed. It was then that she took 8cd
> their forms and made love with Agni. The sages abandoned all their wives 33ea[3]
> but Arundhatī, knowing that they had become impure. Although their *tapas* 33ea[6]
> was great enough to burn the universe, the wives did not curse Svāhā [for 8d
> taking their forms with Agni] for she had done a favour for them [by taking
> the seed from them].
> Then Agni was full of remorse and wished to die, but a voice from the sky 10cd
> prevented him, saying, 'Do not die. It was fate that made you desire and
> enjoy the wives of other men, and as you only thought that you made love to
> them, you will not suffer. For it was your own wife Svāhā who took the form 33ea[3]
> of the sages' wives, and it was she to whom you made love each time. A son
> has been born to you in a pot on the white mountain.' Then Agni went there
> and saw his son, whom he kissed and embraced. 19e
> Pārvatī and Śiva then went to see the child, and Brahmā said to Skanda,
> 'Go to Śiva and Pārvatī, for you were born of the union of their seed.' They 20ea
> embraced Skanda, but the six goddesses who had been abandoned by their
> husbands claimed him as their son, and Svāhā considered him hers, and Agni
> considered him his. As they argued, Skanda smiled and proclaimed himself
> the son of all of them, and everyone rejoiced. The wives of the sages went to
> heaven and became the Kṛttikās.[94]

The incorporation of the story of Agni and Svāhā in the second paragraph has necessitated certain adjustments in other parts of the story, not all of them successful. There are contradictions: the first paragraph says that the seed in the Ganges became a white mountain, forming the birthplace, but the third reverts to the Agni–Svāhā story and says that from the Ganges the seed entered the Kṛttikās. Moreover, as in other early versions, a third batch of this same seed of Śiva is said to have formed a lake, while the lake that one would expect to find in the second
paragraph is replaced by a golden pot in a clump of reeds. (The clump 26e[1]
of reeds, which forms a hiding-place for the Vedic Indra as well as the 26e[1]
Vedic Agni,[95] remains the birthplace of Skanda in many later Purāṇa 26e[1]
texts.[96] Moreover, in South Indian mythology the reeds revert to their
original role as a lake called 'Forest of Reeds', which Śiva creates with 7cd[1]
his third eye or which is filled with the milk flowing from Pārvatī's 26e[1]
breasts at the birth of Skanda or, finally, which serves as the receptacle 19e

44e for the fiery seed of Śiva which engenders Skanda.[97] The reed forest is
44ea also the site of Īḷa's interruption of Śiva and Pārvatī,[98] a multiform of the Agni episode.) To complicate this myth further, a fourth seed is introduced: that of Agni, carried away by the Gāruḍī bird as in the original Svāhā story. To accommodate this quadruplicate of seed, the Purāṇa becomes involved in yet another contradiction: Svāhā receives the seed of Agni and places it in a pot (paragraph two), but she receives the seed of Śiva from the Kṛttikās (paragraph three). And Svāhā makes love with Agni after she has taken the seed from the Kṛttikās, who neither nurse Skanda nor bear him but are nevertheless translated to heaven as the usual curse/reward for their part in his birth. As a result of this multiple parentage, the Purāṇa describes an actual argument over the matter, in which a compromise must be reached. This argument occurs in several other versions as well, even where the parents are more logically accounted for.[99]

C. 2. *The Seven Sages and their Wives*

While Svāhā is omitted from most of the later myths of the birth of Skanda, the Seven Sages and their wives remain essential both to the Skanda myth and to the story of Śiva in the Pine Forest. Some versions merely call the Pine Forest ascetics great sages or householder sages, but several texts identify them as the Seven Sages,[100] the sons of Brahmā. These are the same sages who did *tapas* instead of marrying and procreating, and against whom Śiva in his erotic aspect had occasion to act. There is therefore precedent for his appearance in the Pine Forest in an unmistakably erotic aspect—naked, charming, singing and dancing, ithyphallic—to oppose them and to turn them from their *tapas* to their marital duties. Yet there is equal precedent for Śiva in his ascetic aspect to oppose Brahmā and his sons when they are erotically inclined. The Seven Sages are the enemies of Śiva in the Pine Forest, but they are such an integral part of the myth of Skanda's birth that they remain in that myth as the *assistants* of Śiva, who sends them to ask for Pārvatī on his behalf. Yet there is a touch of irony in this, for when he sends them to *test* her for him, the words that they speak in simulated derision
24a of Śiva[101] are the exact sentiments that they express in earnest in the Pine Forest story.

The wives of the Seven Sages are the embodiment of chastity and marital fidelity, and in spite of their involvement in the birth of Skanda they are never actually seduced. When they become involved it is the result of a minor mistake (bathing, or warming themselves before the

fire, or drinking what they suppose to be water), or simple slander.
Yet the taint of sin remains attached to them in contemporary Indian
folk-lore, where the Pleiades are said to be six repudiated wives or seven
illegitimate children.[102] In only one Sanskrit text is there a hint of 33ea[6]
possible sexual involvement: Indra causes the seed of Śiva to enter
them, and they give birth in a lying-in house.[103] In most versions, the 35ea
Kṛttikās find Skanda and nurse him, thus adopting him; in one text,
he is adopted by only one Kṛttikā, a reversal of the usual situation in
which only one Kṛttikā does *not* adopt him.[104] The most thoroughly
rationalized explanation states that the Kṛttikās gave Pārvatī the seed
of Śiva, in return for which they were explicitly designated the mothers 20ea
of Skanda.[105]

In some of the latest versions of the Skanda story the Kṛttikās' role is most clearly preserved. Because of an actual moral lapse, they become physically pregnant by Agni:

> When Śiva had placed his seed in the mouth of Agni, Agni was ashamed and 44a
> heated by the seed, and he threw it into the waters of the Ganges. She, burnt 16c
> by the seed, placed it on her bank, and the six wives of the Seven Sages came 44e
> there to bathe. Pained by the cold, they thought the blazing seed was fire, 17c 7c
> and they warmed themselves, but the seed entered them through their 20ea
> buttocks. Then, because of its great *tapas*, the seed broke out of their stomachs 7d
> and the six parts joined as one six-headed child. They were all very worried 20ea
> and afraid of the sages, because they had gone before the fire, and they threw 33ea[6]
> the child on the top of the white mountain among the reeds.[106] 26e[1]

In another version, the apparent moral lapse implied here ('They were all very worried and afraid of the sages because they had gone before the fire') is more explicit:

> Agni ate the seed of Śiva and returned to the gods. They all became preg- 16c
> nant by the seed that was in Agni's mouth, just as they all receive the oblation 32ea
> that is placed in Agni. Tortured by the seed, they sought help from Śiva, who 10c
> told them to vomit forth the seed. They did so, and the seed formed a great 9cd
> mountain of burnished gold, but in Agni alone the seed remained, burning
> like a comet. Śiva told Agni to release the seed into the womb of those who 8cd
> are heated every month. That dawn, the Kṛttikās came to bathe, and when 17c 15cd
> they were pained by the cold they warmed themselves before the blazing 7c
> fire, though Arundhatī tried to prevent them. The tiny particles of the seed
> entered through the pores of their skin. Agni, bereft of the seed, was ex- 20ea
> hausted, and the sages' wives went home and were cursed by their husbands 33ea[6]
> to become constellations. In their misery, they released the seed upon a slope 44e
> of Himālaya, where the parts came together and fell into the Ganges, encased 26e[1]
> in bamboo. There it became a six-headed boy, Skanda, and at that moment 20ea
> Pārvatī's breasts began to flow with milk, and she went where Nārada told 19e
> her that the boy was, and she found him and nursed him.[107]

The Kṛttikās' usual role in the birth—the nursing of Skanda—is here explicitly usurped by Pārvatī, whose breasts flow with milk for 'her' son. Though it is not clear what transgression it is that distinguishes the women who must receive the seed, it is obviously some sort of fault which makes them susceptible, as is clear from the pattern of the distribution and transference of sin and from Arundhatī's attempt to prevent them from warming themselves. The recurrence of the word for 'month' in the curse of the women suggests the possibility that they may receive the embryo when they bathe at the end of their monthly period. This is a common method of impregnation in South Indian mythology, and a similar idea, still more closely related to the episode of the Kṛttikās, appears among the Baiga tribe, who believe that men-
15cd struous women must be protected from the sun lest they be impregnated
$5c^3$ by his rays.[108]

In Greek mythology, the seventh Pleiad sometimes vanishes (often said to be the result of a sexual offence), and this ambiguity is found in the Indus Valley as well: there are seven goddesses worshipped at Mohenjo-Daro and six at Harappā. Thus the Seven Sages are married to the six Kṛttikās. These circumstances have led one scholar to suggest that the myth of the birth of Skanda may derive from an Indus Valley myth celebrating the birth of the year (Skanda) with its six seasons (six heads) during the new moon at the Spring equinox, when the sun is in the Pleiades (i.e. when Agni is 'in' the Kṛttikās); these extremely rare astrological conditions did in fact occur during the third millennium B.C., the period of the Indus Valley Civilization.[109] (In the light of this hypothesis, the references to the 'month' in the Kṛttikās' curse in various Sanskrit texts may assume a more specific, temporal connotation.)

A tale recorded among the Gonds, which has been analysed structurally, bears a striking resemblance to the story of the Kṛttikās, including the reversal of nursing roles as it appears in the Sanskrit version described above:

17c [When Kalinkali was twelve years old, she went to bathe in a river, and
28ea Śiva and the other gods saw her naked. She was disgraced, and her father
23a drove her out. Nine months later she gave birth to the gods, whom she
19a abandoned. Śiva and Pārvatī, who were roaming about the world on his bull,
$45e^2$ Nandin, saw the gods crying. Pārvatī suckled them, but the Gond gods
19e 15cd sucked her right breast until blood came, and they continued to suck blood
30e 44ea until the breast shrivelled up. Śiva, angry, trapped the Gond gods in a cave.
4 He made two birds, male and female, with long beaks, to guard the entrance
$13cd^{2,3}$ to the cave, for, he said to Pārvatī, 'I cannot master them. Your blood they

have sucked and no one on earth can control them.' He ordered that they 16c
should subsist on *sukra* seed.

After some time, Lingal freed the gods, and, later, Kalinkali became a clump 5cd
of bamboo beside the great ocean.][110] 26e[1] 14cd

Certain elements of this tale are directly derived from the Skanda myth, but they are rearranged in a way which obscures their significance. The drinking of milk is here obviously contrasted with the drinking of blood, but it is less obvious that the drinking of seed forms a third multiform: for the *sukra* seed which the gods drink is not merely the seed of the *sukra* plant but the seed of Śiva, which is often called *śukra* (as in the myth in which the preceptor of the demons obtains the name of Śukra by emerging from Śiva's phallus), and is often carried in the beak of a bird; the birds here guard the door which, in the Sanskrit myth, is entered by a bird who comes to take the seed. Two motifs which make scant sense in the Gond context—Śiva's inability to control the gods who have drunk Pārvatī's blood, and the transformation of Kalinkali into a bamboo clump—are basic to the Sanskrit corpus. Certain factors which the anthropologists have analysed structurally—the oppositions between purity and impurity, immortal and mortal, rejection and rescue—are equally valid for the Sanskrit cycle, but other oppositions (the complementary roles of Kalinkali/Pārvatī and Śiva/Lingal, the first element conceiving and rejecting the Gods, the second rescuing them) only become fully significant in the Sanskrit context. For it is essential for the parents of Skanda (or of the gods, in the Gond myth) to abandon their offspring, since Pārvatī and Śiva represent the asexual, ascetic parents, while the Kṛttikās and Lingal represent the sexual aspects of the two gods; thus the Kṛttikās conceive Skanda and Pārvatī 'rescues' him when they have abandoned him. The vague transgression of the Kṛttikās is more explicit in the Gond myth (Śiva sees Kalinkali bathing naked just as Agni sees the Kṛttikās), while the subsequent pregnancy and disgrace remain ambiguous.

The obscurity of the sexual offence committed by the six Kṛttikās is somewhat illuminated by the contrast with the seventh one, who remains absolutely chaste: Arundhatī, who tries to prevent their contact with Agni and whose form Svāhā is unable to assume in the original story. In several later versions of the Pine Forest story, Arundhatī is singled out as the one who resists the charms of Śiva, and in this way the ambiguous chastity of the Kṛttikās becomes significant: the point of the myth is that even they, the incarnation of fidelity, cannot resist Śiva; their alleged chastity is the very reason for their seduction. Two versions of the myth make Arundhatī the subject of an entire episode which contrasts her virtue with the frailty of the others:

35ea When the women of the Pine Forest saw Śiva begging in their hermitage
24ea[2] they were overcome by desire. Only Arundhatī, the faithful wife of Vasiṣṭha,
28ea resisted. All the others, old women and young girls, threw off their clothing
24a and urged Śiva to make love to them. . . . Then the sages beat and reviled
33ea[5] Śiva, and Śiva went to Vasiṣṭha's house and said to Arundhatī, the daughter
35ea of Dakṣa, 'I have been beaten by the sages in this wood and have come to
you as a guest. Give me alms, fair lady.' Then he showed Arundhatī all his
wounded limbs, covered with blood, and all his body, enticing her, but she
27a bathed his handsome body as if it were the body of her own son, and she said
to him, 'My son, you are welcome here.' Then he was pleased with her, and
he said, 'We ascetics and naked beggars are well pleased with you. May you
18a prosper in your marriage, and may your old husband become young and able
again, with a divine body, never ageing, like an immortal.' Then Śiva left the
house and wandered through the woods with the frenzied women, laughing
35ea and making love to them day and night for twelve years. . . . Then with a curse
32a the sages caused Śiva's *liṅga* to fall. The fiery *liṅga* stretched for many miles
5cd and landed in the body of Satī, but when it had plunged into the ground its
17cd divine energy was withdrawn from the universe, and the world became dark.
5d Then Arundhatī said to Vasiṣṭha, 'I fear that the naked ascetic who came here
was Śiva, for he did not lose his control or become angry although he was
struck by hundreds of weapons. And the mountain woman with him was my
23e[1, 2] sister, Pārvatī. May we two who participate in the householder stage heal the
body of Śiva and cause this darkness to vanish.' Vasiṣṭha said, 'So be it', and
because of that Śiva's body was restored. . . . Thus Śiva revealed the fickleness
34e 34a of the lustful sages and their wives and the firmness of the faithful women.
35e He proved the strength of those who were householders and the foolishness of
34ea those who took the vow of nakedness.[111]

Arundhatī here represents the good wife, the householder's virtuous woman, in contrast with the fickle wives of the sages. But the story of the good woman whose inviolable virtue resuscitates her *ascetic* husband is also brought into the myth, and this is a story usually told of the sage Atri (Cyavana) and his wife Anasūyā. It seems probable that this part of the story was added through the mediation of a third episode in which, after Śiva has been healed by Arundhatī and then castrated, Anasūyā, the wife of Atri, sees in a dream that it was Śiva who had come to beg from them.[112] As it is Arundhatī who recognizes Śiva in the later version, it would seem that she assumes the resuscitation theme associated with Anasūyā because she assumes Anasūyā's specific role in the Pine Forest myth. This possibility is supported by another text which states that, of all the Pine Forest women, only Anasūyā and Arundhatī remained true to their husbands.[113]

But Arundhatī is the subject of a similar myth in her own right:

> During a drought, the Seven Sages departed to do *tapas*, leaving Arundhatī 15d
> behind. Śiva came to her in the shape of a Brahmin and begged alms from 33ea5
> her. She had no food but jujubes, but she cooked these for twelve years, and 35ea 16cd
> the drought passed. Then the Seven Sages returned, and Śiva revealed him- 15c
> self and said that her *tapas* was greater than theirs, and he rewarded her.[114] 35e

The similarity of this myth to the tale of Anasūyā would be yet another reason for the introduction of the theme of the rejuvenated ascetic in the tale of Arundhatī. Moreover, Arundhatī is particularly suited for the role of the virtuous wife because of her past relationship with Śiva, for in her former incarnation she was Sandhyā, who, after desiring the sons of Brahmā (i.e. the Seven Sages), established the law of chastity by performing *tapas* for Śiva. All three of the female protagonists of the different levels of the myth—Svāhā, Arundhatī, and Satī—are further connected by their common father, Dakṣa,[115] and Arundhatī actually refers to Pārvatī as her sister.

Thus Arundhatī is first lustful and then chaste, famous for her chastity and equally famous for the loss of it on special occasions. Menā, furious because of the match that the Seven Sages and Arundhatī have made between her daughter Pārvatī and Śiva, cries out, 'Where have the Seven Sages gone? I'll tear their beards out! And that ascetic wife of theirs, that fraudulent hussy!' And Mandapāla justifies his hostility towards marriage by saying, 'Even the virtuous Arundhatī became jealous of her husband Vasiṣṭha and dishonoured him among the sages.'[116] An interesting insight into the symbolism of Arundhatī may
be derived from one text of the Ṛṣyaśṛṅga myth which states that Śāntā 1
served Ṛṣyaśṛṅga faithfully, just as Śaci served Indra, Lopamudrā served Agastya, and Arundhatī served Vasiṣṭha;[117] each woman represents the ideal of faithfulness to her husband—but it is a faithfulness marked by strong sexual overtones. Just as Sandhyā's relationship with Śiva is ambiguous (for in some versions of the myth she remains chaste, protected by Śiva, while in others she herself becomes excited and is admonished by Śiva), so too in the Pine Forest Arundhatī alone resists Śiva's wiles, an act which is both hostile to his ostensible purpose and helpful to the true lesson which he hopes to teach.

c. 3. *Śiva and Pārvatī as the Parents of Skanda*

The Seven Sages and their wives thus remain central to both the Pine Forest myth and the story of Skanda. In order to retain them in the latter in spite of the increasing obscurity of their role and the corresponding magnification of the roles of Śiva and Pārvatī, complex rationalizations took place. Many of these adjustments involve the mediation of Agni; usually it is simply stated that after Śiva shed his seed, Agni swallowed it and re-emitted it (thus establishing his parentage), and then passed it on to the Kṛttikās (establishing their role). Often an overt equation is made: thus it is said that Skanda was born from Rudra (when he entered Agni), in Pārvatī (when she entered Svāhā).[118] A similar identification appears in a text which further employs a series of incarnations to justify the multiforms:

> Śiva released the female creative power from his own body and agitated it
> 20ea for the sake of a son. As he did this, a youth, Skanda, broke out of it, blazing
> 5c^3 like a fire or the sun. His birth takes various forms in various eras. He is also
> known as the son of the Kṛttikās and as the son of Agni, because in his second
> 1 incarnation the Kṛttikās and Pārvatī and Agni were the causes of his birth.[119]

A still simpler method merely states the identity of the two fathers and consequently the identity of the two myths:

> Brahmins call Agni Rudra, and therefore Skanda is the son of Rudra. Rudra released his seed and this became the white mountain. And the seed of Agni was formed by the Kṛttikās on the white mountain. . . . This child was produced by Rudra when he entered into fire. Since Skanda was born from it, Skanda was the son of Rudra, and, being born from Agni [who is] Rudra, and from Svāhā and the six wives [of the sages], Skanda was born the son of Rudra.[120]

Another version of the story combines the two parents in yet another way: it tells of the marriage of Śiva and Pārvatī and of Śiva's promise not to beget a son in her. Then:

> 29a Pārvatī was angry because she had been denied children, and she said to
> 2 the gods, 'Since you restrained my husband when he desired to beget off-
> 29a spring, you will all be without offspring.' At the time of the curse, Agni alone
> of all the gods was not present. But when Rudra restrained his seed, a little
> 44a bit spilled and fell on the earth, falling in Agni, fire laid in fire. Meanwhile
> the gods were oppressed by the demon Tāraka, until Brahmā told them that
> Agni was the only god who, not having been present at the time of Pārvatī's
> curse, could beget a son to kill Tāraka. Brahmā said, 'Since Śiva's seed fell
> 44e in Agni, let Agni cause it to be born in the Ganges.'[121]

In almost all the other versions of this myth, Agni appears *before* the curse. In fact, he is the cause of it, for he is the one who prevents Śiva from begetting a child in Pārvatī, thus prompting her to curse the gods to be sterile; Agni is then subjected to the additional curse of bearing the seed of Śiva. Yet this text unites the two sets of fathers by introducing Agni *after* the curse takes place and thus exempting him from it.

Another text also exempts Agni from the curse, but the episodes are awkwardly combined, for Agni releases first Śiva's seed to form the birthplace (the white mountain and the forest of reeds), and then his own seed to produce the actual child. There are two forms of the mountain, one golden and one white, a duplication necessitated by the whole double birth:

Śiva and Pārvatī married, and Śiva promised the gods that he would not 36e
beget a son in her. He released his seed upon the surface of the earth, and the 21a
earth was pervaded by his seed. Agni entered into it, and the seed became 29a
the white mountain and the forest of reeds where Skanda, the son of Agni, 21e 7d 44a
was born. Then the gods rejoiced, but Pārvatī said, 'Since you stopped me 8cd
when I was with Śiva, and desirous of a son, you will beget no offspring in 26e[1]
your own wives, who will be barren. And the Earth, who prevented me from 2
having a son, will never enjoy a son herself.' The gods were ashamed, and 29a
Śiva took Pārvatī and went to do *tapas* on a mountain peak. Then the gods 27ea
and sages went to Brahmā and said, 'The general that you promised us [to 19e
defeat Tāraka] has not been born, and Śiva, who is to be his father, is now
doing *tapas* on a peak of Himālaya with Pārvatī.' Brahmā said, 'Pārvatī's
curse must come true, but Agni will beget a son in the Ganges, to be the 44e
general of the gods. Ganges, the elder daughter of Himālaya, will consider
this son to be the son of Pārvatī.' Then the gods went to Agni and said, 'Release
your great *tejas* [fiery seed] in the Ganges.' Agni sprinkled the Ganges with 44e
his seed, filling all her streams, and when she was no longer able to bear it 7d
she released it with her floods on the slope of Himālaya. It turned the moun- 8cd
tain to gold, and Skanda was born from the seed, and all the gods gave him 9cd
to the Kṛttikās to nurse.[122] 20ea

This version tells of the releasing of the seed before the curse, but it is only a curse upon the wives of the gods, Agni is free to produce the son by himself. The female agency is supplied by another explicit agreement ('Ganges, the elder daughter of Himālaya [and hence Pārvatī's sister], will consider the son to be the son of Pārvatī'), which awkwardly resolves the curse with the necessary birth. In fact, the link is never properly made, for the son is justified as Pārvatī's but not as Śiva's.

It is Pārvatī, however, who is usually most difficult to establish as
a parent of Skanda, because of Śiva's explicit promise not to beget
a son in her. Sometimes, like Agni, she drinks the seed and thus con-
ceives, but even this degree of participation is usually denied her by the
belief that she is unable to bear the *tejas* of Śiva in any way. Thus, even
though in one text the seed is first placed in her, she cannot bear it and
must hand it over to the Kṛttikās,[123] thus maintaining their role in the 7d 8cd
myth although she has supplanted them in their biological function.

Skanda is sometimes said to be born of the seed of Śiva and Pārvatī,[124]
i.e. born of Śiva's seed, spilt after he had made love to Pārvatī. Pārvatī
herself has 'seed', though it never becomes involved in the birth of
44ea Skanda. Once, after the interruption of their love-making, Śiva gave
his seed to Agni to produce Skanda, but from Pārvatī's seed Bhairava
was born to become her gate-keeper and prevent such interruptions in
9cd the future.[125] On another occasion, the seed of Śiva and Pārvatī merged
to form a stream of gold.[126]

Once, Pārvatī actually brought forth the child herself, but she did not receive all of the seed directly from Śiva:

> 36e Śiva made love to Pārvatī for a thousand years, without pause, and when
> 44ea the gods came to see Śiva, the gate-keeper dismissed them and sent them back.
> 44ea After another thousand years, the gods were frightened and sent Agni to find
> 30e out what Śiva was doing. Agni took the form of a parrot and entered and saw
> Śiva lying on the bed with Pārvatī. When Śiva saw the parrot he was a bit
> angry, and he said, 'I have shed half of my seed in Devī, but now that she has
> 16c 44a become embarrassed she is no longer passionate. You, Agni, must drink the
> 8cd other half of the seed since it was you who caused the obstacle.' Agni drank
> 32ea the seed of Śiva and distributed it among the bodies of all the gods, but the
> 9cd 9c seed split open their stomachs, and the hot golden liquid spread out in Śiva's
> 26e hermitage and formed an enormous lake full of golden lotuses. Hearing of
> 17c this, Pārvatī was full of curiosity and went there to play in the water. Then,
> 16c wishing to drink the sweet water, she said to the six Kṛttikās, who were bath-
> 17c ing there, 'I want the water that you have taken up in that lotus petal and are
> bringing home.' They said to her, 'If we give you this water, a child will be
> 20ea born from it. Let him be our son, too, and bear our name.' Pārvatī said, 'How
> can one born from my body be your son?' They said, 'Let us create his upper
> limbs.' She agreed, and she took the golden water and drank it, and it broke
> out through the right side of her womb as a six-headed boy, Skanda.[127]

This is the version that connects Pārvatī most closely with the birth of Skanda, and even here she drinks half of Śiva's seed (after receiving half of it directly), for Śiva's son cannot be born naturally. It is interesting to note that an early version of this text[128] omits the references to Śiva shedding half of his seed in Pārvatī, attributing her impregnation solely to the drinking of the seed. This myth also grapples with the problem of multiple parentage: 'How can one born from my body be your son?' but its solution is rather unconvincing: the child is divided in half just as the seed is usually divided. Here, too, the usual situation is reversed: Pārvatī bears the child but lets him keep the name of the Kṛttikās, while it is usually Pārvatī who is 'called' the mother of Skanda when he is actually born from the bodies of the Kṛttikās.

The confusion surrounding the relationship of Pārvatī and Agni, and the difficulty of resolving this relationship in the light of Agni's seduction of the sages' wives, is revealed by a popular legend of 'the infidelity of Pārvatī':

> During her husband's drunken orgies, [Pārvatī] listened to the burning 4
> words of Agni. [When Pārvatī, in the amorous embrace of Agni, heard Śiva 7c 16d
> coming, she concealed Agni in her body,] just as if it was a wardrobe in vaude- 23ea
> ville. [Because of the fire inside her, Pārvatī writhed in pain, and Śiva was so 35ea 44ea 44a
> miserable and so drunk that he wept, and his tears produced a little man who 11cd 7d
> used a torch and incense to smoke Agni out of the body of Pārvatī.][129] 11d

Pārvatī here assumes the role of Agni as well as that of the Kṛttikās; instead of the fiery seed of Agni–Śiva, she receives Agni himself within her body, and writhes in pain as he does when carrying Śiva's seed. The child is then born neither from her nor from Agni, but from Śiva himself, whose tears often perform the function of seed.

C. 4. *The Golden Seed of Fire*

This protean seed, the most essential element of all the Skanda stories, is also the most ancient. Although it is associated with Agni and Śiva throughout the later mythology, originally it was the golden seed of Brahmā (Prajāpati), who is called Hiraṇyagarbha ('The Golden Womb') in the Ṛg Veda to denote his creative powers.[130] The cosmogonic myth then postulated a golden egg instead of a golden womb,[131] and this symbol was replaced in turn by the image of the god of the golden seed, an epithet of Agni and of Śiva.[132] By the time of the Epic, Śiva was also given the original Vedic epithet of Hiraṇyagarbha, together with the golden seed.[133] One of the Purāṇas transfers the entire cosmogonic myth from Brahmā to Śiva:

> Śiva is the seed of everything. During the primeval creation, the seed arising
> from his *liṅga* was placed in the womb of Viṣṇu, and in the course of time that 21e
> golden seed became an egg and floated in the cosmic waters for a thousand 5cd
> celestial years. Then a wind split it into two, and the top half became the sky, 9c
> the lower half the earth, and the yolk the golden mountain. Then, at sunset, $14c^{I}$
> the Lord of the Golden Womb was born, and from him all the ascetics 30ea
> appeared.[134] 8c 9cd

Another cosmogonic myth links Śiva not with Brahmā or Viṣṇu but
with the usual god of gold, Agni: 'First Śiva created the waters and $14c^{I}$
released his seed in them, and that became the golden egg. In the form 9c 9cd
of Agni he created the golden universal egg by shedding his seed.'[135] 21e
As the passage implies, the golden egg was the earlier concept, and the golden seed was transferred from Agni to Śiva. But another text

describes the process in reverse, maintaining that when Agni bore Śiva's
9cd seed for 5,000 years (before the birth of Skanda) his body became golden,
and so Agni became known as the bearer of the golden seed.[136]

9cd Gold forms a constant tie between Agni and Śiva in the Skanda story.
The seed is placed in a golden pot (i.e. golden womb), or in a forest of
26e^{1} golden reeds,[137] or on a golden mountain, or in a golden lake.[138] Some-
9c times it is placed on a white mountain,[139] which is thereby turned to
gold.[140] The water that Pārvatī drinks, containing Śiva's seed, is golden
16c water,[141] and the seed which the gods vomit forth when they have been
impregnated with Śiva's seed forms a golden mountain or a golden pool
26e^{2} full of golden lotuses.[142] Śiva's seed turns the reeds, trees, and animals
in Skanda's birthplace to gold.[143] 'Gold' is the name of the twins born
of the magic seed.[144]

The motif appears in associated myths as well:

36e 38ea In order to increase the creation of Prajāpati, Śiva made love to Devī.
21e 30ea A stream came from the seed of the couple. The wind ignited a fire which
10c 13cd^{3} drank the seed, and that which the fire vomited forth from its mouth became
16c 9cd a special kind of gold.[145]

9cd Śiva's seed turns into gold and silver when it falls on the ground as he
9cd pursues the *apsaras* Mohinī,[146] and this same seed is also said to have
5cd become *liṅgas* and gold.[147] All of these episodes are multiforms of the
Skanda myth, which is described in these terms: 'Skanda is gold, the
child of Agni—for gold is Agni.'[148]

C. 5. *The Birth of Skanda and the Birth of the Maruts*

The miraculous development of the seed, and in particular its growth
in fire and water, is an element of the Skanda myth which is elaborated
upon in a series of variations of the story of the birth of another group
of Vedic gods associated with Rudra–Śiva: the Maruts. The multiforms
1 of the story are explicitly attributed to a cosmic factor which is also
operative in one of the Skanda myths cited above: seven births are said
to have taken place in seven different eras. The first episode narrated
is the result of Diti's foetus being cut to pieces by Indra, which is in
fact the seventh birth of the Maruts. In the first era, their birth came
about in this way:

A king died childless, and his wife wept bitterly and embraced his corpse
6d until a bird told her that she would have seven sons if she mounted her hus-
30e band's funeral pyre. She obeyed, and as she entered the fire the king arose
6c and flew into the sky with her, by his power of yoga. When the queen entered
18a 22e her fertile period, the king felt it his duty not to neglect her. He made love to

her in the air, and his seed fell down from the sky. Then he went with her 21e
to the world of Brahmā to dwell eternally. 20a
But the wives of the Seven Sages saw the cloud-like seed falling from the 15c
sky into a flower, and they thought it was Soma. Wishing to be young for 26e[2]
ever, they bathed ritually, honoured their own husbands, and drank the king's 14c[2]
seed. The moment that they drank it [having thus unconsciously violated 18e 17c
their chastity] they lost their holy lustre, and all their husbands abandoned 16c 33ea[6]
them immediately as sinners. They gave birth to the seven Maruts.[149] 25e 20ea

In this tale, Agni (again in his elemental form) and the Seven Sages bring about the birth of Śiva's sons, as usual. The particular form of Agni—the funeral pyre—further links this series with the Skanda myth through the character of Satī, the archetypal suttee. The wives of the Seven Sages drink the seed, as they often drink the seed of Śiva, and are abandoned by their husbands for a falsely alleged adultery. The bird, too, is still present, though in a new role.

The second birth of the Maruts adds several more motifs:

The seven sons of a king performed great *tapas* in order to obtain Indra's 8d
place. Indra, learning of this, sent an *apsaras* to impede their *tapas*. She 45a
bathed in the river near them, and when they saw her they were aroused and 17c 21ea
released their seed. A female water demon swimming in the river drank the 21e 16c
seed, and the seven ascetics, whose *tapas* was destroyed, returned to their 25e
palace. After a long time, the female water demon was caught by a fisherman 23e[2]
and brought to the palace, where, swimming in a lovely tank, she brought
forth seven sons, the Maruts.[150] 20ea

This time there are seven fathers rather than seven mothers (all seven being necessary for the seven Maruts, in contrast with the Skanda story in which only six must be involved, one for each of Skanda's six heads).

The third version combines the motifs of the first two in yet another way:

A king and his wife performed *tapas* together in order to obtain a son. The 25ea[3]
Seven Sages promised the queen seven sons and she became pregnant, but 27ea
the king died before she gave birth to them. She mounted his funeral pyre 6d
and a piece of flesh fell from the flame into some cold water. It split into seven 9c
parts, and the Maruts were born.[151] 6c 20ea

Although the Seven Sages are not sexually active in this version, merely granting the boon of pregnancy, the pattern demands their presence as proxy fathers in some way. The next story of the birth, however, omits the sages and reverts back to the original parent, Agni, who is here conveniently divided into seven parts:

A king who desired a son sacrificed his own flesh into the fire. When he had 19e

10c offered his flesh, bones, hair, blood, and sinew, he sacrificed his seed into the
6d fire and he died. As his seed fell upon the seven rays of the flame, the seven
6c 20ea Maruts were born.[152]

The fifth version is essentially the same as the first, but the Seven Sages play in it the role that they play in the third:

25ea[3] A king performed *tapas* to obtain a son. He obtained a girl instead, and
19e took her home with him. When he died, she wished to kill herself, and
10cd although the Seven Sages, who had fallen in love with her, tried to prevent
27e 6d her from entering the funeral pyre, she entered it and died. Seven little boys
6c 20ea came out of the fire, the Maruts.[153]

Again the Seven Sages are not explicitly involved in the birth, but they 'fall in love' with the mother of the Maruts and as a result she bears seven sons. There can be no other fathers of the Maruts, for she is herself unmarried, the man in the pyre being her own father (a possible remnant of the incest motif associated with an early form of this myth).

The final version is much like the second, but as there is only one father and one mother the magical seven is produced in the form of the Saptasārasvata, the part of the sacred river Sarasvatī where there are seven branches:

8d An ascetic named Maṅkaṇaka performed great *tapas* at the holy place on
21ea the Saptasārasvata. The gods sent an *apsaras* to pose an obstacle to his *tapas*,
21e and she excited the sage so that his seed fell into the water. He cursed her
9c 13cd[1] to be destroyed by a horse and then he returned to his hermitage. The seven
3 Maruts were born in the Saptasārasvata.[154]

Here, as in the first version, the sons are born from the river, just as Skanda is born in a lake or in the Ganges; in other versions, fire is the instrument of birth. Thus the basic elements of the Skanda story—the seduction, the Seven Sages, the birth from fire and water—are dispersed among seven versions of the Maruts' story, each one a complete tale but all together telling a single myth, reinterpreting the birth of a group of Vedic gods in terms of the patterns of Purāṇic mythology.

IV

ŚIVA AND BRAHMĀ
OPPOSITION AND IDENTITY

A. ŚIVA AS SEXUAL CREATOR

THE golden seed which Agni–Śiva sheds in the Skanda myth was originally the characteristic of Brahmā, the Creator, from whose early mythology many of the elements of the Skanda story may be derived. Śiva attracted to himself many of the roles and characteristics of the creator god, the giver of seed; Brahmā says, 'Two things are capable of
bearing the seed of Śiva and my seed: Pārvatī may bear Śiva's seed, and 36e
Śiva's form as water may bear my seed.'[1] The *Mahābhārata* inserts the 13c
myth of Brahmā's seed shed as an oblation as an episode in the birth of 9c 10c
Skanda, an explicit multiform.[2] In many of the creation myths, Śiva 1
appears to help Brahmā, usually in the form of an androgyne, but 38ea 32e
Brahmā himself was the original androgyne.[3] One text combines the
early and late traditions: first Rudra appears as an androgyne to assist
Brahmā, and then Brahmā himself creates the androgynous pair from 32e
whom creation proceeds[4] [Plate 8]. In other myths, Śiva begins the 38ea
process of creation by becoming Brahmā's own son: 32e

> Śiva commanded Brahmā to create, but Brahmā did not. He meditated 40e
> upon Śiva for the sake of knowledge, and Śiva was pleased by Brahmā's *tapas* 39ea
> and gave him the Vedas. But since Brahmā still could not create, he again per- 38ea
> formed *tapas*, and Śiva offered him a boon, and Brahmā asked Śiva to be 39ea 38ea
> his son.[5] 18e

This is a reversal of the pattern in which Brahmā's sons, devoted to *tapas* for Śiva, refuse to participate in the creation which Brahmā demands. The role played in those myths by Brahmā is here taken by Śiva, while
Brahmā himself acts as the unwilling son. Another version of this story 8d
states that Brahmā's creatures failed to increase until, in order to assuage 18e 38ea
Brahmā's sorrow and to increase progeny, Rudra became his son in age
after age.[6] *Tapas* here is rewarded, though not in itself sufficient:

> Brahmā praised Śiva and Śiva said, 'I will do what you ask. I will become 39ea
> your son and create the universe. And this aspect of myself, the Lord of 38ea
> Yogis, will help you, by my command.' Brahmā then began to create creatures,

8d but they did not increase. Śiva appeared and said to Brahmā, 'I know the
40e cause of your sorrow and I know what will remove it.' Then he became the
32e[1] androgyne, and from his female half he created Devī as a separate being.
5c[1] Brahmā asked her to become the daughter of his son Dakṣa, in order to
37ea increase creation, and she created a goddess like herself from between her
32e brows. She re-entered Śiva's body, Śiva became the androgyne again, and
5c[1] from that time forth creatures were made by intercourse.[7]

Śiva appears in his anti-ascetic aspect to help Brahmā in the end, but Brahmā must first obtain Śiva's help by performing *tapas* for the Lord of Yogis. In this cycle, in which Rudra takes over the creative function from the unsuccessful ascetic Brahmā, Śiva's sexual creation is taken for granted. Among the tribe of Gonds, Śiva (Mahadeo) is responsible for creation by intercourse just as he is in the Purāṇas, and his methods are graphically described:

7cd[1] [Men used to have their phallus in the middle of the forehead, like the
trunk of an elephant. Then one day, by an accident, all but four fingers'
32a breadth was cut off.] But now the stump sticking out from the forehead did
not look nice, and men went to Mahadeo and begged him to put it somewhere
5c[1] else. He placed it between the thighs. [Then the sexual organs of the women,
in the middle of their chests, were found to be inconveniently located, so
Mahadeo kicked Pārvatī between the thighs and made an opening there.][8]

5c[1] The Gonds also attribute the invention of creation by intercourse to
5cd Lingo—the chaste but priapic counterpart of Śiva.[9] In the beginning
there were a man and a woman with no knowledge of sex until Lingo
filled two pills with love charms, and when they ate the pills they felt de-
16cd sire and produced children.[10] In all of these myths, Śiva is the primeval
45e[1] sexual creator.

B. THE INCEST OF ŚIVA

In a creation myth told in Orissa, Śiva plays the central role:

39a [Mahadeo told Bhimsen to make separate houses for the primeval brother
and sister. He did so, and as they were separated they could not produce
children. Bhimsen went to Mahadeo and complained, and Mahadeo took the
29ea form of black ants, scorpions, and cobras to frighten the girl into her brother's
30a bed. Then Mahadeo invented tickling, and as the brother and sister tickled
5c[1] each other, lust came into them. She became pregnant, and the world was
39e peopled.][11]

In this, as in so many myths throughout the world, original creation involves incest. Śiva at first opposes it—placing the siblings in different houses—but in the end he supports it. Nevertheless, instead of assuming an erotic form to promote the incestuous union, he uses his yoga to transform himself into the snakes usually associated with his yogic aspect. Another tribal creation myth retains this slight ambivalence:

> [In the beginning, a brother and sister would not marry, for fear of the 27e 27a
> sin of incest. Then the goddess of smallpox scarred their faces so that they 29ea
> did not recognize one another, and they married. But still they had no know- 33ea3
> ledge of sex, and so Lingo gave them love charms. Since the woman took 16cd
> more of them than she gave to the man, women are more passionate than 17d
> men. But the man took some of the potion too, and] so strong was their 16d
> passion that the very next morning a child was born.[12] 29e

Here again Lingo (Śiva) encourages the incestuous union by means of a horrible rather than an erotic element. The ascetic viewpoint is also manifest in the misuse of the potion, making the woman into the insatiable and dangerous creature that the misogynist tradition considered her to be.

Thus Śiva appears in the popular tradition as an incestuous creator.[13]
Bengali literature in particular links him explicitly with Brahmā in this 39e
crime: 'For after all, if such illustrious personages as Brahmā, Mahā-
rudra [Śiva], and Parāśara, the father of the sage Vyāsa, were lustful, in 39e
fact so lustful that they pursued their own daughters, what can you expect of unreconstructed man?'[14] Śiva inherits the motif of incest when he assumes the position of a father-god, a process which can be traced in Bengali literature. In a medieval Bengali text, Dharma is the incestuous father, and Śiva the son who later marries the daughter of Dharma:

> [Dharma created Brahmā, Viṣṇu and Śiva, and the three sons went to per- 40a
> form *tapas*. Dharma missed them, and he sighed, and from his sigh there
> appeared an androgyne whom he changed into a beautiful girl and called 32e
> Manasā. He fell in love with her and] married her with the approval of his 39e
> three sons. After sexual intercourse between father and daughter, the latter
> slept very deeply and the father repented of his actions. [Before killing him- 10cd
> self, he tested his three sons, and Śiva proved superior. Then Dharma entered
> Śiva's mouth, after Śiva had agreed to be Manasā's husband. Manasā threw 6c 6d
> herself on the pyre and was reborn as Pārvatī, who eventually married Śiva.][15] 36e

Manasā dies and is reborn, like Sandhyā, but here the father dies as well. A more significant deviation from the classical model is the approval of the sons, whose disapproval in the Sanskrit versions is based upon the traditional punishment of Brahmā by Rudra and/or his ascetic sons. But this disapproval would be out of place in the Bengali story, where Śiva is so completely reconciled with his father.

In the second layer of the Bengali myth, Śiva himself is the father of
Manasā and lusts for her. She wishes to accompany him home, but Śiva 39e

23ea fears the jealousy of his wife Caṇḍī and conceals Manasā in a flower
36a 22a basket, where Caṇḍī finds her and showers abuse upon her.[16] In a related
39e 4 text, Śiva tries to make love to Manasā and is struck down by the deadly
7cd[2] glance from her eye.[17] Thus Manasā, belatedly experiencing a sense of
43a moral indignation, takes from the Śiva–Kāma story the motif of the
ascetic eye and punishes Śiva for his incest.

But the folk tradition of Śiva's incest is not limited to Bengal. In Middle India there are myths in which the primeval incestuous couple are Mahadeo and Pārvatī, sometimes regarded as son and mother,[18] and sometimes as brother and sister:

> [Mahadeo and Pārvatī were born from the two fruits of a single lotus.]
> 43ea When Mahadeo grew up, he could not control his desire for his sister, so he
> 36a turned his back on her and refused to see her face. But when Pārvatī too
> 36ea[2] became mature, she also was filled with desire and begged her brother to look
> 39e 21e at her. At last he turned round and as he did so his seed sprang from him.
> 20ea Pārvati caught it in her hand and held it in her clenched hand. Soon she was
> 5c[1] pregnant and after that children were born in the world.[19]

In this myth, a multiform of the seduction of Śiva by Pārvatī, Śiva turns away from her because he is her brother, rather than because he is a yogi, but she succeeds in stirring his desire. The motif of Śiva's initial disinclination toward incest is retained in Gond mythology, where the Śiva figure, Lingal, is accused of incest with his sister. Although in some versions the incestuous contact is purely accidental, Lingal sometimes foresees the consequences. He objects that such a contact would be
25a a sin, but his sister replies, 'I shall teach you the means to blot out the
sin.'[20] Thus even in these tales Śiva retains his anti-incestuous attitude, however much his participation in original creation necessitates his involvement in the act of incest.

C. ŚIVA OPPOSES THE INCEST OF BRAHMĀ

Just as the procreative aspects of Śiva's character (and hence his incest) tend to be emphasized in popular religion and mythology, so in traditional Sanskrit literature, with its strong philosophical background, the ascetic Śiva is more prominent, and Śiva is famed as the chastiser of the incestuous Prajāpati. The Vedic incest myth does not mention Rudra, but the commentators identify him with the avenger in the original myth, and he is specifically active in the later versions. Moreover, the incest myth supplies much of the imagery of the Skanda birth story (in which Śiva assumes the role of the primeval Prajāpati), as well as the plot elements of the later addition to that story, the conflict between Śiva and Kāma (in which Śiva maintains his role as the opponent of Prajāpati). Thus the Purāṇic tradition rearranges elements of the Vedic myth in such a manner that Śiva plays both the role of the original sexual protagonist and that of the ascetic antagonist.

The original myth, told in rather vague terms, may refer not to Brahmā and his daughter but to heaven and the dawn:

When the father, bent upon impregnating his own daughter, united with 27e
her and discharged his seed upon the earth, the benevolent gods generated 21e 40a
prayer. They fashioned Vāstospati, the protector of sacred rites.[21] 39a

The father and the protector are not identified, but the commentator
elaborates: 'Rudra Prajāpati created Rudra Vāstospati with a portion of 39e 39a
himself', thus identifying Rudra with both the protector and the creator. Other verses in the Ṛg Veda seem to refer to this myth and to connect it with Agni:

[As] he [Agni] made the seed for the great father, heaven . . . the hunter 10c
shot him as he embraced his own daughter. Heaven laid the bright seed aside 39e 39a
and Agni brought forth a youth. The father, heaven, impregnated his own
daughter, earth. The sacrificer into the fire committed incest with his own
daughter.[22] 10c

The connection with Rudra is made explicit later in the Brāhmaṇas,
which retain all the essentials of the Ṛg Vedic story—the incest, the seed
shed upon the earth or into fire, the beast symbolism of the participants
(originally present in the verb which usually connotes the covering of 33ea^{4}
a cow or mare by a bull or stallion),[23] and the punishment—and which 45e^{2} 13cd^{1}
apply the myth to Prajāpati:

Prajāpati desired his own daughter and went to her. His seed fell, and he 39e
shed it in her. Then he heated it so that it would not spoil. He made all the 10c
animals out of it.[24] 33ea^{4}

This brief story is expanded in another Brāhmaṇa:

Prajāpati desired his daughter. She took the form of a doe and he the form 39e 33ea^{4}
of a stag. The gods said, 'Prajāpati is doing something that is not to be done.' 40a
They assembled various dreadful forms and made a god to punish Prajāpati. 39a
He pierced him, and Prajāpati fled upwards, becoming the constellation of the
deer, while the doe became the constellation Rohiṇī. The seed of Prajāpati
poured out and became a lake. The gods said, 'Let not the seed of Prajāpati 9c
be spoiled.' They surrounded it with fire. The winds agitated it, and Agni 10c
made it move. The kindled seed became the sun. The blazing sparks became 30ea
Bhṛgu and the other sages, and the ashes became various animals. Rudra 5c^{3} 8cd 6cd
claimed that what remained was his, but the gods deprived him of a claim.[25] 24a

Several elements of the Skanda story are already present in this myth. The seed falls first in a woman who cannot bear it (the commentator says that the seed was spilled by the stag in the doe, but because of the excessive amount it fell upon the earth and became a great lake), and the seed is then transformed into a lake and placed in fire.

The *Śatapatha Brāhmaṇa* version is slightly more sophisticated and introduces several more Śaiva themes:

39e Prajāpati desired his daughter and made love to her. This was a sin in the
33ea[4] 40a eyes of the gods, who said to the god who rules over beasts [Paśupati, Rudra],
'He commits a sin, acting in this way towards his own daughter, our sister.
21e 38a[1] Pierce him.' Rudra took aim and pierced him. Half his seed fell to the ground.
39a The gods cured Prajāpati and cut out Rudra's dart, for Prajāpati is the sacrifice. To utilize [the seed], the gods said, 'Take care that this may not be lost,
10c but that it may be less than the oblation.' They gave it to Bhaga to eat, but
16c 7cd[2] 7d it burnt his eyes and he became blind. Then they gave it to Pūṣan to eat, but
5c[3] 8cd 44a it knocked out his teeth. At last they gave it to Savitṛ [the sun] and it did not
13d injure him, for he appeased it.[26]

The seed, divided in half (as in several of the Agni–Svāhā stories), instead of producing sages, destroys them. The exception is Savitṛ, a form of the sun, who is created from the kindled seed in one Brāhmaṇa and survives the seed in another; as he is a form of fire, he is immune to its destructive force and is able to absorb it. The destructive power of the fiery seed injures Bhaga's eyes and Pūṣan's teeth in many
38a[1] versions of the story of the destruction of Dakṣa's sacrifice, including another Brāhmaṇa text in which Rudra's portion of the sacrifice is treated like the dangerous seed and is even placed in the mouth of
44a Agni.[27] Even in the *Śatapatha* version it is the sacrifice (explicitly identified with Prajāpati) that Rudra pierces. The multiform is clear from such repeated motifs as the deer whose form is assumed by
33ea[4] Brahmā/Dakṣa, shot by Rudra/Śiva, and translated to heaven as a constellation Rohiṇī/Mṛgaśiras ('Deer's Head').[28] Moreover, Rudra is deprived of a share of the sacrifice, an insult which is the ostensible cause of his fight with Dakṣa, although their enmity is in fact based upon the earlier incest motif.

In yet another Brāhmaṇa text, the disapproving gods are replaced by other sons (including Agni), who participate in the sin themselves. They are the familiar ascetics of the Purāṇas, whose *tapas* leads them to sexual creation:

8c Prajāpati desired to produce progeny, and so he performed great *tapas*. As
7c he became heated, Agni, Wind, the Sun, the Moon, and Dawn were born.
11c 30ea He said to them, 'You should also do *tapas*', and they did so. But Dawn, the

daughter of Prajāpati, took the form of an *apsaras* and appeared before them. $5c^3$
They shed their seed, and then they said to Prajāpati, 'We have shed our seed. $14c^3$ 4
Let it not be lost.' Prajāpati made a sacrificial vessel out of gold, and he placed 8c 21ea
his seed in it. There arose in it a creature with a thousand eyes, a thousand 21e 10c 9cd
feet, and a thousand arrows. He was Rudra.[29] $7cd^2$ 40a

This is the first Brāhmaṇa version in which Śiva appears as the son born of the incestuous seed in the golden bowl rather than as the enemy of the seed and of its source. Agni himself not only incites Prajāpati and saves the seed, but actually sheds the fiery seed himself in this text, which clearly contributes much to the later mythology of the composite Śiva/Agni/Brahmā. Yet even here Rudra has the arrows of the avenging god and uses them against Prajāpati.

D. BRAHMĀ VERSUS KĀMA

In the creation myths composed at the time of the Epic, the 'desire' which Brahmā felt for his daughter was personified as Kāma. Kāma then took the responsibility for the incestuous act (which even at the time of the Brāhmaṇas was hard for some to accept as the fault of Brahmā himself),[30] and Kāma was punished by Śiva as Brahmā/Prajāpati was punished by Rudra. The punishment of Kāma by Śiva is generally implied but not narrated in the Brahmā–Kāma story, and it is in fact a separate motif, one which was known at the time of the Epic but only incorporated into Brahmā's story by the time of the Purāṇas. Later texts then omit the causal link but emphasize the
similarity of motifs: the gods are confident that Kāma will be able to 1
excite Śiva just as he excited the old Prajāpati and caused him to pursue 43ea
his own daughter, stag pursuing doe.[31] 41ea

A typical version of this myth relates it to the theme of androgynous creation:

In order to create, Brahmā meditated and prayed. He broke his body into 8c
two parts, half male and half female. When he saw the woman, who was 32e
Sāvitrī, Brahmā marvelled at her beauty and was excited by the arrows of 39e
Kāma, the male half of the androgyne. His sons reviled Brahmā, saying, 'This 41e 41ea
is your daughter.' But Brahmā continued to gaze at her face and even sprouted 4 40a $7cd^2$
five heads in order to see her better. All the *tapas* that Brahmā had amassed
for the sake of creation was destroyed by his desire for his daughter. Then 25e
Brahmā said to his sons, 'Create gods and demons and men', and when they 8c
had gone to create, Brahmā made love to his daughter. After a hundred years 39e
she gave birth to a son, Manu. Then Brahmā was ashamed of his excessive $5c^1$
desire for his own daughter, and he cursed Kāma, saying, 'Since your arrows 41a
excited my heart, Rudra will soon reduce your body to ashes.' Then Kāma 41ea

2 appeased Brahmā, arguing that he had merely acted as Brahmā had instructed
3 43a him to do. Brahmā promised Kāma that he would become incarnate again,
20e and Kāma departed, in sorrow because of the curse and in joy because of the
remission.[32]

Considerable rearrangement has been made in the casting of the original roles. The male half of the androgyne, who was originally Brahmā, then Rudra, is now Kāma. In keeping with his new character, he incites but does not participate in the act of incest. Kāma replaces Rudra in another sense as well, for just as Rudra pierces Prajāpati with an arrow to punish him for his incestuous act, so Kāma pierces Brahmā with an arrow to cause that act. Brahmā also fills several of the roles of Rudra, for he acts as chastiser (of Kāma) as well as chastised (by Śiva), bringing upon Kāma the curse of a punishment that Śiva will later fulfil. Rudra does not revile Brahmā, for this part of the role is played by Brahmā's sons, who act on behalf of the ascetic, anti-erotic Śiva as they often do. The daughter in this version is Sāvitrī, the female counterpart of Savitṛ, who is central to the Brāhmaṇa myth of the golden seed.

The actual seed, absent from this version of the myth, reappears in a text closer to the Brāhmaṇas in its basic casting, for it includes the sons in the guilt of Brahmā's incest, while Śiva himself comes to censure them all:

8c Brahmā created all the gods and all the *prajāpatis*, including Dakṣa. Then
21ea a beautiful woman named Sandhyā was born from his mind. Her beauty,
39e 40a which deluded the hearts of sages, aroused Brahmā, but he was paralysed by
41e 41ea indecision, realizing that his sons were present. Then from his mind was
26e[1] born Kāma, with his five marvellous flower arrows. Dakṣa and the others
were excited by desire and could not remain calm, but Brahmā regained control of his emotions and said to Kāma, 'Enchant men and women with your five flower arrows and your own beauty, maintaining creation eternally. No one will be able to withstand you—not even Viṣṇu and Śiva and I.' Then Kāma decided to begin his work right then and there, starting with Brahmā,
41ea and he excited Brahmā and all the sages with his arrows. As Brahmā gazed
upon Sandhyā, his senses became aroused, and she too showed the signs of
40a desire. Brahmā's body was overflowing with heat. But as Dharma saw this,
39a he summoned Śiva to protect him from evil, and Śiva appeared and saw the
condition of Brahmā and the others. He roared with laughter, and he called them to shame, saying, 'Brahmā, how can you show such evidence of desire? How can you have forgotten the established law of the Vedas, which came
27a from your very own mouth: "One must never gaze sinfully upon one's mother,
42a sister, brother's wife, or daughter"? Kāma is lowly, small-minded, and does
not know the proper time for such things. How can he drive you and these single-minded yogis to such lust?' Hearing this speech, Brahmā became so
11c ashamed that his sweat doubled in his thwarted desire to seize Sandhyā, and

a drop of sweat fell from his body and produced a group of sages. All but six
of his sons, the sages, let their seed fall upon the ground, producing many 21e
more sages, and from Dakṣa's sweat as he restrained his seed Rati was born. 11c
Śiva then vanished, having protected Sandhyā from sin, but Brahmā was 41e 4
ashamed, remembering the words of Śiva, and he blazed with anger like
a fire and said, 'Kāma will be burnt by the fire from Śiva's eye.' Kāma was 3 41a
frightened and said, 'Brahmā, why have you cursed me so terribly? I merely 2 43a
did what you commanded me to do, and as I have not transgressed, I do not 7cd[1]
deserve this curse.' Brahmā then said, 'I cursed you because you attacked me
in the presence of my own daughter. But now my anger is past, and I promise
that, though Śiva will burn you to ashes, you will obtain a body again when Śiva 20e
takes a wife and household.' Then Brahmā vanished and Dakṣa said to Kāma, 36e
'Take this daughter of mine for your wife.' Seeing her beauty, Kāma forgot 23e[2]
the terrible curse that Brahmā had given him, and a great celebration took
place.[33]

The daughter here is Sandhyā ('Twilight'), a variation of the Vedic Dawn. She represents a meteorological mediation—half day, half night—just as she is a sexual mediation when, having been involved in incest, she is reborn as the incarnation of chastity, Arundhatī. Rati, who appears as the female half of the androgyne in another version of this myth cited above, appears here as the daughter of Dakṣa (who thus acts as a multiform of Brahmā), and is given in marriage to Kāma, as she is in the other version where Kāma is the male half of the androgyne, and as another daughter of Dakṣa (Satī) is usually given to the earlier male half of the androgyne—Śiva himself. Kāma's marriage thus foreshadows Śiva's marriage and the consequent removal of the curse. The extreme forms of sexuality and chastity prove to be once again interchangeable in the context of a creation myth: Rati (the incarnation of sexual pleasure) is replaced by the chaste Sandhyā/Arundhatī as the female half of the androgyne just as Kāma alternates with Śiva as the male half. Dharma appears here as the incarnation of the moral law, rather than as the incestuous creator that he is in the Bengali tradition, and Śiva appears in his ascetic aspect as the enemy of all of them—Brahmā, the lustful sons of Brahmā, and especially Kāma.

A later text introduces certain changes which involve Śiva still more
intimately in the myth: instead of being summoned by Dharma, Śiva
observes the incestuous scene himself as he flies by in the air; when he 39a
reviles Brahmā and Kāma he adds, 'Shame on Kāma. He is even stirring
up lascivious thoughts in [my] firm heart'; when Brahmā becomes 43ea
ashamed and blazes like a fire, he says to Śiva, rather than to Kāma,
'Since Kāma struck me with his arrows in front of you, you will burn 41ea
him with the fire from your eye.' And finally, when Kāma is given Rati 7cd[1] 43a

as his wife, he is so enchanted with her beauty that he forgets the curse, thinking, 'With this lovely woman as my companion I will be able to
43ea delude even Śiva.'[34] All of these adjustments transfer an implication of sexual vulnerability to Śiva as well as to Brahmā and foreshadow Śiva's eventual conquest by Kāma. Moreover, the myth implies that this conquest will be a direct result of Śiva's (superficially) anti-erotic behaviour in the present episode. In the sequel to this part of the myth it is frequently stated that Brahmā is angry not only with Kāma for his part in the shameful incident but also with Śiva for his derision, and Brahmā sees to it that Śiva is vanquished by Kāma as well as the reverse.

The woman who assists Brahmā in his revenge against Śiva embodies both sexuality and chastity: she is Devī, who assumes the role of Kāma to delude Śiva. Devī tells this story to explain to her parents why she is intent upon performing *tapas* in the forest:

> 25ea[2] I am going to do *tapas* in Śiva's presence. When Brahmā was deluded by
> 41ea Kāma and began to rape his own daughter, Śiva appeared in the sky and
> 39e 24a mocked him. Brahmā was full of shame, and he propitiated me and said, 'Take
> 21ea 39a a lovely form and delude Śiva, who is averse to worldly ways. He saw me
> 22ea 37a when I was full of lust and he mocked me and made me ashamed.' I agreed,
> 36ea 34a 3 and now Śiva, tortured with longing for Satī, is doing *tapas* to obtain me.
> 25ea[2] I will go there and delude him so that he will abandon his yoga and take me
> 36ea as his wife.[35]

The willing participation of Devī in the seduction of Śiva is reminiscent of the seduction of Brahmā by Mohinī, and both women are the instruments of Kāma. But in one interesting variant of this myth, Kāma and Brahmā are opposed not in their usual way—where Kāma brings about a sexual act which Brahmā regrets—but quite the opposite: it is Brahmā who is pro-sexual and Kāma for once anti-sexual. This strange reversal may best be understood in the light of the framework of the plot: it is essentially the story of Brahmā and his ascetic sons, and Kāma plays the part of the sons (or of Śiva, a frequent though paradoxical reversal):

> 8c Brahmā was meditating, desiring to create, and from him there was born
> 41e 4 a handsome man, who was Kāma. Brahmā said to him, 'Those *prajāpatis*
> 8d whom I made when I was desirous of creating are not able to produce
> 40e creatures, yet they are satisfied. You should create as I command you.' But
> 41a Kāma vanished, and Brahmā cursed him in anger, saying, 'You will be
> 3 destroyed by the fire from Śiva's eye, since you did not do what I com-
> 43a 7cd[1] manded.' Then Kāma prostrated himself before Brahmā and prayed, and
> 41e Brahmā granted him the boon that he would have Rati as his assistant, to
> 5c[1] delude and deceive everyone in the universe.[36]

The command which Brahmā gives Kāma in the incest myth—and

which Kāma reminds him of at the time of the curse—is the same as the command which Brahmā gives his ascetic sons: to increase progeny. Here it is repeated in the form of a 'boon' at the end of the myth as well as being stated in its more general form at the beginning. And just as Brahmā curses the ascetic sons to become involved or sexually active, so he curses his other son, Kāma, to be burnt by the erotic Śiva. When the forces are reversed, he curses the anti-erotic Śiva to be 'burnt' by Kāma and the erotic Kāma to be burnt by the ascetic Śiva.

An interesting interpretation of the confusion in Brahmā's mind regarding Śiva and Kāma appears in David Stacton's novel:

> [Brahmā saw his daughter, the Dawn, and was overcome with desire.] 39e
> Unable to contain himself, he split in two, that half of him which was the All 32e
> Wise Creator and that half of him which had to have the girl or else, fighting 24ea[1]
> the thing out. It was touch and go, but austerity finally managed to kill desire. 41ea
> Before desire died, the sweat transuded from it left the cold body like fleas 43ea
> deserting a corpse, and became, each drop, the spirits of the dead . . . and yet 11c 43a
> they, too, had been born of desire. . . . Perhaps because he *had* conquered the 10cd
> enticements of the flesh, Brahmā was still angry to have been caught out,
> and since he did not dare to curse Śiva, instead turned on the God of Love, as 4
> the only defenceless person there.[37] 3 41a

Stacton interprets the motif of the androgyne in terms of the ascetic/erotic ambivalence of the creator/yogi himself, rather than the male/female duality usually described in the Sanskrit texts. Yet he recognizes the transference of Brahmā's enmity from Śiva to Kāma.

Kāma elsewhere expresses an awareness of the conflict between Brahmā and Śiva and the similarity between their curses against himself:

> [Brahmā told Kāma to excite Śiva with his arrows. Kāma at first refused, 37a
> remarking that this would provoke Śiva into harming him, but Brahmā 41a
> threatened Kāma with a curse. Kāma obeyed, for he preferred to be Śiva's 43a
> victim rather than Brahmā's.][38] 1

E. ŚIVA VERSUS BRAHMĀ AT THE WEDDING OF SATĪ/PĀRVATĪ

Brahmā's incestuous act, and Śiva's punishment of it, reappear in Śaiva mythology not only in the destruction of Dakṣa's sacrifice but also in the myth of Brahmā's illicit desire for Śiva's bride. The basic myth is closely linked with the latter: Brahmā's incest, punished by Śiva, leads Brahmā to curse Kāma and Śiva to react in a manner that eventually results in Śiva's marriage; at that marriage, Brahmā re-enacts his act of desire, but this time Śiva forgives him. The myth specifically

1 recognizes the tie between the two incidents, for when Brahmā is over-
37a come by desire for Śiva's bride he says, 'As I wished to delude Śiva by
a trick [i.e. trap him into a marriage caused by lust], so even now Śiva
has deluded me with his magical game.' And in one recent English
translation of this myth by a Hindu, Brahmā blazes like a fire and says,
1 43a 'After playing this same trick on Śiva, Kāma will be consumed in the
37a fire of Śiva's eye.'[39] Certain texts retain elements of the incest myth in
41a the wedding episode, such as the unfailing fertility of the seed and the
chastity of the resulting sons:

36e Brahmā saw the beautiful face (or feet) of Pārvatī at the wedding, and
39e he became excited and shed his seed upon the ground. In fear of Śiva, he
21e 29a began to make the seed barren, but Śiva said, 'Brahmā, you should not kill
37e 21a Brahmins, and these are great sages.' Then 88,000 *tapasvins* were born from
19a the seed, and they ran around Brahmā calling him 'Daddy, daddy!'[40]

The sages are born from the seed just as other sages are born from the sweat (a form of seed) shed in the incest myth. They are the 88,000 chaste sages who go by the path of the flame.

Other Vedic elements reappear in another text:

After spilling his seed like water from a broken pot, Brahmā offered it into
10c the fire, taking it with his left hand and offering it as an oblation. From it
21e 21a there arose 88,000 ascetics, passionless, shining like fire, their seed drawn
up in chastity.[41]

The offering of the seed into the fire is familiar from the mythology of Brahmā, Agni, and Śiva. Here the oblation is offered with the left hand because it is impure, but it is nevertheless valid and produces pure sons, their chastity a reflection of the lust which begat them.

The most complex form of the wedding episode occurs as part of the marriage of Śiva and Satī:

36e When Brahmā shed his seed at the wedding, Śiva attempted to kill him,
21e for he remembered that when Viṣṇu had given Satī to him at the beginning
39e 38a[1] of the wedding he had said, 'If any man looks upon Satī with desire, you must
10cd kill him.' But the gods pleaded with Śiva to spare Brahmā, and Viṣṇu said,
'Brahmā was born to perform creation. If he is killed, there can be no other
natural creator. It was he who made Satī to be your wife.' Śiva replied, 'Viṣṇu,
37e I must kill this terrible sinner, but I myself will then create all beings, and
by my own *tejas* I will create another creator.' Hearing this, Viṣṇu smiled
13d and reminded Śiva of the unity of the three of them, and Śiva became calm
38ea and did not kill Brahmā. He told Brahmā to place his hand on his head, and
45e[2] immediately there appeared there the image of Śiva riding on his bull. As
25a expiation, Śiva instructed Brahmā to wander on earth in human form, since

he had shed his seed as human men do, and to perform *tapas* with the image 2
of Rudra on his head, a source of instruction and ridicule among men in the 20e 33ea[5]
world, for Brahmā himself would be blamed and censured. Then the seed 39ea 24a
that had fallen on the altar became the clouds of doomsday in the sky. Brahmā 15c 14d
performed the rest of the marriage ceremony and a great celebration took 36e
place.[42]

This is one of the few versions in which the seed does not produce ascetic sages, but the clouds are a closely related motif. There are strong overtones of the incest myth here, and Śiva's censure of Brahmā is almost verbatim the same as the one that he utters in the earlier myth.

F. THE BEHEADING OF BRAHMĀ BY ŚIVA

Certain elements of the marriage myth refer back to another part of the incest myth, the beheading of Brahmā by Śiva (Rudra). Viṣṇu's command that Śiva should kill anyone who looks with passion upon Satī is an attempt to rationalize this part of the Vedic myth, a command derived on the one hand from the Sandhyā story (for Śiva granted her the boon that anyone who looked upon her with desire would become impotent), and on the other hand utilized as a rather awkward justification of Śiva's brahminicide, which is a sin. The vow of expiation that Brahmā is taught by Śiva, with the image of Rudra on his head, is a copy of the vow of expiation performed by Śiva himself, carrying Brahmā's severed head, in the myth of the beheading.

This myth is very popular in India, primarily because it extols the
virtue of the Kāpālika ('Skull-Bearer') cult and of Benares (Kapālamo- 38a[2]
cana, 'Skull-Releasing') as a shrine of expiation.[43] In most versions the
conflict between Śiva and Brahmā is based upon a contest of supremacy,
which is also the basis of an even more famous myth, the story of the
appearance of the great *liṅga*, in which Śiva takes the form of an 5cd
infinitely high and deep pillar of flame to prove to Viṣṇu and Brahmā
that he is the supreme lord. One text of the flame-*liṅga* myth supplies
a link with the beheading theme: Brahmā's fifth head (the one that 5cd
Śiva chops off) lies, saying that he succeeded in flying to the top of the 38a[2]
liṅga, and then, frightened because of its sin, the head becomes a river.[44] 14c[1]
Yet another variant of the same myth may be seen in the Pine Forest, where the sages (Brahmā appearing here represented by his sons) deny the greatness of Śiva until the flame pillar (the castrated fiery *liṅga*) threatens to destroy them. Moreover, in most of the Pine Forest stories, Śiva enters the forest in the form of a Kāpālika, following the vow of

expiation that he must undergo because of the beheading of Brahmā.
He begs from the wives of the Seven Sages just as one who has killed
a Brahmin must beg from seven houses.[45] Often the Pine Forest adven-
38a[1] ture is explicitly said to follow the beheading, and on several occasions
38a[2] Śiva produces a mountain of skulls in the midst of the Pine Forest.[46]
Moreover, the motifs of beheading and castration share the important
element of physical mutilation inflicted because of a sexual crime. Thus
the myth of the beheading of Brahmā, the Pine Forest story, the flame-
liṅga myth, and the myth of Dakṣa's sacrifice (as well as the Skanda
story and the myth of Brahmā's lust for Śiva's bride) are all derived
from the obscure Ṛg Vedic myth of primeval incest.

One Purāṇa explicitly combines the myth of the beheading with the myth of the flame-*liṅga*:

> Once when Brahmā and Viṣṇu were arguing, each saying that he was the
> 5cd supreme god, a great light appeared between them, illuminating the earth
> 7cd[1] and the heavens, and a man appeared within it, three-eyed and adorned with
> 30a snakes. Then Brahmā's fifth head said to the man, 'I know who you are. You
> are Rudra, whom I created from my forehead. Take refuge with me and I will
> protect you, my son.' When Śiva heard this proud speech he blazed with
> anger, and his anger engendered a man, Bhairava, whom Śiva commanded,
> 38a[1] 'Punish this lotus-born god named Brahmā.' Bhairava cut off Brahmā's head
> with the tip of the nail of his left thumb, for whatever limb offends must be
> punished. Then Brahmā and Viṣṇu were terrified, and they praised Śiva,
> who was pleased and said to Bhairava, 'You must honour Viṣṇu and Brahmā,
> 38a[2] and carry Brahmā's skull.' Then Śiva created a maiden named Brahminicide
> and said to her, 'Follow Bhairava until he arrives at the holy city of Benares,
> after wandering about, begging for alms with this skull and teaching the world
> the vow that removes the sin of brahminicide. You cannot enter Benares, so
> leave him there.' Śiva vanished, and Bhairava wandered over the earth,
> pursued by Brahminicide. He went to Viṣṇu, who gave him alms and said to
> Brahminicide, 'Release Bhairava', but she said, 'By serving him constantly
> 20a under this pretext [of haunting him for his sin], I will purify myself so that
> 38a I will not be reborn.' Then Bhairava entered Benares with her still at his left
> side, and she cried out and went to hell, and the skull of Brahmā fell from
> Bhairava's hand and became the shrine of Kapālamocana.[47]

This version has exalted the position of Śiva in several ways. Whereas in the classical myth Śiva himself is burdened with the skull and forced to wander about, haunted by Brahminicide, here the sin is transferred to an aspect of himself, Bhairava, whom he punishes with the spectre of Brahminicide which he himself creates. Śiva now objects to being called 'Son' by Brahmā, though he willingly plays that role in earlier creation stories.[48]

The father–son relationship is the basis of another version of the myth of the beheading:

Śiva created the five-headed Brahmā, commanded him to perform creation, 8c
and vanished. Brahmā performed *tapas* and Śiva gave him the Vedas, but 39ea
Brahmā was still unable to create. Śiva offered him a boon, and Brahmā asked 38ea
Śiva to become his son. Śiva said, 'Since you wish for me as a son, I will cut 8d
off your head and your glory.' Then Brahmā created a son, Rudra, who was 3
five-headed, carried a trident, and wore a snake for his sacrificial thread. 30a
Brahmā sent Rudra to Himālaya, but then Brahmā became foolish, proud,
and passionate, thinking that he alone had created everything. His fifth head
produced a *tejas* so great that it destroyed the wits of his sons, just as lamps do 7d
not glow when the sun has risen. His sons took counsel together and sought $5c^{3}$ 40a
refuge with Śiva, telling him how Brahmā's fifth head had destroyed their
tejas and asking him to restore things as they had been. Śiva went to Brahmā,
who, overwhelmed by darkness, did not know him. Śiva's *tejas* overcame
Brahmā, deluding him, and Śiva cut off Brahmā's head with the nail of his $38a^{1}$
left thumb.[49]

Both gods here are five-headed, and each is in some way the father of the other. Another multiform of the conflict between creative father and ascetic sons appears in the form of the sons whose *tejas* is overwhelmed by their father's *tejas*, just as Brahmā is overwhelmed by the *tejas* of Śiva's flame-*liṅga*.

The explicit purpose of the myth of the beheading is to justify and exalt the shrine at Benares and the vow of expiation that Bhairava 'taught the world', and there would be no reason to connect it with the myth of Brahmā's incest were it not for the implications and clear connections in other, earlier versions of the beheading. The head that Śiva removes is the fifth head of Brahmā, which appeared in the first place because of Brahmā's incestuous lust, just as the superfluous eyes and heads of Indra and Śiva were caused by their lust. And it is because of lust that the fifth head is destroyed:

Brahmā was dwelling in a lotus, trying to create. When a beautiful woman 8c
appeared from his mouth, Brahmā was overcome by desire; he grabbed her 39e
by force and demanded that she relieve his agony by making love with him. 24e
In anger she said to him, 'This fifth head is inauspicious on your neck. Four
faces would be more suitable for you.' Then she vanished, and the fire of
Brahmā's anger burnt all the water on earth. Rudra then appeared and 12d
attacked the fifth head of Brahmā with his nails. He took up the severed head $38a^{1}$
and became known as the Kāpālika. He wandered over the earth until he 38ea
came to Kapālamocana in Benares, where the skull fell from his hand and $38a^{2}$
he was purified. The gods praised him, and Śiva the Kāpālika created from

8c his own mouth a part of himself, born without a woman, an ascetic who
34a wandered over the earth, teaching the Kāpālika way.[50]

The woman in this myth is created by Brahmā and must be his daughter, though she is not explicitly described in those terms, and Rudra punishes Brahmā for his incest, not for his impiety or pride as in the later versions. But the framework of the story is that of the creation myth in which Brahmā attempts to create, fails, and then is assisted by Rudra —who *helps* Brahmā by cutting off the head that interfered with the process of creation.

In another version, Brahmā's incest is a more direct cause of the severing of the fifth head:

39e Brahmā desired Sarasvatī and went to her, asking her to stay with him. She,
2 being his daughter, was furious at this and said, 'Your mouth speaks in-
auspiciously and so you will always speak in a contrary way.' From that day,
Brahmā's fifth head always spoke evilly and coarsely. Therefore one day
when Śiva was wandering about with Pārvatī and came to see Brahmā,
24a Brahmā's four heads praised Śiva but the fifth made an evil sound. Śiva, displeased with the fifth head, cut it off. The skull remained stuck fast to Śiva's
hand, and though he was capable of burning it up, Śiva wandered the earth
with it for the sake of all people, until he came to Benares.[51]

The ambivalent relationship between Brahmā and Śiva is represented here by the way in which some of Brahmā's sons praise Śiva while some insult him. The secondary cause of the beheading—the insult to Śiva—is combined with the primary cause—the daughter's curse—and the pious storyteller justifies Śiva's expiation by attributing it to his willing submission 'for the sake of all people', his attitude of *bhakti*. Here again, Śiva's aggressive act is not only justified but considered a favour to Brahmā—ridding him of an inauspicious head.

In one interesting variant, Śiva's beheading of Brahmā again ultimately increases Brahmā's erotic powers:

39e 33ea^{4} Brahmā desired his daughter and took the form of a stag to pursue her as
40a a doe. The Brahmins called him to shame, and Rudra shot him with an arrow.
38a The deer's head came away from Brahmā's body and became a constellation
in the sky. But then Gāyatrī and Sarasvatī [the wives of Brahmā] had no hus-
25ea^{2} band. They performed *tapas* for Śiva, and he agreed to revive their husband,
38e giving Brahmā the four heads of Nandin and others of his hosts. Brahmā
45e^{2} 33ea^{4} arose and praised Śiva.[52]

Although Śiva beheads Brahmā, he replaces the (single) head with four others, just as he replaces the heads of Dakṣa and Gaṇeśa, and as he revives Kāma at the request of his wife, Rati.

The act of beheading, however, is antagonistic, as is obvious from the context as well as the background myth of incest. The Abbé Dubois recorded another version which restores the sexual basis of the antagonism:

> Brahmā . . . was born with five heads, but he outraged Pārvatī, the wife of 39e 4
> Śiva, and Śiva avenged himself by striking off one of the heads of the adul- 37e
> terous god in single combat.[53] 38a

There does not seem to be any Sanskrit version of this myth, but Brahmā's lust for Satī, and the shedding of his seed at the sight of her, supplies a close multiform. Moreover, the process of substituting Pārvatī for the original daughter is reflected in the popular tradition which makes Pārvatī (instead of the sages' wives) the object of Agni's adultery. As Brahmā and Agni are often confused with Śiva in the mythology, such a transference is not surprising. In fact, the confusion of Śiva with Brahmā is the *explicit* cause of the beheading in a South Indian version of the myth:

> [Long ago, Brahmā and Śiva both had five heads. One day Brahmā came 37e
> to Pārvatī and she, mistaking him for Śiva because he had five heads, fed him. 39e
> Śiva returned and criticized Pārvatī for feeding Brahmā before his return, 16cd
> and Pārvatī asked Śiva to cut off one of Brahmā's heads so that she could dis- 36a 38a[1]
> tinguish between them. He did so, and, holding the head in his hand, he 38a[2]
> became mad and roamed through the burning-places. Then Pārvatī took the 6d
> head in her own hand and became mad, dancing with it until Śiva told her 31a
> to go to earth. After a fight between them, Śiva began to run from her, and 36a
> although she created a fire in his path and then a large ocean, he crossed them 5d 14cd
> both. Then she agreed to go to earth, where Śiva comes to see her on the 36e
> morning of every Śiva Ratri.][54]

Śiva is often called Pañcavaktra ('Five-Headed') and is so portrayed in the iconography, but it is unusual to see such an explicit reference to the coincidence of attributes in two different gods. Brahmā is only given five heads in relatively late texts, and this attribute was probably introduced long after the myth of Śiva's beheading of Brahmā became prevalent; a nineteenth-century painting portrays a composite image of a five-headed Brahmā/Śiva.[55] The real basis of the beheading is retained as an undercurrent of the myth, however, for Pārvatī's inability to distinguish between the two gods would give rise to a sexual conflict between them (here masked by the reference to her 'feeding' Brahmā), similar to the incestuous conflict which underlies the Sanskrit versions of the tale.

G. THE BEHEADING OF DAKṢA BY ŚIVA

The story of Brahmā's rape of Pārvatī is all the more comprehensible in the context of the final multiform of the incest story—the sacrifice of Dakṣa—which connects the *prajāpati* with the wife of Śiva. The *prajāpati* is Dakṣa in this story, the wife is Satī, and the incest is thoroughly veiled, yet the identity of Dakṣa and Brahmā is clear from the pattern of the myth. When Śiva is about to kill Brahmā at the wedding Viṣṇu says to him, 'You must not kill Brahmā, for it was he who made Satī to be your wife',[56] a statement which further links Dakṣa and Brahmā as parents of Satī. Dakṣa's particular contribution as a *prajāpati* is the creation of wives for the gods and the invention of sexual intercourse as a method of procreation.[57] Since Śiva is often credited with this idea, the conflict between the two gods is based upon competition as well as opposition, as is the case with Śiva and Brahmā. Moreover, the 'invention' of intercourse is tantamount to the 'invention' of Kāma, the latter being the immediate cause of Brahmā's incest.

But incest is attributed specifically to Dakṣa in his own right as early
39e as the Ṛg Veda,[58] and the Purāṇas indicate that this incest is necessary
for Dakṣa for the same reasons that it is necessary for Brahmā himself:

> 32e Dakṣa divided his body in two, and obtained a beautiful woman, upon
> 39e whom he begat many daughters. Then he abandoned the female part of his
> 23e[1] form and gave his daughters to the gods for wives.[59]

Androgynous creation is by nature incestuous, whether it be by Brahmā,
2 Dakṣa, or Śiva. Dakṣa is cursed to be attached to country pleasures, to
33ea[4] lust for women, and to have the head of a goat, while Śiva himself curses
39e Dakṣa to beget a son upon his own daughter in a future life.[60] Both are
examples of the curse which exaggerates the sin for which the curse is
given, rather than the curse which brings about the opposite condition.
The ram or goat is the symbol of lust in Hindu mythology; when Indra
32a is castrated, his testicles are replaced with those of a ram or goat; Indra
33ea[4] takes the form of a ram to rape a Brahmin woman. Prajāpati's seed is
33ea[4] said to have fallen and turned into the billy-goat; therefore, when Śiva
38e 38a[1] beheads Dakṣa he replaces Dakṣa's head with that of a goat.[61] This is
derived in part from the prototypal myth in which the sacrifice which
Rudra pierces or burns with his glance is personified as the sacrificial
33ea[4] animal,[62] though the lecherous nature of the goat is pertinent here as
well. Yet the head of Dakṣa is cut off and cast as the oblation into the
10c fire, like Brahmā's seed, and in this one may see a myth based on ritual.

The later mythology of Dakṣa is complicated by the fact that Śiva, rather than Dakṣa, marries the daughter, Satī, and in some ways the giving of the daughter heals the rift between them. But most of the enmity between Dakṣa and Śiva is derived from their relationship as in-laws, rather than solved by this relationship. Śiva is certainly not the ideal son-in-law, and the parents of his wives object to him primarily because an ascetic is not considered the right man to be a husband. The traditional conflict between ascetic and erotic creation is personified in the Dakṣa myth (as in the myth of Brahmā) as the conflict between Śiva the ascetic and Dakṣa the *prajāpati*.

One Purāṇa establishes firmly the tie between the Dakṣa myth and the myth of primeval creation:

> Brahmā created various creatures, but when they failed to increase he 8d
> became angry and began to do *tapas*. Rudra appeared and Brahmā said to 39ea
> him, 'Produce creatures to fill the universe, for you are able to do this.' When 8c 40a
> Rudra heard this, he plunged into the water and began to do *tapas*, and while 10d
> he was in the water Dakṣa began to create mentally, and his sons created 37e
> mentally. When Rudra emerged from the water, ready to begin creation, he 8c
> made the sacrifice and the gods, but then in fury he said, 'Who has insulted
> me and superseded me, creating all this universe and this lovely maiden?'
> Flames came out of his mouth and turned into demons and ghosts and yogis, 13cd[3]
> who pervaded the earth. Then Rudra made a marvellous bow and other 38a[1]
> weapons, and he attacked the gods and knocked out the teeth of Pūṣan and
> the eyes of Bhaga, and he cut off the testicles of Kratu ['The Sacrifice'], and 32a
> Kratu fell to the ground, his seed pierced. Then Rudra demanded a share of
> the sacrifice, and the gods praised him, and he restored all those whom he had 38e
> maimed.[63]

It is not stated here that the sacrifice is Dakṣa's, but Dakṣa is the one who has usurped Śiva's position as creator and Śiva's anger is directed against him. Dakṣa is not beheaded, but Kratu, the sacrifice, is castrated,[64] his seed pierced like that of the primeval Brahmā. And although 32a
Śiva does not marry Satī in this version, he comments on her beauty and knows that she has been made by Dakṣa.

Satī's role is clearer in a longer version of this myth:

> Brahmā wished to create, but he did not know how to do it. He became 8d
> angry, and Rudra was born from his anger. Brahmā gave Rudra a beautiful
> maiden for his wife, named Gaurī [Pārvatī], and Rudra rejoiced when he 36e
> received her. Then Brahmā forbade Rudra to do *tapas* at the time of creation,
> saying, 'Rudra, you must perform creation.' But Rudra said, 'I am unable', 36a
> and he plunged into the water, for he thought, 'One without *tapas* is not able 40a
> to create creatures.' Then Brahmā took Gaurī back, and, wishing to create, 8c 10d
> he made seven mind-born sons, Dakṣa and his brothers. He gave Gaurī to 37e
> Dakṣa for a daughter, though she had been formerly promised in marriage

to Rudra, and Dakṣa rejoiced and began a great sacrifice which all the gods
attended. Then, after 10,000 years, Rudra rose from the water, and by the
power of his *tapas* he saw all the world before him with its forests and men
and beasts, and he heard the chanting of the priests in Dakṣa's sacrifice. Then
he became furious, and he said, 'Brahmā created me and instructed me to
perform creation. Who is doing that work now?' Flames issued forth from
his ears and turned into ghosts and goblins and various weapons. Rudra
38a[1] destroyed Dakṣa's sacrifice, but he restored it again when the gods praised
38e him. Dakṣa gave his daughter to Rudra as Brahmā asked him to do, and Rudra
36e took her with him to Kailāsa.[65]

The role of Dakṣa is much expanded from the shorter version of the myth cited above. Here Dakṣa, rather than Śiva, creates the gods and the sacrifice, and Dakṣa offends Śiva by taking away his wife, a thinly veiled remnant of the incest myth. Śiva's position here is unambiguous: he rejects the wife he has been given (though he is said to have rejoiced upon obtaining her) and does *tapas* because he is unable, rather than unwilling, to create without it.[66] In the shorter version, Brahmā takes care to tell him, 'Produce creatures to fill the universe, for you are able to do this',[67] but Rudra disobeys him and clearly disagrees with him. Brahmā 'takes back' Rudra's wife (hence, perhaps, the popular myth that he committed adultery with her), and then—a simple multiform—Dakṣa takes her as well, as a daughter, only to give her back to Śiva. The rejection of Dakṣa's daughter, a manifestation of Śiva's ascetic character, is one of the sources of conflict between the two gods. Yet Śiva does not reject her outright, nor does he reject creation—merely a particular aspect of it at a particular time.

H. THE CASTRATION OF ŚIVA

Yet another version of this creation myth emphasizes Śiva's refusal to create by describing his self-castration:

Brahmā and Viṣṇu asked Rudra to create. He said, 'I will do it', and then
8c 10d he plunged into the water for a thousand years. Brahmā and Viṣṇu began to
worry, and Viṣṇu said, 'There is not much time left. You must make an
40a effort to create, for you have the ability and I will give you the female creative
37e power.' Brahmā then created all the gods and other beings, and when Śiva
emerged from the water, about to begin creation, he saw that the universe
was full. He thought, 'What will I do? Creation has already been achieved by
8d Brahmā, and therefore I will destroy it and tear out my own seed.' He released
13cd[3] a flame from his mouth, setting the universe on fire, but eventually Brahmā
39ea 5d propitiated Śiva, who broke off his *liṅga*, saying, 'There is no use for this *liṅga*
5cd 32a except to create creatures.' He threw the *liṅga* upon the earth, and it broke

through the earth and went down to hell and up to the sky. Viṣṇu and Brahmā failed to find the top and bottom of it, and they worshipped it.[68]

Brahmā here usurps Śiva's position, a reversal of the situation in most myths and in actual historical development. Death is necessitated by the fullness of the universe, which is closed ('The Egg of Brahmā'), so that there can be no creation without mortality. When Śiva discovers that he is not needed as a creator, he becomes a destroyer, and his refusal to create is symbolized by his castration, but this too is ambivalent, for it results in the fertility cult of *liṅga*-worship.

This paradox is justified both by the ascetic character of Śiva's creation and by the implications of fertility in the act of castration:

Brahmā told Śiva to perform creation immediately, but Śiva saw the fault
of creatures and he did *tapas* for a long time, submerged in water. Brahmā 10d
waited for a long time, and then he mentally created another creator of all 40a
beings and said, 'Sthāṇu ["The Pillar", Śiva] is in the water. You must per- 37e 26a
form creation.' Then the other creator produced Dakṣa and the others, who
were hungry and increased when Brahmā gave them food. Śiva arose from the 16cd
water and saw them and became angry. He tore out his *liṅga* and placed it in 32a
the earth. To calm him, Brahmā said, 'What did you do all that time in the
water? And why did you tear out your *liṅga* and put it in the ground?' Śiva
said, 'Another created all creatures, so what use was the *liṅga* to me? I under- 8c 16cd
took my *tapas* in order to obtain food for all creatures, and medicinal herbs,
for otherwise they would die.' And then, in anger, Śiva went to perform *tapas* 26a
on the mountain.[69]

In this multiform of the myth of ascetic versus sexual creation, the act of castration is both the cause and the result of asceticism. Yet even here it is a creative asceticism, and as such it is part of the mythology of the fertility god whose personal sexuality must be sacrificed for the sake of the fertility of the universe. The creative aspect of the act is indicated by Rudra's concern for the food which will prevent death.

The creative implications of castration are emphasized in another version of the myth:

Rudra was calm, controlled, and without desire. From him Viṣṇu was born 8c
and was instructed to perform creation. Then [Rudra] thought, 'After doing
tapas I will perform creation', and when he was exhausted from performing 10d
tapas he slept in the ocean of milk for a long time. Meanwhile, as Rudra could
not be found, Viṣṇu and Brahmā performed creation. When Rudra arose, he 37e
wandered about, desirous of creating, and he saw that the universe was filled
with pairs of various creatures and that there was no space left. Then he, who
is the cause of creation, became angry, and he cut off his marvellous *liṅga*, 32a
thinking, 'What use is it?' It was made of great flames, terrible, without base 5cd

5c[2] or middle or end. Brahmā and Viṣṇu saw the *liṅga*, sought in vain the top and
13d bottom of it, and worshipped it. Rudra's anger was assuaged and he vanished.[70]

Here Śiva's destructive and ascetic aspects are attributed to a frustrated or sublimated creativity. The central image is that of fiery power that may be used creatively or destructively and which must be controlled.

Much of the imagery of the myth is shared with that of the Pine Forest. The castrated *liṅga* becomes a destructive fire until it is placed under control, a flame *liṅga* extending to heaven and hell until it is worshipped. The reason for the castration here—that Śiva has 'no use' for his *liṅga*—is given in a slightly modified form in one of the Pine Forest myths, in which Śiva says:

> I abandoned my *liṅga* when I was suffering from longing for Satī, and
> 32a merely on the pretext of the curse of the sages. For who could cause my *liṅga*
> to fall, in all the universe? I will not take the *liṅga* up from the earth or bear
> it, for what would I do with it without my wife?[71]

Other versions of the Pine Forest myth attribute the castration to Śiva himself rather than to the sages:

> 28ea 24a When the sages saw Śiva naked and excited they beat him and they said,
> 'Tear out your *liṅga*.' The great yogi said to them, 'I will do it, if you hate my
> 43ea 32a *liṅga*', and he tore it out and vanished.[72]

In these myths, the castration does in fact bring an end to Śiva's sexual activity, as it does in the creation myths. Kāma is unable to excite Śiva after Śiva has lost his *liṅga* in the Pine Forest.[73]

There is other evidence for this view that castration is anti-erotic in
cause as well as in effect. In an instance of the curse that exaggerates
the fault for which it is given, Devī indirectly describes the fate of Śiva
2 when, after she revives Kāma, she says to him, 'By my grace, whoever
32a reviles you or turns away from you will be a eunuch in birth after birth,
25e and you will cause those evil wretches who oppose my devotees to fall
for unapproachable women and thereby to be destroyed.'[74] Śiva is
'destroyed' by his attachment to the Pine Forest women, and he becomes
a eunuch, for he is the one who did the original injury to Kāma which
underlies the curse of Devī. His anti-eroticism is the source of his
castration in this context. A similar fate for a similar reason befalls
3 Arjuna, who is cursed to be a eunuch because he would not seduce an
32a *apsaras*.[75] Brahmā narrowly escapes this punishment, for when he spurns
24e Mohinī she says to him, 'Any man who is enticed over and over
24a again by a woman tortured by lust, but does not make love to her—he
32a is a eunuch.'[76]

Yet, in another series of myths, castration does not prevent lust. 'Even
when Śiva had no *liṅga*, Kāma did not leave him. . . . Even when his 32a
liṅga had fallen, Śiva remembered Kāma. . . . [Śiva] was beyond sensa- 43ea
tion, but beginning to miss his lingam all the same.'[77] One implication
of sexuality may be seen in the fact that castration, like other ascetic
practices, is traditionally a punishment for a sexual offence, and therefore implies at least the former lust of the god. Many folk-tales explain
the present shape or placement of the genitals by incidents of castration
resulting from sexual transgressions; a typical example is this tale:

> [Men had long penises. One day a man got drunk and wanted to lie with 26ea 16d
> his wife in the presence of their child. She cut off his penis.][78] 27e 32a

In ancient India, a Śūdra who committed adultery was to be castrated,[79] 32a
the king was instructed to mutilate and banish an adulterer or anyone 32a
who raped a virgin,[80] and Śiva himself castrated Kāma when he sus- 42ea
pected him of adultery.[81] More pertinent still to the mythology of Śiva 43a
is the law that a man who had seduced his guru's wife or any maiden 32a
or low-caste woman[82] was to castrate himself, cutting off both testicles 32a
and the penis, taking them in his hand, and walking until he fell.[83] Śiva 25a
in some versions of the Pine Forest myth is castrated by the sages, who
make specific reference to the fact that there is no king to punish him,[84] 32a
and in other versions he castrates himself.[85] In addition to the king and 32a
the offender himself, other chastisers appropriate to Śaiva mythology
are mentioned in the lawbooks: 'One can be made a eunuch by the fire-curse of an angry guru or god.'[86] The sages in the forest quote the legal
texts when they punish Śiva:

> You false ascetic, let your *liṅga* fall to earth here. A shameless and evil man
> who has seduced another man's wife should be castrated; there is no other 32a
> punishment ever. A man who has seduced his guru's wife should cut off the
> *liṅga* and testicles himself and hold them in his hands and walk until he dies.[87] 25a

But there is a more specific mythological background for the castration of Śiva, which reveals still more clearly the manner in which the
punishment increases rather than diminishes Śiva's sexuality: the myth
of the castration of Indra. One version of the Pine Forest myth contrasts
the two episodes explicitly: 'The *tapas* of the sages was powerless
against Śiva, although the gods themselves are usually helpless against
the curses of sages. Indra was cursed by Gautama and lost his phallus 1 45a
and testicles.'[88] Although Śiva is here considered invulnerable, it is 32a
evident that in the basic form of the myth he was treated as Indra was,
and for the same reason. Indra seduced Ahalyā, the wife of the sage

32a Gautama, and was cursed to be castrated,[89] but Agni then replaced
43e 33ea[4] Indra's testicles with those of a ram,[90] the animal sacred to Agni himself. A late Purāṇa describes the episode in considerable detail and
connects it with Śiva through Devī:

33ea[2] Indra took the form of Gautama to seduce Ahalyā, saying to her, 'I am in
the power of Kāma. Give me a kiss and so forth.' But as she was worshipping
the gods she told him that he had chosen an inappropriate time. He said,
'Enough of this talk of what is done and what is not done. You should obey
your husband, especially in matters of sex. Give me an embrace and so forth.'
Then he embraced her and had his pleasure of her, but Gautama knew what
had happened by his powers of meditation, and he hurried home and cursed
2 Indra, saying, 'Since you have acted in this way for the sake of the female
3 sexual organ, let there be a thousand of them on your body, and let your *liṅga*
17cd 32a fall.' Then Gautama went to do *tapas*, and Indra, full of shame, stood in the
10d water for a long time, praising Devī in her aspect of Indrākṣi ['Eyes of Indra'].
25a When she offered him a boon he asked to have his deformity cured, but she
45ea 7cd[2] said, 'I cannot destroy the evil born of a sage's curse, but I can do something
33ea[4] so that people will not notice it: you will have a thousand eyes in the middle
43e 17cd of the female organs, and you will have the testicles of a ram.'[91]

Devī restores Indra's virility as a reward for his *tapas*, curing both the castration of the original myth and the deforming *yonis* of the later versions. The sexual connotations of the ram have been noted in the context of the myth of Dakṣa's beheading; the particular qualities which link the ram to Indra are apparent from a Brāhmaṇa reference to the Indra myth:

32a Indra lost his virility. The gods used the ram, the male goat, and the bull
45e[2] 33ea[4] as recompense. And therefore the bull is sacred to Indra.[92]

Although Śiva's *liṅga* is not replaced by the organ of any animal, there
is an interesting parallel to this detail of the Indra story in the episode
33ea[4] in which Śiva's testicles are fed to the hungry goddesses because he
smells like a goat and is a goat.[93]

43e In some late versions of the Pine Forest myth, the *liṅga* is restored
to Śiva's body.[94] In Stacton's novel, when Kāma inspired Śiva with irresistible desire for Pārvatī, 'Siva's lingam sprang up at once and rooted wavering where it belonged.'[95] Although the actual Kāma–Pārvatī episode takes place before the castration in the Sanskrit cycle, Kāma does in fact inspire Śiva with desire after the castration in many texts. Usually, however, the *liṅga* takes on life and becomes sexually active without being rejoined to Śiva's body, just as Kāma himself remains effective even when he is disembodied. In this way, Śiva's sexuality can be satisfied and controlled only when the phallus ceases

to be a part of him and becomes depersonalized, iconized. That this is
a satisfaction rather than an obstruction of his lust is evident from the
way in which Śiva himself causes the *liṅga* to fall because it is lusting 32a
for a womb.[96] The lusting phallus is also the cause of the castration
from the standpoint of Śiva's enemies: he is punished for his adultery
just as Indra was.

This aspect of the Pine Forest castration is emphasized in one tribal myth:

> [Linga's phallus was two and a half cubits long.] Linga was very embar- 26ea
> rassed by it and he left his parents to go and live alone on Suranpahar. There 25a
> he lived the life of a saint and never looked into the face of a woman. [A twelve- 26a
> year-old girl] met Linga in the forest and he liked her and forgot his saintliness. 21a
> He tried to take her by force, but she ran away. [He chased her and she] cut 21ea
> two cubits off his organ. Full of rage and pain, Linga cut off the girl's nose 32a
> and she turned into Nakti Devi. . . . Linga's organ turned into a stone, and
> those who have no children go there to offer sacrifice.[97] 5c²

Many elements of the Sanskrit myth are transformed here. The chastity of the 'saint' is both a reaction from and a prelude to his excessive sexuality. The stone worshipped by those wishing for children is the Śiva-*liṅga*, which becomes a source of universal fertility as soon as it has ceased to be a source of individual fertility.

For in the myth castration is never a final act; it is merely a cyclic
occurrence, part of one phase that is followed by another. In almost all
versions of the myth—the creation story as well as the Pine Forest tale—
the *liṅga* falls into the earth when it has been cut off, an indication of
the fertility inherent in the act. In this it is reminiscent of the *brahma-*
cārin of the Atharva Veda, who, after performing *tapas* in the waters, 10d
introduces his phallus into the earth.[98] Although the Śiva-figure of
Lingo is associated with castration in tribal mythology, Śiva himself
appears there as a great creator and as the restorer of castrated man.[99]
So, too, in the Sanskrit mythology of Śiva, the castration is inevitably
reversed or transmuted, increasing the fertile powers of the god, however it may diminish him as an anthropomorphic lover in a particular
myth. In later mythology, the castrated *liṅga* in the earth is replaced
by the seed of Śiva, which falls upon the earth (often personified as
a woman) to produce the child Skanda. The pro-sexual nature of the
act of castration is indicated by the fact that the falling of the *liṅga* is 32a
often equated with the falling of the seed, just as the drawing up of the
seed is equated with the raising of the phallus, and the shedding of the 21e 21a
seed produces new *liṅgas*.[100] In one version of the Pine Forest myth 21e

21e the seed of Śiva actually falls in place of the *liṅga*; Viṣṇu takes the seed
20ea and produces a son from it.[101] But even in the original form, the falling
of the *liṅga* does not render Śiva asexual but extends his sexuality to
the sages and to the whole universe. As Satī describes it to Dakṣa:

33ea[5] Formerly Śiva went begging in the Pine Forest, and the 'beggar' was
32a cursed by your friends. Then Śiva filled the whole universe with his mere
5cd limb, and the whole universe became a *liṅga* at that moment.[102]

I. THE COMPETITION BETWEEN ŚIVA AND BRAHMĀ

The basis of the feud between Śiva and Brahmā in the castration myths is not in this instance the conflict between the incestuous creator and the ascetic destroyer, but between the two different valid forms of creation. Śiva opposes Prajāpati because he is himself a *prajāpati*. This
is implied in the myth of Brahmā's lust for Satī, when Viṣṇu begs Śiva
38a[1] not to kill Brahmā and Śiva replies, 'I will kill the evil wretch and I myself will then create all creatures, or else by my own *tejas* I will create
37e another to perform creation.'[103] This is precisely what Śiva does in one
creation myth:

8c 39ea 8d When the creatures that Brahmā had produced mentally failed to increase,
25ea[3] Brahmā performed *tapas* for Śiva, who broke out from the middle of Brahmā's
32e 7cd[1] forehead and said, 'I am your son.' Becoming an androgyne, he then burnt
37e 38a[1] Brahmā up, and then by the path of yoga he enjoyed the female half of him-
36e
38e self. In her he created Viṣṇu and Brahmā.[104]

When Brahmā's *tapas* fails to create, Śiva introduces sexual creation; yet Brahmā wins Śiva's help by means of *tapas*, and Śiva enjoys his wife 'by the path of yoga'. Though Śiva kills Brahmā, he recreates him. Similarly, when Śiva delays by performing *tapas*, Brahmā creates another creator in his place. This competition is clarified in another cycle of creation myths in which Brahmā produces mortal creatures (or death itself) and is opposed by Śiva, who represents perfect creation—the creation of immortals by means of *tapas*—as opposed to the creation of mortals by means of intercourse. Although superficially the roles seem reversed (Śiva representing life, Brahmā representing death), they are appropriate in the Hindu context, where Śiva represents *tapas* and immortality, Brahmā intercourse and mortality.

One of the earliest versions of this story, in the *Mahābhārata*, deals primarily with death rather than creation:

The earth became overloaded with living creatures. Brahmā created from
11c 5d his sweat and anger a great fire to destroy them, but Śiva appeared as Sthāṇu

and said, 'The fire of your anger has burnt all living creatures to ashes. Have 4 26a
mercy. Restrain your fiery anger and let it subside. Instead [of killing them 6cd 13d
all now], let all creatures be absorbed into a period of quiescence.' Brahmā 20e
then restrained his fiery anger and made the process of cyclic action and
quiescence, the chain of rebirth. Then he vanished, but from his restrained
fire of anger and from his sweat there appeared a woman, the spirit of death 11c
and universal dissolution, and he instructed her to kill living creatures 10cd
periodically.[105] 37ea 17d

Among the many reversed roles in this myth, it is interesting to note that the woman born from Brahmā's sweat—Death—replaces Rati, who is born from the sweat of Brahmā/Dakṣa in other creation myths. In the later mythology, Śiva is begged by Brahmā to restrain his fiery anger, but in this myth Śiva appears as Sthāṇu, his chaste and quiescent form, and restrains Brahmā by establishing a basic resolution of the Śaiva paradox: the cycles of action and quiescence. In this context, periodic death is a favour granted by Śiva in his peaceful form as an alternative to the total death here represented by Brahmā (though usually represented by Rudra). These reversals are far from arbitrary, for they attribute to each god an aspect consonant with his general personality.

Death is regarded as a favour from Śiva in the tribal tradition as well:

[The sixty-four *yoginīs* bathed in the sea while they were menstruating. 17c
A girl was born from a drop of their blood on which the shadow of a hawk had 15cd
been cast. She was given men for her food, but the men were excreted and 30e 17d
revived, because they kept the Water of Immortality in a hollow bamboo. 20ea 16cd
She complained of this to the *yoginīs*, for she was always hungry, and they 14c[2]
told Mahadeo about it. He stole the water from the men and from that time 26e[1]
forth there was death.][106] 10cd

The necessity for an ambiguous, imperfect, mortal creation is the basis of many variants of the myth in which Brahmā prevents Śiva from
creating immortals.[107] Though it is Brahmā who introduces death, Śiva's 4
subsequent refusal to create mortals produces a kind of preventive euthanasia, a reversal of the reversal, so that he ends up creative after all. One version of this myth comments, 'Out of his compassion, Rudra gives final peace to all creatures, effortlessly, by the power of his magic yoga, for he gives passionlessness and release.'[108] Death rather than immortality is here regarded as Śiva's gift to mortal mankind.

The connotations of mortality in Rudra's conflict with Brahmā are evident from yet another variant of this myth:

Brahmā performed *tapas* and created Rudra the androgyne, who divided 39ea
himself as Brahmā commanded him to do. Dakṣa then took the female half 32e
of the androgyne to be his daughter, and he gave her to Rudra. Brahmā said 36e

40a to Rudra, 'Śiva, lord of Satī, perform creation', but Rudra said, 'I will not
26a perform creation. Do it yourself, and let me destroy. I will become Sthāṇu.'
37ea And thus having commanded Brahmā to create, Śiva went to Kailāsa with
Satī.[109]

The theme of androgynous creation is combined with the Dakṣa–Satī myth, and Śiva rejects sexual creation even though he accepts a wife. There is no argument about immortal versus mortal creation, but Śiva expresses the necessity for a god of destruction, just as Brahmā in other myths explains to Śiva the need for death.

J. THE COMPLEMENTARITY OF BRAHMĀ AND ŚIVA

Several texts combine the Sthāṇu myth with the related theme of the
sons of Brahmā who refuse to create. Often the sons are forms of
40a Śiva,[110] and a strong Śaiva bias usually prevails, so that Śiva is not con-
demned for his passionlessness as the sons of Brahmā usually are. This reversal is made possible by the fact that the second path—sexual creation—is understood to be practised by someone else (Brahmā, in this case). Thus Hinduism in this context divides into different aspects—and personifies as separate gods—the roles which appear in other texts as different phases of a single god. Brahmā accomplishes sexual creation and Śiva devotes himself to asceticism, so that the universe is supplied with mortality and immortality.

This division of roles is apparent from certain versions of the Sthāṇu-ascetic-sons myth,[111] and the complementarity of the two creative methods is clear from this variation:

40a Brahmā created the mind-born sages, who remained celibate and refused to
36e create. Brahmā then created Rudra from his anger, and he gave him various
5c[1] wives and told him to become a *prajāpati* and to create progeny with the wives
7d he had received. Rudra created creatures like himself, who swallowed up the
universe on all sides, burning up the skies with their blazing eyes. Brahmā
4 was frightened and said, 'No more of these creatures. Do *tapas* for the sake
26a of all creatures and create the universe as it was before.' Śiva agreed, and he
37ea went to the forest to do *tapas*. Then Brahmā created his mental sons and
41e Kāma.[112]

Here Śiva's creation is directly connected with death, his sexuality producing destructive, fiery sons that rage out of control. Only creation by *tapas* is acceptable from Rudra in this myth, and Brahmā supplements this method with his sexual creation and with the creation of Kāma, to preserve the balance.

By refusing to participate personally in the process of creation, Śiva assists that process. On a cosmic level, his function is to make creation constantly possible by producing periodically the dissolution of the universe, destroying so that creation may take place. On the human level, each person has his own *svadharma*, his personal role to play; Śiva's *svadharma* causes him to disobey Brahmā's request for sexual creation, but he allows Brahmā to use this method—for sexual creation is Brahmā's *svadharma.*

A final version of the myth begins with the premiss of an unproductive death but concludes with an acceptance of the creative aspect of death:

> Brahmā began the process of creation but succeeded only in producing 8d
> delusion, suffering, death, disease, old age, sorrow, and anger. These offspring 29a
> were miserable and they had no wives or children. Then Brahmā said to
> Rudra, 'Create creatures', and Rudra meditated upon his wife Satī and 25ea^3
> mentally created creatures like himself, blazing with *tejas*, carrying skulls and 7d
> drinking Soma, their seed drawn up in chastity, having thousands of eyes, 14e^2 38a^2
> of such terrible gaze that one could not look upon them, great yogis of great 21a 7cd^2
> *tejas*. They were the Rudras, who devour oblations. When Brahmā saw them 10c
> he asked Śiva to create instead beings who would be subject to death, for, 4
> said Brahmā, 'Creatures free from death will not undertake actions.' Śiva 10cd
> refused and remained thenceforth Sthāṇu, his seed drawn up in chastity.[113] 26a

Death is associated with the asexual creation of Brahmā, while Śiva
uses his wife (although he merely meditates upon her) to produce a
deathless creation. Neither combination is successful, and in the next
episode Śiva must revert to the androgynous form and supply wives 32e
in order for creation to proceed.[114] Brahmā states the need for an 5c^1
ambiguous creation, brought about by an ambiguous method: 'Creatures 37ea
free from death will not undertake actions.'

In writing about the relationship between Brahmā and Śiva, Alan Watts has personified each one unequivocally:

> The polarity of Brahma and Shiva thus finds its expression in what at times seems to be the extreme ambivalence of Hindu culture—extreme in its asceticism as in its sensuality. . . . One might almost say that India has set herself the problem of exploring these two attitudes to their extremes and then of finding the synthesis between them. The problem, stated in mythological terms, is the recurrent theme of a type of popular Hindu literature known as the Puranas.[115]

The two aspects are there as Watts describes them, but the line that he draws between Brahmā and Śiva does not exist. The two gods participate in aspects of each other so deeply that they exchange roles almost at random. The synthesis that the Purāṇas seek takes place not merely in the interaction of two diametrically opposed gods, but in a far more complex manner within the character of the single god, Śiva himself.

Śiva often acts in place of Brahmā, and his opposition to Brahmā is frequently based upon similarity of purpose. In many of the later myths, sexual creation is personified as Kāma, and just as Brahmā opposes Kāma and curses him, so Śiva brings about the realization of that curse partly as the ascetic in opposition to Brahmā (resisting the attacks of Kāma that Brahmā has directed) and partly as an extension of Brahmā (chastising Kāma as Brahmā cursed him to be chastised). Moreover, just as Brahmā both curses Kāma and restores him, so Śiva too destroys Kāma but simultaneously participates in Kāma's nature and increases his power. In this way, the complex identity/opposition relation between Brahmā and the various aspects of Śiva underlies much of what appears to be paradoxical in the later mythology of Śiva.

V

ŚIVA AND KĀMA

THE conflict between Śiva and Kāma is the central point of the Śaiva Purāṇas. In the later texts, Kāma is sent by Brahmā to attack Śiva, out
of spite and in revenge against Śiva (for opposing Brahmā's incestuous 37a
behaviour) as well as against Kāma (for causing this behaviour).[1] In the earlier Purāṇas, however, Kāma is sent by Indra to cause Śiva to marry and beget the son needed by the gods. And in a still earlier era, before Śiva became the ascetic *par excellence*, Indra sent Kāma (or his assistants, the *apsarases*) to seduce ascetics in order to reduce the threat of their powers. In the context of the Skanda story, where the Kāma–Śiva conflict takes place, this episode is late,[2] for the birth of Skanda resulted first from the incestuous seed of Prajāpati, then from Agni's seduction of the sages' wives, and finally from the gods' need of a general. Yet most of the Purāṇas include the episode of Kāma, and the interaction of the forces which Śiva and Kāma represent is central to Indian culture from the time of the Vedas. Because of the remarkable continuity of that culture, the more elaborate and explicit myths of the Purāṇas may in fact capture and explain, as they purport to do, the often obscure meaning of the ancient tales.

A. THE CHASTITY OF ŚIVA—AND ITS CONTRADICTION

Śiva is the natural enemy of Kāma because he is the epitome of chastity, the eternal *brahmacārin*,[3] the very incarnation of chastity.[4] When Himālaya tries to bring his daughter Pārvatī to Śiva, Śiva objects with the traditional misogynist argument:

> This girl with her magnificent buttocks must not come near me. I insist 36a
> upon this. Wise men know that a woman is the very form of Enchantment, 25e
> especially a young woman, the destruction of ascetics. I am an ascetic, a yogi, 21ea
> so what need have I of a woman? An ascetic must never have contact with 34a
> women.[5]

Because of his chastity, Śiva is considered to be the one man in the universe who can resist Kāma. When Brahmā plots to have Śiva seduced he says, 'But what woman in the three worlds could enter his heart,

cause him to abandon his yoga, and delude him? Even Kāma will not
be able to delude him, for Śiva is a perfect yogi and cannot bear even
42a to hear women mentioned.'[6] Kāma is at first unwilling to attack Śiva,
for this very reason:

> 34a Don't you know how hard Śiva is to overcome? When one would conquer
> lechery, one thinks of Śiva. . . . Śiva takes pleasure in *tapas*, and all the Brahmins
> 7c revile me over and over again, saying, 'That Kāma is very evil, a great fire
> that envelops the knowledge of the wise and is their constant enemy. There-
> 30a fore Kāma must always be avoided like a serpent.' How then could Śiva be
> 42a pleased with me, my nature being such as it is?[7]

Śiva's reaction to Kāma in one Sanskrit play is much as Kāma fears it
30a will be: 'You stupid, vile Kāma, I see that some holes harbour vipers
9d as well as harmless snakes. Well, I will draw your poison.'[8] As lord of
ascetics, Śiva has shamanistic powers over serpents, which serve him as personal adornments; this and his fame as a drinker of poison lend special weight to his threat against Kāma.

But each of these statements is merely a thesis to be answered with an antithesis: Śiva's chastity is set against his lust, his invulnerability against his susceptibility. Many of the myths illustrating the chastity of Śiva appear in a mirror image as well, or contain within themselves implications of his lust. One such tale is an elaboration upon the myth in which Śiva enlightens Viṣṇu and causes him to leave the form of the boar in which he has married the Earth. In this version, the Earth is replaced by a group of demon women, but the troublesome sons remain:

> When Viṣṇu had driven the demons back down to hell, he happened to see
> 21ea there a group of beautiful women. Struck by the arrows of desire, he stayed
> 19a there and made love to the women, engendering in them sons that troubled
> 33ea[4] the world. To save the gods, Śiva took the form of a bull, who entered hell,
> 45e[2] bellowing, and killed Viṣṇu's sons. Then he enlightened Viṣṇu, saying, 'You
> 34a must not indulge yourself sexually here, a slave to desire.' The other gods
> 3 wished to enter hell to see the voluptuous women, but Śiva pronounced
> 19a a curse, saying, 'Except for a perfectly controlled sage or a demon born of me,
> 24ea[1] whoever enters this place will die.' Thus Viṣṇu the supreme womanizer was
> 10cd 34a chastised by Śiva, and the universe rejoiced.[9]

Śiva's position in this myth is fairly unequivocal in its chastity, but even here he assumes the form of a bull, the emblem of sexuality, instead of the *śarabha* beast of the boar myth, and he cleverly words the curse to allow himself (the 'perfectly controlled sage') and his sons to enjoy the demon women.

The second variant elaborates upon this aspect of Śiva until the whole point of the myth is reversed. After repeating the myth with some minor variations it continues:

After Śiva had pronounced the curse and the gods had returned to heaven,
some time passed. Then one day, when Śiva was rapt in thought and Pārvatī
happened to ask him what he was thinking about, he said, 'I am thinking 23ea
about the beautiful women of hell, the most beautiful women in the universe.' 21ea
'You fool,' said Pārvatī, 'you are so easily deluded. I will see for myself.' 'Go
ahead', said Śiva, and so she went to hell, and when she saw the beauty of the 22a
women there she said to them, 'Your beauty is of no use, like that of poisonous 22e
vines. Prajāpati created women for the sake of the sexual enjoyment of men, 9d
but Śiva cursed your husbands, forbidding them to enter here. Now let my 19a
sons, Śiva's hosts, wise ascetics, be your husbands, and make love with them.' 24ea^{2}
Then she vanished. Thus Viṣṇu the great womanizer made love with the 21ea
demon women in hell.[10]

The reversal of the myth is clear from the reversal of the final line, where Viṣṇu's love-making, rather than his chastisement, is made the point of the story. Śiva cannot help thinking about the demon women. His susceptibility is commented upon by his wife, and the ambivalence of his position is revealed in the multiform of his sons, who are allowed to make love to the demon women because of their status as ascetics and their supposed chastity.

Indeed, it is almost impossible to find a myth in which Śiva *remains*
chaste throughout, though many myths are based upon the initial premiss of his chastity. Even in the *Mahābhārata* passage which describes
Śiva as the chaste *brahmacārin*, Śiva is praised as the god who 'sports 35ea
with the daughters and the wives of the sages, with erect hair, a great 26ea 28ea
phallus, naked, with an excited look. . . . The universe was created from 21e
the seed that poured out of the *liṅga* of Śiva during the sexual act, and 36e
the gods worship that *liṅga*.'[11] 5c^{2}

B. THE BURNING OF KĀMA—AND ITS REVERSAL

The destruction of the god of desire would seem to be an unequivocally antisexual act, and that is in fact its original significance. One late text goes to elaborate lengths to make this clear; Pārvatī explains to the Seven Sages:

You imagine that [Śiva] has only now burnt up Kāma and until this day 43a
has been a prey to desire. But I believe that Śiva has always been an ascetic, 43ea
unborn, irreproachable, free from lust and sensual desire. . . . When you said
that [Śiva] had burnt up Kāma, you were displaying profound ignorance.
Fire, my good sirs, is of such a nature that snow can never approach it; if it 12d
comes near it, it is sure to be destroyed; and so it is with Kāma and [Śiva].[12]

In this context, Śiva's destruction of Kāma is the inevitable result of his
34a perfect chastity. The *Mahābhārata* says, 'The great *brahmacārin*, Śiva,
36e did not devote himself to the pleasures of lust. The husband of Pārvatī
43a extinguished Kāma when Kāma attacked him, making Kāma bodiless.'[13]
Yet even here, the chastiser of Kāma is simultaneously called the husband of Pārvatī, the erotic aspect of Śiva.

Even when Śiva expresses strong anti-erotic sentiments, he is forced to acknowledge Kāma's value, to act against his better judgement and to restore Kāma to life. When, after Śiva has burnt Kāma, the gods beg him to marry Pārvatī and to beget a son to slay the demon Tāraka, he replies:

36e If I were to marry Pārvatī, who is the most beautiful woman in the world,
all the gods and sages would be full of desire and incapable of the highest path,
43e 43a for Devī would revive Kāma for the wedding. But I burnt Kāma for the
34a success of all creatures and as a great favour for the gods. Let everyone
remain without desire, as I am, and do *tapas* passionlessly, and by this medita-
20a tion without desire you will obtain supreme bliss. Remember what Kāma
1 did to Brahmā in former times, and how he used to disturb everyone's medita-
25e 41ea tion and cause people to fall to hell. . . . The practice of marriage is not
36a suitable for me. There are many evil attachments in the world, but the
attachment to a woman is the worst, a great shackle that cannot be broken.
A wise man wishing for happiness should abandon all objects of the senses,
9d which kill as surely as poison. But even though I know all this, I will do what
1 9d you ask, for I am ever in the power of my devotees. I drank poison for the
19e 36a sake of the gods, and I will always remove their misery. I never take any
36e pleasure in marriage, but I will marry Pārvatī just in order to beget a son.[14]

The solution here is one which appears often in the later Purāṇas: the irrational power of love and devotion overcomes the rational arguments, and Śiva manages to save face by assuring the gods that although he will *do* what they ask, he won't *enjoy* it. Śiva's objection to Kāma is given a rational answer in a text which draws upon the ancient anti-ascetic tradition, just as Śiva draws upon the ascetic canon for his denunciation of Kāma:

The gods asked Śiva to revive Kāma, and they said, 'Without Kāma the whole universe will be destroyed. How can you exist without Kāma?' But
43a Śiva replied in anger, 'The universe must continue without Kāma, for it was
45e[1] 1 he who caused all the gods, including Indra, to fall from their places and to
become humble, and it is Kāma who leads all creatures to hell. Without
Kāma a man can do no evil, and even Tāraka will be without desire from now
on, although he used to be evil. I burnt Kāma in order to give peace to all
creatures, and I will not revive him, since he is the evil at the root of all
34a misery. Now all of you should set your minds on *tapas*.' The gods and sages
said, 'What you have said, Śiva, is no doubt the very best thing for us, but

nevertheless, all of this universe was created by means of desire, and all of it
is the form of desire, and that desire cannot be killed. How can you have burnt
Kāma? You yourself made him and gave him the ability he has just used.' 42e
But Śiva merely scowled and vanished.[15] 42a

C. THE LUST OF THE CHASTISER OF KĀMA

In spite of his anti-erotic reputation and sentiments, Śiva ultimately acknowledges the power of Kāma. Throughout the Purāṇas, the meaning of the conquest of Kāma by Śiva is undercut by qualifying episodes and even complete reversals: Śiva burns Kāma but is nevertheless sexually aroused; Śiva burns Kāma only to revive him in a more powerful form; Śiva burns Kāma and is therefore a desirable lover; and, the final Hindu complication, Śiva *is* Kāma.

The Purāṇas differ greatly in their attitude to the effect of Kāma upon
Śiva immediately before the burning takes place. In several texts, Śiva
is said to faint with lust, to be full of desire, or to be tortured by Kāma:[16] 43ea
'Śiva was a *brahmacārin* on Himālaya, but he left his *brahmacarya* when 34a
he was tortured by Kāma's arrows.'[17] Śiva himself muses upon the 43ea
phenomenon of his excitement: 'How can I lust to make love to Pārvatī
when she has not performed a vow of *tapas*? And how is it that I wish 43ea
to rape her? How can I have been excited by desire when I do not wish
it now? For some reason I seem to be attracted to this young girl and to
wish to unite with her.'[18] Overcome with passion, he places his hand
inside Pārvatī's garment and moves it about until she draws away in
shame.[19]

The later Purāṇas and poetry actually describe Śiva's erotic affliction in explicit detail, while the earlier works merely relate his eventual marriage. One Purāṇa adds the following passage to embellish the statement, in an earlier text, that Śiva asked Satī to marry him and that the flavour of desire entered their minds:[20]

Śiva desired her for his wife and offered her whatever she wished. At this 36e
moment, while Śiva's eye was attached to a beautiful woman, Kāma found an
opportunity in this improper behaviour, and he shot the arrow called Thrilling 43ea
into Śiva's heart, so that Śiva's hair stood on end when he looked at Satī and
he forgot all thoughts of the highest godhead. Then Kāma shot him with the
arrow called Delusion, and Śiva was deluded and revealed his emotion. Satī
overcame her bashfulness and said to Śiva, 'If you wish to give me a boon that
I desire—' and then as she paused in her speech Śiva blurted out, 'Be my
wife.' She rejoiced, seeing Śiva standing before her full of desire, and Kāma
rejoiced, and Satī asked Śiva to marry her with her father's permission, and
he agreed. He summoned Brahmā and said, 'All that you said before in praise

35e of a wife and household now seems very true. Satī propitiated me and I gave
36ea her a boon, and when I was near her Kāma wounded me with his arrows so
23e 43ea that I cannot bear to wait. Go quickly to Dakṣa's palace and ask for her on my
behalf.'[21]

42a In the earlier text, Brahmā then goes to Dakṣa and says, 'He in whose
armour Kāma could find no chink for his flower arrows, he, though
36ea unpierced by Kāma's arrows, has abandoned his meditation and thinks
only of Satī, stirred like a natural man.'[22] The later text, however,
simply removes the negatives and says, 'For Kāma found a chink in his
43ea armour and pierced him with all his arrows, and thus wounded, Śiva
has abandoned . . .'[23] The actual situation is the same: Śiva *is* wounded
by Kāma, but the later text is more consistent in its details, and it glosses
over the paradoxes of the earlier version.

In some texts, Śiva himself describes his affliction and attempts to justify himself: 'My heart being burnt by Kāma—and for the sake of the good of all, and for the increase of progeny—I have had the idea of taking a wife.'[24] But just a few lines later, waiting for the wedding to begin, Śiva simply confesses, 'I have been burnt by Kāma.'[25] In a late Sanskrit play, Śiva says that he is haunted by the image of Pārvatī as she appeared at the moment when Kāma's arrow of Delusion wounded him.[26] The comparison between Śiva and the 'natural man' appears frequently:

> Even the Lord of Creatures spent those days with difficulty,
> longing to unite with Pārvatī.
> 43ea If such emotions touch even one who is self-controlled,
> how must they excite another man who is not his own master?[27]

Śiva himself is upset by the contrast, and the Purāṇa writer makes explicit the moral:

> Śiva looked at Pārvatī and thought, 'What pleasure it would be to embrace
> 36ea her', but in a moment he realized, 'If I, thus deluded, desire the joy of touch-
> 36a ing a woman's body, then what can one expect of a mere lowly man?'[28] . . .
> 43ea Waiting for the wedding, even Śiva the lord of all was in the power of Kāma,
> deluded by Kāma just like a natural man. For Kāma is powerful among men
> and has conquered the whole universe. He is the king.[29]

This comparison plays upon the supposed invulnerability of Śiva in order to magnify the power of Kāma, just as the supposed chastity of the Seven Sages' wives emphasizes the irresistibility of Śiva. A similar technique may be seen in this description of Kāma's power over Śiva:

> 31e One day as Śiva was dancing and laughing, sporting erotically, the un-
> 43ea conquered Kāma glanced upon him and he became intoxicated in his erotic

play. He sent Nandin to bring Pārvatī to him from Kailāsa immediately, but
Pārvatī delayed to adorn herself as Śiva had requested her to do, and Śiva 28e
became greatly aroused waiting for her. Nandin, sent to hurry her, said to
Pārvatī, 'You must hurry, for your husband is tortured by desire. Śiva is surrounded by *apsarases*, and the woman whom he, the enemy of Kāma, chooses 21ea
for himself is indeed the queen. The goblins who serve him are saying to one 43a
another, "Kāma is killing this Enemy of Kāma."'[30] 43ea 43a

The Purāṇa delights in referring to the supposed destruction of Kāma in situations like this, when Kāma is clearly supreme. It lends great force to the irony of Śiva's seduction:

'So now this [Śiva], whose asceticism is known through all the world, 34a
fearful of absence from his mistress, bears her in his very form. 32e
And they say that we were overcome by him!' 43a
Victory to Love, who with these words
presses [Rati's] hand and falls to laughter.[31]

This assumption that Kāma in fact conquered Śiva, rather than the
reverse, appears in another early Sanskrit work: 'Whose son is this,
a second Kāma humbling the pride of Śiva's roar?'[32] And it remains 43ea
a basic motif of Sanskrit poetry: 'We bow to . . . Kāma, who makes the
gods Śiva, Brahmā, and Viṣṇu slaves in dark chambers of doe-eyed 43ea
women.'[33]

The Purāṇas attempt to reconcile the lust of Śiva with his famous
emotional control, sometimes merely by a statement of both aspects of
the god: 'Kāma shot Śiva and Śiva was deluded. Even though he had 43ea
conquered his senses and was without emotional excitement, he became 34a
eager to make love.'[34] The usual rationalization for this conflict is that 36e
Śiva consents to marry in order to do a favour for the gods.[35] As the
Seven Sages say to Himālaya, 'Śiva is the best of yogis. He does not
desire to unite with a wife, but at the urging of Brahmā he will marry
your daughter.'[36]

A doctrine related to the *bhakti* argument is used to reconcile the supposed indifference of Śiva with the obvious signs of lust which he displays. This is the concept of *līlā*, or divine play:

All the time that Śiva made love with Satī, it was just his divine play, for 33ea[7]
he was entirely self-controlled and without emotional excitement the whole 36e
time. . . . When Satī died, Śiva, the great yogi, wept like a lover in agony, but 34a
this is just his divine play, to act like a lover, for in fact he is unconquered 11cd
and without emotional excitement. . . . Though Śiva was devoid of passion
and the enemy of lust, he himself came into the power of Devī by his own
divine play. Then, though he was without desire, he became full of desire
because of her loveliness.[37]

Pārvatī uses this doctrine as an inducement to get Śiva to marry her:
'You are indeed without emotional excitement, but nevertheless, for
the sake of your devotees, you assume emotional characteristics, for you
33ea[7] are clever at various divine sports.'[38] And this very philosophy is used
to explain the power that Kāma has over Śiva: 'This is just Śiva's divine
33ea[7] play, to act like a lover, for were he not unconquered and free from
43ea emotion, what need would there be for Kāma to delude him?'[39]

The logical inversion in this reasoning betrays the fact that the *līlā*
argument is a late rationalization. If there is any divine play-acting in
the original myth, it is more akin to the human variety: at the wedding,
33ea[7] Śiva is said to have rejoiced greatly, full of excitement at the thought of
24ea obtaining Pārvatī, but he hid the signs of desire in his heart.[40] From the
plot of the myth, the motives are clear: he marries her because he is
overcome by love for her and is shaken from his yogic trance. This is
all the more evident from the fact that the myth is a reworking of the
story of Svāhā and Agni, where there is no attempt to conceal the erotic
intention of the god. Moreover, when the explicit 'intention' of a character in a myth is contradicted by his actual behaviour, it is almost always
the case that the behaviour *is* the myth, the 'intention' a subsequent
justification.

D. THE VICTORY OF KĀMA IMPLICIT IN THE BURNING OF KĀMA

Even without the descriptions of the manner in which Śiva is 'burnt'
by Kāma before he can return the attack, the very act of burning Kāma
betrays Śiva's vulnerability and his innately erotic nature. In glossing
24e 43a the epithet Kāmanāśana ('Destroyer of Kāma'), the *Mahābhārata* commentator says, 'He destroys the desire by giving the enjoyment of the
desired thing',[41] an interpretation directly opposed to the explicit meaning of the word but implicit in the action of Śiva. The myth of the
43ea burning of Kāma has been interpreted as a myth of sublimation, in
43a which Śiva suppresses through the heat of his asceticism the inclination
to lust that has arisen within him.[42] R. K. Narayan describes the burning
of Kāma in this way: Śiva says to Rati, '[Kāma] is not destroyed, but
exists in a sublimated state.'[43] Narayan further developed this theme in
a novel in which a group of modern Hindus attempt to produce a commercial film based upon the cycle of Śiva myths:

> 33ea[7] Srinivas read a symbolic meaning in this representation of the power of
> love, its equipment, its limitation, and saw in the burning of Kāma an act of
> sublimation. . . . [The actor playing the part of Śiva began to notice the

beauty of the actress playing Pārvatī.] He pulled himself up. It seemed 1
a familiar situation: he recollected that in the story Shiva himself was in a 43ea
similar plight, before he discovered the god of the sugar-cane bow [Kāma] 26e
taking aim. He seemed to realize the significance of this mythological piece
more than ever now. And he prayed: 'Oh God, open your third eye and do 7cd[1]
some burning up here also. . . . Mankind has not yet learned to react to beauty 43a
properly', he said to himself.[44]

In this modern version of the myth, in which the 'divine play' is transferred to the human level, the burning of Kāma is clearly the last resort of a thoroughly conquered ascetic.

In the Purāṇas, the battle rages back and forth between Śiva and Kāma on various magical, mental, and physical levels:

Kāma entered Śiva's heart through his ear in the form of the humming of 43ea
bees, and when Śiva heard this sweet, erotic sound he remembered Satī and 30e
his heart became empassioned. But by his power of meditation he closed his 34a
mind to this obstacle, and by will power he awakened from the emotional 42a
change that Kāma had wrought. Then he expelled Kāma by his power of
yoga. Kāma, now on the outside of Śiva, approached him and shot him with 43ea
the arrow of Fascination. Śiva was pierced in the heart and became inclined
to desire, even though he was as firm as a mountain, but by great effort he
expelled Kāma and blazed with anger.[45] 43a

A more psychological explanation of the struggle within Śiva appears in another Purāṇa:

Kāma assumed the form of a very subtle creature and entered Śiva's heart. 43ea
Then Śiva was heated by a desire for sexual pleasure, and he thought of Devī,
and his perfection vanished. Thus maddened and emotionally stirred by 25e
Kāma, Śiva made a great effort and regained his firmness. Then he saw Kāma 42a
in his heart, and he thought, 'I will burn Kāma out of my body by means of
withdrawal from worldly objects. If he should enter a yogi, then the yogi will
burn him out of the body by concentrating on the external fire.' Kāma was 8d
terribly heated by Śiva, and he left Śiva's body in a mental form. Taking 26e[2]
refuge at the foot of a mango tree, he shot the arrow of Delusion into Śiva's 43ea
heart, and in anger Śiva burnt Kāma to ashes with the fire from his third 43a
eye.[46] 7cd[1]

The subduing of lust is an important part of the philosophy of yoga,
which emphasizes that the lust must be present in the first place for
the yogi to work upon: 'Once the mind has stimulated the power of sex,
the yogi cannot recover his mastery over himself, the brilliance of his
inner light, until he has burned up lust by bringing the power of his 43a
seed up to the fifth centre.'[47] Just as Kāma's body is preserved in its 10c
essence, so the power of lust within the ascetic is not fully destroyed but
is transmuted into ascetic power.

The fact that Śiva finds it necessary to burn Kāma is thus proof that Śiva was affected by lust. A Ceylonese version of the burning of Kāma makes explicit this vulnerability of Śiva:

> 4 Maha Ishvara (Shiva) is God. [Pārvatī] his wife lives in his turban because
> 36e from the turban it is very easy to have sexual intercourse. One day [Pārvatī]
> 42ea saw a man of great beauty. She had sex relations with the man. When Maha
> 7cd[1] Ishvara heard of this he was angry and gazed on the man with his third eye.
> 43a The man was reduced to ashes. [Pārvatī] craved Maha Ishvara's pardon and
> 6cd begged him to recreate the man. The man was recreated but he was without
> 43e 32a genitals.[48]

Like Brahmā and Agni, Kāma is said to have committed adultery with Pārvatī in the popular tradition, though never in the Sanskrit tradition. The Purāṇas do supply precedents for another unusual aspect of the
4 Ceylonese story, the fact that Śiva injures Kāma not because Kāma has
42ea tried to inspire lust in him but because he has tried to interfere with
it.[49] The reversal of the usual roles is revealed by the nature of the punishment inflicted upon Kāma: castration, a theme appropriate to the fertility god, be it Śiva or Kāma. Śiva's jealousy of Kāma as the immediate cause of the castration is a motif supported by the corpus
38a[1] of Gaṇeśa myths, in which Gaṇeśa is beheaded and his head is replaced
38e with that of an elephant because he has come between Śiva and Pārvatī
33ea[4] 44ea in some way.[50] In one modern variant of this myth, Śiva beheads
38a[1] Gaṇeśa in anger when he sees Gaṇeśa playing with Uṣā, who is here
39e 39a said to be Śiva's daughter;[51] this text appears to have confused the
Gaṇeśa myth with the myth of Brahmā's incest with his daughter Uṣas and Śiva's beheading of Brahmā. Here, as in many Sanskrit texts, Śiva plays both the role of the incestuous father (father of Uṣā/Uṣas) and the anti-incestuous avenger (beheader of Gaṇeśa/Brahmā). In another ver-
42ea sion of the myth, Gaṇeśa is actually said to have made love with Pār-
43a 32a vatī and to have been castrated by Śiva in a fit of jealousy.[52]

Thus the punishment of Kāma by Śiva is due as much to Śiva's own sexuality as to that of Kāma. Another weakness in Śiva implicit in his burning of Kāma is noted in a Buddhist poem:

> 25e Love and anger both are states
> hostile to self-control.
> What then did Śiva hope to gain
> 43a by slaying Love in anger?
> Rather may he who by forbearance
> 13d quelled Love together with a hundred foes,
> that chief of saints, the Buddha,
> point you to your welfare.[53]

The true ascetic remains impervious and does not retaliate. This very
fact is used by Arundhatī to identify Śiva in the Pine Forest, for she
says, 'I fear that Śiva was that naked beggar, for he, though beaten by 28ea
the weapons of the sages, did not lose his control and did not become 13d
angry or attack in return.'[54] Yet in the Kāma myth, Śiva does become
angry, reacting just as Indra traditionally would wish him to do; Śiva
dispels *tapas* through anger if not through lust. Śiva's weakness is mentioned explicitly in one Purāṇa: '[Rudra] burnt Kāma with a glance of 43a
anger, but he could not burn up his anger.'[55] 7cd[1]

E. THE SEDUCTION OF ŚIVA BY PĀRVATĪ

The vulnerability of Śiva to anger as well as to lust causes him to play
directly into the hands of Indra, who ultimately conquers him not
through Kāma but through his other servant, Pārvatī. This is evident
from a recent Hindu interpretation of the myth: 'Although Kam was
burnt by the fire issuing from Shiv's third eye, finally Shiv himself was 43a
conquered, if not by the Fascination-tipped arrow of Kam, certainly 7cd[1]
by that personification of Fascination, Parvati.'[56] The myth of Kāma 43ea 36ea[2]
and Śiva is thus merely a variant of the myth of the seduction of an
ascetic by a princess or a prostitute sent by Indra.

Though Indra and Śiva share their fertility aspects, nevertheless
Indra as enemy of ascetics is the enemy of Śiva, and he is responsible
for Śiva's seduction in almost all versions of the myth. When Indra
summons Kāma to seduce Śiva, Kāma says, 'If anyone is doing terrible
tapas in order to usurp your position, I will cause him to fall from virtue 25e 8d
in a moment, using the sidelong glance of a beautiful woman as my 45a
weapon. I can shatter Brahmā and Viṣṇu, and even Śiva.'[57] This is 21ea 43ea
a true description of the state of affairs from Indra's standpoint and
from the pattern of the myth. In many ways, Śiva's *tapas* proves a 8d
threat to the whole universe, and he must be shaken from it,[58] even 36ea[2]
when there is no need to make Śiva beget Skanda or marry Pārvatī:

> Śiva was performing *tapas* at the confluence of the Ganges and another 8c 8d
> river. His *tapas* created the worlds, but then it began to heat them, and every- 10d
> one begged Indra to prevent Śiva from thus heating the universe. Indra 7d
> thought of an obstacle to Śiva's *tapas*: he sent Kāma, Spring, and all the 45a
> *apsarases* to shake Śiva, but Śiva burnt Kāma to ashes. When everyone 21ea 43ea
> became depressed, saying, 'Everything proceeds by intercourse, and without 43a
> Kāma all creatures are drying up', Śiva gave Kāma a body, and Kāma per- 43e
> formed *tapas* until Śiva, pleased, made Kāma's body more beautiful than ever 25ea[1]
> before and removed all obstacles for him.[59] 42e

The role of Pārvatī is here assumed by the more traditional assistants
of Indra, the *apsarases*. These nymphs seduce Śiva in another context,
21ea in a version of the Pine Forest myth in which they replace the Pine
Forest sages' wives.[60]

An interesting variation on this theme appears in a tribal myth:
8d Lingo performed *tapas* for twelve months until the golden seat of
7d 9cd Mahadewa began to shake, and Mahadewa agreed to Lingo's requests.[61]
34e 34a Here Śiva appears simultaneously on the two sides of the myth that he
occupies separately in the Sanskrit tradition: as Mahadewa he turns the ascetic from his asceticism, and as Lingo he is the ascetic who must be turned in this way.

The ancient folk-motif of the seduced ascetic is transferred to a higher, more cosmological level in the myth of Śiva and Kāma, and the conflict is one of powers rather than of personalities. The enemy of the ascetic is therefore, in the early Śaiva Purāṇas, not a woman, the object of desire, but Desire incarnate. But the later texts, particularly under Tantric influences, magnify the status of Pārvatī until she surpasses both Kāma and Śiva and assumes the central position of the *apsaras* in the original motif. These myths then reinterpret the *tapas* of Śiva in an entirely new light:

> The gods, troubled by Tāraka, wished to have Śiva marry and beget a son
> 19e to save them. But Indra said, 'Śiva is a yogi, always averse to worldly ways.
> 34a Who could stand before him and say, "Take a wife"?' Then Bṛhaspati [the
> 25ea² guru of the gods] said, 'There is a way. Śiva is doing *tapas* in order to obtain
> 45a a wife, Pārvatī. Why else could he be doing such terrible *tapas*? For he has
> conquered the Self, and he is the one on whom the yogis meditate. Pārvatī
> is always near him, but Śiva has been immersed so long in the meditation of
> yoga that all his desires have been destroyed, and he will never marry her.
> 36a Therefore you must summon Kāma to break his meditation. When Śiva is
> 43ea pierced by Kāma's arrows, he will marry Pārvatī, for he will then be averse
> 36e to thoughts of yoga.'[62]

The motif of *tapas* performed in order to obtain a wife, when applied to the myth of Kāma, produces a reversal of the concept underlying Śiva's *tapas* and must ultimately be re-reversed to restore the original basis of that *tapas*: though his *tapas* has an erotic purpose, its effect is to destroy his desire, and therefore he must be re-excited. The cycles of yoga and sexual activity are so closely intertwined that the logical causation is almost destroyed: Śiva must be seduced from the *tapas* which he is performing in order to be seduced.

The logic of the myth is better supported by the mirror-image motif: the *tapas* performed by Pārvatī. The two are closely related conceptually:

'We praise the ancient pair, the parents of the universe. Each is the end 25ea² 36ea
attained by the penance of the other.'[63] In most versions of the seduction 35ea
episode, Kāma alone is not sufficiently powerful to move Śiva from *tapas* to desire, for Śiva must be moved not by the force of the stage he is moving toward, but by the power of his present stage, asceticism. Pārvatī wins him by her *tapas* as well as by her beauty, as Śiva himself
admits.[64] The two paths are inseparable. Even when Śiva is drawn to 36ea
her by the power of Kāma, the second path must also be satisfied:

> Arjuna asked, 'Since Śiva knew that Satī was his own wife and he was 36e
> tortured by longing for her, why did he burn Kāma? For he performed *tapas* 43ea
> because of his longing for her, in order to win her again.' Nārada said, 'Śiva 43a
> was thinking, "I cannot unite with her unless she has performed *tapas*. With- 25ea²
> out *tapas* the body is never purified, and I cannot unite with a woman whose 27ea
> body is not purified."'[65]

In another text, Śiva is said to be without desire, and he wishes Pārvatī
to perform *tapas* for her own sake. He thinks, 'If she undertakes a vow 36ea
of *tapas*, then I will marry her, when she is devoid of the seed of pride.'[66] 27ea
Later in this myth, Nārada explains this to Pārvatī: 25ea²

> Pārvatī, you served Śiva without *tapas*, and you were proud. But Śiva is 36ea 34a
> a passionless ascetic, a great yogi, who expelled Kāma and burnt him, and so 25ea² 43a
> you must propitiate him with *tapas* for a long time, and when you have been 27ea
> thus purified he will accept you.[67] 36e

The 'pride' of Pārvatī is described in another text, in which she at first refuses to do *tapas*, feeling certain that Śiva will be overcome by her beauty.[68] Yet, whether or not Śiva desires her, she must perform *tapas* for her own sake and the sake of the world, as well as to satisfy him.

Pārvatī's *tapas* is occasionally described in terms that suggest the traditional pattern but given another twist: she is the ascetic whose
tapas forces the (erotic) god (Indra or Śiva) to seduce her. Her *tapas* 7d
heats the universe so that Brahmā is forced to grant her a boon when 8d
she seeks to obtain Śiva for her husband.[69] When Śiva refuses to marry 25ea²
Pārvatī, her *tapas* is so great that he is frightened by it and is shaken 8d
from his own meditation.[70] Her *tapas* causes the entire universe to 25ea² 36ea
smoke, until Brahmā promises her that Śiva will come to her, and Indra 8d
sends the Seven Sages to her when she has heated all the creatures in 25ea²
the universe with the fire of her *tapas*.[71] The limbs of all creatures are 8d
burnt by her *tapas*, so that Viṣṇu asks Śiva to marry her, and she even 25ea²
heats the seat of Śiva on Kailāsa, so that he is forced to appear before 36ea
her.[72] In this, as in the Lingo episode, Śiva himself suffers from the 35ea

very condition that he brings upon Indra, and Pārvatī acts simultaneously as the ascetic who must be seduced from her *tapas* and as the woman who seduces Śiva; she uses her *tapas* to shake him from his own.

One late text reverses the episodes, and Pārvatī performs *tapas* before
4 Śiva has burnt Kāma.[73] Although Brahmā grants her a boon and the
36ea Seven Sages, having tested her, report favourably to Śiva, he neverthe-
24a 36a less returns to his *tapas*. When Indra then sends Kāma to attack him,
45a this too proves ineffective, and only the importunity of Viṣṇu can stir
43a 36e Śiva from his asceticism. The Seven Sages are then sent once more to
24a Pārvatī (an awkward multiform to which they make explicit reference:
1 'Last time you would not heed our words'). Thus, by reversing the
episodes in which Śiva's involvement is sought by the force of *kāma*
or *tapas*, the text nullifies the effect of Pārvatī's asceticism. Although
this version then resorts to Vaiṣṇava devotionalism (its underlying spirit)
to supply Śiva's motivation, the archetypal myth in fact suggests that
Pārvatī's *tapas* is causally superfluous, that her essential role is not that
of a *yoginī*, but that of an *apsaras*.

Certainly it is not Pārvatī's *tapas* alone which seduces Śiva, for the other path constantly reasserts itself. The voluptuous description of Pārvatī as she is brought to Śiva by her father is clearly that of an *apsaras*, and Śiva immediately recognizes her as such:

> 21ea Seeing the beauty of the full-breasted, sensuous girl, which stole the hearts
> 36ea^{2} of those who meditate, Śiva, the great yogi, quickly closed his eyes and
> 36a meditated on his own form.[74]

Pārvatī is the natural enemy of his *tapas*, constantly attempting to interrupt his meditations for one reason or another after they have been married. Yet in a late text which exalts Devī, she seduces him only to test him:

> Devī created Brahmā, Viṣṇu and Śiva. Then she divided herself into three
> 19ea parts, and promised to become the wife of each of them. She instructed them
> 37ea to create, preserve, and destroy the universe, and she promised to bear them
> 19e all children. But Śiva wished to obtain her for his wife alone, and so he began
> 25ea^{2} to propitiate her with *tapas* and *bhakti*. Viṣṇu and Brahmā then also stopped
> 29ea creating and performed *tapas*, and to test their *tapas* Devī assumed a terrifying
> 4 form and appeared before each one. Brahmā became four-faced in order to
> 21ea turn away from her, and Viṣṇu closed his eyes and plunged into the water,
> 10d thus breaking his *tapas*, but she was unable to turn Śiva from his *tapas*, for
> 36e he was a great yogi. Then she was pleased with him and promised to become
> Satī to marry him.[75]

Although she is said to assume a terrifying form, the reactions of

Brahmā and Viṣṇu are the reactions which they display elsewhere when faced with a seductress: Brahmā sprouts four heads as he does in order to see Mohinī, and Viṣṇu plunges into water as Śiva does when refusing a wife. Moreover, the terrifying form of Devī frequently has erotic connotations in its own right. Here, she tests Śiva just as, in the earlier texts, he tests her before agreeing to marry her. In both versions, the object of the *tapas* is marriage, which amounts to the seduction of the ascetic.

In a variant of this story, the sexual implications of the seduction are clear at the end:

> After appearing before Brahmā and Viṣṇu in the form of a worm-infested 29ea
> corpse, Devī went to Śiva and was at first unable to shake him from his medita- 21ea
> tion. She released a perfumed wind which carried atoms from her body to 10cd
> Śiva's nose. Śiva perceived the perfume, broke his trance, and took the corpse 30ea 36e
> upon his breast. Then he returned to his meditation, and Devī was pleased 5cd
> with him and recognized him as Śiva. He took the form of the *liṅga* and she 17cd 36a
> the form of the *yoni*. She placed the *liṅga* within her and plunged into the 5c[1, 2]
> water to create progeny.[76] 13c

In addition to the explicit transition to creative sexuality at the end of the myth, there are several motifs of the traditional seduction, in spite of the anti-erotic form that Devī assumes. To attack Śiva, she takes the form of a perfumed wind, the very method used by Kāma, and Śiva at first responds to her but then returns to his meditation, as he does when faced by Kāma. Even the corpse is an erotic motif in Śaiva mythology, which preserves a strong tie between love and death, for Devī appears as a corpse when Śiva, mad with passion, takes up the body of Satī and dances with it; Viṣṇu then dismembers the corpse, and the place where the *yoni* falls becomes particularly sacred, just as in the present myth the corpse of Devī turns into the *yoni*. In this context, it is apparent that Devī is successful in seducing Śiva and causing him to leave his meditation to marry her, in spite of the superficial statement that he did in fact return to his meditation, a statement which is ultimately contradicted, just as it is in the Kāma myth.

F. THE REVIVAL OF KĀMA BY PĀRVATĪ

In addition to 'seducing' Śiva by causing him to marry her, Pārvatī aids Kāma explicitly in one essential way: she is responsible for his revival.[77] 43e
In order to make love to her, Śiva must revive the deity of sexual pleasure. One text seems to contradict this:

> At the wedding of Śiva and Pārvatī, the goddesses urged Rati forward, as 36e

she lamented her widowhood, and they said, 'Now is the time.' Then they said to Śiva, 'Formerly Rati came to you, but now she does not appear,
42a because she has lost Kāma.' But Śiva made a sign to Rati with the finger of
his left hand, and spoke to her, keeping her away, for he was anxious to see Pārvatī.[78]

This episode is omitted in another version of this text and it is unclear to the Hindu translator, who reverses the meaning by adding, 'Śiva gave her hopes, raising his left hand.'[79] Śiva's desire for Pārvatī here seems to prevent or at least postpone the revival of Kāma, yet usually this desire is the immediate cause of the revival: 'Viṣṇu flattered Śiva,
43e telling him how handsome he looked, and then asked him to revive
Kāma. Then Śiva, eager to see Pārvatī's lotus face, created Kāma, by his own wish.'[80]

Even when Śiva points out that Kāma is perfectly effective in his dis-
43e embodied form, he promises him reincarnation as well,[81] primarily for
20e the sake of Rati, the one who most directly benefits from the restoration
of the anthropomorphic as well as the abstract Kāma. Sometimes this reincarnation is *only* for the sake of Rati, as when Śiva revives Kāma but renders him corporeal and visible only to Rati, incorporeal and imperceptible to all others.[82] As Rati is frequently a multiform of Pārvatī, it is only reasonable that she obtains her husband when Pārvatī obtains hers, and at the request of Pārvatī.

In addition to her implicit influence, Pārvatī frequently makes an explicit request that Kāma be revived:

25ea^{1} Pārvatī propitiated Śiva with her *tapas*, and when he offered her a boon she
36ea^{1} 43a said, 'Now that Kāma has been killed, what good to me is a boon from you?
24a Without Kāma there can be no happiness for men and women.' Śiva said,
7cd^{1} 'It was not I who killed Kāma, but my eye which is fire. Choose a boon.' She
43e said, 'Let Kāma live to stir fire in all people. I want nothing but Kāma.' Śiva
said, 'Let Kāma be bodiless and shake the world in that form, to please you.'
Then Pārvatī returned to her father and said, 'I have propitiated Śiva with
25ea^{2} my *tapas* and obtained the boon that he will be my husband. Now I am
fulfilled.'[83]

Pārvatī considers the revival of Kāma—even without a body—to be the equivalent of obtaining Śiva for her husband, even though Śiva does not actually promise to marry her, so strong is the tie between the two episodes in terms of the pattern of the myth. The gods are given the
43e promise that Kāma will be reborn when Śiva marries, or when he takes
36e a wife and household, or when he becomes impassioned—that is, when
23e Kāma reasserts his power over Śiva.[84] When Pārvatī inspires Śiva with
43e desire she is said to 'revive Kāma again and again', so that all the

animals in Śiva's hermitage are full of passion.[85] Similarly, after the wed- 25ea[1]
ding, at the request of the widow Rati, Pārvatī performs *tapas* and 're- 43e
ignites' Kāma, and then Śiva and Pārvatī begin to make love.[86] 7c 36e

Śiva revives Kāma in order to make love to Pārvatī, a causal link established by the chain of events in many Purāṇas.[87] In one text, Rati makes clear to Śiva where his interests lie:

> 'Now that you have Pārvatī, why have you reduced the lord of my life to 36e
> ashes when it was not for your own advantage? By reviving my husband now,
> you will enjoy his influence yourself and banish the discomfort of longing. All
> creatures rejoice in your wedding. Let me rejoice too, and once my husband
> is alive, your love-making will be complete.' Then she gave Śiva the ashes of 6cd
> Kāma, and Śiva gazed upon Kāma with his Soma glance, and from the ashes 7cd[1]
> Kāma appeared, smiling, bearing the scar on the place where the fire of Śiva's 14c[2]
> anger had entered him.[88] 43e

This same self-interest is used by Brahmā, with a kind of reversed logic, to convince Kāma to attack Śiva in the first place:

> For the sake of the universe, my child, you must excite Śiva so that he will 2 37a
> take a wife and household with a happy heart, even though he is now a self- 36e
> controlled woman-hater. When Śiva becomes impassioned, then your curse 34a
> [just given him by Brahmā] will be ended. Therefore you should do this for
> your own sake. When Śiva is full of passion and wishes to enjoy your pleasures 43ea
> he will cause you to exist again.[89] 43e

Pārvatī participates in the revival of Kāma in yet another, more direct manner: she *is* the essence of Kāma even when he himself is destroyed. Sometimes this is expressed literally: when Kāma was burnt and became
bodiless, his essence entered the limbs of Devī.[90] Usually, however, the 43a
reincarnation is taken in a more metaphorical sense: 8cd

> May the dark neck of Śiva, which Kāma has surrounded with nooses in the 9d
> form of the alluring glances of Pārvatī who lies against his chest, bring you 36e 36ea
> happiness. 43ea 8cd
>
> May the water of Śiva's sweat, fresh from the embrace of Pārvatī, which 11c 43ea
> Kāma employs as his aqueous weapon because of his fear of Śiva's eye, 36e 8cd
> protect you.[91] 7cd[1]

Pārvatī is a particularly apt form for Kāma to assume, as it was for her sake that he was burnt and her lover who burnt him, but the poetic
image is extended to other women as well.[92] Thus, just as she is said 26e[2]
to be a medicinal herb for the revival of Kāma,[93] so it is said of an 43e 8cd
anonymous woman:

> Did the Creator grind all the digits of the harvest moon 14c[3]
> and carefully compound them with ambrosia 14c[2]
> to make for Love, when Śiva's roar consumed his limbs, 8cd
> this revivifying medicine?[94] 43a 43e

Another verse describes rather more specifically the feminine abode of the burnt Kāma, here dynamically equated with the flame-*liṅga*:

> 43a Burning from Shiva's wrath, the god of love
> 13c 17cd Plunged in the lake between my lady's thighs
> 42e 5cd To quench the flames; and hence as smoke arise
> The curling hairs on Venus' mount above.[95]

26e[2] A woman who flirts with Śiva in the Pine Forest, strewing flowers
8cd before him, is described as 'the flower-bow of Kāma, which had assumed
7cd[1] 43a another form when it was frightened by the eye in [Śiva's] forehead'.[96]
7cd[1] Another woman teases Śiva, saying, 'Did you open the fiery eye in
43a 43e 7cd[2] your forehead and burn Kāma?' To which Śiva replies, 'I am indeed
8cd made a laughing-stock when he is reborn in your gaze, lovely one.'[97]
The play upon the contrasting eyes appears in another verse:

> 7cd[1,2] I sing the praise of lovely-eyed women,
> 43e victorious over three-eyed Śiva,
> who by their glances resurrect
> 43a that Love which he consumed by his.[98]

The ambiguous glance may belong to Śiva alone, who is said to resurrect
43e 14c[2] Kāma with his Soma glance (the elixir of immortality which is con-
7cd[1] trasted with the fierce fire of the destructive glance).[99] While the fiery
glance is Śiva, the Soma glance is Pārvatī, who revives Kāma when Śiva has burnt him.

G. KĀMA REBORN AS A TREE—REBIRTH FROM FIRE

Sanskrit poetry delights in describing a number of aphrodisiacs, in addition to certain features of beautiful women, as the reincarnations of Kāma, more powerful than the dead god himself. The moon, said
14c[2] to consist of various creative substances including Soma and semen, is
8cd a form of Kāma.[100] In one Purāṇa, Śiva places the fire of Kāma in the
moon, but he distributes it elsewhere as well:

> 26e[2] 7cd[1] 7d Śiva reduced Kāma to ashes, and the fire from his third eye then yawned
> 14e[3] 5d wide to burn the universe. But then, for the sake of the universe, Śiva divided
> 30e 43a that fire among the mango and Spring and the moon and flowers and bees
> 7c 8cd and cuckoos—thus he divided the fire of Kāma.[101]

The substances in which the fire of Kāma lodges are all of erotic significance in Hindu culture and are usually personified as Kāma's assistants. Among these, the most frequently used is the flower, the very substance of which Kāma's weapons are made. In a reversal of this motif, Kāma is said to reject this weapon in favour of his other arsenal—women:

> The mind-born god [Kāma], as he was about to perish,
> burned by the flame from the eye of Gaurī's lord, 36e 43a
> looked first upon his useless shaft of flowers 26e[2]
> and then in anger made an all-compelling weapon, 8cd
> this weapon, whence the fame of fair-browed women,
> has conquered all the world.[102]

The image of the flower-like face is here replaced by the metaphor of the bow whose shape may be seen in the arched brows of beautiful women.

More frequently, Kāma is pictured as a tree whose sprouts are women. 8cd
Śakuntalā's hand is said to be a new sprout from the tree of Kāma, which 26e[2]
had been burnt by the fire of Śiva's anger and revived by a chance rain 43e 43a 15c
of Soma; Pārvatī herself, making love with Śiva, is said to be a new 14c[2]
sprout from the burnt tree of Kāma.[103] The lotus appears most often 36e 26e[2]
in these metaphors, and its connotations are somewhat ambiguous: the 43e
flower itself is usually likened to the face of a woman, and in Tantric 26e[2] 17cd
symbolism the lotus represents the *yoni* ('The jewel is in the lotus').
Nevertheless, the *stalk* of the lotus appears in Śaiva Purāṇas in place 26e[2] 5cd
of the *liṅga*, and the seed of Śiva which is placed upon a lotus leaf (the *yoni*) travels through its stalk (the *liṅga*). The latter aspect of the lotus symbolism is manifest in the symbolism of the tree of Kāma.

The power of Kāma only enters the tree when Kāma himself has been burnt:

> When Śiva left the Pine Forest, Kāma tried to excite him once again, but 43ea
> Śiva saw him and looked at him with an angry glance and burnt him to ashes 7cd[1]
> as if he were a forest of dry wood. As his feet caught fire, Kāma dropped his 43a
> bow, which broke into five parts, these turning into five trees and flowers, and, 26e[2]
> by the grace of Śiva, all his arrows turned into flowers and Kāma himself 8cd
> died.[104] 26e[2]

The dry tree of the living Kāma is transformed by fire into the flowering tree of the disembodied Kāma. An inscription of A.D. 473 employs
a metaphor in which, when Kāma's body is burnt by Śiva, Kāma forms 43a
his arrows by uniting with five blossoming trees and shrubs.[105] Thus the 8cd 26e[2]
erotic fire becomes incarnate in a tree, just as the Vedic Agni often hides 5cd
in plants, particularly in bamboo, and the *śamī* tree, from which the 26e[1]
Vedic fire-sticks are made, is said to contain fire.

Yet another tree—the pine—is associated with Kāma in several ways. Many of the versions of the Pine Forest myth take place immediately before or after the burning of Kāma by Śiva and of Śiva by Kāma, and

Kāma often chases Śiva into the Pine Forest. When Śiva wanders about
in an erotic frenzy, carrying the corpse of Satī, one of the pieces of her
dismembered body falls into the Pine Forest, and when Kāma attacks
Śiva the tree which he hides behind is sometimes explicitly said to be
26e^2 a pine tree.[106] Śiva himself is connected with the pine tree in a different
19e creative metaphor: Pārvatī sometimes uses a pine tree as a substitute
33ea^7 for Skanda, watering it with pitchers just as she would nourish Skanda
with milk from her breasts.[107]

It has been suggested that the burning and resuscitation of Kāma has
its basis in a fertility ritual in which either Kāma's image or a tree is
burnt. The significance of the burnt tree, and of its relationship with the
45e^1 Dionysian aspect of Śiva, may be seen in the parallels between the phallic
5cd 26e^2 26a Indra-pillar, the Śiva-*liṅga*, and the tree of Kāma.[108] The myth of the
burning of Kāma by Śiva may stem from the Indo-Germanic rite of
burning the tree that symbolizes the demon of fertility, a rite which was
32a later replaced by the self-castration of the god.[109] In this context, Śiva's
burning of Kāma (equated in folk-legend with the castration of Kāma
by Śiva) is equivalent to the sages' castration of Śiva, and the revival of
26e^2 Kāma is a multiform of the restoration of Śiva himself. Śiva is 'reborn'
26a as a tree, a transformation expressly considered to be a *prevention* of his
2 fertility, in one version of the Skanda myth in which Pārvatī curses all
29a the gods to become barren trees.[110] Yet, just as Śiva's self-castration is
ultimately procreative, so his burning of Kāma is ultimately conducive
to fertility.

It is interesting to note here that the burning itself is celebrated as
equivalent to the resuscitation. Epigraphical evidence suggests that an
effigy of Kāma was burned, in commemoration of his destruction by
Śiva, at the close of the Holi festival, a rite which persists in a form of
26e^2 mystery play commemorating the death of Kāma.[111] Nathurām, a folk
45e deity considered to be a form of Kāma, is also burnt in effigy as a tree.
5cd He is 'a phallic fetish' whose image is made 'of a most disgusting shape',
35ea a god who is said to have seduced a number of women until he was put
32a to death, whereupon he became a ghost who can only be appeased by
'indecent songs and gestures performed by the women'.[112] The description of Nathurām's activities could apply to the myth of Śiva in the
Pine Forest as well as to Kāma: he annoys the women until he is killed
(castrated), and then continues to plague them until he is worshipped
as a phallus.

That Kāma should be reborn after having been burnt to death is quite
6c natural in the context of Hindu mythology, in which rebirth from fire is

a generally accepted theme. In Indian folk-lore also, rejuvenation by 6cd
burning and resuscitation from ashes are recurrent motifs.[113] One
Brāhmaṇa states that ashes which are thrown into water reproduce from 12c 6cd
the water what there was in them of Agni's nature, and a dead man is
reborn out of the fire, which only consumes his body, just as he is born 6c
from his parents.[114] This phoenix symbolism underlies the identification of ashes with the seed of Śiva:

> Śiva said, 'I am Agni and [Devī] is Soma. The ashes are my seed, and 7c 12cd
> I bear my seed on my body. I am Agni the maker of Soma and I am Soma who 14c² 6cd 21a
> takes refuge in Agni. When the universe is burnt by my fire, and reduced to 9c
> ashes, I establish my seed in ashes and sprinkle all creatures.'[115] 10c 5d 12c 6d

The ashes are the spark of life suspended in water until the universe is
ready to be reborn. The ashes which Śiva bears on his body are the 8cd 6cd
ashes of the burnt Kāma, and once placed on Śiva's body they act as 43ea
Kāma himself does, to burn Śiva and stir his desire.[116] Śiva says to 6cd
Pārvatī, 'Kāma who was burnt by me lives in the form of ashes on my 43ea
body, acting against me and trying to burn me in your presence. Draw 7c
me out of Kāma as if out of a fire, and save me with the Soma of your 14c²
body.'[117] The ashes upon Śiva's body are sometimes said to arise from 13c 24e
a different but related source: when Satī has burnt herself, Śiva smears 6d
his limbs with her ashes.[118] The model for this episode is the mourning 6cd 28a
of Rati, who takes the ashes of her husband Kāma and smears them upon 6cd
her body, preserving them in order to revive him later,[119] and at last 28a 6c
presenting them to Śiva himself,[120] so that he may produce Kāma from 43e
them. In a variant of this myth, Śiva uses the ashes of Kāma to produce
a demon who troubles the earth until he is killed by Devī.[121] From these 6cd
overtones and associations stemming from a fairly extensive Śaiva
mythology of ashes, it becomes almost inevitable that Kāma will be
revived from his own ashes.

Even without his suspension in ashes, between life and death, Kāma's
power remains when Śiva burns him. He is called 'Bodiless' (Anaṅga),
but retains his function:[122] Śiva says, 'Although Kāma has no body, he 43e
will still do all that is to be done at the time of sexual intercourse, do not 43e
fear.'[123] In only two of the many versions of this myth in the Sanskrit
texts is Kāma in any way diminished by the burning. In one text, after
Śiva has burnt Kāma and Rati has begged him to revive her husband,
Śiva replies, 'At a certain time, Kāma will come to life, but not a single 43e
creature here [in the grove on Himālaya where Śiva had done his *tapas*] 42a
will ever be shaken by the wiles of Kāma.'[124] And once, Śiva revives 43e
Kāma but says to Rati, 'You must teach your beloved Kāma that he

42a must never thus offend against the great.'[125] These are anomalous instances in which Kāma does not at least maintain his strength or even increase it ultimately as a result of his burning by Śiva.

H. THE REVIVED KĀMA'S POWER OVER ŚIVA

The revival of Kāma by Śiva indicates that Śiva has undergone a change of heart, and so it is not surprising that the reborn Kāma has powers over Śiva that he did not have before Śiva destroyed him.[126] This would follow merely from the general growth of Kāma's powers arising from the process of death and revival, for Kāma's magic is made stronger by the advantages of invisibility, no longer concentrated in one anthropomorphic form but diffused into the world, like the demons released from Pandora's box. This belief underlies a poem which plays upon the fact that the word for oil (*sneha*) also signifies love or affection:

7cd[1] False is the tale, my love, that once the flame
43a From Śiva's third eye burned to ash the frame
8cd Of Kāma. Nay, his body, through that heat,
42e Melted to oil, which now inflames our hearts.[127]

The particular application of Kāma's new power over Śiva is often
42e described in the Purāṇas: Śiva reincarnates Kāma with a half of Śiva's
embodied essence in him, and Kāma is revived and made one of Śiva's
servants.[128] Śiva promises that Kāma's powers will be doubled, and he
43ea 43a remarks, when he is overcome with lust for Sāvitrī, 'Kāma is attacking
me, remembering our former enmity.'[129] Thus Śiva admits that his
'destruction' of Kāma has merely added to Kāma's power over him.
43ea Similarly, Kāma's effect upon all of Śiva's subjects is a form of revenge
against Śiva: 'Kāma has disturbed the world, the creation of Śiva,
43a making woman his weapon, as if recalling Śiva's enmity.'[130]

One myth uses the enmity of Rati to explain the subsequent 'weakening' of Śiva:

43a When Kāma had been burnt by the fire of Śiva's anger, Rati lamented until
Kāma's friend, Spring, and his five assistants (Delusion, Deception, Anger,
Greed, and Disputation) offered to help her. Rati said, 'The murderer is
24a honoured everywhere. Let an obstacle be made to destroy his worship by any
25ea[1] means possible, and then my sorrow will be assuaged a little.' Spring and the
others performed great *tapas*, frightening everyone, until Brahmā appeared
to them and offered them a boon. They said, 'Our dear friend, Kāma, has
been destroyed by Śiva. As reprisal for this, we wish to revile Śiva so that he
24a is no longer worshipped.' Brahmā agreed to let this take place in the Kali age,

and that is the cause of the reviling of Śiva. Thus Spring and the others consoled Rati.[131]

Although Kāma is not revived in this episode, Rati enjoys her own vengeance upon Śiva.

More often, however, Śiva's new 'weakness' corresponds to Kāma's
new strength. At the end of the wedding, Śiva revives Kāma and gives 43e
him permission to use his arrows, even against Śiva himself.[132] In one 43ea
text, Śiva qualifies this dispensation somewhat: 42e

When Kāma had been burnt, Pārvatī did *tapas* in order to obtain Śiva for 43a
her husband, though he had been doing *tapas* for a long time, his seed drawn 25ea[1,2,3]
up in chastity. She wished to have a son and to revive Kāma, but she forgot 36ea[1] 34a
to worship Gaṇeśa to obtain success. When Śiva discovered Pārvatī's desires, 21a 19e
he said to her, 'I burnt Kāma because of a curse laid upon him formerly by 43e
Brahmā, a curse due to Kāma's excessive pride. But I will beget a son by means 41a
of your creative power and mine, for I do not have offspring as ordinary 20ea
people do, from the force of lust.' Then Śiva promised to create a natural son 29e
in Pārvatī, and he gave permission for Kāma to be born, bodiless, in the 43e
minds of all embodied creatures. He even gave Kāma a place in his own 42e
heart. Then Pārvatī rejoiced, and Śiva made love to her for a thousand years.[133] 36e

Even though Śiva does not give Kāma a body, he revives him and grants the other parts of Pārvatī's request (that he marry her and give her a son), and he grants Kāma power over himself, a direct contradiction of his boast that he does not need lust to beget children as ordinary people do. These powers that he officially grants to Kāma are described in action in another Purāṇa:

When Śiva had burnt Kāma to ashes, the gods asked Devī to revive Kāma, 43a
to relieve Rati of her widowhood and to cause Śiva to marry Pārvatī and 43e
engender the son to kill Tāraka. Revived by Devī, Kāma arose more glorious 36e
than before. Then she said to him, 'You are my son. By my grace you will 19e
delude the whole universe. Śiva will lose his control because of you, and 42e
though he will be angry because of his hatred of passion, he will not be able 43ea
to burn you, and he will marry Pārvatī. Whoever reviles you or turns away 34a 36e
from you will be impotent in birth after birth.' Then Kāma went with Spring 2
to Śiva's hermitage and inflamed all the creatures there with passion. Śiva 32a
abandoned his *tapas*, lost all his scruples, and thought only of Pārvatī. Tor- 43ea
tured by desire, his body heated by Kāma's arrows, he could not extinguish 7c
the flame of Kāma, and he determined to marry Pārvatī in order to cure his 24e
passion. Kāma, thus having deluded Śiva, then aroused Pārvatī, who longed 36e
for her husband and burned with the fire of desire. Himālaya advised her to 7c
do *tapas* in order to obtain Śiva, and she satisfied Śiva with her *tapas* and 25ea[2]
he agreed to marry her. The Seven Sages made the necessary arrangements, 36ea
Śiva and Pārvatī were married, and Śiva took Pārvatī to Kailāsa and made 36e
love to her.[134]

Here the *tapas* with which Pārvatī wins Śiva is superfluous, for Kāma is successful in wounding Śiva the second time. Revived, Kāma is more glorious than before, and Śiva cannot resist him although he continues to hate passion. The curse of impotence against the enemies of Kāma (such as the castrated Śiva) appears in reverse in another passage, where Kāma's friends (such as the phallic Śiva) are cured of impotence:

> The gods sent Kāma to arouse Śiva, but Śiva ran away in fear when he saw
> 7cd[1] Kāma. After many years of wandering, he opened his third eye and burnt
> 43a Kāma to ashes, and when he had burnt Kāma his anger was assuaged. But
> 13d Rati lamented until a voice promised her that Śiva would revive her husband.
> 43e All the gods bowed to Śiva and said, 'For the sake of the gods, you should
> take a wife. You burnt Kāma in anger, and without him all creation on earth
> is ruined.' Then Śiva said, 'Let Kāma wander bodiless among men. Even
> without his body he will have his seed and his power.' But the gods said,
> 'Śiva, remember Kāma for the sake of all creatures', and so Śiva himself
> 42e remembered Kāma, and because of that his eternal *liṅga* arose on earth.
> 26ea When Kāma was remembered, he became powerful, though bodiless, and
> 5cd 43ea because of him Śiva married Pārvatī and Skanda was born. And because Śiva
> 36e had remembered Kāma even when his *liṅga* had fallen, he is known in the
> 19e world as the Rememberer of Kāma [Kṛtasmara]. And no man seeing Śiva thus
> 5c[2] [i.e. seeing the *liṅga*] is impotent or blind or sick.[135]

This passage depends upon a pun: Kāma's epithet of Smara is also the word for memory. This pun is often used with irony: when Śiva burns Kāma he makes him 'nothing but a memory'.[136] Indra and Śiva are sometimes said to 'remember Smara',[137] and Kāma's arrows cause Śiva to 'remember' Satī or to remember the Seven Sages (as go-betweens for the wedding).[138] When Śiva married Satī and took her to Himālaya, 'he remembered Kāma of his own accord, and Kāma came there and spread his presence, and Śiva and Satī made love there for a long time'.[139] The other significant point in the narrative cited above is that Śiva 'remembers' Kāma when his *liṅga* has fallen, and because of that his *liṅga* arises on the earth. This may be a reference to the Pine Forest story (which precedes this incident in the text), in which Śiva's *liṅga* falls from his body and then arises from the earth. Thus, just as Kāma's power is not limited by his lack of a physical body, so his power over Śiva is not even limited by Śiva's lack of a sexual organ.

I. THE EROTIC APPEAL OF THE CHASTISER OF KĀMA

There is yet another reversal of the initial assumption of the anti-erotic significance of the burning of Kāma by Śiva: as the greatest of all yogis,

Śiva is the obvious subject for a seduction. This concept supports the
irony of those verses which refer to Śiva's supposed conquest of Kāma
while describing his erotic behaviour, and it is based upon the satire
of the false ascetic. Because of his reputation for chastity, Śiva's seduction is all the more to the credit of Kāma and the seductress. An *apsaras*,
about to try to seduce Nārada, boasts, 'I could wound with the arrows 43ea
of Desire even Brahmā or Viṣṇu, or even the blue-necked Śiva',[140] and 21ea
in praising Pārvatī's beauty Nārada says, 'She caused Śiva, who is with- 9d
out passion and is the enemy of Kāma, to wander like a minnow lost in 43a
the depths of her loveliness.'[141] This 'lack of passion' makes Śiva even 43ea
more desirable, as it does the conventional ascetic. The women of 36ea^{2}
Himālaya's city marvel at Śiva's beauty and say, 'Kāma's body was not
burnt by Śiva when his anger mounted, but I think that, out of shame 43a
when he saw Śiva, Kāma himself burnt his body.'[142] 42ea

It is Śiva's supposed invulnerability to desire that causes Pārvatī to
desire him. Although everyone cites the burning of Kāma when trying 43a
to dissuade her from her love of Śiva,[143] Pārvatī's desire only intensifies.
At first, though she desires him, she despairs of success, thinking, 'Śiva
is by nature hard to obtain, and now he is performing *tapas*. He has
burnt Kāma and is without desire. How can a girl like me win such as 43a
him?'[144] But then she takes heart, even when her parents say to her,
dissuading her, 'What use have you for this Rudra who burnt Kāma?
Because of his lack of emotion he will certainly not take you as his wife.'
But Pārvatī merely laughs and replies, 'This passionless Śiva, who burnt
Kāma, will be won by my *tapas*, for he is loving to his devotees.'[145] The 43a
psychological truth inherent in these passages, that Śiva's asceticism 36ea
inspires Pārvatī with love, is hinted at by a companion of Pārvatī: 36ea
'Pārvatī is performing *tapas*, for she wishes to win Śiva for a husband. 25ea^{2}
She went back to her father's house because of the enmity of the Burner 43a 24ea
of Kāma, but she is strongly attracted to him.'[146] A poem expresses this
causal relationship in a metaphor:

> Though Kāma's body was destroyed by Śiva's eye, 7cd^{1}
> his arrow, unable to reach its goal 43a
> and repelled by Śiva's unbearable cry of defiance,
> wounded Pārvatī deeply in her heart.[147] 24ea

Thus Pārvatī desires Śiva because he has destroyed Desire. And when
she has won him, the poet describes her as 'naïvely smiling when they 43ea
say that he hates Love'.[148] Once again the burning of Kāma has an 43a 24ea
effect directly opposite to its superficial connotation.

J. KĀMA AND AGNI TRANSPOSED

In view of the intimate connection between the burning and the revival
of Kāma, it is not surprising to find several Sanskrit texts which confuse
36e or reverse these two episodes. In one of these myths, the gods beg Śiva
19e to marry and beget a son, and although Śiva refuses to have anything to
21e 36a 44a do with a woman, he gives them his seed (*tejas*), placed in Agni, and
21a returns to his *tapas*. Only at this point does Kāma appear:

> When the gods went with Śiva's seed and told Brahmā what had happened,
> 41e 37a Brahmā laughed, and from his mouth Kāma appeared, born from Brahmā's
> 8c creative heat [*tejas*]. Kāma's power [*tejas*] caused men and women every-
> 7c 41ea where to unite, tortured by lust, but Śiva created a great ascetic fire [*tejas*]
> 7cd[1] from his third eye and assuaged that sickness. Kāma became angry at this,
> 4 43a and, taking up his arrows, he filled Śiva with desire. Śiva married Pārvatī,
> 43ea the *yoginī*, and made love to her for a thousand years. The gods, afraid that
> 36e 27ea 5d the world would be destroyed, went there and praised Śiva. Śiva and Pārvatī
> 31e 7d were ashamed and angry, and a great heat arose from them. The gods fled,
> 44ea 7d but Kāma alone remained there, unafraid. The fire of Śiva's anger burnt
> 42e 43a Kāma to ashes, but Rati propitiated Śiva so that he promised to revive Kāma
> 43e 44a with a half of his own essence.[149]

Almost every element of the basic myth has been transposed. The giving of the seed comes first instead of last; Kāma is created when Brahmā laughs at the way in which Śiva has shed his seed, instead of when Śiva laughs at the shedding of Brahmā's seed; Kāma attacks Śiva because Śiva has burnt the essence of Kāma, instead of the usual situation in which Śiva burns Kāma because Kāma has attacked him. And after the wedding, when Śiva usually restores Kāma, he finally burns him up—not for stimulating desire but for interrupting it, as Agni usually does. In fact, the burning of Kāma replaces the 'burning' of Agni (i.e. the cursing of Agni to bear the burning seed), which has already taken place at the beginning of the whole sequence, where the burning of Kāma usually occurs; the two episodes are reversed. The complexity of the manner in which Kāma, Śiva, Brahmā, and Agni—all representing different aspects of creation—assume one another's roles evolves from the basic similarity and flexibility of the characters involved, all of whom epitomize some aspect of *tejas*, the fiery power to create or destroy. *Tejas* is Agni; it is the burning seed of Śiva, the creative laugh of Brahmā, the power of Kāma to inspire desire, the power generated by the love-making of Śiva and Pārvatī or by their anger, and it is the fire of Śiva's third eye. All of these are essential to the myth and are preserved, but the individual episodes of the plot are topsy-turvy.

Another Purāṇa contains only one of these reversals: the burning of Kāma takes place after the wedding, when the revival usually occurs:

> After the wedding ceremony, Śiva dismissed the gods. Then the evil- 36e
> minded, crooked, and cruel Kāma wished to wound Śiva, for Kāma is always 44ea
> doing improper things, making obstacles for sages who have taken vows of 4
> chastity. Kāma took the form of a *cakravāka* [ruddy goose] and came there 43ea
> with Rati to wound Śiva, but Śiva looked at him with disapproval and burnt 30e
> him up with his third eye. Rati lamented, and Śiva consoled her, promising 43a
> her that Kāma would be reborn. And then, having burnt Kāma, Śiva made 43e 7cd[1]
> love to Pārvatī, rejoicing in the lovely groves and caves and cascades.[150] 36e

Since Kāma appears in the episode of Agni (at the moment in the myth when Agni usually appears), he takes the form that Agni usually takes: a bird, the descendant of the Gāruḍī bird of the Svāhā myth. The particular bird used in this episode—the *cakravāka*—is most appropriate, for according to Indian folk-lore the *cakravāka* is a lovebird who becomes separated from his mate every night and cries mournfully for her until dawn, thus symbolizing erotic love in separation. The burning of the Kāma/Agni bird by an ascetic's glance appears in another myth as well:

> A forest-dweller of great *tapas* was resting under the branches of a tree
> when a female crane released her droppings on him. The sage became enraged 30e
> and burnt the bird to ashes with a glance.[151] 7cd[1] 43a

The bird motif links Agni with Kāma, as well as with Śiva, in yet another
way, for Kāma is often said to ride upon a peacock, which is the form
that the 'Blue-necked One' (Śiva) assumes when he swallows poison,[152] 30e 9d
and the peacock is also the vehicle of Skanda. An obvious sexual symbol,
the peacock is a recurrent motif in Indian erotic painting and poetry.

In spite of these symbolic ties, there is obviously confusion regarding the role that Kāma plays when he is substituted for Agni in the Purāṇa myth. Kāma is chastised in his own right, not for interrupting the love-play but for attempting to stimulate it, but as soon as Śiva has burnt Kāma he does what Kāma was attempting to make him do anyway. This may be a reflection of the Tantric doctrine of intercourse devoid of desire, the conquest of a sensual act by indulging in it without being 'attached' to it, but in terms of the myth it is the simple confounding of two motifs: the burning of Kāma (inappropriate at the point where it takes place) and the revival of Kāma. These two episodes alternate here because they are, in the Hindu view, inevitably linked, even to the point of identity: the burning implies the revival.

Minor rearrangements of this sort occur in yet another text, which tells of the marriage of Śiva and Pārvatī, omitting the episode in which Śiva burns Kāma, but then continues:

> 4 After the wedding, Kāma came within Śiva's range of vision when Śiva
> 44ea was united with Pārvatī. Kāma took the form of a breeze and asked Śiva to
> 43e 30ea restore his body. Śiva said, 'When I burnt your body before, in Pārvatī's
> 43a presence, I promised that you would be re-embodied in her presence again.'
> 36e 43ea Then Kāma had his body, and he entered the bodies of Śiva and Pārvatī, and
> they made love for many years. The gods then sent Agni to Śiva, and Agni
> 30e 44ea took the form of a turtledove.[153]

Here the Kāma and Agni episodes are thoroughly confused. The text has not described the burning of Kāma, yet Śiva refers to it. Kāma takes the form of a breeze and comes within Śiva's range of vision just as he does when Śiva burns him up, but he is revived. And although Kāma replaces Agni in the episode of interruption, Agni himself then appears as well. Kāma enters into the bodies of Śiva and Pārvatī to inspire them with passion, but they are already united at the moment when he arrives; his effect is then delayed until after the Agni episode, when it leads not to the birth of Skanda but to the erotic behaviour of Śiva (Agni) in the Pine Forest, which follows immediately in this text.

The interaction of the various fires is noted by the *Mahābhārata*,
44a which describes the placing of Śiva's seed in Agni as '*tejas* laid in *tejas*'.[154]
In another version, the fire appears in six forms before it is finally controlled:

> 44a Having received the seed of Śiva, Agni went in great pain to Indra and
> 30e told him what had happened: 'Śiva saw me disguised as a bird, and he recog-
> 10c nized me and, furious, wished to burn me as an oblation in the fire of his
> 7cd[1] blazing forehead. I praised him and begged him to protect me, for I was
> 43a 44ea terrified of being swallowed up by that blazing fire of his anger which is so
> 36a hard to restrain. But Śiva restrained his passionate embrace of Pārvatī and
> stopped making love to her, because he was embarrassed. Then he placed in
> 44a my body the seed which had fallen when I interrupted them, and that seed
> 10c 5d 7d is never in vain, very hard to bear, and capable of burning the universe. I am
> 44e 8cd now burnt by that unbearable *tejas*.' Indra thought of a way to assuage Agni's
> 9c 45a pain, and he said, 'If you plunge into the Ganges, your pain will disappear.'[155]

The first fire is the ritual flame which receives the oblation. The second is the fire of Śiva's forehead-eye, the same angry fire that had burnt Kāma, and the third is the fire of Śiva's passion, the fire of Kāma. All of these are restrained, but the fourth fire—the seed—assumes the aspect of the doomsday flame and is placed within Agni, the sixth and archetypal form, who finds his final rest in water.

K. THE PARTIAL IDENTITY OF ŚIVA AND KĀMA

The overlapping of the functions of Agni and Kāma which results in these transposed episodes also contributes to the ambiguous relationship between Śiva and Kāma in the normal course of the myth. The synthesis of all three gods may be seen in one description of the burning of Kāma:

> Śiva reduced Kāma to ashes, and the fire from his third eye then yawned 43a
> wide to burn the universe. But then, for the sake of the world, Śiva dispersed 7cd^{1} 5d
> that fire among mangoes and the moon and flowers and bees and cuckoos— 8cd
> thus he divided the fire of Kāma. That fire which had pierced Śiva inside and 26e^{2} 14c^{3}
> outside, kindling passion and affection, serves to arouse people who are 30e
> separated, reaching the hearts of lovers, and it blazes night and day, hard 7c
> to cure.[156] 43ea

The full power of Kāma is the more compelling as it is augmented by contact with Śiva's own force. The interaction of the two supposedly opposed fires—the fire of desire and the fire of asceticism—is clear: the ascetic fire from Śiva's eye merges with the fire with which Kāma pierced Śiva and finally lodges in the hearts of lovers. The phrase 'the fire of Kāma' is a pun, denoting the fire used *by* Kāma and *against* him as well, a flame composed of two sparks. The image of the intermingling fires appears in a classical verse:

> Within the wood the cuckoos charm the heart 30e
> with warbling of their throats grown strong 26e^{2}
> from eating of fresh mango buds.
> What here pretend to be their eyes, 7cd^{2}
> if but the truth were known, are sparks 8cd
> fanned by the flames of Śiva's glance 7cd^{1}
> from the coals of burning Love.[157] 43a 6cd

The cuckoos and mangoes are again considered the receptacles of the combined erotic/ascetic fire. This same interaction underlies a verse
which states that Śiva 'kindled' Kāma—burnt him up, but reignited him 7c 43a
with his own fire,[158] just as Pārvatī 'reignites' Kāma when she revives 42e
him. Similarly, Śiva is said to have 'extinguished' Kāma's fire with the 7c 43e
fire from his third eye, and Kāma's weapon is extinguished when it 42a
strikes Śiva.[159] The fires clash and mingle, so that when Śiva attempts 43a
in vain to disperse his erotic fever he is said to be aflame with the fire of Śiva, Kāma, and Agni.[160]

In this way, Agni supplies a link between Kāma and Śiva which supports their partial identity, reinforcing the link supplied by Indra's phallic/castrated aspects. As a result, in a relationship similar to that

which characterizes his conflict with Brahmā, Śiva opposes Kāma, in part from their opposition as ascetic and erotic gods, but in part also because of their competition as fertility gods. The symbolism and mythology of Śiva and Kāma are largely shared. The *liṅga* is basically associated with Śiva, but Kāma is connected with this symbol in the Holi festival, where he appears as the tree/phallus of fertility, and the motif in both Śiva and Kāma may be traced back to the 'Indra-poles' of an earlier era. The belief that Kāma was the son of Śiva appears in several Purāṇas; indeed, the very argument used to make Brahmā retract his curse against Kāma is used to make Śiva revive him: 'Have
41e 42e mercy upon Kāma, for it was you who created him and who instructed him in the very action which he has performed, using the ability that you gave him.'[161] According to the South Indian tradition, Śiva created
41e 42e Kāma and gave him the boon of exciting love among all creatures, when Kāma had adored the Śiva-*liṅga*.[162]

Śiva, in his turn, partakes of the nature of Kāma. He is actually called
42e Kāma in the *Mahābhārata*, an epithet which is explained thus: 'He is desired and has the form of women and other objects of the senses.'[163]
42e A similar explanation is given elsewhere: 'He is Kāma, because he is desired by the great yogis',[164] combining his two functions. Another text states, 'He who is known as Smara [Kāma] is Śiva, whose nature is
42e bliss. One who desires happiness should remember [*smara*] Śiva born in his body in the form of Kāma.'[165] In the Pine Forest, Śiva behaves like Kāma and is described as more beautiful than Kāma, indis-
42e tinguishable from Kāma, the very form and image of Kāma, or so hand-
24ea some as to destroy the pride of Kāma.[166] When Pārvatī asks Śiva to seduce the women of the Pine Forest, she asks him to become Kāma
42e to do it, and he resembles Kāma when he seduces a group of *apsarases*
42e and mortal women.[167] Śiva is a master of the *Kāmasūtra*, and he is the
42e Lord of Kāma when he marries.[168]

In many myths, Śiva's role develops parallel to that of Kāma. Dakṣa gives his daughter Rati to Kāma and his daughter Satī to Śiva.[169] Śiva makes love to Pārvatī in the forest when Kāma makes love to Rati.[170] One passage links Śiva with Kāma in the seduction of a number of sages, including several who are aspects of Śiva or his enemies:

> 42e Śiva, assisted by Kāma, deluded many heroes by his powers of magic,
> 45e[1] causing Viṣṇu to rape the wives of other men, Indra to sin with Gautama's
> 7c 35ea wife and to be cursed, Agni to be conquered by Kāma, the Sun to be over-
> 5c[3] 13cd powered by passion and to assume the form of a stallion when he saw a mare,
> 40e 39e Dakṣa and his brothers to lust for their sister, Brahmā to wish to make love

to his daughter, Cyavana the great yogi to fall in love with Sukanyā—and 25a
all of these were deluded by Śiva.[171]

These myths, which all involve some multiform of Śiva either as
seducer or seduced, are grouped together to glorify his erotic aspect.
As Śiva and Kāma are both creators, their roles are closely intertwined
in the creation myths. In one version of the androgynous creation, Kāma 32e
is the male half instead of Śiva,[172] and Brahmā creates Kāma in order 42e
to proceed with eternal creation, just as he enlists the aid of Rudra when
his ascetic sons fail him.

Yet, in spite of all the examples of the interchanging roles of the two
gods and the intermingling of their powers, it is clear that whereas Kāma
is merely one aspect of Śiva, the reverse is not true. Śiva is Kāma, but
he is more as well, and it is this 'more' that opposes Kāma. Śiva is the
god of virility, Kāma the god of sensuality.[173] Śiva burns Kāma because 42ea
of Kāma's frivolous approach to a matter which for Śiva involves the
procreation of the cosmos rather than the titillation which is Kāma's
stock-in-trade. In Stacton's novel, when Kāma and the Dawn (Rati)
appear before Śiva he is 'contemptuously amused. He had asked for 42ea
a wife, not for those pretty little nothings, love and desire.'[174] When
Pārvatī accuses Śiva of taking no pleasure in Desire, Śiva replies: 'Our 42ea
love is more than Desire. How could it be born of mere Desire? For- 41e
merly I made the universe by giving birth to Desire, and I myself made
Desire for the sexual pleasure of each person. How then can you re-
proach me for burning Desire? Kāma thought that I was just like the 43ea
other gods, and he disturbed my mind, and so I burnt him to ashes.'[175] 43a

From this it appears that Śiva objects not to Kāma's essence, which he accepts as his own, but to Kāma's particular way of manifesting it. Both Śiva and Kāma are fertility gods, but Śiva is ascetic and destructive as well. Moreover, Śiva has not merely assimilated the character of Kāma, for Kāma is a comparative latecomer to the Indian mythological scene; Śiva's creative aspect is taken from Indra and Agni and Brahmā long before the advent of Kāma. Above all, Kāma's straightforward symbolic essence limits his religious role to fable and metaphor, while Śiva's complexity allows him to penetrate into the deepest corners of Hindu devotion.

VI

ŚIVA IN THE PINE FOREST

In the Pine Forest myth, Śiva retains his ambiguous status as the god who is both seducer and seduced. As a true ascetic, he is tempted by the wives of the sages, and as a hypocritical ascetic he seduces them, while as the supreme god he himself brings about the seduction of the sages. Much of this ambivalence results from the combination of different elements of the story of Agni and Svāhā: the sage (Agni) seduces the women, while the woman (Svāhā) seduces the sage. Even the central
33ea[6,7] element of doubt and mistaken accusation is derived from the older myth: just as the Kṛttikās are wrongly accused of adultery by their husbands, so in many versions of the Pine Forest myth Śiva is punished for a seduction which he does not in fact bring about.

Within the pattern of the ancient plot, there are three progressions that one might expect to find in the character of Śiva: (1) Śiva is full of desire and intentionally seduces the wives of the sages. (This follows directly from the Agni myth.) (2) Śiva enters the forest full of chastity and remains chaste in spite of the enticements of the women. (This follows from Svāhā's unsuccessful temptation of Agni as well as from Śiva's reputation for invulnerability.) (3) Śiva enters the forest chaste but succumbs to the charms of the sages' wives. (This follows from the Agni myth as well as from the myth of Śiva and Kāma.) It is therefore worthy of note that this third possibility *never occurs* in the Sanskrit texts. No change ever takes place in the character of Śiva during the course of this myth, a complete contrast to the Śiva–Kāma myth in which Śiva's attitude towards Kāma changes almost constantly. In the Pine Forest, Śiva is depicted either as lustful throughout or as chaste throughout. The *semblance* of change, however, appears in a frequent variant which serves as a complement to the non-occurring
33ea[6,7] third possibility: (3A) Śiva *appears* to be lustful but is ultimately revealed to have been chaste. The purpose of this masquerade is twofold: sometimes he pretends to seduce the sages' wives in order to reduce their *tapas*, sometimes in order to teach them a lesson. The myth is primarily concerned with the sages' transformation, rather than with any transformation of Śiva, who merely acts as a pivot around whom the other

characters revolve. When this unchanging Śiva assumes his erotic aspect, the myth is fairly straightforward and close to its ancient prototype. When Śiva appears in his ascetic aspect, however, complex rationalizations must take place.

A. ŚIVA, THE FALSE ASCETIC, SEDUCER OF THE SAGES' WIVES

The question of Śiva's intention and state of mind in the Pine Forest is explicitly discussed in one version of the myth: 'In order to judge whether or not Śiva's mind was aroused by the erotic gestures of the 35ea
Pine Forest women, I shall tell what the women said and what he replied.'[1] The ensuing conversation is overwhelmingly erotic, even salacious, on the part of Śiva as well as the women. Even in texts which develop the second plot line—that Śiva remained chaste throughout—there are frequent overtones of the first, more basic theme. Thus, in a text which describes Śiva's steadfast meditation in spite of the enticements of the women, Śiva is described as possessing a phallus which lusts for a womb and as being maddened with passion.[2] Another text glorifying the steadfastness of Śiva nevertheless introduces the myth as one in a series of tales in which great sages overcome (sinful) gods with 1 45a
their *tapas*, as Gautama overcame and castrated Indra. The Purāṇa 32a
hastily adds that Śiva is greater than all of these,[3] and the victory of the sages over him proves only temporary, but it is a victory all the same, undisputed in other versions of the story.

At the time of the Epic, Śiva's behaviour in the Pine Forest was hardly 35ea
that of a proper ascetic: 'He sports with the daughters and the wives of 26ea
the sages, with erect hair, a great penis, naked, with an excited look. 28ea
He laughs, sings, dances charmingly, speaks like a madman, speaks 31e
sweetly, laughs horribly.'[4] A later text is more blunt: Śiva violated a thousand sages' wives.[5] Since he comes to the Pine Forest ostensibly 24ea
to beg for alms, he plays the role of the false ascetic, a term which the 35ea
sages actually apply to him and which is substantiated by the accompanying description:

> When Śiva failed to be satisfied by making love to Gaurī, his wife, he then 23ea 24ea[1]
> went naked into the Pine Forest in the guise of a madman, his *liṅga* erect, his 28ea
> mind full of desire, wishing to obtain sexual pleasure with the wives of the 33ea[5]
> sages.[6] 26ea 35ea

This lends weight to the sages' accusation: 'He came like a thief into our hermitage, for the sake of his *liṅga*, stealing the wives of other men. 23ea
. . . He came like a madman into our midst, for the sake of the women 24ea[1]

who are here.'[7] Śiva himself confesses to being a false ascetic when he replies to the taunts of the women in the forest:

> *The women*: You are the foremost of wantons. How can you wander begging without embarrassment?
> 24ea *Śiva*: There is no expedient but wandering as a beggar in order to reveal
> my own songs, gazes, and words among women in different places.[8]

The *Mahābhārata* commentator is equally blunt in his assessment of
28ea Śiva's intentions: 'It is known that Śiva entered the Pine Forest naked
35ea in order to entice the wives of the sages.'[9] And Nārada, when praising
7cd^{1} sensual pleasures, says, 'It is known that Śiva, the three-eyed, went to
35ea the Pine Forest in order to make love with the daughters of the sages.'[10]
In one of the many quarrels between Śiva and Pārvatī, she accuses him of ascetic hypocrisy:

> 33ea^{7} Śiva and Pārvatī were playing dice, and she won from him all his ornaments
> 28e 28ea 28a and even his loincloth. Then all the hosts and attendants were embarrassed
> 36a and turned their heads away, and Śiva was ashamed and angry. He said to
> her, 'All the sages and gods are laughing at me. Why have you done this?
> If you have won, at least let me keep my loincloth.' But Pārvatī laughed and
> 28ea said, 'What need have you for a loincloth? You went naked into the Pine
> 24ea^{1} Forest and seduced the wives of the sages, on the pretext of begging. And
> 35ea then when you had gone they gave you great honour. The sages there caused
> 32a your loincloth to fall, and therefore you must cast it off now, for you have
> lost it at dice anyway.'[11]

The castration of Śiva is thus awkwardly equated with the falling of the loincloth (as it is equated, more appropriately, with the falling of the seed in other contexts), which here indicates merely the shameless lust of Śiva.

It is evident that Śiva is under the influence of lust from the moment that he enters the forest, and indeed several versions of the myth imply that this emotion stems from a time before he ever cast eyes on the Pine Forest women:

> 27ea Śiva taught Pārvatī the merits of *tapas* and instructed her in it. Then she
> 43ea went away to do *tapas*, but Śiva was overcome by desire, and he wandered
> 13c over the earth. Everywhere he sprinkled his body with water, but he found
> 34e no peace anywhere. . . . Then Śiva went among the houses of the sages,
> 35ea revealing their fickleness. . . . Thus Śiva was tortured with desire for the wives
> of the sages.[12]

Often Śiva is said to enter the Pine Forest full of longing after the death
10cd of Satī.[13] Although ostensibly he seems to change from ascetic mourning

to lust, the actual mourning is erotic in the context of Śaiva mythology and his behaviour speaks for itself in one modern version of the myth:

> [After the death of Satī, Śiva wandered] like a demented creature. While he
> was passing through a forest in this state, the young wives of the sages who
> lived there happened to meet him and asked him the cause of his distress.
> Shiva told them that he had a beautiful wife who had immolated herself to 6d
> avenge a slight he suffered at the hands of her father, and he was mourning 23a
> her death. On hearing this lamentable story a gay young lady laughed aloud. 10cd
> Shiva wished to know the cause of her hilarity and was told by the fair mocker
> that he looked indeed a man for whom a beautiful young woman would 24a
> commit suicide! This taunt so infuriated the god of virility that he violated 35ea
> her. Her husband came on the scene and cursed the god to be worshipped as 2
> the Lingam.[14] 5c^2

This is the only version of the myth in which the sexual encounter takes place because of the unattractiveness of Śiva's form. In all the Sanskrit texts, though Śiva is described sometimes in conventionally handsome terms and sometimes in the less obviously attractive form of a naked ascetic, the women desire him and he does not need to take them by force. European standards have distorted an essential motif here, yet even so Śiva is described as the god of virility.

Śiva's role of the false ascetic in the Pine Forest is supported by various other stories in which he behaves in the same way:

> On the stony shores of Lake Sipra, Śiva looked every inch the yogin, but
> was actually whiling away the time by the invention of the 84,000,000 sexual 24ea^1
> postures, of which 84,000 survive, of which 729 are possible and practicable,
> given block and tackle; and by meditation upon the unreliable nature of the 16d
> drug cantharides; the fatigues subsequent upon a well-spent youth; and other
> subjects more appropriate to the bedroom than the study.[15]

A Purāṇa states, 'Once, Śiva saw some beautiful women and was overcome by desire for them. He invited them to go far away in the sky with 21ea
him. Pretending to do *tapas*, the god in fact intended to make love to 24ea^1
them.'[16] This background and the evidence of the underlying myth of the lustful Agni seem to show that the original state of Śiva was the one indicated by the pattern of the myth rather than by the subsequent explicit rationalizations.

B. ŚIVA, THE PASSIVE ASCETIC, UNMOVED BY THE SAGES' WIVES

One version of the Pine Forest myth states that the wives of the sages attempted in vain to seduce Śiva:

> When the wives of the sages saw Śiva they fell in love with him and forgot 35ea

21ea about bringing the fuel (home to their husbands from the forest), but Śiva
42a was engaged in meditation and did not notice the women. They remained
there all day, waiting for him to stop meditating and notice them, but still he
did not stop meditating. Finally, when the sun set, the women took up the
fuel and flowers and returned home to their hermitage.[17]

Śiva remains passive in this way until the sages castrate him for estranging their wives. Another version also stresses his innocence:

43ea When Satī had died, Kāma took his bow and attacked Śiva, who fled in
24ea^2 fear. He reached the hermitage of the sages, and when the women saw him
28ea 35a naked, they desired him and were overcome by lust. Śiva, who was without
42a desire, ran away from them.[18]

Although this encounter is directly preceded by an encounter with Kāma—a remnant of the earlier pattern—Śiva is said to have escaped him (presumably unwounded) and to be without desire.

An interesting body of support for Śiva's passive innocence in the Pine Forest myth is supplied by the Gond myths of Lingo or Lingal, who is an aspect of Śiva; this is clear from his name (which in Gond mythology is attributed to the erection of his *liṅga* or to the *liṅgas* with which he is covered) and from his close association with Mahādeva (Śiva). The myth is of particular interest because, although in most versions Lingo is chaste and innocent, seduced or falsely accused by the women, there is, nevertheless, evidence that he is sexually active in the story and that his sexuality, resulting from and conflicting with his chastity, cannot be accepted by the Gond myth-makers. There are many variants of the Gond tale, and many interpretations have been offered,[19] but a fairly typical composite version might be summarized thus:

[All but the youngest of seven brothers married. The six wives fell in love
24ea with the youngest brother and stayed to listen to his music when they brought
31e 16cd lunch to their husbands in the fields. The brothers, angry, drove him away.
33ea^6 He wrestled with a tiger they sent against him, and then, under the instruc-
8c tions of Viṣṇu, he killed a demon and spent twelve years in *tapas*, playing his
31a instruments in a solitary place. He took two buffaloes and tied them to the
28ea harrow with his own loincloth. As he was driving the buffaloes he came face
16cd to face with his sisters-in-law who were bringing him his food.] His *ling* stood
26ea up stout and strong before him, and when the girls saw it they said, 'Look
how stout and strong is his *ling*, from today his name must be Lingo.' [Lingo
31e· then put on his clothes and played music for them. Then the brothers
33ea^6 thought,] 'Surely this fellow is up to some mischief with our wives, or why
should they be so late?' [The women scratched their bodies with thorns and
33ea^6 said,] 'Look how that scoundrel has treated us.' For they were angry that
35a Lingo had not made love to them. [The brothers tried to kill Lingo and failed.
Then they put him to the ordeal of boiling oil, but Lingo played his music
13c 11d inside the cauldron, and it became cool. The six sisters wept, begging him

to emerge from the pot.] Lingo's mother's brother's daughter said, 'If you are 31e
impotent you will sit there, but if you are a man you will come out.' Lingo 32a
at once stood up [and emerged from the cauldron.

He married his mother's brother's daughter, but she was carried away by 36e 16d
a demon who made a love charm for her. She had a child and Lingo heard 22a
the child crying. He found his wife and killed her, and she became a goddess, 19a
and Lingo then married seven wives.][20] 36e 35ea 36a

The wives who delay with their husbands' lunches (food being a metaphor for sex), the battle with the tiger and the demon, the cooling of boiling water—all are taken from the Sanskrit versions of the myth. The twelve years' vow of *tapas* is the Kāpālika vow that Śiva performs before he enters the Pine Forest. More significant is the ithyphallic nature of Lingo and the erotic quality of his music, taken from the Dionysian Śiva of the *Mahābhārata*. The thinness of the euphemism of Lingo's music is indicated by the manner in which, after the women admire Lingo's erect phallus, he plays music for them. This side of Lingo emerges more clearly at the end of the myth, where the ambiguous seventh sister inspires him to demonstrate that he is not impotent and then marries him. (The question of impotence combined with Lingo's punishment for alleged adultery links that punishment with the traditional one of the Pine Forest—castration.) The ascetic background of Lingo suddenly re-emerges—he kills his wife—and is finally replaced by the dominant erotic aspect: Lingo marries seven wives (the original wives of his brothers?), as Agni seduces the Kṛttikās.

Yet the story-teller takes pains to show that Lingo's nakedness was not meant to be provocative, that Lingo just happened to have taken off his loincloth to harness oxen. He explicitly states that the women accused Lingo because he did *not* seduce them (a phenomenon with precedents in mythology, as well as in feminine psychology), and this motif of the false accusation appears in many Sanskrit versions as well. Two other tribals myths[21] relate the seven sisters to a boy whose sexuality is ambivalent. Although the boy is not directly connected with Śiva, certain other motifs link the myths to the Śiva cycle:

[A boy refused to marry any of seven sisters. Then he went to look for the 21a
eighth, a spirit girl who lived in the forest and talked to the gods. He over- 30e
heard seven parrots talking and realized that they were the seven sisters.
From their hints, he went to ask the help of an ascetic named Virabadra who
had the girl but who said,] 'I am a jungle man and I have always lived in the 24ea[1]
jungle. How should I have a girl with me?' [But when he knew that the boy
had understood the parrots talking, he gave him the spirit girl as his wife.] 19ea

The ambiguous chastity of the boy (who refuses to marry the seven sisters but then seeks the eighth) is offset by that of the ascetic (whose name is an epithet of Śiva). An ambiguity more closely related to that of the Gond Lingo motivates the second version of this tribal myth:

19e [Seven sisters were without husbands. The youngest asked Nanga Baiga
24ea[2] to give her a child. After twelve months a son was born to her, and the six
22e 20ea 19a other sisters were jealous and pronounced a curse: 'Let all childbirth cease
2 29a throughout the world.' And it was so, until Nanga Baiga propitiated them and
5c[1] childbirth began again.]

As in the Gond cycle, the sisters are angry with the hero for his (implied) refusal to impregnate them as well as the unique seventh sister. Their curse is the curse given by Pārvatī to the gods: barrenness, the female counterpart of the castration curse of the Pine Forest. This condition is overcome by Nanga Baiga, who here plays a predominantly sexual role in spite of the non-sexual character one would expect from the pattern of the myth of the seven sisters 'rejected' by him.

In this way, the Gond cycle of Lingo illustrates one reading of the Pine Forest myth—that Śiva (Lingo) is innocent—while maintaining certain hints of the opposite reading—that he merely pretends to be chaste, while intentionally exciting, if not satisfying, the desire of the women.

C. THE APPARENT LUST OF THE ASCETIC ŚIVA

Whereas the false ascetic pretends to be chaste when he is lustful, the Pine Forest masquerade is frequently the reverse: Śiva pretends to be lustful though he is actually chaste. As a technique of myth construction, this masquerade very cleverly resolves the two basic versions of the myth: the secondary version (the chastity of Śiva) is taken as the true state of affairs, while the primary version (the lust of Śiva) is merely a bit of play-acting, a manifestation of the divine play which rationalizes other Śaiva paradoxes. Within the myth itself, however, the masquerade of Śiva serves two important purposes: his feigned lust, stimulating lust in the sages' wives, serves to destroy the *tapas* of his enemies, transferring their powers to him, and by demonstrating to the sages the frailty of their wives and themselves he teaches them a valuable lesson.

C. 1. *The Destruction of the Sages' Powers by the Seduction of their Wives*

In one group of Pine Forest myths, Śiva seduces the sages' wives in order to disperse the powers of the sages, powers thought to be inherent

in the chastity of the wives. The antecedent god for this aspect of the
myth is not Agni but Indra, who would send a woman to seduce a
dangerous sage (just as Śiva uses Pārvatī or Viṣṇu's female form in some
late versions of the Pine Forest myth). Sometimes, however, Indra himself would seduce the wife in order to reduce her husband's powers, as 45e[1] 45a
in the tale of Gautama and Ahalyā, and this is the model which applies
most closely to the behaviour of Śiva in most of the Pine Forest stories.

The usual technique is simply a variation of the general method of
subverting virtue or *tapas*. When Viṣṇu seduces the wife of the demon
Jalandhara he states the necessity for the seduction: 'We will follow
the path that he himself has shown us [by attempting to rape Pārvatī]. 25e
Otherwise, he cannot be conquered, for he is so well protected by the 34e
chastity of his wife.'[22] In another version of this myth, it is Pārvatī who
makes the suggestion to Viṣṇu, adding, 'You must break the fidelity of 25e 34e
his wife, for there is no dharma like the dharma of wifely fidelity.'[23]
According to one South Indian myth, in order to reduce the power of 18a
a hundred and one kings who had been granted immortality, Śiva 35ea 29a
resolved to destroy the chastity of their wives, who had no children. 26e[2]
He took the form of a sacred fig tree, which the women embraced in 25e
order to have children. They gave birth to a hundred and one girls, and 5c[1] 10cd
thus they destroyed their husbands' powers.[24] Although the women
wish to have children, the connection between procreation and the loss
of immortality is well-established. And although the method of their
impregnation would seem to be devoid of moral stigma, it is no more
far-fetched than the moral lapses of the Kṛttikās. The fig-tree plays the
same role in another myth in which immortality is replaced by unlimited sexless procreation which is, nevertheless, destroyed in the same
way: the gods formed a fig-tree for demon women to embrace, 'to 26e[2]
induce the sexless Rakshasas [demons] to propagate in the same way 5c[1] 8c
that men do. They would then lose their power of limitless increase.'[25] 25e
The apparent reversal (unlimited progeny replacing the childlessness
of the first myth) is in fact thematically related (ascetic creation replacing
ascetic immortality), and both powers are susceptible to destruction by
loss of chastity.

The technique is complicated by a characteristic of *tapas* which, when applied to the exigencies of plot in the Śaiva myth, results in an apparent paradox: although by seducing a woman Śiva loses his own powers of *tapas*, he thereby also destroys the powers of the woman's husband. Śiva may rebuild his powers by more *tapas*, but the enemy remains suppressed for ever. Similarly, when anyone attempts to seduce Pārvatī, the

powers of the seducer are destroyed while Śiva remains intact, having
tricked his enemy and protected the virtue of Pārvatī. The god always
emerges from the final conflict strengthened; even when he is punished
for a sexual transgression, that very punishment becomes a source of
32a his power. In this way, when Sāvitrī has cursed Śiva to be castrated in
3 the Pine Forest because of his assistance to Brahmā in committing
bigamy, the woman whom Śiva had procured as Brahmā's second wife
32a turns the curse into a boon, saying, 'When your *liṅga* has fallen, men will
5c^2 do honour to you and will thereby win heaven. You will exist for ever
9c 2 by the banks of the Ganges in the form of a *liṅga*.'[26] This ambiguity
about Śiva's castration in the Pine Forest is basic to the mythology: in
2 some versions, Śiva is said to be cursed to be worshipped as the *liṅga*,
5c^2 while in others he himself curses the sages to worship him as the *liṅga*.[27]

The Baiga tell a version of the Pine Forest myth which illustrates the manner in which Śiva's sexual sin and its punishment are the source of his power. Śiva is not mentioned by name, but the pattern of the myth suggests his character:

> 33ea^{5,6} [Two Baiga discovered that their wives were having an intrigue with
> 35ea a Brahmin beggar, and decided to make a trap for him.] They made nooses
> 17d of their hair and tied these in the organs of their wives. . . . The noose [of the
> 32a first woman] tightened round his penis and cut it off, but he did not cry out;
> 16c he said to one of the women, 'I have dropped my medicine on the ground.
> Give it to your husband to eat and he will get great strength.' [The man
> 5cd swallowed it whole. That night it broke out of his stomach and entered his
> 10cd 17d wife's vagina. He went to her and the double length killed her.][28]

The rather bizarre Freudian elements of this myth are merely an anthropomorphic form of the episode in the Sanskrit versions of the myth in which Śiva's severed phallus moves about causing damage to the sages. The Baiga myth also expresses the basic concept underlying the corpus of seduction myths: that the sexual act is dangerous, causing the loss of power and sometimes of life itself.

In several of the Pine Forest myths, it is stated that by seducing the
wives of the sages Śiva has destroyed some aspect of the sages' power.
The sages worry about the prolonged absence of their wives: 'With
them gone, the oblation is destroyed and our sins are upon the family.
What can we do? We cannot marry again. . . . Our wives are our
assistants in the sacrifice.'[29] Śiva's reason for thus reducing their ritual
power is the same as Indra's, and is even expressed in the same meta-
8d phor: 'Sages in the Pine Forest were performing *tapas* without knowing
7d the true nature of God. Smoke arose from their heads as they tortured

themselves with *tapas*, and that great smoke filled the temple of the uni- 45a
verse.'[30] A similar method was used by Śiva, with the help of Viṣṇu and
Brahmā, to solve a similar problem: when the *tapas* of Atri began to 8d
trouble the world, they seduced his wife.[31] 25e

A myth recorded in the eighteenth century describes the dangerous 35ea
powers of the sages and the method by which these powers were reduced:

[Certain ascetics had obtained great powers by their prayers and their
sacrifices, but in order to conserve them it was necessary for their hearts to 8d
be pure always, as well as the hearts of their wives. Śiva, having heard of the 25e
beauty of their wives, wished to seduce them; he took the form of a young 35ea
beggar, of perfect beauty, and he made Viṣṇu take the form of a most beautiful 43ea
young woman. Then he told Viṣṇu to go to the ascetics and arouse them. . . . 33ea[5, 1] 21ea
Viṣṇu excited all of them. They abandoned their sacrifices in order to run 7c 10cd
after the woman, as moths fly about the light which they see in the night. . . .
Meanwhile, Śiva came there begging. The women ran after him, half un- 35ea
dressed, and abandoned their housework, begging him to remain there with 28ea
them. He left, and they followed him. Then the sages noticed that their 25e
sacrifices did not have the usual effects, and that their powers were no longer
what they had been. After a few moments of consideration, they realized that
it had been Śiva who had made the disorder among the women, having taken
the form of a handsome young man, and that Viṣṇu had seduced them themselves in the form of a young woman. They tried in vain to kill Śiva by means 24a
of a sacrifice, a tiger, serpents, a disembodied head, a giant, fire, and, finally, 30a
they sent all the power of their prayers and *tapas* against him. These forces 38a[2]
came forth like a mass of fire which beat against the genitals of Śiva and 8d
detached them from his body. Śiva, full of indignation against the sages, 5d 32a
wished to burn up the entire earth with his genitals, but Viṣṇu took the form 5cd 5d
of the female genitals and received those of Śiva, thus preventing the general 33ea[1]
conflagration. Moved by their prayers, Śiva consented to refrain from burning 17cd
up the world, on the condition that all men would adore the genitals that had 13c 13d
been detached from his body.][32] 5c[2]

Although there are traces of the original motivation—'Śiva, having heard of the beauty of their wives, wished to seduce them'—the effective pattern of this version is implicit in the way that the sages' powers set the stage for the myth, and by the fact that when they have been seduced their sacrificial powers dwindle. They actually abandon their sacrifices in order to pursue Viṣṇu, but the mere act of that pursuit would be sufficient to destroy their sacrificial powers, as is clear from the introduction: their hearts, and the hearts of their wives, must remain pure. Another text of this same variant remarks that the fire of their passion
made them lose their prestige.[33] Thus Śiva uses the power of lust to 25e
disperse the dangerous *tapas* of an ascetic.

C. 2. *The Transference of the Sages' Powers to Śiva: The Pāśupata Cult*

By seducing the sages or their wives, Śiva not only causes them to lose their powers, but also transfers those powers to himself. In the closed Hindu universe, often described as an egg, nothing is ever lost, but things are merely transferred, reborn, or transmuted. The law of *karma* is based upon this world view: one's personal merit and demerit, the sum of past actions, is embodied in the force of *karma* (literally, 'action'), which is considered a discrete, transferable quantity. One Upaniṣad describes a mystic view of the sexual act and then concludes: 'The man who practises intercourse while knowing this formula takes
8cd to himself the good *karma* of the woman; he who does it without know-
25e ing the formula loses his good *karma* to her.'[34] A similar notion may be
8cd traced back to an early law book: 'When a *brahmacārin* becomes un-
25e 45a chaste, his *tejas* enters the Maruts, Indra, Bṛhaspati, and Agni.'[35] Pār-
8cd vatī transfers her *tapas* to Śiva when he is disguised as a water demon,[36]
8cd and the sage Gālavi obtains half the *tapas* of the woman he marries.[37]
After Jalandhara and his wife have been killed, having first been
8cd weakened by means of seduction, the *tejas* of the wife emerges from her
25e body and enters Pārvatī, and the *tejas* of Jalandhara enters Śiva.[38]
8cd A later version of this tale says that the soul of Jalandhara, taking the
5cd form of a flame, united with the Śiva-*liṅga*,[39] the image of the soul
being a multiform of the power (the flame of *tejas*) which Śiva steals from his enemy.

At first, the law of *karma* was accepted as an accidental, immutable law of cosmic fate. Later, it came to be considered a force that one might purposely turn to one's own benefit. Believing that if anyone should happen to injure another he would lose his good *karma* to the injured person, a Hindu sect began to cultivate such situations rather than to leave the matter to chance. These were the Pāśupatas, a sect which came into existence sometime around the beginning of the Christian era.[40]
38a[2] The Kāpālikas were derived from them,[41] and both sects are closely linked with yoga and Tantra. It is as a Pāśupata or a Kāpālika that Śiva enters the Pine Forest.

The Pāśupata was instructed to 'play the lecher' in order to stimulate slander, acquiring *tapas* by this means:

> 24ea[1] He should take up his stand by a group of women . . . Turning his atten-
> 33ea[6, 7] tion to one of them that is young and pretty he should stare at her and act as though he were setting his desire upon her and honouring her. When . . . she looks at him, he should act out the symptoms of love such as straightening
> 24ea[1] his hair, etc. Then everyone, women, men, and eunuchs, will say, 'This is no

man of chastity; this is a lecher.' By this false accusation their merit comes 24a
to him and his bad *karma* goes to them.[42] 8cd

This would serve as a description of Śiva in the Pine Forest: by his erotic appearance and gestures (his nakedness and his dancing) he excites the women and infuriates their husbands, but he does not actually *do* anything. He is a man of chastity, making others believe him to be a lecher, a false ascetic in reverse. The sect itself reflects two historical levels which are parallel to those of the myth: the original cult probably used more blatant forms of sexuality to obtain magical ends, later rationalized into a mere masquerade of lechery,[43] just as the 'erotic' behaviour of Śiva is derived from the actual adultery of Agni.

The transference of *karma* is mentioned in one version of the myth,
when Brahmā says to the sages, 'You have ill-treated Śiva himself, and
turned away a guest at midday. One must never mistreat a guest, for
the guest then takes the good *karma* of the host and leaves his own bad 8cd
karma behind.'[44] This is not merely a Pāśupata tradition; the law books
state that if a guest is allowed to depart unfed he takes with him the good
karma of his host,[45] and the motif of allowing the guest to enjoy one's 8cd
wife plays a part in the Pine Forest myth. But other Pine Forest texts
refer explicitly to the Pāśupata cult; Śiva says to the sages, 'Formerly
I proclaimed the Pāśupata vow which should be performed with a con- 6cd
trolled mind and a body smeared with ashes, chaste, naked or with 21a
a loincloth.'[46] 28ea

The typically Pāśupata concept of false accusation is central to the myth. In only one version, a modern one, does Śiva actually seduce the women, and even this is uncharacteristically euphemistic:

> [The beggar (Śiva) went from one street to another. The sages' wives 33ea[5]
> followed him and then lost their chastity. Conception took place in them and, 35ea
> without the pain of pregnancy, they gave birth to 48,000 sons, who im- 20ea
> mediately devoted themselves to *tapas* on the advice of their father.][47] 19a 21a

Usually, the injustice of the sages' accusation is made clear, as it is in two late versions of the myth, one noted by Alberuni in the eleventh century and one by Francis Wilford in the eighteenth:

> A rishi [sage], on seeing Mahadeva with his [the rishi's] wife, became 33ea[6]
> suspicious of him, and cursed him that he should lose his penis. At once his 35ea
> penis dropped, and was as if wiped off. But afterwards the rishi was in 32a
> a position to establish the signs of his innocence and to confirm them by the
> necessary proofs. The suspicion which had troubled his mind was removed
> and he spoke to him: 'Verily, I shall recompense thee by making the image
> of the limb which thou hast lost the object of worship for men, who thereby 5c[2]
> will find the road to God, and come near him.'[48]

28ea One day, as Mahádéva was rambling over the earth, naked, with a large
26ea club in his hand, he chanced to pass near the spot where several *Munis* [sages]
34e 24a were performing their devotions. Mahádéva laughed at them, and insulted
24ea[1] them in the most provoking and indecent terms, and lest his expressions
33ea[7] should not be forcible enough, he accompanied the whole with significant
32a signs and gestures. The offended *Munis* cursed him and the *Linga*, or *Phallus*,
fell to the ground. Mahádéva, in this state of mutilation, travelled over the world, bewailing his misfortune. His consort, too, hearing of this accident, gave herself up to grief, and ran after him in a state of distraction, repeating mournful songs. This is what the *Greek* mythologists called, the wanderings of Damater and the lamentations of Bacchus.

The world being thus deprived of its vivifying principle, generation and
31ea[2] vegetation were at a stand; Gods and men were alarmed, but having dis-
5cd covered the cause of it, they all went in search of the sacred *Linga*; and at last
found it grown to an immense size, and endowed with life and motion.

5c[2] Having worshipped the sacred pledge, they cut it, with hatchets, into one
32a and thirty pieces, which Polypus like, soon became perfect *Lingas*. The
Devatas left one and twenty of them on earth, carried nine into heaven, and removed one into the inferior regions, for the benefit of the inhabitants of the three worlds.[49]

The 'large club' which Śiva carries is the emblem of Lakulīśa, the ithyphallic yogi. The 'significant signs and gestures' and 'provoking and indecent terms' of Wilford's version are very like the suggestion
24ea[1] that the Pāśupata 'should act improperly . . . He should speak im-
33ea[6, 7] properly.'[50] The false suspicions and recompense of Alberuni's version
seem thoroughly Pāśupata. Other elements, such as the cutting up of the *liṅga* and its extension to heaven and hell, are familiar from the Sanskrit tradition as well. But the concept of chastity purposely masquerading as lust is central to the myth. When the sages insist that Śiva's 'wife' (impersonated by Viṣṇu) misbehaved, Śiva replies, 'It only appeared to
33ea[6,7] you [that she misbehaved]. What I said [that she did not] is true.'[51]
The baselessness of their suspicions protects Śiva from the counter-curse, enabling him to take their powers from them without losing his own in a true sexual encounter.

D. THE SEXUAL DESTRUCTION OF DEMONS BY ŚIVA

Even when actual sexual encounters do take place, when seduction is used both by Śiva and by his enemy (usually a demon rather than a sage), Śiva emerges supreme by virtue of the special nature of his sexual powers, derived from his incomparable *tapas*. The element of masquerade is essential to these competitions, a motif which recurs in

Indian folklore as well: seduction by masquerading as a woman's hus- 33ea^2
band.[52] When Śiva undermines Jalandhara's power by bringing about
the rape of the demon's wife, Jalandhara's retort is unsuccessful because
he cannot duplicate Śiva's powers:

> Jalandhara deluded Śiva in the middle of the battle by creating an illusion
> of beautiful *apsarases*, on whom Śiva's attention was riveted. Then Jalandhara 21ea
> desired to see Pārvatī. He assumed a form like Śiva's, with ten arms, five 25e
> heads, three eyes, and matted locks, mounted on a bull. By the power of his 33ea^2
> demon magic Jalandhara became the image of Śiva. When Pārvatī saw him, 7cd^1
> she ran out to meet him, but when Jalandhara saw the beauty of Pārvatī's 45e^2
> body he released his seed and became immediately spent. Then Pārvatī 21e
> recognized the demon, and she vanished, and Jalandhara returned to the 25e
> battle.[53] 24e

At the beginning of this episode, Jalandhara has the upper hand by virtue of his great chastity. He is faithful to his wife, so that Nārada must go to great lengths to stir Jalandhara's desire for Pārvatī,[54] while Śiva is immediately put *hors de combat* by the elementary trick of the illusion of *apsarases*. But by shedding his seed, Jalandhara loses his supremacy. The statement that Pārvatī recognized the demon when he had shed his seed may be a reference to the belief that after intercourse a demon in disguise will inadvertently reveal his true form, as he does when asleep, dying, angry, afraid, or joyous; for this reason, Jalandhara's wife recognizes Viṣṇu (disguised as Jalandhara) one day after he has made love to her.[55] But even this may be considered a reflection of Śiva's powers, for he is noted for his ability to draw up his seed for thousands of years, and to make love to Pārvatī for equally long periods. Therefore the premature shedding of the seed reveals Jalandhara to be someone other than Śiva and thus protects Pārvatī and, by extension, Śiva himself.

This interpretation is supported by another version of the myth:

> Jalandhara deluded Śiva in the middle of the battle by creating an illusion
> of beautiful *apsarases*, on whom Śiva's attention was riveted. Then, oppressed 21ea
> with desire, Jalandhara went to see Pārvatī, assuming the form of Śiva. When 25e
> he asked Pārvatī to make love with him, she was uncertain, and she said to 33ea^2
> her friend Jayā, 'Take my form and find out if he is Śiva or someone else. 33ea^2
> If he embraces and kisses you, it must be a demon using magic powers of
> delusion.' Jayā went to the demon, who was full of lust. He embraced her
> and released his seed and became quickly spent, and she said to him, 'You 21e
> cannot be Śiva; you have little virility. And I am not Pārvatī, but her friend.' 25e
> Then she told Pārvatī what had happened, and Pārvatī hid. But Jayā resumed
> her own form and said to Jalandhara, 'By this fall of strength you have been
> killed by Śiva.'[56]

In this version, the act of intercourse actually takes place, and to avoid involving Pārvatī in it, a substitute for her is introduced into the myth, to counteract the impersonation of Śiva by the demon. Jayā makes a specific reference to the parallel masquerades. The demon's lack of virility, rather than his lust (of which it is a direct result), brings about the fall of strength which is his undoing.

In a multiform of the Jalandhara myth, Viṣṇu betrays himself much as Jalandhara does, but since Viṣṇu is acting on behalf of Śiva he wins the ultimate victory, though he is also punished:

> Śiva knew that he could not kill the demon Śaṅkhacūḍa as long as the demon's wife remained faithful. He commanded Viṣṇu to take the form of
> 33ea[2] Śaṅkhacūḍa and to deposit his seed in the womb of the demon's wife. Viṣṇu
> 21e did this, and at the moment that he deposited the seed, Śiva raised his trident
> 25e 10cd and killed Śaṅkhacūḍa. While making love to Śaṅkhacūḍa's wife, Viṣṇu com-
> mitted certain excesses, and the good woman realized everything and said, 'You have tricked me into letting you make love to me. By breaking my virtue,
> 2 you have killed my husband.' And she cursed him to become a stone.[57]

Viṣṇu is cursed to be a stone (just as Śiva is cursed to be a stone *liṅga*), in part because he betrays himself by committing 'certain excesses', as Jalandhara does, but in part because, unlike Jalandhara, Śaṅkhacūḍa has not committed any rape of Pārvatī to justify Viṣṇu's actions in the name of revenge. Even in the Jalandhara story, this is a fairly thin excuse, as Jalandhara is noted for his fidelity to his wife and has to be tricked into seducing Pārvatī. The weakness of Śiva's moral position in this respect is betrayed by the fact that in both myths he feels it necessary to get Viṣṇu to do the job for him—and to receive the punishment.

D. 1. *The Sexual Death of Āḍi*

When his enemy is a sage, Śiva uses lust as a weapon merely to reduce his threatening powers, in order to avoid the sin of brahminicide. But when threatened by a demon, Śiva usually kills him after weakening him in this way. In a number of myths, the actual manner of the
10cd demon's death is sexual, often at the request of the demon, who may
33ea[1,2] wish to die in the embrace of Devī.[58] The inverse motif, essential to the
10cd Āḍi variant, appears in contemporary Indian folklore as well: 'transformation to resemble a man's mistress so as to be able to kill him'.[59] The motif of the *Liebestod* may also be seen in the longing of the demon women for an erotic death by fire, and the connection of this longing with Śiva is quite appropriate. Death and sex are two motifs thoroughly

interwoven in the mythology of Śiva: as god of destruction, and simply as the hero who must kill demons, Śiva brings about the death of his enemies; as god of the *liṅga*, he uses sexual methods to achieve his ends. Sir Alfred Lyall composed some doggerel about Śiva which describes this double function in a Swinburnian manner:

> I am the lord of delights and pain, 29ea
> Of the pest that killeth, of fruitful joys;
> I rule the currents of heart and vein; 5cd
> A touch gives passion, a look destroys. . . . 7cd[1]
> I am the God of the sensuous fire, 7c
> That moulds all nature in forms divine,
> The symbols of Death and of man's desire.[60] 10cd

These myths assume two basic forms: in one, a woman is killed by
the phallus used as a weapon, as in the Baiga tale of the Pine Forest; the
more usual form (also part of the Baiga myth) is that in which a man is
killed (or castrated) by contact with a woman. Thus a demon who interrupted a Brahmin couple in the act of love (by eating the husband) was 44ea 10cd
cursed to die in the act of love himself.[61] Similarly, Pāṇḍu, having shot 16cd 17d
a female deer who was united with an ascetic who had assumed the form 44ea 10cd
of a stag, was cursed to die in the embrace of his wife.[62] Elwin gives 33ea[4] 17d
several tribal versions of the myths of *vagina dentata* or *penis aculeatus*
and relates them to the natural sadistic element of sex (particularly the 29ea
kind of biting and scratching described in the *Kāmasūtra*), to castration
as a sexual punishment, and to fears of castration, impotence, defilement 32a
by menstrual blood, etc.,[63] several of these themes being pertinent to 15cd
Śaiva mythology. Certainly the motif is related to the fear of harm
or defilement by sex which plays such an important part in Hindu
chastity and the closely related misogyny of Hindu asceticism. Two
versions of one myth support this view: when Śiva has killed the demon
Āḍi he shows him to Vīraka, who becomes worried and puts no trust in
women thenceforth; then, when Śiva sees Pārvatī he says, 'Shame on all 25e
women', and she replies, 'You are right. Women deserve to be reviled.'[64]

Closely related to the motif of a sexual death is the theme of the
'Poison Damsel', a young girl fed on poison and sent to destroy an
enemy who would die in her embrace, the poison being transferred by 9d
a kiss, a bite, a scratch, or by the sexual act. This motif has been 17d
explained in terms of the fear of snake-bite and the motif of the snake- 30a
maiden.[65] The latter is of particular interest in this context, for Āḍi
takes the form of a serpent to enter Śiva's bedroom before assuming the
form of a woman in order to kill him. Perhaps the most famous example

of this theme in India appears in a Bengali tale in which the goddess of snakes becomes a female black cobra to bite a young man on his wedding
30a night. The cobra weeps when she sees the beauty of the bridegroom's
10cd body, and does not wish to kill him, but his foot strikes her fang and he
dies.[66] The motifs of the *Liebestod* are obvious here.

The most primitive and least subtle of these myths is the tale of Āḍi, in which sex is literally the death of the demon:

36a Śiva once teased Pārvatī about her dark skin, and Pārvatī resolved to per-
25ea[1] form *tapas* to obtain a golden skin. As she departed, she said to her son
Vīraka, 'My son, I am going to do *tapas*, but Śiva is a great woman-chaser,
23ea and so I want you to guard the door constantly while I am gone, so that no
44ea other woman may come to Śiva.' Meanwhile, Āḍi, the son of the demon
Andhaka, learned that Pārvatī had gone to do *tapas*, and he resolved to con-
8d quer all the gods, for he remembered his father's death. Āḍi did *tapas* and
18a won from Brahmā the boon that he would only die when he had transformed
himself twice. Then he came to Śiva's door and saw Vīraka there, and to
33ea[4] delude him he changed himself into a serpent, forgetting the prediction about
30a the manner of his death. Once inside, he took the form of Pārvatī in order to
33ea[1,2] deceive Śiva, and he placed teeth as sharp as thunderbolts inside her vagina,
36e 17d for he was determined to kill Śiva. When Śiva saw him he embraced him,
thinking him to be Pārvatī, and Āḍi said, 'I went to do *tapas* in order to be
dear to you and lovely, but I found no pleasure there and so I have returned
to you.' When Śiva heard this he was suspicious, for he knew that Pārvatī
would not have returned without completing her vow, and he looked closely
for signs by which to recognize her. When he saw that the illusory Pārvatī
did not have the mark of the lotus on the left side of her body, as the true
Pārvatī did, he recognized the magic form of the demon, and he placed
5cd a thunderbolt in his own phallus and wounded the demon with it, killing him.
10cd 33ea[6] When Vīraka saw this, he thought that Śiva had killed a woman, and
20e 2 Pārvatī heard of this and cursed Vīraka to be born as a mortal, for she thought
44ea that he had allowed a woman to make love with Śiva. Then she resumed her
tapas, obtained the boon of a golden skin from Brahmā, and returned to the
palace. Vīraka shut the door against her and cried out, 'You cannot enter here.
A demon came here to deceive Śiva, assuming the form of Pārvatī, and Śiva
killed him. Then Śiva told me not to let you enter until he himself sees you
at the door.' Pārvatī realized that she had cursed her son unjustly, and she
limited the period of the curse. Then she entered the palace, and when Śiva
saw her he was full of desire but also troubled by doubt. He smiled and
29ea assumed his terrifying form, but she too assumed a terrifying form to match
36e his. Then Śiva recognized her and rejoiced, and quickly he made love to her
24e to assuage his longing.[67]

A number of masquerades occur in this myth: Āḍi masquerades as a snake and as Pārvatī; Pārvatī disguises herself with a golden skin and then with a terrifying form; Śiva indulges in play-acting when he pretends not to recognize the demon, and finally he disguises himself in his terrifying form to test Pārvatī. Three other Purāṇas follow this text closely, but they all differ slightly on the details of the death of the demon and the attack upon Śiva, the main peculiarities of the myth. In one variant, Āḍi places the adamantine teeth in his mouth, a misunderstanding of the point of the encounter.[68] Another text differs more extensively:

> Śiva embraced his 'wife' [Āḍi in disguise] joyously, for he was full of 36e
> longing. He made love to her at first artificially and externally, and then he
> entered her. Then he discovered a marvellous golden *liṅga* inside her, with
> a trident in the middle. Although he was a little worried, Śiva was so tortured
> by desire that he continued to make love to her. But then the womb of the
> demon turned to adamantine, and the demon in the form of a woman made 17d
> a staff and a cudgel in order to cut off Śiva's *liṅga*. Śiva perceived this magic
> and created tridents and other weapons and emitted them from the tip of 5cd
> his *liṅga*, and when Śiva had finished making love to the demon, the demon 10cd
> gave up his female form and died.[69]

The inconsistencies of this text, which attributes to the demon peculiar anatomical features more appropriate to Śiva, are glossed over by the commentator: 'Śiva recognized the false form, but he embraced her and attached his *liṅga* to her. He, the bearer of the trident, made love with his *liṅga* to the demon.' Unfortunately, the Sanskrit text does not allow of this construction, and all that is certain is that Śiva's phallus was somehow the instrument of death. Although here, as in the Jalandhara myth, the demon is ultimately recognized and killed, Śiva's excessive lust delays the recognition (*pace* the commentator), and makes it possible for the demon to approach him; even though he is suspicious, Śiva is so full of desire that he continues to make love to Āḍi. In the end, however, his lust gives him the weapon with which to kill the demon.

The Āḍi story may be traced back to the myth in which Indra attempts
to kill the embryo in Diti's womb by entering the womb and cutting
up the foetus with a thunderbolt. The thunderbolt, Indra's weapon, 45e[1]
comes to be specifically identified with the phallus,[70] and it is also 5cd
associated with castration as early as the time of the Brāhmaṇas: 'With
that thunderbolt, the gods cut away manhood from [those who later 14c[2]
became their] wives.'[71] The curse of the Pine Forest sages takes the 32a
form of a thunderbolt to castrate Śiva,[72] and the thunderbolt is said to 32a
be adamantine, like the teeth in Āḍi's womb. In the Āḍi myth, the con- 17d
cept of the dangerous phallus appears with its complementary motif,

the concept of the dangerous womb. The latter is the basis of another rather grossly anatomical myth:

During a battle between the gods and the demons, Śukra, the guru of the
18a demons, continually revived all the demons who were slain. Śiva knew that
25e Śukra could not be killed because he was a Brahmin, and so he resolved to
7cd[1] throw Śukra into the vagina of a woman. From Śiva's third eye there appeared
a horrible woman with flowing hair, a great belly, pendulous breasts, thighs
7cd[2] like plantain tree trunks, and a mouth like a great cavern. There were teeth
17d and eyes in her womb. Śiva said to her, 'Keep the evil guru of the demons in
1 your womb while I kill Jalandhara, and then release him.' She ran after Śukra
21ea and grabbed him and embraced him after stripping him, and she held him
in her womb. She laughed and vanished with him.[73]

In this variant of the myth of Śukra and the daughter of Indra, the
anatomical details are particularly appropriate to the characters, for
Śukra's very name ('The Seed') is said to be derived from a time when
16cd Śiva placed him in his own (Śiva's) belly and emitted him through his
phallus like seed.[74] In that myth, Śiva was acting for Śukra's benefit;
in the episode with the female demon, Śiva acts against Śukra, but he
takes pains to put him out of action in a way that will not harm him.

D. 2. *The Death and Transfiguration of Andhaka*

The myth of Śiva's encounter with the demon Andhaka is at first glance simpler than the tales of Jalandhara and Āḍi, for the sexual initiative is Andhaka's alone, and the attempted seduction involves no lurid details. The myth is also probably older than either of the other two, for it appears in a wider range of older texts and in combination with a number of other ancient episodes [Plate 6]. There are few contradictions between the different versions of the Andhaka myth, and taken in combination they supply numerous mutually supporting details of complex implication:

34a Once when Śiva was performing *tapas*, Pārvatī closed his three eyes, and
36ea out of the resulting darkness a son was born, named Andhaka ['Blind'], who
7cd[1, 2] 5d was blind because of the darkness in which he was born. Śiva knew that he
27e 19a would commit evil deeds some day and would desire his own mother, but
19e 9cd Śiva gave Andhaka to the prayerful demon Hiraṇyākṣa ['Golden Eyes'] for
7cd[2] his son, promising that some day he would himself purify Andhaka's body.
18a Andhaka obtained from Brahmā the boon that no one but Śiva could slay
27a him. Moreover, he said to Brahmā, 'Of all the women in the universe, the
27e 10cd most beautiful is like a mother to me and cannot be approached by me even
24ea[1] in thought. When I desire her, let me die.' Then Andhaka made love to all
44ea 32e the women in the world, until one day he chanced to see Śiva making love
with Pārvatī (or: he saw the androgyne), and he became blind with lust. His

ministers tried to dissuade him from this infatuation by several means: they 25e 1
told him of the general dangers of adultery, illustrating this with many stories; 23ea
they reminded him that his own son, Kanaka, had been killed by Indra because
Kanaka was in love with another man's wife; they reminded him that the wife
of Śiva was the mother of the universe and therefore should not be desired
by him; they insisted that it was better to be a eunuch than to seduce another 32a
man's wife, that even an ordinary woman could cause a man to burn, let alone
Pārvatī herself; and finally they reminded him that Pārvatī was his own 25e
mother. But Andhaka merely shouted, 'She is the mother of my enemy!' and 27e
he was so blind with lust that he sent an insulting messenger to Śiva saying, 24a
'You fraudulent ascetic, what need have you for this firm-breasted woman? 24ea[1]
Give her to me and stick to your *tapas*.' Śiva replied, 'I am performing the
Pāśupata vow and she is my wife, but you may take her and protect her.' 36a
Pārvatī herself sent a message, saying, 'Tell Andhaka that I will belong to
any man who will conquer me in battle.' Andhaka then prepared for battle, 29ea
and Śiva went to restore his powers by means of *tapas* (or: he went to the 25a
Pine Forest). In his absence, Pārvatī summoned Viṣṇu and the other gods,
who came there and assumed the forms of women. Andhaka arrived and 33ea[1,5]
demanded Pārvatī, but Viṣṇu created a hundred Pārvatīs (or: Pārvatī herself, 33ea[1,2]
frightened, assumed the form of a hundred goddesses, and Andhaka, wander- 33ea[3]
ing about like an elephant in rut in a forest full of female elephants, could not
tell which was the true Pārvatī. Nor is this surprising, for equally unable to
'see' truly is one who is blind from birth, blind with passion, blind with mad- 7cd[2]
ness, or blind with greed) (or: Andhaka assumed the form of Śiva and went
to Pārvatī, but she examined his body for the birthmarks of Śiva, and, failing 33ea[2]
to find them, she disappeared in fear). Andhaka fled, but still his lust drew
him back again, and Śiva came to do battle with him. Śiva impaled Andhaka
upon his trident and burnt him with his third eye for a thousand years until 7cd[1]
he was nothing but skin and bones, and his sins were all burnt away by the 43a
fire of Śiva. Then Śiva gave Andhaka a form with three eyes, blue neck, and 7cd[1]
matted hair, and Pārvatī adopted him as her son.[75] 43e 9d 19e

The underlying themes of battle and power are still present, though somewhat submerged: Andhaka's weakness is his lust, the specifically weakening and endangering nature of which is pointed out by his ministers; yet he himself wishes to use this very lust to weaken Śiva through Śiva's wife. While Śiva strengthens himself by performing *tapas*, Andhaka destroys himself through an unsuccessful seduction. The motifs of masquerade, superfluous to the plot, are nevertheless retained as the usual ornaments of the basic theme: in addition to the first masquerade (Andhaka as Śiva), which is penetrated exactly as Āḍi's transformation is penetrated, all the gods masquerade as women, and in addition Pārvatī produces multiforms of herself, just as she produces a single multiform (Jayā) to confuse Jalandhara. But superimposed upon this ancient pattern is a more metaphysical thread, in which the demon's death is a form of enlightenment which he himself requests and which Śiva grants as a supreme favour. The motifs of blindness are particularly appropriate to the enlightenment theme: Andhaka (who was created from Śiva's third eye) is born blind and is blinded with lust; he cannot 'see' Pārvatī for both of these reasons, as well as because of the illusion of the hundred Pārvatīs. Finally, Andhaka is purified by means of Śiva's third eye and is himself given a third eye, the outward manifestation of his inner enlightenment. Together with this thread, the myth unfolds a series of hints of incest (the parallels with the transferred parentage, unconscious incest, and blinding of Oedipus are intriguing): Pārvatī is his mother as well as the mother of all men; Andhaka asks to die when he desires his own 'mother', and when he has become purified she adopts him as her son. A Freudian interpretation is not entirely justified here; Andhaka requests from Brahmā not an incestuous *Liebestod* that he actually hopes for, but circumstances of his death so apparently impossible that he will in fact be immortal. He attempts to seduce Pārvatī not because his ministers claim that she is his mother but because he is so blind with lust that he cannot see this truth for himself. In this way, the sexual encounter frees Andhaka from his lust and reveals to him the true nature of the universe.

E. THE ENLIGHTENMENT OF THE PINE FOREST SAGES

According to one group of texts, Śiva seduces the wives of the sages in order to demonstrate a metaphysical truth. This motif as it appears in the Pine Forest stories is a late one, a fairly sophisticated rationalization of a myth which has its basis in conflicts of power or conflicts of social roles, and its supplementary nature is evident from the fact that there is grave disagreement in the texts themselves as to the nature of the error in the sages' behaviour that Śiva wishes to correct. In some texts, he opposes their *tapas* not out of fear of its power, as in the earlier versions, but out of a belief that *tapas* alone is insufficient as a path to Release. In other versions, he opposes their involvement with their wives and treats the sages like false ascetics who pretend to perform *tapas* while enjoying the pleasures of the flesh. Thus the ambiguity of Śiva's role is further confused by the ambiguous status of the sages, who are sometimes considered virtuous and innocent victims of a lascivious Śiva, but sometimes regarded as wicked enemies to be chastised or wrong-headed mortals to be enlightened.

The social level of the myth, dealing with the forest-dwellers and their wives, is treated sketchily and inconsistently. The problem is heightened by the innate character of myth, which strives in vain to resolve an insoluble contradiction. The law books could come to no clear reconciliation of the married life and the ascetic life, and although the myth is free to pursue certain solutions impossible in the world of reality, it too must falter when dealing with human situations. Śiva himself combines the characters of ascetic and husband either by eternal cycles or by an extreme heightening of the double powers of ascetics. He never tries to effect a compromise, and therefore he tends to oppose the life of the forest-dwellers, the intermediate stage. Sometimes his visit is designed to make them give up their wives, sometimes to make them abandon their *tapas*, but always it serves to destroy the uneasy balance that they have striven to maintain before his visit there.

E. 1. *Śiva opposes the Forest-dwellers'* kāma

Śiva's opposition to the wives of the ascetics is based in part upon his
character as the chaste, misogynist ascetic, but also upon the more
general view that women cannot but cause trouble when they accompany their husbands to the forest, a theory which Śiva proves by
seducing them. That the sages are in fact trying to have it both ways is
clear in many versions of the myth. One text describes the violence
of their *tapas* at great length, yet they themselves refer to themselves as 35a
householders; in another, they are called forest-dwellers, and their
wives are referred to as *tapasvinīs* when they are overcome with lust 27ea
for Śiva.[76] Śiva's disapproval of the wives is clear: they are said to live
by lust, and Śiva describes them as princesses proud of their beauty,
who befoul the sages' minds so that the sages curse whatever man enters
the woods, in fear of the infidelity of their own wives; similarly, Brahmā
says to the sages, 'You say that you have set aside all desires, but look
at this disturbance caused by your wives.'[77] Śiva refers to the sages as 35a
'those ascetics who lust for their wives' lotus mouths',[78] and the sages
themselves attribute their shortcomings to their marital status: 'We 35a
have the wits of fools, and we are evil. The Self has not been revealed
to the householder.'[79] In many versions of the myth, the disruption 35a
which Śiva causes seems specifically directed against the marital state,
for he causes the women to abandon their household duties and their 35a
vows of marital fidelity.[80]

Although the sages accuse Śiva of being a false ascetic, they themselves play this role at times. And Śiva, as lord of true yogis, is traditionally

opposed to the hypocrites of his sects. When Himālaya asks Śiva why
he will not allow Pārvatī to serve him while he performs *tapas*, Śiva
24ea[1] explains at length, smiling and demonstrating to Himālaya the behaviour
34a of bad yogis in the world.[81] He condemns ascetics who consort with
women and he says, referring to the sons of Brahmā who lust for
24a Sandhyā, 'These single-minded yogis here, Dakṣa and the others, how
35a can they be so ardently full of desire for a woman?'[82]

The Pine Forest sages appear to Śiva as inadequate, if not actually false, ascetics. When Pārvatī asks Śiva why he does not reward their fierce *tapas*, he replies:

> These men do not know dharma, nor are they free of lust. They are not
> 34a without anger, but merely stupefied.[83] . . . They still bear the triad of desire,
> 35a anger, and greed. They are fools, who have undertaken their vows out of
> 24a senility, but they remain attached to the enjoyments of lust, these worms of
> 24ea[1] sages.[84]

When Pārvatī doubts the truth of this, Śiva proceeds to seduce the
sages' wives, who immediately abandon their chastity and embrace him
passionately. The sages thereupon attack Śiva and try to kill him,
24ea abandoning their dignity because of their mad lust.[85] The sages' hatred
of Śiva's virility may be based upon their own repressed sexuality[86]
24ea[1] (even as Śiva's opposition to Kāma reveals his own sexual nature), and
one purpose of Śiva's visit to the forest is to force the sages to admit
their sexuality and to deal with it realistically rather than to stifle it
with *tapas*.

It has been suggested that this contrast between the omniscient god and the misguided ascetics is depicted in the main iconographical groups at Khajurāho, in which a serene, four-armed god (Śiva) stands alone, surrounded by various erotic couples (the sages and their wives):

> The presence of the ascetics touches on a comic note. Jealous husbands and
> penitents too sure of their merits, they have not been depicted to their
> 24a advantage. The ridicule of their role has been emphasized. Far above these
> 35a transports of passion and anger, Śiva is the beautiful god, calm and seductive.
> He has made sport of the ascetics and their wives, but he is the refuge sought
> by all beings, who are drawn to him.[87]

Yet Śiva himself is surely depicted in the erotic figures at Khajurāho as well as in the calm, mocking bystander. It is by behaving erotically himself that he demonstrates to the sages the flaws in their own false chastity. This process may be seen at work in a popular myth from northern India, in which Bhagwan (God) may be Śiva:

> [There was a sage who was one day reading the *śāstras*, and he came across

a verse which taught that even ascetics are enamoured of the beauty of 21ea
women. He would not believe that this could be true, so Bhagwan determined 34e
to teach him not to distrust the Scriptures. One night he sent a lovely maiden 21ea
to the hermitage of the sage, who let her in but locked the door to her room,
giving her a key and warning her, 'An evil demon sometimes at night assumes 33ea[2]
my form. Should he come to the door and desire admittance, open not to
him.' She sang that night, and he became full of desire for her. Remembering
his words, she did not let him into her room, but other ascetics, hearing the
noise, came and saw the condition of the sage. Then they said, 'This will be 24a
a lesson to you not to doubt the truth of Holy Writ.']88

The sage seems to suspect the truth of the 'Holy Writ' even before the actual temptation, for he takes suitable precautions against his own lower nature by invoking the familiar theme of the demon who seduces women by means of impersonation. Yet Bhagwan sends an *apsaras* to teach him a lesson.

A similar lesson is taught to the sage Nārada, also in the form of a sexual encounter involving a masquerade:

One day Nārada and Pārvata saw a beautiful princess named Śrīmatī, and 24ea[1]
both of them fell in love with her. Each went secretly to the king and asked 21ea
for her, but the king said that she would choose her husband herself. Then 23a
each went secretly to Viṣṇu and asked him to give his rival a monkey face. 33ea[4]
On the day set for Śrīmatī to choose her husband, both sages approached her,
each thinking that only the other had a monkey face. Śrīmatī was frightened
of both of them and chose a handsome youth who stood between them—
Viṣṇu himself in disguise. The sages complained to Viṣṇu, who merely 33ea[5]
laughed and said, 'What is this great lust in you, who are supposed to be
sages?' Then Nārada and Pārvata were full of sorrow and resolved to have 24a
nothing more to do with women, but to remain pure as before. And then, 21a
scorning the tricks of Viṣṇu, they both became devotees of Śiva.[89]

On to the basic motif of the lustful ascetic and the king's daughter the Purāṇa has grafted a lesson in misogyny. Another Purāṇa retells this story at greater length:

The great sage Nārada once practised *tapas* in a cave on Himālaya. Seeing 21a
this, Indra trembled and thought, 'The sage desires my kingdom', and he sent 8d
Kāma to delude and intoxicate Nārada, but Kāma was unable to shake the 45a
sage, for this reason: this was the place where Kāma had been burnt by Śiva, 43ea
who had then revived Kāma at the request of Rati but only on the condition 1 42a
that no one in that particular place would ever again be shaken by the wiles 43a 43e
of Kāma. When Kāma failed to arouse Nārada, he went back to Indra, and 42a
Indra was amazed and praised Nārada. Then Nārada thought that it was he
who had vanquished Kāma, and he became proud. He went to Kailāsa and
told Śiva how he had conquered Kāma, and Śiva cautioned Nārada not to
boast, but Nārada did not take this advice, and he went to Brahmā's world
and Viṣṇu's world, telling everyone how he had conquered Kāma.

33ea[7] Śiva then commanded Viṣṇu to create an illusion of a city in which a
beautiful princess named Śrīmatī was to choose a husband. Spurred on by
24ea[1] Kāma, Nārada went to the palace and fell in love with the princess. He said
21ea to the king, 'Your daughter is greatly endowed. Her husband will certainly
24ea[1,2] be one who, like Śiva, has conquered Kāma.' Then he asked Viṣṇu to give
43a him a handsome form so that Śrīmatī would choose him. Viṣṇu smiled and
said, 'I will do what is best for you, to remedy your suffering.' Viṣṇu gave
33ea[4] Nārada the face of a monkey, but Nārada thought he had been given the form
33ea[5] of Viṣṇu. Viṣṇu himself appeared before the princess, who chose him, for
2 she was frightened of the sage with the monkey face. Nārada cursed Viṣṇu
20e to become incarnate as a man [Rāma], to have a monkey as his ally [Hanuman], and to suffer for the sake of a woman [Sītā]. Then Śiva withdrew his illusion, and Nārada came to his senses and worshipped Śiva, and he wan-
21a dered over the earth until he came to Benares, where he learned the true
20a nature of Śiva.[90]

Although Śiva is here the supreme god who designs the lesson, Viṣṇu remains the one who actually causes the seduction and takes the punishment, 'by the command of Śiva'. The parallel with Śiva and Kāma is used to frame the story and to furnish a contrast: Śiva has truly conquered Kāma, but Nārada merely thinks that he has, until he is taught that only by the grace of Śiva can anyone overcome his erotic nature. Nārada thinks that he is as good as Śiva, for he has himself in mind when he predicts that the king's daughter will marry 'one who, like Śiva, has conquered Kāma'. He uses these words when he describes to Himālaya the future husband of Pārvatī, and he must be punished for applying similar terms to himself. Śiva alone can fully combine his sexual and ascetic nature; though he sets an example, it is one which cannot be matched by any mortal. Thus in the Pine Forest Śiva himself may behave lustfully, but only to show the sages the folly of their belief that they are above such behaviour.

E. 2. *The Temptation of the Devotee by God*

Śiva's behaviour in the Pine Forest may be viewed as a kind of temptation of the sages, and many of the texts refer to this when they
35ea say that Śiva came there in order to test them.[91] But this is not temptation by a deity in the Western sense of the term, for it seems fairly clear that Śiva tempts the sages with the full hope, and indeed the certain knowledge, that they will succumb. Although this serves as an excuse for Śiva's own licentious behaviour or for his Machiavellian measures against the threatening ascetics, it is also the basis for their own eventual enlightenment. Certainly in many stories Hindu gods seduce women

simply because of their own lust, but in other ancient myths they do it in the hope that they will be resisted.

The mythology of Śiva contains another episode of temptation in which the intention is fairly unambiguous: the scene in which Śiva comes in disguise to Pārvatī to tempt her to abandon the *tapas* which she is performing for his sake. Here he does not wish her to succumb to his blandishments, and he rewards her for her steadfastness by granting her a boon. This boon, however, results eventually in the very abandonment of *tapas* with which he had tempted her. This is a typical pattern of temptations: the reward for resistance is simply a heightened form of the temptation itself, just as the reward for asceticism is an eternity of sensual pleasures, far greater than those that the yogi forsakes in order to perform his vow. Thus, in a sense, Śiva does succeed in seducing Pārvatī from her *tapas*, but the explicit purpose of the temptation is both to tease her into admitting her passion for him (as an erotic god) and to make certain of the steadfastness of her devotion to her *tapas* for him (as an ascetic god). Here the opposing aspects of his nature merge perfectly in a situation that may be understood in terms of either aspect alone or both together.

Both forms of Śiva play a part in another level of the Pine Forest temptation which assumes the form of another traditional Indian motif: the god tests his devotee's chastity by asking him to give him his wife. The request is accepted in Hinduism as the strongest test of devotion, and one that must be honoured, although the literature also tends to treat the one who makes the request as a false ascetic who uses his status to gratify his lust:

> Sudarśana, the son of Agni and Sudarśanā, married and led the life of
> a householder, thinking, 'As a householder, I will conquer death.' He vowed 18e
> never to disregard a guest, and he instructed his wife to obey this vow, too.
> One day Dharma came in the form of a Brahmin and asked the wife to give 33ea[5]
> herself to him. Remembering the command of her husband, she complied. 35ea
> When Sudarśana returned and called for his wife, the Brahmin called back,
> 'Your wife is pleasing me with the various guest-rites. Her mind is firm and
> honest.' Sudarśana smiled and said, 'May you enjoy your love-making. The
> pleasure is mine.' Then the Brahmin revealed himself to be Dharma and he 27ea
> said, 'I came to test the truth of your vow. Your wife is chaste and cannot be 25a
> defiled, for she has mastered yoga. She will become a river, and you have 14c[1] 18e 18a
> conquered death by adhering to the duties of a householder and by conquering 18ea
> your passions, desires, and angers.'[92]

Many of the Pine Forest motifs occur in this myth, which extols the virtue of the householder who conquers his passion, and one Purāṇa

actually relates the story of Sudarśana in order to illustrate the folly of
the Pine Forest sages. After Śiva is castrated and terrible omens appear,
1 the sages seek refuge with Brahmā, who tells a story to them in order
to show them that they must give their wives to any guest who demands
them, especially if that guest happens to be Śiva:

The Brahmin householder Sudarśana told his wife, 'All guests are really
forms of Śiva himself, and so you must give anything, even yourself, to a guest.'
33ea[5] Then one day Dharma took the form of a Brahmin in order to test their faith.
16cd He came to Sudarśana's wife and said, 'Never mind preparing food for me,
35ea just give me yourself.' She was ashamed, but she determined to do as he
wished. As she was doing so, her husband came to the door and said, 'Wife,
where are you?' Dharma replied, 'I am right now in the very act of making
love to your wife, and I am quite satisfied.' Sudarśana was delighted, and he
said, 'Enjoy her as much as you wish.' Then Dharma revealed himself and
18e 18a said, 'I did not really make love to her, even in thought. I came here to test
18ea your faith. By this *tapas* you have conquered death.'[93]

This version is more explicit, but the basic theme remains unchanged, and Dharma considers the hospitality of the householder to be a kind of *tapas*. The justification of Dharma's behaviour is more explicit, too, but there are other myths of this pattern in which his action is less laudable. When he comes to 'test' a woman who is performing *tapas* in order to marry Viṣṇu, the Purāṇa comments, 'Thus Dharma spoke in order to seduce her by a trick, not to test her true nature or to know her goodness.'[94] Similarly, when Dharma 'tests' the fidelity of Padmā, the wife of Pippalāda, his motives are openly challenged.

In the later mythology of Śiva, the original lust of the god is almost always replaced by his pure wish to test the devotee by asking for his wife:

There was a tribal mountaineer who lived with his wife; both were devoted
33ea[5] Śaivas. Śiva came one day in the form of an ascetic, in order to test the house-
35ea holder. He said to him, 'Give me a place to sleep', but the man complained
23e[2] that his house was too small. Then his wife said, 'My lord, you must give
a place to the ascetic. Do not turn away a guest, or you will violate the dharma
of a householder. You stay inside the house with the ascetic, and I will sleep
outside.' He did not consider this proper, but he realized that it was equally
improper to dismiss the ascetic. 'I will stay outside the house', he decided.
6d In the night he was devoured by cruel beasts. At dawn, the woman prepared
to enter her husband's funeral pyre, but Śiva revealed himself and promised
6c 18a that she would be reborn as Damayantī and her husband as Nala [two famous
lovers].[95]

The more specifically sexual nature of Śiva's demand becomes apparent in a very similar story in which some roles are transposed:

One day when a certain king, a fervent Śaiva, was making love to his wife 44ea
in a deep forest, Śiva decided to test the firmness of his dharma. He took the 35ea
form of a Brahmin, and Pārvatī took the form of his wife, and they created 33ea^5
an illusion that Pārvatī was devoured by a tiger in the presence of the king.
The king, feeling that he had failed in his royal duty to protect his subjects,
offered the 'Brahmin' his kingdom as reparation, but Śiva replied, 'What good
is a house to one who lives on alms? Since my wife has been killed, I will never 23e^2
again enjoy any pleasures, but I desire your queen. Give her to me.' The king
said, 'I will give you all the wealth of my kingdom, and even my own body,
but not my wife. The sin incurred by enjoying the wife of another man cannot 25e
be erased even by a hundred expiations.' But Śiva said, 'I can scatter with my 23ea
tapas the sin of the slaughter of a Brahmin, so what is adultery to me? Give 25a
me your wife or you will go to hell for having failed to protect my wife.'
Terrified, the king considered the sin of giving away his wife less than the
sin of failing to protect his subjects. He gave his queen to Śiva and kindled 6d
a fire, thinking to enter it. But Śiva revealed his true form and explained the
illusion that he had created to test the king, and he granted the king and queen
eternal devotion to him.[96] 6c 18a

Here the tiger eats the wife of Śiva instead of the wife of the devotee, and the *svadharma* of the householder is replaced by the *svadharma* of a king. Each of these codes produces a quandary when it comes into conflict with the need to revere the ascetic, and the prevalence of the latter is evident in each case when the *tapas* of the householder (or the corresponding motif of self-immolation) is rewarded by the god.

A similar tale appears in a South Indian text:

[A Brahmin gave everything he had to the Śaiva yogis. Then Śiva himself
appeared as a Brahmin Śaiva devotee in the guise of a libertine and asked for 33ea^5
the man's wife. Although his relatives disapproved and fought with him, the 35ea
man gave her to Śiva. While he was escorting this pseudo-yogi into the woods, 23a
the yogi assumed the form of Śiva mounted on the bull.][97] 24ea^1 45e^2

The conventional *svadharma* of the householder appears here as the social pressure exerted by the devotee's relatives, yet it is also part of the householder's dharma to revere the ascetic and to give him his wife. It is noteworthy that Śiva is described as a pseudo-yogi and has 'the guise of a libertine', for in the prototype of all these myths it was in the *character* of a libertine, rather than as an impartial judge, that Śiva demanded the wives.

E. 3. *Śiva opposes the Forest-dwellers'* tapas

Although Śiva demands the devotee's wife in order to prove to him the dangers of attachment to *kāma* (or attachment to the wife), many myths of this genre exalt the dharma of the householder. This aspect of the myth is developed explicitly in a number of texts in which Śiva comes to the forest to teach the sages to give up their *tapas* and devote themselves to their wives.

The sages are sometimes described as great Brahmins who follow the four stages of life with great devotion, each delighting in his own dharma,
32a and they castrate Śiva by taking an oath on the four stages of life that
18ea they have followed faithfully.[98] But when Śiva praises them, he says,
'This is the great Pine Forest where many Brahmins live following the
household dharma. All their women are devoted to serving their hus-
35e bands and know no other god or dharma.'[99] In this text, Śiva believes
in the virtue of the sages and only agrees to disturb them because Pārvatī
insists upon it; this is a complete reversal of those versions in which Śiva
35a objects to the lust of the sages and Pārvatī pleads with him to reward
34ea their *tapas*.[100] The virtue of the householder and his wife is lauded in
35e the episode of Śiva and Arundhatī,[101] in which Śiva reveals 'the fickle-
34e ness of the lustful sages and their wives, and the firmness of the women
35e true to their husbands, . . . the virtue of the women who were house-
28ea holders and the absurdity of those who had taken the vow of nakedness'.[102] The householders' chastity is contrasted with the lust of the
23e^{2} ascetics in a speech by Brahmā to the sages: 'You live in a hermitage but
34e 34ea you are overcome with anger and lust. Yet the true hermitage of a wise
35e man is his home, while for the man who is not a true yogi even the
hermitage is merely a house.'[103] As a modern Hindu commentator para-
phrased the point of this myth, Brahmā taught them the doctrine of the
18ea four stages of life, 'according to which one performs the ordained duties
34ea of the householder's life and thus obtains the objective of true renuncia-
35e tion'.[104] This is Śiva's anti-ascetic role, the Dionysian aspect that he
assumes in order to oppose the *tapas* of the sons of Brahmā (who are the
40e Pine Forest sages)[105] and to send them back to the world of normal
social involvement.

In one text, Śiva explains the insufficiency of *tapas* alone:

> 34e 6cd The smearing of ashes on the body, the wearing of great matted locks, the
> 38a^{2} bald head, animal skin, pot, rosary, garland of skulls, nakedness, the ochre
> 28ea robe—the whole vow is made vain by desire and anger. Being in such a state,
> 25e they will not obtain Release by means of *tapas*, which merely dries up the
> 8d body.[106]

Śiva gives a similar lecture to the gods who have sought immortality by drinking Soma (as the sages seek it by *tapas*) without true regard for him: 'What good are sacrifices and *tapas* and rituals, if you do not know the Self?'[107] Here he demands not the supplement of *kāma* but the Upaniṣadic ideal of knowledge to enrich action.

The flaw in the sages' method of *tapas* is described at some length:

> Formerly in the Pine Forest there were Brahmins doing *tapas*, vying with
> each other in various ways, but they did not achieve success. Then they 8d
> thought, 'The sages did not speak the truth when they said that success in everything is obtained by *tapas*.' Overcome by impatience, they put aside their *tapas* and became atheists. But at this time a voice said to them, 'Do not despise the scriptures, do not blame *tapas* or dharma, but blame yourselves. You strive against each other, desiring success, and because of that your *tapas*
> is fruitless, destroyed by desire, egoism, anger, and greed. A man achieves 25e
> perfection in *tapas* only when he looks upon another man's wife as if she were 27a
> his mother. Propitiate the *liṅga* of Śiva and you will obtain success.' The 5c²
> Brahmins obeyed the voice and obtained success.[108] 18ea

Tapas as a whole is certainly not condemned here, merely *tapas* performed with the wrong attitude, in the false confidence that it alone will suffice to obtain everything.

E. 4. *The Balance:* Śānti *and* Liṅga-*worship*

Tapas does not succeed unless desire is conquered, yet it is by means of *liṅga*-worship that the unsuccessful ascetics eventually obtain salvation. These theological standpoints are usually personified in the myth: the sages use their *tapas* to castrate Śiva, only to learn that they can only function if the *liṅga* is restored to him and worshipped, signifying their acceptance of the cult of fertility.

Both points of view are often expressed side by side in a single version, and almost all versions agree on a somewhat modified form of each
extreme: Śiva praises *śānti*, calm self-control and lack of passion, even 34a
in versions which condemn extreme *tapas*,[109] and he teaches the value 18ea
of *liṅga*-worship even when criticizing excessive attachment to one's 34e 5c²
wife.[110] Though he may speak against the sages' wives, he never actually 18ea
causes the sages to leave them. He condemns and praises in a single 35a
phrase the wives' role in the religion: 'Those ascetics who lust for their
wives' lotus mouths will worship my *liṅga* and do honour to me with 35a 5c²
their wives, and they will regain their sight.'[111] Similarly, he condemns 34ea
the sages' jealous passion for their wives but then adds, 'As sick men 35a 34ea
do not enjoy food set before them, even so these men who have under- 24e
taken vows (do not enjoy) union with their beloveds',[112] a metaphor 16cd 35e
which seems to imply that if they were not sick (i.e. performing *tapas*) they would not neglect the nourishment that their wives offer them, and

that superficial, physical chastity has merely created the disease of lust in their minds.

The attempt to combine both paths sometimes produces apparent contradictions. In one text, although Śiva is said to have been satisfied with the sages who were practising *tapas* in the woods with their wives and children, he nevertheless goes there to teach them the knowledge based on withdrawal from the world, and he is satisfied with their wives and children but opposes their worldly involvement.[113] Another version of this same text adds to the confusion by reversing the initial premiss:

> In the forest of Dāruvanam [Pine Forest] even women and children took
> to the performance of austerities and forgot the worldly ways of living. . . .
> 35e To make them feel the need also of the worldly ways, Śiva started out to beg
> 33ea[5] in their quarters. For this purpose, he became a black, ugly-looking being
> 28ea and naked he went into their midst. Through his *māyā* [power of delusion]
> the residents of the forest took to all sorts of bad ways of this world. Angered
> 24a by the bad example set by the newcomer, the *rishis* cursed him, but instead
> of being affected by it he disappeared.[114]

Although he intends to encourage worldly ways as well as *tapas*, Śiva does this by setting an example of 'bad ways of this world', which would tend to drive them toward withdrawal. This is more consistent in another version of the text in which Śiva's express purpose is to move them away from worldly ways toward withdrawal:

> 35a Śiva would always discuss the fault of those sages in the woods who per-
> formed worldly rituals, sacrifices, and *tapas*, their minds ever set on worldly
> 34a ways. He went there in order to establish the knowledge of withdrawal from
> 18ea the world. . . . Śiva said to the sages, 'Yoga [i.e. ritual action] and meditation
> together give salvation, but you devoted yourselves to yoga alone, abandoning
> meditation and wearing yourselves out.'[115]

In this speech, which models its compromise upon the *Bhagavad Gītā*, Śiva stresses the necessity to follow both the path of meditation (i.e. *jñāna*, Sāṅkhya, or *tapas*) and that of ritual (i.e. *karma*, Yoga, or *liṅga*-worship).

Śiva's apparently contrary behaviour serves as a catalyst. In order to force the sages to attend to *tapas* as well as to their wives, Śiva behaves not as an ascetic but as a phallic god. And to teach them not to be too attached to their wives, he brings his own wife, to whom (as he actually says to the sages) he is deeply attached. He thus teaches them a deeper realization of both roles, and both views of married ascetic life emerge in their conversation:

> 19ea Śiva said, 'I have come here to perform *tapas* with my wife.' Then the sages

said, 'Leave your wife and perform *tapas*.' Śiva laughed and said, 'You are
so eager to support your own wives, so how can you tell me to abandon mine?' 24a
The sages said, 'Women who like to misbehave must be abandoned by their
husbands, but we are adored by our wives and so we must not abandon them.'
Śiva said, 'My wife never desires another man, and so I will never leave her', 35e
but the sages replied, 'You liar, we have seen her misbehaving. Go away.'
Śiva said, 'I spoke the truth; it only appeared to you otherwise', and he
left them.[116]

The sages do not realize which are the good wives and which the wicked wives, a classical point of contention for forest-dwellers. Ultimately, Śiva does not ask them to abandon their wives as they asked him to do, but merely to balance their excesses. Brahmā tells the sages:

> You have ruined everything, with your vain *tapas*. Make an image of the 8d
> *liṅga* and worship Śiva with it, along with your wives. You must maintain 34ea
> chastity and establish the highest *tapas*.[117] 5c[2] 18ea

Desire must be conquered, not denied. By means of *liṅga*-worship, *tapas*
becomes successful. The sages must worship the *liṅga* with their wives, 5c[2]
yet they must maintain true chastity and great *tapas*.[118] When each is 8c 21a
done in the proper way, they sustain rather than oppose each other. 18ea

At the end of the myth, however aggressively Śiva may have acted toward the sages, he always shows them his favour. Although he is sometimes praised as the Destroyer of the Pine Forest,[119] he is also noted for his grace toward the sages there. He enters the forest in order to enlighten and instruct the forest-dwellers, and to favour them; he removes their delusion and gives them peace.[120] The aggressive and gracious aspects merge in two of his epithets:

> He is called 'Greatly Reviled' because he was reviled by the sages, who said, 24a
> 'He came into the Pine Forest, assuming a handsome, naked form, in order 28ea
> to bewitch the minds of our wives, for he is an evil wretch.' He is called 'Giver 24ea[1]
> of Peace' because after the sages had reviled him he gave them peace by
> destroying their doubts and giving them knowledge of the true nature of
> things.[121]

The initial aggression is necessary, for only by spending their wrath on him can they be enlightened:

> The sages of the Pine Forest, fearing lest their wives lose their chastity, 33ea[6]
> became angry at Śiva. They did not recognize him, for he had taken the form 24a
> of a naked beggar in order to demonstrate to Pārvatī the lack of quiescence in 28ea
> the sages. As soon as they had cursed him, they knew him to be the lord, and 33ea[5]
> they sought refuge with him.[122] 34e 35a

F. ENLIGHTENMENT BY SEXUAL IMPERSONATION

Whatever lesson Śiva wishes to teach the sages, he teaches it to them by
means of a sexual encounter involving a masquerade. This is a common
33ea[2, 3] technique of Śaiva mythology,[123] at least as old as the Epic myth of
Svāhā. It is used by Pārvatī to teach a lesson to her own son:

When Skanda had killed Tāraka, Pārvatī told him to amuse himself as he
23ea pleased. Skanda made love to the wives of the gods, and the gods could not
prevent it. They complained to Pārvatī, and she took the form of whatever
33ea[2] woman Skanda was about to seduce. Skanda summoned the wife of Indra,
27e and then the wife of Varuṇa, but when he looked at each one he saw his
27a mother's form, and so he would let her go and summon another. She too
became the image of his mother, and then Skanda was ashamed and thought,
'The universe is filled with my mother', and he became passionless. When
he found out that his mother had thus tricked him in order to turn him from
his worldly ways and to make a laughing-stock of him, he was full of shame,
but he realized that he must treat all women as he would treat his mother.[124]

Here the motif of impersonation is used to prevent sexual encounters, rather than to promote them, dramatizing the common Hindu saying that a righteous man treats every woman like a mother, a point which is also illustrated by the tale of Andhaka.

One late Vaiṣṇava text, which tells the story of Śiva and Pārvatī only
as an embellishment of the myth of Rāma and Sītā, describes an episode
33ea[2] in which Satī masquerades as Sītā in order to test the greatness of
Rāma; Rāma immediately penetrates her disguise, but Satī lies to Śiva
36a to conceal her failure, and Śiva is forced to abandon her to teach her
a lesson.[125] Śiva himself is enlightened by a similar impersonation:

33ea[7] Śiva was beaten at dice by Pārvatī, and they quarrelled. Śiva then went
36a naked and alone into the woods. When he was gone, Pārvatī was tortured by
28ea longing and thought only of Śiva. Her friend said, 'You won Śiva by perform-
1 ing great *tapas*, but you cheated at dice with him. You must ask him to
25ea[2] forgive you.' Then Pārvatī took the form of a voluptuously beautiful mountain
36ea woman, and when Śiva saw her he tried to grab her by the hand, for he arose
33ea[3] from his meditation and was full of desire, but she vanished. Then he wan-
22ea dered about in delusion, full of lust and longing, and he saw the mountain
43ea woman and asked her who she was. She said, 'I seek a husband who knows
36ea everything, is independent, and is free from emotions.' Śiva said, 'I am the
24ea[2] husband that you seek', but she smiled and said, 'You are quite different from
the man I seek. You have abandoned in the forest the woman who won you
36a with her *tapas*.' Śiva said, 'I never abandoned her', but she said, 'You are rich
in *tapas*, great lord of yogis, without passion, and you burnt Kāma. You are
43a too great for me to win.' Then Śiva, the killer of Kāma, said, 'Be my wife',
and he tried to take her by force, but she said, 'Release me. It is not proper
25e for you to take me by force through the power of your *tapas*. Ask my father

for me.' Śiva agreed, and she led him to her father, Himālaya, and Śiva asked 25a
Himālaya for her. Hearing this, Himālaya said, 'Why are you prattling like 23a
this? It does not befit the lord of the universe.' Then Nārada came and 24a
laughed, saying, 'Contact with women always makes men ridiculous', and
he enlightened Śiva. When Śiva realized how he had been tricked by his 36a
own wife he laughed and went away to perform terrible *tapas*, but Pārvatī 36ea
prostrated herself before him and Śiva returned with her.[126] 36e

The misogynist lesson which Śiva sometimes teaches Nārada by means of a masquerade is here pointed out to him by Nārada, though staged by his own wife. In an attempt to reconcile his yoga and his marital status, Śiva leaves his wife but is merely tricked by her into proposing all over again. The masquerade teaches him that women are a trap, but a trap in which he is inexorably caught, as the repeated, cyclic episodes of the myth demonstrate.

In another version of one of their quarrels, the masquerade is accidental and takes a more conventional form: instead of mistaking his wife for another woman, he mistakes another woman for his wife:

Pārvatī left Śiva to perform *tapas* in order to obtain a golden skin, and Śiva 25ea[1, 2]
was tortured by longing and sought her, but in vain. One day, deluded by 43ea
Kāma, Śiva saw the beautiful Sāvitrī, who resembled Pārvatī in all her 33ea[2]
qualities, and mistaking her for Pārvatī, he begged her to make love with him 24e
as an antidote to the attacks of Kāma. He tried to take her by force, and she,
a chaste woman, mocked him, saying, 'You fool, you should apologize to your 24a
wife, instead of trying to take another man's wife. Since you have tried to 23ea
seduce me, behaving like a human man, you will make love to a human 2
woman.' Then Śiva was ashamed, and he returned home, and because of this 20e 33ea[5]
curse he became incarnate as Candraśekhara, a human man, and he made
love to a human woman.[127]

Śiva seeks his wife and intends to disturb her *tapas*, just as she seeks and disturbs him when she takes the form of a mountain woman. Deluded and cursed, victimized by Kāma, Śiva sees Pārvatī here where there is no masquerade, while in the story of Āḍi (which takes place in the same situation, where Pārvatī goes away to perform *tapas* for a golden skin), Śiva remains in control and recognizes the true nature of 'Pārvatī' in spite of the disguise.

The motif of 'penetrating the disguise' is basic to Hindu thinking, for the universe itself is merely an illusion wrought by god. Our failure to perceive the true nature of the world is often expressed by the metaphor of a man who sees a rope and thinks that it is a snake. We must be taught to see properly; just as Skanda learned to see his mother in all women, and the sages at last recognized Śiva, so the worshipper must learn to see Śiva in all men and Pārvatī in all women. This moral is revealed by a myth of complex impersonations which begins with one of the episodes related above: as a result of Sāvitrī's curse, Śiva was born on earth as Candraśekhara and enlightened two mortals by means of a sexual encounter with the god in disguise:

19e 25ea[3] A king propitiated Śiva, who gave him a fruit which was divided into three
16c 16cd parts, one to be given to each of the king's wives. They ate the fruit and,
22e when the king had made love to each wife at the proper season, all three
20ea brought forth a third of a child, and the three portions united and became
a son known as Tryambaka ['Possessing Three Mothers', an epithet of Śiva],
or Candraśekhara ['Possessing the Moon as his Diadem', another epithet of
18a Śiva]. When Candraśekhara grew up, the old king went to the forest to per-
23e[1] form *tapas*, and Candraśekhara married Tārāvatī, an incarnation of Pārvatī.

36e One day when Tārāvatī was bathing in the river, she was seen by a sage
17c 21ea named Kāpota, who was overcome by lust for her. He said, 'You must be
24ea[1] a goddess or a demon woman who has become mortal in order to enjoy the
33ea[5] pleasures of the flesh. You must be Pārvatī or Śaci.' She said, 'I am not
a goddess but merely a mortal queen, Tārāvatī, wife of king Candraśekhara.'
14cd Kāpota said, 'I fell into the ocean of desire the moment that I saw you. Save
24e me with the boat of your thighs. You will have two strong and handsome sons
19e by me.' Tārāvatī was very unhappy, and she said, 'You should not speak to
25e me like that. This is improper for you, for such an act would destroy your
tapas.' Kāpota said, 'Whether or not the destruction of my *tapas* or some other
43ea evil may befall me, I must make love to you. You must save me from Kāma
8d or he will burn me, and then I will burn you with a curse.' Tārāvatī was
afraid of the sage's curse, but she devised a trick. She sent her younger sister
33ea[2] Citrāṅgadā, dressed in the ornaments of Tārāvatī, to Kāpota. The sage was
23ea 25a deluded with lust and made love to her, resolving, 'Afterwards, by my powers
20ea of *tapas*, I will release her from the sin of adultery.' Immediately she gave
birth to a pair of sons, whom Kāpota raised while she stayed with him, and
Tārāvatī returned to the palace.

17c Some time later, when Tārāvatī came again to bathe in the river, Kāpota
discovered the deception, and, furious, cursed Tārāvatī, saying, 'Since you
3 humiliated me, thinking yourself so virtuous and inviolate, thinking yourself
36e too good to desire me, therefore Śiva will make love to you by force, coming
24ea[1] 29ea 28a to you wearing terrifying garments, bearing a skull, deformed, poor, and you
33ea[4] 38a[2] will immediately bear him a pair of monkey-faced sons.' Tārāvatī said, 'I swear
by my true vows to Candraśekhara that I will never allow any man but him
to make love to me, even in a dream. I swear this by the vows that my father
made to Pārvatī when he obtained me for his daughter.' Kāpota then meditated and learned the true nature of Tārāvatī and Candraśekhara, and he took
Citrāṅgadā home with him and honoured her.

23e[2] Tārāvatī told Candraśekhara what had happened, and he made a high
terrace on the top of the palace in order to protect her, an impenetrable place
where he always made love to her. After a year, as Tārāvatī was standing upon
the terrace one day thinking of the king, she worshipped Śiva and Pārvatī,

and as she thought of Candraśekhara and Śiva she did not distinguish between the two of them. Then Śiva came with Pārvatī, to whom he said, 'Tārāvatī is your human incarnation. As I wish to make love to no woman but you, enter 33ea[5]
into her form now so that I may beget the two sons in you.' Pārvātī did so, 19e
and Śiva then approached Tārāvatī to make love to her, in the form of a 33ea[5]
Kāpālika wearing a garland of bones and disgusting clothing, with a deformed 38a[2]
and evil-smelling body. But Tārāvatī, having been entered by Pārvatī, 28a
received him with great joy and afterwards gave birth immediately to two 36e
sons with monkey faces. Then Pārvatī left the body of Tārāvatī and deluded 20ea 33ea[4]
her so that she did not recognize herself [as an incarnation of Pārvatī]. When
Tārāvatī saw the two sons she thought that she had violated her vow of faith- 19a
fulness to her husband, and as she saw Śiva standing before her in his loath- 33ea[6]
some clothing she realized that the sage's curse had come true. Śiva said to 28a
her, 'Your vow to Kāpota—never to desire any man but Candraśekhara—is still true, for I am Śiva, and I am Candraśekhara. Do not grieve.' But when Śiva vanished, Tārāvatī was again overcome by delusion, and she wept in grief and anger.

When Candraśekhara arrived and heard Tārāvatī's tale, he thought, 'How can this be? Śiva loves no woman but Pārvatī, and therefore he would not
make love to anyone else. The sage's curse is so powerful that some demon 33ea[2]
must have come here magically disguised as Śiva and defiled my dear wife, 33ea[6]
begetting these demon sons in her. Why else would they have monkey faces?' 33ea[4]
But Sarasvatī came to him and assured him that it was Śiva himself who had 19a
begotten the sons in Tārāvatī, and Candraśekhara took the sons and raised them. Then Nārada came to him and explained how Śiva was born as Candraśekhara and Pārvatī as Tārāvatī because of Sāvitrī's curse, and the king realized that he was Śiva incarnate. Nārada said, 'Take Tārāvatī upon your
lap and close your eyes and let her close her eyes, and when you open them 7cd[2]
you will see your divine nature.' They did so, and they saw that Tārāvatī had the form of Pārvatī and Candraśekhara the form of Śiva, wearing a tiger
skin, riding on a bull, with matted locks. When they knew who they were, 45e[2]
and had arrived at perfect understanding, Nārada said, 'Now you must close your eyes and return to mortal understanding until you give up your bodies.' Then they closed and opened their eyes and they thought, 'We are mortals.'

As time went by, Candraśekhara favoured his three other natural sons over 19a
the two boys engendered by Śiva, for he feared that the twins would harm
his sons. Śiva's sons went away and performed *tapas*, and then they married 19e 19ea
and begat sons, and Śiva came to them and gave them the elixir of immortality 18e
to drink, and they became immortals, leaders of Śiva's hosts, Vetāla and 14c[2]
Bhairava.[128]

Śiva's incarnation is born, as Skanda is, from the joining of several
portions of seed in several different mothers. The monkey faces[129] and 33ea[4]
the mortal incarnations[130] are curses related to a punishment for sexual 20e
crimes. But mortal incarnation is at the same time a reward for sexuality, as well as a punishment, for Kāpota suggests that Tārāvatī is the wife of Śiva or Indra, who has become a mortal in order to enjoy the pleasures

of the flesh. This concept underlies the statement in one Purāṇa that all the goddesses, having seen Kṛṣṇa's love-play with the cowherd girls, were inflamed with the fire of Kāma and immediately made themselves
33ea[5] born as little girls in all the houses of the kings of India.[131]

20e The impersonations in the myth of Candraśekhara function on two levels, one a multiform of the other. The episode in which Citrāṅgadā impersonates Tārāvatī is an old Indo-European motif, but in this myth it is simply an appendage, introducing the pertinent but superfluous motif of the lustful ascetic. Kāpota's attempted rape of Tārāvatī is merely a multiform of Śiva's successful rape of her (the direct result of Kāpota's curse). This then is the first impersonation: Citrāṅgadā explicitly impersonates Tārāvatī and Śiva implicitly appears as Kāpota, begetting twins upon Citrāṅgadā as he begets them upon Tārāvatī.

The higher level of impersonation is that of Śiva and Pārvatī in Candraśekhara and Tārāvatī, and this in turn functions on two planes: the specific impersonation necessitated by the curse, and the implicit metaphysical incarnation based on the belief that all men and women are forms of Śiva and Pārvatī. The series of sexual adventures used to demonstrate this moral is particularly appropriate in the context of a religion where sexual union is a frequent metaphor for union with god. The Kāpālika in a Sanskrit play says, 'He who resembles the god who
36e has the moon as his diadem, and who with delight embraces women as
20a beautiful as Pārvatī—he sports, having obtained Release.'[132] The parallel is complete even to the particular epithet of Śiva, wearing the moon on his head, Candraśekhara. Similarly, in certain Tantric sects, ritual intercourse was performed with a female devotee who was considered to represent Devī.[133] Another example may be taken from the
32ea Tamil Śaiva tradition: a saint imagined himself and other devotees to be women, with Śiva as their lover.[134]

The sexual nature of man is used as a specific argument that Śiva is the supreme god:

> Since human children bear neither the mark of the lotus [the emblem of
> 5cd Brahmā] nor the sign of the discus [Viṣṇu's], nor of the thunderbolt [Indra's],
> 17cd but are marked with the male and female organs [i.e. the *liṅga* and *yoni*], therefore Śiva is the author of all men, and Devī of all women.[135]

The mortal who recognizes his sexual nature sees his divine identity with Śiva. This is what Tārāvatī must learn, though she at first denies it. When Kāpota suggests that she may be Pārvatī incarnate, she refuses to accept it—whereupon he attempts to rape her. She then makes a vow to protect herself from the rape predicted in Kāpota's curse, but her

ignorance of the identity of Śiva (Candraśekhara) and her husband
(Candraśekhara) causes her to word her vow in such a way that it fails
to protect her from the curse, even though she reveals in that vow the
clue that should teach her her own identity: the fact that she was born
when her father propitiated Pārvatī. When Śiva makes love to her, she
learns who she is, only to forget again when she returns to the mortal
world and is left holding two monkey-faced sons to explain to her husband. He, too, fails at first to believe that it was Śiva, suspecting instead
a demon disguised as Śiva (i.e. a third level of impersonation), and he is
only persuaded when Nārada tells him the story of Śiva and Sāvitrī, yet
another case of mistaken identities to illuminate his own. Finally, Nārada
enlightens them by means of a purely mortal sexual encounter, when
Candraśekhara takes Tārāvatī upon his lap and they close their eyes,
but the vision is a momentary one and cannot be sustained. Conventional life obscures it, and though Candraśekhara knows that the boys
are the sons of Śiva and at first treats them well, in time the human ties
of his natural sons supersede the dim mystical vision, and Candraśekhara
rejects the sons of his god. In the same way, Pārvatī herself sometimes
places conventional considerations above her love for Śiva, and Kṛṣṇa's
mother, once having glimpsed the whole universe, including herself,
within the mouth of her baby son, is unable to bear the vision, and
Kṛṣṇa, out of pity for her, allows her to forget that he is anything more 33ea^{5}
than a mortal child.[136] When Candraśekhara and Tārāvatī have played
their part in Sāvitrī's curse, there is no further need for them to have
pure understanding; in fact, it is as a favour to them that the vision is
withdrawn, for it would make normal life intolerable.[137] Yet they retain 7d
a part of the vision: after they have opened their eyes and consider themselves mortal, they still know that the sons are the sons of Śiva, and the
king makes love to his queen, thinking, 'I am a portion of Śiva, and
Tārāvatī is a portion of Pārvatī.'[138] This much of the truth is tolerable 33ea^{5}
and accessible to all mortals, revealed to them particularly at the moment
of sexual experiences, without the need for the actual encounter with
Śiva himself which is enacted in the myth.

VII

SIVA AS ASCETIC AND HOUSEHOLDER

A. ŚIVA'S FAILURE TO RECONCILE HIS TWO ROLES

ŚIVA shares with the Pine Forest sages the classical problems of married ascetics, but he has a wider scope and greater powers with which to resolve them. The initial attempt at resolution may at first result not in a successful embodiment of both aspects but rather in the achievement of neither one. Menā, the mother of Pārvatī, scorns Śiva because he is penniless and makes love to Pārvatī constantly[1]—that is, she sees him as a bad husband (poor) and a bad yogi (lascivious), rather than as a good husband (virile) and a good yogi (indifferent to material objects). Similarly, Dakṣa views Śiva as neither one thing nor the other:

> 24a He is not primarily an ascetic, for how can an ascetic bear weapons as he
> 23a does? And he cannot be counted among the householders, for he lives in
> 24ea[1] a burning-ground. He is not a *brahmacārin*, since he has married, and how
> 23e 6d could he be a forest-dweller, since he is deluded with pride in his supreme
> 19ea lordship [and a forest-dweller must give up all material ties]? He belongs to
> 32e none of the four classes, and is neither male nor female [because he is an
> 5c[2] 32a androgyne]. And he certainly cannot be a eunuch, for his *liṅga* is an object
> of worship.[2]

A similar objection to Śiva's unique behaviour in the Pine Forest is the basis of the sages' curse: 'This is not the kind of behaviour proper for householders like us, nor is it the manner of those who are fond of chastity, nor of those who dwell in the forest. It is not the dharma of ascetics, either. It is not done anywhere.'[3] The problem underlies the statement made by the Seven Sages to test Pārvatī: there are two kinds
18ea of pleasures in the world, mental and physical; Śiva, being a disgusting
beggar, is of no use for pleasures of the body, and, being inauspicious because of his necrophilic associations, he cannot even satisfy the longings of the mind.[4]

It is frequently said against Śiva in the myths that he is a bad, or even a false, ascetic because of his involvement with Pārvatī. A certain
24a demigod was cursed to be reborn as a demon because he mocked Śiva,
24ea[1] casting aspersions on his virility, saying, 'This is the guru of the world,
44ea the teacher of dharma, making love to his wife in the midst of an

assembly. He wears matted locks and does fierce *tapas*, but he takes
a woman on his lap shamelessly like a natural man. Even common men
enjoy their wives in privacy, but this great ascetic does it in public.'[5]
This sexual involvement makes Śiva vulnerable to his enemies and 25e
reduces his ascetic powers.

The combination of roles works against him in the opposite way as
well: a number of texts point out that, being an ascetic, Śiva is a somewhat unsatisfactory husband.[6] When he first describes the conditions 36a
under which he will marry, the ascetic Śiva demands that his wife be
a *yoginī* when he performs yoga and a lustful mistress (*kāminī*) when he 27ea
is sexually inclined. But then he adds: 'If she impedes me when I am
meditating, I will kill her, and if she has no confidence in what I say, 36a
I will abandon her.'[7] Pārvatī does in fact interrupt his meditations
frequently, as well as argue with him and even mock him, and although
he does not kill her he does occasionally abandon her. He himself makes
ironic reference to this situation when he comes to Pārvatī in disguise
and says, 'Why do you do *tapas*? Are you a *tapasvinī*, the companion of 27ea
some ascetic who does not support you and who has gone away?'[8] This 36a
is not the reason for her *tapas* at that time, but it is an accurate description of her condition during their future married life. When Pārvatī
leaves him after one of their frequent quarrels and then meets him in
the forest, she says to him, 'You have abandoned the woman who won 36a
you with her *tapas*. You are rich in *tapas*, lord of yogis, without passion, 43a
and you burnt Kāma. You are too great for me to win.'[9]

In addition to his many diatribes against Kāma and women in
general, Śiva offers explicit arguments against the possibility of his
marriage: 'I am the greatest of the eleven Rudras, the lord of yoga. How
can I take a beautiful wife, a woman who is the very form of Illusion? 36a
Any yogi ought to regard every woman as if she were his mother. I am 27a
a yogi: how can I marry a woman, my mother?'[10] The classical prob- 27e
lems of the married yogi are sometimes complicated rather than simpli-
fied by Śiva's immortality:

> Pārvatī wished to have a natural son, but Śiva said, 'I am not a householder, 19e
> and I have no use for a son. The wicked gods presented me with a wife, but 19a
> a wife is the most useless thing for a man who is without passion. Offspring 36e 36a
> are a noose and I will have none. Householders have need of a son and wealth: 18e
> for them, a wife is necessary for the sake of a son, and sons are necessary to 19e
> give the oblations to the ancestors. But I never die, and so I have no need for 18a
> a son. When there is no disease, what use is medicine?' Still Pārvatī insisted, 19a
> 'What you say is true, but nevertheless I wish to have a child. When you have 19e
> begotten a child, you can return to your yoga. I will take care of the son and 19a

you can be a yogi as you wish. I have a great desire for the kiss of a son's
22e mouth, and since you have made me your wife you should beget a child in
me. If you wish, your son will be averse to marriage, so that you will not
20a establish a whole lineage.' Still Śiva was angry, and he said, 'I will give you
20ea a son you can kiss if you wish', and so saying he pulled at her red sari and
said, 'Now make a son out of that and kiss it.' She said, 'Do not tease me. How can I enjoy a son who is a piece of cloth?' But she took the cloth and played with it as if it were a child, swinging it and talking to it, saying, 'Live, live', and it came to life. She gave it her breast to suck and she kissed the baby, and he smiled at her.[11]

Śiva here avoids a son for the very reason that mortals usually need one: for the sake of immortality through progeny. The conflict cannot be resolved in cycles, as Pārvatī attempts to do in suggesting that the son will be chaste to make up for the sexual lapse of the father, because this involves the very chain of rebirth from which Śiva, as the epitome of the yogi, has divorced himself and of which he, as a god, has no need. Nor can it be solved simply by the shorter phases of sex and yoga which alternate in the life of Śiva (as she suggests, after begetting the child he may return to his yoga, as he does after the birth of Skanda), for, as a mythological and symbolic figure, Śiva is simultaneously yogi and husband. The depth of the conflict is indicated by the tender desperation with which Pārvatī seeks a child and the grim determination with which Śiva opposes one. In this particular instance, the solution is the creation of Gaṇeśa, an unnatural child for Pārvatī, as the mortal solution was often the birth of an illegitimate child from the unnaturally shed
seed of the yogi. The problem endures in tribal mythology: when Pār-
19a vatī becomes pregnant, Mahadeo tricks her and kills all her children.[12]

In the many speeches which Śiva (in disguise) makes to dissuade Pārvatī from her *tapas*, he points out his flaws as a husband:

A husband who makes women happy is always fond of sexual pleasures,
but Śiva has no such qualities. Kāma is contrary, it is true, but how can Śiva
28ea be a suitable husband? He is naked, covered with snakes, and he lives in the
30a burning-grounds. The virtues which are usually sought in a bridegroom—
6d family, good nature, etc.—are all absent in him. People will laugh at you when
45e[2] you ride on his bull, and how will you bear to touch the ashes on his body?
6cd Śiva has not a single one of the qualities that suitors ought to have to give
43a happiness to women. Kāma is dear to you, and Kāma was burnt by Śiva, who,
36a showing disrespect for you, abandoned you and went away. He is always
34a alone and without passion, and therefore you should not desire him.[13]

In a similar genre are the speeches of the Seven Sages sent to test Pārvatī on behalf of Śiva (though their traditional opposition to him, in their role of Pine Forest sages, puts a possibility of direct criticism into their words as well):

> He for whom you do this *tapas* is the passionless yogi who killed Kāma. 43a
> He has no shame, wears filthy clothes, or goes naked. What happiness would 25ea^2 34a
> you have with such a husband? When he married Satī, he did not support 28ea 28a
> her, and then he insulted and abandoned her. What use is he to a woman?... 36a
> Śiva only married Satī to satisfy public opinion, and then he deserted her and
> brought about her death.[14]

An obvious occasion for such condemnations is provided by the
speeches of the demons who hope to take Pārvatī away from Śiva. It is
in their best interests to point out his inadequacies as a husband, and
they do so. One demon says that Śiva's *tapas* has made him impotent, 32a
while the demon himself, on the other hand, is tortured with desire for
her and would make her give up her *tapas* in a minute; another demon
says to Śiva, 'It is not proper for you to have this firm-breasted woman. 24ea^1
Give her to me. Why do you do *tapas* with a woman, you fool? You have
no use for her, for you are better suited for *tapas* and fasting.'[15] Almost
as if to justify these accusations, Śiva does agree to give up his wife,[16]
and the demons' speeches, though prompted by self-interest, are never- 36a
theless supported by the conventional view of the incompatibility of
asceticism and married life.

A similar encounter takes place with Jalandhara, whose desire is excited by Nārada's reply to Jalandhara's request for a description of Śiva's possessions:

> Śiva has some ashes, a begging-bowl, an old bull, lots of serpents, and two 6cd
> sons—one with the head of an elephant and the other with six heads.... Oh, 45e^2 38a^2
> and he has a high-breasted wife, so beautiful that he desires her constantly, 20ea 30a
> though he burnt Kāma.[17] 36e 36ea 43a

Jalandhara takes the bait and sends several messages to Śiva:

> How can you live on alms and yet keep the beautiful Pārvatī? Give her to 24ea^1
> me, and wander from house to house with your alms-bowl. You have broken 38a^2
> your vow.... You are a yogi. What need have you for a wife? You live in the
> woods, attended by goblins and ghosts, and as you are a naked yogi you should 28ea
> give your wife to one who will appreciate her better than you do.[18]

B. ŚIVA'S TROUBLE WITH HIS PARENTS-IN-LAW

The outlook of the demons is unfortunately shared by the parents of Śiva's prospective brides. They behave like in-laws the world over, and worry about his ability to support their daughter (a princess) in the manner to which she is accustomed. Śiva asks Himālaya for Pārvatī in

these words: 'I have no mother or father, nor any relatives or friends.
23a Without possessions I dwell on the peaks of mountains, but I want your
daughter, O King of Mountains.'[19] Śiva's earlier father-in-law, Dakṣa,
24a voices strenuous objections on these very grounds. He complains, 'Śiva
16cd 23a lives on alms. How will he be able to offer food to Satī? I gave my
6d daughter to Śiva against my will, for he wanders in the horrible burning-
28ea 38a² grounds like a madman, naked, his hair disarranged, laughing, weeping,
garlanded with bones. I gave her to that madman because Brahmā urged
me to do it, but I did not like it.'[20] The element of social conformity in
Dakṣa's outlook is evident from another of his complaints:

31e 31a Śiva always wanders about dancing and singing and doing other despicable
24a things. This makes me ashamed, and besides he does not even have a proper
23a house. Because of this, and being embarrassed before society, I have not
23e² invited him to my sacrifice, but afterwards I will bring him here and honour
him privately.[21]

Dakṣa's more particular hatred of Śiva is based on the older conflict in which Śiva the ascetic opposes Dakṣa the incestuous creator, and there are overtones of this conflict in the personal enmity as well:

36a [When Satī returned to Dakṣa and complained about Śiva, Dakṣa said,]
23a 'My poor child', and stroked her hair, perhaps too much. He had been lonely;
39e he had missed her; and besides, he did not care for Śiva so very much. . . .
38a² 'He carries a skull for a begging bowl', said Daksha, as additional information,
'and it is empty. But that he should corrupt my daughter too fills me with
grief.'[22]

A final bone of contention between Śiva and Dakṣa is provided by the ancient social tradition of the law books, which prefer a virile bridegroom to an ascetic.[23]

These same objections are responsible for the less virulent strife
between Śiva and Himālaya, which begins when Nārada predicts as the
24a husband of Pārvatī one who is still unborn, who will have his hand out
23e² 23a always, a naked yogi, poor and homeless. Seeing the alarm of Pārvatī's
28ea parents, Nārada then explains that they have misunderstood him, that
the husband is Śiva himself and that he will have his hand out not to
beg (as they imagined), but rather to offer boons. This satisfies them
all for the time being.[24] Although in several of the later versions Himālaya is said to rejoice in the prospect of Śiva for a son-in-law,[25] his basic
43a antipathy to Śiva emerges clearly in the early texts. He says to the Seven
34a Sages, 'Śiva killed Kāma and is the best of ascetics, without passion.
23a How can he be a worthy husband, he who made Kāma disembodied?
24a One must not give one's daughter to anyone very rich or very poor,

a fool or an idiot or a madman, nor to one who is free from passion or sick. Therefore I am uncertain whether or not I should give her to Śiva.'[26] The conventional rules override even the spirit of worship. To give Pārvatī to Śiva of course violates the rule against giving a daughter in marriage to one who is passionless or an ascetic, and Śiva may also come under the rubric of 'very poor' or even an idiot or a madman, as he is often described as mad. Sometimes Himālaya cites other
Hindu law books which state that a eunuch, a man without a livelihood, 32a
one who is deformed, or a madman, may not be the bridegroom, and Menā describes the perfect son-in-law—of good family, high birth, the right age, handsome, wealthy, and powerful—and then remarks, 'How
can my daughter go to a man who is horrible because of his great 23a
tapas?'[27]

A Sanskrit play describes at great length the deceitful measures that the gods find it necessary to employ in order to be sure that Himālaya will allow his daughter to marry Śiva. A servant of Indra, disguised as
a Śaiva sage, tells Himālaya that an ascetic died by falling into one of 33ea^{5}
Himālaya's snowdrifts, thus casting the sin of brahminicide on to
Himālaya. Because of this, he says, Himālaya will lose his kingdom and 23a
all his wealth. When Himālaya cries out in agitation, 'Oh no!' the sage 8d
assures him that if he can get Śiva to marry his daughter his sins will
be cured. Himālaya despairs of doing this, since Śiva is without passion, 34a
and he contrasts the attributes of Śiva and Pārvatī: she lives in a palace, 23e^{2} 6d
he in the burning-grounds; she is covered with sandalwood paste, he 6cd 28e 30a
with ashes; she wears pearls and silks and carries a lotus, while he wears 28a
snakes and bloody elephant skins and carries a skull; she has lotus eyes 26e^{2} 38a^{2} 43e 7cd
and is ever intent upon the lord of Rati, while he gazes at the tip of his 43a
nose and is intent upon *tapas*.[28] In order to maintain his kingdom, however, Himālaya arranges the match, just as other kings offer their daughters to appease irate ascetics.

Himālaya's wealth is used to prevent, or rather to delay, the match in a Purāṇa which offers an elaborate rationalization for Himālaya's embarrassing lack of devotion to Śiva:

When Indra and the gods learned of the great devotion to Śiva which filled 45a
Menā and Himālaya, they were afraid that Himālaya might obtain Release 7d
and leave the earth, taking with him all the jewels of the earth [which are 20a 28e
believed to originate in the caves of Himālaya]. So they asked Śiva to malign 24a
himself before Himālaya, for Śiva alone could censure himself and still avoid the destruction which would come upon anyone else who reviled him. (Moreover, as they remarked, 'Rebuking others is conducive to destruction, but rebuking oneself is conducive to fame.') Śiva took the form of a Vaiṣṇava

33ea[5] Brahmin and repeated before Himālaya and Menā the list of horrible qualities
24a of Śiva that he had detailed to Pārvatī. When he had gone, Menā refused to
23a let her daughter marry Śiva. Śiva then summoned the Seven Sages and sent
them to enlighten her and Himālaya, and to persuade them to give Pārvatī to him.[29]

The cause of this blasphemy is not unprecedented in Hindu mythology (for heresies are taught to keep people out of heaven when it is overcrowded),[30] but it does seem superfluous here, the more so as it merely necessitates yet another episode in which Himālaya and Menā are taught to give their daughter to Śiva after all. The motif of Himālaya's wealth, which represents all the conventional values that are rejected by Śiva's way of life, appears in yet another multiform of this incident:

21ea Both Rudra and the sage Bhṛgu desired Pārvatī, but Himālaya said, 'Rudra
3 is the bridegroom that I want.' In anger, Bhṛgu cursed Himālaya to be with-
28e out precious jewels.[31]

Here Bhṛgu rather than Śiva is the sage who curses the king for failing to give him the princess, and Himālaya favours Śiva.

23a Himālaya's wife, Menā, is more difficult to win over. She vows that
9d she will take poison or drown herself before she will give her daughter
to Śiva.[32] She is closely tied to the conventional anti-ascetic view, for when Nārada praises Śiva she, 'being a woman, takes no heed of the words', and she herself says to Himālaya, 'Being a woman, I have taken no heed of Nārada's words. Marry our daughter to some handsome suitor. Let her find a *good* husband.'[33] Menā never learns to accept Śiva on his ascetic level, but in order to please her Śiva transforms himself into a god that she can understand on a conventional level. Śiva first antagonizes her with his erotic form and then charms her with his ascetic form; then he reverses the process and antagonizes her with his ascetic form, only to appear in his conventional erotic form to win her approval for the last time:

31e Once when Himālaya had gone to bathe in the Ganges, Śiva took the form
33ea[5] of a graceful dancer and danced before Menā. On hearing his beautiful song,
6cd Pārvatī fainted, and in her heart she saw Śiva smeared with ashes, garlanded
7cd[1] 38a[2] with bones, three-eyed, covered with snakes. She chose him for her husband
24ea[2] 30a and the vision passed. Then Menā, who saw only the graceful dancer, was
25ea[2] enchanted by him and offered him jewels, but he did not accept them. He
28e asked only for Pārvatī as alms, and then he began to sing and dance again.
24a Menā was angry and abused him and tried to throw him out, and Himālaya,
23a 8d on his return, tried also, but no one could touch the beggar, who blazed like
5c[3] a great fire. He displayed his various forms, appearing as Viṣṇu and the sun,
36e and as Śiva with Pārvatī, and finally as formless *tejas* itself, marvellous and

ineffable. He then resumed the form of a beggar, asking for Pārvatī as alms. 7d
When Himālaya refused this request, the beggar vanished and Himālaya 33ea[5]
realized that it had been Śiva, and a great devotion to Śiva was born in 25ea[2] 23a
Himālaya and Menā.[34]

This episode bears a resemblance in many details to the myth of the Pine Forest: Śiva waits until the husband is absent performing a ritual, begs and dances before the wife, enchanting her and angering her husband, manifests his form of pure *tejas* when he is punished, and is at last worshipped. His Dionysian aspect appeals to Menā when she fails to be won by any metaphysical argument.

Menā's attitudes toward the two aspects of Śiva are played upon in a multiform of Śiva's apparent self-revilement. This time, he does not describe his ascetic attributes but actually demonstrates them, and here again he must in the end revert to his erotic form to win back Menā's devotion:

Menā was anxious to see the form of Śiva, and she stood at the door of the
palace with Nārada, waiting for Śiva to arrive at the wedding. As each god 23e[2]
arrived she asked Nārada, 'Is this Śiva?' and Nārada would reply, 'This is
only one of his servants. Śiva is far more glorious than this', and Menā's
pride in her good fortune swelled. Knowing of her egotism, Śiva decided to
reveal himself in such a way as to break her heart and remove her pride. He
arrived surrounded by ghosts and goblins, riding on a bull, three-eyed, 45e[2]
smeared with ashes, carrying a skull, wearing an elephant skin. Menā was 7cd[1]
terrified, and just then Nārada said to her, 'This is Śiva himself, for whose 6cd 38a[2] 25ea[2]
sake Pārvatī did her lonely *tapas*.' Menā fell to the ground like a vine struck 36ea[1]
down by the wind, crying, 'I have been deceived!' When she regained consciousness, she reviled Pārvatī, threatened to kill herself and her daughter, 23a
and refused to let the marriage take place. Though Nārada said to Menā, 'It 33ea[7]
was in sport that Śiva took this improper form instead of the beautiful, 28e 28a
proper form', and Himālaya assured her, 'Śiva bears many forms. The
monstrous form that you saw was just a game of his', she was resolute: 'How 33ea[7]
can I give my daughter to such a terrible husband, deformed and naked? 28ea
What kind of a husband is he? He has no parents or caste, no good looks, 23e[2]
cleverness, clothes, house, ornaments, servants, no elegant mount, no youth
or wealth or knowledge. He would make a laughing-stock of me and the whole
family. If Śiva has a handsome form, I will give my daughter to him, but not
otherwise.' Hearing this, Śiva assumed a marvellous form, magnificent in all
his limbs, gorgeously adorned, smiling sweetly and attended by all the gods. 28e
Thus he came to Himālaya's door, and Menā stared at him and said, 'How
fortunate my daughter is to have brought the great Śiva to my house with her 25ea[2]
tapas. Forgive me, Śiva, for having reviled you just now', and she fell before 36ea[1]
him and praised him.[35]

In this episode, Śiva assumes a form that is 'improper' for Menā—the ascetic form—in order to teach her a lesson. It is not an improper form

in the eyes of those who know Śiva truly, but it is inappropriate for his mother-in-law, who represents conventional religion, and he retracts it after he has made his point. As the supreme god, assuming all forms, he may appear to each worshipper as he is desired to appear, just as in other contexts he purposely assumes the most antagonistic and con-
7cd[1] trary form. In a late version of the wedding transformation, Śiva appears
28a at first three-eyed and garlanded with human heads, a form which
38a[2] terrifies the children of the city and causes the horses to shy, but the
parents, who understand Śiva, reassure their children. The women, and
23a particularly Menā, are repulsed and frightened, and Menā refuses to
consent to the marriage until Nārada enlightens her, this time not with an actual transformation of Śiva but merely with an explanation of his greatness.[36]

The transformation of Śiva for the sake of his in-laws is joined with the closely related motif of the rejuvenation of the ascetic (who usually antagonizes his father-in-law because of his senility) in this South Indian myth:

[A Brahmin had a daughter named Gaurī who was devoted to Śiva. Her
23a parents gave her in marriage to a Vaiṣṇava, but her in-laws treated her very
badly when they saw the Śaiva signs on her. One day they all went to a
33ea[5] wedding and left her behind. Śiva took the form of an old Śaiva devotee and
16cd came to her. She fed him, and suddenly he changed into a handsome young
18a 28e 28a man. His rosaries turned into jewels and the ashes on his body into sandal-
6cd wood. Just then the in-laws returned home, and in order to save her from
19e embarrassment Śiva turned into a baby, with ashes on his forehead. The
19a mother-in-law chased Gaurī out of the house, accusing her of having an
23a affection for Śiva who dances, adorned with bones, in the burning-grounds.
31a 38a[2] Gaurī took the child in her arms and thought of Śiva, and the child dis-
45e[2] 6d appeared and Śiva came through the air mounted on his bull. Gaurī assumed
36e the form of Pārvatī and Śiva carried her away.][37]

The rejuvenation is here carried one step further than usual, through youth to infancy, and then further still—to immortality. Gaurī here attracts several motifs usually applied to Śiva: she is reviled by her in-laws and given no invitation to the wedding/sacrifice. Yet even here it is still the ascetic aspect of Śiva which antagonizes the mother-in-law, while his conventional form of beauty (jewels and sandalwood instead of rosaries and ashes) transforms him into the perfect bridegroom.

C. THE HOUSE OF THE ASCETIC ŚIVA

The bourgeois quality of Menā's thought is revealed by her repeated complaints about Śiva's poverty, about the laughing-stock that he will

make of her family, and in particular about the importance of houses,
the symbol of married life (the 'householder' stage). When Pārvatī sets
out to perform *tapas* in the woods to win Śiva, Menā says, 'Do *tapas*
here in the house, if you must, but do not go out. There are gods here 23e[2]
in the house, and shrines and holy places. It is not the done thing for
a woman to go out of the house to perform *tapas*.'[38] Menā's insistence 24a
upon the necessity of a proper house leads Pārvatī to make this demand
of Śiva: 'Why, when you have so many lovely dwellings, do you live 23e[2]
in the burning-grounds, which are terrifying and horrid?'[39] In the Epic, 6d
this question receives a metaphysical answer, and Pārvatī is satisfied,
but in the Purāṇas she causes considerably more trouble for Śiva:

One day when Śiva and Pārvatī were together, Menā took Pārvatī aside and 23a
said, 'Your husband is so poor that he has no house, and he plays all the 23e[2]
time.' Pārvatī was sad, and she asked Śiva to take her somewhere else to live.
Śiva laughed and said, 'How can you be angry? I live in the burning-grounds, 6d
with no house but the forests and caves and mountains, where I wander naked 28ea
with my troops. Your mother spoke the truth.' Still she asked him to do what
would make her happy, and so Śiva left the mountain Himālaya and took her
to Meru to live.[40]

Śiva's position is unequivocal: he is a yogi and cannot have a house.
As he himself remarks in another context, 'What good is a house to a
man who lives on alms?'[41] The problem raised by Menā seems to be 23e[2]
solved in this episode merely by taking Pārvatī away from her mother's
influence, for there is no indication of a house being built on Meru. In
another Purāṇa, this is the explicit purpose of Menā's complaints: to get
Śiva and Pārvatī out of her house:

One day Menā said to Pārvatī, 'You did great *tapas* to win a husband with- 25ea[2]
out family or virtues or youth. You never leave him, day or night, and you 24a
live in my house, supported by your father's wealth. In all the universe, 23e[2] 23a
a married girl is adorned by her husband and goes forth to her husband's 28e
house.' Hearing her husband thus reviled, Pārvatī went angrily and silently 22a
back to Śiva and said a harsh speech prompted by love: 'It is not right for us
to live with my parents. Is there not some other place suitable for us to dwell
in?' Then Śiva took her to Benares, and she forgot her mother and father.[42]

In another version of the story, Śiva does attempt to supply a house,
but with ultimately unsatisfactory results:

Śiva married Pārvatī and lived in the presence of the gods. His attendants, 36e
rich in *tapas*, pleased Śiva and Pārvatī, but they did not please Menā, who 23a
said to Pārvatī, 'Your husband does not behave properly in my presence. He 24a
is entirely penniless, shameless, and makes love to you tirelessly.' Pārvatī, 24ea[1]
unable to listen to this, asked Śiva to take her to his own home. Śiva searched
the world and chose Benares as the most pleasant place to live, but Pārvatī 23e[2]

22a was not happy there because she was unsatisfied with the house. Śiva, how-
36a ever, laughed and refused to leave Benares, saying, 'I will never abandon this
house. You may go, but I like it here.'[43]

Benares is the holy city of Śaiva ascetics, and it is to this connotation that Pārvatī objects.

Another story based on the problem of Śiva's houselessness has a somewhat more satisfactory resolution:

5d One day Satī said to Śiva as they sat on Mount Mandara, 'The hot season
7d is almost here and I have no house to enter when the hot winds and sunlight
$5c^3$ become oppressive.' Śiva said, 'I am always without a house, for I wander in
30ea
$23e^2$ the forest.' And so they spent the hot season in the shade of the trees. Then
$26e^2$ came the season of monsoon, when no one went outside, and the sky was
covered with dark thunderclouds. She said to him, 'The winds are blowing
15c 14d and the clouds roar. Lightning flashes through the dark blue clouds and the
30e peacocks scream. This is a terrifying season, hard to live through. Make
$23e^2$ a house where I may be secure.' Śiva said, 'I have no wealth to accumulate
30a houses. I wear a tiger skin, and snakes are all my ornaments.' Then Satī was
frightened and angry and ashamed, and she said, 'How can I pass the rainy
season? Shall I stand at the foot of some tree?' Śiva said to her, 'We can stay
above the clouds, and then the rain will not fall on you.' Then Śiva mounted
a high cloud with her, and they passed the rainy season there. When it was
over, they returned to Mandara.[44]

Pārvatī learns here to value the special qualities of Śiva, his mastery of fire (summer) and water (monsoon), his ability to command the clouds or to fly above them, and she places these qualities above the conventional qualities which he lacks (the money to buy a house). But the problem is not usually so easily resolved:

$23e^2$ [Śiva married Satī and took her home to his house.] 'Does it have a roof?'
asked Satī, in a tone he had not heard her use before. 'It is the roof of the
world.' She did not find this explanation reassuring, and had the first of her
36a second thoughts about the Great Ascetic. . . . Śiva permitted himself a
superior smile. 'An ascetic has no home', he explained. 'Surely you knew
29ea that when you married me? I thought it was why you *had* married me. Out
of admiration, you know. An ascetic is content to storm the wilderness. It is
romantic.' Seeing the expression on her face, he consented to move under the
$26e^2$ 30a shade of an adjacent tree. . . . Śiva, who had stepped into the menhir dangling
a few pit vipers and other trophies, could not see why [a house] was needed.
The rainy season would pass. Since it was one of his days for desire, he took
36e her up above the clouds and stayed there with her until autumn, so she did
not get wet after all, so no complaining . . .[45]

When the metaphysical arguments fail to amuse or convince Satī, Śiva falls back upon his erotic aspect ('Since it was one of his days for desire . . .'), thus avoiding, though not really solving, the problem of the house.

D. PĀRVATĪ'S CONFLICT WITH THE UNCONVENTIONAL, ASCETIC ŚIVA

The attitudes of the mother are thus reflected in the daughter, and
although Pārvatī's relationship with Śiva is complex, there is in it an
element of the conventional anti-asceticism of Menā. In Bengali literature there is an entire genre of songs in which Menā bemoans her ill- 23a
fortune in having married her daughter to Śiva. She complains because 16d
her son-in-law is a beggar who drugs himself with marijuana and sells
Pārvatī's jewels to buy marijuana, because he haunts the foul burning- 6d
grounds, goes about naked, and fails to feed Pārvatī properly. Pārvatī 28ea 16cd
then reproaches her mother for giving her in marriage to a beggar.[46] 36a

Pārvatī usually reacts to Śiva as a woman rather than as a goddess,
and, like her human incarnation, Tārāvatī, she fails to accept fully the
implications of allowing the divine level to penetrate into conventional
life. As one modern Hindu scholar translates a remark made by the
Seven Sages to Pārvatī regarding Śiva, 'He is after salvation, O gentle
lady, how can a woman put up with him?' Pārvatī is capable of defend- 22a
ing Śiva on a metaphysical level against the criticisms of the Seven Sages
or Śiva himself in disguise, but nevertheless she wishes to have him
satisfy her conventional longings as well:

> Again and again she had begged him not to use that disgusting begging 38a^2
> bowl. It was just the sort of thing a man who refused to shave in the morning
> would refuse to give up. Appearances meant nothing to him. And as she had 22a
> feared, it had led to ostracism: it was not like everybody else's begging bowl.[47]

Even at the moment of her greatest triumph, when Śiva reveals himself to her and asks her to marry him, she shows concern for human conventions:

> When Pārvatī heard Śiva's proposal, she rejoiced, but then she said, 'By
> the moral convention, Śiva should ask my father for my hand in marriage,
> for a girl is given by her father, not by her *tapas*. If I am given by my *tapas*, 36ea
> then my father will also give me. Let Śiva ask Himālaya for me and marry 23e
> me by the rituals.'[48] 23a

In another story of the wedding, Śiva asks Pārvatī to marry him by simple physical union and mutual consent, a form of marriage accepted in ancient Indian literature. When she asks him to marry her in the conventional way he is disappointed but he agrees, saying, 'So be it. Let not convention be scorned.'[49] In one version, he wishes to marry her by *tapas*; in the other, by sexual union. Conventional ritual acts as a link between the two, and he consents to it.

Pārvatī demands other conventional pleasures connected with wealth,
for she is after all the daughter of the King of Mountains. Thus when
Menā tries to get Pārvatī to approach Nārada (when Pārvatī is still just
a little girl), she says, 'Honour the sage, my daughter, and you will
19ea obtain a husband rich in *tapas*', but Pārvatī, unimpressed, merely hides
in her mother's skirts. But when Menā says, 'Honour the sage and
28e I will give you a lovely jewelled toy that I have been keeping for some
time', Pārvatī goes quickly and bows at Nārada's feet.[50] Even in married
life there are indications that she values the *tapas* of her husband not for
its own sake but for the special powers—magical as well as sexual—
that she sees in it:

36e One day when Śiva was sitting with Devī on a bed, making love to her, he
untied the knot of her waistcloth and placed his hands under it, but she said,
22a 'What's this?' and tied it up again. Then he gave her a pearl for a nose-
28e ornament, but as it was covered with turmeric and did not shine she said,
28a 'I will not wear this pearl, because I do not like it. Śiva, your house is full of
28e 38a[2] wealth and I used to think it would be used for ornaments, but you adorn
30a your head with a garland of Brahmins' skulls and wear poisonous serpents
9d for your bracelets.'[51]

28e 28a Śiva's unique ornaments disgust Pārvatī, but his attempt to supply conventional jewels is hardly more successful. In the Bengali tradition, she
22a quarrels with him because he is too poor to buy bracelets for her.[52]

These domestic problems are the natural outcome of the conflict between asceticism and married life. Pārvatī is noted for her attempts to seduce Śiva from his asceticism and for her interruptions of his meditation. This is a familiar theme in Sanskrit court poetry:

May Śambhu's [Śiva's] customary prayer to twilight bless you,
36a a prayer wherein his hands deceive his wife,
folding in imitation of the closing lotus
as if to say, 'See, goddess, as the sky grows red
26e[2] these lotuses that would have matched your face
have come to this.'

19a 'Mother—' 'Darling—'
'What is that hidden in Father's hands?'
'A fruit, my child.' 'And won't he give it me?'
22ea 'Yes, go yourself and take it.'
36ea[2] Guha [Skanda], so spoken by his mother,
13d pulls wide the hands of Śambhu clasped in evening worship.
His meditation broken, Śambhu stills his wrath and laughs.
May this his laughter save you.[53]

One of the most beautiful passages in Sanskrit poetry, Kālidāsa's

description of the sunset over Himālaya, is prompted by Śiva's attempt
to pacify Pārvatī, who disregards him, pouts, chatters aimlessly with her 22a
friends, and generally sulks when Śiva performs his sunset worship.[54] 36ea^{2}

After one of their frequent quarrels at dice, Pārvatī tries unsuccessfully to seduce Śiva:

> Once when Śiva and Pārvatī were playing dice, Śiva lost and went, ashamed, 33ea^{7}
> to hide in a ketaki forest. Pārvatī took the form of a beautiful young woman 26e^{2} 33ea^{3}
> and tried to entice him back. He ignored her, until he smelled the fragrance 28e 36ea^{2} 42a
> of the ketaki flowers she wore. Annoyed at the disturbance of his prayers, 43ea 41a
> Śiva cursed the ketaki flowers.[55]

As usual, Śiva is particularly annoyed by Pārvatī's use of erotic ornaments. His displeasure is all the more intense here since the ornaments are flowers, the very form of Kāma; and indeed he treats them as he treats Kāma, first responding to them (for his prayers are disturbed), and then cursing them.

Another quarrel at dice begins with the conventional argument about jewels but moves on to more cosmic matters:

> Śiva wagered his crescent moon and his earrings against Pārvatī's pearls 14c^{3} 33ea^{7}
> and golden ornaments. When he lost, however, he refused to pay her, saying, 28e 28a
> 'I am invincible. Let us play dice as much as you wish, and I will win back
> all I have lost.' She mocked him, said that he was *not* invincible, and demanded 22a
> that he pay her, since she had beaten him. One of Śiva's servants then said to
> Pārvatī, 'You have said many things you must never say again. My master is
> indeed invincible, but because you are a woman you do not know the highest
> god. Formerly, placing Kāma foremost, you united with the terrible Śiva. 43e
> But you should recall what Śiva has done—he destroyed Kāma's body, and 36e 1 43a
> burnt the forests on Himālaya.'[56] 23a

Pārvatī, being a woman who places Kāma foremost, cannot fathom the ascetic nature of the 'terrible' Śiva. She sees the mortal, domestic, superficial level—that she has just beaten him at dice—but is ignorant of the immortal, cosmic, inner level—that god is invincible.

A similar argument ensues when, playfully covering up Śiva's eyes, 7cd^{1}
Pārvatī inadvertently plunges the universe into darkness and almost 5d
destroys it. Śiva then rebukes her, 'You silly girl, without thinking you 36a
have done something that could destroy the universe. I myself will
destroy it at doomsday, at the right time, but you, in your foolishness, 33ea^{7} 5d
have done it at the wrong time, and in jest.'[57] The gap between the
terrible god in all his awesome destructive power and the playful young
wife cannot easily be bridged. A popular myth tells that Śiva tried to
explain the Vedas to Pārvatī, but, noting her inattention, he became 36a 27ea
angry and complained, 'It is clear that you are not a suitable wife for 19ea

a yogi.'[58] Of course, there *is* no such woman, as Śiva himself realizes, and so it is he who capitulates in the end, lowering himself to her level as he cannot raise her to his.

In one late text, he punishes her severely for her spiritual shortcomings. When she fails to accept his explanation of Viṣṇu's incarnation
36a as Rāma, Śiva remarks that she is 'just like a woman' and he thinks,
'Dakṣa's daughter will come to no good.' He then undertakes a vow 'not to touch her' and treats her so coldly that she eventually commits suicide.[59] Usually, however, the quarrels end in some sort of reconciliation.

E. THE QUARRELS OF ŚIVA AND PĀRVATĪ

In the incidents described above, it is Śiva who causes the trouble, objecting to his wife's anti-ascetic presence. In other quarrels, however, it is she who objects to his unconventional and ascetic behaviour. As a modern Bengali scholar has described the situation:

> [Śiva] is rather an impecunious god. In truth, mendicancy is his only
> means of subsistence. The miserable condition of his household is further
> 16d aggravated by his fondness for drugs and low company. Domestic quarrels
> naturally break out often, in these circumstances, and in these quarrels the
> 22a poor old god is worsted by his young wife.[60]

Śiva's 'fondness for drugs' is a frequent source of discord, epitomizing
the ecstatic ascetic behaviour most directly opposed to conventional
married life. According to tribal tradition, when Gaura (Pārvatī) married
30e 16d Mahadeo she sent her parrot to spy on him when he drank opium and
smoked bhang. The parrot, sent on an anti-ascetic errand, here assumes the role of Kāma and serves Pārvatī. Another tribal myth uses the smoking of tobacco (perhaps bhang) to resolve the conflict between the ascetic and his wife as well as the confusion between hunger and sexual appetite:

> From the day of his birth, Father Mahadeo was a little mad. [One day he
> 16cd came home hungry and kept asking Pārvatī for food.] She was young and
> thought that Mahadeo desired to take his pleasure with her. [She kept
> smiling at him instead of preparing his food, and after ten years had passed,
> 20ea Gaṇeśa was born. Still Śiva continued to ask for food, and Pārvatī, becoming
> 19a weary of him and of the child, went to the forest and said to the forest deity,
> $26e^2$ 22a 'Make my husband love me.' The deity gave her tobacco, which she brought
> $25ea^2$ 16d home to Śiva. He smoked happily and stopped asking for food.][61]

Even here, Śiva's addiction to tobacco solves only one of the problems—

9. Agni swallowing the seed of Śiva. Bhuvaneśvara, Orissa. Eighth century. MOTIF: 10c, 16c, 44a.

10. Śiva, three-eyed, wearing snakes, in a burning-ground, threading skulls with his sons, Gaṇeśa and Skanda. Kangra painting. 1790. MOTIF: 6d, 7cd, 19e, 19ea, 29ea, 30a, 36e, 38a², 45e².

11. Śiva embracing the Ganges. Kangra painting. Eighteenth century. MOTIF: 9c, 14c, 23ea, 44e.

12. Śiva as Bhikṣāṭana, the beggar, wearing skulls, seducing the wives of the sages. Pahārī painting, Basohlī style. Eighteenth century. MOTIF: 35ea, 38a².

his request to be fed. There is no evidence in this myth that he ever comes to love her, as she wishes, nor anything but the unexplained birth of Gaṇeśa to indicate that he ever responds to her hopeful and seductive smiles.

Most of the arguments are simply reversals of the episode in which Śiva, in disguise, reviles himself while she defends him. All the ascetic peculiarities which he mentions to test her before the wedding—and which she earnestly accepts—are condemned and thrown back in his face by Pārvatī when she has to live with them. The most obvious of these arguments—the fact that by burning Kāma Śiva has demonstrated himself to be an unlikely lover—is used frequently by Pārvatī against
Śiva, who is unable to defend himself as eloquently as she did in the
reverse situation. When she asks him why he has burnt Kāma, he 22a 43a
answers lamely that it was not *he* who burnt Kāma, but merely his third 7cd[1]
eye; and when she teases him, she says, 'You did *tapas* for a long time 25ea[2]
in order to obtain me as your wife. Then why did you destroy Kāma? 43a
With Kāma destroyed, what use have you for a wife? This is the act of 34a
a yogi [not of a husband]. . . . If you take no sexual pleasure in me, how 29e
have you managed to make love to me? But sexual pleasure cannot make 43a
you happy, for you burnt Kāma to ashes.'[62] Since Śiva is a yogi (and has burnt Kāma), he is at least theoretically averse to sexual pleasures, and his *tapas* does in fact cause the gods to interrupt his love-play, whereupon Pārvatī weeps and says, 'Among all the pleasures of women,
the greatest pleasure is to unite with a good man in private, and the 44ea
misery that arises from its interruption is not equalled by any other. The 21a
second greatest misery is the falling of the seed [in vain], and the third 29a
is my childlessness, the greatest sorrow of all.'[63]

Many of their arguments arise when Śiva teases her by calling her 'Kālī' ('The Black One',) and she takes umbrage, retorting with a catalogue of his faults:

> This is the reward for all my *tapas*, that I am dishonoured at every step. 25ea[2]
> I am not the one who is insincere or crooked, but you are famous for your 36a
> poisonous attachments and your sins. I am not the one who destroyed the 9d
> teeth of Pūṣan or the eyes of Bhaga. You call me dark, but you are yourself
> famous as the Great Dark One. . . . You revile me but disregard your own
> faults. Because of your serpents you speak with many tongues; because of 30a
> your ashes, you oppose love [*sneha* means love or oiliness, the opposite of 6cd
> ashes]; because of your bull, you are stupid; because you live in the burning- 45e[2]
> grounds you are fearless, shameless because you are naked, merciless because 6d
> you carry a skull. Why should I live here to be insulted by a worthless 28ea 38a[2]
> adulterer?[64] 23ea

A similar invective based upon verbal ambiguities and puns appears in a classical poem:

36a 'Why are you hard-hearted, Pārvatī?'
'This is the nature of those born of a rocky mountain.'
'Why have you no love [or oiliness] for me?'
6cd 'A man of ashes could bear no oiliness.'
'Your anger against me will bear no fruit [will get you nowhere], darling.'
26a 'How should there be fruit on a *sthāṇu* ["post", also a name of Śiva]?'
May Śiva, thus dumbfounded by his mountain-born queen, long protect you.[65]

The particular qualities that she chooses to tease him about are those most suited for this sort of word-play, but they are all aspects of his asceticism (the serpents, ashes, nakedness, burning-grounds, and skull), while the Sthāṇu or pillar aspect of Śiva is the symbol of his eternal chastity. She holds his asceticism responsible for the anti-erotic turn of mind that leads him to insult her sexual pride by calling her 'Kālī'. Her resentment of his *tapas* is reflected in the belief that South Indian yogis, snake-charmers, and scavengers 'account for their condition as resulting from a curse that was imposed because of some slighting remarks made regarding Pārvatī's breasts'.[66]

F. THE ADULTERY OF ŚIVA

23ea In one of the 'Kālī' arguments, Pārvatī calls Śiva an adulterer, and his
lascivious behaviour causes as much trouble with her as does his
asceticism, though for the opposite reason: he is guilty of adultery,
incest, and general profligacy. He refers to himself as a voluptuary, and
on several occasions Pārvatī calls him a woman-chaser.[67] When leaving
her house, she posts a guard at the door to keep other women from
43a entering and making love with Śiva, for, as she says, 'Śiva is a great
44e 23ea womanizer, and although he is the enemy of Kāma he is the lover of the
23ea Ganges and full of passion for Sandhyā.'[68] Śiva is said to have attempted
21e to seduce Sāvitrī, to have spilt his seed at the sight of some nymphs
21ea 17c bathing, and even to have begotten a saint in a cow.[69] In addition to the
45e²20ea seduction of the wives of the Pine Forest sages, Śiva begets a son upon
Atri's wife Anasūyā, an episode to which one Purāṇa attributes the
origin of *liṅga*-worship:

19ea 27ea One day the sage Atri was performing *tapas* with his wife Anasūyā. Brahmā,
35ea 45a Viṣṇu, and Śiva came and offered him a boon, but Atri remained silent,
26ea meditating. Then the three gods went to Anasūyā. Śiva had his *liṅga* in his
43ea hand, Viṣṇu was full of erotic feeling, and Brahmā was beside himself with

desire, saying to Anasūyā, 'Make love with me or I will die.' When she heard 24e
this coarse speech, Anasūyā made no reply, for, although she feared the anger
of the gods, she was true to her husband. But they were overcome with
delusion, and they raped her by force. Then she became angry and she cursed 2
Śiva to be worshipped as a *liṅga*, Brahmā to be worshipped in the form of 5c[2]
a head, and Viṣṇu to be worshipped as feet, in order to ridicule them all, and 38a[2]
she cursed them all to be reborn as her sons. Because of this, Śiva was reborn 2
as Durvāsas.[70] 20e

Although Śiva is not alone in this adultery, the curse applies particularly well to him, and although the episode may be viewed as an exaggeration of the motif of the temptation of the devotee's wife or the destruction of a sage's *tapas* by the corruption of his wife, rape is by no means out of character for Śiva.

In fact, by means of the theme of seduction in disguise, the Purāṇas
depict several incidents in which Śiva manages to rape or seduce his
own wife. The basic motif recurs in Indian folk-lore: a disguised husband visits his wife, sometimes to show her that he is not as repulsive 33ea[3]
as she thinks him[71] (as Śiva appears to Pārvatī when she performs *tapas*
for him). In the myth of Candraśekhara, Śiva disguises himself as a
Kāpālika and casts a metaphysical haze over the mind of his reincarnated
wife in order to rape her. Candraśekhara reasons, 'Śiva has no beloved
but Pārvatī, and therefore he would not make love to anyone else.'[72]
This is technically true in this particular instance, though not always
true. Pārvatī herself does not have Candraśekhara's faith, for she makes 22a
a terrible fuss when she happens to see her own reflection on Śiva's 33ea[3]
chest and thinks that he loves another woman,[73] mistaking herself for 23ea
his concubine just as Śiva mistakes her for a beautiful mountain woman.
In Bengali mythology, Pārvatī disguises herself to seduce Śiva in order
to punish him for his adulteries:

[Śiva went every day to pick flowers. Out of feminine curiosity, Chaṇḍī
(Gaurī, Pārvatī) followed Śiva secretly in the guise of a *dom* (untouchable) 33ea[3]
woman beautifully dressed and ornamented. She stationed herself as a ferry
woman.] Śiva came and asked the ferry woman to carry him across. He fell 17c
in love with the *dom* girl at first sight and proposed to enjoy her. Gaurī 43ea
vehemently protested on the ground that she was a woman of low origin, 23ea
whereas Śiva was a great god, as he himself said. But finally Śiva purchased
her beauty at the price of a diamond ring. After that Gaurī revealed herself 28e
and berated Śiva for his licentious behaviour. 22a

Śiva made a plan to humiliate Gaurī for thus humiliating him. He became
a mouse and chewed her bodice. Then Śiva in the guise of an old itinerant 33ea[4]
tailor appeared in his own house, [darned the bodice], and then refused to 33ea[3, 5]
be satisfied until Chaṇḍī had allowed herself to be enjoyed by him. Then 28e
Śiva threw off his disguise and berated Chaṇḍī as she had done him.[74] 23ea 36a

In this turnabout, Śiva himself has the last word with the method that is his own, even when usurped and used against him. Yet the basic technique, and even the particular incident, appears elsewhere in Indian folk-lore: a woman in disguise is wooed by her faithless husband, and
33ea[3] a husband who has teased his wife about a 'bought kiss' is approached
by her, in disguise, and made to buy a kiss from her.[75] Śiva even goes
33ea[3] so far as to take the form of a Muslim sentry in order to rape his own
wife, rather than possess her simply in the lawful manner.[76]

Just as Śiva seduces the Pine Forest women in the presence of Pārvatī, so she also witnesses his seduction of Mohinī, an episode which is in many ways a multiform of the Pine Forest myth:

33ea[1] Viṣṇu took the form of the *apsaras* Mohinī in order to beguile the demons
21ea and to steal the Soma back from them. Having accomplished this, Viṣṇu was
14c[3] approached by Śiva and Pārvatī, and Śiva asked him to display the seductive
21ea form which he had assumed for the demons. Viṣṇu became Mohinī, and Śiva
23ea immediately ran after her, abandoning Pārvatī who stood with her head
36a lowered in shame. Śiva embraced Mohinī by force, and his seed fell upon the
21e ground. Mohinī disappeared and Śiva returned to Pārvatī.[77]

Two other Purāṇas elaborate upon the myth and conclude:

21ea Mohinī freed herself and ran away, but Śiva followed her, and his seed fell
21e 9cd upon the ground and turned to gold and silver. His seed became the place
5cd of *liṅgas* and of gold. When the seed was shed, Śiva realized his delusion,
24e became cool, and turned back from his evil act.[78]

The golden seed, here fruitless, is productive of a son, Skanda in the
20ea South Indian tradition[79] and Hanūman in one Purāṇa:

33ea[1] One day Śiva saw the Mohinī form of Viṣṇu. He was struck by Kāma's
43ea arrows and let fall his seed. The Seven Sages put the seed in a pot and they
21e 20ea infused it into the daughter of Gautama through her ear. In time, Hanūman,
33ea[4] the monkey-god, was born from it.[80]

The ties with the Skanda myth are obvious. Another version also links the Mohinī story with the myth in which Viṣṇu assumes the form of a seductive woman in order to save Śiva from the demon Bhasmāsura:

6cd [Śiva hid from the demon Bhasmāsura ('Demon of Ashes'), who had
8d threatened to burn him to ashes. Viṣṇu took the form of Mohinī and tricked
33ea[1] the demon into reducing himself to ashes. Then Śiva asked Viṣṇu to assume
21ea the form of Mohinī again.] Viṣṇu did so, and found himself a prey to the
uncontrollable passion of Śiva. The result of this incestuous connection be-
20ea tween Hari and Hara [Viṣṇu and Śiva] . . . was Aiyanār.[81]

Yet another text assimilates the Mohinī story to the Pine Forest myth, in which Viṣṇu saves Śiva not from a demon but from the angry sages:

38a [Śiva beheaded Brahmā, whose skull then stuck fast to his hand. Śiva then

vowed to beg until the skull was full. He begged, but the fiery rays from the 7cd[1]
eye in his forehead consumed all that was put into the skull and reduced it 6cd
to ashes. Śiva then came to the hermitage of the sages, whose wives came 16cd
running with ladles full of butter to fill the skull. When they saw Śiva, they 10c
lost control and let their ladles fall from their hands and their clothes from 35ea
their bodies. The sages returned and saw their wives naked. Full of jealousy, 28ea
they wished to kill the yogi Śiva. Viṣṇu, knowing the state his brother Śiva 33ea[6] 33ea[1]
was in, wished to help him; he changed himself into a beautiful young virgin 21ea
and appeared to the sages. They were affected as their wives had been, lost
control, and fell to the earth. Although Śiva did not fall to the ground, his
seed fell from him to the ground. Viṣṇu took it in his hands and made a son. 21e
After twelve years of begging, Śiva went to Viṣṇu and begged from him. 20ea
Viṣṇu blinded the (forehead) eye and then wounded himself in his little finger. 7cd[1]
The blood flowed into the skull and filled it, producing a child whom Brahmā, 15cd
Viṣṇu, and Śiva each claimed as his own. Indra declared him to be the son of 20ea
all three.][82]

The motifs from the myth of Skanda are framed by a multiform of the burning and resuscitation of Kāma (here, the burning and quenching of the flame of the third eye within the skull), but the Mohinī episode is placed within the Pine Forest, and it is she, and not Śiva, who stirs the sages so that they lose their *tapas* and Śiva sheds his seed, as he loses his *liṅga* in the usual course of the myth.

In another version of the Mohinī myth, without the Pine Forest context, the connection between the seed and the *liṅga* is more direct:

Vishnu, at Shiva's request, manifested himself as a female (Mohinī). Shiva, 33ea[1]
enraptured at the sight, had an ejaculation. He caught the divine sperm in his 21ea
hand. This turned into a linga which was the godling Aiyanar. Mohinī 21e
changed back into Vishnu.[83] 5cd 20ea

The Mohinī and Pine Forest myths are explicitly combined in one South Indian text:

[When Viṣṇu had taken the form of Mohinī to get the Soma back from the 33ea[1]
demons, he maintained that form to demonstrate the manner in which, once, 14c[2]
he had taken the form of a woman in the Pine Forest. Śiva seized Viṣṇu, took 1
him under the shade of a tree by the seaside, and united with him. The saliva 21ea
that they spat out was transformed into a great river, and from their union 23ea
there was born a child with red hair and a black body, called Hariharaputra 14c[1]
(the son of Viṣṇu and Śiva).][84] 20ea

In addition to Mohinī, the Ganges and Sandhyā are the objects of
Śiva's extramarital lust. Śiva's adultery (or, in some instances, bigamy) 23ea
with the Ganges is the result of the Ganges' presence in the story of the birth of Skanda from Agni. Originally merely a river, the Ganges becomes personified as a wife when her own cult grows in importance

[Plate 11]. Two fairly late Purāṇas attribute to the wish of Devī herself
10cd the duplication of wives: when, after the death of Satī, Śiva begged
Devī to marry him, she agreed to divide herself into two parts, one half
14c[1] made of water (the Ganges), to reside on his head as the corpse of Satī
had done, the other half to be reborn as Pārvatī.[85] The *Rāmāyaṇa* absorbs Gaṅgā (the Ganges) into the Skanda story by making her the sister of Pārvatī:

> Menā married Himālaya and bore him two daughters, the elder named Gaṅgā and the younger Pārvatī. The gods asked Himālaya to give Gaṅgā to
> 36e them and he did, and the other daughter undertook a terrible vow of *tapas*,
> 2 and Himālaya gave her to Rudra. . . . Brahmā said, 'Pārvatī's curse must come
> 29a true [that all the gods would be barren], but Agni will beget a son in Gaṅgā,
> 44e the elder daughter of Himālaya, and Gaṅgā will consider this to be the son
> of Pārvatī.'[86]

Another Purāṇa accounts for Śiva's relationship with Sandhyā ('Twilight') as well as with the Ganges, simply by adding a third sister, Rāgiṇī ('The Red'), who is cursed to become the redness of twilight as punishment for trying to receive Śiva's seed when her *tapas* was insufficient. (She is also cursed to be conjoined with the Kṛttikās in her and their astrological aspect, thus involving yet another set of Skanda's foster-mothers.) The Ganges, who appears here as the river Kuṭilā, is
2 cursed for the same reason but with an inverse effect: she must become
44e a river in order to bear Śiva's seed.[87] (Pārvatī, the only sister whose
tapas is considered sufficient, is completely excluded from any contact with Śiva's seed, though she alone marries him.)

The myth in which Śiva receives the Ganges upon his head is widely known but not usually interpreted in terms of marriage or adultery:

> 9d King Sagara ['Poisonous'] performed a horse sacrifice, but the horse was
> 13cd[1] stolen by Indra and hidden in the ocean, which was at that time devoid of
> 14cd water. The king sent his 60,000 sons to find the horse; they dug down into
> 45a 18e hell, where they saw the horse wandering about, but the sage Kapila, who was
> 7cd[1] performing *tapas* there, released a flame from his eye and burnt the sons to
> 43a ashes. Sagara's one remaining son propitiated Kapila and obtained the horse,
> with which the king performed his sacrifice, and the ocean became Sagara's son, called Sāgara.
>
> Many years later, Bhagīratha, the great-grandson of Sagara, propitiated
> 43e 34a Śiva and the Ganges. The Ganges fell from heaven [where she is the Milky
> 14c[1] Way] to earth, flowing over the ashes of the 60,000 sons and reviving them,
> 12c and Śiva received the first torrents of the Ganges upon his head, breaking the
> 44e 6cd 6c fall so that it would not shatter the earth.[88]

The Ganges here reverses the usual Hindu procedure and is transformed *from* a heavenly constellation to an earthly figure. Śiva here appears not only explicitly in the benevolent role of reviver of the sons, but also implicitly as the sage Kapila who destroys them with the fire of his eye. The boon which he gives—that he will receive the Ganges on his head—is reversed in one text in which he grants a boon to another sage to take the Ganges from him:

Śiva married Devī, but, although he was passionate, he was unable to 36e
stimulate her passion, for she kept looking at the Ganges that Śiva had hidden 23ea
in his matted locks. She took Skanda and Gaṇeśa aside and said to them, 'Śiva 4
is the lover of the Ganges and will not abandon her.' Then Gaṇeśa tricked 44ea
Śiva into offering a boon to the sage Gautama, who asked for the Ganges,
thus removing Devī's cause for jealousy.[89]

The reversal of the boon is matched by the reversal of Gaṇeśa's usual role of interfering with the love-making of Śiva and Pārvatī, for here he assists them by removing the river whose presence is given unmistakable sexual overtones.

Yet the general view is that the Ganges remains for ever on Śiva's
head. In iconography, when Śiva appears with the Ganges, 'on the left
of Śiva there should be Umā [Pārvatī] standing in a state of mental 23ea
uneasiness; this is the feeling of jealousy due to Śiva trying to favour
another lady with his attention'.[90] Dakṣa criticizes Śiva for having one 24a
woman on his head and another on his body,[91] as Pārvatī herself com- 23a
plains. The manner in which the icon (in the hair) and the personifica- 23ea
tion (in the myth) may be combined is evident from representations of
Śiva with a woman (the Ganges) peering out from the folds of his
turban,[92] a concept reminiscent of the folk tradition that Śiva keeps
Pārvatī in his turban 'because from the turban it is very easy to have
sexual intercourse'.

Yet another combination of the iconic or symbolic aspect of the
Ganges (i.e. her personification as a river) and her anthropomorphic
effect upon Pārvatī may be seen in one variant of the myth in which 35ea
Śiva sends a flood to wash away Pārvatī's sand *liṅga*, which she protects $5c^{2}$
by clasping it to her breasts. In this variation, Śiva sends not merely $14c^{1}$ 14d
a flood but the Ganges, whom he summons forth from his own hair and 23ea
sends to frighten and test Pārvatī. In anger and jealousy, Pārvatī then 3
curses the Ganges to become as untouchable as a Caṇḍālī woman. The
Ganges is burnt by the curse, her water dries up, and only after lengthy 12d
expiation is she purified.[93] (The curse of untouchability is also given to
other women whom Pārvatī considers her rivals and to certain *apsarases* 3
and *gandharvas* whose erotic behaviour offends Pārvatī when she is 20e
overcome by longing for Śiva during his absence.)[94] 36a

In the Bengali tradition, Gaṅgā is the first wife and Pārvatī the usurper. This influenced one Purāṇa composed in Bengal:

6c When Satī had died, she was reborn as a pair of daughters, Gaṅgā and
36e Pārvatī. Śiva married Gaṅgā and received her on his head. Later the gods
19e asked Śiva to marry Pārvatī and beget Skanda, but he replied, 'I obtained
23ea Satī in the form of the Ganges: whom else did you have in mind?' They per-
25ea[2] suaded him to marry Pārvatī, and he rewarded her *tapas* with a promise to
marry her, but, having obtained the Ganges upon his head, the great yogi
36a was without any desire for a wife. As he remained in meditation, Pārvatī
36ea[1] 34a resolved to perform *tapas* again to obtain him.[95]

The reversal of the positions of Pārvatī and Gaṅgā makes it possible for Śiva to bolster his usual arguments against marriage with his disinclination to commit bigamy. Although this reversal avoids the double birth that occurs in the *Rāmāyaṇa*, it introduces another multiform: Pārvatī must do *tapas* twice, as Śiva's marriage to Gaṅgā invalidates her first boon.

Even in the Bengali texts, where Durgā (Pārvatī) is not his first wife, it is she who bears Śiva his two sons:

Durgā, who grew up in the family of the sage Hemanta, made love secretly
23ea with Śiva, who finally married her with the consent of his first wife Gaṅgā.
36e [He stayed in a garden for twelve years, and] Durgā twice visited him in dis-
33ea[3] guise and had intercourse with him, which resulted in the birth of Gaṇeśa
20ea and Kārtikeya.[96]

In another Bengali version, 'the consent of his first wife Gaṅgā' is not so easily obtained, causing one of their frequent quarrels:

36e [Śiva married Gaṅgā. He built a garden in order to make love in it to Durgā.
23ea Durgā came there and Śiva made love with her for several days. Gaṅgā was
14d informed by Nārada of Śiva's secret love; she became angry and sent her two
sons to drown Durgā, but they did not succeed. When Durgā arrived home,
33ea[6] her father Hemanta tested her, for he doubted her chastity, but Durgā
25a magically restored her own virginity and successfully passed the tests he set
22a for her. Śiva then asked Gaṅgā to let him marry Durgā. Gaṅgā abused him
and declared that he was too old and poor to take a second wife, but finally
36e she reluctantly agreed, and Śiva, assisted by Nārada, took Durgā as his second
wife.][97]

Gaṅgā tries to drown Durgā just as she attempts to flood Pārvatī and the *liṅga*. In this version the sons are Gaṅgā's rather than Durgā's, and they act to get rid of her rival even as they sometimes help Durgā to dispose of Gaṅgā. In keeping with these reversals, it is Gaṅgā rather than Durgā with whom Śiva quarrels, but the accusations are the usual

ones (he is old and poor, a senile ascetic), even when the occasion for the
quarrel arises from his other, lecherous aspect.

The other woman who causes Pārvatī to be jealous of Śiva is the third
sister—Sandhyā. Usually Sandhyā represents an anti-erotic threat,
being the embodiment of the evening worship which takes Śiva from
Pārvatī's presence, but she is personified as a woman, and so the threat
becomes erotic as well:

> One day Pārvatī saw Śiva bowing and praying to Sandhyā, with his eyes 33ea[6]
> closed, and she thought, 'What lovely woman is he meditating upon now? 23ea
> The affection that he shows me is mere deception. How can one know the
> devious minds of men? Śiva, the enemy of Kāma, deceived me when he 43a
> promised to be my slave. Because I lack beauty, Śiva thinks of other women.
> I will perform *tapas* to become beautiful.' Thus her mind was sullied by 25ea
> jealousy.[98]

Even when she performs *tapas*, Pārvatī worries about Śiva's possible
infidelity during her absence, basing her fears upon his established
liaisons with the Ganges and Sandhyā. On another occasion she says to
Śiva, 'You rogue, you carry the Ganges and bow to Sandhyā. You were 23ea
never won by me.'[99] These two women, though mere personifications,
are her eternal rivals.

G. THE RECONCILIATION OF ŚIVA AND PĀRVATĪ

Quarrels are an important part of the mythology of Śiva and Pārvatī,
not only because they demonstrate the conflict between the aspects of
Śiva, but also because, in the Hindu view, quarrels, violence, and separation are an essential part of any sexual relationship, enhancing rather 29ea
than impeding it.[100] The lover's infidelity and the subsequent quarrel
and separation provide a more ardent spur to love, and the theme of
love in separation is used by the court poets to heighten the erotic 29ea
mood.[101] Physical violence and sex are closely intertwined in the *Kāmasūtra*, which devotes an entire chapter to the technique of biting and
scratching, and Kālidāsa explicitly mentions this part of the love-play 29ea
of Śiva and Pārvatī: although when he first made love to her there was
no biting of her lips and scratching of her breasts, later her hands were 29ea
tremulous with pain, her lips marked with bites, and her thighs scored
with the traces of his nails.[102] The violence of Pārvatī's *tapas*, with its
icy baths and scorching fires, is an initiation into this kind of passion, 27ea
preparing her for her physical union with Śiva even as it purifies her
for her spiritual union with him. And it sweetens the final union by its

contrast, by the denial of love, just as Śiva's ascetic nature inspires her to seek that union and to overcome that denial.

Only through constant discord and reconciliation can Pārvatī accept Śiva as both her husband and her god. Moreover, for the ultimate product of their union—the birth of their son—it is necessary for them to quarrel and separate:

When Pārvatī was about to be born, Brahmā summoned Night, his
40a daughter, and said to her, 'Śiva and Pārvatī, both with great powers of *tapas*,
19ea will be united, but there must be a small argument between them. You must
27ea bring about an obstacle to separate them when they are making love. Colour
36a her when she is still an embryo, so that later, when Śiva is tired after making
44ea love to her, he will laugh at her and mock her, and she will become angry and
25ea^{3} go to do *tapas* again. By this *tapas* she will obtain the necessary power to
bring forth the son begotten by Śiva.'[103]

The golden skin which Pārvatī is driven to seek is symbolic not only of conventional beauty (which in India has always been considered to favour light-skinned women) but also of creative powers—the golden seed, the golden egg. The quarrel brings about a hiatus in their sexual union that makes it possible for Śiva and Pārvatī to replenish their powers by means of *tapas*. Then, reconciled, they can apply these powers to the process of procreation, which can only take place when the
32e 36a primeval androgyne is separated into its two contrary principles.[104] In
44ea the cosmic, cyclic view, therefore, the quarrel is ultimately a sexual
stimulus. This is graphically illustrated by another version of the 'Kālī' argument:

36a Śiva called Pārvatī 'Kālī' and a terrible quarrel took place. The universe
5d shook and all the gods were frightened. Then the uproar from that quarrel
5cd burst through the ground and became a *liṅga* which the gods named the
5c^{2} 36a Liṅga of the Lord of Quarrels, and whoever worships it is free for ever from
36e quarrels in his house.[105]

The quarrel produces the symbol of sexual union which prevents quarrels, a most concise example of the workings of cyclic Śaiva myth-
33ea^{7} ology. Similarly, after a quarrel at dice, the forest of Kāma is said to
26e^{2} 36a have arisen in the place of reconciliation.[106]

36e One such reconciliation results in the androgynous form, the ultimate reunion and the starting-point for new separations:

Shiva, as a mendicant, supported the family by begging; but one day, due
16d to excessive smoking [of marijuana] he could not go on his daily rounds.
24a [Nārada came and teased Pārvatī about Śiva, saying,] 'It pains me to say so,
8d noble lady, but there is no getting away from the fact that the tendencies of
36a your husband are essentially destructive, and he cares not for his wife and

children.' Pārvatī brooded over the words of Nārada and decided to desert 19a
her husband. [She set out to go, taking the children, but Nārada told her to 22a
beg for food. She did so and returned home, and then Śiva returned with 27ea 38a^{2}
an empty begging-bowl.] Pārvatī now fed him with the food she had collected, 16cd
and Mahādeva was so pleased with her that he embraced her violently and 32e
became one with her. Pārvatī feeding her husband is known as Annapūrṇā
Devī [the goddess full of food].[107]

Śiva quarrels with Pārvatī in his ascetic aspect and reunites with her in his erotic aspect; the myth begins with fasting and ends with feasting.
In another myth, after an argument about his asceticism, Śiva becomes 31e
a dancer in order to propitiate Pārvatī,[108] just as he does to propitiate her mother.

But the *rapprochement* may come about from the opposite direction: Śiva remains an ascetic and Pārvatī comes to accept him in this aspect. In this way, she accepts the clouds and mountains as a more wonderful kind of house than the conventional one which Śiva lacks, and she herself defies convention to be with him. She defends Śiva's houselessness 23e^{2} 23a
when her parents try to dissuade her from doing *tapas* in the forest to 25ea^{2}
marry him,[109] and she answers all the arguments which point out his flaws as a husband. Śiva knows that she will withstand all the criticisms and denunciations, for he comes in disguise and says to Himālaya:

> Śiva has no wealth, no attachments, no good looks or qualities. He is an 24a
> old man, free from passion, a wanderer and a beggar, not at all suitable for 34a
> Pārvatī to marry. Ask your wife and your relatives—ask anyone but Pārvatī.[110] 24ea^{2}

And there is a similar implication in the speech that Śiva makes, in disguise, to Pārvatī herself:

> Śiva is devoid of all pleasures, has no house or relatives or enjoyments or 24a
> erotic life, and never has a wife or son. Yet for some reason you want him for 34a
> your husband. . . . Why should a woman want for her husband a man who 24ea^{2} 10cd
> destroys everything?[111] 29ea

When Śiva learns that she is to choose her husband, he says, 'How could you turn down a handsome man and choose such as me?' But she,
thinking of his importance and his grace, replies, 'I will choose you, and 24ea^{2}
there is nothing marvellous in that.'[112] 29ea

Indeed, it is *not* marvellous, in the context of the Śaiva Purāṇas. Her attachment to Śiva is unconventional, and incomprehensible to her parents, but it is not without cause. She loves him for the very reasons that are usually cited against him. Even the smoking of marijuana
endears him to her: 'Bhola ['The Fool', a name of Śiva] is ever laughing 16d

and weeping and knows no one save me. He is always eating hemp, and I must stay near him. I cannot keep from worrying . . . about this madman.'[113] When Dakṣa reviles Śiva, Satī persists in her love:

> Why she loved such a peculiar god, going about with goblins and demons,
> 24ea[2] indifferent to comfort and pleasure, was a mystery. But there is no accounting
> 29ea for love. And Satī not only loved Shiva, she was obsessed by him.[114]

'Obsessed' is an appropriate word to describe Satī's love for Śiva, for
she is almost morbidly attracted to his anti-erotic qualities. She defends
Śiva before his accuser, saying, 'Whether he be auspicious or in-
29ea auspicious and terrifying, wealthy or poor, adorned or unadorned—
24ea[2] whatever he be like, he will be my husband.'[115] When Śiva came in dis-
38a[2] guise to Pārvatī, waved 'a yellow skull from which the flesh still hung',
and denounced himself, Pārvatī's reply was unmistakable: '"We have
29ea always desired", croaked Pārvatī, her tongue cracked, "a real man."'[116]

H. THE HORRIBLE AND THE EROTIC

When Śiva reviles himself before her, he means it ostensibly as a de-
terrent to her love for him, but there is in all the wine and wildness
which he seems to censure the Dionysian quality of life that strengthens
10cd her love even as he speaks of horrible things. Many of the superficially
anti-Śiva speeches—the speech of Śiva himself in disguise, of the Seven Sages to Pārvatī, of Nārada to Menā, of Śiva (disguised as the Vaiṣṇava Brahmin) to Himālaya—are made in the spirit of what the Hindus call 'blame-praise'. Śiva speaks thus to Pārvatī not only to test her but also to praise himself before her while seeming to blame; for all the qualities that he describes, inappropriate as they may be for a conventional bridegroom, are not only symbols of his greatness but also symbols of great erotic appeal. The snakes, the bloody elephant skin, the third eye in his forehead—all may transcend their conventional and literal repulsiveness and exert a magical erotic power. When Nārada predicts as Pārvatī's husband a naked yogi without parents or erotic tendencies, Menā and Himālaya are downcast, but Pārvatī delights in her heart, for she recognizes Śiva by his signs,[117] and she sees the erotic aspect of the ascetic symbols. His horrible ornaments fascinate her, revealing the hidden desire in destruction, just as he shows, in the burning of Kāma, the destruction that may pervade desire.

The interplay of the erotic and the horrible in Śiva is based in part upon the more elemental interplay of sex and death. An interesting discussion of this motif appears in the last novel of Aldous Huxley, based upon an imaginary Tantric Indian society:

> The yoga of the jungle, the yoga that consists of being totally aware of life
> at the near-point, jungle life in all its exuberance and its rotting, crawling 29ea
> squalor, all its melodramatic ambivalence of orchids and centipedes, of leeches 26e^{2}
> and sunbirds, of the drinkers of nectar and the drinkers of blood. . . . Beauty 30e 30a
> and horror. And then suddenly . . . you know that there's a reconciliation. 14c^{2} 15cd
> And not merely a reconciliation. A fusion, and identity. Beauty made one
> with horror in the yoga of the jungle. Life reconciled with the perpetual
> imminence of death in the yoga of danger.[118] 10cd

The fusion of beauty and horror in Śaiva religion is indeed related to
the reconciliation of life and death: 'Rudra inspires terror and, most
paradoxically, a fascinated tenderness for the terrible.'[119] The presence 29ea
of horror to enhance love is an important motif in Indian miniature
painting: a woman steals out to meet her lover at night in spite of the
dangers of darkness, lightning, snakes, ghosts, and jungle plants that
tear her sari and pluck off her golden ornaments. The same psychology
is at work in the disgusting Kāpālika form which Śiva assumes in order 29ea
to rape Tārāvatī[120] and to seduce the women of the Pine Forest. The
canons of Hindu iconography state that when Śiva carries the skull he 38a^{2}
must be surrounded by beautiful women in erotic attitudes,[121] and the
Pine Forest women fall in love with Śiva because they are 'incurably 29ea
attracted to any dangerous thing'.[122]

The motifs of love and death are at the heart of the myth in which Śiva wanders, mad with love and grief, carrying the corpse of Satī. In later Tantric art, the imagery is reversed, and Devī embraces the corpse of Śiva. Both of these episodes emphasize the interplay between the erotic and the anti-erotic aspects of death [Plates 4 and 10].

Pārvatī fears and loves Śiva simultaneously. A Sanskrit poet notes that
Śiva is never left by Pārvatī, 'for though she draw away in fear / she is 32e
bound to the dexter part, which ever draws her back'.[123] The combina- 29ea
tion of love and fear in Pārvatī on the wedding-night aroused Śiva's 29ea
desire,[124] and the ambiguous nature of Śiva's appeal is illustrated by
a poem in which desire masquerades as fear:

> 'Whence comes this perspiration, love?' 11c
> 'From the fire of your eye.' 7cd^{1}
> 'Then why this trembling, fair-faced one?'
> 'I fear the serpent prince.' 30a
> 'But still, the thrill that rises on your flesh?'
> 'Is from the Ganges' spray, my lord.' 44e

33ea^7 May Gaurī's hiding thus her heart
for long be your protection.[125]

This sentiment appears in a short benedictory stanza: 'I worship Pārvatī, whose eyes are closed with the delight of grasping Śiva's neck as if
9d she were fainting at the touch of the Kālakūṭa poison which stains it.'[126]

A similar juxtaposition of emotions underlies a Tamil song in praise
23a of Śiva. In it, 'the mother is apparently perturbed that the daughter has
24a lost her heart to a weird character like Śiva; yet her catalogue of his
qualities brings out his unique greatness':

What made you fall in love with him? . . .
Was it for the wedding gifts his non-existent parents will bring?
14c^3 7cd^1 Or for the moon in his locks and the blazing eye in his forehead?
43a Or for killing Kāma, or for swallowing poison? . . .
9d Was it for the tiger-skin he stripped and wore as a shawl?
6cd Or his foolhardy courage in holding blazing embers in his strong hands?
30a Or for grabbing the big snakes to drape around his neck as garlands?
28e Or for the sari he would get you by begging?
35ea Or for the deeds he wrought or his lovesports?
What made you fall in love?[127]

The conventional concerns of Menā—the wedding gifts, the sari—are mingled with the yogic aspect of Śiva in the blame-praise motif. Ostensibly, it is a speech against Śiva, but certain words betray great admiration for him: he has 'foolhardy courage' and 'strong hands', and the final reference to his lovesports, though spoken in sarcasm, is nevertheless a reference to actual feats performed in his erotic aspect. In this way even Śiva's enemies are made to realize, in spite of themselves, the unity of his seemingly contradictory forms.

I. THE TRANSFORMATION OF ŚIVA'S ORNAMENTS

The mediation between Śiva's horrible and erotic forms is expressed
throughout the Purāṇas by the transformation of his ascetic accoutrements into beautiful ornaments. Details of dress are significant throughout ascetic mythology in this way; Lopamudrā is desired by the sage
28e only after she has put off her royal garments for the bark dress of the
28a *yoginī*, but, on the other hand, she makes Agastya produce rich garments
28e to replace the ascetic garb before she will make love with him.[128] Of
these two concepts, the first—based upon the subtle connection between the erotic and the horrible, as well as upon the sexuality of the ascetic tradition—is the more sophisticated; the second is the conventional view of which the other is an inversion.

This second, more elementary attitude appears frequently in the
Śaiva myths. Śiva in disguise emphasizes the unseemly contrast between
his bloody elephant skin and Pārvatī's silken sari, his funeral-pyre ashes 28e 28a
and her yellow sandalwood paste, his three eyes and her two fawn 6cd
eyes.[129] The skulls that he wears are considered inauspicious and 7cd[1,2]
frightening,[130] and Pārvatī says that Śiva is horrible because of them.[131] 38a[2]
The inappropriateness of skulls as ornaments is demonstrated when they 38a[2]
are compared with Pārvatī's pearls or placed next to the crescent moon 28e
or made into a garland.[132] This natural contrast underlies the humour 14c[3]
of the passage in which Ṛṣyaśṛṅga describes the 'rosaries' (bracelets) and
'matted locks' (coiffure) of the 'ascetic' (prostitute). The essence of this 28e 28a
contrast is the Śaiva androgyne, with the male half nude and wearing 32e
skulls, the female half clothed and wearing a garland of lotuses.[133] 28ea
Kālidāsa plays upon the negative connotations of Śiva's ascetic apparel 26e[2] 38a[2]
when he says that, after the gods had interrupted the love-play of Śiva 28e
and Pārvatī and deprived her of a child, she wept and he consoled her 44ea 29a
by wiping away her tears with the end of his loincloth.[134] Although the 11cd
loincloth represents the aspect of Śiva responsible for her present sor- 28a
rows, it is nevertheless successful here as an erotic instrument, for Śiva
then continues to make love to Pārvatī, and tears upon a loincloth are
creative in other contexts.

This ambiguous attitude toward Śiva's ascetic clothes, still based upon a primarily negative view of asceticism, appears in a Bengali poem:

> 'Why do you burn my body, Madana [Kāma]? 43ea
> I am not Śaṅkara [Śiva], but a delicate girl.
> This is not his matted locks, but a neatly-done braid. 28e 28a
> Not Gaṅgā, but a mallikā-garland is on my head. 44e
> A pearl tiara this and not the crescent moon; 14c[3]
> Not an eye on my forehead but a vermilion spot. 7cd[1]
> I have no poison on my neck but musk 9d
> And a necklace on my breast, not the king of snakes. 30a
> A blue silk sari I have on, not a tiger-skin;
> A lotus in my hand, not a death skull.' 26e[2] 38a[2]
> Vidyāpati says in this fluent meter,
> This is powdered sandalwood, not ashes on her body.[135] 6cd

The natural aversion to Śiva's ascetic ornaments contributes to
Dakṣa's disapproval of his daughter's transformation from a princess 28e
into a *yoginī*: 'In my house, you were lovely, golden, and you wore 28ea
heavenly garments. Now you are black, naked, terrible.'[136] Therefore
when Śiva changes his aspect, he usually changes his ornaments into

the conventional ones with which they are often compared. When he
30a prepares to marry Pārvatī, all the serpents that adorn his body are bound
9cd with gold, his matted locks become a coiffure, he becomes two-eyed, the
7cd[1] eye in his forehead becomes a fabulous gem or a *tilaka* (an auspicious
6cd dot applied to the forehead with vermilion pigment), and the streaks of
28a ashes on his body turn into perfumed sandalwood paste. By Śiva's wish,
28e all his accoutrements become conventional ornaments.[137]

This process is a transformation, not a substitution. When the god-
28e desses laid out ornaments suitable for marriage, Śiva rejected them, and
28a his own apparel underwent a change, becoming suitable for a bride-
38a[2] groom: the skulls became a tiara, the ashes a pale ointment, the third
6cd 7cd[1] 30a eye a *tilaka*, and the serpents became ornaments, changing only their
28e bodies and retaining the jewels in their hoods.[138] According to another
text, Brahmā brought jewels in order to adorn the bridegroom, but Śiva
merely touched the jewels and said, 'I am pleased with your loving
30a offering. Consider it as if I had worn these jewels on my body', and he
caused the serpents on his body to change into various beautiful jewels,
28e so that all who looked on were struck with astonishment and admiration.[139] Śiva transforms himself in this way not for the sake of his bride
23a but for the representative of the conventional world: his mother-in-law,
Menā.[140] Brahmā makes explicit this reason for the transformation when
he approaches Śiva before the wedding:

28a 'Śiva, this is your highest form, beloved of yogis, your form that is streaked
6cd with ashes, four-armed. You should reabsorb this form and assume a lovelier,
7d gentler one, so that your father- and mother-in-law will rejoice to see how
28e 23a handsome you are, and so that no woman will be frightened of you.' Then
13d Śiva assumed an anthropomorphic form, with two arms, and his matted locks
9cd 40a became a golden diadem, and his fire became calm.[141]

40a In another text, Brahmā again convinces Śiva to change his form to make
sure that Devī will choose him for her husband, and Śiva becomes so
42e handsome that he is called the Lord of Kāma, and Devī thinks him to be
Kāma incarnate and is overcome with desire for him.[142]

This process appears in one text in a double reversal: it applies not
to Śiva but to Pārvatī, and includes a transformation first from the erotic
28e to the ascetic (when Pārvatī puts off her royal clothes in order to perform
28a *tapas*) and then back again:

25ea[2] Śiva said to Pārvatī, 'You have now been purified [*saṃskṛtā*] by *tapas*, and
28a I am your slave. I will adorn [*saṃskāraṇaṃ*] your limbs and decorate your
28e matted locks, replacing your bark garments with lovely silks. I will give you
pearl anklets and bracelets and golden jewels.'[143]

13. Kāma wounding Śiva. Kangra painting, eighteenth century. MOTIF: 43ea.

14. Rati begs Śiva to revive Kāma; she smears the ashes of Kāma on her body. Kangra painting, eighteenth century. MOTIF: 6c, 6cd, 6d, 43e.

15. Agni, in the form of a parrot, and the gods interrupting Śiva and Pārvatī; Vīrabhadra guards the door. Kangra painting, eighteenth century. MOTIF: 30e, 36e, 44ea.

16. The birth of Skanda in a forest of reeds, while Śiva, Pārvatī, and Kṛttikās watch. Kangra painting, eighteenth century. MOTIF: 19a, 20ea, 26e[1].

The same word is used to describe the inner adornment of Pārvatī by *tapas* and her external adornment by jewels: *saṃskṛ*, to purify, adorn, perfect. The first process takes place in the realm of the ascetic, the second in the world of the householder, but they complement each other and each has its proper costume.

In this context, the ornaments of Śiva are considered superior rather
than inferior to the conventional ones. Pārvatī says that only creatures
overcome with delusion take pleasure in ornaments, while Śiva is without delusion and therefore without desire for adornments, and she
appreciates his true form without any need for transformation.[144] She
accepts the snakes of Śiva not because they are like golden bracelets
but because a god who wears snakes is far more wonderful than one
wearing ordinary jewels, and in her eyes the eventual transformation is
no more than a revelation. In this way, when Menā sees the graceful 31e
dancer she fancies, Pārvatī sees the true Śiva—three-eyed, covered with 7cd^1
snakes—and chooses him for her husband.[145] 30a

Several of the Purāṇas describe the 'transformation' from Pārvatī's point of view: the objects are not changed into their conventional counterparts, but are rather considered to act as substitutes for them unchanged:

> The seven goddesses came to adorn Śiva in the conventional way, but how 28e
> can anything be done for one who is perfect? His own natural garb became 14c^3
> a kind of adornment. The moon took its place in the position of a diadem, 7cd^1
> the third eye was a lovely *tilaka*, and the streaks of ashes were the sandalwood 6cd
> paste. The serpents, with their various jewels, became ornaments. By Śiva's 30a
> power, all these natural qualities were transformed. It is difficult to describe
> the beauty of such a form.[146]

The transformation is not merely from the common to the royal, but
from the royal to the magical. Other texts substantiate this point of
view: Śiva wore a great bone for a diadem, dark blue serpents for brace- 38a^2
lets;[147] his elephant skin, serpents, matted locks, and crescent moon all 30a
served as ornaments;[148] he appeared to Satī three-eyed, smeared with 14c^3 7cd^1
ashes, lovely in all his limbs; and Indra anointed Śiva with ashes that
shone like silver.[149] In this set of texts, when Śiva politely rejects the
festive wedding garments brought to him, instead of changing his own
features he merely uses his ashes, skulls, elephant skin, third eye, ser- 6cd 38a^2
pents, and crescent moon for his adornment.[150] 14c^3 7cd^1 30a

Śiva even uses his ascetic jewels to satisfy the conventional wish for ornaments that occasionally makes Pārvatī a nuisance to him: when she asks him repeatedly for jewels—'a desire he considered a mere frivolity

28e 28a on her part'—he at last gives her *rudrākṣas* (rosary beads), out of which
she makes necklaces, bangles, armlets, and ear-rings.[151] In tribal mythology, Śiva is said to have employed even more bizarre ornaments:

> 28e [At the wedding, Pārvatī asked Mahadeo what ornaments he had brought
> 9d her.] Mahadeo had gathered all the poisonous things in the world and made
> 30a ornaments from them. [He had made snake-armlets from the dirt of his
> thighs, hornet-nose-studs from the dirt of his chest, scorpion-ear-rings from
> 28a the dirt of his eyes.] He took the dirt from his penis and made a toad to serve
> 29ea as a spangle in the middle of the bride's forehead. Thus adorning Pārvatī in
> 36e things of poison, he took her home to Madhuban.[152]

As if the ascetic ornaments themselves were not sufficiently repellent, the author of this myth has gone out of his way to extend the extremes, to emphasize the contrasts and to show that, even so, Śiva is an acceptable bridegroom to Pārvatī. Moreover, the particular articles that he
29ea employs—snakes, scorpions, and toads—are used as erotic stimulants
30a by Mahadeo in another context.[153]

A development from the conventional to the ascetic point of view may be seen in the manner in which three closely related texts treat the same passage describing Śiva's wedding preparations. The first resolves the conflict by combining Śiva's ascetic accoutrements with conventional ornaments but retaining horrible adornments in his entourage:

> 38a[2] Śiva's garland of skulls was strung together with many pearls, and the
> 30a serpents on his body became golden ornaments. He was adorned with many
> 28e jewels. The *yoginīs* came to accompany him, adorned marvellously with ser-
> 30a 10cd pents and scorpions, wearing for ear-rings the hands and feet of heroes slain in
> 38a[2] battle, with garlands made of their severed heads.[154]

A second version describes the ascetic ornaments as they are, but adds as a leaven a few conventional gems in the entourage (on the bull), and one ambiguous jewel:

> 14c[3] Brahmā fixed the crescent moon in Śiva's matted locks, and Cāmuṇḍā
> 38a[2] tied a garland of great human skulls upon his head. The Sun gave Śiva a shin-
> 5c[3] 7d ing red gem with great blazing flames, and all the snakes served as ornaments,
> 30a blazing with their own *tejas*. The winds adorned his bull with various jewels.
> 30ea 45e[2] Indra gave him an elephant skin. The Lord of Ghosts smeared funeral ashes
> 6cd of silver upon the skull he carried and bound a garland of human skulls upon
> 33ea[4] 38a[2] him. Agni gave him a goat skin.[155]

The ruby, though a jewel, is transformed by its association with the Sun into a thing of *tapas* and fire, a magical rather than conventional gem.

A more explicit resolution appears in the third text, which begins

almost word for word the same as the second, with certain noteworthy
exceptions and additions: the sun, moon, and fire shine forth from Śiva's $5c^{3}$ $14c^{3}$
three eyes, and Yama (the god of death) places a necklace of serpents 7c $7cd^{1}$
on Śiva's neck. This replaces the serpents who serve him of their own 30a
accord in the other two texts, but the serpents reappear at the end of the
passage:

> Putting aside the ornaments of great jewels of various forms which Kubera 28e
> [the god of wealth] had brought, Śiva with his own hand made ear-rings out
> of the two great serpent kings.[156] 30a

Śiva clearly rejects the conventional ornaments offered to him and adorns himself only with his ascetic attributes in this third phase of the passage.

In several myths, Śiva appears with both traditional and ascetic
ornaments in order to please the different levels of his worshippers.
When he visits Himālaya, he appears adorned with snakes, ashes, and 30a
three eyes, but when Menā enters he becomes handsome and his tiger 6cd $7cd^{1}$
skin becomes a silken garment, the ashes sandalwood paste, the poison 28e 9d
on his body turns to musk, his goblin attendants become dancers, and 31e
he has one head with a pair of lotus eyes.[157] He enters the Pine Forest
first as a filthy madman, and then he returns as a handsome dancer, but 31e
the women love him in either form.[158] Pārvatī also loves him in both
aspects: 'Shining with ornaments, or with snakes; wearing an elephant 28e 30a
skin, or silk; with skulls or the moon as his diadem—no one can compre- $38a^{2}$
hend Śiva, who takes all forms.'[159] $14c^{3}$

I. I. *Snakes and Nakedness*

The mediating role of Śiva's ornaments turns upon the ambiguity of the symbols themselves as well as upon the reversal of an unambiguous symbol. For example, the serpents and nakedness which are a basic part of all the anti-Śiva speeches are frightening and disgusting on one level, but they are erotic symbols as well. Less obvious, but equally forceful, is the erotic significance of the ashes and the third eye. The question of the actual or metaphorical transformation of the ornaments is thus complicated by the erotic overtones of their unchanged forces, in addition to the general erotic value of the horrible and ascetic elements in them.

The snakes that serve as Śiva's sacred thread, necklace, bracelets,
bowstring, and even the warp and woof of his clothes, are superficially
disgusting and frightening to Pārvatī, who attributes Śiva's 'crooked-
ness' to them,[160] but they have other uses and meanings. In their natural 30a

28e form, cobras are said to bear rubies in their hoods, and the jewelled
30a heads of cobras serve as lovers' lamps for Śiva and Pārvatī in the night.[161]
The general sexual significance of snakes is of course well known; the
5c² 30a excited cobra with expanded hood is often found encircling the *liṅga*,
17cd the tail carried down into the *yoni*[162] [Plates 8, 10, 12].

28ea Similarly, on a superficial level Śiva's nakedness is said to be improper,[163] a disgraceful indication of his poverty,[164] or proof of his lack
28ea of modesty.[165] Pārvatī throws all of this in his face when she strips him
of his loincloth in the course of a game of dice.[166] Metaphysical justifica-
28ea tions are often proffered on Śiva's behalf, and he himself says, 'I am
naked because all the sages and gods and men are born naked, and a man
with uncontrolled senses is naked though he be clothed in silk. A man
should clothe himself in patience and passionlessness.'[167] A rationalization more closely related to the Tantric ideal of sublimation was noted
but rejected by the Abbé Dubois, who spoke of naked ascetics, 'the
28ea object of this indecent practice being to convince the admiring public
that they are no longer susceptible to the temptations of lust'.[168]

The sexual aspect of Śiva's nakedness is particularly apparent in the
28e Pine Forest. He is naked in the earliest *Mahābhārata* reference to his
love-play with the wives and daughters of the sages,[169] and the commentator uses the Pine Forest myth to explain the epithet 'Clothed-in-
the-Skies' (i.e. naked):

> 28ea It is known that Śiva entered the Pine Forest naked in order to entice the
> 43a wives of the sages; but actually he is clothed in the infinite skies. . . . When
> 27ea Śiva had slain Kāma, he went begging with his wife. He was naked. One day
> 28ea the wife of a sage said to him, 'Let your uncovered *liṅga* fall to the ground.'
> 32a 36ea 5d Then Śiva's *liṅga* fell, and the three worlds were greatly upset, until Devī,
> 17cd who had been burning with desire for a long time, took the form of a *yoni*
> 5c² 5cd and received the *liṅga*.[170]

These obvious erotic connotations which are mingled with the ascetic
practice of nudity may be traced back to an Atharva Veda hymn, possibly
the basis of the concept of Śiva as the great naked god, in which a great
28ea nude man with matted locks is pursued by a great nude woman who
7c 21ea says that her limbs are burning with desire as if with a forest fire and
16cd begs him, 'Eat this dish of boiled rice and fuck me [*yabha mā́m*].'[171]
24ea² The Pine Forest women say that Śiva is a 'charming ascetic' because of
26ea 28ea his naked *liṅga*,[172] unlike the anomalous sage's wife who takes offence
at his exhibitionism. And in addition to these particular erotic and
ascetic connotations, nakedness forms a theoretical mediating motif as
a transitional phase between ascetic clothes and erotic clothes.

The complete resolution of the erotic and ascetic elements of Śiva's nakedness may be seen in a verse which treats the nakedness as other ascetic elements are sometimes treated, reducing it to a level of playfulness and humour:

> When the snake that forms his girdle starts away 30a
> from the emerald of the bowing Indra's crown 28e 45ea
> in terror of that ornament; 30e
> may he, at whom the mountain daughter smiles with sidelong glance
> to see him on his deerskin mat
> thus forced to cover up his slipping loincloth, 28ea
> may Śiva, bring you purity.[173]

The emerald, being the emblematic gem of the Garuḍa bird who is the enemy of snakes (and a gem used as a protection against snake-bite), frightens Śiva's serpent. And the serpent contributes to the scene by exposing the very part of Śiva which, in other contexts, he himself represents.

1. 2. *The Ashes of Śiva*

The ashes of Śiva, though often transformed into their conventional 6cd
counterpart—sandalwood paste—are by nature capable of sustaining
a number of implications.[174] On an explicit, superficial level, the ashes
are ascetic, disgusting (being the ashes of corpses), and simply anti- 6cd
erotic.[175] But, for all their apparent loathsomeness, the ashes assume an 6d
erotic and creative significance upon Śiva by their association with
the burning and resurrection of Kāma and Satī [Plate 14].

An important Epic myth is predicated upon the primary, ascetic significance of Śiva's ashes:

> The sage Maṅkaṇaka, seeing some vegetable sap fallen from his hand, 26e[2]
> began to dance. To stop his dancing, Śiva broke off his own finger, which 15cd
> turned to ashes. Seeing this, the sage realized, 'One's own body is only made 31e
> of ashes.' Thus, Śiva is called Bhasmabhūta ['Made of Ashes'].[176] 34e 6cd 34a

The myth is told in greater detail elsewhere in the Epic and in several Purāṇas, which offer a less metaphysical and more typically Śaiva explanation:

> The sage Maṅkaṇaka, having performed *tapas* for many years, cut his 26e[2]
> finger on a blade of grass one day and saw vegetable sap flowing from the 15cd
> wound. He danced for joy, and the dance disturbed the universe until Śiva, 31e 7d
> at the request of the gods, took the form of a Brahmin and approached the 34e
> sage, saying, 'It is against the dharma of sages to dance with the lust of passion
> or to sing and dance, as it is pleasant to young women and breaks the *tapas* 33ea[5]
> of a Brahmin.' Maṅkaṇaka explained the reason for his dance, but Śiva merely 25e

6cd laughed and struck one of his thumbs against the other, and ashes pale as
snow flowed from his wound. When the sage saw this he was ashamed, seeing
such a miracle of asceticism, and he said, 'You must be Śiva, for no one else
has such a power. Forgive me for what I did in ignorance, dancing and thus
34a destroying the *tapas* amassed for many years.' Śiva was pleased and told
18a Maṅkaṇaka that, as a special boon, his *tapas* would be increased rather than
$5c^2$ destroyed, if he worshipped the *liṅga*.[177]

Śiva acts here as the anti-erotic ascetic, opposing the dance which symbolizes the breaking of Maṅkaṇaka's vow. Yet this is the very dance
which he himself performs in the Pine Forest with the same ultimate
result: to teach a proud ascetic to worship the *liṅga*. The ashes here
represent his blood, his life force, rather than the funeral pyre from
which they are derived. According to a contemporary Hindu inter-
$14c^2$ pretation of this myth, the sap from Maṅkaṇaka's hand is Soma, the
15cd 7c 12cd sap from Śiva's hand is Agni, and both are essential for creation.[178]

The fact that ashes were used in rites of expiation suggests one of
their erotic connotations. Ashes were the traditional remedy for a fever,
13c especially the fever of love, and they were to be used in place of sandal-
6cd wood paste upon the bodies of a couple who had performed Tantric
ritual intercourse.[179] A similar use is apparent in several myths:

> Formerly the gods lusted for Gautama's wife and raped her, for their wits
> 25e were destroyed by lust. Then they were terrified and went to the sage Dur-
> 25a vāsas [an incarnation of Śiva], who said, 'I will remove all your defilements
> with the Śatarudrīya Mantra [an ancient Śaiva prayer].' Then he gave them
> 6cd ashes which they smeared upon their bodies, and their sins were shaken off.[180]

Seen in the light of this concept of expiation, the ashes smeared on
Śiva's body may bear witness to his past sexual excesses rather than to
his steadfast asceticism. This is substantiated by the commentary on
another epithet of Śiva, Bhasmaśaya ('Lying on Ashes'), which cites
a law book: 'Anyone who has committed a theft, seduced his teacher's
wife, drunk wine, or killed a Brahmin, should cover all his limbs with
6cd ashes . . . and lying on a bed of ashes, meditating upon Rudra, he is
25a released from all sins.'[181] It is clear from the glossed epithet that Śiva
himself is considered to lie upon ashes in such an expiation.

The image of the ash as seed, as the essence of the dead lover, the
pyre as a bed, and ashes as sandalwood paste—all of this is present in
a verse expressing the erotic longing for union with god:

> 6d Let me become a pyre of sandalwood;
> 6cd Light it with your hand.
> 6c And when [it] burns to a heap of ashes,
> 28e Apply [it] to your body.[182]

Classical Sanskrit verses take the transfer one step further, describing the ashes on Śiva's body—originally taken from the body of Kāma or Satī, or merely used as a contrast to the sandalwood paste on Pārvatī's breasts—placed in turn upon the breasts of Pārvatī:

Upon the morrow noticing 36e
that the son-in-law bears kohl upon his lip 28e
and the bride's young breasts are sealed with ash, 6cd
the women smile with rising joy.
Long live the many words they speak,
sweet to the ear of Gaurī's mother. 23a

May the breasts of the mountain daughter save you,
swelling like the temples of Indra's elephant,
coated with ashes for cosmetic 28e 6cd
from the pressure of her tight embrace of Śambhu.[183] 36e

The erotic use of Śiva's ashes is more than a late poetic fancy, for it is
inherent in the nature of the ash itself. As early as the time of the Epic, 26ea
Śiva was worshipped as the god upon whose erect phallus ashes were 6cd
smeared.[184]

I. 3. *The Third Eye*

The third eye is a natural symbol for extraordinary or magical vision, and as such it appears throughout world folk-lore. In India, it is the attribute of the great Indian magician, the yogi. This is its primary connotation as an attribute of Śiva, an ascetic and anti-erotic force which is used to burn Kāma. Pārvatī complains about the eye in the course of their dicing argument:

When Pārvatī won his loincloth at dice, Śiva looked at her in fury with his 33ea[7]
third eye, and the hosts of Śiva were terrified and thought, 'Now Rudra is 28ea
angry with Pārvatī and will burn her as he burned Kāma.' But Pārvatī smiled 7cd[1]
and said to Śiva, 'Why do you look at me with that eye? I am not Death, nor 1 43a
Kāma, not the sacrifice of Dakṣa, nor the triple city, nor Andhaka [all of 38a
whom were burnt by the third eye]. What good will it do you to look at me
with that thing? You have become three-eyed in my presence in vain.' Hearing this, Śiva decided to go alone to a deserted wood.[185] 36a

The anti-erotic nature of the third eye is an important element in another version of the quarrel at dice:

Once when Śiva and Pārvatī played at dice, Śiva won and laughed at 33ea[7]
Pārvatī, who grew angry and said, 'You should not laugh simply because you 36a
have won at dice, especially since you used loaded dice.' Śiva, smiling, said, 22a
'Are you saying that my dice are crooked?' and she, laughing, replied, 'Not 24a
just your dice, either, Three-eyes. All your names, forms, and actions are 7cd[1]

38a[2] crooked. You are called Ugra ["Horrid"], Kāpālika, Tryambaka ["Three-
6cd Eyed"], Vāmadeva ["Crooked God"]. And you are smeared with ashes and
have three eyes, and I cannot even describe what you *do*.' Then Śiva cursed
2 his wife, saying, 'Since you have mocked me, you yourself will have three
7cd[1] eyes and be black and reviled.' Then she held her tongue and prostrated her-
24a self before him, in terror, begging his forgiveness. He told her how to free
25ea[1, 2] 43e herself of the curse, and she became Kāmākṣī ['Having the Eyes of Kāma'].[186]

The motif of the grotesque, destructive eye is closely associated with
the myth of the Seven Kṛttikās in two tribal myths which incorporate
several related motifs of fire and water and resuscitation from ashes.[187]
Even without these associations, a third eye in the middle of the forehead produces a reaction of horror and aversion as a mere physical
monstrosity. This is brought out in the Purāṇa passages which contrast
7cd[1] Śiva's three eyes with Pārvatī's lotus-petal eyes, his deformed eyes with
her wide eyes, his monkey-eyes with her fawn eyes.[188] The inappropriateness of the third eye in an erotic context is expressed in this verse
describing Śiva in the Pine Forest:

7cd[1] As the third eye saw the body of Śiva, which, though the body of the
43a enemy of Kāma, was arousing passion throughout the three worlds, the eye
42ea was ashamed of its former deed [the burning of Kāma], and hid.[189]

Yet the eye is capable of transformation; at the wedding it serves as
7cd[1] the *tilaka* mark on Śiva's forehead and is called 'beautiful' and 'shin-
28e ing':[190]

7cd[1] The eye that blazed in the middle of his forehead,
its pupil red and yellow from the fire within,
28e performed the office of a *tilaka*
9cd made of golden pigment.[191]

On the wedding night, the eye is put to striking erotic uses, arousing in
Pārvatī the very desire that it had formerly destroyed incarnate:

28e When her silken gowns were drawn away for love-making,
28ea Pārvatī covered Śiva's eyes with her hands.
7cd[1] But to her dismay her efforts were in vain,
for Śiva gazed at her with the eye in his forehead.[192]

In addition to these erotic uses, the third eyee has rotic origins, some
of them derived from the mythology of Indra. One myth states that
21ea when Tilottamā danced before them, Indra sprouted extra eyes and
45e[1] 7cd[2] Śiva extra heads to see her.[193] Another version of the Tilottamā story
omits Indra but is more closely related to the origin of Śiva's third eye:

Brahmā created Tilottamā, an *apsaras* so beautiful that she aroused even
39e Brahmā himself. He sent her to Kailāsa to bow to Śiva, who saw her but did

not dare to look carefully at her, for Pārvatī was there by his side and he was 21ea
afraid of her. As Tilottamā walked around Śiva, he made a head facing in 23ea
each direction. Then Nārada said to Pārvatī, 'Look what a despicable thing 7cd
your husband has done. You will be laughed at by all the wives of the gods 24a
when they know that Śiva is attracted to another woman. You can imagine 23ea
what Śiva is thinking about this prostitute who is reviled by wise men.' Then 21ea
Pārvatī was angry and covered up Śiva's eyes. Darkness came over the world, 7cd[1]
and all the mountains were shattered, and the oceans left their beds; it was 22a
like doomsday. Nārada was afraid, and he said, 'Release Śiva's eyes now or 5d
everything will be destroyed.' Yet Pārvatī did not uncover the eyes, and so,
out of pity for the world and in order to protect it, Śiva made an eye in his 7cd[1]
forehead.[194]

The fire of the third eye and the absence of the eye (darkness) produce two equivalent extremes: doomsday. The myth combines two versions of the origin of the eye, one from the desire to see Tilottamā and one from the touch of Pārvatī's hands. The latter origin is derived from a myth which appears in the *Mahābhārata*, where it is already connected—though not explicitly—with the tale of Tilottamā, which follows it immediately in the text:[195]

Pārvatī once covered Śiva's two eyes in play, and darkness fell until a 7cd[1] 5d
flaming third eye appeared in Śiva's forehead, setting the forests and moun- 7cd[1] 5d
tains on fire. As the fire began to burn the mountain who was Pārvatī's father, 7d
Śiva controlled it and restored all to its natural state.[196] 23a 13d

This myth is a multiform of Śiva's burning and restoration of his other
father-in-law, Dakṣa; the parallel is brought closer by the *Mahābhārata*'s
statement that Dakṣa himself by means of *tapas* produced the third eye
in Rudra's forehead after the destruction of his sacrifice. As he acted 7cd[1]
in anger, the third eye must have been produced in order to deform 38a[1]
Rudra, much as Gautama deformed Indra. Yet other texts usually state 32a
that Śiva used his third eye to destroy Dakṣa's sacrifice.[197] 45a

In another version of this story, Pārvatī's gesture is used to explain not the origin but the function of the third eye, which is here considered to be benevolent[198] (as in the Tilottamā myth), rather than malevolent (as in the destruction of Dakṣa or Himālaya):

One day on Mount Mandara, in playful jest, Pārvatī covered Śiva's (two) 33ea[7]
eyes with her lovely hands. When his (three) eyes were covered, great dark- 7cd[1] 5d
ness arose, and from the touch of her hand Śiva's sweat of passion was shed. 11c
A drop of it fell into the fire [of the third eye] on his forehead, and it became 10c
heated. From it a child appeared, singing and dancing and laughing, wearing 20ea
matted locks. Śiva asked Pārvatī to release his (three) eyes; she released his 31e
(two) eyes and light shone forth again. but the child was blind because of the
darkness in which he was conceived, and so he was called Andhaka.[199]

The myth imperfectly combines several earlier versions and retains certain inconsistent details. Pārvatī covers only two eyes, as in the *Mahābhārata*, and the Purāṇa does not mention the origin of the third, but it refers to the third eye and even uses it to explain the birth of the child. This confusion is heightened by the natural tendency to refer to eyes in the dual, in spite of the fact that Śiva must be three-eyed throughout this myth.

A South Indian version resolves several of these inconsistencies:

7cd[1] [On Kailāsa, for a joke, Pārvatī closed Śiva's two eyes with her hands. The
33ea[7] 5d universe was plunged into darkness, and everyone was afraid. Śiva created
7cd[1] a third eye in his forehead. Pārvatī trembled and removed her hands from his
11c eyes, and drops of sweat fell from her ten fingers, forming ten rivers, all forms
44e of the Ganges. They flowed in all directions, flooding everything, until the
14d gods begged Śiva to stop their flow. He called them and put them in his hands
12cd and on his head, where they all united.][200]

Here the two episodes are clearly separated: the eye is first created as a reaction to Pārvatī's touch, and then it in turn creates not a child but a river. The sweat is transferred from Śiva to Pārvatī, and although the text does not state whether or not the sweat fell into the fiery eye before creating the rivers, the water behaves destructively exactly as its natural partner (the fire) behaves in the earlier version of the myth, raging out of control until Śiva regains power over it. Sweat here has a doubly ambivalent function: it produces either fire or water, which is either creative or destructive. The myth is then assimilated to the pattern of the Skanda birth story (a fiery seed [the sweat] placed in the Ganges, a multitude of streams uniting to form one as the parts of Skanda merge after the Kṛttikās have found him) by virtue of another myth which
7cd[1] may be seen as a link: Śiva is said to have created the demon Jalandhara
9c 13cd[1] or the submarine mare when the fire of his third eye was placed in the
44e 20ea ocean.[201] When the third eye is covered, the universe is plunged into
14cd darkness, being deprived of its triple source of light, or it is set on fire
(or, by another reversal, the universe is flooded) by the creation of that same source. The resulting omens are closely related to those which appear in the Pine Forest when Śiva has been castrated, for the eyes of Śiva are thematically related to the phallus.

These are just a few of the conflicting overtones of the third eye, all of which play a part in the myth of Śiva and Kāma, in which Śiva, after
7cd[1] burning Kāma to ashes with his fiery glance, then revives him by gazing
14c[2] upon him with his Soma glance, the gentle gaze made of the elixir of
43e 7cd[1] 6c immortality.[202] This same Soma glance is used by Śiva to revive

Himālaya after his third eye has burnt him to ashes.[203] The interrelation- 14c[2]
ship of these aspects is beautifully expressed by a Purāṇa verse: 6c

> May the three eyes of Śiva protect you 7cd[1]
> when at the time of his meditation they are divided into three moods:
> one is closed in yogic meditation; 34a
> the second, however, lusts greatly 43ea
> while looking at the hips and breasts of Pārvatī, 36e 36ea
> and the third blazes with the fire of anger against Kāma, 43a
> who has thrown his bow far away.[204]

In this way, the ambiguous symbols of Śiva express in a static form the resolution of the mythological paradoxes, for the symbol represents simultaneously the conflicting aspects which appear in series in the myths. Thus where the myth, which functions in terms of action, must describe first one and then another aspect of the god, resorting to cyclic activity, the symbol juxtaposes them so closely as to superimpose them, forming the moment of complete resolution which the episodes of the myth approach but never reach.

J. ŚIVA AS ASCETIC AND HOUSEHOLDER: THE RECONCILIATION

Just as the transformation of Śiva's ornaments expresses symbolically the resolution of his conflicting aspects, so too on a narrative level the asceticism which seems at first to interfere with his life as a householder ultimately enhances it. It is therefore not surprising that Śiva often
appears as the householder *par excellence*.[205] The marriage of Śiva is 36e
contrasted with the illicit sexuality of Brahmā: 'Śiva enters into a 36e
regular marriage for the sake of *Maithunī-sṛishṭi* [creation by inter- 5c[1] 21e
course], whereas Brahmā emits his energy at the sight of Sarasvatī or 27e
Sāvitrī or Śatarūpā.'[206] Śiva is also capable of the illicit spilling of the 39e
seed (and even shares with Brahmā, on occasion, an uncontrollable lust for Sāvitrī), but he does enter into 'regular marriage' as well. He is said
to have married Satī and become a householder,[207] to have become 36e
incarnate as a householder,[208] to have married with the proper rituals 23e
and to have lived as a householder with Pārvatī, building a house and thus following the path of tradition,[209] and to have envied Brahmā and Viṣṇu their married lives.[210]

Moreover, although Śiva cannot have a conventional son, he is nevertheless capable of enjoying the conventional pleasures of paternity.
Pārvatī adopts Vīraka as a son (for she cannot have a son by Śiva), but 20ea
then her breasts flow with sweet milk because of her love for him, and 19e

she takes him on her lap and kisses him and says, 'Go now and play with
Śiva's hosts, but don't play roughly. And don't go into the Ganges,
where it's rough, and don't go into the forest, where there are many
tigers.'[211] Her breasts begin to flow with milk at the moment when
20ea Skanda is born, even though his birth takes place without her agency
19e and far away from her. Puzzled, she asks Śiva the reason for the milk,
but he too is ignorant of the cause, until Nārada comes and announces
19e the birth of Skanda.[212] Then Śiva takes Skanda on his lap, and Skanda
30a plays with the snake that serves Śiva as a necklace, counting the fangs
or hoods with childish inaccuracy, '1, 3, 10, 8', so that Śiva and Pārvatī
laugh.[213] This is a popular motif in Sanskrit poetry, which uses the
ascetic and horrible accoutrements of Śiva as instruments of childlike
humour even as they are used in other contexts as erotic stimuli. In
these verses, Skanda romps among the serpents and other ascetic
symbols:

19e May Guha [Skanda] save you from misfortune,
who rolls at will upon his father's chest
6cd until his limbs are whitened from the funeral ash;
44e who from the headdress then dives deep into the Ganges
at the coldness of whose stream he cries aloud,
till trembling and with chattering teeth
7cd[1] he holds his hands before the blazing eye.[214]

In another verse, the horrible ornaments are 'mistaken' for toys:

19e 38a[2] He touches the garland made of skulls
30e in hope that they are geese
14c[3] and shakes the crescent moon with eagerness to grasp
a lotus filament.
7cd[1] Thinking the forehead-eye a lotus flower,
26e[2] he tries to pry it open.
May Skanda thus intent on play
within his father's arms protect you.[215]

These verses show that the ascetic motifs can be as easily assimilated to a mood of tenderness as they can to one of passion [Plate 10].

Thus the ascetic and householder meet in Śiva without contradiction or compromise, though not without a certain amount of conflict. This tension, expressed by the mythology in terms of marital discord and unnatural children, is ultimately obviated by the attitude of Pārvatī, as it is accepted in the mind of the worshipper, through *bhakti*, a deep love for the god, transcending all reason. The Purāṇas abound in explicit statements of Śiva's reconciliation of the two roles: 'When Śiva became incarnate as Rudra on Kailāsa, he was a yogi, free from any emotions.

He then became a householder, marrying the best of women. Though
he was an ascetic, he married her, herself an ascetic, at the importunity 19ea
of Viṣṇu.'[216] This importunity is described in detail:

> Kṛṣṇa summoned Śiva and said, 'Marry the goddess Devī.' Śiva smiled
> and said, 'I will not take a wife like a common man. A woman is an obstacle 35a
> to knowledge and salvation, an instrument of lust and delusion. I do not want 25e
> a household wife, for I wish to remain free of all enjoyments and sexual 21ea
> pleasures.' Kṛṣṇa said, 'You are the greatest of ascetics and yogis, but now 23e 36a
> you must marry and enjoy erotic pleasures for a thousand years. You must 34a 36e
> not be merely an ascetic. In time you will be a householder and a man of *tapas* 18ea
> as you wish. And only an evil woman brings the misery that you see in union
> with a wife, not a chaste woman. Satī will be your wife, and men will worship 5c^2 5cd
> your *liṅga* placed in the *yoni* of the goddess.'[217] 17cd

Kṛṣṇa here convinces Śiva to avoid being 'merely' an ascetic or a
householder. The argument—that a virtuous wife is a boon and only
a wicked woman a burden—is used for the opposite purpose against
Śiva by the Pine Forest sages.[218]

Without any feeling of contradiction, the devotee sees in Śiva the
realization of all possibilities: he is an ascetic and a householder at once;
of course he is the eternal *brahmacārin*; and he is a forest-dweller in all
those myths in which he performs *tapas* with Pārvatī. A passage similar
to Dakṣa's diatribe against Śiva appears in a hymn in praise of Śiva: 33ea^5
'You are not a god or a demon, nor a mortal, nor an animal. You are not 33ea^4
a Brahmin nor a man nor a woman nor a eunuch.'[219] Even the accusa- 32e 32a
tions of Dakṣa and the sages are based not on the absence of any particular requirement for any particular stage, but rather on the presence
of qualities from other stages which seem to conflict with the stage in
question. He does not lack asceticism, but he has weapons as well. He
does not lack a wife, but he lives in the burning-grounds (rather than 18ea
in a house) as well. The *Mahābhārata* reference to Śiva as 'having tufted 19ea
hair, bald, and with matted locks' is interpreted by the commentator 34ea
to imply that Śiva is a householder, an ascetic, and a forest-dweller,
even though he is eternally a *brahmacārin*.[220] A hymn of praise invokes 18ea
him as the dweller in the forest, the householder, the ascetic, and the 19ea
brahmacārin.[221] The two conflicting paths merge in Śiva through the 34ea
extraordinary level of his *tapas*. When he has married Pārvatī, he carries 19ea
her into the bedroom 'with powers made great by his meditation', 25ea^1
powers particularly useful for sexual enjoyments.[222] Śiva is said to make 24ea^2
love to Pārvatī particularly well because of his *tapas*,[223] and when he
looks upon her with desire and begins to make love to her for a hundred
years, he is described as having great *tapas*.[224] In the context of Indian

asceticism there is no conflict at all between the two opposed stages within Śiva.

The stages of life meet in two ways in Śaiva mythology: Pārvatī herself brings elements of the householder ethic into the world of asceticism when she leaves her father's palace to marry Śiva, and he introduces elements of *tapas* into the tradition of married life by accepting her. This mirrors the symbiotic relationship of conventional and ascetic thought in the actual social order. Both Śiva and Pārvatī transgress normal conventions in order to unite the superficially opposed elements of *tapas* and *kāma* that are reconciled in the religious sphere and that, by implication, ought to be combined in ordinary life as well. The image of Śiva shows that the conflict between worldly joy and the joy of devotion is a positive one, a tension between two desiderata rather than between a Scylla and a Charybdis. Its resolution is represented by the many beautiful descriptions of the forest hermitage in which Śiva meditates—a lush landscape of birds and flowers and magical beings: even in his asceticism, Śiva is *in* the world. The two joys are the same joy, however much they may appear—even to the god, at times—to be separate. They are two aspects of one life force.

But in the more banal versions of the myth it is more difficult to transcend the superficial level on which the two paths conflict. The opposition on the mortal level is between the two goals: it is best to be a holy man, to give up sensual pleasures, and it is best to beget sons, to fulfil one's duty to society. This is of course a problem known to other cultures as well, but in Hinduism it is exaggerated, because passionless sages are so deeply venerated, and the ties of family and children, strengthened by caste strictures and the importance of rituals for the dead, are so very compelling. Man himself must be both procreative and ascetic; so god must be the most ascetic of ascetics, the most virile of lovers. Śiva resolves the paradox in his own character by embodying a philosophy found throughout Hinduism: that chastity and sexuality are not opposed but symbiotic, that the chaste man is procreative by virtue of his chastity, and that the man who lives happily with his wife is performing a sacrament in his very life, if he but realize it.

VIII

THE CONTROL AND TRANSFORMATION OF DESIRE

ON the human level as well as the divine, one solution to the conflict
between sexual and ascetic behaviour was to equate them completely,
playing upon the basic function of power which they share in Hindu
thought, qualifying sexual activity in such a way as to make it entirely
yogic in its application. This solution underlies the Tantric theory of
sublimation, by which desire itself, subjected to ascetic discipline, is
used to conquer desire. The conventional ascetic viewpoint opposes the
method of sublimation; desire must be conquered by chastity, by firmness, by resistance to temptation. As Śiva himself explains, 'The desire
for desires is increased rather than assuaged by the enjoyment of them, 10c
just as a dark flame is increased by oblations poured upon it.'[1] But the
fire which is increased by oblations may be channelled and controlled
by submersion in water, and desire may be controlled not by un-
disciplined licence but by the careful application of sexual stimuli.

The Tantric element in medieval Śaiva mythology is undeniable, but it is false to seek the *origins* of Śiva's sexual ambiguity in this comparatively late development, as some scholars have done:

> Śiva is the tutelary deity of all monks and of all ascetic orders; he stands 34a
> for complete control of the senses, and for supreme carnal renunciation. His 26ea
> phallic representation would be an inane paradox unless we take into account 5cd
> the tantric ideological background of this symbolism, which is truly profound.
> . . . The paradoxical situation, then, is that the tantric appears to the orthodox 24ea[1]
> Hindu and Buddhist as a libertine, whereas in reality he preserves a state of 33ea[6]
> complete celibacy.[2] 21a

The particular element described here as a quality of the Tantric—the masquerade of a chaste man as a libertine—may be traced back to the Pāśupatas of a much earlier period. Another element of this 'ideological background' of Tantrism is described more explicitly by Alan Watts:

> [Śiva] lived with Satī upon remote mountain peaks, and went naked and 36e
> ash-smeared like a yogi. This would seem surprising in view of his abandon- 28ea
> ment of the ascetic life for Satī, unless we bear it in mind that certain forms 6cd
> of Indian Yoga, in common with Chinese Taoism, employ motionless sexual 36ea 34a
> union as a form of meditative discipline.[3] 31ea 21a

This doctrine of *coitus reservatus* has long been a source of embarrass-
21a ment to Hindus.[4] It has a place in Śaiva mythology, neither so central as Western Tantricists would have it, nor so distant as some Hindu scholars might wish. It explains only one of the numerous manifestations of the Śaiva paradox.

In the Tantric view, sex is a cure for desire. Śiva justifies his behaviour in the Pine Forest by saying, 'The wise consider union with a young
24e woman to be the medicine for the fever of old men',[5] thus supplying the erotic parallel to ascetic rejuvenation. In glossing Śiva's epithet of 'Destroyer of Kāma', the commentator says, 'He destroys the desire by
24e giving the enjoyment of the desired thing',[6] thus reversing the explicit meaning of the epithet by interpreting it in terms of Tantric sublimation. A sexual ritual is prescribed to purify a woman who has committed sexual sins:

> 24e 25a A woman who has been unchaste should worship Śiva in his calm aspect,
> 42e Śiva who is Kāma. Then she should summon a Brahmin and give herself to
> 21ea him, thinking, 'This is Kāma who has come for the sake of sexual pleasure.'
> 33ea[5] And whatever the Brahmin wishes, the sensuous woman should do. For
> 35ea thirteen months she should honour in this way any Brahmin who comes to
> 27ea the house for the sake of sexual pleasures, and there is no immorality in this
> for noble ladies or prostitutes.[7]

The Brahmin guest represents Śiva/Kāma, who purifies the woman whom he seduces, for extreme sexual licence may remove sexual stigma, just as extreme *tapas* does.

A. SEXUAL SATIETY: THE *LIṄGA* IN THE *YONI*

43ea When Kāma has aroused Śiva by shooting him with the arrow of
36e 24e Fascination, Śiva resolves to marry Pārvatī in order to cure himself of
43ea the disease born of desire.[8] He says, 'I burn day and night because
24e 13c of Kāma. I will find no peace [*śānti*] without Pārvatī.'[9] The symbolism which expresses this cure is that of the *liṅga* and the *yoni*. Śiva with Pārvatī, the *liṅga* with the *yoni*, and fire in water—the three images of satisfaction on the levels of the myth, the cult, and the symbol—combine in Gāyatrī's curse of Śiva:

> 3 When you are in the Pine Forest, the sages will become angry and curse you,
> 35ea 38a[2] saying, 'Kāpālika, you lowly creature, you wish to carry off our women.
> 13c 5cd Therefore that *liṅga* which you are so proud of will fall upon the ground.'
> 24e 17cd 32a 36e Deprived of your virility by the sages' curse, tortured, you will seek consola-
> 44e tion from your wife on the banks of the Ganges.[10]

Although in the myths the origin of *liṅga* worship is sometimes thus

ascribed to a curse, it is more frequently the result of measures taken
to cure Śiva of his destructive sexual fever:

> The sages cursed Śiva's *liṅga* to fall to the earth, and it burnt everything 32a
> before it like a fire. Never still, it went to the underworld and to heaven and 5cd 5d
> everywhere on earth. All creatures were troubled, and the sages went in 31e
> desperation to Brahmā, who said to them, 'As long as the *liṅga* is not still,
> there will be nothing auspicious in the universe. You must propitiate Devī
> so that she will take the form of the *yoni*, and then the *liṅga* will become still.' 17cd
> They honoured Śiva, and he appeared and said, 'If my *liṅga* is held in the 13c
> *yoni*, then all will be well. Only Pārvatī can hold the *liṅga*, and then it will
> become calm.' They propitiated him, and thus *liṅga*-worship was estab- 5c[2]
> lished.[11]

The solution to Śiva's dangerous sexuality is not to impose chastity
upon him—as the sages attempt to do, and fail, merely exacerbating
the danger—but to satisfy him. Desire must be controlled, not denied,
and in certain extreme situations the only possible control is release.

Lust remains a threat only until it is answered. Satī says to Śiva, 'My
lord, having made love to you for many years, I am satisfied, and your 24e
mind has withdrawn from these pleasures. I wish to know your true
nature, that frees one from rebirth.'[12] As Stacton comments upon the 20a
episode in which Śiva and Pārvatī become bored with sex and invent
the Tantras, 'Your true eunuch is the man who goes to a brothel once 32a
a week. It is an emotional matter.'[13] For this reason, Indra doubts that 24e
he will be able to disturb Śiva's *tapas*, for Śiva has fulfilled all his 45a
desires.[14] 24e

Iconographically, the image of the androgyne is the symbol of sexual
union but also representative of a situation in which union is physically
impossible:

> The meaning of this imagery must be plus rather than minus, suggesting 32e
> that innocence is not the absence of the erotic but its fulfilment. . . . Herma-
> phroditic imagery suggests, rather, that there is a state of consciousness in 24e
> which the erotic no longer has to be sought or pursued, because it is always
> present in its totality.[15]

Moreover, in a purely mechanical way, the hermaphrodite is incapable
of sexual activity, being paralysed in a position which denies any action
of the man and woman relative to one another. This problem is recognized by a classical Sanskrit verse which pities Śiva for his inability to
see Pārvatī when they form the androgyne,[16] and a book entitled *The* 32e
Thirty-Two Positions of the Androgyne illustrates graphically the attempts 36a
of the two members of the pair to separate so that they may unite.[17] The 32e 36a
conquest of desire is the satisfaction of desire: 'In the life of sentient

24c beings, only the state of total sexual consummation is desireless, hence
13c again the symbolism of the *liṅga*.'[18]

B. YOGA AND *BHOGA*

The terms yoga and *bhoga* (the latter indicating sexual enjoyment) appear often in Tantric texts to represent the extremes of the two paths:

21a If a man is a yogi, he does not enjoy (sensual pleasures); while one who
21e enjoys them does not know yoga. That is why the Kaula [Śaiva Tantric]
24ea[2] doctrine, containing the essence of *bhoga* and yoga, is superior to all (other
18ea doctrines).[19]

This Tantra goes on to explain its central doctrine: 'In the Kaula
20e 20a doctrine, *bhoga* turns into yoga directly. What is sin [in conventional
religion] becomes meritorious. *Saṃsāra* [worldly life] becomes Release.'[20]
Yet another paraphrase of this concept appears in other Tantric texts:

20a Where there is worldly enjoyment there is no Release. Where there is
20e Release there is no worldly enjoyment. But both enjoyment and Release are
5c[1] in the palm of the hand of those who are devoted to Devī. . . . Sexual union
20a is an auspicious yoga which, though involving enjoyment (of sexual pleasures),
gives Release.[21]

On one level, this is a simple conjunction of opposites, enhanced by a felicitous assonance (*bhoga*–yoga, *bhokṣa*–*mokṣa*)—the sort of proposition which is not uncommon in the crude system of the Tantras. But it contains the seed of metaphysical as well as psychological truth, and this is developed in the mythology.

Tantrism seeks to employ the devotee's natural dispositions to raise him from the level of sin to the level of the divine.[22] These natural dispositions are natural in the sense of animal and also in the sense of common, present in all men, as opposed to the higher spiritual qualities needed for non-Tantric yoga. It was in view of this aspect of man's nature that Śiva is said to have invented one Tantric doctrine for the benefit of the Śūdras (the lowest of the four classes):

Śiva knowing the animal propensity of their common life must lead them to take flesh and wine, prescribed these rites with a view to lessen the evil and to gradually wean them from enjoyment by promulgating conditions under which alone such enjoyment could be had, and in associating it with religion. 'It is better to bow to Nārāyaṇa with one's shoes on than never to bow at all.'[23]

But it is not enough merely to incorporate into the ritual that which one is naturally inclined to do; this oversimplification led an English writer to remark that 'the bent toward religion of some sort is so strong in India that some of its people even "sin religiously"'.[24] Every ritual of sexual union must be performed correctly, so that a man does not offer his sin to the deity; the natural, animal functions must be converted into acts of worship.[25] Thus what may appear to be a doctrine which allows immorality to members of a religion is considered by the Hindus themselves to be a doctrine which allows religion even to those who are immoral—that is, to those who acknowledge the natural immorality of the flesh.

The application of this doctrine to Śiva, the greatest of yogis and the
greatest of *bhogins* (i.e. those who indulge in sensual enjoyments), is
obvious. Śiva is the narrator of most of the Tantras, explaining them
to Pārvatī, and he himself is usually regarded as the author of their
doctrine: 'This homeopathic system of Shiva is infallible and yields 24e
speedy results. He who thirsts for wine or lusts after women can be 2
cured by this treatment within a very short time.'[26] A Śaiva yogi in 16d
a Sanskrit play sings this verse:

> Gods Vishnu and Brahm, and the others may preach
> Of salvation by trance, holy rites and the Vedies. 18a
> 'Twas Uma's [Pārvatī's] fond lover alone that could teach 36e 20a
> Us salvation plus brandy plus fun with the ladies.[27] 34ea 16d

A similar sentiment is expressed by the Kāpālika in another play:

> Ho, don a right jolly and quaint attire, 28a
> Drink brandy and gaze in your wenches' eyes: 16d
> Long life to our Lord of the Trident [Śiva], who found 34ea
> That the road to salvation this way lies![28] 20a

As propounder of this doctrine, Śiva is also the greatest of its examples.
Brahmā cites this in criticism of Śiva when Śiva has censured him for
his attempted incest: Brahmā says that Śiva considers himself to be
a wise yogi and a *bhogin* with conquered senses.[29] 34ea 24ea²

C. THE TRANSFORMATION OF DESIRE BY SELF-TEMPTATION

It is significant that Śiva, even when a *bhogin*, an enjoyer of sensual
pleasures, has 'conquered senses', for this distinguishes him from the
false ascetic. In a myth which seems to suggest that mere indulgence may 43ea
cure desire, Śiva's lust for Mohinī deludes him until he spills his seed; 21e
then he realizes his delusion, becomes spent, and refrains from his low 24e
act, whereupon Viṣṇu praises him for being the only one ever to have 42a
conquered his delusion in this way.[30] The release—the shedding of the

seed—is not in itself a sufficient cure; it must be accompanied by the conquest of delusion, the attainment of indifference. When this is attained, the devotee who indulges in sexual pleasures is saved rather than damned by them:

> He who thirsts for pleasures in order to enjoy them becomes addicted to desire. But the sage who partakes of sensual pleasures as they happen, with a detached mind, without desire, he becomes free of desire.[31]

This is the justification which Śiva uses frequently in the Purāṇas to retain his status as a yogi while participating in sexual experiences urged by the gods: he does what they ask but he does not enjoy it. The dichotomy between the Tantric's thought and action (like that of the Pāśu-
33ea[7] pata), the inverse of the dichotomy of the false ascetic, appears on the divine level as the masquerade of *līlā*, divine play. Physical involvement without emotional involvement makes the yogi even stronger than he would be if he merely remained for ever in his meditation. For this reason, Śiva is said to have conquered Kāma, not in spite of the fact
43ea that Kāma first stirred his senses greatly, but *because* he was greatly
43a aroused. By conquering his incipient desire,[32] by burning up *his* Kāma, he shows his control, like an alcoholic who is finally able to have just one drink, far more difficult than total abstention.

This kind of self-temptation underlies the episode in which Śiva allows Himālaya to bring Pārvatī to him when he is performing *tapas*. Śiva receives her not because he is a false ascetic but because he is so great an ascetic that he is in no danger from women, or so he thinks:

> 36e Because of his respect for Himālaya, Śiva accepted his daughter, even
> 21ea though he realized that her beauty was a source of great passion, an obstacle
> 42a to anyone meditating upon *tapas*. For this is even greater firmness, to be able
> to remain firm when there is an obstacle. The *tapas* that is done in a place
> without obstacles is greatly increased when done in a place with obstacles.
> 36e . . . Śiva received her even though she was an obstacle to his meditation, for
> 21ea those whose minds are not disturbed even when temptation is near—they
> 42a are truly firm.[33]

Pārvatī taunts him to prove his invulnerability by exposing himself to her temptation, for she says that if he is truly beyond the power of women, he will have nothing to fear from her presence.[34]

This psychology underlay Mahatma Gandhi's habit of sleeping beside a young girl in order to expose himself to temptations so that he might conquer them. He himself defined the true *brahmacārin* in these terms: 'One who never had any lustful intention, who by constant attendance upon God has become capable of lying naked with naked women, however beautiful they might be, without being in any manner whatsoever sexually excited.'[35] Similarly, the Bengali Vaiṣṇava saint, Viśvanātha Cakravartī, married a beautiful girl with whom he lay, but after he had been 'transformed' he did not touch her, as it had been his custom to do, but simply lay with her according to the instructions of his guru, thus controlling his senses.[36] An insight into the success with which such vows were usually performed may be inferred from the Sanskrit term for the vow to sleep with a young wife without touching her, a term which came to denote 'any hopelessly difficult task'.[37]

The explanation which Edward C. Dimock offers for the Viśvanātha story illuminates one aspect of the temptation: 'If one is continually exposed to a given sexual situation, passion gradually drains away; desire loses its significance, perhaps even being replaced by boredom.'[38] Boredom is very close to the indifference sought by the Śaiva devotee. Dimock has pointed out the importance of self-temptation in the Tantric Sāhajiyā sect of Bengal:

> It is necessary to transform desire into true love, or *prema*, before ritual union can be effective. And the Sāhajiyās consider that chastity, especially under extreme temptation, has the power to transform desire into love. . . . Desire, called *kāma*, is dangerous only when it is considered as the end. The truth is that *kāma* is the beginning.[39]

The initial impulse to chastity (which is always visualized as an active state, a method) is a sexual impulse.

D. THE RETENTION OF THE SEED

Eventually, the Tantras refined the doctrine of ritual chastity to allow the man who had conquered his desires to perform the sexual act itself, merely retaining his seed to demonstrate the complete control of his senses. This further confuses the subtle line between free licence and controlled release, for with this sanction sexual play (or mere *rati* in Śaiva mythology, as opposed to the fully consummated act, *mahāmaithuna*) becomes the supreme demonstration of the control of passion. This is the ultimate variation upon the theme of temptation, for in
physiological terms the 'extreme temptation' is the erotic impulse that 21a
stirs the seed so that it can rise through the spinal cord to the brain,[40] 18a
a process which renders the yogi immortal:

> Loss of semen is loss of power. . . . Exposure to sexual stimulation arouses 21a
> this power; controlled, the power is like steam in a boiler, no longer random.[41] 21ea

The seed must be stirred sexually before it can be absorbed mentally. 13cd^{1}

The model *brahmacārin* is the man whose virile energy has been stirred up.[42]

The upward motion of the seed—as in the figure of the ithyphallic
ascetic—represents the channelling of the life forces, and in order for
18a the ritual to be effective it was essential for the yogi to restrain his seed.
24ea[1] For, as Mircea Eliade remarks, 'Otherwise the yogin falls under the law
of time and death, like any common libertine.'[43] In Tantric terms, this
is what distinguishes the false ascetic ('any common libertine') from the
true yogi, as Śiva insists that he is distinguished from the other targets
of Kāma.[44] The seed must be rechannelled, not held motionless; this
is in keeping with the mythological concept of power which cannot be
destroyed but must be set in motion in a safe direction.

21a Tantric texts describe the manner in which the yogi may even control
21e the seed after it has been emitted.[45] In the mythology, this takes the
16c form of numerous incidents in which the seed of the yogi is swallowed,
10c 20ea or cast into a fire, or redirected in other unnatural ways.[46]

One interesting result of the technique of *coitus reservatus* is that the
yogi is able to combine the alternating phases of sexuality and chastity
just as Śiva does in his symbolic aspects, restoring his spent powers
even as he spends them. Śiva himself is noted for his ability not only to
draw up his seed in chastity but to draw it up in sexuality as well, to
21a make love to Pārvatī for many years without shedding his seed.[47] The
gods complain about this, saying, 'For a thousand years as the gods
31ea 21a count them, Śiva has made love to her, motionless; and, being a yogi,
he does not stop.'[48] Since he never sheds the seed which would naturally
put an end to the act, he must be interrupted by some external force,
and this is an important motif in the mythology. On the emotional level,
Śiva rises above his act by continuing to make love to Pārvatī when he
no longer desires her, thus producing the state of indifference to sensual
stimuli sought by the yogi: 'Even when his passion was spent, Śiva con-
29e tinued to make love to Pārvatī.'[49] Śiva is so famous for this ability that
Pārvatī is able to see through Jalandhara's impersonation of Śiva immediately when he sheds his seed and becomes quickly spent.

D. 1. *The Separation of Fertility and Eroticism*

In one Purāṇa, Śiva points out the irrationality of the gods' conflicting requests concerning the restraint of his seed:

44ea Brahmā and the gods interrupted Śiva and Pārvatī in their love-making.
Then Śiva said to the gods, rather hastily, 'Why have you come?' They said,
31e 7d 'Your great sexual activity disturbs the universe. The earth trembles, and

none of the gods can find any peace. Take pity on us all and abandon this
great sexual act [*mahāmaithuna*] and indulge in mere love-play [*ratimātra*].' 21a
Śiva was not particularly happy about this, and he said, 'If the sexual act is
abandoned and mere love-play employed, there will be no son born in Pārvatī. 29a
But it is expressly in order to engender a son that this effort is being made, for 19e
the son born of my seed in Pārvatī's body will slay your enemies and cause you to prosper. Therefore do not worry about me when I am making love to Pārvatī. Go home and leave it to me.'[50]

When the gods insist that he do as they wish, Śiva complies, but Pārvatī's curse of barrenness inflicted upon the gods reflects the basis of their request, which is in fact betrayed by the distinction between the sexual act and love-play: only the first produces a child. The gods are thus rather explicitly asking Śiva to use *coitus reservatus* as a method of contraception. Knowing this, Pārvatī curses them, saying, 'Since you
have interrupted Śiva and me in our sexual act and caused me to be 44ea
barren, therefore all the gods will be denied sexual intercourse with their 29a
wives and will be without sons as I am.'[51] Her curse covers both aspects 29e 2
of the act, the erotic and the procreative, but the quality of fertility is emphasized in most versions of the curse, which merely state that the wives of the gods must be barren.

Yet it is precisely because they *do* want Śiva to beget Skanda that they persuade him—against his will, as he points out—to marry. And it is for this very reason that they then interrupt the love-making of Śiva and Pārvatī: because Śiva, being a great yogi, can make love indefinitely without letting his seed fall, therefore his sexuality must be thwarted in order that his fertility may function. While Śiva makes love to Pārvati,
the gods wonder, 'What will Śiva do? Why does he delay? . . . Śiva, the 34a
lord of yoga, married for our sake, for he is without emotion, but no son 36e
has been born of him. Why is he procrastinating?'[52] When they send 19e 29a
Agni to interrupt the couple, they thereby interrupt the very act which is to produce the general that they need. This inconsistency in the gods' attitude causes Pārvatī's servant to say to her, 'I had to laugh today,
because although Śiva himself said that you were to have a son, and he 19e
himself desired a son, he was today prevented by the gods from begetting 44ea
one.'[53] 29a

The irony of this situation was apparent to the authors of several Purāṇa texts, who were forced to invent unlikely explanations for the unique physical properties of Śiva's love-making:

> Śiva and Pārvatī made love for a thousand years, every day, but Pārvatī 36e
> did not become pregnant by Śiva. The gods became worried and said, 'Just 29a
> as Kāma is attached to Rati, so is Śiva to Pārvatī, but our need is not fulfilled, 42e

29e because the embryo keeps flowing out. We must see to it that their love-play
44ea [*rati*] does not recur.' They said to Agni, 'Go to Śiva and Pārvatī at the end
of their love-play, and show yourself, preventing them from beginning again.
22a When Pārvatī sees you she will be ashamed and will depart in order to practise
25ea[3] *tapas*. Then, since you are his pupil, ask the chastiser of Kāma about some
43a metaphysical question, and delay him for a long time on this pretext. After
19e 20ea a long time has passed, Pārvatī will give birth to Skanda.' Agni agreed to this
44ea and went to Śiva, but he arrived during their love-play, right before the
28ea releasing of the seed. Seeing him, and being naked, Pārvatī was ashamed and
36a departed. Śiva, thus abruptly caused to cease making love to her, was furious,
44a and he deposited his seed in the mouth of the oblation bearer. Agni went to
10c the gods, who were full of both joy and sorrow, thinking, 'We have the seed,
16c but how can we obtain a son from it?' The embryo grew in Agni's stomach
32ea for ten months, and then the gods went to the Ganges and said, 'The embryo
44e is within Agni, but it will not be born without a woman.' She agreed to
12d receive the embryo, but after several months she could bear it no longer, for
15cd her water was all gone, her body was trembling and bloodied, and she was
33ea[6] worried about her fidelity to her husband. At last she released the embryo
26e[1] from her belly and threw it into a clump of reeds, where the child was found
20ea by the six Kṛttikās and eventually given to Śiva and Pārvatī.[54]

The gods in this version wish to have a son, and wish to have him born in Pārvatī. They send Agni neither to prevent Śiva from letting his seed fall in her nor to cause his seed to fall, but merely to prevent him from making love to her *after* the seed has fallen. (This seems to be the implication of the statement that the embryo keeps flowing out.) Agni's interruption is meant to result in Pārvatī's increased *tapas* and the subsequent birth of her son, just as Night's obstacle to their love-making is intended to do. Since this does not happen, it is then necessary to stipulate that Agni, by accident, arrives *before* the seed has fallen and therefore receives it himself contrary to the wishes of the gods. Their ambivalence is clearly expressed—they rejoice at having the seed but despair at having no woman to place it in, for they state explicitly their belief that it is in fact necessary to have a woman in order for the birth to take place. The Ganges is then given unusually anthropomorphic qualities in order to justify her role as the mother: she bears the seed in her belly and worries about her marital fidelity as the Kṛttikās usually do.

The gods' ambivalent attitude towards Śiva's fertility, and the conflict between his fertility and his eroticism, produce similar contradictions in another text:

19e The gods asked Śiva to beget a son for them, and he agreed. He went to
25ea Kailāsa with Gaurī and performed *tapas* in the manner suitable for *kāma*.
27ea 36e Then the gods were frightened, thinking, 'Śiva has been making love for

a thousand years, but our need is not fulfilled.' In misery, they went to see 29e 29a
him, but Nandin prevented them from entering. They sent Vāyu (the Wind) 44ea
to find out what Śiva was doing, and he arrived when Śiva, making love to 30ea
Pārvatī, had reached the supreme bliss. Then Śiva's seed was shaken forth 43ea 21e
from its place, but it did not reach the womb. Śiva saw Vāyu close by and, 29a
becoming ashamed, he stood up quickly, leaving his dear wife although she
was full of love and asked him not to stand up. Śiva said to Vāyu, 'Why have 4
you come here?' and, upon learning about the fears of the gods, he summoned them and said, 'The great action which I undertook for your sakes,
and for the sake of a son, has been made vain by Vāyu, since my seed was
shaken from its place. By my firmness I caused my seed to remain stationary 21a
in the middle of the *liṅga*, and it is always fruitful. Where shall I put it so 26ea
that a son will be born to conquer the demons? No one but Agni can bear it.' 19e
The gods told Agni to bear Śiva's seed in his mouth, and Śiva, tortured by the 44a
arrows of Kāma, placed the seed in Agni and, thinking of Pārvatī, obtained 16c 43ea
supreme bliss. Agni was burnt greatly by that seed which was like the dooms- 5d
day fire, and he threw it into a clump of reeds, whence it was taken by the six 26e[1]
Kṛttikās. Indra caused the seed to enter them, and they prepared a lying-in 45a
house, and on the next day a boy was born.[55] 20ea

Agni is here replaced by Vāyu, perhaps through association with the breeze whose form Kāma assumes to elude Nandin in order to disturb Śiva's *tapas*. As Agni has not offended, he cannot be cursed to bear the seed, but Śiva specifies that no one else can bear it and the gods see to it that Agni takes the seed. As in the previous version, the gods inadvertently interrupt the sexual act and unintentionally bring about a form of contraception: here, apparently, Śiva's seed is shaken forth and is about to enter the womb when, seeing Vāyu, he stands up and thus withdraws from Pārvatī, who protests. Yet, according to Śiva, it was by *retaining* the seed that he intended to produce the son, for he accuses the gods of having made vain his act of procreation by shaking the seed from its place. The element of eroticism is then reintroduced at the end, when Śiva is said to be tortured by the arrows of Kāma and finally to obtain 'supreme bliss' when placing the seed in Agni. (The identical phrase—'supreme bliss'—is used to describe the moment when the seed first falls, at Vāyu's entrance, a repetition which may indicate the Paurāṇika's confusion of the two episodes of the seed.)[56]

Thus the conflict between the gods' wish to have Śiva beget a son by making love to Pārvatī and their wish to have him beget a son by *ceasing* to make love to her is rationalized by their 'accidental' interruptions of his love-play. The paradox is further complicated, however, by a related turnabout on the part of the gods: though they have asked Śiva to marry Pārvatī in order to beget a son, as time goes by they decide that they do *not* want Śiva to beget Skanda in Pārvatī, and they send Agni to prevent the birth rather than to hasten it. At times this pair of contradictions makes nonsense of the Skanda myth, revealing its patchwork as the combination of a myth of the seduction of an ascetic (the Kāma–Pārvatī episode, a myth of eroticism) and a myth of the miraculous birth from the seed of a yogi (a myth of fertility). That these episodes are discrete, that the seduction is not necessary for the birth but is a separate myth, is clear from the manner in which they remain separate in several early versions of the myth. In one text, Devī shows an awareness of the dichotomy between her role as seducer of Śiva and her (thwarted) role as the mother of Śiva's child:

> 23a When Satī was dishonoured by her father, Dakṣa, she wanted to kill her-
> 6d self, but she remembered that she had become incarnate in order to give Śiva
> 19e a son. 'Yet a part of this has not come about', she thought. 'Śiva has not had
> 36ea 29a a son. Nevertheless, a part of it has happened, for Śiva has become passionate
> toward a woman. No other woman can cause his passion to grow great, and
> 6c he will marry no one but me. I will be reborn as Pārvatī and marry Śiva,
> 36e and surely by this means I will fulfil the purposes of the gods.'[57]

Although Devī divides her two roles between two births, even in the second birth the dichotomy remains, as she is allowed to stimulate Śiva's passion but not to receive the risen seed. She is the only woman in the world whose *tapas* is great enough to win Śiva as her lover, but she has too much *tapas* to be allowed to bear his child.

Throughout the Skanda story, eroticism and fertility perform separate, even opposed, functions: Śiva retains his seed during the sexual act and spills it in order to produce a child after he has left his wife, thus indulging in what amounts to a combination of natural contraception and artificial insemination. The notion of fecundity is secondary to the sacred value which Hindus attribute to eroticism: 'The character of participation with the divine which is attributed to the sexual act does
29e not come from its procreative use but from its voluptuous character.'[58]
5c^{2} On the other hand, the cult of fertility as represented by the *liṅga* is
29e primarily procreative and not erotic.[59] According to the Bengali Sāhajiyā Tantrics, '*Svakīyā* love (with one's legal wife) . . . is meaningful only
29e when procreation is the end in view; it is worthless for emotional or
religious purposes',[60] while *parakīyā* love (adultery) corresponds to the
path of non-involvement in the world and contact with god, being solely
18e for erotic purposes. Procreative, *svakīyā* love, conventional love, produces immortality through progeny; erotic, *parakīyā*, religious love
18a offers immortality through Release.

The separation of eroticism and fertility is not merely a by-product
of the yogic technique, but an essential part of its philosophy. Eliade
has interpreted the method of seminal retention as an attempt to recover 21a
the primordial powers that men had before the Light was dominated by
Sexuality; by defeating the biological purposes of the sexual act, one 29e
ceases to act in instinctual blindness like other animals.[61] The conquest
of the biological purpose corresponds to the yogi's conquest of the
emotional purpose—desire. In the mythology of Śiva, the restraint of
the seed serves a double purpose: on the one hand, it makes possible the
birth of a son who must not be born in Pārvatī but who must be inspired
by Śiva's union with Pārvatī; that is, Śiva must make love to Pārvatī in
order to stir the seed up, but he must not place it in her. And in addition,
by separating the functions of eroticism and fertility in this way, the
technique of *coitus reservatus* also allows Śiva to maintain his ambivalent 21a
status as yogi and lover.[62] 24ea^{2} 26ea

Yet the emphasis on Śiva's retention of the seed as a justification for
his sexual involvement is too simple and cannot be made to bear the
burden of the resolution. In the first place, Tantric methods are later
than the ambiguous myths of Śiva, and, in the second place, perhaps
the most important of all the aspects of Śiva, and one of the oldest, is his
role as the giver of the seed.

D. 2. *The Unnatural Creation of Śiva's Son*

The shedding of the seed is not a negation of Śiva's status as a yogi.
Like the episode of Kāma, the engendering of Skanda turns on the
question of Śiva's emotion at the time: was he in full control, acting out
of concern for his devotees, or was he overcome by passion? And, as in
the Kāma episode and the Pine Forest myth, there is evidence to support
both points of view. According to one late Purāṇa, Śiva decided to emit
his seed for the sake of the gods and the universe, long after he had 21e
parted from Devī.[63] Yet in other texts it is clear that Śiva's seed is shed 21e
because of his passion for Pārvatī, the only woman in the world capable 36ea
of making Śiva, who has drawn up his seed in chastity, shed his seed, 21a
and Śiva places his seed in Agni when his passion has risen.[64] In other 21e 44a
contexts, Śiva spills his seed at the sight of Mohinī and even in the 21e
embrace of his own sister.[65] 27e 23ea

The seed of the ascetic is never shed in vain, and therefore once shed
it must be safely disposed of lest it become destructive instead of
creative. It is fertile in itself, without any female agency; the seed is
more important than the womb.[66] A child unnaturally produced in this

way may grow to be either a great hero or, as is more usual in Hindu
mythology, a dangerous monster. The ascetic's son is frequently a source
19a of danger to his father and may even have to be killed; Śiva and Pārvatī
27ea themselves, in the tribal tradition, are said to have killed the children
19a of their unnatural union.[67] Their cumulative *tapas* is so great that it is
29a 7d necessary for Śiva to engender a son from his seed shed somewhere
other than in Pārvatī, whom the gods do not wish to bear a natural son:[68]

36e When Śiva began to make love to Pārvatī, the gods were worried and said
24ea[2] to him, 'This union of a *tapasvin* and a *tapasvinī* produces an excess of *tejas*.
27ea 7d Your seed is never in vain, and if you have a child in Pārvatī it will be so
19a powerful that there will be nothing left in the universe. Therefore restrain
25ea[3] 5d your great seed from producing progeny.' Śiva agreed to this and drew up his
21a 26a seed in chastity.[69]

The danger of the son combines with the danger of the sexual act itself to produce evil omens:

36e Śiva and Pārvatī made love with great *tapas* for a thousand years for the
25ea[3] sake of the gods, in order to engender a son to kill Tāraka, and they were full
19e 27ea of lust. Terrible omens arose—a rain of bloody bones fell and fierce winds
15c 5d blew, comets fell and no one read the Vedas. When Pārvatī and Śiva trembled,
15cd the whole universe trembled. The gods asked Nārada the cause of these omens
38a[2] 31e and he said, 'Śiva and Pārvatī make love night and day, and so these omens
7d 44ea have arisen. You must interrupt them if you wish to be happy, for the child
19a who will be born in Pārvatī is far more powerful than anyone else, and the
7d earth could not bear him.'[70]

The causal link between the dangerous act and the dangerous child is evident from another text:

36e In order to beget a son to kill Tāraka, Śiva made love to Pārvatī for a
hundred celestial years. Seeing their unbearable activity, the gods became
31e 7d frightened and considered the sexual ritual unbeneficial to them. 'Who could
19a bear the son born of someone who makes love for a hundred celestial years?'
44ea they reasoned, and so they sent some Brahmins to interrupt the love-making.[71]

The gods in one South Indian text are still more blunt: 'My lord', they
36e say to Śiva, 'we are happy with your married life, but we would not like
29e 29a it if Pārvatī were to conceive.'[72] Here the act itself is acceptable, but
its fruit is not.

In addition to the danger posed by the *tapas* of his parents, the unborn child is a threat to the gods by virtue of the ancient Indo-European concept (perhaps even an 'archetype' of the universal subconscious) in which the father fears his unborn son and seeks to destroy him. Thus Chronos swallows his children, and Indra produces the Maruts (sons of Śiva, like Skanda) by destroying the embryo of the potential Indra-killer in the belly of Diti. An early version of this story supplies additional links with Śiva:

The Sacrifice lusted after Speech [Vāc] and united with her. Indra was 39e
worried that a monster would spring from their union, so he himself became 19a
an embryo and entered into that union. After he was born, he feared that 45a
a monster might be born after him, so he tore out the womb and placed it 39a
on the head of the Sacrifice.[73] 17cd

Indra acts like Śiva in opposing a union which is in other versions incestuous, for the Sacrifice is Prajāpati, and Vāc is his daughter. This reason for the threat of Skanda—Indra's fear of usurpation by a monster—remains in several early versions of the Skanda birth story:

Śiva made love to Pārvatī for a thousand years, disregarding dharma, and 36e
the worlds trembled and the oceans shook. The gods were afraid, thinking, 31e 7d
'Let us do something so that this act of love is not completed, for if it is then 19a
the son who will result from it will surely steal away Indra's place as king of 45a
the gods.' . . . Indra, knowing that the union of the passionate Śiva and
Pārvatī might produce a child, and fearing the child that might arise from 25ea[3]
two so great in sexual powers, was frightened and sent Agni to interrupt 27ea
them.[74] 44ea

In another Purāṇa, Indra is still more explicit about his fears, even admitting the paradoxical position in which he places the gods:

Indra and the other gods begged Śiva to beget a son to slay Tāraka, and 19e
Śiva began to make love to Pārvatī, but the years passed and he was still 36e
unsatisfied. The earth shook and the gods were greatly upset, and Indra said, 31e 7d
'I am terrified, for the son born of such a sexual ritual will surely overcome 19a
me. I am even more afraid of that son than I am of Tāraka. Brahmā must see 45a
to it that their son does not overcome me and all the gods.'[75]

Thus Indra fears the result of Śiva's extreme *kāma* even as he fears the extreme of his *tapas*, and he sends Agni to interrupt the former as he sends Kāma to interrupt the latter. Indra himself plays a part in the interruption in some versions of the myth, one of which combines a number of the negative aspects of Śiva's sexuality:

When Pārvatī had married Śiva, Śiva took her to a deserted forest and made 36e
love to her for a thousand years. Śiva swooned with lust merely from the touch
of her body, and she was so ecstatic that she knew neither night nor day. 43ea
Seeing their great erotic play, the gods were worried and said to Viṣṇu, 'Śiva,
being a yogi, never ceases to make love, and he does not engage in any (other) 24ea[2]
activity. When they finally stop, what sort of a creature will be born of such 31ea[1]
a couple?' Viṣṇu said, 'Devise some means by which his seed may fall upon 29a
the ground, for if it should fall in the womb of Pārvatī a child would be born 45a
who would destroy the gods and demons.' The gods were worried and afraid. 19a
Indra then went to the door of Śiva's house and stood with his face averted,

45a and he said, 'What are you doing, great lord, master of yogis? Honour to
44ea you.' Then Indra went away, and the Sun came and said the same thing,
5c[3] 14c[3] and then the Moon came, and finally Agni. When Śiva heard this praise, he
44ea wished to stop making love to Pārvatī, but he did not stop, because of his fear
29e of her. But when he saw all the gods standing there in terror and about to
21e begin to praise him all over again, Śiva stopped making love, and as he stood
20ea up his seed fell upon the ground, and Skanda was born from it. Then, in fear
36a of Pārvatī, he said to the gods, 'Flee!' and they all fled in terror of Pārvatī's
curse, and Śiva, the destroyer of the whole universe, trembled. The Goddess
5cd arose from the bed and a great pillar of fire and anger came out of her body,
2 29a and she cursed the gods to be barren.[76]

In this late, Śākta-influenced text, it is Pārvatī rather than Śiva who poses the threat to the gods, and even in other versions the measures undertaken by Indra serve not to prevent Śiva from having a son but to prevent him from begetting a son in Pārvatī.

For these various reasons, the children of Śiva and Pārvatī are never
said to be born in the natural manner. Although in some versions the
gods say that they wish Śiva to beget a natural son, they usually take
19a steps to prevent such a birth, and although Pārvatī begs Śiva to engender
19e 29a a son in her, he refuses.[77] Even when he does not object to the birth
19e of a son, he refuses to allow her to participate in the birth: he desires
29a to have a son born to his wife without having her become pregnant.[78]
The wife of the yogi must always be barren, even though the yogi is the
most procreative of men. Thwarted in this way, Pārvatī seeks revenge
29a by cursing the wives of the gods to be barren, and she herself is mocked
19a for having nothing but 'artificial' sons.[79] In only a very few versions of
the Purāṇa myths are there any indications that Śiva's seed is placed
21e in Pārvatī, although she is said to be the only receptacle for his seed,
8cd and even in these texts the seed is not allowed to develop. The seed
which Śiva sheds in the womb of Pārvatī falls upon the mountainside
21e 7d and is distributed;[80] he sheds his terrible seed in her, but she cannot
8cd bear it and spills it on the ground.[81] Śiva spills half of his seed in her
21e but is then interrupted by the gods and gives the other half to Agni;[82]
44ea 44a nothing further is said of the seed shed in Pārvatī, but Agni's half of the
seed ultimately produces Skanda. Other texts state that Devī gave birth
to Skanda, but they do not describe her impregnation.[83]

Pārvatī's exclusion from the birth of Skanda is historically derived from her comparatively late introduction into the Agni–Svāhā myth, but the persistence with which the Purāṇas refuse to assimilate her may be attributed to the insurmountable problem of accounting for the yogi's wife and child. The myth presents the impossible situation and

then reveals the dangers attendant upon it, as well as the absurdities.
Śiva boasts to Pārvatī of his ability to engender a son by unnatural
means, considering it a talent rather than a curse: 'I will beget a son by
your creative power and my own, for I have no offspring as ordinary 20ea
people do, born through the force of lust.'[84] 29e

The seed of Śiva develops in a variety of unnatural ways to produce
his sons, but they may be divided into two basic groups: some other
substance may be substituted for the seed itself, or the womb in which
the seed is placed may be replaced by a pot, fire, the earth, a river, or
even the mouth of a god. (Even when Pārvatī receives the seed, she
receives it not in her womb but in her mouth or her hand.) Yet the
sexual element is usually present in the form of the stimulation provided by the wife so that the seed may be stirred up. Skanda and the
other sons are born from various liquid substances that pour out of the
bodies of Śiva and Pārvatī after the sexual act. Pārvatī herself sometimes
produces the 'seed' without the agency of Śiva: Skanda is born when
she spits upon the earth,[85] and Gaṇeśa is born from the water she uses 20ea
to wash herself after she has made love with Śiva, water mixed with her 20ea
own seed,[86] or from the rubbings of her body when she anoints herself 17c 20ea
in her bath.[87] Her daughter Kālī is born when she urinates after making 17c
love with Śiva, and nine female deities are born from her images 20ea
reflected in the gems of her necklace, scattered when the gods interrupt 28e
her love-play with Śiva.[88] Gaṇeśa, born from the sweat of Śiva and Pār- 44ea
vatī, is said to be named Vināyaka because Pārvatī created him without 11c
a husband (*vinā nāyakena*).[89]

D. 3. *Creation by Blood, Sweat, and Tears*

Although Śiva is the source of the creative seed, he often employs other substances in order to produce a child. This is a cosmogonic motif used throughout the world to explain the creation of the universe directly from the body of a divine being.[90] In Hindu mythology, the unilateral creation is all the more acceptable because the seed, or seed-substitute, is simultaneously fire and water, male and female—it is liquid flame,
molten gold. Śiva produces a son from the blood of Viṣṇu in the Pine 15cd
Forest,[91] and blood is also the source of a number of demons.[92] In con- 15cd
temporary Indian folk tradition, semen rather than blood is said to flow from the wounds of a *brahmacārin*. But more common in the mythology is creation from sweat or tears.

Sweat is compared to seed in a negative way: 'The drops of semen of 11c
a man who is always excessively attached to women are as unconducive 25e

to happiness as if they were born of sweat.'[93] But the converse is equally true: the drops of sweat of a man of chastity are as productive as seed. The idea of creative *tapas* itself stems from the early Vedic
11c belief in the efficacy of the heat generated by the priest during the ritual,[94] and sweating appears throughout the Vedas as a product of
11c yogic activity.[95] Śiva wanders naked, doing *tapas*, and when he sheds
28ea 11c a drop of sweat from his forehead the Earth nourishes it and raises the
20ea child born from it,[96] just as she receives Śiva's seed to bear Skanda. The sweat of anger is as destructive and creative as the sweat of *tapas*: the
11c demon of fever is born when Śiva sheds a drop of sweat at Dakṣa's
38a[1] sacrifice.[97] And of course the sweat of lust is particularly creative, born
39e of a heat opposed to, though similar to, that of *tapas*. When Brahmā
11c desired Sandhyā, but managed to control his lust, his sweat fell to the ground to produce a multitude of sages, and at the same time the sweat
11c of Dakṣa produced Rati.[98] Similarly, the sweat of Śiva or Pārvatī pro-
11c duces Andhaka, Skanda, Gaṇeśa, and other creatures,[99] and a drop of Andhaka's sweat begets another demon.[100] The relationship between sweat and seed is apparent in a Bengali tale:

> 21e After the discharge of semen Śiva sweated and he washed the sweat away
> 11c with a piece of cloth which he threw away. Out of this sweat a girl was
> 20ea born.[101]

11c In a tribal myth, the first two creatures are born of sweat, but incest presents a barrier to subsequent creation, which is finally accomplished by another seed-substitute:

> 27e [She objected that she could not marry him because they were siblings.]
> 24a This she followed with taunting remarks about his ugly shape. [He wept and
> 11cd she picked up the tear-drops.] The tears penetrated her womb and she became
> 20ea pregnant.[102]

Creation by tears is particularly central to the early mythology of Rudra:

> 11cd After his first unsuccessful creation, Prajāpati wept, and his tears became
> 20ea Rudra, with his hundred heads and thousand eyes, and all the other Rudras.
> 16cd 7cd 7d Rudra sought food, and the gods were afraid of him. They gathered food and
> 13d appeased him.[103]

11cd Usually it is Rudra who weeps until he is fed or named;[104] his name is
11cd said to be derived from *rud*, to weep.[105] Another myth relates tears to the creation of the moon, the receptacle of Soma:

> 8c Brahmā told Atri to create, and Atri performed great *tapas* for creation. By
> 36e this *tapas* a great bliss entered his eye, in which Śiva dwelled together with
> 11cd Pārvatī, and tears flowed down from Atri's eyes, flooding the universe with

light. The ten quarters of the sky, taking the form of a woman, received that
embryo in their belly, and after three hundred years, when they could bear 14c[2,3]
it no longer, they released it and Brahmā made it into a youth, Soma.[106] 20ea

Śiva and Pārvatī dwell together in Atri's eye, as Indra and Indrāṇī are 7cd[2]
said to dwell in the eyes of the yogi, where they shed their seed, and as 36e 21e
Śiva and Devī dwell in the yogi's head, where they cause Soma to 36e
flow.[107] Atri's tears are simultaneously Soma and seed, unbearable like 14c[2]
the seed of Śiva, received by the skies as Śiva's seed is received by the constellation of the Kṛttikās. Another tribal myth describes the creative power of Śiva's tears:

> There never used to be tears. When Sahadeo, the father of Mahadeo, went 11cd
> to his wife he was able to continue for six months without rest. As a result 21a
> Sahadeo's wife conceived. [When she gave birth she was in pain and her eyes 19e 7cd[1]
> flashed fire. Sahadeo threw magic water into her eyes and water began to flow 5c[1] 11d
> from them. Mahadeo was born.] After that people began to cry.[108] 20ea 11cd

The traditional motifs are here deprived of their causal relationship, but the fiery liquid (tears, sweat, seed, or Soma) still results in primeval creation.

D. 4. *The Drinking of the Seed*

In addition to the substitution of some other fiery liquid for the seed, the magical birth often proceeds by placing the seed somewhere other than in the womb. Usually, the seed of Śiva is said to have been drunk by Agni, and the image of thirst, and of the seed as a delicious liquid,
recurs in the Purāṇas: 'Śiva emitted his seed, and Agni swallowed it as 21e 44a
a man tortured by thirst swallows water mixed with sesamum.'[109] Even 16c
when Agni is not involved in the birth, the seed is associated with thirst:

> When Śiva and Pārvatī were making love together, Viṣṇu took the form 36e
> of a Brahmin with matted locks, oppressed by thirst, and he went to the bed- 33ea[5]
> room door and said, 'What are you doing, Śiva? Arise and give me food and 44ea 16cd
> water, for I am an old man oppressed by thirst.' Śiva arose, and his seed fell 21e
> on the bed instead of in the womb of his wife. Then Śiva and Pārvatī offered
> the Brahmin food and water, and he vanished and took the form of a child 20ea
> and went to Pārvatī's bed. There he became mixed with the seed of Śiva that was on the bed, and he was born like an engendered child. Pārvatī found the child and nursed him, naming him Gaṇeśa.[110]

In spite of the thematic importance of this motif, in anthropomorphic terms the drinking of the seed is a sin. Śiva says to Agni, 'You did
a perverse thing, to drink my seed.'[111] The law books prescribe an 16c
expiation for a man who has unwittingly swallowed semen,[112] and even 16c

the permissive *Kāmasūtra* has nothing but blame for this particular
16c perversion, which is confined to eunuchs and prostitutes.[113] Thus it is
16c 10c said, 'He who performs sexual intercourse in the mouth of his wife
18e causes his ancestors to eat his seed for a month.'[114] Here the prohibition
on the human level is combined with a parallel description of the supernatural level. Agni is commanded to drink the seed in order to resolve
the ambiguous fatherhood of Agni and Śiva, to maintain the ritual
symbolism of the seed placed in fire, and to ensure an unnatural birth
of Śiva's son. (The fiery seed is placed in Agni's mouth both because of
the ancient belief that Agni receives the oblation in his mouth and
because of the ancient motif of mythical people and animals with fire
coming out of their mouths, a motif epitomized by the submarine mare
13cd[3] who is called Fire-Mouthed [Jvalamukhī].) Nevertheless, Agni must be
2 punished, by being cursed to suffer from the burning seed, to be omni-
44a vorous, to eat ordure, or to suffer from leprosy.[115] The human and
divine planes cannot be resolved in any other way; so, too, Viṣṇu is
punished for seducing the wife of Jalandhara, and Śiva himself performs
a vow of expiation for beheading Brahmā.

In spite of the fact that one of the purposes of the drinking of the seed
is to allow Śiva to beget a child without the agency of Pārvatī, this very
same method is used in several versions of the myth to place the embryo
16c in Pārvatī after all. When Agni has drunk the seed and the gods have
44a been impregnated, the seed bursts forth from their stomachs to form
32ea 9cd a golden lake, whose water Pārvatī drinks. She then gives birth to a son,
16c but only after the intervention of enough other agents to prevent the
20ea child from being considered the direct product of Śiva and Pārvatī.[116]
9cd Another version of this episode makes explicit this last condition: after
16c Agni has vomited forth the lake and Pārvatī asks the Kṛttikās for some
20ea of the water to drink, they at first object, saying, 'If we give it to you,
7d then let the child who will be born from it be our son too. For the seed
19a of you and Śiva would be hard for the universe to bear.'[117] The lake of
seed is assimilated to a motif of the 'natural' motherhood of Pārvatī in
one South Indian tale:

> 19e [When Pārvatī found Skanda, she picked him up to nurse him, and her
> 9cd breasts began to flow with milk so abundantly that it flowed like a river into
> 33ea[4] the lake called Forest of Reeds. Six sons of a sage, who were in this lake in the
> 26e[1] 20e form of fish because of a curse given by their father, swallowed this milk
> 16c 20a and gained their true form.][118]

The six sons replace the six Kṛttikās who find the seed/milk in the
forest/lake of reeds. Motifs of divine (unnatural) birth and rebirth

alternate with those of conventional parentage, such as the milk in Pārvatī's breasts.

A Bengali version indicates that the drinking of the seed, even without the intervention of the Kṛttikās, is considered sufficiently removed from the sexual act to allow the yogi to beget an unnatural child in a woman:

> [Dharma once wiped the sweat off one side of his body, and it became the 11c
> goddess Ādyā.] She went to Kāmadeva and advised him to disturb Dharma's 20ea
> undivided religious meditation. Dharma then felt amorously inclined. He 39e 21ea
> deposited his seed on a vessel and went to the river to get a leaf, how- 43ea
> ever, his seed, which was mistaken for poison by Ādyā. 'I shall make an end 21e 26e²
> to myself by swallowing the poison', she thought, suffering from remorse. 9c 10cd 9d
> She swallowed it but became quick with child, [and she then gave birth to 16c
> Viṣṇu (who appeared from her navel), Brahmā (who came out through the 20ea
> crown of her head), and Śiva (who emerged 'in the natural way').][119]

Another version of this myth adds certain significant details:

> [Kāma was born from the passionate thoughts of Ādyā when she reached 41e
> puberty. Dharma was so aroused at the sight of her that he spilled his seed, 39e
> which an owl collected in a pot and brought to her. Then he went out to 21e 21ea
> search for a bridegroom for her (or: Dharma himself married Ādyā and then 30e
> left her, to do *tapas* as before).[120] As time passed, Ādyā felt the wounds of 23e 43ea 36a
> Kāma so deeply that she drank what she thought to be poison in order to 36e 10cd
> end her life. She became pregnant instead, however, giving birth to Brahmā, 16c 20ea 9d
> Viṣṇu, and Śiva. In time, Dharma tested Śiva and told him to marry Ādyā,
> which he did.][121] 36e

Several motifs are reversed in these myths, but the elements of the plot
remain almost intact. Sometimes the seed is mistaken for Soma and 14c²
drunk to ensure immortality;[122] here it is mistaken for poison and drunk 16c
to ensure death. In the first version Ādyā wishes to die because (like
Sandhyā) she is ashamed of her desire; in the second she wishes to die
because she is under the influence of that desire. In the first she is
involved incestuously with her father; in the second with her son. But
in each case Kāma excites an illicit desire which results in an unnatural
birth. The third child, Śiva, said to emerge 'in the natural way', is
nevertheless conceived unnaturally. In another Bengali incest myth, the 27e
sister becomes pregnant when, repulsed by her brother, she 'unknow- 27a
ingly' drinks the semen which he has discharged into a river when 16c 21e
sexually aroused; she then marries her brother.[123] The primeval pair 9c
in this story are birds, who are frequently involved in myths of the 30e
drinking of the seed: a king hunting in the forest, separated from his 30e
wife when she is in her fertile period, sends his seed to her in a leaf- 22e
packet carried by a falcon.[124] In another Bengali story, Śiva is excited 21e 26e²

30e 44ea by the sight of birds mating, casts his semen upon a lotus leaf, and the
21e 26e[2] seed passes down through the stalk of the lotus into hell, where it
5cd eventually engenders his daughter Manasā.[125] The lotus—whose hollow
20ea stalk relates it in function to the reed—here fulfils the role of the flame
liṅga which plunges down to hell.

16c Impregnation by drinking semen is a world-wide theme,[126] and it is
particularly well developed in India. In the Vedic story of Saṃjñā, the
13cd[1] mare becomes pregnant by smelling or absorbing through her nostrils
16c 33ea[4] the seed of her husband.[127] Ṛṣyaśṛṅga was born when a female gazelle
16c drank the seed shed by the sage Kāśyapa (or Vibhāṇḍaka) when he was
21e 21ea excited by an *apsaras*,[128] and Nārada was born when a woman begged
24ea[2] Kaśyapa to impregnate her, was refused, and then drank the seed which
21ea 16c Kaśyapa shed at the sight of another *apsaras*[129] (just as Svāhā took the
21ea seed which Agni shed at the sight of the sages' wives). Still more closely
related to the Skanda myth is the story of Yuvanāśva, who accidentally
16c drank the consecrated water which his wife was to have drunk in order
32ea 45e[1] to enable her to bear a son; Yuvanāśva himself became pregnant and
32ea bore a son who was suckled upon Indra's thumb,[130] a reversal of the
normal sexes in both pregnancy and nursing. Since Agni is the messenger
between gods and men, the seed which he drinks is automatically transferred to all of the gods, who are said to be pregnant with the seed of
Śiva. This is generally accepted as a metaphor, but one Purāṇa takes it
literally and treats it with humorous common sense:

32ea The gods came to Śiva and said, 'We have all become pregnant and are
44a lactating. Your seed is burning our bodies and we are a laughing-stock, for
7d we are men who have become pregnant. Help us.' Śiva smiled and said, 'But
29a this is what you wanted. You did not want a son born in the belly of Devī,
and so you yourselves have become the place of the embryo.'[131]

The impregnation of the gods by Śiva balances their wives' barrenness
due to Pārvatī's curse, but it is also a manifestation of the transformation
of the sex of the male worshipper in order to enjoy union with god.

16c Less obviously fertile substances may prove productive when
17c ingested: Gaṇeśa is said to have been born to a female demon who had
drunk the unguents mixed with body rubbings discarded by Pārvatī.[132]
In another tale, Pārvatī is said to have miscarried and thrown the
9c embryo into a stream; the seven daughters of Jalandar Guru bathed
17c 8cd there and became infected with various diseases including syphilis,
15cd gonorrhea and menstrual problems.[133] This is a reversal of the myth
in which Pārvatī receives the embryo from the wives of the Seven Sages,
17c bathing in the river, but the bathing itself is a widely accepted method

of impregnation.[134] The sages' wives become pregnant with Rudra's seed
by bathing in the Ganges[135] or by warming themselves by the fire after 17c
bathing.[136]

E. THE SEED AS SOMA AND POISON

The drinking of the seed is all the more appropriate in the light of the
connection between the seed and Soma. The yogi causes his seed to rise 14c^{2} 21a
to his head, where it becomes Soma.[137] The love-making of Śiva and 36e
Pārvatī sustains the moon, the source of Soma.[138] Soma is seed stored 14c^{3,2} 14c^{2,3}
in the moon, and when the moon is full the gods drink it to gain immor- 16c 18a
tality.[139] The image of Agni as the bird (parrot, goose, swan, or turtle- 30e
dove,[140] and once as an owl[141]) with seed in his mouth is derived from 14c^{2}
the Vedic myth of the bird who stole the Soma,[142] combined with the 30e
related Indo-European motifs of Agni as a Fire-bird (the Russian 7c
zharptitsa) and the tale of the bird who brings ambrosia or fire from 14c^{2}
heaven, usually within a hollow reed.[143] The sexual significance of birds 26e^{1}
in India may also be related to the ancient Greek tradition of the winged 5cd
phallus or phallic-headed bird (particularly the goose or swan, as in the 30e
myth of Leda); in this context, it is natural for the bird to carry seed. 10c
Agni is thus both the bird who carries the seed and the sacred fire into 14c^{2}
which the Soma is offered: 'Agni is Gāyatrī . . . and since Gāyatrī, as
a falcon, fetched Soma from heaven, therefore she is (called) the Soma-
bearing falcon.' Indra is called the eagle who bears Soma, and he is said 45e^{1} 33ea^{4}
to have changed himself into a falcon once during a rivalry over the 30e
Soma.[144] The image of the seed as Soma persists in Śaiva symbolism, 16c
for when Pārvatī drinks the seed she is the snake goddess coiled around 14c^{2} 30a
the *liṅga*, drinking Soma through the mouth of the *liṅga*.[145] 5cd

The seed placed in Agni is the Soma used as an oblation in fire. In the 10c
Vedas, the seed of Prajāpati serves creation in this way;[146] it forms a pond
which is preserved by being surrounded by fire, and it is offered as an
oblation into the sacrificial fire.[147] This story is inserted as a conscious 10c
multiform within the myth of the begetting of Skanda in the *Mahā-* 1
bhārata:

Formerly all the sages and gods came to a great sacrifice. Śiva himself came
there and offered himself as an oblation into himself. Then all the goddesses 10c 44a
came there, and when Brahmā saw them he shed his seed upon the earth; 39e 21ea
then Pūṣan took up in his hands the dust which was mixed with Brahmā's 21e
seed and he cast it into the sacrificial fire. And as Brahmā offered the oblation, 10c
acting as the priest, he took up the seed with a sacrificial spoon and offered

20ea it as if it were consecrated butter. From that seed Brahmā created the various
orders of creatures.[148]

The primeval incest, the shedding of Brahmā's seed at Satī's wedding,
the destruction of Dakṣa's sacrifice (here linked by the character of
Pūṣan), and the creation of Skanda—all these motifs unite in the ritual
image of the oblation, explicitly identified with Śiva himself. Himālaya
will give Pārvatī only to Śiva, for only fire is worthy to receive the puri-
44a fied oblation, and the *Mahābhārata* says, 'Was not the seed of Śiva
10c poured as a libation upon the fire?'[149] The sexual image may be used
in either direction: just as the sexual act may be considered an oblation,
10c the oblation may be a sexual act, in which the fire is likened to the
17cd *yoni*,[150] a reversal of the usual imagery of the fiery seed in the liquid
yoni. In the Pine Forest, the women use this reversed image to entice
Śiva, but he turns their metaphor against them:

17cd The women said to him, 'The Vedas say, "Fire is the woman, the fuel is
6cd her lap; when she entices, that is the smoke, and the flames are her vulva.
What is done within is the coals, and the pleasure is the sparks. In this
10c Vaiśvānara fire [within the human body] the gods always offer seed as oblation." Therefore have pity. Here is the sacrificial altar.' But Śiva, the ascetic
24ea² who is always gracious to women, smiled and said, 'This *tapasvinī* [Pārvatī
27ea in the form of a mountain woman beside him] serves me as a well-stoked
10c sacrificial fire. And into this fire I sacrifice my seed as an oblation for the
perfection of creation.'[151]

The women are quoting fairly directly from a text which appears in
several Upaniṣads and Brāhmaṇas.[152] This ancient imagery is used in the
Tantras, which liken the act of ritual intercourse to the oblation into
the sacred fire. Śiva himself tells Pārvatī in one Tantric text, 'I take my
10c seed and at the end of the oblation I sacrifice it into the fire.'[153] The
liquid seed in fire is the mirror-image of the fiery *liṅga* plunged into the
liquid *yoni* of the goddess.

14c² The gods offered Soma into the fire and made Agni immortal, thereby
10c 18a making themselves immortal,[154] just as they make Agni and themselves
pregnant (the alternative to ritual immortality, involving immortality
through progeny) with Śiva's seed. The parallel is stated in one text:

14c² Agni said, 'Release your seed, the heavenly Soma, into my hands, and let
16c the gods drink it immediately.' Then from his *liṅga* Śiva released his perfect
21e seed which had the fragrant perfume of jasmine or the blue lotus. Agni took
44a it in his hands and drank it, rejoicing, thinking, 'Elixir!' and then Śiva
vanished.[155]

In many of these myths, Soma is closely related to poison. The

Kṛttikās are burnt by Śiva's seed as if they had plunged into an ocean 9d
of poison.[156] The Soma/poison opposition may be understood in terms
of the simple conjunction of opposites, but a more specific background
may be seen in the myth of the churning of the ocean, in which Śiva 14cd
is the drinker rather than the source of the drink.[157] One version of this 16c 9d
myth relates the poison to the *tejas* of Śiva:

> When the gods churned the ocean for Soma, a flaming poison emerged $14c^{2}$ 14cd 9d
> and threatened to burn the universe. The gods sought refuge with Śiva, say- 5d
> ing, 'We strove for immortality, but we found death. When in our greed we 18a 8d
> began to churn excessively, the poison emerged. Protect us.' Śiva took the 30e 7d
> form of a peacock and held the poison in his throat. 16c
>
> When Devī saw this she was terrified and vanished, and Śiva was sad. He 22a
> asked the Ganges to carry the poison to the ocean but she refused, saying that 14cd
> the poison would burn her. He asked all the other rivers, and finally the Siprā 44e 12d
> agreed to take the poison to the Mahākāla ['Great Black'] forest and place it
> on the Lord of Kāma *liṅga* there. She did this and it became a poison *liṅga* 5cd
> which killed several ascetics who gazed upon it. Śiva then revived them and $14c^{2}$ 9d
> made it into a *liṅga* which bestowed health upon its worshippers.[158] $5c^{2}$

The motif of the blazing substance which is transferred from one place
to another appears in the Skanda story and in the myth of the submarine 13cd
mare, which emerges from the ocean immediately before the poison and 9d
is eventually carried back into the ocean by the one river willing to 14cd 44e
undertake this dangerous task.[159] The *liṅga* here produces not the seed
(as it does in nature) nor the Soma (as it does in Tantric symbolism),
but poison. The *liṅga* then restores the poison to its original beneficial
state (medicine, the equivalent of Soma), resolving the danger in a cyclic
transformation just as the *liṅga* of quarrels becomes a cure for quarrels.

Śiva inherits one aspect of his fame as a drinker of Soma from Indra, $45e^{1}$
who is the great Soma-drinker of the Vedas. Śiva's drinking of poison $14c^{2}$ 16c
may be traced back to the Vedic sage who drinks poison with Rudra, an 9d
ecstatic practice which remained a part of Hindu yoga: the yogi is said
to have the power to digest deadly poison as if it were nectar.[160] Similarly 9d
it is said, 'By the poison which kills all animals, by that same poison the $14c^{2}$ 2 9d
physician destroys disease. . . . Here Shiva (the propounder of the $14c^{2}$ 2
Tantric system) prescribes poison which eradicates poison.'[161]

F. FOOD AND SEX

The drinking of the seed is further supported by the connection
between eating and sexual activity, an analogy which Lévi-Strauss has 16cd

discussed at considerable length[162] and which is of great significance in Hinduism:

> *Bastu* or *birya* [seed] is generated inside the body of a man and *rati* [the
> 21e 21a seed of a woman] is generated in the body of a woman after the intake of food.
> 16cd Food is converted into blood, and from the blood itself are generated *birya*
> 15cd and *rati*.[163]

15c This is based upon the Upaniṣadic concept of the generation of seed
16cd from rain through the medium of ingested plants,[164] and it is related
26e to the general belief in the interdependence of the digestive and repro-
21e ductive tracts. In this way, Śukra, trapped inside Śiva's stomach after
16cd having been eaten, emerges as seed from his *liṅga*.[165]

The concept of Śiva's seed as food is employed in one variant of a group of myths in which enemies can be destroyed only by voracious demons who then must be fed to be controlled:

> The demon Ruru with his army attacked the gods, who sought refuge with
> 13cd[3] Devī. She laughed, and an army of goddesses emerged from her mouth. They
> 16cd killed Ruru and his army, but then they were hungry and asked for food.
> 33ea[4] Devī summoned Rudra Paśupati and said, 'You have the form of a goat and
> 7d you smell like a goat. These ladies will eat your flesh or else they will eat
> 1 everything, even me.' Śiva said, 'When I pierced the fleeing sacrifice of Dakṣa,
> 38a which had taken the form of a goat, I obtained the smell of a goat. But let the
> 8cd goddesses eat that which pregnant women have defiled with their touch, and
> newborn children, and women who cry all the time.' Devī refused this dis-
> gusting food, and finally Śiva said, 'I will give you something never tasted by
> 5cd anyone else: the two balls resembling fruits below my navel. Eat the testicles
> 16cd that hang there and be satisfied.' Delighted by this gift, the goddesses praised
> 32a Śiva.[166]

The goat is introduced into this myth for several reasons: Śiva in his identity of Agni has the form of a goat or ram, the animal noted for its virility and therefore used to supply testicles for the castrated Indra, just as it supplies a head for Dakṣa (an incident explicitly mentioned in the myth); it is therefore in his goat aspect and as Lord of Animals (Paśupati) that Śiva offers his testicles here. The close connection between the goat and the testicles is revealed by the fact that another version of this myth, in which the goddesses are satisfied with the 'disgusting food' and do not eat any part of Śiva, does not refer to the testicles or to the goat.[167]

Lust and hunger are closely related in Śaiva mythology. In one of the
many myths which deal with the satiation of Rudra's hunger, Prajāpati
7d fears that Agni will eat him, as there is no other food, and he satisfies

Agni by offering him a wife—Svāhā, the oblation, the food of fire.[168] 16cd
Elsewhere Śiva supplies a sexual panacea to satisfy hunger: 10c

> [A man saw a beautiful maiden] and he wanted to devour her, for he had 16cd
> no penis and he could only find pleasure in swallowing. [Mahadeo came there] 32a
> and between her legs with his nails he made an oval opening. [He made a penis 17cd 5cd
> and testicles for the man out of his own thumb and the two swellings on his 5c[1]
> ears.] The world was saved.[169]

The reversal of this situation—food used to satiate a sexual appetite—appears in the *Rāmāyaṇa*, where the demon Rāvaṇa threatens to eat Sītā if she refuses to satisfy his desire.[170] Both appetites are considered potentially destructive forces that must be controlled or channelled, usually by eating. A Hindu scholar discusses the interrelationship of sexuality and hunger in Śiva:

> Agni without food or fuel becomes finally extinguished and black ashes 7c 11d
> (*bhasma*), but if it is supplied with its daily food or offering it is converted 6cd
> into the radiant flame of life. Food is called Soma and that represents the 12c
> female or Mother principle whereas Agni represents the male or Father 14c[2] 17cd 7c 5cd
> principle. When Agni is satiated with Soma that is the normal order of Yajña 10c
> [the sacrifice]. In Rudra–Śiva mythology, that is represented as Ardha- 13c
> nārīśvara, the half-male and half-female aspect of Śiva.[171] 32e

The symbol of sexual satiation is the image of the fire fed and assuaged with a liquid representing a female power.

In one myth, Śiva uses the hunger itself to solve the problem:

> When Śiva heard the message of Jalandhara, he frowned in anger, and from
> between his brows there appeared a terrible man with the face of a lion, hair 33ea[4]
> standing on end, and blazing eyes. The man tried to eat Rāhu, the messenger 7cd 7d
> of Jalandhara, but Śiva prevented him. Then the man complained of his
> constant hunger and asked for food, and Śiva said, 'If you are hungry, eat 16cd
> the flesh from your own limbs.' The man devoured himself until only his head 38a
> remained. Śiva was pleased and made him his doorkeeper.[172]

Rāhu, the messenger who is almost devoured, appears as the devourer
in the myth of the churning of the ocean from which this motif is taken.
When Śiva drinks the poison and keeps it in his neck, Rāhu steals the 9d
Soma and only manages to swallow it as far as his neck when he is 14c[2]
beheaded. The head—being immortal by virtue of the Soma which has 38a
passed through it—is thenceforth responsible for lunar eclipses (i.e. the 14c[3]
periodic devouring of the Soma) as well as solar eclipses. 5c[3]

Eating (frequently with sexual overtones) is thus a frequent solution
to the problem of chain reactions which threaten to become intermin-
able. When Śukra revives the demons slain in battle, Śiva eats him, and
when demons arise from each drop of Andhaka's blood, goddesses are 15cd

16cd created to devour them; when the goddesses in turn prove a threat to
7d the universe, Viṣṇu creates yet another band of goddesses from parts
32a of his body, including his genitals. When the secondary goddesses have
disposed of the first group, Viṣṇu reabsorbs them into himself (i.e.
eats them).[173]

G. THE CONTROL OF EXCESS

There are many similar myths, in which Śiva is called upon to restrain or control some force which has reached the level of excess and threatens destruction. One version of the myth of the beheading of Brahmā falls into this pattern:

Brahmā's fifth head was helping the demons to devour the gods, who asked
5d Viṣṇu to cut it off. He said, 'If the head is cut off it will destroy the universe.'
38a Then they praised Śiva, and he agreed to cut off the head and hold it, since
12d the earth could not bear it and the ocean would have been dried up in a
minute. Śiva held the head, out of pity for the world, until he placed it in
Benares.[174]

The danger posed by the head is clearer in another text:

7d Brahmā's fifth head had such excessive *tejas* and shone so brilliantly that
5c[3] all the gods and demons were unable to see or move, for it was far brighter
than the sun, and it swallowed up the *tejas* and the power of the gods.[175]

From this it is apparent that the destructive force may not even be a negative one; the excess of anything, bad or good—such as the virtue of an ascetic—poses a threat to the balance of the closed universe.

Śiva controls the power of Viṣṇu in a myth which demonstrates the danger of powers created for a specific destruction and enduring beyond their particular need:

33ea[4] Viṣṇu took the form of the Man-lion to kill a demon who harassed the gods.
7d But then the Man-lion continued to capture and harass the whole universe
33ea[4] himself. The gods sought refuge with Śiva, who assumed the form of a *śarabha* beast, killed the Man-lion, and enlightened Viṣṇu.[176]

5d Another Purāṇa says that the flame of the Man-lion pervaded the uni-
1 verse until the gods sought refuge with Śiva, saying, 'Formerly you
9d protected us when we churned the ocean, for you swallowed the poison
that would have burnt us to ashes. Now we are oppressed by the flame
13d of the Man-lion, and only you are capable of quenching it.'[177] As usual,
destructive power takes the form of a flame whose control is visualized
33ea[4] in terms of quenching. Śiva also takes the form of a *śarabha* to oppose
Viṣṇu in another animal incarnation, that of the boar, in which his

excesses are sexual rather than murderous;[178] in this myth, the chain 7d 19a
is extended by one more link, for the gods, fearing yet another reper-
cussion, approach Śiva and say, 'You must abandon this *śarabha* form
which terrifies people.' Śiva then distributes the *śarabha*'s limbs, and 33ea^4
the torso becomes a Kāpālika.[179] 8cd 38a^2

H. THE DISTRIBUTION OF ŚIVA'S *TEJAS*

This method of dismemberment or distribution is often resorted to in myths which cannot be resolved by eating or similar methods, particularly when the problem is caused by a form of energy rather than matter. Fire is the substance used to destroy all things, to destroy the whole universe at the end of an aeon, but when fire itself becomes uncontrollable it can only be redirected or redistributed. In this corpus of myths, Śiva is the threat more often than he is the saviour; although he resolves certain conflicts by developing them to their extremes, in others he himself creates the extremes for others to resolve.

The distribution of Śiva's forms of *tejas* is a motif inherited from
Indra, who was pursued by the Fury of Brahminicide after he killed
a demon, just as Śiva was pursued after beheading Brahmā. Indra finally 8cd
divided his sin among fire, the waters, the grasses, trees, and the 7c 14c^1
apsarases, this last portion to be transferred to any man who made love 26e^2 21ea
to women during their menstrual period.[180] In another myth, the sin of 15cd 8cd
Indra's brahminicide (a fever) was divided among trees, rivers, moun- 30e 38a^2
tains, birds born of heads or blood, earth, fire, and women, the latter 26e^2
portion to appear in the blood of the menstrual flow.[181] Women are also 14c^1 7c 21ea
said to have received a portion of another of Indra's problems: once 15cd
when Indra refused to give the Soma to the Aśvins, Cyavana (Atri) 45a 14c^2
conjured the demon of intoxication to devour Indra; when Indra granted 16d
the Aśvins their portion of the Soma, the demon of intoxication was 8cd
distributed among women, drinks, gambling, and hunting.[182] Often the 21ea 16d
sin is taken up by sinful or procreative women, just as the goddesses in
the Ruru myth are given as their food women associated with childbirth.
These myths then serve to explain the origin of certain sins in the
world.[183] Thus when Indra had seduced Ahalyā, her husband said to
him, 'This emotion which you have shown here will also appear among
men in the world, and the man who [commits adultery] will have half 8cd
the sin, and you will have half.' And he cursed mortal women to have 2
the beauty of Ahalyā, the cause of the trouble.[184]

The essence of Indra's brahminicide is said to be derived from a force originally created by Śiva, partially distributed but later transferred to Vṛtra, whence (it may be surmised) it entered Indra and was yet again transferred to living creatures. In the course of narrating the myth of the distribution of Indra's brahminicide, the *Mahābhārata* relates this Śaiva origin:

38a When Śiva destroyed Dakṣa's sacrifice, a drop of sweat fell from his fore-
11c 5d head and became a great fire like the doomsday fire; then it became a man
7d named Fever, short, red-eyed, red-bearded, hair standing on end, very hairy,
dark-skinned, wearing red garments. Brahmā said to Śiva, 'All the gods will
give you too a share (in the sacrifice), for they can find no peace because of
your anger. If this man born of your fever wanders among men in one piece,
13d the whole world will not be able to bear him. Restrain (him), and let him
8cd be divided into many.' Śiva, thus implored, said, 'So be it', and for the peace
33ea[4] of all creatures he distributed Fever among the headaches of elephants, slough
45e[2] 30a of serpents, sore hooves of bulls, blindness of cattle, constipation of horses,
30e 7cd moulting of peacocks, red eyes of cuckoos, disturbances in sheep's livers,
13cd[1] hiccups of parrots, fatigue of tigers, and fever among men.[185]

One variant of the theme of the distribution of Śiva's fiery *tejas* is an
elaboration of one of the most ancient Vedic motifs of fire and water:
9c Agni hides in the waters and the plants until the gods find him. This story
44e 26e[1] is told in the Vedas and Brāhmaṇas,[186] where Agni hides in a hollow
44ea reed. In the Epic, Agni is cursed by Bhṛgu to become omnivorous;
2 hoping to avoid this curse, Agni hides in a *śamī* tree (used to make ritual
26e[2] fire-sticks and therefore said to contain fire), but the gods find him and
the curse takes effect.[187] It is significant that the curse which Agni fears is precisely the curse which he receives in punishment for swallowing Śiva's seed in later myths, and, moreover, that Bhṛgu, who curses him, is the sage who curses Śiva in the cycle of myths in which Bhṛgu replaces Agni as the one who interrupts Śiva and Pārvatī in their love-play which produces that seed. The episode of the *śamī* is thus closely tied to the Śaiva cycle.

Elsewhere in the *Mahābhārata*, the myth of Agni hiding is further expanded and revised to include another of Śiva's Vedic precursors, Indra, who hides from the gods in order to escape from a dangerous demon:

33ea[1] Agni searched for Indra, assuming the form of a woman. Finally only the
4 waters were left to search, and Agni was afraid to enter them, for fire is
9c 11d destroyed by water. 'My *tejas* which goes everywhere is extinguished in the
27e waters which are its womb', he said. At last Bṛhaspati strengthened Agni with
44e magic spells and persuaded him to enter the waters.[188]

Here Agni is the seeker, rather than the sought. A later part of the

Mahābhārata restores the Vedic motif of hiding to Agni and inserts the entire episode as a conscious multiform within the story of Skanda's birth. The 'dangerous demon' from whom Indra hides is replaced by Śiva himself, from whom Agni hides, not in fear of the consequences of interrupting Śiva's love-play with Pārvatī, but after the interruption, in fear of having to rid himself of the very seed which is the punishment he avoids in other versions:

> The gods, realizing that Agni must place Śiva's seed in the Ganges, sought 4
> him, but Agni had hidden in the water. The water creatures were tortured by 44e
> Agni's *tejas*, and a frog told the gods that Agni was hiding in the subterranean 9c 7d
> waters, heating them so that they issued forth as hot springs. Agni then hid 12d 13cd^1
> in an *aśvattha* tree, but an elephant betrayed his hiding-place. Finally he hid 26e^2
> within the *śamī* tree, but a parrot betrayed him. Agni cursed all three animals 30e 2
> and then reluctantly agreed to place Śiva's seed in the Ganges.[189] 44e 3

The entire episode of Agni hiding within the waters is a multiform of the episode of the placing of the seed in the Ganges, though the first is carried out in order to avoid the second. The parrot that Agni curses is the very form he assumes in other versions to receive the seed, and the 'discovery' of Agni's watery hiding-place is a further variant of the 'discovery' (or interruption) of Śiva when he is with Pārvatī (thematically equivalent to fire under water). The other hiding-places (the trees) reappear in the myths of the distribution of Indra's sin and replace the reeds of the Brāhmaṇa version, the traditional Indo-European hiding-place of fire as well as the site of the golden seed.

Other distributions follow the model of Indra: the poison left over 9d
from the churning of the ocean, after Śiva had drunk most of it, was 8cd
given to the serpents, and Śiva promised Agni that he would be relieved 30a
of the torture of the seed if he released it in the body of those women 8cd
who warm themselves each month,[190] a possible reference to the sin 15cd
associated with the menstrual flow. Śiva's seed is placed in fire, earth,
and water, as well as in trees (reeds), mountains, and women. The seed
left over from the begetting of Skanda is distributed in bloody water
(as the sin is placed in menstrual blood), in the rays of the sun (like the 15cd
tejas of the castrated *liṅga*), in earth (like the seed), in trees (like the fire 5c^3
of the eye that burnt Kāma), and on the mountain on which the sun 26e^2
sets in the West (like the seed).[191] A similar cluster appears in an ancient 13cd^1
text in which the gods deposit their weapons in Agni, who places them 14c^1
in cattle, water, and the sun,[192] three constituent elements of the fiery 5c^3
mare beneath the sea. The pattern of the distribution of Indra's sin is
also followed in the burning of Kāma. After burning Kāma, the fire 43a 7cd^1

43ea from Śiva's third eye, augmented by the fire of Kāma himself, threatens
7c 26e^{2} 5d to burn all the universe until it is distributed among the mango tree,
14c^{3} Spring, bees, the moon, flowers, cuckoos, and the passion of lovers;
30e among proud men, a certain melody, and pleasure-gardens.[193] The fever
8cd of Kāma tortures Śiva until he transfers it to the son of Kubera, to
whom Śiva gives the ability to drive men mad,[194] just as Indra transfers his sin to passionate women.

In several myths, Śiva states explicitly the problem of disposing of a destructive or creative fire once it has been aroused:

> 37e 5d Once, when Śiva had begun to destroy all that Brahmā had made, Brahmā
> 37ea propitiated him and asked him to spare the universe. Śiva replied, 'But what
> 7d 8cd will I do with the *tejas* that I released in order to destroy your creation?'
> 5c^{3} Brahmā said, 'Place your *tejas* in the sun, and we will all live by the glory of
> the sun. And at the end of the aeon, you can take the form of the sun and burn
> 5d everything.'[195]

The fire is suppressed by fire, delayed until a time more appropriate for
10c universal destruction. The kindled seed of the incestuous Prajāpati is
5c^{3} 15c 14d also placed in the sun or in the god of the sun,[196] or it forms the clouds
5d of doomsday in the sky,[197] latent destruction like the *tejas* of Śiva.

But in most of the myths of Śiva, the fire cannot be returned to the sun, which is its source. Śiva refuses to take back his phallus, saying,
32a 'The sages cursed my *liṅga* to fall when I was not emotionally aroused.
How then can I take it back again? It would not be pure. The immov-
13c able *liṅga* cannot be taken up, but if you honour it the universe will find
5c^{2} peace.'[198] Similarly, a place of rest must be found for Śiva's fiery seed,
21e 5d for he warns the gods, 'My seed is never shed in vain, for it would
destroy the triple world and burn it to ashes. Therefore you must make
13c use of it quickly for the sake of peace.'[199] Once released, the power must
be distributed or used, for the finite amount of *tejas* in the closed universe cannot be increased. There is a careful balance between the two extremes which shifts from moment to moment, constantly recontrolled, as the balance between the sexual and ascetic powers of the yogi must be constantly readjusted within the microcosm of his body.

I. ŚIVA AS FIRE UNDER WATER

The image of fire placed in water is used throughout Indian mythology to express the control of indestructible excess energy. Although in Western thought water brought to fire usually results in the extinction

of fire, in India the fire almost always emerges intact from the combination, merely controlled or transformed, like uranium in which blocks of cadmium have been suspended. (The aptness of this apparently anachronistic image of harnessed nuclear energy emerges from two modern ironies: that J. Robert Oppenheimer, upon seeing the first atomic explosion, recalled the *Bhagavad Gītā* verses describing the doomsday conflagration, and that the atomic reactor at Trombay in India is in the unmistakable shape of the *liṅga* within the *yoni* [as, for example, the reactor is depicted on the 10-rupee stamp] [Plate 3].) The force continues to generate energy, but there is no explosion. Śiva's association with this symbolism may be traced back to an early period.
In the Atharva Veda it is said that Rudra is in fire and water;[200] in the 12cd
Brāhmaṇas he is born from fire and water.[201] In the *Mahābhārata*, 12cd 5d
Śiva's terrible form is fire and the sun, which devours the world, while 5c[3]
his auspicious form is water and the moon, Soma and chastity.[202] Śiva 14 14c[2]
is Agni with Soma and Soma with Agni.[203] 7c

This statement is often modified in a significant way: Śiva himself
is merely Agni, of great *tejas*, and his wife is Soma.[204] The first four lines 5cd 17cd
of a Sanskrit poem refer to his Agni aspect, the last four to the attributes 14c[2]
of Soma associated with him:

> He who, though gifted with the power
> to stomach deadly poison, to burn to ashes Love 9d
> and metamorphose doomsday's fire 43a
> to his glowing forehead-eye, 5d 7cd[1]
> still bears the ambrosial moon, 14c[2,3]
> the mountain daughter and the heavenly stream, 36e
> so wondrous is his skill of policy, 44e
> may he, great Śaṅkara, protect you.[205]

A complex interpretation of these symbols appears in one Purāṇa:

> Agni is the glorious form of Śiva and Soma his calming form. The *tejas* 5c[3] 5d
> form is sun and fire; the liquid form is Soma and water. Everything is made 14c[2]
> of a combination of *tejas* and liquid. From fire Soma arose, and fire is kindled 9c
> with Soma. Fire flows upwards and Soma downwards. The universe is 10c 5d
> periodically burnt by the doomsday fire and reduced to ashes, the seed of fire. 12c 6cd
> Then this seed of fire is again flooded with Soma.[206] 14c[2]

In both the Skanda myth and the Pine Forest myth, Śiva's lust is controlled by submersion in water. There is general precedent for this
in the *Mahābhārata*: 'Let a man in whom passion has arisen enter the 13c
water.'[207] Śiva pleads with Pārvatī to draw him out of Kāma as out of 7c 24e
a fire, to save him with the Soma of her body.[208] He seeks relief in the 13c 17cd

14c^{2} waters of two rivers, which appear as substitutes for Pārvatī as the Ganges
does in the Skanda myth:

> 43ea Śiva was overcome with desire and he wandered over the earth, sprinkling
> 13c his body with water, finding no peace. One day he saw the Yamunā river
> 44e and he plunged in, trying to assuage the torture of his heat, but the water of
> 12d the river became black by contact with the fire of Śiva and Kāma. . . . He fell
> 44e into the Kalindī river, and the waters were burnt up and became as black as
> 12d collyrium, but still he found no peace.[209]

Water does not quench the fire of Kāma but is burnt instead. The waters
12d of the Yamunā and Kalindī are burnt dry when Śiva wishes to bathe
8cd away his sin of brahminicide, which he tries, in vain, to wash away in
various rivers, as he tries to wash away the fire of Kāma; and the world
is troubled by the fire of *tapas* when Śiva immerses himself in the
10d Sarasvatī river.[210] Śiva's failure to quench the fire of Kāma is described
in another Purāṇa:

> 43a After Kāma had been burnt by Śiva and revived by Devī, he went and
> 43e 43ea assailed Śiva with arrows. Śiva was tortured by Kāma's arrows and could not
> 13c 14c^{2,3} assuage the heat of his body with the coolness of the crescent moon or the
> 44e Ganges, nor by the Soma dripping from the moon, nor by lying in snowy
> 15c waters.[211]

Pārvatī uses this metaphor to express her passion: 'Even if fire were to
11d become cool, I would not stop loving Śiva'; but when, spurned by him,
she enters a fire, her ascetic powers make it become as cool as sandalwood paste.[212]

11d The unquenchable fire appears in the Pine Forest as the flame *liṅga*
5cd which often comes to rest in a river, just as the castrated phallus of
9c Ouranos falls into the sea.[213] The concept of the fiery phallus placed in
water appears in a dream related by one Agaria:

> 5cd I made my forge and began to fashion iron tools. A spark fell on me. I got
> 9c 17cd up and waved my hands to put it out. My wife threw water on my penis.
> 13c 'There is the fire', she cried.[214]

This natural symbolism is thus psychologically attested in India, and
17cd it is intrinsic in the mythology of the flame *liṅga*. Brahmā instructs the
5cd sages to beg Pārvatī to take the form of the *yoni* to receive the *liṅga* and
13c 9c to sprinkle the *liṅga* with consecrated water to make it peaceful.[215]

5cd This is reflected in actual cult practice: 'The *liṅga* of Mahādeva,
16c 13c a thirsty deity, who needs continued cooling to relieve his distress, must
15c 15d be kept continually moist to avoid drought.'[216] Although thirst and
drought are motifs related to this symbolism, it is primarily the lust of

Śiva which must be controlled in this way. The Abbé Dubois similarly misinterpreted the nature of Śiva's heat:

> Sometimes during the periods of excessive heat, the Hindus suppose that 5d
> Śiva, from whom it emanates, is more than usually inflamed. Consequently,
> fearing lest he should set everything on fire, they place over the head of his 5cd
> idol a vessel filled with water. In this vessel a little hole is pierced, so that the 17cd
> water may, by falling on him drop by drop, refresh him and abate the burning
> heat that consumes him.[217]

The water controls but cannot quench this consuming heat. This is expressed by a verse that combines the symbols of Pārvatī and Śiva as water and fire with the central image of their balance: the fiery mare at the bottom of the sea:

> United with Pārvatī, Śiva spent the days and nights 36e
> of a thousand years as if it were a single night. 14cd
> But the joys of love-making did not satisfy his thirst, 13c 12d
> just as all the floods of the ocean do not quench 12cd
> the fire blazing beneath it.[218] 13cd

J. ŚIVA AS THE SUBMARINE MARE

The fire of doomsday, having originated from the chaste anger of a 13d
terrible sage, is said to repose in the mouth of a mare who wanders at 21a 14cd 8d
the bottom of the ocean, drinking the sea waters (the floods of dooms- 13cd 12d
day) while she awaits the moment when she will re-emerge to destroy 14d
the universe with the fire from her mouth.[219] The balanced extremes 5d
implicit in this image are evident from a Sanskrit aphorism which
stresses the less obviously destructive of the two excesses: kings even
having great *tejas* should not over-indulge in drink, for the mare-fire 16c 16d
herself, through excessive drinking, was rendered powerless to burn
even a blade of grass.[220] Śiva is said to have engendered the mare with 26e
the fire of his third eye (a multiform of the sage's chaste anger). This 13cd
fire, although distributed in various ways in other myths, is described 7cd^1
as the fire of doomsday and therefore has but one inevitable resting-
place—the ocean:

> Kāma deluded Śiva, arousing him, and when Śiva realized that Kāma was 43ea
> attacking him he released a fire from his third eye, burning Kāma to ashes. 7cd^1
> Having come from Śiva's eye, the fire could never return to Śiva; moreover, 43a
> Brahmā had paralysed the fire in a vain attempt to shield Kāma. When Śiva 41e
> had vanished, the fire began to burn the gods and all the universe. The gods 5d
> sought refuge with Brahmā, who made the fire into a mare with ambrosial 13cd^1
> [*saumya*] flames issuing from her mouth. Then Brahmā took the mare to the 14c^2
> ocean and said, 'This mare is the fire of Śiva's anger. Having burnt Kāma, it 14cd

wished to burn the entire universe. Now you must bear it until the final
14d deluge, at which time I will come here and lead it away from you. It will
12d devour your water, and you must make a great effort to bear it.' The ocean
12cd agreed to this, and the fire entered and was held in check, burning quietly
with its halo of flames.[221]

A very similar myth is told about a conflict with Indra in place of Kāma. Again the uncontrollable flame from Śiva's eye is placed in the ocean, but this time instead of producing the mare it produces the demon Jalandhara:

28ea 45a Once Indra saw a naked yogi on Kailāsa, and he reviled him and struck him
6cd 24a with his thunderbolt. But the thunderbolt was reduced to ashes, and the
33ea[5] 9d man's neck turned blue where it struck, for the yogi was Śiva himself. Then
7cd[1] 45ea 43a Śiva glanced at Indra with the fire of his third eye and was about to kill him,
13d but Bṛhaspati begged him to restrain his fire. Śiva said, 'How can I take back
30a the anger that has issued from my eye? How can a snake put on again the
8cd skin that he has sloughed off?' Bṛhaspati asked him to throw the *tejas* some-
14cd where else, and Śiva took it with his hand and threw it into the salt ocean at
44e 20ea the confluence of the Ganges, where it took the form of a child, Jalandhara.[222]

Skanda is produced in a similar manner in another myth:

19e [The sages were molested by a demon and they begged Śiva to produce
7cd[1] a defender for them. Then, opening his third eye, he plunged its glance into
9c the lake called Forest of Reeds, and at once there arose from the bottom of
26e[1] 20ea the waters six infants who were suckled by the wives of the six sages.][223]

A South Indian version of this episode remains closer to the traditional Sanskrit elements of the myth but incorporates the motif of the third eye within the lake called Forest of Reeds:

36e [Śiva married Pārvatī and made love to her for many years, but no child
29a was produced. The gods became anxious and sent Vāyu, in the form of
30ea a breeze, to find out what Śiva was doing, but Nandin did not let Vāyu enter
44ea the bedroom. Then the gods themselves went there and were admitted by
19e Nandin. They saw Śiva seated with Pārvatī and they asked him to beget
a child to chastise the demon who was tormenting them. Śiva assumed a form
21e 7cd[1] with six heads, and a spark came forth from each head. The air dried up and
14cd 12d the oceans lost their waters. Pārvatī and the gods at first fled in terror, but
22a when they returned and implored Śiva to protect them, the three-eyed god
13d caused his five new heads to disappear and he took the sparks in his hands.
44a He gave them to Agni and Vāyu to place in the Ganges so that she could carry
them to the lake called Forest of Reeds. Agni and Vāyu at first hesitated, for
9c 13d they feared the sparks, but Śiva made them invulnerable to the fire. Vāyu
44e carried the sparks and then gave them to Agni, who left them in the Ganges.
12cd 12d The river dried up, but by the grace of Śiva she again abounded in water, and
20ea she carried the sparks to the lake, where the six-headed Skanda was born.][224]

Vāyu here assumes the role of interrupter (as he does when Kāma takes the form of a breeze to interrupt Śiva's *tapas*) and the role of creative mediator, the wind that moves upon the waters, as it does in other creation stories. The sparks which come out of Śiva's six heads are multiforms of the blaze of his third eye and of the fiery seed. The destruction which they cause—burning up first the ocean, then the Ganges—is immediately rectified by Śiva, so that there is no need to create the submarine mare or Jalandhara, and the only result of the combination of the destructive fire and the unwilling water is the long-awaited child, Skanda. In several of these variants, the flame is the fire of anger, which alternates with the fire of lust as the heat of *tapas* does.
In one variation, Jalandhara is born when the fire emanating from Śiva's
forehead at the time of the destruction of the triple city of the demons 7cd[1]
enters the sea at the confluence of the Ganges.[225] The Jalandhara story 9c 14cd
is connected more explicitly with the submarine mare by two incidental 44e
references: Indra, trying to justify to Jalandhara the churning of the
ocean (Jalandhara's father), says, 'Formerly the ocean offered a refuge 14cd
to my enemy Mainaka [a son of Himālaya], and also to the fire in the 13cd[1]
form of a horse that burnt all creatures. Therefore we punished him.' 13cd[1]
And Jalandhara himself boasts, 'I obstructed the mouth of the mare-fire 12d
and flooded the whole universe',[226] an indication of the need for the 14d
fire to consume the ocean water, just as it is necessary for the ocean waters to subdue the mare.

In addition to these myths, there are scattered references to Śiva as the mare-fire throughout Sanskrit literature. 'Jwala Mukhi' ('Mouth of
Fire') is the name of a holy place in the Himālayas where fire comes out 13cd[1]
of the ground; Satī is said to have created this fire and immolated her- 6d
self within it.[227] The *Mahābhārata* says, 'Śiva's mouth is the mare's 13cd[1]
head', and P. C. Roy translates this passage, 'Thou art the Barabanala [Vaḍavānala, 'mare-fire'] Mare's head that ranges within the ocean,
ceaselessly vomiting fire and drinking the saline waters as if they were 12d
sacrificial butter',[228] thus playing upon the symbolism of the oblation 10c
in fire that is the inverse of the submarine mare. The three eyes of Śiva 7cd[1]
in his *śarabha* form are said to be the sun, moon, and fire, while his 5c[3]
tongue is the submarine mare.[229] The fire of Śiva's anger, the mare-fire, 14c[3] 7c
and the fire of Kāma combine in a verse addressed to Kāma: 13cd[1]

> Surely the fire of Śiva's anger still burns in you today, 43a
> like the fire of the mare in the ocean; 13cd[1]
> for how else, Kāma, could you be so hot 43ea
> as to reduce people like me to ashes?[230] 7c 6cd

The mare is used to express the image of fire within water because of
the connotations of fertility, royalty, and power which the horse embodied in ancient India and in Indo-European civilization in general
45e (notably in Ireland). Indra (the phallic god of rain) approaches the
14c^{2} 13cd^{1} Soma (the fiery liquid) as a stallion comes to his mare.[231] As a sacrificial
animal, the horse is often represented by its head alone, the part used
33ea^{4} as an offering; moreover, animal-headed mortals, as transitional figures
38a mediating between animals and humans, abound in Indian mythology;
cf. the deer head of Dakṣa's sacrifice, Saṃjñā, Dadhyañc, Gaṇeśa,
Narasiṃha, Ṛṣyaśṛṅga, Nandin, the Kiṃpuruṣa or Aśvamukha ('Horse-
head'), etc.

The Indo-Aryans were the great horse-tamers of the ancient world, and the mare-fire is the epitome of taming: the horse remains wild and fiery, the incarnation of beauty and strength, but its wildness is placed in a delicate control, reined in so that it is creative rather than destructive, just as fire is harnessed by its sea change. This imagery is particularly appropriate to Śiva, for Śiva is Lord of Animals (Paśupati),
13cd^{2} and he is said to be the god of wild and tame animals.[232] The Brāhmaṇas
refer to Rudra as the tamer of horses.[233]

Śiva himself is half fire and half water; he is fire and Pārvatī is water, and they are one. He is the ascetic fire that rages against the erotic power, and he is the fire of passion that cannot be extinguished by asceticism. He is the seed placed in fire and the spark within the cosmic floods. He is thus the image of the balance of powers in the universe, and his flame blazes eternally, unquenched by all the floods of nature,[234] like the flame within the sea.

IX

CYCLES OF ASCETICISM AND SEXUALITY

THE control of *tejas* on the macrocosmic and microcosmic level is ultimately realized neither by distribution nor by sublimation, both of which merely represent temporary phases of a more general waxing and waning. As the danger is one of energy, the ultimate solution is one of motion, not a static condition but a continuous transmutation which harnesses destructive fiery forces to drive forward the life processes. As long as they are in motion, caught up in the myth, these forces are benign, whatever their source or nature, no matter how extreme their power may be.

The mortal man resolves his chastity and eroticism through various cycles. One must store up powers of chastity to gain erotic powers, which are spent and then followed by expiatory *tapas* which is a source of rejuvenation. One prepares in chastity (*brahmacarya*) to become a householder, only to revert eventually to chastity (*sannyāsa*). Unlike the mortal yogi, Śiva need not always alternate phases of sexual activity and yogic restoration, but may exist in both states simultaneously, renewing his lost powers at the very moment that he spends them. He cannot merely go from one phase to another, because he is not subject to birth or death or growth; he has no childhood, as Kṛṣṇa has, for he is always complete. This frees him from the mortal cycles but involves him in cosmic cycles on a different scale, alternations of sexuality and chastity without development and often without apparent purpose.

As Śiva embodies the extremes of each aspect, he explores each one to its fullest, even absurd extension. In so doing he himself becomes involved in the problem of uncontrollable excesses and extremes, and although the ultimate result of the myth is a balance, before that is reached it may approach dangerous extremes in either or even both of its components. Both Śiva's sexuality and his chastity pose certain threats to the balance of the universe, and the ambiguous figure of the erotic ascetic is, among its many other functions, the only possible continuous manifestation of Śiva which can hold these two extremes in suspension.

A. THE DANGER OF ŚIVA'S EXCESSIVE CHASTITY

In spite of the importance of chastity in Indian religion, and in spite of the logical analogy between chastity and quiescence, Hinduism presents an equally strong case for the view that chastity, suppressing and building up a pressure of thwarted powers, is far more dangerous than the sexuality which releases them naturally. The Tantric theory of sublimation is the paramount expression of this viewpoint. Of the four heads
36e which Śiva sprouted in order to see Tilottamā, the northern head loves
21a 5d Pārvatī and is mild, while the southern head is chaste, terrible, and
5cd destructive.[1] When Śiva's *liṅga* falls in the Pine Forest, it burns every-
21a 5d thing because the seed which has been stored up for thousands of years
9c pervades the earth until the sages place it in the Narmadā river.[2]
13c Śiva's *tapas* generates great heat which menaces the world, and Pārvatī also is capable of generating a dangerous amount of *tapas*. When
27ea both of them performed asceticism together, after a quarrel at dice, 'the
24ea^2 7d fires which they kindled blazed so vehemently as to threaten a general
5d conflagration'.[3] Another myth illustrates the interrelationship of the two dangers: Śiva's sexuality leads to an argument with Pārvatī which causes her to perform destructive *tapas*; one extreme leads to the other:

21ea Mahádéva was so struck with the beauty of some of the *Apsaras* [*sic*] and
23ea his looks were so expressive of his internal raptures, that Pārvatī, unable to
22a conceal her indignation, uttered the most virulent reproaches against him.
26e [Śiva could not pacify her, and she hid in the hollow of a *śamī* tree and per-
27ea formed *tapas* for nine years. A terrible fire arose from her and pervaded the
7d 5d mountains, terrifying everyone until she recalled the fire and placed it in the *śamī* tree.][4]

Another kind of danger results from the fact that, since Śiva embodies the forces of nature, the universe ceases to function when he withdraws from worldly activity:

31ea^2 [Śiva remained immobile and silent during his *tapas*, and the people of
29a heaven and earth renounced conjugal life and lived like ascetics. This would
21a 5d have led to the gradual extinction of beings, who no longer multiplied. . . .
36e After the wedding of Śiva and Pārvatī, the people of heaven and earth renounced their asceticism, and, taking up again their former manner of life,
5c^1 became happy and tranquil.][5]

This is another expression of the concept implicit in the gods' statement that, when Kāma has been destroyed by Śiva, all the universe ceases to continue. Another manifestation of this causal relationship appears in the Pine Forest myth:

32a The sages said, 'May the lingam of this man fall to the ground.' The lingam

fell to the ground: love was now impotent. This was more than the gods 29a
bargained for, and they asked Śiva to resume it. 'If gods and men will worship $5c^{2}$
my lingam I will resume it, not otherwise.' They could not bring themselves
to do this, though it was the sole generative principle of the universe, so it lay
there in the snow, frost-bitten, knobby, and black as a lemur's, glistering in 15c
the spring thaw, and besieged by flies, while Śiva passed over the final ridge 13c
of grief and was lost to the world on the far side. There then ensued 3,600
years of peace and quiet, which would be with us yet, had there not arisen
a puritan monster called Taraka.[6]

Although Śiva's chastity here results in 'peace and quiet', as in the
normal Hindu point of view, it is clear that the negative aspects are
disquieting: love is impotent, and 'the sole generative principle of the
universe' is incapacitated. The direct link between this 'principle' and
the regeneration of the universe is expressed in one version of the Pine
Forest myth by a simple transference of the central image: Śiva danced
in the forest and seduced the sages' wives; the sages cursed him and his 31e
liṅga fell to the ground, but the *liṅgas* of the sages fell simultaneously. 35ea 32a
Frightened, they worshipped Śiva, who restored them when they had 38a
agreed to worship his *liṅga*.[7] 38e $5c^{2}$

When Śiva was castrated, 'all generation and vegetation was at a 32a
stand'.[8] The effects of his chastity are the same as one of the dis- 29a
advantages of his sexuality: he neglects all other duties.

To satisfy Devī and restore all things to their former situation, [Śiva $33ea^{5}$
became incarnate as a king. He ruled well, chastising the wicked, but] he 31ea
entirely neglected every other pursuit. His indifference for the female sex 34a
alarmed his subjects; he endeavoured to please them; but his embraces were 19e
fruitless. This is termed Asc'halana in Sanskrit [*askhalana*, the failure to shed 21a
the seed]. . . . The *Apsaras*, or celestial nymphs, tried in vain the effect of
their charms. [Then Devī came there, but Śiva was deluded and did not 21ea
recognize her. Nevertheless,] suspecting that the person he was speaking to $33ea^{3}$
might be a manifestation of Pārvatī, he thought it advisable to marry her.[9] 36ea

The role of Pārvatī is here explicitly compared with that of the celestial prostitutes, who attempt to seduce Śiva not because his *tapas* is dangerous in a positive way, but merely because he is not doing anything else.[10] Similar considerations appear throughout the Purāṇas whenever the gods begin to worry about Śiva's continued chastity:

Brahmā worried, 'As long as Śiva is averse to worldly ways, solitary and 37a
passionless, he will certainly undertake no action.' . . . Brahmā said to Devī, 31ea
'As long as Śiva has no mistress, how can creation take place? . . . Śiva, your 34a
husband, is a great yogi performing *tapas* alone, without a wife, without 29a 19ea
emotion. As long as he has no wife, how can there be any auspicious creation? 36a
For he, though passionless, is the cause of it all.' . . . The gods came to Śiva 34a 29a

and said, 'There are many demons to be killed, some by Brahmā, some by
19e Viṣṇu, some by you, and some by a son who is to be born to you. But as long
34a as you perform yoga, free of passion and hatred, you cannot kill the demons
37e and save the universe. Viṣṇu and Brahmā have wives and act for the benefit
36e of the universe; now you must marry some beautiful woman for the sake of
us all.'[11]

36e Śiva himself says that his love-play with Pārvatī maintains the uni-
36e verse,[12] and his sexual activity is also said to sustain the moon, which
14c[3] wanes when he is separated from Pārvatī and is full when he returns to
her and makes love to her.[13] Moreover, Śiva's chastity not only fails to
produce a demon-killing son but prevents Śiva from using one of his
own most effective demon-deterrents: the weapon of lust.

B. THE DANGER OF ŚIVA'S EXCESSIVE SEXUALITY

Yet the great majority of the Hindu myths depict Śiva's sexual activity
as dangerous and his chaste aspect as a refuge. Where sexual activity is
5c[3] 5d motion and fire, chastity is quiescence and cool water. 'There are two
7c forms of Śiva, one terrible and one mild. The terrible form—fire,
14c[3] lightning, and the sun—destroys the universe. The auspicious form—
21a dharma, water, and the moon—performs chastity.'[14] Śiva's excessive
sexual behaviour weakens him so that he is unable to conquer demons,
just as his excessive chastity places him *hors de combat*:

36e After marrying Pārvatī, Śiva made love to her for a thousand years, but
25e then he lost all of his *tejas* and his virility was reduced. Seeing himself thus
25a diminished, Śiva resolved to perform *tapas*, and he undertook a great vow,
38a[2] wandering on earth, carrying a skull.[15]

While Śiva is away on his pilgrimage, the demon Andhaka attacks Pārvatī, and Śiva uses the powers obtained by his recent vow to overcome him. In another version of this story, the demon attacks first, when Śiva's powers have been reduced by his sexual indulgence, and Śiva must perform *tapas* specifically to overcome him:

Andhaka took his weapons and the battle began. Then Śiva said to Pārvatī,
'My dear, the vow that I performed formerly gave me powers which I have
25e now exhausted. Therefore I, an immortal, have been attacked by mortals
36e [demons]. And this strife has come about because I lost my ascetic merit by
25a making love to you day and night. Now I must again enter the terrible forest
and perform a great vow of *tapas*.' Then he went away and performed *tapas*
for a thousand years.[16]

As Śiva's powers decline, so the gods who derive their powers from him are weakened, and the powers of vegetation which he represents are depleted when he is drained,[17] just as they cease when he withdraws completely. Moreover, although the ultimate result must be to his advantage, Śiva is often weakened at first by his sexual encounters. In one myth, his sexual nature—here manifest in his devotion to his frivolous wife—places him in a difficult situation, from which that same sexuality eventually rescues him:

A demon [Bhasmāsura] performed *tapas*, and Pārvatī urged Śiva to grant 8d
him a boon, but Śiva said, 'What you have said does not please me. When- 36ea[1]
ever one does anything because of the wish of a fool, a woman, a child, or an 36a
enemy, there are dire consequences.' But she said, 'A woman whose husband
will not do what she asks him has no dignity. I will kill myself if you do not 43e
respect me.' So Śiva granted the demon the boon that he asked: that he could 42e
burn to ashes anyone on whose head he placed his hand. The demon im- 6cd
mediately started to test his power by placing his hand over Śiva's head. Śiva 43ea
fled in terror and sought refuge with Viṣṇu, saying, 'There is no happiness
for a man who has been conquered by a woman.' Viṣṇu told Śiva to wait on 13c
the banks of a river, where Śiva made love to the *apsarases*. Meanwhile Viṣṇu 21ea
took the form of a beautiful woman to entice the demon, who was overcome 33ea[1]
by lust and begged her to marry him. She told him that the custom in her 21ea
family was to marry by placing one's hand over one's own head. The deluded 43a
demon, blinded by desire, did this and was burnt to ashes, and all the gods 6cd
rejoiced.[18] 17d

A whim of Pārvatī causes the initial problem as it does in some of the Pine Forest stories, and Viṣṇu extricates Śiva by assuming the form of a beautiful woman as he does in other versions of that myth. The demon burns Śiva with the very boon he has just received from him, to test it, just as Kāma 'burns' Brahmā and Śiva with his newly received powers, and the demon of ashes, like Kāma, is ultimately burnt by Śiva after Śiva has been seduced by the *apsarases* or Pārvatī. Pārvatī herself participates in another version of this myth, and it is specifically her form which Viṣṇu (Lakshmañjati) impersonates, while the demon assumes still more of the characteristics of Kāma:

Basamkara Deo [Bhasmāsura] was in love with Mahadeo's beautiful wife 42ea
Pārvatī and was ever trying to seduce her. [He wished to burn Mahadeo to 43ea
ashes with an amulet and then to take Pārvatī away. Mahadeo fled and hid 6cd
in a cave, but Basamkara Deo followed him there. Lakshmañjati then took 33ea[1]
Pārvatī's form and led Basamkara away.] There Basamkara prepared to fulfil 21ea
his desire, but Lakshmañjati in the form of Pārvatī said, 'My Maharaja first
dances, then he does it.' [Basamkara danced, and Lakshmañjati told him to 31e
place his hands on his head. Basamkara did this, the amulet touched his head, 43a
and he was reduced to ashes.] But as he was dying, his seed came out from 21e 10cd
him, and Lakshmañjati caught it in his hand and put it in a hollow bamboo. 26e[1] 17d
Then he took his own form and went home. [Two girls were born from the 20ea

seed. Mahadeo and Pārvatī found them and Mahadeo said that since they
8cd were born of evil seed they would give gonorrhea and syphilis to any man
25e 17d that made love to them.][19]

The obvious parallels between Viṣṇu's role here and his role of Mohinī in the Pine Forest has attracted several of the subsidiary motifs of that myth, but the result of the myth is altogether different. In addition to weakening him personally, Śiva's sexuality (here embodied in the beautiful wife who provokes the demon) results ultimately in the destructive sexuality of mortals (embodied in women who transmit venereal diseases). In many similar instances, Śiva's sexuality causes harm to mortals with whom he comes in contact, in spite of the tradi-
25a tional power of yogis to restore the purity of the women they seduce:[20]

21ea One day Śiva saw a group of beautiful young women, and he invited them
24ea[1] to go far away in the sky with him. Pretending to do *tapas*, he intended to
23ea seduce them, and, overcome with passion, he made love with them, but
36a Pārvatī's mind was worried, and by her yoga of meditation she saw him there
30e 22a with the women. Furious, she took the form of an eagle and entered the hut
42e where Śiva, looking like Kāma himself, was ardently embracing and kissing
the beautiful women. The eagle swooped down and grabbed the women by
the hair and kicked them in the eyes and threw them down to earth, where
3 their faces were deformed and their bodies burnt by Pārvatī's curse. They
became Cāṇḍālī women, untouchables who make love with libertines when
33ea[3] they have been widowed. Then Pārvatī divided herself into a hundred women
36e and made love with Śiva on Kailāsa. This is the eternal nature of lust, by
43ea which even Śiva was deluded.[21]

This same excessive sexuality, bringing on a curse from Pārvatī, makes
the Ganges into a Cāṇḍālī woman and is used to explain the ugliness of
3 the women of a certain tribe: a Hindu god fell in love with one and his
jealous wife cursed them all to be ugly.[22] Similarly, the eternal childlessness of the gods is their punishment for attempting to control Śiva's sexual behaviour in the absence of Pārvatī.

In this way, Śiva's lust brings indirect harm to the gods and to mortals, but far more common is a more direct danger, the actual friction or heat generated by the activity itself, like the dangerous *tapas* of chastity; once again, the effect of the extreme form of either of the opposed forces is the same. Śiva in his erotic aspect dances and disturbs the world:

6d When Satī had killed herself, Śiva took up her corpse on his head and
10cd danced fervently with it. The earth trembled and the tortoise and serpent
31e 31a 7d supporting the earth could not bear it, but Śiva kept dancing in joy, his eyes
30a whirling. All the gods wondered how he could be made to calm down, and

then Viṣṇu cut the body of Satī into pieces with his discus, and as Śiva continued to dance he felt the body become light and he realized that all the limbs
had been cut off. He asked Nārada where Satī was and Nārada replied, 'You
will find Satī, but now you have been causing an untimely destruction with
your dance.' Śiva said, 'I am calm now. Where is Satī's body?' Nārada told 5d 13d
him what Viṣṇu had done, and Śiva looked about and saw the *yoni* in Kāma- 17cd
rūpa [Assam], and his flesh thrilled to see it. Then he saw the *yoni* break
through the earth and start falling towards hell, and he took the form of
a mountain and supported the *yoni*, and wherever there was a part of Satī
he became a *liṅga*.[23] 5cd

This myth is in many ways a variant of the two great myths of Śiva's excessive sexuality: the birth of Skanda and the Pine Forest story. The motion of Śiva's dance/love-making/castration shakes the earth; Satī's body is dissected as the *liṅga* is castrated (and, in one version, cut into pieces);[24] and the *yoni/liṅga* falls to hell, resulting in the cult of *liṅga*-worship.

Another version of the episode of Satī's corpse adds other motifs from the related myths:

When Satī had killed herself, Śiva destroyed the sacrifice of Dakṣa. Then 6d
he found the corpse of Satī and he wept like a common man. When Kāma 38a^1 10cd
heard of this, he went there and wounded Śiva with all five arrows at once. 11cd
Then Śiva was half out of his mind with grief and terribly agitated by the 43ea
arrows of Kāma, and he mourned and raved and wandered about embracing
her corpse. As he wept, his tears fell upon the earth and threatened to burn 5d
it up, and the gods begged Śanaiścāra to hold the tears of Śiva as he had held
the rain for a hundred years in his clouds. Śanaiścāra said, 'I will do what you 15c
ask, but you must distract Śiva so that he will not notice me and destroy me 9c
in anger.' The gods did so, and Śanaiścāra took up the rain of tears, but he
was unable to bear them and threw them on the great mountain Jaladhāraka
['Water-Bearer' or 'Cloud']. They split the mountain and flowed into the 44e 14cd
ocean in the form of a river.

Śiva continued to mourn, mad with grief, and as the corpse had touched
his body it did not decay and could not be destroyed. Then the gods entered
the corpse and caused it to fall in pieces in various places. Wherever a part
of the body fell, Śiva took the form of a *liṅga*, and the gods came and honoured 5cd
Śiva and Devī there, praising him. Śiva assumed his own form again, and 5c^2
Brahmā enlightened him and persuaded him to stop troubling the earth with
his tears and sighs, which were scalding the earth and tearing up mountains 11cd
and forests. Brahmā promised Śiva that Satī would be his wife again after
a hundred celestial years, and Śiva went away and awaited her rebirth.[25] 6c

The specifically sexual nature of Śiva's tears and dancing in this context is made clear by the presence of Kāma, who wounds Śiva as he does in the myths of Skanda and the Pine Forest. The episode of the scalding tears attracts several motifs from the Skanda story; the seed/teardrop is taken up by Agni/Śanaiścāra (the latter more successful than the former in avoiding the wrath of Śiva which both fear) and thrown upon a mountain and into a river. The fiery liquid is basically creative but it is able to cause destructive heat when thwarted:

> 11cd [Śiva's] eyes wept fire and vitriol. 'If that fire fall, the earth burns, the
> 5d second storey heaven will catch, and we shall be roast pig', said the gods. . . .
> 'Satī's body cannot decay. We must dismember it. . . . The great cry-baby must be given nothing to cry over, or we shall be scorched.'[26]

The destructive tears are a multiform of the destructive corpse, and the double danger is averted on three levels: the fiery tears in the ocean, the *liṅga* in the *yoni*, and the god with his wife.

The Skanda myth offers the classic form of the image of dangerous
31e sexuality: when Śiva and Pārvatī make love, it is like a great, unwanted
7d 5d doomsday about to destroy the universe,[27] shaking the earth and the
universe.[28] But the love-making of Śiva and Pārvatī can be dangerous for the opposite reason, like their chastity—not because it generates too much activity, but because it causes them to withdraw from all other
31ea activity, so that the universe is in danger of running down.[29] When
31ea locked in Pārvatī's embrace, Śiva performs no sacrifice or *tapas*, does
31ea nothing at all, and deprives the gods of the sight of his person.[30] In
31ea a modern Punjabi version of the myth, the world simply begins to end
44ea without the activity of Śiva and Pārvatī, and so Nārada is sent to
4 interrupt them.[31] In one Sanskrit version, no physical danger arises, and it would seem that mere prurient curiosity inspires the gods:

> The gods wished to see Śiva, and they asked Nārada, 'What is Śiva doing?
> 14c[3] And should we go there or not?' Nārada said, 'The moon is waning . . . and
> 36e so Śiva is involved in the ritual of love-making.' Indra said to Agni, 'Take
> 33ea[5] the form of an ascetic beggar, a Brahmin, because then you cannot be slain
> or beaten. Go into Śiva's presence and tell us what to do.' Agni went there and saw Śiva with Pārvatī, and when Pārvatī saw him she became ashamed
> 44ea and stopped making love. She asked, 'Who are you?' and Agni said, 'I am
> 16cd a hungry beggar, old, poor, and blind. Give me food.' Pārvatī thought, 'Then
> 44ea he did not see', and she fed him. Agni went back and reported, and Nārada
> 7cd[2] then came secretly to Pārvatī and, covering his eyes with his hands, averting
> 45a his head, weeping and stammering, he stood at her feet and said, 'Indra has
> 24a described your love-play to the gods, and you have both been laughed at and
> criticized. Then they sent Agni in the form of a Brahmin to interrupt your pleasure. I feel terrible about this. How can they laugh at you so?' Pārvatī
> 4 was furious; her eyes were red, her lower lip trembled. Then Nārada went
> to the gods and said, 'Śiva has ceased making love. Come and see him.' Hearing this speech of Agni [*sic*], the gods went and praised Śiva. Pārvatī

said to Indra, 'Lover of Ahalyā, marked with a thousand female organs, evil 1
one, you laughed at me. Now obtain the fruits of that action. All the wives 17cd
of the gods—all the gods and their wives will become trees, ignorant of the 26e 2 29a
pleasure of women.' Then Śiva became a fig tree, Indra a mango tree, and all
the gods became trees and the goddesses became vines.[32]

As there is no reference to the dangerous seed in this version, Agni's role is largely usurped by Nārada, who is simply a trouble-maker and bearer of tales; yet Agni appears as well, and the two roles are somewhat confused. The only reference to the effect of Śiva's sexual activity is the obscure implication that it causes the moon to wax full, a positive effect. Yet there are hints of more serious and traditional grounds for the gods' discomfort: Agni takes the form of a Brahmin beggar, as Viṣṇu does when the gods expressly wish to take Śiva's seed from him, and Pārvatī's curse seems to begin with the traditional imprecation against the goddesses, whom she curses to be barren in the myths in which the interruption is expressly designed to make her barren.

The curse of barrenness is conjoined with two other famous curses in another myth involving Śiva in a sexual transgression:

Once Brahmā took a second wife, though he was already married to
Sāvitrī. Śiva and the other gods helped him to procure and marry his new 38ea
wife, and when Sāvitrī found out about this she cursed Śiva to be castrated 3
in the Pine Forest; she cursed Agni to swallow Śiva's seed; and she cursed 32a
all the wives of the gods, including Pārvatī, to be barren.[33] 44a 4 29a

Here Pārvatī receives the curse which she usually gives, and there are
other reversals as well: the sexual activity for which Śiva is punished
(the abetting of Brahmā against Sāvitrī) is a reversal of his ascetic stand 4
on behalf of Sāvitrī against her incestuous father. Moreover, Śiva himself is guilty of a sexual transgression against Sāvitrī, for which he is 23ea 33ea[2]
cursed not to be barren but to beget a son.[34] 2

The possibility that Śiva's sexuality (like his chastity) will prevent him 19e
from undertaking other duties appears also when he is involved in
another aspect of household life, the pleasures of children:

The gods sought refuge with Śiva, for they were troubled by the demons
of the triple city, and Śiva agreed to slay the demons. But just then Devī said
to him, 'See how Skanda is playing', and Śiva looked at his son's mischief 19e
and did not tire of watching him and listening to him, and he forgot the gods
who were oppressed by the weapons of the demons. He embraced Skanda and 31e
danced with him, crying, 'My son', and the little boy danced and played, and
all the world danced, and Pārvatī rejoiced. The gods stood beside the door
in misery, and they praised Śiva, but they looked at each other as if to say, 44ea
'But—!' And they said, 'We are unlucky. The demons have all the luck.' 31ea
They said, 'Honour to Śiva', but they honoured him less in their hearts.[35] 25e

Śiva dances here in joy rather than in grief, but it is the same erotic
dance. The gods take exception not to his dancing but merely to his
delay in fighting, and because of his involvement they honour him less,
31e 25e just as they disdain him for his sexuality and laugh at him for dancing
and singing to please Pārvatī.[36]

C. THE INTERRUPTION OF SEXUAL ACTIVITY

Thus the extreme forms of Śiva's asceticism and sexuality pose certain closely related dangers to the universe, resulting from excessive activity or withdrawal from activity in either case. Various methods are employed to cause a transition from one phase to another: the natural process of synthesis may provide an internal stimulus, one extreme leading naturally to its antithesis, or a curse may bring it about, or the gods may plead with or enlighten Śiva when he has become too deeply involved in any one phase. To move Śiva from chastity to fertility, the gods send Pārvatī and Kāma, using elements of both his present stage (*tapas*) and the desired stage (*kāma*) to move him. To bring him from fertility to chastity, the usual method is to interrupt the couple in the midst of their love-making; this intervention is doubly necessary as Śiva, being able to restrain his seed for any length of time, need never stop making love to Pārvatī. Being above desire, he need not move into a phase of chastity when his desire is satisfied, as a common man must do: the interruption of his sexual act (*coitus interruptus*) is made necessary by his ascetic powers (*coitus reservatus*).

The interruption motif, like the seduction motif, works in either direction: the gods must send Kāma to interrupt Śiva's trance and Agni to interrupt Śiva's sexual activity, motifs so closely interrelated that they are occasionally interchanged. The two actions also share the paradox that, although they are necessary in cosmic terms, they are sinful in human terms; the result is that they must be done, but the agent must be cursed. Just as Kāma is burnt in spite of the fact that he is merely helping the gods, so Agni and the gods are burnt or cursed to be barren. The curse here acts not as a catalyst but as a resolution; it is the price paid for the compromise between the theoretical level and the emotional level which meet in the myth, and it serves also as the bridge into the next episode of conflict, for it predicts and limits the chain reaction. Furthermore, it serves to resolve the conflict between the real and the ideal which underlies the myth.

That the Hindus considered it a sin to interrupt a couple in the act of

love is well documented.[37] Arjuna Kārtavīrya was killed by Viṣṇu for 44ea
interrupting Indra when he was with Śaci,[38] an episode which Biardeau 44ea
remarks upon: 'When Indra stays with his wife in a loving mood, things
must be in order in our human world. To come and disturb this happy 45e^{1}
occasion is a dreadful act in itself, as well as having dire consequences.'[39]
These considerations apply equally well to Śiva and Pārvatī, as Agni
points out:

> One must not interrupt even a common man when he is making love with
> his wife, let alone Śiva, who is the lord of all. Who could look upon him when 44ea
> he is engaged in love-making? And he is united with Pārvatī for the sake of
> the gods. It is a disgraceful, evil, and dangerous act, to interrupt them, for
> Śiva would mutter, 'Shame on the wretch', and he would kill me straight away
> with a glance if I should enter the bedroom and look upon the Goddess when 4
> she is naked.[40] 7cd^{1}

Similar misgivings are voiced by Kāma before he is persuaded to interrupt the phase of *tapas*. Here, Agni fears that Śiva will burn him as he burnt Kāma, and Viṣṇu answers the objection with the very argument given by Indra to Kāma: 'What you say is true. It would be wrong if done for one's own sake, but there is no evil in it when it is for the sake of someone else.'[41] In another version of the myth, Viṣṇu himself offers a long argument against the interruption, citing the histories of several gods who interrupted couples and were cursed to be separated from their wives. He concludes: 'Who is capable of stopping Śiva from taking his pleasure? He will stop of his own accord after a thousand years, but not now. No one must separate a man and a woman. . . . The act of love is a means of impregnation, and impregnation is very powerful.'[42] A similar argument is given by Gaṇeśa when Bhṛgu tries to
interrupt Śiva and Pārvatī: 'When a man and a woman are joined
together, whoever interrupts their joy goes straight to hell and is 44ea
separated from his wife in seven rebirths.'[43] Since Agni knows that he
will be exposed to both sin and danger in this way, he takes great pains
to hide from the gods, but in vain.[44] Śiva curses Agni for thwarting his
sexual enjoyment, and Pārvatī curses the gods to remain barren as 44ea
she is.[45] Lack of progeny is a curse which can be given to an immortal 2
but which corresponds most closely to the usual curse given to mortals 29a
who commit the same sin: death. Gaṇeśa mentions another aspect of
this curse: instead of being denied sons by their wives, the offending
gods are denied the company of their wives for a period of time.

Yet another variant of the curse appears in the related myth of Īḷa, in which the offenders are cursed to be transformed from men into women, a curse which in effect denies them both the pleasures of children and the pleasures of their wives. Moreover, the fact that by this curse the offender is technically 'unmanned' relates it to the cycle of castration myths as well as to the sexual transformations of Ādi, Viṣṇu, Indra, and Śiva himself. The story of Īḷa exists as a myth separate from the Skanda myth,[46] but the scene often takes place in a forest of reeds and the similarities between the two myths were noted by the author of one late Purāṇa, who combined them:

36e The gods were worried about the protracted love-making of Śiva and
44ea Pārvatī, so they sent a group of Brahmins to interrupt them. When Pārvatī
28ea saw the Brahmins, she was ashamed of her nakedness and she closed her gar-
32ea ment. Then, to please her, Śiva placed a curse on that place, so that any man
who came there would be transformed into a woman.[47]

Although Śiva and Pārvatī are interrupted by Brahmins rather than by Agni, Agni himself takes the form of a Brahmin in some versions of the Skanda birth story. Other Purāṇas tell a similar story but do not connect it with the gods' fears about Śiva and Pārvatī or with their intention to interrupt them:

7d One day the sages came to see Śiva in the woods, illuminating the skies
28ea with the lustre from their bodies. Pārvatī was naked, and when she saw them
44ea she became ashamed and arose from Śiva's embrace, tying her waist-cloth
around her loins. The sages, seeing that the couple were making love, turned
back and went to the hermitage of Viṣṇu. Then, to please his beloved, Śiva
32ea said, 'Whoever enters this place will become a woman.'[48]

A variant of this story states that Pārvatī herself, embarrassed at having
44ea been seen by the sages while in the embrace of Śiva, proclaimed that
32ea any man entering that place would become a woman as beautiful as an
apsaras, and so all creatures there—demons and goblins and ghosts—
21ea became women and sported with Śiva like *apsarases*.[49] Another, probably older, Purāṇa tells the latter part of this version in identical words
32ea but omits the beginning—the interruption by the sages—which supplies
21ea 44ea the point of the myth.[50] Yet another text also omits the specific motive,
the interruption:

36e One day when Śiva and Pārvatī were making love, Pārvatī said, 'It is the
nature of women to wish to hide their sexual pleasure. Therefore, give me
a special place, called the Forest of Pārvatī, in which, except for you and
32ea Gaṇeśa and Skanda and Nandin, any man will become a woman.'[51]

Several other texts use the story of Śiva's previous curse upon that particular place in order to explain the fact that King Īḷa, upon entering

the forest, was transformed into a woman, and his stallion into a mare.
In some versions the curse upon him is modified so that he is a woman 13cd[1]
for a month and then a man for a month, or so that he is a Kiṃpuruṣa 32ea
(literally, a 'What?-Man'), usually described as half man, half horse,[52] 32e 33ea[4]
a boon which he obtains by means of a horse sacrifice. Thus his curse is 13cd[1]
halved temporally or spatially.

One Purāṇa uses the entrance of Īḷa as the cause as well as the effect of the curse:

> One day when Śiva was making love to Pārvatī in a forest, King Īḷa came 36e
> there hunting. When he saw that Śiva was naked, he closed his eyes, but Śiva 44ea
> saw that Pārvatī was embarrassed, and so he said, 'In this place, all creatures 28ea
> but me will become women.' And as he said this, all male creatures were 32ea
> transformed, and Īḷa became a princess, and his horse became a mare.[53] 13cd

In another text, Īḷa interrupts Śiva and Pārvatī, but the sexual transformation takes place before he appears:

> Īḷa went hunting one day and came to the place where Śiva was making 44ea
> love with Pārvatī. Śiva had taken the form of a woman to please Pārvatī, and 36e
> everything in the woods, even trees, became female. As Īḷa came to that place, 32ea
> he was turned into a woman, and when he approached Śiva to seek relief from 26e[2]
> his misery, Śiva laughed and said, 'Ask for any boon except masculinity.'
> Īḷa pleaded with Pārvatī, who granted half of his boon and made him a man 32e
> for one month, a woman for the next. She also granted that, when he was a
> man, he would forget his existence as a woman, and the reverse. Later, Īḷa
> performed a horse sacrifice for Śiva, who restored his masculinity.[54] 32ea

The confusion in chronology here produces the paradoxical statement that Śiva himself became a woman while making love with Pārvatī, a situation expressly avoided by the wording of her request in other versions. In these two latter texts, Īḷa fills the role of the interrupting sages as well as his own role.

The sages are the central figures, however, in another important version of this myth, a story of the origin of *liṅga*-worship, which further identifies the sages as the inhabitants of the Pine Forest, who are, as usual, scandalized by Śiva's sexual behaviour:

> The gods and sages asked Bhṛgu to decide for them who among the three
> great gods was the greatest. Bhṛgu went to see Śiva, but when he asked
> Nandin, who was guarding the door, to let him enter, Nandin said, 'Śiva is 44ea
> making love to Pārvatī. Turn back if you wish to live.' Bhṛgu stayed at the 36e
> door for many days, and finally he said, 'Since Śiva is immersed in the 2
> embrace of a woman and therefore dishonours me, let his form be that of 5cd
> the *liṅga* in the *yoni*, and let his worshippers be heretics, outside the pale of 17cd

$5c^2$ 6cd the Vedas, smeared with ashes.' Thus having cursed Śiva, Bhṛgu went to see
Viṣṇu and Brahmā.[55]

As often happens in the Pine Forest myth, the curse to be worshipped as the *liṅga* is transmuted into a blessing. In a version of the tale recorded in the mid seventeenth century, the sage comes to see Śiva when he is with Pārvatī ('Therefore the sage came at quite an inopportune moment'), is made to wait, and curses Śiva to become that with which he is at the moment involved; later, however, the sage ordains that anyone who worships the *liṅga* in the *yoni* will be blessed.[56] Both the curse and the blessing appear in the version of the myth recorded by the Abbé Dubois:

[Brahmā, Viṣṇu, and Vasiṣṭha, with many sages, came to visit Śiva on
44ea Kailāsa one day] and surprised him in the act of intercourse with his wife.
He was not in the least disconcerted by the presence of the illustrious visitors,
and so far from showing any shame at being discovered in such a position,
continued to indulge in the gratification of his sensual desires. The fact was
that the shameless god was greatly excited by the intoxicating liquors which
16d he had drunk, and with his reason obscured by passion and drunkenness, he
was no longer in a state to appreciate the indecency of his conduct. At sight
24a of him some of the gods, and especially Vishnu, began to laugh; while the
rest displayed great indignation and anger, and loaded the shameless Śiva
2 with insults and curses. [They cursed him to be banished from the society of
honest folk, and they retired, covered with shame. When Śiva had recovered
his senses a little and learned from the guards what had taken place] the words
of the guards fell on Śiva and his wife Durgā like a clap of thunder, and they
10cd both died of grief in the same position in which the gods and the penitents had
surprised them. Śiva desired that the act which had covered him with shame,
and which had been the cause of his death, should be celebrated among mankind. 'My shame', said he, 'has killed me; but it has also given me new life,
5cd and a new shape, which is that of the lingam!' [And he ordained that men
$5c^2$ should offer him worship in that form.][57]

The good Abbé takes a dim view of the circumstances of Śiva's 'death', and seems to sympathize with the gods and sages who interrupt the 'shameless' Śiva rather than with the god whose cosmic love-play is disturbed by his impatient congregation.

A rather loose variation of Dubois's version of the myth was narrated recently by a Brahmin:

44ea Śiva had been discovered in bed with his wife Durgā by Brahma, Vishnu,
16d and other gods. He had been so drunk that he had not thought it necessary
to stop. The majority, all except Vishnu and a few of the broader-minded,
24a thought them nasty and brutish and said so. Śiva and Durgā died of shame
10cd in the position in which they were discovered; but before they expired Śiva

expressed the wish that mankind should worship the act manifest in the form 5cd
which he now took to himself, the lingam.[58] 5c[2]

Another contemporary version of this myth incorporates other elements of the Pine Forest story:

> Shiva one day roamed into a forest with his wife where some Rishis were
> practising austerities and, forgetting that the spot was sacred to the sages, 35ea
> suddenly became amorous. In the heat of the moment he lost all sense of 43ea
> decorum and embraced his spouse in an open place. As ill-luck would have 36e
> it some of the sages who inhabited the woods came that way, and saw Shiva 44ea
> and his wife in each other's arms. The outraged saints converted Shiva into 2
> a Lingam by a curse.[59] 5cd

Since the Pine Forest myth, like the Bhṛgu story, accounts for the origin of *liṅga*-worship, and since Bhṛgu is one of the Pine Forest sages, it is easy to see how elements of the former would be transferred to the latter in this manner. Moreover, one Purāṇa tells another story which combines the motif of interruption with elements of the Pine Forest story, though it does not mention the *liṅga*:

> One day in the presence of the sages Śiva said to Pārvatī, 'This is the lovely
> house of some Brahmin. Go and anoint yourself with sandalwood paste, and
> while the bees hum and the sun sets, we two will make love on a delightful bed 28e
> strewn with flowers, and I will kiss your red lips.' Hearing this, the sages were 36e 44ea
> angry and said, 'Why, this is a lovely speech to say in front of us.' Then Śiva 24a
> became angry, and from his mouth there appeared a flame-woman with an 13cd 5d
> enormous mouth. She attacked the wife of one of the sages, who fled to Viṣṇu
> for refuge, but suddenly the flame disappeared, and Śiva explained that the
> flame-woman had been an illusion wrought by his magical powers.[60] 33ea[7]

Here, in addition to the angry sages in the forest and the sexual activity of Śiva in their presence, the Pine Forest myth appears in the motif of the fire which appears from Śiva, replacing the usual image of the flame-*liṅga* with the related image of the fiery-mouthed mare.

Another interruption episode substitutes for the *liṅga/yoni* motif (itself a surrogate for the anthropomorphic sexual embrace) the image of the androgyne:

> [Once when Śiva was seated with Pārvatī on Kailāsa, all the gods and sages 36e
> came there to pay homage to him. All but the sage Bhṛṅgin circumambulated
> both Śiva and Pārvatī, but Bhṛṅgin had vowed to worship only Śiva. Pārvatī 35a
> became angry with Bhṛṅgin and cursed him to become a skeleton immediately, 2
> devoid of all flesh and blood. When Śiva saw that the sage was unable to stand 28ea 38a[2]
> up in this condition, he gave him a third leg, and Bhṛṅgin danced for joy. 7cd[1]
> Pārvatī, angry once more to see her curse thus thwarted, performed *tapas* for 31e 31a 36ea[1]
> Śiva, who granted her the wish of being joined to his own body. But Bhṛṅgin 32e 33ea[4]

44ea then assumed the form of a beetle and pierced a hole through the composite
form of the androgyne and thus circumambulated Śiva alone. Pārvatī admired
him and showed her grace to him.][61]

Two elements taken directly from the episode of Agni's interruption of
Śiva and Pārvatī are the motif of transformation into an animal and the
emphasis upon the enmity of Pārvatī. The presence of Bhṛṅgin may
result from a misunderstanding of the name of Bhṛgu, who usually participates in this episode. As Bhṛṅgin is a skeleton (an aspect of Andhaka,
who also opposes the union of Śiva and Pārvatī and receives a third eye
from Śiva, while Bhṛṅgin receives a third leg), the myth is twisted to
include an explanation of his form, utilizing (and reversing) elements of
the myth of Maṅkaṇaka, the dancing ascetic [Plate 8].

Yet another variation of the interruption motif is associated with the
Pine Forest myth through a complex series of reversals, in the myth of
Viṣvaksena. This is a multiform of the myth of the beheading of Brahmā
38a by Śiva in which Śiva, afflicted with the skull of Brahmā and the Fury
25a of Brahminicide incarnate, assumes the form of a beggar and seeks alms
not from the sages' wives but from Viṣṇu, as he does in certain other
4 late versions of the Kāpālika–Pine Forest myth. In this version, how-
44ea ever, Śiva is stopped at Viṣṇu's door by the doorkeeper, Viṣvaksena,
38a whom he beheads as he has just beheaded Brahmā, and when Śiva is
then garlanded with the skull and bones of Viṣvaksena he is known as
Kaṅkāla, another form of the Kāpālika.[62] Since Viṣvaksena plays the
role of Nandin, Śiva himself for once is the interrupter rather than the
interrupted, assuming the role of Kāma–Agni as he often does in other
contexts. This version of the motif of interruption is an Indian variant
of the widespread myth of the slaying of the guardian (usually a dragon)
at the door. Metaphysically, it is an expression of the breaking down of
barriers; the interrupter is a messenger who unites the worshippers with
their god.

37a The motif of interruption appears throughout the mythology of Śiva.
41a When Brahmā went to Kāma in order to request him to interrupt Śiva's
44ea trance, he found Kāma and Rati together, and he 'materialized, as luck
4 would have it, just in time to create *coitus interruptus*, to the same effect
13c as if he had flung a bucket of pepper water over the neighbours' dogs'.[63]
The motif is easily transferred from Śiva to Kāma, as it is transferred
20e from the interruption of *kāma* to the interruption of *tapas*. Thus Pārvatī
28ea curses Bhairava to become a mortal because he interrupts her in a state
44ea of erotic dishabille:

44ea When the gods interrupted Śiva and Pārvatī, two sons were born of drops

of Śiva's seed. These sons were then posted at the door to prevent further 21e
interruptions while Śiva made love to Pārvatī, having promised the gods that 20ea
he would not spill his seed in her. One day Pārvatī came out of the bedroom 21a
in great dishabille, half naked, her breasts scored with teeth marks. The two 28ea
sons chanced to see her like that, and they were upset, but Pārvatī became 27e 44ea
angry and said, 'Why have you looked at me when I was not in a state to be 2
seen by anyone but my husband? You should have closed your eyes. Since
you have done this immoral thing, you will be reborn as mortal men with the 20e 7cd^2
faces of monkeys.' Then they were miserable and protested that it was her 33ea^4
fault for having come out so suddenly, and they cursed her to become a mortal 2
queen (Tārāvatī) and Śiva to be her husband (Candraśekhara) so that they 20e
themselves might be born again as their sons, Vetāla and Bhairava.[64] 19e

The sons born of the first interruption are inadvertently responsible for a second one. For this transgression they are cursed to be reborn (with the monkey faces often associated with sexual curses), but Śiva and Pārvatī are also cursed to become incarnate (a related punishment associated with sexual excesses).

The sons in this myth are not only the interrupters but also the
guards, who often are cursed in this way. Thus, in a typical reversal, 2
Vīraka is cursed by Pārvatī not for interrupting a sexual encounter but 20e
for failing to guard Śiva from such an encounter, for allowing a woman 44ea
(Āḍi in disguise) to enter Śiva's bedroom; and the curse is that Vīraka 4
will be born as a mortal.[65] Similarly, although Nandin, the doorkeeper, 43ea
is usually instructed to prevent Kāma from interrupting Śiva's *tapas*, 4
according to one South Indian text Śiva gives Nandin express instruc- 42e
tions not to allow anyone *except Kāma* to enter while he is meditating.[66] 4
Nandin is also given the usual curse of incarnation for permitting the
interruption of Śiva's love-play:

When Śiva married Pārvatī, he made love to her for a hundred celestial 36e
years, for he was under the control of his passion, tortured by desire. Seeing 43ea
this great love-play, the gods were worried that the son born of such a union 19a
would destroy the universe. They went to Śiva, but Nandin guarded the door 5d
and would not let them enter while Śiva was with Pārvatī. Then Agni took 44ea
the form of a swan and eluded Nandin, and he whispered in Śiva's ear, saying, 30e
'Indra and the other gods are standing at the door.' Śiva went to the door, 4
and the gods bowed to him and begged him to abandon his terrible love-play. 3
Śiva agreed, and the gods returned to heaven, but Śiva cursed Nandin to be 20e
born on earth immediately. When Nandin had fallen, he wandered to the 5c^2 33ea^5 38a^2
Mahākāla forest in the form of a Kāpālika, and he worshipped the *liṅga* and 20a
was released from the curse.[67]

Here Nandin receives the punishment which in other versions of this episode is given to Agni, occasionally to Kāma, and on rare occasions

to Vāyu or Nārada. The curse which these gods receive, however—to carry the burning seed—is here replaced by the curse usually associated with an excess of *kāma* rather than with the prevention of *kāma*—the curse of rebirth. Yet the motif of the burning seed attracts to this version the closely related motif of the flaming *liṅga* in the Pine Forest, which Nandin enters (as Śiva does) in the form of a Kāpālika. The Pine Forest
44ea is associated with Nandin in yet another variant, in which Nandin tries
26e to prevent the demon Rāvaṇa from entering a forest of reeds where Śiva
and Pārvatī are making love.[68]

So widespread is the motif of interruption that even the interruption of the *narration* of a sexual scene is regarded as a sin. Most manuscripts of Kālidāsa's poem, *The Birth of Kumāra*, omit those cantos which describe the love-play of Śiva and Pārvatī; this literary tradition is
3 explained as the result of a curse given to Kālidāsa by Pārvatī, who was
44ea embarrassed at having her erotic behaviour described in such detail.[69]
A similar variation on the interruption motif accounts for the incarnation of another poet:

> 36e While Śiva was telling Pārvatī the story of the birth of Skanda, Puṣpadanta
> 44ea came to see him. Nandin did not let him enter, but Puṣpadanta took the form
> 30ea of a breeze, entered, and listened to the story. When Devī discovered what
> 20e 2 had happened, she cursed Puṣpadanta to become a mortal.[70]

Puṣpadanta eludes Nandin as Kāma does, by taking the form of a breeze, but he receives the usual curse given to one who interrupts erotic play. In these various ways, the motif of interruption acts as the transition between cycles of sexuality and asceticism.

D. QUIESCENCE AND ENERGY

In Hindu mythology, the two forces interact in a constantly shifting balance, vibrating from one phase to another, approximating but never attaining the point of simultaneous existence of the two extremes. Chastity builds into desire, and the fulfilment of desire leads to chastity. In one Purāṇa, the specific episodes of Śiva's marriage are in an inap-
21e propriate order, but the alternation of cycles is preserved: Śiva gives
34a 36a away his seed (*kāma*), but refuses to marry and returns to his asceticism
43ea (*tapas*); Kāma inspires passion (*kāma*), but Śiva assuages it (*tapas*);
42a Śiva marries (*kāma*), then burns Kāma (*tapas*), then revives him
36e 43e 43a (*kāma*).[71] The alternation of phases in the myth of the dicing quarrel

provides a fairly close parallel to the Kāma story but in a completely reversed order:

Dicing Quarrel[72] ↓		*Marriage of Śiva and Pārvatī* ↑	
Śiva and Pārvatī play dice	= *kāma* =	Śiva and Pārvatī marry and make love	36e 33ea[7]
They quarrel and part	= *tapas* =	Śiva (disguised) argues with Pārvatī and they separate to prepare to wed	36a 33ea[3]
Pārvatī, disguised as a mountain woman, seduces Śiva	= *kāma* =	Pārvatī (with Kāma) seduces Śiva	33ea[3] 36ea 43ea
Śiva returns to *tapas*	= *tapas* =	Śiva performs *tapas*	34a 36a

Similar transitions take place in the Pine Forest myth. Unsatisfied lust 36e
for his wife (or susceptibility to her demands) leads Śiva to wander alone 36a
as an ascetic in the woods; this leads to the seduction of the sages' wives, 35ea
which leads in turn to the castration of Śiva (the essence of chastity) 32a
and the ultimate restoration of the *liṅga* in the *yoni* (the essence of sexu- 5c[2]
ality). The castration functions, like most curses, as a catalyst to the
inevitable transition: the imprecation may function homoeopathically 2
(as when a lustful man is cursed to commit incest), producing a situation
in which the extreme form of the sin will of itself eventually bring about
the reversal; or the curse may explicitly impose a change of phase upon 3
the offender (as when a vow of chastity is imposed upon one who has
committed a sexual transgression).

The changes in Śiva are sometimes brought about by another external factor: the aspect of the other characters in a particular myth. Edmund Leach has noted this variation in the mythology of Gaṇeśa:

> Ganesha's broken tusk is a phallic emblem and . . . its detachability denotes 5cd
> a certain ambivalence about Ganesha's sexual nature. There are contexts in 32a
> which the *lingam*-phallus, which is properly an emblem of Shiva, may serve 24ea[2]
> as a manifestation of any one of Shiva's sons, Ganesha included. In such
> a context Ganesha may be virile and potent. But there are other contexts 26ea
> where Ganesha seems to be an effeminate eunuch. 32a
>
> This ambivalence is not haphazard. Ganesha does not exist by himself but in association with other members of Shiva's family. The sexual qualities which are attributed to Ganesha depend upon context, and, generally speaking, are the opposite of those attributed to his father (Shiva) or to one of his two brothers Skanda and Aiyanar. As Shiva varies, so also Ganesha varies, but in the inverse direction.[73]

In this way, Śiva himself varies in opposition to the qualities of other gods and sages, as if to set up a thermostatic control on their excesses, just as they do on his. When Brahmā is incestuous, Śiva appears as an ascetic to oppose him, but Śiva himself sheds the golden and incestuous seed of Prajāpati in other contexts. Śiva is responsible for the seduction of the dangerous ascetic, but he is himself an ascetic so seduced. The extreme of one force is the extreme of its opposite; *tapas* and *kāma*, interchangeable forms of cosmic heat, replace and limit one another to maintain the balance of the universe.

In some myths, energy (activity, worldly involvement [*pravṛtti*]) is
contrasted with quiescence (withdrawal, release [*nivṛtti*]), the former
identified with sexual activity and the latter with asceticism. When Śiva
26a ceases to create and becomes a pillar of chastity, he is said to have
31ea quiescence as his nature.[74] As an ascetic, he dwells in quiescence and
24e 31ea shuns a wife and involvement. His mind is quiescent when, after making
love for many years, he is satisfied.[75]

However, since both *tapas* and *kāma* are forces of energy, together
they may be contrasted with their true opposite: quiescence. And
although this quiescence is what Śiva usually *teaches* (for it is the
favourite path of the ascetic Upaniṣadic schools which he represents),
he himself usually *embodies* pure life energy. Like the Mahāyāna Buddha,
34a he teaches rest but is not himself at rest.[76] Thus, though he is said to
31ea go to the Pine Forest to teach the sages to leave activity and devote
31e 28ea themselves to quiescence,[77] he does this by dancing in wild, naked
35ea abandon with their wives. Although he says that he will not marry and
36a 31ea that he delights only in *tapas* and quiescence, with no use for activity
36e and the ways of mistresses,[78] he does in fact marry, and he seduces
35ea 31e a number of women. The famous dancing Śiva, Nāṭarājā, is the very
embodiment of energy, haloed in a circle of flames, constantly in motion,
destroying, exciting [Plate 7].

The cycles of activity and quiescence play an important part in Tantric philosophy:

> [One] attempt to make the Universe intelligible regards it as an eternal
> 18e rhythm playing and pulsing outwards from spirit to matter (pravritti) and
> 18a then backwards and inwards from matter to spirit (nirvritti). . . . The Tantras
> 18ea recognize and consecrate both movements, the outward throbbing stream of
> energy and enjoyment (bhukti) and the calm returning flow of liberation and
> peace. Both are happiness, but the wise understand that the active outward
> movement is right and happy only up to a certain point and under certain
> restrictions.[79]

During the Tantric rite, the devotee exhausts the forces of activity, the

outgoing path, and begins to cultivate quiescence.[80] Śiva too must use 18ea
both paths, must follow the outgoing path to prevent the accumulation of too great a power and then replenish that power by the path of
quiescence. At Śiva's request, Brahmā substitutes for universal death 37ea
the process of periodical action and quiescence.[81] Śiva himself is the source of both action and quiescence,[82] passion and peace.

For quiescence is not the end, not the final goal; it is merely the temporary goal for one who is involved in activity. Nor is quiescence in Śiva merely a negative quality, an absence of power; it is the ultimate solution to the problem of cycles. The moment at which the two extremes of chastity and sexuality cancel each other out is the moment of quiescence, the hiatus between the episodes of energy (chaste or sexual). It has been suggested that this appearance of stillness resulting from two equal and opposite forces underlies the symbolism of the mathematical zero, which the ancient Indians invented:

> Zero is the transition-point between opposites, it symbolizes the true balance within divergent tendencies. Zero has now taken on, in a more deepened and philosophical way, the functions earlier assigned to the number Three. Zero is the productive All and None, the matrix of positive and negative, of addition and subtraction, of generating and destroying capacities. It is the productive point of indifference and balance . . . between the two opposites of extreme greatness (*ākāśa*) and extreme smallness (*aṇu*).[83]

In Indian mythology, too, quiescence is an apparent calm which is in fact a perfectly balanced tension.

X

CONCLUSION: THE PENDULUM OF EXTREMES

At the end of almost every myth told in the Purāṇas there appears a statement of the advantages that one can hope to gain by listening to the tale: 'Whoever hears [or, in later times, reads] this story will be freed from the flames of hell, purified of the stigma of adultery, received into the presence of Śiva. . . .' Although such extravagant claims cannot be made for the present work, the reader may, at least, have gained an understanding of the central concerns of the Śaiva myths. Each reader will draw his own conclusions, and those expressed below are merely the author's personal response to the corpus of myths.

First of all, there is something to be learned about the form and structure of Hindu mythology and mythology in general, and its relation to content. 'Form' is perhaps a misleading word to use here, for Indian mythology impresses us with its apparent formlessness; there is no one 'myth' but rather a vague, ectoplasmic substance whose outlines constantly change, containing somewhere within it the essence of the myth. Physicists now tell us that, because of the constant motion of the surface atomic particles of a table, the table has no permanent form, but can only be located 'somewhere' within a statistical area; so too the myth has no final delineation, for there will always be yet another variant containing some motifs which, like electrons escaping from the surface of the table, extend the myth beyond the bounds established by all other variants.

The staggering variety of Indian mythology is significant not only from an artistic point of view, where it reveals a perhaps unparalleled gift of imagination and originality, but from the psychological standpoint as well. By noting the points that are most often changed, elaborated upon, and, in particular, 'mistakenly' interpreted (i.e. confused with irrelevant stories or modified in such a way as to destroy the logic of the myth), one comes to understand the true crux of the mythology. This recurrence and constant revision is in part a result of the long historical development and structural expansion of an oral tradition, but it may also reveal a preoccupation almost equivalent to a neurotic *idée fixe*. Just as Mr. Dick could never manage to keep the head of King Charles the First out of his petition, so the Hindus cannot seem to leave alone certain aspects of their own mythology.

A related formal aspect of myth which has philosophical implications is the use of detail. Indian literature—classical poetry and drama, as well as the popular literature of the Purāṇas and Epics—abounds in descriptions which betray a taste for the almost mathematical systematization of any activity. In battle scenes, there are weapons of infinite variety, and the poet dwells with such relish upon the minute details of beheadings and maimings that they become aesthetically fascinating; there are tales describing the thousand different delicious dishes that a clever woman can prepare when given only a few grains of rice with which to begin; scientific treatises enumerate the ways to judge and train elephants; pandits argue over the endless permutations of metaphysical doctrine and social law; there are dissertations on the numerous possible (and impossible) positions of sexual intercourse; the mathematical proportions of temples—all of this is developed with an obsession for detail. The ancient Indian knew well the Faustian lust for the full experience of the most diverse possibilities of human life; the Buddha saw this thirst as the cause of all human misery, but the Hindus did not dismiss it so easily. They recognized a constant tension between the desire to sample every aspect of experience and the desire to exhaust at least one by plumbing its extreme depths. Thus every human action involves a choice, and every choice implies a loss.

In the sphere of human society, the choice implicit in this conflict was simply denied by the caste system with its doctrine of *svadharma*, one's own particular duty in life: each person could perform one role fully and must let the rest go untried, at least in this existence. But these frustrations are relieved in the myths, where Śiva embodies *all* of life, in *all* of its detail, at every minute. He alone need make no choice; through him all of the conflicting challenges are accepted at once. In reading the myth, we too embrace the preciousness of life; we, too, lose nothing. Yet even the myths cannot fully slake this thirst; hence each story is told again and again, each time with new detail—a new character, a different episode, an expanded description—for no single myth can capture all the richness; each is merely a hint, a promise, a symbol of all that life can be.

Another structural element—the interplay of microcosmic and macrocosmic scales—arises in response to another philosophical quandary which might be formulated, in personal terms, as a question: How can one fully savour the joys of the most trivial moments—a child's laugh, the first snowfall, the scent of flowers at dusk—while remaining aware of cosmic and metaphysical dimensions—the distance of the stars, the randomness of death—which threaten to reduce such moments to insignificance? This question is implicit throughout Hindu mythology, which at one moment seems to function on a purely mundane level but then unexpectedly blossoms out into infinity and, equally abruptly, returns to the banal. The gods who represent the awesome powers of nature are suddenly revealed as petty and confused pawns like ourselves, while the apparently insignificant mortal is transformed into the instrument of divine grace or wrath. Indra, puffed up with pride in his might and power, is made to see that he is merely one of a series of Indras who trail through the aeons like a parade of ants;[1] and Kṛṣṇa's mother, thinking to chastise her naughty son for eating mud, looks into his mouth and sees within him the whole universe, and herself, and him.[2] This double vision is a quality of myth in general—the sudden epiphany, the revelation of the sacred in the profane—but it is portrayed with characteristic extremity in the myths of Śiva, who uses his magic eye to bring about the final conflagration of the universe and is then berated by his wife for using it to cheat at dice. In this manner, the structure of the myth expresses the conflict between the scales on which human life may be viewed.

The formal points of repetition, variation, detail, and scale thus assume a dimension of content as well. The myths structured in this way are of great importance to the Hindus, for they resolve, at least on an artistic level, certain contradictions that are logically irreconcilable. The corpus of Śaiva myths returns again and again to the age-old quandaries about the way in which men ought to live: how can one live *in* the world, enjoying the pleasures of life and perpetuating these in one's children, and yet renounce the world, thus freeing the spirit? This dilemma is treated in other cultures as the struggle between the values of God and mammon, spirit and flesh, the hereafter and the present moment, the sacred and the profane.

In the course of more than three millennia of recorded Indian religious speculation, different mythological figures emerged to catalyse these conflicts. The permutations of the central myth thus supply a touchstone upon which we can judge something of the *Zeitgeist* of each subsequent age of metaphysical thought: Rudra, Indra, and Agni of the Vedas (*c.* 1200 B.C.) provide a skeletal archetype of certain patterns of creation and destruction; Brahmā Prajāpati of the Brāhmaṇas (*c.* 900

B.C.) furnishes a more complex philosophical treatment of the conflicting patterns of creation and the self-contradiction inherent in the concept of ascetic creation; Agni and the many ascetics of the *Mahābhārata* (*c.* 300 B.C.–A.D. 300) demonstrate the paradoxical nature of the life of the married ascetic; and Śiva and Kāma in the Purāṇas (*c.* 300 B.C.–A.D. 1000) interact and replace one another in such a way as to demonstrate the extraordinarily flexible state of mind which the Hindu mythmaker ultimately developed in his attempt to view simultaneously every possible solution to his dilemma. The comparatively late developments of Tantrism and devotionalism (*c.* A.D. 1000) provided further philosophical rationalizations: the Tantric ascetic, by reversing certain traditional values, maintained the identity of the two extremes of asceticism and sensuality, control and release; and the devotee (*bhakta*) believed that any action of the god or his worshipper could be justified if performed in a spirit of absolute and compelling love.

The combination of so many different facets of the paradox was made possible largely through the use of recurrent symbols. This process was facilitated by the manner in which Hindus tended to view as the interplay of natural powers problems which we might see in moral, ethical, or philosophical terms. These elemental powers influence divine and human individuals by embodying the impulses of passion, self-control, desire, anger, asceticism, etc., and they are constantly in flux. The control or transmutation of these forces may be seen on the cosmic level, where the continual interaction of the natural elements (primarily fire and water) animates the flow of vital forces within the universe. Each force must be allowed to develop to its extreme, and then a balance is sought by the rechannelling or transformation of any force which is out of control; in this way, the universe pulses from extreme to extreme like a pendulum. Since a perfect balance can never be reached, the pendulum can never be at rest, but moments of apparent peace occur from time to time as the wave crosses from one phase to another. On the symbolic level, these are the moments when the forces of fire and water are simultaneously present but not mutually destructive; on the divine level, these are the undertakings in which creative and destructive divinities reinforce one another; on the human level, these are the episodes in which ascetic and sexual impulses combine within an individual, each impulse allowed to develop the full expression of its power without impeding the expression of the contrasting impulse.

These fleeting moments of balance provide no 'solution' to the paradox of the myth, for, indeed, Hindu mythology does not seek any true synthesis. Where Western thought insists on forcing a compromise or synthesis of opposites, Hinduism is content to keep each as it is; in chemical terms, one might say that the conflicting elements are resolved into a suspension rather than a solution. The aesthetic satisfaction of the myth lies here, where the god seems to savour fully and perfectly both of the extremes. The mortal worshipper uses the myth in an attempt to freeze this moment of balance, to capture a point of time that is perfect; he shares Faust's vain plea to the supreme moment—'Linger a while, thou art so fair.'[3]

But time flows; the pulse of the myth constantly reasserts itself; there is no true peace. As the Buddha pointed out, nothing is permanent but change itself; matter constantly transforms itself, and death is no more significant than any other change from one moment to the next. The myth has no beginning or end; it begins in the middle, as there is always some unknown episode from the past which shapes the events of the present, and there is always an unsatisfied curse, an unfulfilled prediction to carry us forward into the next episode.

By refusing to modify its component elements in order to force them into a synthesis, Indian mythology celebrates the idea that the universe is boundlessly various, that everything occurs simultaneously, that all possibilities may exist without excluding each other. The myths rejoice in all the experiences that stretch and fill the human spirit; not merely the moments of pure joy that we want to capture, nor the great tragedies and transitions that transform and strengthen us, but all the seemingly insignificant episodes and repetitious encounters of banal reality which the myth—with its minute detail and its awareness of simultaneous scales—teaches us to sanctify and to value. Untrammelled variety and contradiction are ethically and metaphysically necessary; this constitutes the peculiar charm and strength of the Hindu world-view.

In many myths Śiva is merely erotic or merely ascetic, as a momentary view of one phase or another. But in the great myths, transcending the limits of mundane causality, he participates in cycles of cosmic dimensions which melt into a single image as they become ever more frequent, making an almost subliminal impression in their brief symbolic appearances, creating an infinitely complex mosaic. The conflict is resolved not into a static icon but rather into the constant motion of the pendulum, whose animating force is the eternal paradox of the myths.

APPENDIX A

CONNECTIONS BETWEEN EPISODES IN THE ŚAIVA CYCLE

This list does not contain an exhaustive treatment, but merely sufficient examples to establish each link. References are to texts in which two episodes are juxtaposed, rather than those in which one episode contains a reference to another (conscious multiforms, motif 1). A diagram of the cycle follows the list.

1. Brahmā's incest → Śiva beheads Brahmā.
   Numerous examples; cf. Chapter IV and motifs 38 and 39.
2. Śiva beheads Brahmā → Pine Forest.
   Sāmba 16–17; *Skanda* 5. 2. 8. 1–14; *Skanda* 5. 3. 38. 6–68; *Varāha* 97. 1–18; *Skanda* 1. 1. 6. 2–68; Jouveau-Dubreuil, ii, 32; Baldaeus, pp. 17–18; Dessigane (1967), pp. 84–5 (2. 32. 6–47); *Padma* 5. 17. 35–55; MhB XIII. 329. 21.
3. Brahmā's incest → Brahmā curses Śiva and Kāma.
   Numerous examples; cf. Chapter IV and motifs 39e, 37a, and 41a.
4. Brahmā curses Śiva and Kāma → Kāma wounds Śiva → Śiva burns Kāma → Śiva marries Satī → Brahmā sheds seed at wedding → Śiva destroys Dakṣa's sacrifice → Satī kills herself.
   Śiva 2. 2. 8–20. Others contain all episodes but Brahmā's seed.
5. Śiva beheads Brahmā → Pine Forest → flame *liṅga*.
   Skanda 1. 1. 6. 2–68.
6. Flame *liṅga* → Śiva beheads Brahmā.
   Brahma 135. 1–25; *Śiva* 3. 8. 36–66, 3. 9. 1–57.
7. Śiva beheads Brahmā → Pine Forest → Mohinī.
   Baldaeus, pp. 17–18; Churchill, p. 737; Rhode, p. 236; Dessigane (1967), pp. 84–5 (2. 32. 6–47).
8. Satī kills herself → Kāma wounds Śiva.
   Kālikā 18. 1–117.
9. Satī kills herself → Pine Forest.
   Skanda 7. 3. 39, 5–12; *Kālikā* 18. 1–111.
10. Kāma wounds Śiva → Śiva burns Kāma → Pārvatī performs *tapas* → Śiva marries Pārvatī → Śiva revives Kāma → Birth of Skanda.
    Most texts.
11. Śiva marries Pārvatī → Brahmā sheds seed at wedding.
    Śiva 2. 3. 1–55.
12. Kāma wounds Śiva → Śiva burns Kāma → Śiva creates mare-fire.
    Śiva 2. 3. 20. 1–23; *Kālikā* 44. 124–36; *Mahābhāgavata* 22. 108–11, 23. 1–4.

13. Kāma wounds Śiva → Pine Forest.
Kālikā 44. 110–12; *Mahābhāgavata* 24. 28, 25. 25; *Vāmana* 6. 36; 6. 93–6; *Skanda* 7. 3. 40. 4–23; 7. 1. 100; 7. 3. 39. 5–38; 3. 3. 26. 1–10. Nīlakaṇṭha on MhB XIII. 17. 39 and 42.

14. Pine Forest → Kāma wounds Śiva.
Vāmana 6. 60–93; *Skanda* 7. 3. 40. 4–33.

15. Kāma wounds Śiva → Pine Forest → flame *liṅga*.
Vāmana 6. 60–93.

16. 'Kālī' argument → Āḍi → Pine Forest.
Śiva, Dharmasaṃhitā, 10. 28–77 and 10. 79–215.

17. 'Kālī' argument → Āḍi → Birth of Skanda.
Matsya 158. 1–23; *Padma* 5. 41. 1–117; *Skanda* 1. 2. 29. 82–210.

18. Andhaka → Pine Forest.
Bṛhaddharma 1. 16. 19–123; *Kūrma* 1. 16, 123–240; *Skanda* 7. 2. 9. 151–63; *Śiva*, Dharmasaṃhitā, 4. 4–208.

19. Andhaka → Maṅkaṇaka.
Vāmana 59–70.

20. Pine Forest → Śiva beheads Brahmā.
Varāha 21 and 22.

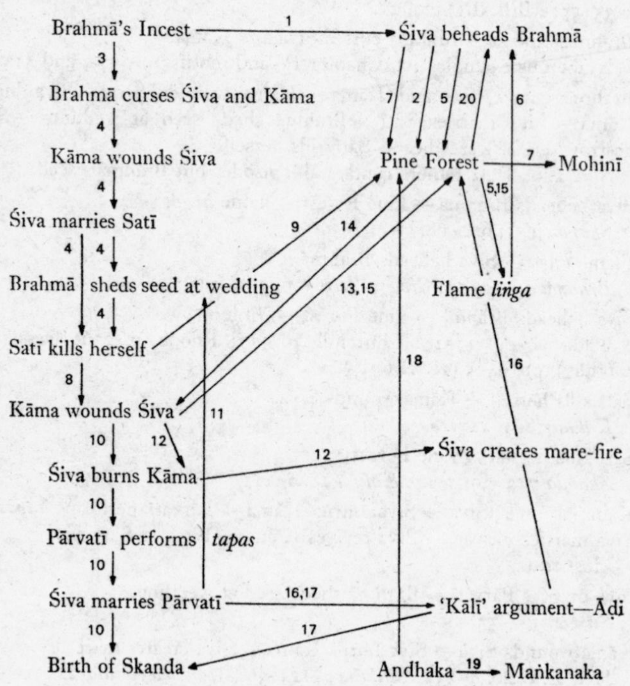

APPENDIX B

MAJOR OCCURRENCES OF THE MAIN EPISODES

It is unfortunately impossible to offer here the full texts of the Śaiva cycle, as this would run to hundreds of pages. For the use of readers who wish to consult the texts, however, this appendix indicates the Sanskrit passages containing significant treatments of the central episodes (the conflict between Śiva and Kāma, the birth of Skanda, and the Pine Forest). Non-Sanskritists may consult the available translations of these passages as well as the texts recorded only in European languages (Part II).

I. SANSKRIT TEXTS

A. ŚIVA AND KĀMA

1. *Bhaviṣya* 3. 4. 14. 9–85.
2. *Brahma* 34. 42–101, 35. 1–63, 36. 1–135, 37. 1–23, 38. 1–20.
3. *Brahma* 71. 1–42, 72. 1–33.
4. *Brahmāṇḍa* 4. 11. 1–34, 4. 30. 30–99.
5. *Brahmavaivarta* 4. 38–45.
6. *Bṛhaddharma* 2. 53. 1–49.
7. *Devībhāgavata* 7. 31. 4–64, 7. 40. 38–40.
8. *Haracarita* 9. 16–195.
9. *Kālikā* 4–13.
10. *Kālikā* 42–6.
11. *Kumārasambhava* 1–8.
12. *Liṅga* 1. 101–3.
13. *Mahābhāgavata* 12, 14–15, 20–8.
14. *Manmathonmathana*.
15. *Matsya* 148. 17–24, 154. 1–495.
16. *Padma* 5. 40. 46–450.
17. *Pārvatīpariṇaya*.
18. *Rāmāyaṇa* 1. 34. 13–20.
19. *Saura* 53–9.
20. *Śiva* 3. 33. 1–63, 3. 34. 1–35, 3. 35. 1–36.
21. *Śiva*, Jñānasaṃhitā 9, 10, 13–18.
22. *Śiva* 2. 2. 8–20.
23. *Śiva* 2. 3. 1–55.
24. *Skanda* 1. 1. 20–7.
25. *Skanda* 1. 2. 22–6.
26. *Skanda* 2. 7. 8. 1–96.
27. *Skanda* 5. 1. 34. 1–58.
28. *Skanda* 5. 2. 13. 23–55.
29. *Skanda* 5. 3. 150. 7–35.
30. *Skanda* 7. 1. 200. 1–30.
31. *Skanda* 7. 3. 40. 4–23.
32. *Vāmana* 6. 26–107.
33. *Vāmana* 25. 1–20, 31. 1–18.
34. *Varāha* 22. 1–45.

B. THE BIRTH OF SKANDA

1. *Brahma* 128. 3–46.
2. *Brahmāṇḍa* 4. 30. 98–101.
3. *Brahmavaivarta* 3. 1, 3. 2, 3. 8, 3. 9, 3. 14.
4. *Brahmāvaivarta* 4. 46. 9–61.
5. *Bṛhaddharma* 2. 53. 50–63.
6. *Haracarita* 9. 196–221.
7. *Kālikā* 48. 12–96.
8. *Kathāsaritsāgara* 3. 6. 60–88.
9. *Kumārasambhava* 9–11.
10. *Mahābhāgavata* 29. 1–35, 30. 1–37.
11. *Mahābhārata* XIII. 83. 40–57, XIII. 84. 1–76, XIII. 86. 5–15.
12. *Mahābhārata* III. 213–16.
13. *Matsya* 158. 25–50.
14. *Padma* 5. 41. 118–42.
15. *Rāmāyaṇa* 1. 36. 6–28, 1. 37. 1–28.
16. *Saura* 60. 1–66, 61. 2–89, 62. 1–33.
17. *Śiva*, Jñānasaṃhitā 19. 7–15.
18. *Śiva* 2. 4. 1. 1–55, 2. 4. 2. 1–73.
19. *Skanda* 1. 1. 27. 1–110.
20. *Skanda* 1. 2. 29. 82–210.
21. *Skanda* 2. 7. 9. 1–94.

22. *Skanda* 3. 3. 13–14 (= Hatakeśvara Māhātmya 245. 1–46, 246. 16–22, 264. 3–16).
23. *Skanda* 3. 3. 29. 3–34.
24. *Skanda* 5. 1. 34. 58–80.
25. *Skanda* 5. 2. 20. 1–25.
26. *Skanda* 6. 70. 24–68, 6. 71. 1–20.
27. *Vāmana* 28 and 31.
28. *Varāha* 25. 15–46.
29. *Vāyu* 72. 6–40 (= *Brahmāṇḍa* 3. 10. 16–48).
30. *Viṣṇudharmottara* 1. 228. 2–11.

C. THE PINE FOREST

1. *Bhikṣāṭanakāvya*.
2. *Brahmāṇḍa* 2. 27. 1–127.
3. *Darpadalana* 7. 17–71.
4. *Haracarita* 10. 3–188.
5. *Kūrma* 1. 16. 19–123.
6. *Kūrma* 2. 37. 1–151.
7. *Liṅga* 1. 29. 1–83, 1. 31. 21–45.
8. *Padma* 5. 17. 35–84.
9. *Sāmba* 16. 24–33, 17. 1–22.
10. *Saura* 69. 34–54.
11. *Śiva*, Dharmasaṃhitā 10. 79–215.
12. *Śiva*, Jñānasaṃhitā 42. 1–51.
13. *Śiva* 4. 12. 1–54.
14. *Skanda* 1. 1. 6. 2–68.
15. *Skanda* 3. 3. 26. 1–30, 3. 3. 27. 1–75.
16. *Skanda* 5. 2. 8. 1–45.
17. *Skanda* 5. 2. 11. 1–25.
18. *Skanda* 5. 3. 38. 6–68.
19. *Skanda* 6. 1. 5–64.
20. *Skanda* 6. 258. 1–48, 6. 259. 1–77.
21. *Skanda* 7. 1. 187. 14–40.
22. *Skanda* 7. 3. 39. 5–38.
23. *Vāmana* 6. 60–93.
24. *Vāmana* S. 21–2.
25. *Yāgīśvaramāhātmya* 24–34.

II. NON-SANSKRIT TEXTS

A. ŚIVA AND KĀMA

1. Dessigane (1967), pp. 6–15.
2. P. Thomas (1958), p. 32.
3. Tulasī Dās, pp. 36–53 (C. 65–103).

B. THE BIRTH OF SKANDA

1. Baldaeus, p. 27.
2. Dessigane (1960), No. 11.
3. Dessigane (1964), No. 25.
4. Dessigane (1967), pp. 16–19.
5. William Taylor, p. 62.

C. THE PINE FOREST

1. Alberuni, ii, 103.
2. Baldaeus, pp. 17–18.
3. Churchill, p. 737.
4. Dessigane (1960), No. 32.
5. Dessigane (1964), No. 59.
6. Dessigane (1964), No. 40.
7. Dessigane (1967), pp. 84–5.
8. Dessigane (1967), pp. 192 ff.
9. Dubois, pp. 629–30.
10. Rao, ii, 1, 302.
11. Rhode, p. 236.
12. Roger, pp. 247–8.
13. Sonnerat, pp. 176–9.
14. P. Thomas (1959), p. 114.
15. Wilford (1795), p. 397.

APPENDIX C

GLOSSARY

apsaras: A celestial nymph, dancer, or prostitute. A water-nymph.

aśvattha: The sacred fig-tree.

Atharva Veda: The fourth Veda, said to have been composed by the fire priest and consisting chiefly of formulas and spells. Probably written about 900 B.C.

bhakti: Loving devotion of the worshipper to the god and tender love of the god for his devotees.

bhasma: Ashes, particularly the ashes from the funeral pyre, placed upon the bodies of certain Śaiva sectarians.

bhikṣu: A beggar or monk.

bhoga: Enjoyment, particularly of sensual pleasures or food.

bhogin (sometimes *bhogi*): One who enjoys sensual pleasures.

brahmacārin: One who practises *brahmacarya*, the first of the four stages of life. A chaste young student.

brahmacarya: The first stage of life, literally 'moving in *brahma*'. Usually it merely denotes chastity.

Brāhmaṇas: Appendixes to the Vedas, consisting of rules for the conduct of the sacrifice, with explanations and legends. Probably composed between 1000 B.C. and 700 B.C.

Brahmin: A priest, member of the first of the four classes.

cakravāka: A love-bird that becomes separated from its mate at night.

dharma: The righteous performance of one's traditional duty in life.

gandharva: A handsome celestial musician and dancer.

Jātakas: Buddhist stories, in Pali, based on a folk tradition of considerable antiquity.

kāma: Desire, particularly sexual desire.

Kāmasūtra: The textbook of erotic science.

kāmin: One who has desire, a lover.

kāminī: A woman who has desire, a mistress.

Kāpālika: A member of the Śaiva sect which carries a skull (*kapāla*).

karma: Action. More particularly, the law of retribution by which one's past action, good or bad, determines one's future fate.

Kiṃpuruṣa or Kinnara: Literally 'What?-man', a horse-headed musician.

līlā: Celestial sport, the playful spirit in which Śiva participates in meaningless actions. Play-acting. Erotic play.

liṅga (sometimes *lingam*): The phallus, particularly of Śiva.

mahāmaithuna: 'Great' or 'complete' intercourse, including ejaculation.

maithuna: Sexual intercourse.

Mahābhārata: The great epic of India, probably composed between 300 B.C. and A.D. 300.

Meru: The golden mountain at the centre of the world.

mohana: Delusion, enchantment, mental error.

muni: An ascetic sage.

nivṛtti: Cessation of action, quiescence, peace. Opposed to *pravṛtti*.

Parakīyā: The woman of another man, i.e. an adulterous mistress; adultery.

prajāpati: A Vedic creator.

pravṛtti: Action, involvement, energy. Opposed to *nivṛtti*.

prema: Affectionate, long-enduring, sympathetic love.

Purāṇas: Collections of legends and ritual instructions in Sanskrit. Difficult to date (see Introduction).

Paurāṇika: A bard who recited the Purāṇas, composing them orally.

Rāmāyaṇa: The epic story of Rāma, composed between 200 B.C. and A.D. 200.

rati: Sexual pleasure. Love-play.

ratimātra: 'Mere' love-play, i.e. intercourse without ejaculation.

retas: The seed.

sādhu: A sage.

Śaiva: Pertaining to the worship of Śiva. A worshipper of Śiva.

Śākta: Pertaining to the worship of Devī.

śamī: A tree used to make the ritual Vedic fire-sticks, said to contain fire.

saṃsāra: The wheel of birth and rebirth. Worldly involvement.

śānti: Peace, the state in which the passions are extinguished.

sannyāsin (sometimes *sannyāsī*): An ascetic, one engaged in the fourth stage of life.

śarabha: A mythical beast, said to have eight legs and wings.

śāstra: A textbook, particularly of sacred law.

Sāyaṇa: A commentator on the Ṛg Veda.

Soma: The elixir of immortality, food of the gods, used in Vedic ritual.

Śūdra: The lowest of the four classes.

svadharma: One's own caste duty, one's preordained role.

Svakīyā: One's own woman, one's lawful wife; marital love. Opposed to Parakīyā.

Tantras: Religious works, medieval, involving the use of ritual sexuality.

tapas: The heat of asceticism.

tapasvin: One who has *tapas*, an ascetic.

tapasvinī: A female ascetic.

tejas: Fiery splendour, glory, fiery destructive power. Energy.

tilaka: An auspicious mark painted in vermilion on the forehead.

Upaniṣads: Philosophical works, appended to the Vedas, composed from about 700 B.C. to 300 B.C.

ūrdhvaliṅga (or *ūrdhvameḍhra*): Having a raised phallus, ithyphallic.

ūrdhvaretas: Having the seed drawn up in chastity.

vaḍavā: A mare, particularly the submarine mare-fire.

vaiśvānara: The fire within the human body, digestive fire.

vāmācāra: The 'left-hand' or orgiastic path of the Tantras.

vānaprastha: A forest-dweller, member of the third stage of life.

Vedas: The four holy books of the ancient Indians. Most important is the Ṛg Veda, a collection of hymns composed *c.* 1200 B.C.

vrātya: An early ascetic, probably Aryan but non-Vedic.

yati: An ascetic.

yoga: The practice of asceticism by physical mortification and meditation.

yogi (sometimes *yogin*): One who practises yoga.

yoginī: A woman who practises yoga.

APPENDIX D

BIBLIOGRAPHY

I. ABBREVIATIONS

ASS	Ānandāśrama Sanskrit Series
Bib. Ind.	*Bibliotheca Indica*
BSOAS	*Bulletin of the School of Oriental and African Studies*
ERE	*Encyclopedia of Religion and Ethics* (ed. Hastings)
HOS	Harvard Oriental Series
HR	*History of Religions*
IA	*Indian Antiquary*
IHQ	*Indian Historical Quarterly*
JAOS	*Journal of the American Oriental Society*
JBBRAS	*Journal of the Bombay Branch of the Royal Asiatic Society*
JBORI	*Journal of the Bhandarkar Oriental Research Institute*
JBORS	*Journal of the Bihar and Orissa Research Society*
JOIB	*Journal of the Oriental Institute of Baroda*
JRAS	*Journal of the Royal Asiatic Society*
JRASB	*Journal of the Royal Asiatic Society of Bengal*
SBE	Sacred Books of the East
SBH	Sacred Books of the Hindus
WZKM	*Wiener Zeitschrift zur Kunde des Morgenlandes*
ZDMG	*Zeitschrift der Deutschen Morgenländischen Gesellschaft*

II. SANSKRIT TEXTS AND TRANSLATIONS

ALPHABETIZED BY TITLE

* Denotes primary edition, cited in bibliographic notes unless otherwise indicated.

Abhijñānaśākuntala of Kālidāsa. Bombay, 1958.

Agni Purāṇa (cited as *Agni*). ASS 41. Poona, 1957.

—— Trans. M. N. Dutta. Calcutta, 1901.

**Aitareya Brāhmaṇa*, with the commentary of Sāyaṇa. ASS 32. Poona, 1896.

—— Ed. and trans. Martin Haug. Bombay and London, 1863.

—— Trans. Arthur Berriedale Keith. HOS 25. Cambridge (Mass.), 1920.

Amarakośa of Amarasiṃha, with the commentary of Maheśvara. Bombay, 1896.

Aṅguttara Nikāya. Pali Text Society. London, 1883.

Āpastambīya Dharmasūtra [*Aphorisms on the Sacred Law of the Hindus, by Apastamba*]. Ed. Georg Bühler. 2nd ed. Bombay, 1892.

Arthaśāstra of Kauṭilya. Punjab Sanskrit Series 4. Lahore, 1923.

Atharva Veda, with the commentary of Sāyaṇa. Bombay, 1895.

—— Ed. Rudolph R. Roth and William Dwight Whitney. Berlin, 1855.

—— Trans. Maurice Bloomfield. SBE 42. Oxford, 1897.

—— Trans. William Dwight Whitney, ed. Charles Lanman. HOS 7–8. Cambridge (Mass.), 1905.

Avadānakalpalatā of Kṣemendra. Buddhist Sanskrit Texts. Darbhanga, 1959.
Baudhāyana Dharmaśāstra. Bombay, 1938.
Bhagavad Gītā, with the commentary of Śaṅkara. Poona Oriental Series 1. Poona, 1950.
—— Trans. and ed. Franklin Edgerton. HOS 38–9. Cambridge (Mass.), 1946.
**Bhāgavata Purāṇa* (cited as *Bhāgavata*). Gorakhpur, 1962.
—— With the commentary of Śrīdhara. Bombay, 1832.
—— Trans. Eugène Burnouf. 5 vols. Paris, 1840–98.
—— Trans. J. M. Sanyal. Calcutta, 1930–4.
Bhaviṣya Purāṇa (cited as *Bhaviṣya*). Bombay, 1959.
Bhikṣāṭanakāvya of Utprekṣavallabha. Kāvyamālā Series 12. Bombay, 1895.
Brahma Purāṇa (cited as *Brahma*). Calcutta, 1954.
Brahmāṇḍa Purāṇa (cited as *Brahmāṇḍa*). Bombay, 1857.
Brahmavaivarta Purāṇa (cited as *Brahmavaivarta*). ASS 102. 4 vols. Poona, 1935.
—— Trans. Rajendra Nath Sen. SBH. 2 vols. Allahabad.
Bṛhaddevatā, attributed to Śaunaka. HOS 5. Cambridge (Mass.), 1904.
—— Trans. Arthur Anthony Macdonell. HOS 6. Cambridge (Mass.), 1904.
Bṛhaddharma Purāṇa (cited as *Bṛhaddharma*). *Bib. Ind.* Calcutta, 1888–97.
Bṛhannāradīya Purāṇa (cited as *Bṛhannāradīya*). *Bib. Ind.* Calcutta, 1891.
Bṛhatkathāmañjarī of Kṣemendra. Kāvyamālā Series 69. Bombay, 1931.
Bṛhatsaṃhitā of Varaha Mihira. *Bib. Ind.* Calcutta, 1865.
Caturvargacintāmaṇi of Hemādri. *Bib. Ind.* Calcutta, 1873.
Darpadalana of Kṣemendra. Kāvyamālā Series 6. Bombay, 1890.
Daśakumāracarita of Daṇḍin. Bombay, 1928.
—— [*The Ten Princes*]. Trans. Arthur W. Ryder. Chicago, 1927.
Devī Purāṇa (cited as *Devī*). Calcutta, 1896.
Devībhāgavata Purāṇa (cited as *Devībhāgavata*). Benares, 1960.
—— Trans. Swami Vijñānanda. SBH. Allahabad, 1922.
Drāhyāyaṇa Śrautasūtra. London, 1904.
Gautamapraṇītadharmasūtrāṇi. ASS 61. Poona, 1910.
Gṛhastharatnākara of Candeśvara Thakkura. *Bib. Ind.* Calcutta, 1928.
Haracaritacintāmaṇi (cited as *Haracarita*) of Jayaratha. Kāvyamālā Series 61. Bombay, 1897.
Harivaṃśa, with commentary. Bombay, 1927.
—— Trans. (into French) by Simon Alexandre Langlois. London, 1834–5.
Harṣacarita of Bāṇa. Delhi, 1965.
—— Trans. E. B. Cowell and F. W. Thomas. London, 1929.
Haṭhayogapradīpikā of Svātmarāmayogīndra. Text, with trans. by Shrinivas Iyangar. Bombay, 1815.
Jaiminīya Mīmāṃsā Sūtra of Śabara. Benares Sanskrit Series. Benares, 1903.
Jaiminīya [*Talavakara*] *Brāhmaṇa* of the Sāma Veda. Sarasvatī-vihara Series 31. Nagpur, 1954.
Jātaka, with commentary. Ed. Viggo Fausbøll. 7 vols. London, 1877.
—— Trans. E. B. Cowell *et al.* Cambridge, 1895–1913.
Kālikā Purāṇa (cited as *Kālikā*). Bombay, 1891.
Kālīvilāsa Tantra. Tantrik Texts 6. Calcutta, 1917.
Kāmakalāvilāsa. Text, with commentary of Natanānanda-nātha and trans. by Arthur Avalon. Tantrik Texts 10. Calcutta and London, 1922.
Kāmasūtra of Vatsyāyana. 2 vols. Bombay, 1856.
—— Trans. Sir Richard Burton. London, 1883/1963.
Kāñchīmāhātmya (*Brahmapurāṇāntargata*). Śāstramuktāvalī 26. Conjeevaram, 1906.

Karpūramañjarī of Rājaśekhara. Ed. Sten Konow, trans. Charles Lanman. HOS 4. Cambridge (Mass.), 1901.

Kārttika Māhātmya of the *Sanatkumāra Saṃhitā*. Bombay, 1912.

Kaṭhaka [*Die Saṃhitā der Kathā-Çākha*]. 3 vols. Leipzig, 1900.

Kathākośa [*The Kathakoça or Treasury of Stories*]. Trans. C. H. Tawney. London, 1895.

Kathāsaritsāgara of Somadeva. Bombay, 1930.

—— [*The Ocean of Story*]. Trans. C. H. Tawney and ed. N. M. Penzer. 10 vols. London, 1924.

Katyāyana Śrautasūtrāṇi. Part III of the White Yajur Veda. Berlin, 1859.

Kauṣītaki Brāhmaṇa [*Śaṅkhāyana Brāhmaṇa*]. ASS 65. Poona, 1911.

—— Trans. Arthur Berriedale Keith. See *Aitareya Brāhmaṇa*.

Kṛtyakalpataru of Bhaṭṭa Lakṣmīdhara. *II: Gṛhasthakhaṇḍa*. Oriental Series 101. Baroda, 1944.

Kulārṇava Tantra. Tantrik Texts 5. Calcutta and London, 1917.

Kumārasambhava of Kālidāsa, with the commentary of Mallinātha on the first 8 cantos and the commentary of Sītārāma on the last 9. Bombay, 1955.

—— (first 7 cantos). Trans. S. R. Sehgal. Delhi, 1959.

**Kūrma Purāṇa* (cited as *Kūrma*). Bombay, 1926.

Kūrma Purāṇa. *Bib. Ind.* Calcutta, 1890. Also (in Bengali script) Calcutta, 1818.

**Liṅga Purāṇa* (cited as *Liṅga*). Calcutta, 1812.

Mahābhāgavata Purāṇa (cited as *Mahābhāgavata*). Bombay, 1913.

**Mahābhārata* (cited as MhB), attributed to Kṛṣṇa Dvaipāyana Vyāsa. Critically edited by Vishnu S. Sukthankar, *et al.* Poona, 1933–59.

Mahābhārata, with the commentary of Nīlakaṇṭha. Bombay, 1862 (and 1876).

—— Trans. Pratap Chandra Roy. 11 vols., 2nd ed. Calcutta, 1927–32.

Mahānirvāṇa Tantra, with the commentary of Hariharananda Bharati. Tantrik Texts 13. Madras, 1929.

Majjhima Nikāya. Pali Text Society. London, 1888.

Mānavadharmaśāstra (cited as Manu). London, 1887.

—— Trans. Georg Bühler. SBE 25. Oxford, 1886.

Manmathonmathana of Rāma. *ZDMG* lxix (1909), 409–37, 629–54.

**Mārkaṇḍeya Purāṇa* (cited as *Mārkaṇḍeya*). With commentary. Bombay, 1890.

—— *Bib. Ind.* 29. Calcutta, 1862.

—— Trans. Frederick Eden Pargiter. *Bib. Ind.* 2 vols. Calcutta, 1888–1904.

Mattavilāsaprahasana of Mahendravikramavarman. Trivandrum Sanskrit Series 50. Trivandrum, 1917.

—— Trans. L. D. Barnett. *BSOAS*, v, 4 (1930), pp. 699–717.

**Matsya Purāṇa* (cited as *Matsya*). ASS 54. Poona, 1907.

Matsya Purāṇa. Calcutta, 1876. Also Calcutta 1890.

—— Trans. S. Vidyārṇava. SBH XVII.

Naiṣadhacarita of Śrīharṣa. Calcutta, 1875–6.

Nārada Pañcarātra. *Bib. Ind.* Calcutta, 1865.

Nāradasmṛti. Calcutta, 1885.

**Padma Purāṇa* (cited as *Padma*). ASS 131. Poona, 1893.

—— Calcutta, 1958.

—— Bombay, 1927.

—— *Pātāla Khaṇḍa* of the *Padma Purāṇa*. Bodleiana, Wilson 111–16. Transcribed by Lüders, p. 99.

Pārvatīpariṇaya of Bāṇabhaṭṭa. Text, with trans. by T. R. Ratnam Aiyar. Madras Sanskrit Series 1. Madras, 1898.

Pāśupata Sūtras, with the commentary of Kauṇḍinya. Trivandrum Sanskrit Series 143. Trivandrum, 1940.
Prabodhacandrodaya of Kṛṣṇamiśra. Bombay, 1935.
—— Trans. John Taylor. Bombay, 1872.
Rājataraṅginī of Kalhaṇa. Bombay Sanskrit Series XLV. Bombay, 1892–6.
**Rāmāyaṇa* of Valmīki. Baroda, 1960.
Rāmāyaṇa of Valmīki. 2nd ed. Madras, 1958.
Rasikarañjana of Rāmacandra [*Rāmacandra's Ergötzen der Kenner*]. Text and (German) trans. Richard Schmidt. Stuttgart, 1896.
Ṛg Veda, with the commentary of Sāyaṇa. 6 vols. London, 1890–2.
—— Trans. (into German) Karl Friedrich Geldner. 3 vols. HOS 33–5. Cambridge (Mass.), 1951.
—— Trans. Horace Hayman Wilson. London, 1866.
Saddharmapuṇḍarīka. *Bibliotheca Buddhica*. St. Petersburg, 1908.
Sāmavidhāna Brāhmaṇa. London, 1873.
Sāmba Purāṇa (cited as *Sāmba*). Bombay, 1942.
Saṃskāraprakāśa of the *Vīramitrodaya* of Mitra Misra. Chowkhamba Sanskrit Series 139. Benares, 1913.
Śaṅkhāyana Brāhmaṇa. See *Kauṣītaki Brāhmaṇa*.
Sarvadarśanasaṃgraha of Mādhava. *Bib. Ind.* Calcutta, 1858.
Śatakatraya of Bhartṛhari. Singhi Jain Series 23. Bombay, 1948.
—— Trans. Barbara Stoler Miller. New York, 1967.
Śatapatha Brāhmaṇa of the White Yajur Veda, with the commentary of Sāyaṇa. *Bib. Ind.* Calcutta, 1903.
**Śatapatha Brāhmaṇa* of the White Yajur Veda, in the Madhyaṇḍina Śākha. Chowkhamba Sanskrit Series 96. 2nd ed. Benares, 1964.
—— Trans. Julius Eggeling. SBE 12, 26, 41, 43, 44. Oxford, 1882.
Saura Purāṇa (cited as *Saura*). Calcutta, 1816.
**Śiva Purāṇa* (cited as *Śiva*). Jñānasaṃhitā, Dharmasaṃhitā, and Vāyavīya Saṃhitā, cited by name. Bombay, 1884.
**Śiva Purāṇa* (cited as *Śiva*), with the *Śiva Purāṇa Māhātmya* of the *Skanda Purāṇa*. Cited by Saṃhitā number. Benares, 1964.
—— Trans. J. L. Shastri, in *Ancient Indian Tradition and Mythology* (i–iv). Delhi, 1970.
Skanda Purāṇa (cited as *Skanda*). Calcutta, 1959.
**Skanda Purāṇa* (cited as *Skanda*). Bombay, 1867.
Stotrasamuccaya. Adyar Library Series 99. Madras, 1969.
Subhāṣitaratnakoṣa of Vidyākara. HOS 42. Cambridge (Mass.), 1957.
—— Trans. Daniel H. H. Ingalls. HOS 44. Cambridge (Mass.), 1965.
Subhāṣitāvalī of Vallabha. Bombay, 1886.
Taittirīya Brāhmaṇa of the Black Yajur Veda, with the commentary of Sāyaṇa. *Bib. Ind.* Calcutta, 1859.
Taittirīya Saṃhitā of the Black Yajur Veda, with the commentary of Madhava. *Bib. Ind.* Calcutta, 1860.
—— Trans. Arthur Berriedale Keith. HOS 19. Cambridge (Mass.), 1914.
Talavakara Brāhmaṇa. See *Jaiminīya Brāhmaṇa*.
Tāṇḍya Mahābrāhmaṇa, with the commentary of Sāyaṇa. *Bib. Ind.* Calcutta, 1869–74.
—— Trans. W. Caland. *Bib. Ind.* Calcutta, 1931.
Tantropākhyāna [*Ten Tales from the T.*]. Text and trans. by George T. Artola. *Adyar Library Bulletin*, xxix, 1–4. Madras, 1965.

Upaniṣads: One Hundred and Eight Upanishads (Īsha and Others). 4th ed. Bombay, 1913.

Vaikhānasasmārtasūtra. Calcutta, 1927.

Vaiṣṇava Upaniṣads, with the commentary of Śrī Upaniṣad Brahma-yogin. Adyar Library Series 8. 2nd ed. Madras, 1953.

—— Trans. Robert Ernest Hume [*The Thirteen Principal Upanishads*]. 2nd ed. Oxford, 1931.

Vāmana Purāṇa (cited as *Vāmana*). Ed. and trans. by Anand Swarup Gupta. Varanasi, 1968.

Varāha Purāṇa (cited as *Varāha*). *Bib. Ind.* 110. Calcutta, 1893.

Vāśiṣṭhadharmaśāstra. Bombay Sanskrit Series 23. Bombay, 1883.

**Vāyu Purāṇa* (cited as *Vāyu*). ASS 49. Poona, 1860.

—— Bombay, 1867.

—— *Bib. Ind.* Calcutta, 1880.

Viṣṇu Purāṇa (cited as *Viṣṇu*). Gorakhpur, 1962.

—— Trans. Horace Hayman Wilson. 3rd ed. Calcutta, 1961 [London, 1840].

Viṣṇudharmottara Purāṇa (cited as *Viṣṇudharmottara*). Bombay (no date).

Viṣṇusmṛti. Ed. Julius Jolly. Calcutta, 1880.

Yāgīśvaramāhātmya. India Office Manuscript No. 3719. Reproduced by Wilhelm Jahn, *ZDMG* lxx (1916), pp. 310–20.

Yājñavalkyasmṛti. ASS 46. Poona, 1904.

III. SECONDARY SOURCES

ALPHABETIZED BY AUTHOR

Agrawala, Vasudeva Sarana. *Matsya Purāṇa: A Study*. Benares, 1963.

—— *Śiva Mahādeva, The Great God: An Exposition of the Symbolism of Śiva*. Benares, 1966.

—— *Vāmana Purāṇa: A Study*. Benares, 1964.

Alberuni. *Alberuni's India*. Trans. Edward Sachau. London, 1888.

Anand, Mulk Raj. *Kāma Kalā: Some Notes on the Philosophical Basis of Hindu Erotic Sculpture*. Geneva, 1960.

Apte, Vaman Shivram. *The Student's Sanskrit–English Dictionary*. Delhi, 1963.

Arbman, Ernst. *Rudra: Untersuchungen zum altindischen Glauben und Kultus*. Uppsala, 1922.

Auboyer, Jeannine. *Daily Life in Ancient India*. London, 1965.

—— and Zannas, Eliky. *Khajuraho*. The Hague, 1960.

Aufrecht, Theodore. *Catalogus Codicum Manuscriptorum Sanscritorum Post-vedicorum quotquot in Bibliotheca Bodleiana adservantur*. Oxford, 1859.

—— 'Ueber die Paddhati von Çārṅgadhara.' *ZDMG* xxvii (1873), pp. 1–120.

Avalon, Arthur (translator). See *Kāmakalāvilāsa*.

—— See Woodroffe, Sir John George.

—— *The Serpent Power*. 3rd ed. London, 1931.

Ayyar, C. V. Narayan. *Origin and Early History of Śaivism in South India*. Madras, 1936.

Baldaeus, Philippus. *Naauwkeurige beschryvinge van Malabar en Choromandel, der zelver aangrenzende Ryken en het machtige Eyland Ceylon, & Afgoderye der Ost-Indische Heydenen*. Amsterdam, 1672.

Balys, Jonas. See Thompson, Stith.

Banerjea, Jitendra Nath. *The Development of Hindu Iconography*. Calcutta, 1956.

Banerjea, R. D. *The Eastern Indian School of Medieval Sculpture*. Archaeological Survey of India, No. 47. Delhi, 1933.

Barnett, L. D. (translator). See *Mattavilāsaprahasana*.

Barua, B. K. 'The Kālikā-Purāṇa on Iconographical Representations of some Śākta Goddesses and their Worship in Medieval Assam.' *P. K. Gode Commemorative Volume*. Poona, 1960. iii, 1–18.

Beal, Samuel (translator). *Si-yu-ki: Buddhist Records of the Western World*. London, 1884.

Beswick, Mrs. Ethel. *Tales of Hindu Gods and Heroes*. Delhi, 1959.

Bhandarkar, D. R. 'An Eklingji Stone Inscription and the Origin and History of the Lakulīśa Sect.' *JBBRAS* xxii (1905–7), pp. 150–67.

—— 'Lakulīśa.' *Report of the Archaeological Survey of India*, 1906–7, pp. 169–92.

Bharati, Agehananda [Leopold Fischer]. *The Ochre Robe*. London, 1961.

—— *The Tantric Tradition*. London, 1965.

Bhattaśali, Nalini Kanta. *Iconography of the Buddhist and Brahmanical Sculpture of the Dacca Museum*. Dacca, 1929.

Biardeau, Madeleine. 'Some More Considerations about Textual Criticism.' *Purāṇa* x, 2 (July 1968), pp. 115–23.

—— 'The Story of Arjuna Kārtavīrya without Reconstruction.' *Purāṇa* xii, 2 (July 1970), pp. 286–303.

Blair, Chauncey. *Heat in the Rig Veda and Atharva Veda*. American Oriental Society Publication No. 45. Cambridge (Mass.), 1961.

Bloomfield, Maurice (translator). See *Atharva Veda* (1897).

—— 'On False Ascetics and Nuns in Hindu Fiction.' *JAOS* xliv (1924), pp. 202–42.

Böhtlingk, Otto. *Indische Sprüche*. St. Petersburg, 1870.

Bosch, F. D. K. 'The God with the Horse's Head.' In *Selected Studies in Indonesian Archaeology*. Koninklijk Institut voor Taal-, Land-, en Volkenkunde. Translation Series No. 5. The Hague, 1961.

—— *The Golden Germ: An Introduction to Indian Symbolism*. The Hague, 1960.

—— 'Het Linga-Heiligdom van Dinaja.' *Tijdschrift voor Indische Taal-, Land-, en Volkenkunde*, Batavian Society of Arts and Sciences, lxiv (1924), pp. 227–91.

Briggs, George Weston. *Gorakhnath and the Kanphata Yogis*. Calcutta, 1938.

Brough, John. *Poems from the Sanskrit*. Harmondsworth, 1968.

Brown, W. Norman. 'Change of Sex as a Hindu Story Motif.' *JAOS* xlvii (1927), pp. 3–24.

Bühler, Georg (translator). See *Mānavadharmaśāstra* (1886).

van Buitenen, J. A. B. 'Dharma and Moksha.' *Philosophy East and West*, vii (Nos. 1–2, April–July 1957), pp. 33–40.

Burnouf, Eugène (translator). See *Bhāgavata Purāṇa*.

Burridge, K. O. L. 'Lévi-Strauss and Myth.' In Leach (1967), pp. 91–118.

Campbell, Joseph. *Oriental Mythology*. Vol. iii of *The Masks of God*, ed. Joseph Campbell. New York, 1962.

Carpenter, Joseph Estlin. *Theism in Medieval India*. London, 1921.

Chakravarti, Chintaharan. *The Tantras: Studies in their Religion and Literature*. Calcutta, 1963.

Chanda, Ramaprasad. *Explorations in Orissa*. Memoirs of the Archaeological Survey of India, xliv. Calcutta, 1930.

Chandra, Pramod. 'Kāpālika Cults at Khajuraho.' *Lalit Kala* i–ii (1955–6), pp. 98–107.

Charpentier, Jarl. 'Über Rudra-Śiva.' *WZKM* xxiii (1909), pp. 151–79.

Chatterton, Bishop Eyre. *The Story of Gondwana*. London, 1916.

Chattopadhyaya, Sudhakar. *The Evolution of Theistic Sects in Ancient India*. Calcutta, 1962.

Chaudhuri, Nanimadhab. 'Rudra-Śiva as an Agricultural Deity.' *IHQ* xv (1939), pp. 183–96.

Chaudhuri, Nirad. *The Continent of Circe: An Essay on the Peoples of India*. London, 1965.

Chavannes, Édouard. *Cinq Cents Contes et Apologues extraits du Tripitaka Chinois*. 3 vols. Paris, 1910–11.

Churchill, J. *A Collection of Voyages and Travels*. London, 1752.

Clark, T. W. 'Evolution of Hinduism in Medieval Bengali Literature: Śiva, Caṇḍī, Manasā.' *BSOAS* xvii (1955), pp. 503–18.

Coomaraswamy, Ananda K. *History of Indian and Indonesian Art*. New York, 1965.

Cowell, E. B. (translator). See *Harṣacarita* (1929).

Crooke, William. 'Folktales from Northern India.' *IA* xxv (1906), pp. 142–50.

—— *The Popular Religion and Folklore of Northern India*. 2nd ed. 2 vols. London, 1896.

Dahlquist, Allan. *Megasthenes and Indian Religion*. Stockholm, 1962.

Daniélou, Alain. *L'Érotisme divinisé*. Paris, 1962.

—— *Hindu Polytheism*. London, 1964.

Dasgupta, Surendranath. *A History of Indian Philosophy. V: Southern Schools of Śaivism*. Cambridge, 1962.

Dessigane, R., and Pattabiramin, P. Z. *La Légende de Skanda selon le Kāñchīpurāṇam Tamoul et l'iconographie*. Publication de l'Institut Français d'Indologie No. 31. Pondichéry, 1967.

—— —— and Filliozat, Jean. *La Légende des jeux de Çiva à Madurai* [*Hālāsyamāhātmya*]. Publication de l'Institut Français d'Indologie No. 19. 2 vols. Pondichéry, 1960.

—— —— —— *Les Légendes Çivaites de Kāñcīpuram*. Publication de l'Institut Français d'Indologie No. 27. Pondichéry, 1964.

Deutsch, Eliot S. 'Śakti in Medieval Hindu Sculpture.' *Journal of Aesthetics and Art Criticism*. Autumn 1965.

Dikshitar, V. R. Ramachandra. *The Matsya Purāṇa: A Study*. Madras, 1935.

Dimock, Edward C., Jr. 'Doctrine and Practice among the Vaiṣṇavas of Bengal.' In Singer, pp. 41–63.

—— *The Place of the Hidden Moon: Erotic Mysticism in the Vaiṣṇava Sāhajiyā Cult of Bengal*. Chicago, 1966.

—— *The Thief of Love: Bengali Tales from Court and Village*. Trans. Edward C. Dimock, Jr. Chicago, 1963.

—— and Ramanujan, A. K. 'Manashā: Goddess of Snakes.' *HR* i (Winter, 1962), pp. 307–21; iii, 2 (Winter 1964), pp. 300–22.

Douglas, Mary. 'The Meaning of Myth, with Special Reference to "La Geste d'Asdiwal".' In Leach (1967), pp. 49–70.

Dubois, Abbé J. A. *Hindu Manners, Customs, and Ceremonies*. Trans. and ed. Henry K. Beauchamp. 3rd ed. Oxford, 1959 [London, 1816].

Dumont, Paul Émile. *L'Aśvamedha: description du sacrifice du cheval*. Paris, 1927.

Dumont, Louis. 'Définition structurale d'un dieu populaire Tamoul: Aiyanar, le Maître.' *Journal asiatique* ccxlvi (1953), pp. 256–70.

—— 'For a Sociology of India.' *Contributions to Indian Sociology* i (April 1957 [-A]), pp. 1–22.

—— 'A Structural Definition of a Folk Deity of Tamil Nad: Aiyanar, the Lord.' *Contributions to Indian Sociology* iii (July 1959), pp. 75–87.

—— *Une Sous-caste de l'Inde du Sud: organisation sociale et religion des Pramalai Kallar*. Paris, 1957 (-B).

—— 'World Renunciation in Indian Religion.' *Contributions to Indian Sociology* iv (April 1960), pp. 33–62.

Durkheim, Emil. *Les Formes élémentaires de la vie religieuse*. 2nd ed. Paris, 1925.

Edgerton, Franklin (translator). See *Bhagavad Gītā* (1946).

—— 'The Meaning of Sāṅkhya and Yoga.' *American Journal of Philosophy* xlv (1924), pp. 1 ff.

Eggeling, Julius (translator). See *Śatapatha Brāhmaṇa* (1882).

Eliade, Mircea. *Mephistopheles and the Androgyne: Studies in Religious Myth and Symbol*. Trans. J. M. Cohen. New York, 1965.

—— *Yoga: Immortality and Freedom*. Trans. Willard R. Trask. Bollingen Series LVI. New York, 1958.

Eliot, Sir Charles. *Hinduism and Buddhism*. 3 vols. London, 1921.

Elmore, Wilber Theodore. *Dravidian Gods in Modern Hinduism: A Study of the Local and Village Deities of Southern India*. University Series No. XV, 1. Nebraska, 1915.

Elwin, Verrier. *The Agaria*. Oxford, 1942.

—— 'The Attitude of Indian Aboriginals toward Sexual Impotence.' *Man in India* xxiii (1943), pp. 127–46.

—— *The Baiga*. London, 1939.

—— *Folk-Tales of Mahakoshal*. Oxford, 1944.

—— *The Muria and their Ghotul*. Oxford, 1947.

—— *Myths of Middle India*. Oxford, 1949.

—— *Tribal Myths of Orissa*. Oxford, 1954.

Evans-Pritchard, E. *Nuer Religion*. Oxford, 1956.

Farquhar, John Nicol. *An Outline of the Religious Literature of India*. Oxford, 1920.

Fausbøll, Viggo. *Indian Mythology in Outline, According to the Mahābhārata*. London, 1903.

Fergusson, James. *Tree and Serpent Worship*. London, 1868.

Filliozat, Jean. See Dessigane.

—— 'Les images d'un jeu de Śiva à Khajuraho.' *Artibus Asiae* xxiv (1961), pp. 283–99.

Fišer, Ivo. *Indian Erotics of the Oldest Period*. Acta Universitatis Carolinae, Philologica Monographia xiv. Praha, 1966.

Fleet, John Faithfull. *Corpus Inscriptionum Indicarum. III: Inscriptions of the Early Gupta Kings and their Successors*. Calcutta, 1888.

Forster, E. M. *Hill of Devi*. London, 1965.

Foucher, Alfred. *Les Vies antérieures du Bouddha*. Paris, 1955.

Fouchet, Max-Pol. *The Erotic Sculpture of India*. London, 1959.

Fournereau, Lucien. *Le Siam ancien*. Annales du Musée Guimet, 27ᵉ tome, 1ère partie. Paris, 1895.

Frazer, Sir James George. *Adonis, Attis, Osiris: Studies in the History of Oriental Religion*. 3rd ed. 2 vols. Part iv of *The Golden Bough: A Study in Magic and Religion*. London, 1914.

von Fürer-Haimendorf, Christoph. *The Aboriginal Tribes of Hyderabad*. Vol. i: *The Chenchus* (London, 1943); vol. iii: *The Raj Gonds of Adilabad. I: Myth and Ritual* (London, 1948).

von Fürer-Haimendorf, Christoph. Review of Herrenschmidt (1966) in *Man: Journal of the Royal Anthropological Institute*, ii, 2 (June 1967), p. 326.

Gangadharan, N. 'Garuḍa Purāṇa: A Study.' *Purāṇa*, xiii, 2 (July 1971).

Geldner, Karl Friedrich (translator). See *Ṛg Veda* (1951).

Getty, Alice. *Gaṇeśa: A Monograph on the Elephant-faced God*. Oxford, 1936.

Ghosh, Amalananda. 'Śiva: His Pre-Aryan Origin.' *Indian Culture* ii (1936), pp. 763–7.

Ghosh, Oroon. *The Dance of Shiva and Other Tales from India*. New York, 1965.

Ghurye, G. S. *Gods and Men*. Bombay, 1962.

Giteau, Madeleine. 'Une représentation de Śiva à Anghor Vat.' *Arts asiatiques* xi (1965), pp. 133 ff.

Goetz, Hermann. *The Art and Architecture of Bikaner State*. Oxford, 1950.

Goldman, Robert. 'Mortal Man and Immortal Woman, an Interpretation of Three Ākhyāna Hymns of the Ṛg Veda.' *JOIB* xviii, 4 (June 1969), pp. 273–303.

Gonda, Jan. *Change and Continuity in Indian Religion*. The Hague, 1965.

—— 'Einige Mitteilungen über das Altjavanische *Brahmāṇḍa Purāṇa*.' *Acta Orientalia* xi (1933), pp. 218–59.

—— *Die Religionen Indiens*. Vols. xi–xiii of *Die Religionen der Menschheit. I: Veda und älterer Hinduismus. II: Der jüngere Hinduismus*. Stuttgart, 1963.

Grierson, Sir George Abraham. *Linguistic Survey of India. Vol. IX: Indo-Aryan Family, Central Group. Part IV: Specimens of the Pahari Languages and Gujuri*. Calcutta, 1916.

Grousset, René. *The Civilization of India*. Trans. Catherine Alison Phillips. New York, 1931.

Gupta, Shakti M. *Plant Myths and Traditions in India*. Leiden, 1971.

Hackin, J. *Asiatic Mythology*. London, 1932.

Halhed. *Ancient Indian Literature Illustrative of the Researches of the Asiatick Society. I: Summary of the Sheeve Pouran*, from Mr. Halhed's Manuscript in the British Museum. London, 1807.

Hartland, Edwin Sidney. *Primitive Paternity: The Myth of Supernatural Birth in Relation to the History of the Family*. London, 1909.

Hastings, James. *Encyclopedia of Religion and Ethics*. Ed. James Hastings. Edinburgh, 1908–26.

Hauer, Jakob Wilhelm. *Die Anfänge der Yogapraxis im Alten Indien*. Berlin, 1922.

—— *Der Vrātya: Untersuchungen über die nichtbrahmanische Religion Altindiens*. Stuttgart, 1927.

—— *Der Yoga als Heilweg nach den indischen Quellen dargestellt*. Stuttgart, 1932.

Hazra, Rajendra Chandra. *Studies in the Purāṇic Records on Hindu Rites and Customs*. University of Dacca, Bulletin 20. Dacca, 1948.

—— *Studies in the Upapurāṇas: I: Saura and Vaiṣṇava Upapurāṇas. II: Śākta and Non-Sectarian Upapurāṇas*. Calcutta Sanskrit College Research Series 11 and 22. Calcutta, 1958 and 1963.

Heimann, Betty. *Studien zur Eigenart Indischen Denkens*. Tübingen, 1930.

—— *Facets of Indian Thought*. London, 1964.

Henry, Maurice. *The Thirty-two Positions of the Androgyne*. New York, 1963.

Herrenschmidt, Olivier. *Le Cycle de Lingal: essai d'étude textuelle de mythologies: les mythologies des tribus de langue Gondi* (*Inde Centrale*). École Pratique des Hautes Études, VIe section. Paris, 1966.

Hill, W. D. P. (translator). See Tulsī Dās.
Hislop, Rev. Stephen. *Papers relating to the Aboriginal Tribes of the Central Provinces*. Ed. Sir R. C. Temple. Nagpore, 1866.
Hoens, Dirk Jan. *Śānti: A Contribution to Ancient Indian Religious Terminology*. The Hague, 1951.
Hollings, W. *Bytal Pucheesee*. Trans. Captain W. Hollings. 4th ed. Lucknow, 1884.
Hooykaas, C. *Āgama–Tīrtha: Five Studies in Hindu–Balinese Religion*. Verhandlungen der Koeniglichen Academie der Wetenschappen LXX, 4. Amsterdam, 1964.
Hopkins, Edward Washburn. *Epic Mythology*. Encyclopedia of Indo-Aryan Research, ed. Georg Bühler. iii, 1, B. Strasbourg, 1915.
—— 'The Fountain of Youth.' *JAOS* xxvi, 1, 1905, pp. 1–67.
—— 'Indra as a God of Fertility.' *JAOS* xxxvi, 1916, pp. 242–68.
—— *The Religions of India*. Boston, 1895.
Huxley, Aldous. *Island*. London, 1964.
Ingalls, Daniel H. H. (translator). See *Subhāṣitaratnakoṣa* (1965).
—— 'Cynics and Pāśupatas: The Seeking of Dishonor.' *Harvard Theological Review* lv, 4 (October 1962), pp. 282–98.
—— 'Dharma and Moksha.' *Philosophy East and West* vii, 1–2 (April–July 1957), pp. 41–8.
Isherwood, Christopher. *Rama Krishna and his Disciples*. London, 1965.
Jacobi, Hermann. 'Agastya.' *ERE* i, 180.
—— 'Brahmanism.' *ERE* ii, 799–813.
Jahn, Wilhelm, 'Die Legende vom Devadāruvana.' *ZDMG* lxix (1915), pp. 529–57; lxx (1916), pp. 301–20; lxxi (1917), pp. 167–208.
Jesudasan, C., and Hepzibah. *A History of Tamil Literature*. Calcutta, 1961.
Jolly, Julius. 'Expiation and Atonement (Hindu).' *ERE* v, 659.
Jones, Sir William. 'On the Gods of Greece, Italy and India.' *Asiatick Researches* i (1788), pp. 242 ff.
Jouveau-Dubreuil, G. *Archéologie du sud de l'Inde. II: Iconographie*. Paris, 1914.
Kane, P. V. *History of Dharmaśāstra*. Government Oriental Series B. 6. Poona, 1930–62.
Kantawala, S. G. *Cultural History from the Matsya Purāṇa*. Baroda, 1964.
Keith, Arthur Berriedale. *Indian Mythology*. Vol. vi, part i, of *The Mythology of All Races*, ed. L. H. Grey. Boston, 1917.
—— *The Religion and Philosophy of the Vedas and Upanishads*. HOS, Nos. 31–2. Cambridge (Mass.), 1925.
—— 'The Saturnalia and the Mahāvrata.' *JRAS* xxxv (1915), pp. 133–8.
Kennedy, Vans. *Researches into the Nature and Affinity of Ancient and Hindu Mythology*. London, 1831.
Kincaid, Charles August. *Tales of the Saints of Pandharpur*. Oxford, 1919.
Kirfel, Willibald. *Die fünf Elemente, insbesondere Wasser und Feuer*. Beiträge zur Sprach- und Kulturgeschichte des Orients, No. 4. Walldorf-Hessen, 1951.
—— 'Śiva und Dionysos.' *Zeitschrift für Ethnologie* lxxviii (1953), pp. 83–90.
Kittel, F. *Über den Ursprung des Lingakultus in Indien*. Mangalore, 1876.
Kosambi, D. D. *An Introduction to the Study of Indian History*. Bombay, 1956.
Kuhn, Adalbert. *Mythologische Studien. I: Die Herabkunft des Feuers und des Göttertranks*. Gütersloh, 1886.

Lal, Kanwar. *The Cult of Desire: An Interpretation of the Erotic Sculpture of India*. 2nd ed. London, 1967.

Lanman, Charles (translator). See *Karpūramañjarī*.

Leach, Edmund R. 'Genesis as Myth.' *Discovery*, May 1962 (1962-A).

—— *Lévi-Strauss*. London, 1970.

—— 'Pulleyar and the Lord Buddha: An Example of Syncretism.' *Psychoanalysis and the Psychoanalytic Review* (Summer 1962), pp. 81–102 (1962-B).

—— *The Structural Study of Myth and Totemism*, ed. Edmund R. Leach. Association of Social Anthropologists, Monograph No. 45. London, 1967.

Leeson, Francis. *Kāma Shilpa: A Study of Indian Sculptures Depicting Love in Action*. Bombay, 1962.

Lévi, Sylvain. *La Doctrine du sacrifice dans les Brāhmaṇas*. 2nd ed. Bibliothèque de l'École des Hautes Études, Sciences Religieuses, LXXIII. Paris, 1966.

Lévi-Strauss, Claude. 'Conversation with Lévi-Strauss', by George Steiner. *Encounter* xxvii, 10 (April 1966 [-B]), pp. 38 ff.

—— *The Raw and the Cooked. Introduction to a Science of Mythology: 1*. Trans. John and Doreen Weightman. New York, 1969.

—— *The Savage Mind*. London, 1966 (-A).

—— 'The Story of Asdiwal', trans. Nicholas Mann. In Leach (1967), pp. 1–48.

—— *Structural Anthropology*. New York, 1963.

—— 'The Structural Study of Myth.' In Sebeok (1958).

Lommel, Hermann. 'Soma.' *Forschungen und Fortschritte*, xi, 2 (1935), p. 21.

Lord, Albert B. *The Singer of Tales*. Harvard Studies in Comparative Literature No. 24. Cambridge (Mass.), 1960.

Lüders, Heinrich. 'Die Sage von Ṛṣyaśṛṅga.' Nachrichten von der Königlichen Gesellschaft der Wissenschaften zu Göttingen, Philologisch-Historische Klasse, 1897, pp. 87–135.

Macdonell, Arthur Anthony (translator). See *Bṛhaddevatā*.

—— 'Mythological Studies in the Rig Veda.' *JRAS* xxv (1893), pp. 419–96.

—— *Vedic Mythology*. Encyclopedia of Indo-Aryan Research, ed. Georg Bühler, iii, 1, A. Strasbourg, 1897.

MacMunn, Sir George. *The Religions and Hidden Cults of India*. London, 1931.

Maity, Pradyot Kumar. *Historical Studies in the Cult of the Goddess Manasā*. Calcutta, 1966.

Marriott, McKim. 'The Feast of Love.' In Singer (1966), pp. 200–12.

Marshall, Sir John. *Mohenjo-Daro and the Indus Civilization*. 3 vols. London, 1931.

Martin, E. Osborn. *The Gods of India*. London, 1913.

Maspéro, Henri. 'Les procédés de "nourrir le principe vital" dans la religion Taoïste ancienne.' *Journal asiatique* ccxxviii (1937), pp. 177–252 and 353–430.

Mazumdar, B. C. 'Phallus worship in the *Mahābhārata*.' *JRAS* xxvii (1907), pp. 337–9.

Meinhard, Heinrich. *Beiträge zur Kenntnis des Śivaismus nach den Purāṇa's*. Thesis, Bonn, 1928. (Baessler Archiv 12).

Meyer, Johann Jakob. *Sexual Life in Ancient India*. New York, 1930.

—— *Trilogie der Altindischer Mächte und Feste der Vegetation*. Zürich, 1937.

Miles, Arthur [Gervée Baronti]. *Land of the Lingam*. London, 1933.

Miller, Barbara Stoler (translator). See *Śatakatraya*.

Mitra, Rajendra Lala. *Sanskrit Buddhist Literature of Nepal*. Calcutta, 1882.

Mitra, S. C. 'A Note on the Travesty of an Ancient Indian Myth in a Modern Hindu Ceremony.' *Indian Culture* iv (July 1937), pp. 111–13.

Modi, J. J. The Vish-Kanya.' *Folk-Lore* xxxviii, pp. 327 ff.

Monier-Williams, Sir Monier. *Brahmanism and Hinduism*. London, 1891.
—— *Religious Thought and Life in India. I: Vedism, Brahmanism and Hinduism*. 2nd ed. London, 1885.
Mookerjee, Ajit. *Tantra Art: Its Philosophy and Physics*. New York, 1966.
Moor, Edward. *Śrī Sarvadevasabhā. The Hindu Pantheon*. London, 1810.
Narasimmiyengar, V. N. 'The Legend of Rishya Śṛiñga.' *IA*, ii (1873), Bombay, 1874, pp. 140–3.
Narayan, R. K. *Gods, Demons and Others*. New York, 1964.
—— *Mr. Sampath*. London, 1949.
Newby, Eric. *Slowly Down the Ganges*. New York, 1966.
Nivedita, Sister (Margaret E. Noble) and Coomaraswamy, Ananda K. *Myths of the Hindus and Buddhists*. London, 1913.
O'Flaherty, Wendy Doniger. 'Asceticism and Sexuality in the Mythology of Śiva.' *HR* 8, no. 4, May 1969, pp. 300–37; and *HR* 9, no. 1, August 1969, pp. 1–41 (1969-A).
—— 'The Symbolism of the Third Eye of Śiva in the Purāṇas.' *Purāṇa* xi, 2, July 1969, pp. 273–84 (1969-B).
—— 'The Origin of Heresy in Hindu Mythology.' *HR* 10, no. 4, May 1971, pp. 271–333 (1971-A).
—— 'The Submarine Mare in the Mythology of Śiva.' *JRAS* 1971, 1, pp. 9–27 1971-B).
—— 'The Symbolism of Ashes in the Mythology of Śiva.' Purāṇa xiii, 1, January 1971, pp. 26–35 (1971-C).
—— 'The Indian Variants of the Tale of the Horned Ascetic.' In the commemorative volume for Albert E. Lord, ed. David E. Bynum, Cambridge (Mass.), 1973.
Ogibenin, B. L. *Struktura mifologicheskikh tekstov 'Rigvedy'*. Moscow, 1968 (-A).
—— *Sur le symbolisme du type chamanique dans le Ṛgveda*. Tartu, 1968 (-B).
Oman, John Campbell. *The Mystics, Ascetics and Saints of India*. London, 1903.
Oppert, Gustav. *On the Original Inhabitants of Bharatavarsha or India*. London, 1893.
Pandey, S. M., and Zide, Norman. 'Surdas and his Krishna-Bhakti.' In Singer, pp. 173–99.
Pandit, S. M. Natesa Sastri. *Tales of Tennalirama*. Madras, 1900.
Panigrahi, K. D. 'Sculptural Representations of Lakulīśa and other Pāśupata Teachers.' *Journal of Indian History* xxxviii, 3 (1960), pp. 635–43.
Pargiter, Frederick Eden (translator). See *Mārkaṇḍeya Purāṇa*.
Pathak, M. V. S. *History of Śaiva Cults in North India*. Benares, 1960.
Pattabiramin, P. Z. See Dessigane.
Piatigorskii, A. M. 'Nekotorye obshchie zamechaniia o mifologii c tochki zreniia psikhologa', *Semiotiki: Trudy po znakovym sistemam*, 2, Tartu, 1965, pp. 38–49.
Piggott, Stuart. *Pre-historic India*. London, 1952.
Polo, Marco. The Book of Ser Marco Polo. Trans. and ed. Sir Henry Yule. 3rd ed. 2 vols. London, 1903.
Pott, P. H. *Yoga and Yantra: Their Interrelationship and their Significance for Indian Archeology*. Trans. Rodney Needham. Koninklijk Institut voor Taal-, Land-, en Volkenkunde, Translation Series No. 8. The Hague, 1966.
Pusalker, A. D. *Studies in the Epics and Purāṇas of India*. Bombay, 1955.
Raghavan, V. 'Tamil Versions of the Purāṇas.' *Purāṇa* ii (1960), pp. 223–46.
Ramanujan, A. K. See Dimock (1962 and 1964).
Randhawa, V. S. *Kangra Valley Painting*. Delhi, 1954.

Rao, T. A. Gopinatha. *Elements of Hindu Iconography*. 2 vols, 4 parts. Madras, 1916.

Rawson, Philip. *Indian Sculpture*. New York, 1966.

—— *Indian Painting*. New York and Paris, 1961.

—— *Erotic Art of the East*. New York, 1968.

—— *Tantra*. Arts Council of Great Britain. London, 1971.

Regnaud, P. 'Les origines du myth d'Aurva.' *Revue d'Histoire de Religion* xxiii (1891), pp. 308–15.

Rhode, J. G. *Über Religiöse Bildung, Mythologie und Philosophie der Hindus*. Leipzig, 1827.

Rivett-Carnac, J. G. 'The snake symbol in India, especially in connexion with the worship of Śiva.' *JRASB* xlviii (1879), pp. 18 ff.

Rivière, José, 'The Problem of Ganesha.' *Purāṇa* iv, 1 (January 1962), pp. 96–102.

Robinson, Marguerite S., and Joiner, L. E. 'An Experiment in the Structural Study of Myth.' *Contributions to Indian Sociology*, New Series, 1968, 2, pp. 1–37.

Roger, Abraham. *Offne Thür zu den verborgenen Heydenthum*. Nürnberg, 1663.

Roy, Pratap Chandra (translator). See *Mahābhārata* (1927–32).

Ruben, Walter. *Eisenschmiede und Dämonen in Indien*. Internationales Archiv für Ethnographie, xxxvii, supplement. Leiden, 1939.

—— *Kṛṣṇa: Konkordanz und Kommentar der Motive seines Heldenlebens*. Istanbuler Schriften No. 17. Istanbul, 1944.

Sarkar, Benoy Kumar. *The Folk Element in Hindu Culture*. London, 1917.

Sarkār, Sudhīracandra. *Paurāṇik Abhidhan* (in Bengali). Calcutta, 1963.

von Schiefner, Franz Anton. *Tibetan Tales Derived from Indian Sources*. Trans. from the Tibetan of the *Kah-gyur*. [iv. fols 136, 137.] English trans. W. R. S. Ralson, London, 1882 (esp. pp. 253–7).

Schmidt, Richard. 'Kṣemendra's *Darpadalanam*.' *ZDMG* lxix (1915), pp. 1–51.

von Schroeder, Leopold. *Mysterium und Mimus im Rig Veda*. Leipzig, 1908.

Sebeok, Thomas A. *Myth: A Symposium*. Ed. Thomas A. Sebeok. American Folklore Society. Bloomington, 1958.

Sen, Dinesh Chandra. *History of Bengali Language and Literature*. Calcutta, 1911.

Shastri, Hari Prasad. *A Descriptive Catalogue of the Sanskrit Manuscripts in the Government Collection, under the care of the Asiatic Society of Bengal*. Calcutta, 1925.

Shastri, J. L. (translator). See *Śiva Purāṇa*.

Sieg, Emil. *Die Sagenstoffe des Ṛgveda, und die Indische Itihāsatradition*. Stuttgart, 1902.

Singer, Milton. *Krishna: Myths, Rites and Attitudes*. Ed. Milton Singer. Honolulu, 1966.

—— 'The Radha-Krishna Bhajanas of Madras City.' In Singer (1966).

Sinha, Surajit. 'A Note on the concept of sexual union for spiritual quest among the Vaiṣṇava preachers in the Bhumij belt of Purulia and Singbhum.' *Eastern Anthropologist* xiv 2 (1961), pp. 194–6.

Sircar, Dines Chandra. 'The Śākta Pīṭhas.' *JRASB Letters* xiv, 1 (1948), pp. 1–108.

Smith, V. A. 'Celibacy (Indian).' *ERE* iii, pp. 275–6.

Sonnerat, Pierre. *Voyage aux Indes Orientales et à la Chine*. Paris, 1782.

Spencer, Arthur Marshman. See Thompson, Edward J.

Stacton, David. *Kaliyuga. A Quarrel with the Gods*. London, 1965.

Steel, F. A., and Temple, R. C. *Wide-Awake Stories, a Collection of Tales Told by Little Children between Sunset and Sunrise, in the Panjab and Kashmir.* Bombay, 1884.

von Stietencron, H. 'Bhairava.' *ZDMG* 1969, Supplement 1, Vorträge, Teil 3, pp. 863–71.

Tawney, C. H. (translator). See *Kathāsaritsāgara* (1924).

Taylor, John (translator). See *Prabodhacandrodaya* (1872).

Taylor, William. *Oriental Historical Manuscripts, chiefly bearing upon the History of the Kingdom of Madura.* Tamil text and trans. by William Taylor. 2 vols. Madras, 1835.

Temple, Sir Richard Carnac. *The Legends of the Punjab.* 3 vols. Bombay, 1884, 1885, 1900.

—— See also Steel, F. A.

Tendulkar, D. G. *Mahatma, Life of M. K. T. Gandhi.* Vol. vii. New Delhi, 1953, 1962.

Thieme, Paul. 'Agastya und Lopāmudrā.' *ZDMG* cxiii (1963), pp. 69–79.

—— *Gedichte aus dem Rig-Veda.* Stuttgart, 1964.

Thomas, P. *Epics, Myths and Legends of India.* 5th ed. Bombay, 1958.

—— *Hindu Religion, Customs and Manners.* Bombay, 1960.

—— *Kāma Kalpa: The Hindu Ritual of Love.* 11th ed. Bombay, 1959.

Thomas, F. W. (translator). See *Harṣacarita* (1929).

Thompson, Edward J., and Spencer, Arthur Marshman. *Bengali Religious Lyrics, Śākta.* Calcutta and Oxford, 1923.

Thompson, Stith. *Motif-Index of Folk Literature.* Revised ed. 6 vols. Bloomington, 1955–8.

—— and Balys, Jonas. *The Oral Tales of India.* Bloomington, 1958.

—— and Roberts, Warren E. *Types of Indic Oral Tales: India, Pakistan and Ceylon.* F. F. Communications No. 180. Helsinki, 1960.

Tiwari, A. R. G. 'Shiva-Lingam and Phallus Worship in the Indus Valley Civilisation.' *Journal of the Sri Venkatesvara Oriental Institute* xiv (1953).

Trench, C. G. Chenevix-. *Grammar of Gondi. II: Vocabulary, Folk-Tales, etc.* Madras, 1921.

[Tulsī Dās]. *The Holy Lake of the Acts of Rāma, an English Translation of Tulasī Dās's Rāmacaritamānasa,* by W. D. P. Hill. London, 1952.

Venkataramanayya, N. *Rudra-Śiva.* Madras, 1941.

Venkateswaran, T. K. 'Radha-Krishna Bhajanas of South India: A Phenomenological, Theological, and Philosophical Study.' In Singer (1966).

Vidyārṇava, S. (translator). See *Matsya Purāṇa.*

Volchok, B. Ya. 'Towards an Interpretation of Proto-Indian Pictures.' *Journal of Tamil Studies,* ii, 1, May 1970, pp. 29–53.

—— 'Protoindiiskie paralleli k mifu o Skande.' *Proto-Indica* 1972. Institut Etnografii, Akademiia Nauk, SSSR, pp. 305–12.

Watts, Alan W. *The Two Hands of God: The Myths of Polarity.* Vol. iii of *Patterns of Myth,* ed. Alan W. Watts. 3 vols. New York, 1963.

Weber, Albrecht. *Indische Streifen.* Berlin, 1868–70.

Westermarck, E. *The History of Human Marriage.* London, 1921.

Wheeler, Sir Mortimer. *The Indus Civilisation.* 3rd ed. Cambridge, 1968.

Whitney, William Dwight (translator). See *Atharva Veda* (1905).

—— 'On the *Jaiminīya* or *Talavakara Brāhmaṇa.*' *Proceedings of the American Oriental Society,* 1883, pp. cxlii–cxliv.

Wilford, Lieutenant Francis. 'On Egypt and the Nile from the Ancient Books of the Hindus.' *Asiatick Researches* iii (1792), pp. 295–468.

Wilford, Lieutenant Francis. 'A Dissertation on Semiramus, the origin of Mecca . . . from the Hindu Sacred Books.' *Asiatick Researches* iv (1795), pp. 363–84.
Wilkins, W. J. *Hindu Mythology, Vedic and Puranic.* 2nd ed. London, 1882.
Williams, Charles Allyn. *Oriental Affinities of the Legend of the Hairy Anchorite.* Urbana, Illinois, 1926.
Wilman-Grabowski, H. de. 'Brahmanic Mythology.' In Hackin, 100–46.
Wilson, Horace Hayman (translator). See *Viṣṇu Purāṇa* (1961), *Ṛg Veda* (1866).
—— *Essays on the Religion of the Hindus.* 2 vols. Vols i–ii of *Works*, London, 1864.
—— 'Analysis of the Purāṇas. *JRASB* i (1832), pp. 81–6, 217–33, 431–42, 535–43.
—— 'Essays on the Purāṇas.' *JRASB* v (1839), pp. 61–73 and 298–313.
—— 'A Sketch of the Religious Sects of the Hindus.' *Asiatick Researches* xvi (1828), 1–136; xvii (1832), 169–313.
—— *Sketches of the Religious Sects of the Hindus.* Calcutta, 1849.
Winternitz, Moriz. *A History of Indian Literature. I: Introduction. Veda, National Epics, Purāṇas, and Tantras.* Trans. Mrs. S. Ketkar. 2nd ed. Calcutta, 1963.
Woodroffe, Sir John George (Arthur Avalon). *Śakti and Śākta: Essays and Addresses on the Śākta Tantraśāstras.* Madras, 1959.
Yalman, Nur O. '"The raw: the cooked:: nature: culture"—Observations on *Le Cru et le cuit.*' In Leach (1967), pp. 71–90.
Zaehner, Robert Charles. *Hinduism.* Oxford, 1962.
Zide, Norman. See Pandey, S. M.
Ziegenbalg, Bartholomaeus. *Genealogy of the South Indian Gods.* Trans. G. J. Metzger. Madras, 1869.
Zimmer, Heinrich. *Myths and Symbols in Indian Art and Civilization.* Bollingen Series No. 6. New York, 1946.

APPENDIX E

BIBLIOGRAPHIC NOTES

Sanskrit sources are cited here only by title (frequently abbreviated to the first word) and secondary sources by author's last name (and date of publication, in case of several works by one author). Full citations appear in the Bibliography (Appendix D).

CHAPTER I

1. MhB I. 56. 33.
2. Zimmer, pp. 219–21, citing Martin Buber, *Die Chassidischen Bücher* (Hegner, Hallerau, 1928), pp. 532–3.
3. Stacton, p. 30.
4. Douglas, p. 63.
5. Lévi-Strauss (1969), p. 340 and p. 3.
6. Lévi-Strauss (1963), p. 210.
7. Lévi-Strauss (1969), p. 6.
8. Leach (1970), p. 63.
9. Lévi-Strauss (1969), p. 3.
10. Dubois, p. 508.
11. Zaehner, p. 113.
12. Campbell, p. 209.
13. Watts, p. 96; D. C. Sen, p. 72; Bharati (1965), pp. 296–7.
14. *Subhāṣitaratnakoṣa* (Ingalls's translation), verse 103. Cf. *Kumārasambhava* 6. 95.
15. *Kālikā* 42. 71–7.
16. *Skanda* I. I. 21. 70.
17. Atharva Veda XI. 5. 5 and 12. Cf. Charpentier, p. 154, and Bloomfield (1897), p. 627.
18. MhB XIII, Appendix I, No. 5, 47–50. Cf. *Kathāsaritsāgara* 114. I.
19. *Śiva* 2. 2. 16. 39; *Kālikā* 9. 49–50.
20. *Śiva* 2. 5. 18. 44–51.
21. *Mahābhāgavata* 20. 36, 12. 10.
22. *Śiva* 2. 3. 4. 31–40.
23. *Matsya* 154. 332 (1907 and 1876).
24. *Matsya* 154. 332 (1890) and *Padma* 5. 40. 324–5.
25. *Haracarita* 10. 74–5.
26. *Stotrasamuccaya*, verse 37. Vāmadevanavaratnamālikāstuti.
27. *Yogaśāstra*, quoted in the *Tarkarahasyadīpikā*, cited by D. R. Bhandarkar (1906–7), p. 190.
28. B. K. Sarkar, p. 71.
29. Stacton, p. 159.
30. Rawson (1966), pp. 46–7.
31. Piggott, p. 202; A. Ghosh, p. 767; Zaehner, pp. 20 and 110.
32. Wheeler, plate XIX, *c*, p. 90.
33. A. Ghosh, p. 767.
34. Ṛg Veda VII. 21. 5 and X. 99. 3.

35. Personal communication from Dr. James C. Harle of the Ashmolean Museum, Oxford.
36. Rao, i, 22.
37. J. N. Banerjea, pp. 48 and 457, pl. XXXIX, No. 2; Panigrahi, p. 640; Goetz, p. 4, fig. 4; Rawson (1966), p. 46; R. D. Banerjea, pls. LII *a–b*, LIII *a*, LIV *c*, LV *b* and *d*, LVI *b*; Chanda, pls. VII 1–2; p. 117.
38. *Uttarakāmikāgama*, cited by A. Ghosh, p. 766.
39. A. Ghosh, p. 765; Daniélou (1962), pp. 20, 29, and 31; J. N. Banerjea, pl. XXXIX No. 2; Anand, pl. LXIV; *Matsya* 260. 7.
40. Rivière, p. 100.
41. Lal, pp. 79, 95, and 100; pls. VI–VII.
42. MhB XIII. 17. 45, 74, and 83; XIII. 146. 17; X. 7. 37; *Liṅga* 1. 20. 61; *Padma* 5. 17. 57.
43. *Śiva*, Dharmasaṃhitā 10. 79; *Vāmana* S.22. 68–9.
44. MhB XIII. 17. 58; VII. 173. 83–4; VII. 173. 92; XIII. 146. 10–17. But cf. *Tāṇḍya Mahābrāhmaṇa* 17. 14. 1 ('those whose phallus is lowered in self-control').
45. MhB, with the commentary of Nīlakaṇṭha (1862), XIII. 17. 45–6.
46. *Śiva* 2. 3. 16. 31.
47. *Kumārasambhava* 9. 14–15.
48. MhB XIII. 17. 45.
49. *Matsya* 4. 30–2; *Skanda* 7. 2. 9. 5–17.
50. Agrawala (1966), p. 3.
51. Rawson (1966), p. 48; cf. Rawson (1971), fig. 74.
52. Bharati (1965), p. 296.
53. Daniélou (1962), p. 42.
54. Ruben (1939), p. 209.
55. Daniélou (1962), p. 20; J. N. Banerjea, pl. XXXIX, No. 2.
56. *Skanda* 7. 3. 39. 10.
57. *Brahmāṇḍa* 2. 27. 12.
58. *Padma* 5. 5. 45.
59. *Padma* 1. 5. 39 (Bombay, 1927).
60. Elwin (1949), p. 473.
61. Lal, pl. LXXIII.
62. *Arthaśāstra* 4. 13. 41.
63. *Skanda* 1. 3. 1. 4. 1–31.
64. Lévi-Strauss (1969), p. 340.
65. Biardeau (1968), p. 122.
66. Lévi-Strauss (1966-A), pp. 16–22.
67. Moor, p. 36.
68. Douglas, p. 51.
69. Ibid.
70. Lévi-Strauss (1967), p. 21.
71. Watts, p. 2.
72. Lévi-Strauss (1969), p. 56.
73. Leach (1970), p. 57.
74. Heimann (1930), p. iv.
75. Douglas, pp. 65–6; Lévi-Strauss (1969), p. 4; (1966-B), p. 38.
76. Herrenschmidt and Robinson, *passim*. See below, pp. 100–1 and 176–8.
77. Lévi-Strauss (1969), p. 334.
78. Yalman, p. 74.
79. Lévi-Strauss (1969), p. 51 n.

80. Yalman, p. 73.
81. Lévi-Strauss (1969), p. 13.
82. Biardeau (1968), p. 123.
83. Yalman, pp. 74–7.
84. Leach (1970), p. 70.
85. Lévi-Strauss (1969), p. 5.
86. Yalman, pp. 74–7; Lévi-Strauss (1969), p. 13.
87. Biardeau (1970), pp. 293 and 301.
88. Leach (1970), p. 59; also (1962-A), p. 2.
89. Lévi-Strauss (1963), p. 229; (1966-A), p. 22; Leach (1970), p. 71.
90. See Appendix F, motif 1 (conscious multiforms).
91. *Vāmana* 46. 1 ff.; *Liṅga* 1. 11–14.
92. *Śiva* 2. 4. 13. 4.
93. *Śiva* 4. 27. 23–4; cf. *Rāmāyaṇa* VII. 4. 3–4 and VII. 16. 44.
94. Leach (1962-A), pp. 1–2.
95. Lord, chapter 4, 'The Theme'; *Brahma* 35. 31–60.
96. *Kūrma* 2. 37. 1–151; (*Bib. Ind.* 2. 38, pp. 722–43).
97. *Brahmavaivarta* 3. 1, 3. 2, 3. 4, 3. 9, and 3. 14; *Padma* 6. 3–19 and 6. 98–107.
98. Leach (1970), p. 79; Lévi-Strauss (1969), p. 5.
99. Lévi-Strauss (1966-B), p. 38.
100. Lévi-Strauss (1969), p. 32.
101. Lévi-Strauss (1958), p. 64; Douglas, p. 52.
102. Leach (1962-A), p. 4. Cf. MhB, verse inserted before III. 205. 1.
103. Watts, p. 16.
104. Lévi-Strauss (1967), pp. 29–30.
105. Leach (1970), p. 57.
106. Lévi-Strauss (1967), pp. 27–9.
107. Ogibenin (1968-A), *passim*, esp. pp. 51–8.
108. Durkheim, p. 190.
109. Leach (1970), p. 58.
110. Ibid., p. 71.
111. Lévi-Strauss (1963), p. 229; (1966-A), p. 22.
112. Douglas, p. 52.
113. *Haracarita* 10. 75–6.
114. *Śiva*, Jñānasaṃhitā 18. 18.
115. *Mahābhāgavata* 22. 38–9; *Skanda* 1. 1. 21. 15.
116. *Śiva* 2. 2. 16. 30–6; cf. *Śiva* 2. 3. 24. 60, 66–7, and 75.
117. *Śiva* 2. 4. 4. 5.
118. *Bṛhaddharma* 2. 60. 15.

CHAPTER II

1. Ṛg Veda X. 136. 1–7; cf. Hauer (1932), p. 12; Hauer (1922), p. 168; and Briggs, p. 211.
2. Ṛg Veda X. 136. 1–7.
3. Atharva Veda XV. 1; cf. Eliade (1958), p. 103; Hauer (1922), pp. 172 and 184; Whitney (1905), p. 773.
4. *Śatapatha Brāhmaṇa* XI. 5. 4. 16; Manu 5. 159; MhB XIII. 74. 36, XII. 232. 4, and I. 109. 26; and *Mārkaṇḍeya* 47. 59.
5. *Muṇḍaka Upaniṣad* 1. 2. 11; *Chāndogya Upaniṣad* 5. 10. 1–6.

6. *Āpastambīya Dharmasūtra* 2. 9. 23. 4; cf. *Vāyu* 50. 213–20 and *Śiva* 5. 23. 56–9.
7. *Matsya* 3. 38–40.
8. *Matsya* 14. 1–8; cf. *Matsya* 3. 39–40, and Manu 11. 121–2.
9. *Kālikā* 30. 1–42, 31. 1–153.
10. Ṛg Veda x. 129. 3; Atharva Veda xi. 5. 5, 7, 10, and 26; cf. Ṛg Veda x. 34. 10; *Taittirīya Brāhmaṇa* 3. 12. 3. 1; and Blair, p. 63.
11. *Śatapatha Brāhmaṇa* 6. 1. 3. 1–2; cf. *Aitareya Brāhmaṇa* 10. 1. 5 and 11. 6. 4.
12. *Kauṣītaki Brāhmaṇa* 6. 1; and *Taittirīya Brāhmaṇa* 2. 2. 9. 1.
13. Ṛg Veda vii. 103. 8–9; i. 100. 3; vi. 70. 2; v. 58. 7.
14. *Devatattva* 3. 3, cited by Daniélou (1964), p. 106.
15. *Chāndogya Upaniṣad* 5. 10. 3–6.
16. Ṛg Veda v. 58. 7; *Taittirīya Saṃhitā* 2. 4. 10. 2; cf. Blair, p. 5.
17. *Kālikā* 11. 27 ff.
18. *Śiva* 2. 2. 19. 26–34, 68–76; 2. 2. 20. 14–26.
19. MhB xiv. 95. 1 ff.
20. *Alambusā Jātaka*, No. 523.
21. Hollings, pp. 4–5; Grierson, ix, 4, p. 74; *Caitanya Carita Antya* 3. 94, cited by Dimock (1966), pp. 154–5; Briggs, p. 212; *Jaiminīya Brāhmaṇa* 2. 405; *Daśakumāracarita*, pp. 75 ff.; Meyer (1930), p. 548. I have discussed the Ṛṣyaśṛṅga myth at greater length elsewhere (1973).
22. *Naḷinikā Jātaka*, No. 526.
23. MhB iii: 110. 17–36, 111. 1–22, 112. 1–18, 113. 1–25.
24. MhB iii. 110. 3 and 25–6.
25. *Padma Purāṇa, Pātāla Khaṇḍa* 13. 52.
26. MhB iii. 110. 7.
27. *Padma Purāṇa, Pātāla Khaṇḍa* 13. 67; Narasimmiyengar, pp. 140–3.
28. Meyer (1930), pp. 292 and 565; von Schroeder, p. 292 ff.
29. von Schiefner, pp. 254–5.
30. Chavannes, No. 453 (Tripitaka xxxvi, 4, pp. 420), iii, 233–7.
31. Lüders, pp. 111–13.
32. MhB iii. 110. 25–6; *Padma Purāṇa, Pātāla Khaṇḍa* 13. 67.
33. Narasimmiyengar, pp. 140–3; *Naḷinikā Jātaka*, No. 526.
34. MhB iii. 110. 8.
35. *Padma Purāṇa, Pātāla Khaṇḍa* 13. 48 (cf. *Skanda* 6. 70. 46–9: paramam ānandam prāpa); Narasimmiyengar, pp. 140–3.
36. Beal, i, 113.
37. Chavannes, iii, 235–6.
38. Ibid. iii, 233.
39. Narasimmiyengar, pp. 140–3.
40. *Padma Purāṇa, Pātāla Khaṇḍa* 13. 20 and 13. 68–78.
41. MhB iii. 113. 11–20.
42. MhB iii. 113. 21; *Padma Purāṇa, Pātāla Khaṇḍa* 13. 78.
43. *Rāmāyaṇa* i. 8. 7–23, i. 9. 1–14. Cf. i. 7 and i. 10.
44. *Avadānakalpalatā*, No. 65, Ekaśṛṅgāvadāna, vol. 2, p. 411, verses 15–20.
45. Chavannes, iii, 237.
46. *Jātakas* No. 523 and 526; Narasimmiyengar; von Schiefner; *Avadānakalpalatā*.
47. *Rāmāyaṇa* i. 9. 32; *Padma Purāṇa, Pātālakhaṇḍa* 13. 68–78; MhB iii. 113. 24–5.
48. *Avadānakalpalatā* 65. 72–3.

49. von Schiefner, p. 256.
50. MhB III. 110. 17; *Jātakas* 523 and 526; *Avadānakalpalatā*; Beal, i, 113; *Pātāla Khaṇḍa* 13. 10; von Schiefner; Chavannes, iii, 233–4.
51. *Padma Purāṇa, Pātāla Khaṇḍa* 13. 52.
52. Lucien Fournereau, plate XIX (bottom); Narasimmiyengar, from the temple of Gopālasvāmi in Devāṇḍahaḷḷi, Western Ghats; Cunningham, *The Stūpa of Bharhut*, plate XXVI; Fergusson, plate LXXXVI.
53. Epic of Gilgamesh, Tablet I, column 3, lines 42 ff., Heidel edition; also Tablet VIII, column 1, lines 3 ff., Schmökel, p. 76.
54. Williams, ii, 117 and 120; cf. i, 13–25 and 25–36.
55. Lüders, p. 115.
56. Piggott, p. 202.
57. *Mahābhāgavata* 22. 34–43; *Matsya* 47. 113–27; 47. 170–213; *Padma* 5. 13. 257–313; *Śiva* 2. 3. 17. 19–22; *Saura* 53. 48; *Kumārasambhava* 3. 4; MhB V. 15. 2–25.
58. *Manmathonmathana*, Act I, 25–6.
59. *Brahmavaivarta* 4. 31. 22–65, 4. 32. 1–20, 4. 33. 1–76.
60. R. Dessigane *et al.* (1967), pp. 191 ff. (6. 13. 30–45).
61. Eliade (1958), p. 257; von Schroeder, p. 166; Lal, pp. 67, 102, 104; Dubois, p. 310; *Drāhyāyaṇa Śrautasūtra* 11. 3. 9 ff.; Gonda (1965), p. 296.
62. Ṛg Veda I. 179.
63. von Schroeder, p. 160; Geldner, i, 257.
64. Thieme (1964), pp. 75–6; cf. Sieg, p. 124; also Sāyaṇa, on Ṛg Veda I. 179.
65. *Bṛhaddevatā* 4. 57–8; cf. von Schroeder, pp. 159, 161–2; Hauer (1922), p. 38.
66. *Sāmavidhāna Brāhmaṇa* I. 7. 9.
67. Thieme (1963), p. 73.
68. MhB III: 94. 1–27, 95. 1–24, 97. 17–25; cf. Goldman, pp. 273–303.
69. *Bhāgavata* 3. 14. 7–49.
70. *Śiva* 4. 7. 4–28.
71. Dessigane (1967), p. 9 (1. 6. 7).
72. *Yogatattva* 59 ff., cited by Eliade (1958), p. 129.
73. *Kāmasūtra* 7. 2. 55–7.
74. Atharva Veda XI. 5. 12; Whitney (1905), p. 638; Bloomfield (1897), p. 627.
75. *Śiva* 2. 1. 16. 12.
76. *Śiva*, Dharmasaṃhitā 10. 126.
77. Baudhāyana, cited in *Saṃskāraprakāśa*, p. 755; and *Liṅga Purāṇa*, cited ibid., p. 752.
78. *Śiva* 2. 1. 3. 17–18.
79. *Nāradasmṛti* 12. 8–19; *Yājñavalkyasmṛti* 1. 55; Manu 9. 78–9.
80. *Kālikā* 51. 21–3, 44.
81. *Śiva* 3. 27. 39–41.
82. Jouveau-Dubreuil, p. 32.
83. *Sāmba* 16. 24–33; *Skanda* 5. 2. 8. 1–5; cf. *Kūrma* 1. 16. 117–29 (*Bib. Ind.* 1. 16, pp. 184–5); *Vāmana* 6. 87.
84. *Vāmana* 34. 1–4.
85. Manu 11. 123; *Agni* 169. 18; cf. Meyer (1930), p. 257 n.; MhB XII. 159. 27 and XII. 207. 13; Manu 2. 181–2, 11. 106; *Vāyu* 18. 8–9; Bühler, p. 452.
86. MhB XII. 159. 26–7.
87. Manu 11. 106.
88. Bühler, p. 452; he cites Medhātithi, Kullūkabhaṭṭa, Rāghavānanda, and Nārada.

89. MhB XII. 207. 13.
90. *Vāyu* 18. 7, 8, 14, and 17.
91. *Śiva* 5. 12. 45.
92. Ṛg Veda I. 116. 10 and V. 74. 5; Blair, p. 137; Ṛg Veda VII. 1. 7, X. 80. 3, VII. 9. 6; cf. *Bṛhaddevatā* 5. 82–7.
93. Ṛg Veda VIII. 1. 30–4; *Bṛhaddevatā* 6. 40; cf. *Śaṅkhāyana Śrautasūtra* 16. 11. 17.
94. Ṛg Veda V. 78. 5–6.
95. Sāyaṇa on Ṛg Veda V. 78. 5.
96. *Śatapatha Brāhmaṇa* 4. 1. 5. 1–15.
97. *Jaiminīya Brāhmaṇa* 3. 122–6.
98. MhB III: 122. 1–27, 123. 1–23.
99. *Devībhāgavata* 7. 2. 30–65; 7. 3. 1–64; 7. 4. 1–56; 7. 5. 1–57; cf. *Bhāgavata* 9. 3. 11 ff.; cf. *Padma* (ASS) 5. 14. 49–65; 5. 15. 1–19.
100. *Viṣṇu* 4. 2. 69–124; *Haṭhayogapradīpikā* 3. 65.
101. Tale of Tirunīlakaṇṭha Nāyanār, cited by Ayyar, pp. 151–2.
102. *Skanda* 1. 2. 25. 24–84.
103. *Varāha* 22. 8–25; Dessigane *et al.* (1960), No. 23; William Taylor, p. 72.
104. *Rāmāyaṇa* III. 10. 12–17.
105. *Śiva* 3. 25. 2 and 3. 24. 5.
106. *Śiva* 3. 24. 34–64; Sudhīracandra Sarkār, p. 302.
107. *Skanda* 7. 1. 32. 1–128, 33. 1–103; *Brahma* 110. 85–210. Cf. O'Flaherty (1971-B).
108. *Śiva* 2. 3. 33. 22–64, 34. 1–39, 35. 1–62. Cf. *Brahmavaivarta* 4. 41. 103–45, 4. 42. 1–69.
109. *Śiva* 3. 25. 5 and 2. 3. 34. 18; *Śiva* 3. 25. 10–15.
110. Hopkins (1905), pp. 55–6.
111. *Skanda* 6. 257. 11; *Devī* 8, p. 30, line 2; cf. MhB XII. 161. 29, and Meyer (1930), p. 133 n.
112. *Mattavilāsaprahasana*, Act I, verse 8.
113. Atharva Veda IV. 34. 2.
114. MhB III, Appendix I, No. 6, 120–1.
115. MhB IX. 47. 1–27; cf. *Rāmāyaṇa* V. 30. 17–48.
116. *Śiva* 2. 2. 5. 1–68, 6. 1–62, 7. 1–26.
117. MhB XIII. 110. 8; Eliade (1958), p. 152.
118. *Rasikarañjana*, No. 9; cf. *Śatakatraya*, No. 135.
119. *Śatakatraya*, No. 120, translated by John Brough, No. 9; cf. *Subhāṣitaratnakoṣa*, Nos. 562 and 565 and *Śatakatraya*, No. 136.
120. O'Flaherty (1971-A), pp. 276–9; cf. *Rājataraṅginī* 7. 278; and *Kūlārṇava Tantra* I. 79.
121. *Āpastambīya Dharmasūtra* 2. 6. 14. 13.
122. *Majjhima Nikāya*, Culadhammasamadanasutta, i, pp. 305–6; Meyer (1930), p. 160; P. V. Kane, v, 2, 1094; Nirad Chaudhuri, pp. 192, 203.
123. Bloomfield (1924), p. 204; cf. *Mattavilāsaprahasana*; *Kathākośa*, pp. 130–5; *Prabodhacandrodaya* III. 19; *Kathāsaritsāgara* 3. 1. 30–54, 15. 30, 24. 83, 121. 3; *Tantropākhyāna*, No. 1.
124. *Caitanya Carita Antya* 2. 116–18, cited by Dimock (1966), p. 45.
125. *Haracarita* 10. 3–32; *Yāgīśvaramāhātmya* 27b. 10; *Vāmana* S.22–3; *Darpadalana* 7. 17–71; *Saura* 69; *Śiva*, Dharmasaṃhitā 10. 187; 10. 78–80; *Bhikṣāṭanakāvya* 9. 13; *Skanda* 1. 1. 34. 116–30; *Padma* 5. 53. 1–2.
126. Ayyar, p. 16; O'Flaherty (1971-A), pp. 276–9.

127. MhB v. 35. 39–41; cf. Ayyar, pp. 62–3.
128. *Kathāsaritsāgara* 61. 147–252.
129. Dubois, pp. 592–4.
130. Newby, pp. 228–32.
131. Śabara, *Jaiminīya Mīmāṃsā Sūtra* I. 3. 4; *Sarvadarśanasaṃgraha*, p. 3; *Prabodhacandrodaya* II. 26.
132. *Śatakatraya*, 113.
133. *Mārkaṇḍeya* 14. 4; cf. MhB VII. 18. 32 and Manu 3. 46–8.
134. *Padma* 6. 14. 49.
135. Crooke (1896), ii, 22.
136. *Śiva* 3. 14. 32.
137. MhB I. 220. 5–17, 224. 1–32.
138. *Mārkaṇḍeya* 92–5; (*Bib. Ind.* 95–8), cf. *Devībhāgavata* I. I. 4 ff.; *Brahma* 34. 62–73; MhB I. 41. 1–30, 42. 1–20.
139. *Kālikā* 92. 4–22, 93. 1–15.
140. MhB IX. 51. 1–23.
141. *Śiva* 3. 3. 1–29; *Śiva*, Vāyavīyasaṃhitā 7. 15–7. 17; *Viṣṇu* I. 7. 1–19; *Padma* 5. 3. 155–72; cf. Dessigane *et al.* (1964), No. 63, pp. 82–3.
142. *Vāyu* 9. 67–93; *Viṣṇu* I. 7. 1–19; *Padma* 5. 3. 155–72; *Mārkaṇḍeya* 47. 1–17.
143. *Brahmavaivarta* 4. 35. 31–73, 101–2.
144. *Śiva* 7. I. 12. 1–2, 19–22, 44–7; 7. I. 14. 14–21; 7. I. 17. 1–5 ff.
145. *Vāyu* 67. 24–30 and 67. 14–16; *Brahmāṇḍa* 3. 4. 3–27; cf. *Liṅga* I. 20. 80–97.
146. *Brahmavaivarta* I. 8. 10–49.
147. *Nāradapañcarātra* 10. 24–32.
148. *Brahmavaivarta* I. 23. 1–40, I. 24. 1–47, I. 25–I. 28.
149. *Matsya* 5. 2–4.
150. *Śiva* 2. 2. 13. 1–40.
151. MhB I. 70. 5–6.
152. *Bhāgavata* (with Śrīdhara's commentary), 6. 5. 36–8 and 6. 5. 20.
153. *Śiva* 2. 3. 25. 29–38; and Tulsī Dās, p. 41 (C. 78–9).
154. *Vāyu* 65. 121–58; cf. *Viṣṇu* I. 15.
155. MhB I. 70. 5–6; *Bhāgavata* 6. 5. 36–8 and 6. 5. 20.
156. Dessigane (1967), p. 176 (6. 3. I ff.).
157. Dessigane (1964), p. 45, No. 36.
158. Beswick, pp. 92–3; Nivedita, p. 292.
159. *Āpastambīya Dharmasūtra* 2. 9. 24. 1.
160. Ibid.
161. *Śatakatraya*, No. 88, trans. Brough No. 167; cf. *Śatakatraya*, No. 135.
162. Miller, xxiv.
163. *Matsya* 154. 330–41.
164. *Brahmavaivarta* 4. 47. 152–60.
165. Zimmer, p. 22.
166. *Śiva* 7. I. 28. 19.
167. Zaehner, p. 9; van Buitenen, pp. 35–40; Ingalls (1957), pp. 45–8.
168. *Bṛhadāraṇyaka Upaniṣad* 3. 5 and 4. 4. 22.
169. *Devībhāgavata* 4. 13. 32 and 35.
170. MhB XIII. 2. 39–40.
171. *Vaśiṣṭhadharmaśāstra* 11. 48; Manu 4. 257, 6. 33–7; cf. *Taittirīya Brāhmaṇa* 6. 3. 10. 5, and *Śatapatha Brāhmaṇa* I. 7. 2. 1–6.
172. MhB XII. 214. 10; III. 199. 12; cf. *Rāmāyaṇa* I. 8. 9.

173. *Smṛtyarthasāra* p. 2, v. 17, cited by Kane, ii, 929; cf. *Abhijñānaśākuntala* II. 14.
174. Briggs, p. 23; Nirad Chaudhuri, p. 180; Dumont (1960), pp. 46–7; (1957-A), p. 17.
175. *Śiva Saṃhitā*, last 3 verses, cited by Briggs, p. 49.
176. *Vāmana* S.22. 84.
177. Briggs, p. 34.
178. *Bṛhadāraṇyaka Upaniṣad* 3. 5.
179. Gonda (1963), p. 288.
180. Kane, ii, 928–9.
181. Manu 6. 2–3; *Kūrma* (*Bib. Ind.*) 2. 27. 1–17; *Vaikhānasasmārtasūtra* 9. 5; Kane, ii, 918.
182. D. R. Bhandarkar (1906–7), pp. 189–90; Dasgupta, p. 144.
183. Dubois, pp. 505 and 508.
184. *Yājñavalkyasmṛti* 3. 44; *Vaśiṣṭhadharmaśāstra* 9. 5; Manu 6. 26; *Vaikhānasasmārtasūtra* 9. 2–5.
185. *Kūrma* 2. 27. 16–17.
186. Cited by Kane, ii, 920.
187. *Yāgīśvaramāhātmya* 24–34.
188. Elwin (1949), pp. 243–4.
189. MhB III. 116. 1–18.
190. Forster, p. 113.
191. Gonda (1963), p. 287.
192. Dumont (1960), p. 45.
193. Kane, ii, 928–9; *Bṛhannāradīya Purāṇa* 22. 16; *Nārada Purāṇa* 1. 24. 14.
194. Böhtlingk, i, 26, No. 136, from Śārṅgadhara *Paddhanīti* 26 (ati sarvatra varjayet) and i, 27, No. 137 (sarvam atyantagarhitam).
195. *Aṅguttara Nikāya* I, p. 70 (II. 7. 1).

CHAPTER III

1. Arbman, p. 10.
2. Ṛg Veda I. 114. 7; cf. *Taittirīya Saṃhitā* 4. 5. 66.
3. *Brahmāṇḍa* 2. 27. 107–9.
4. *Skanda* 1. 1. 22. 53; *Śiva* 2. 2. 26. 15 and 2. 3. 27. 27.
5. *Vāyu* 23. 219–21.
6. Kosambi, p. 40.
7. Ruben (1944), p. 103; Daniélou (1964), p. 107; Dahlquist, pp. 140–1; Wilson (1866), i, xxvi–xxvii.
8. Macdonell (1897), pp. 79–81; Hopkins (1916), p. 245.
9. Sāyaṇa on Ṛg Veda I. 114. 6.
10. *Bṛhatsaṃhitā* 58. 42–3.
11. *Śatapatha Brāhmaṇa* 9. 1. 1. 6–7; *Kauṣītaki Brāhmaṇa* 6. 1; *Taittirīya Saṃhitā* 4. 5. 5. 5.
12. MhB I. 203. 15–26; cf. *Skanda* 5. 3. 150. 18, 6. 153. 2–27.
13. Ṛg Veda IX. 60. 1.
14. Ṛg Veda VII. 34. 10; Atharva Veda IV. 16. 4; Ṛg Veda I. 79. 12.
15. Personal communication from Mircea Eliade.
16. *Vāyu* 72. 39–40; *Matsya* 3. 30–8.
17. *Daśakumāracarita* II, p. 85.
18. Ṛg Veda X. 111. 2 and II. 33. 4 and 6.
19. MhB I. 57. 1–27.
20. Ṛg Veda IV. 17. 16; Ṛg Veda I. 62. 11.

21. Ṛg Veda VIII. 91. 4; *Vaśiṣṭhasmṛti* 12. 24, citing the *Kāṭhaka*.
22. Daniélou (1964), p. 109.
23. *Garuḍa Purāṇa* III. 28. 50–5, cited by Gangadharan, p. 107.
24. Ṛg Veda X. 171. 2; cf. *Bhāgavata* 4. 19. 1–25; also cf. *Kāthaka Āraṇyaka* (ed. L. von Schroeder, Berl. Sitz. Ber. 137), p. 114.
25. Ṛg Veda X. 86. 16–17; cf. Ṛg Veda VIII. 24. 8.
26. *Śatapatha Brāhmaṇa* 3. 3. 4. 18; MhB V. 12. 6, XII. 329. 4. 1, XIII. 41. 12; *Rāmāyaṇa* I. 47. 15–32, I. 48. 1–10.
27. MhB XII. 329. 14. 1, XIII. 41. 12–23; *Kārttika Māhātmya* 4. 32.
28. *Rāmāyaṇa* I. 47. 27–8; cf. I. 47. 15–32 and I. 48. 1–10; *Padma* (Bombay) I. 56. 15–33; cf. *Śatapatha Brāhmaṇa* 12. 7. 1. 10–12; 5. 2. 3. 8; Ṛg Veda VI. 46. 3 and VIII. 19. 32.
29. *Brahmavaivarta* 4. 47. 31–2.
30. *Kathāsaritsāgara* 17. 137–48; Tawney, ii, 46.
31. Ṛg Veda VI. 46. 3 and VIII. 19. 32.
32. *Jaiminīya Brāhmaṇa* I. 162.
33. Manu 9. 237; *Arthaśāstra* 4. 8. 27–8.
34. von Fürer-Haimendorf (1948), pp. 105 and 128.
35. *Kāṭhaka*, xiii. 5, Berlin, 1868–70; cf. Atharva Veda VII. 38. 2.
36. Kincaid, p. 119.
37. *Padma* I. 56. 15–33.
38. *Brahmāṇḍa* 2. 27. 23.
39. *Viṣṇu* 4. 9. 18; *Bhāgavata* 4. 2. 18; *Śiva* 2. 2. 26. 18; cf. *Tāṇḍya Mahābrāhmaṇa* 14. 11. 28.
40. MhB IX. 42. 28–36; cf. MhB V. 9–14, XII. 273. 26–54; Dessigane (1960), p. 7, No. 1; cf. *Bṛhaddevatā* 6. 149–53; *Śatapatha* I. 1. 3, 5–12.
41. MhB IX. 47. 1–27, 52–5.
42. MhB IX. 47. 30–51.
43. *Śiva*, Dharmasaṃhitā 44. 21–2; cf. *Jātaka* I. 59. 32.
44. *Abhijñānaśākuntala*, I. 2; cf. Hopkins (1915), p. 139.
45. MhB III. 135. 16–42.
46. MhB XII. 11. 1–28.
47. *Rāmāyaṇa* III. 8. 13–23.
48. *Tāṇḍya Mahābrāhmaṇa* 8. 14; *Aitareya Brāhmaṇa* 35. 2.
49. MhB V. 9. 8.
50. Meyer (1930), pp. 260–1.
51. MhB XII. 329. 21 ff.; *Matsya* 61. 21–6; *Bhāgavata* 11. 4. 7.
52. *Śiva* 2. 1. 2. 1–9.
53. MhB I. 120. 1–12.
54. *Rāmāyaṇa* I. 63. 24–7, I. 64. 1–5.
55. MhB V. 15. 2–25.
56. *Matsya* 47. 113–27, 170–213; *Padma* 5. 13. 257–313; *Vāyu* 2. 97–8; cf. O'Flaherty (1971-A), pp. 313–15.
57. *Padma* 6. 18. 82–90.
58. Manu 6. 47–8.
59. *Vāmana* 33. 5–6.
60. *Vāmana* 43. 95 and MhB XIII. 41. 22–4.
61. *Rāmāyaṇa* I. 48. 1–4.
62. *Rāmāyaṇa* I. 63. 1–15; III. 9. 14; VII. 17. 33.
63. *Bhāgavata* 4. 19. 12–20; Hopkins (1915), p. 137; cf. MhB XIV. 54. 12–35; Dessigane (1967), p. 7 (I. 3. 32–5); MhB XIII. 14. 88 ff.; Ruben (1944), p. 158.

64. Nīlakaṇṭha on MhB XIII. 17. 45; *Śiva* 3. 15. 39.
65. Blair, p. 83.
66. Ṛg Veda VIII. 60. 16 and 9, III. 18. 2, X. 87. 14 and 20, VII. 1. 7.
67. *Liṅga* 1. 6. 4.
68. Ṛg Veda III. 29. 1–3.
69. Atharva Veda III. 21. 4; *Taittirīya Saṃhitā* 2. 2. 3. 1.
70. Atharva Veda VI. 130. 4.
71. *Śatapatha Brāhmaṇa* 3. 4. 3. 4–5 and 3. 5. 3. 16; cf. MhB III. 209. 23; Atharva Veda IX. 2 and 52; Bloomfield (1897), p. 592.
72. *Vāmana* 6. 44.
73. Elwin (1949), p. 113.
74. Ibid., p. 109.
75. Nirad Chaudhuri, p. 210.
76. Bosch (1924), pp. 268 and 266.
77. Ibid., p. 249.
78. Ṛg Veda I. 66. 8 and I. 71. 5.
79. *Matsya* 140. 59–65; *Śiva* 2. 5. 10. 37–8; cf. *Subhāṣitaratnakoṣa*, Nos. 49, 61, and 67, and *Matsya* 139. 23.
80. *Brahmavaivarta* 4. 39. 16–21.
81. MhB XIII. 2. 12–35; *Skanda* 5. 3. 33. 2–42.
82. *Kūrma* 2. 38. 42; *Brahmāṇḍa* 2. 27; *Haracarita* 10. 3 ff.; *Yāgīśvaramāhātmya*; *Śiva*, Dharmasaṃhitā 10. 195.
83. *Śiva*, Jñānasaṃhitā 42. 1–51.
84. Elwin (1942), pp. 115, 118, 119, and 98–9.
85. Bosch (1924), p. 249.
86. *Kauṣītaki Brāhmaṇa* 6. 1–9.
87. *Taittirīya Saṃhitā* 5. 5. 4. 1; cf. 6. 5. 8. 1–2.
88. *Taittirīya Brāhmaṇa* 1. 1. 3. 8.
89. *Śatapatha Brāhmaṇa* 2. 1. 2. 4–5; cf. 4. 4. 2. 9 and 6. 1. 3. 7–8.
90. *Śiva* 2. 4. 2. 62–4; *Skanda* 1. 2. 29. 122; 1. 1. 27. 75.
91. MhB III. 213. 41–52, III. 214. 1–17, III. 219. 1–15. N.B. III. 215. 12.
92. *Śiva*, Dharmasaṃhitā 11. 28–35.
93. *Brahma* 128. 3–46.
94. *Skanda* 1. 2. 29. 81–210.
95. MhB V. 16. 11; *Śatapatha Brāhmaṇa* 6. 3. 1. 26.
96. *Skanda* 6. 70. 65–6.
97. Dessigane (1967), p. 3 (1. 7. 57–66); p. 19 (1. 13. 31–4); p. 16 (1. 11. 43–91).
98. *Matsya* 11. 44.
99. Cf. Baldaeus, pp. 17–18; Churchill, p. 737; and Rhode, p. 236.
100. *Vāmana* S.22. 40 ff.; *Liṅga* 1. 33. 20; *Haracarita* 10. 19.
101. *Matsya* 154. 330–4.
102. Stith Thompson (1955–8), motifs A 773.2 and A 773.4.
103. *Skanda* 6. 70. 64–5 and 6. 71. 10.
104. MhB XIII. 86. 5–11; *Rāmāyaṇa* 1. 36. 23–7; *Kathāsaritsāgara* 3. 6. 60–88; *Vāyu* 72. 16–48; *Saura* 60–2; *Brahmavaivarta* 3. 1–14. The exception is *Kālikā* 48. 12–96.
105. *Matsya* 158. 43–6.
106. *Skanda* 5. 1. 34. 60–6.
107. *Skanda* 1. 1. 27. 44–102; cf. *Śiva* 2. 4. 2. 48–54 and 59.
108. Elwin (1939), p. 211 n.; cf. Crooke (1896), i, 11 and 69; Hartland, i, 25 ff.; and Meyer (1930), p. 37.

109. Volchok (1970), pp. 42–3, and (1972), pp. 305–12.
110. von Fürer-Haimendorf (1948), pp. 102, 129–37; Robinson, *passim*; and cf. below, pp. 176–8.
111. *Śiva*, Dharmasaṃhitā 10. 96–8, 163–8, 193–202, 213–14; cf. *Kūrma* (1818), 2. 37. 33–9. (*Bib. Ind.* 2. 38, pp. 727–8.)
112. *Kūrma* 2. 38. 44–5. (*Bib. Ind.* 2. 38, pp. 728–9.)
113. *Vāmana* 6. 61–2.
114. MhB IX. 47. 30–51.
115. *Śiva*, Jñānasaṃhitā 10. 170; *Brahma* 128. 3.
116. *Śiva* 2. 3. 44. 7; MhB I. 224. 27–9.
117. MhB III. 113. 23.
118. MhB III. 220. 9.
119. *Varāha* 25. 31–4, 45–7.
120. MhB III. 218. 27–30.
121. MhB XIII. 83. 48–53, 84. 1–13.
122. *Rāmāyaṇa* I. 34. 12–21, I. 35. 1–26, I. 36. 1–29.
123. *Brahmāṇḍa* 4. 30. 99–101; *Vāyu* 72. 23–40.
124. *Skanda* 1. 2. 29. 200.
125. *Mahābhāgavata* 29–30.
126. *Bhāgavata* 5. 24. 17.
127. *Matsya* 158. 27–50; *Padma* 5. 41. 118–42; cf. *Haracarita* 9. 196–221.
128. *Matsya* (Calcutta, 1876 and 1890) 158. 27–50.
129. Fouchet, p. 8; Miles, pp. 219–20.
130. Ṛg Veda X. 121. 1; Atharva Veda X. 5. 19; *Taittirīya Saṃhitā* 5. 5. 1. 2; *Śatapatha Brāhmaṇa* 6. 2. 2. 5.
131. *Śatapatha Brāhmaṇa* 11. 1. 6. 1 and 6. 1. 1. 10; Manu 1. 8–9.
132. *Amarakośa* 1. 58.
133. MhB I, Appendix 1, No. 28, 188, and MhB XII. 291. 12 and 17; *Liṅga* 1. 20. 80–6.
134. *Liṅga* 1. 20. 80–6.
135. MhB XIII. 17. 40 (1862).
136. *Vāmana* 31. 9–10.
137. *Skanda* 3. 3. 29. 23.
138. *Rāmāyaṇa* I. 37. 18–20.
139. MhB III. 218. 27.
140. MhB XIII. 84. 64–70; Nīlakaṇṭha on MhB XIII. 14. 13 (1862); *Saura* 62. 19.
141. *Matsya* 158. 37–8.
142. *Śiva* 2. 4. 2. 39; *Skanda* 1. 1. 27. 63; *Matsya* 158. 38.
143. *Vāmana* 31. 19.
144. *Brahma* 128. 3–46.
145. *Bhāgavata* 5. 24. 17.
146. *Bhāgavata* 8. 12. 33.
147. *Agni* 3. 20 ff. Cf. *Bṛhaddevatā* 7. 78.
148. MhB XIII. 84. 78–9.
149. *Vāmana* 46. 4–22.
150. Ibid. 46. 24–41.
151. Ibid. 46. 42–55.
152. Ibid. 46. 56–61.
153. Ibid. 46. 63–9.
154. Ibid. 46. 71–5. Cf. also MhB IX. 37. 28–31.

CHAPTER IV

1. *Kumārasambhava* 2. 60.
2. MhB XIII. 85. 1–12.
3. *Vāyu* 9. 75; *Liṅga* 1. 70. 324–7; *Viṣṇu* 1. 7. 12–13; *Śatapatha Brāhmaṇa* 14. 4. 2; Manu 1. 32; *Viṣṇu* 1. 7. 14.
4. *Viṣṇu* 1. 7. 13 and 17.
5. *Skanda* 5. 1. 2. 8–19.
6. *Śiva*, Vāyavīyasaṃhitā 12. 2 ff.; *Śiva* 7. 1. 14. 1–4; *Liṅga* 1. 11–16.
7. *Saura* 24. 55–67, 25. 5–29.
8. Elwin (1949), p. 258.
9. Elwin (1947), p. 239.
10. Elwin (1949), pp. 289–90.
11. Elwin (1954), pp. 422–3; cf. Elwin (1947), pp. 257–8; Dahlquist, p. 75; Ruben (1939), p. 213; Maity, pp. 191–200.
12. Elwin (1947), pp. 257–8; cf. Dimock and Ramanujan (1964), p. 304.
13. Ruben (1939), p. 213.
14. *Ānandabhairava* of Prema-dāsa, in *Sāhajiyā-sāhitya*, edited by Manindramohan Basu (University of Calcutta, Calcutta, 1932), p. 153; cf. Sukumar Sen, *Bangla Sahityer Itihas*, i, 109, cited by Maity, p. 191.
15. *Manasāmaṅgal* of Jagajjīban, ed. S. C. Bhattacharya and A. Das (University of Calcutta, Calcutta, 1960), pp. 1–20, cited by Maity, pp. 199–200.
16. *Manasāvijaya* of Vipra-dāsa, ed. S. Sen (Asiatic Society of Bengal, Calcutta, 1953), cited by Dimock (1964), p. 304.
17. *Manasāmaṅgal* of Narāyan Dev, cited by Dimock (1964), p. 304.
18. Elwin (1939), p. 325.
19. Elwin (1949), p. 293.
20. von Fürer-Haimendorf (1948), pp. 283 and 109; cf. p. 150.
21. Ṛg Veda X. 61. 7, with Sāyaṇa's commentary.
22. Ṛg Veda I. 71. 5 and 8; I. 164. 33; III. 31. 1; cf. *Bṛhaddevatā* 4. 110–11.
23. Ṛg Veda X. 61. 7 (*adhiṣkand*); cf. Atharva Veda X. 10. 16, and Fišer, p. 45.
24. *Tāṇḍya Mahābrāhmaṇa* 8. 2. 10; cf. *Bṛhadāraṇyaka Upaniṣad* 1. 4. 1–4.
25. *Aitareya Brāhmaṇa* 13. 9–10; cf. *Śatapatha Brāhmaṇa* 1. 7. 4. 1–7; Hopkins (1895), p. 463; *Brahmāṇḍa* 3. 1. 29–38; *Maitrāyaṇi Saṃhitā* 4. 2. 12.
26. *Śatapatha Brāhmaṇa* 1. 7. 4. 1–7.
27. *Gopatha Brāhmaṇa* 2. 1. 2. For later versions of the destruction of Dakṣa's sacrifice, cf. MhB XIII. 145. 17–18; XII. 274. 5–59; XII, Appendix 1, no. 28, 1–155; *Kūrma* 1. 14. 53 ff. (*Bib. Ind.* 1. 15, p. 165); *Varāha* 33 and 21. 1–88; *Vāmana* 5. 10–20, 26, 43; *Liṅga* 99. 1 ff.; *Bhāgavata* 4. 24; *Śiva* 2. 2. 26 ff.
28. *Śiva* 2. 2. 37. 45–6; *Vāmana* 5. 26, 43, 32; *Vāyu* 30. 155–9.
29. *Kauṣītaki Brāhmaṇa* 6. 1–9.
30. *Bṛhaddevatā* 4. 110–11; cf. Lévi, p. 21.
31. *Manmathonmathana* 1. 19.
32. *Matsya* 3. 30–44 and 4. 11–21.
33. *Śiva* 2. 2. 2. 15–42, 2. 2. 3. 1–78, 2. 2. 4. 1–34.
34. *Kālikā* 1. 24–65, 2. 1–59, 3. 1–49.
35. *Mahābhāgavata* 21. 35–45.
36. *Skanda* 5. 2. 13. 2–20.
37. Stacton, p. 41.
38. Dessigane (1967), p. 8 (1. 4. 1–76).

39. *Śiva* 2. 2. 19. 17–19; and in J. L. Shastri's translation of 2. 2. 3. 63–4.
40. *Brahma* 72. 18; *Vāmana* 27. 56–9; cf. *Śiva*, Jñānasaṃhitā 18. 62–8; *Śiva* 2. 3. 49. 3–10; *Skanda* 1. 1. 26. 15–22.
41. *Saura* 59. 54–61.
42. *Śiva* 2. 2. 19. 1–76; 2. 2. 20. 2–25; cf. *Skanda* 6. 77. 16–75.
43. *Kūrma* 2. 31. 22 ff.; cf. von Stietencron, *passim*.
44. *Brahma* 135. 1–25.
45. *Baudhāyana Dharmaśāstra* II. 1. 1. 3; Manu 11. 123, 2. 181–2, 11. 106; MhB XII. 159. 27, XII. 207. 13; *Vāyu* 18. 8–9; *Agni* 169. 18; cf. Meinhard, pp. 41–2.
46. *Varāha* 97. 1–18; cf. Jouveau-Dubreuil, ii, 32; Baldaeus, pp. 17–18; *Sāmba* 16–17; *Skanda* 5. 28. 1–14, 5. 3. 38. 6–68, 1. 1. 6. 2–68; *Padma* 5. 17. 35–51; Dessigane (1967), pp. 84–5 (2. 32. 6–47). See Appendix A.
47. *Śiva* 3. 8. 36–66; 3. 9. 1–57.
48. von Stietencron, p. 866. Śiva is Brahmā's son in MhB XII. 349. 67, XII. 351. 11, XII. 352. 30, XII. 166. 16; *Harivaṃśa* 43; *Mārkaṇḍeya* 50. 4; *Viṣṇu* 1. 7. 4; *Vāyu* 1. 9. 61; *Kūrma* 1. 11. 1; *Liṅga* 1. 41. 11. Brahmā is Śiva's son in MhB XII. 14. 4; *Vāyu* 34. 41; *Liṅga* 1. 20. 73, 1. 41. 11.
49. *Skanda* 5. 1. 2. 1–65.
50. *Bhaviṣya* 3. 4. 13. 1–19.
51. *Śiva*, Jñānasaṃhitā 49. 65–80.
52. *Skanda* 3. 40. 1–59.
53. Dubois, p. 613.
54. Told by the temple drummer (Pombaikaran) of Dharanpuram, Kongu; personal communication from Brenda E. F. Beck.
55. Cf. *Liṅga* 1. 85. 11 and 13; 1. 96. 40; von Stietencron, p. 866; Rawson (1961), p. 163: 'A Syncretic Image of Brahma and Siva'.
56. *Śiva* 2. 2. 19. 56; cf. Moor, p. 106.
57. *Liṅga* 1. 63. 2.
58. Ṛg Veda X. 72. 4–5; Agrawala (1966), p. 11.
59. *Harivaṃśa* 3. 22. 1–7.
60. *Bhāgavata* 4. 2. 22–3; *Kūrma* 1. 14. 63 (*Bib. Ind.*, p. 156); cf. *Vāyu* 30. 61; *Skanda* 7. 2. 9. 42.
61. *Śatapatha Brāhmaṇa* 3. 2. 4. 18; cf. Ṛg Veda VIII. 2. 40; *Śatapatha Brāhmaṇa* 6. 2. 2. 6; *Bhāgavata* 4. 7. 3; *Śiva* 2. 2. 42. 22–9; *Skanda* 4. 2. 89 ff.
62. *Tāṇḍya Mahābrāhmaṇa* 7. 9. 16.
63. *Varāha* 33. 1–33.
64. *Varāha* 33. 10 and 31; *Skanda* 4. 2. 87–9.
65. *Varāha* 21. 1–88.
66. Cf. *Vāyu* (*Bib. Ind.*) 1. 10. 42–3.
67. *Varāha* 33. 4.
68. *Śiva*, Dharmasaṃhitā 49. 35–86.
69. MhB X. 17. 10–26.
70. *Śiva*, Dharmasaṃhitā 10. 1–23.
71. *Skanda* 6. 1. 50–2.
72. *Kūrma* 2. 38. 39–41; cf. *Haracarita* 10. 74; *Yāgīśvaramāhātmya* 26a. 14.
73. *Vāmana* 6. 93–6; cf. 6. 82.
74. *Brahmāṇḍa* 4. 30. 62.
75. MhB III, Appendix I, No. 6, 135.
76. *Brahmavaivarta* 4. 33. 5.

77. *Skanda* 7. 3. 40. 4 and 41, and 7. 1. 100; cf. *Pārvatīpariṇaya* 4. 34 and 5. 32. 3; Stacton, p. 116.
78. Elwin (1949), p. 257.
79. Manu 8. 374.
80. Manu 8. 352–3, 8. 364; *Āpastambīya Dharmasūtra* 2. 10. 26. 20–1.
81. Yalman, pp. 89–90.
82. Manu 11. 171.
83. Manu 11. 105; *Agni* 169. 22; MhB XII. 36. 17; XII. 159. 47.
84. *Śiva*, Dharmasaṃhitā 10. 187–90.
85. *Kūrma* 2. 38. 39–41; *Skanda* 6. 1. 49–52; *Haracarita* 10; *Yāgīśvaramāhātmya* 26a. 14.
86. *Nāradasmṛti* 12. 12.
87. *Śiva*, Dharmasaṃhitā 10. 187–90; cf. B. K. Sarkar, pp. 234–5.
88. *Brahmāṇḍa* 2. 27. 23.
89. *Rāmāyaṇa* 1. 47. 15–32, 1. 48. 1–10.
90. *Rāmāyaṇa* 1. 48. 1–10; MhB XII. 329. 14. 1–2; *Śiva*, Dharmasaṃhitā 11. 1–12.
91. *Padma* 1. 56. 15–53.
92. *Śatapatha Brāhmaṇa* 12. 7. 1. 10–12; 5. 2. 3. 8.
93. *Padma* 5. 26. 100 ff.
94. *Skanda* 6. 1. 55–62.
95. Stacton, p. 119.
96. *Yāgīśvaramāhātmya* 26a. 14.
97. Elwin (1949), p. 256; cf. p. 473.
98. Atharva Veda XI. 5. 12.
99. Elwin (1949), p. 258.
100. Agrawala (1964), p. 16; *Nārada Pañcarātra* 3. 1, cited by Daniélou (1964), p. 225.
101. Baldaeus, pp. 17–18.
102. *Skanda* 1. 1. 3. 11–13.
103. *Śiva* 2. 2. 19. 58–60.
104. *Liṅga* 1. 41. 7–12.
105. MhB VII, Appendix I, No. 8, 70–131.
106. Elwin (1949), p. 420.
107. *Matsya* 4. 30–2; *Vāyu* 1. 10. 42–59.
108. *Brahmāṇḍa* 2. 9. 68–92; *Śiva* 7. 14; *Liṅga* 1. 6. 10–22.
109. *Skanda* 7. 2. 9. 5–17.
110. *Kūrma* 1. 10. 17–40; *Śiva* 2. 1. 15. 49–64.
111. *Saura* 23. 16–52, 25. 5–29.
112. *Bhāgavata* 3. 12. 1–26.
113. *Liṅga* 1. 70. 300–24; *Vāyu* 10. 42–59.
114. *Liṅga* 1. 70. 324–39.
115. Watts, pp. 88–9.

CHAPTER V

1. *Bṛhaddharma* 2. 53. 40–1; *Śiva* 2. 2. 8. 12–22; *Skanda* 5. 2. 13; *Kālikā* 4–13.
2. An early reference to the burning of Kāma by Śiva appears in an inscription of A.D. 473–4, cited in Fleet (1888), No. 18, p. 81, pl. XI, 11. 21–3.
3. MhB XIII. 17. 45 and 72.
4. *Kumārasambhava* 5. 30.
5. *Śiva* 2. 3. 12. 28–33.

6. *Śiva* 2. 2. 8. 17–18; cf. *Matsya* 154. 213–16, and *Skanda* 1. 2. 24. 17–20.
7. *Matsya* 154. 213–16; *Skanda* 1. 2. 24. 17–20.
8. *Manmathonmathana* IV, after verse 25.
9. *Śiva* 3. 22. 45–55; 3. 23. 1–36.
10. *Śiva*, Dharmasaṃhitā 9. 46–61.
11. MhB XIII, Appendix I, No. 4, 66–7, and XIII. 14. 101–2.
12. Tulsī Dās, p. 46 (C. 90).
13. MhB XII. 183. 10. 3–5; cf. MhB XIII. 17, 98, and Nīlakaṇṭha on MhB XIII. 17. 101.
14. *Śiva* 2. 3. 24. 18–28 and 2. 2. 16. 30–6, 2. 3. 24. 60–75; cf. *Skanda* 1. 1. 22. 19–27.
15. *Skanda* 1. 1. 21. 82–99.
16. *Bhaviṣya* 3. 4. 14. 56–8; *Śiva* 2. 2. 17. 12; *Mahābhāgavata* 7. 1 and 24. 28; *Śiva*, Jñānasaṃhitā 9–18, 10. 73; *Śiva* 2. 3. 18. 31–43; *Skanda* 1. 1. 21, 5. 2. 13; *Vāmana* 6. 27–48; *Matsya* 154. 237–8.
17. *Skanda* 2. 2. 12. 22; cf. *Śiva* 2. 2. 17. 63–4; *Kālikā* 10. 54–5.
18. *Kālikā* 44. 110–12; cf. *Mahābhāgavata* 25. 23–5; *Vāmana* 6. 36; *Pārvatīpariṇaya* 4. 7.
19. *Śiva* 2. 3. 18. 38.
20. *Śiva* 2. 2. 17. 18.
21. *Kālikā* 10. 1–34.
22. *Śiva* 2. 2. 17. 63–4.
23. *Kālikā* 10. 54–5.
24. *Mahābhāgavata* 24. 28.
25. *Mahābhāgavata* 25. 25; cf. *Vāmana* 6. 36.
26. *Pārvatīpariṇaya* 4. 7.
27. *Kumārasambhava* 6. 95.
28. *Śiva*, Jñānasaṃhitā 10. 73b.
29. *Skanda* 1. 1. 24. 52–5.
30. *Śiva* 2. 5. 51. 35–46.
31. *Subhāṣitaratnakoṣa*, No. 323, Ingalls's translation.
32. *Harṣacarita*, p. 20, line 27 (Kane ed. p. 11, lines 17–18).
33. *Śatakatraya* 112.
34. *Mahābhāgavata* 22. 99–102.
35. *Śiva*, Jñānasaṃhitā 15. 39.
36. *Brahmavaivarta* 4. 41. 44.
37. *Śiva* 2. 2. 24. 16; 2. 3. 4. 32–40; *Padma* 6. 101. 10–11.
38. *Śiva* 2. 3. 29. 33–4.
39. *Śiva* 2. 3. 4. 40–1.
40. *Śiva* 2. 3. 47. 26.
41. Nīlakaṇṭha on MhB XIII. 17. 52.
42. Charpentier, p. 170.
43. Narayan (1949), p. 250.
44. Ibid., pp. 101 and 139.
45. *Matsya* 154. 235–48; *Haracarita* 9. 53–7.
46. *Skanda* 5. 2. 13. 27–35.
47. Daniélou (1964), p. 172.
48. Nur O. Yalman, personal communication based on field work undertaken in central Ceylon in 1954–5; cited by Leach (1962), pp. 89–90.
49. *Bhaviṣya* 3. 4. 14. 45.
50. *Varāha* 23. 16–19; cf. *Śiva* 2. 1. 19. 1–23.
51. Gupta, pp. 103–4.

52. Baldaeus, p. 21.
53. *Subhāṣitaratnakoṣa*, No. 4, Ingalls's translation.
54. *Śiva*, Dharmasaṃhitā 10. 196.
55. *Bhāgavata* 2. 7. 7; cf. *Subhāṣitaratnakoṣa*, No. 420.
56. Lal, pp. 22 and 24.
57. *Subhāṣitaratnakoṣa*, No. 395, Ingalls's translation; cf. *Śiva* 2. 3. 51. 14.
58. Cf. *Skanda* 5. 3. 150. 7–9, and *Vāmana* 34. 19–23, 62. 34–8.
59. *Skanda* 5. 3. 150. 7–35.
60. *Bhikṣāṭanakāvya* 2. 1.
61. Hislop, iii, 29 ff.
62. *Mahābhāgavata* 22. 34–43; cf. 20. 25–38.
63. *Kuvalayānanda* of Appaya Diksita, cited by Rao, ii, 1, 60.
64. *Śiva*, Jñānasaṃhitā 14. 72.
65. *Skanda* 1. 2. 25. 1–5.
66. *Śiva* 2. 3. 13. 51.
67. *Śiva* 2. 3. 21. 26–8.
68. *Brahmāṇḍa* 4. 30. 7 ff.; *Mahābhāgavata* 20. 25–38; *Brahmavaivarta* 4. 38. 15–25.
69. *Skanda* 5. 2. 55. 1–5.
70. *Skanda* 1. 1. 22. 38–40.
71. *Brahma* 34. 94; *Matsya* 154. 310–13.
72. *Śiva* 2. 3. 24. 19; 2. 3. 24. 53; P. Thomas (1959), p. 117.
73. Tulsī Dās, pp. 39–46 (C. 74–89).
74. *Śiva* 2. 3. 12. 6–12, 28–33.
75. *Mahābhāgavata* 3. 15–70.
76. *Bṛhaddharma* 2. 31. 16–36.
77. *Saura* 54. 1–4, 16–20, 55. 1–6.
78. *Matsya* 154. 449–551; *Padma* 5. 4. 346–450.
79. *Matsya*, Vidyārṇava's translation, p. 101, cliv. 451.
80. *Haracarita* 9. 151–4.
81. *Brahma* 38. 10.
82. Dessigane (1967), p. 15 (1. 10. 85–90).
83. *Saura* 54. 1–4, 16–20, 55. 1–6.
84. *Skanda* 5. 1. 34. 36–7; *Śiva* 2. 3. 24. 18–28; *Kālikā* 3. 15, 4. 16–17; *Brahmavaivarta* 4. 39. 57; *Haracarita* 9. 154.
85. *Skanda* 1. 1. 35. 15.
86. *Skanda* 1. 3. 2. 17. 13–23.
87. *Skanda* 6. 245. 32–42.
88. *Śiva* 2. 3. 51. 1–14.
89. *Kālikā* 4. 10–17.
90. *Bṛhaddharma* 2. 53. 44.
91. *Kathāsaritsāgara* 2. 1. 1; cf. 1. 1. 1, 3. 1. 2; and cf. *Kumārasambhava* 1. 41.
92. *Subhāṣitaratnakoṣa*, No. 395.
93. *Bṛhatkathāmañjarī* 1. 1. 49.
94. *Subhāṣitaratnakoṣa*, No. 455, Ingalls's translation.
95. *Subhāṣitāvalī* of Vallabha, No. 1558, translated by Brough, No. 188.
96. *Bhikṣāṭanakāvya* 8. 20.
97. *Bhikṣāṭanakāvya* 9. 6.
98. *Subhāṣitaratnakoṣa*, No. 395, Ingalls's translation.
99. *Śiva* 2. 3. 51. 14.
100. Daniélou (1964), pp. 98–9.
101. *Matsya* 154. 250–2.

102. *Subhāṣitaratnakoṣa*, No. 441, Ingalls's translation.
103. *Abhijñānaśākuntala* III. 20, alternative verse; *Caturvargacintāmaṇi* 2. 2. 366.
104. *Vāmana* 6. 94–107.
105. Fleet, p. 81.
106. *Devībhāgavata* 7. 30. 77; *Skanda* 1. 1. 21. 59. Cf. *Bṛhaddevatā* 7. 78.
107. Gupta, p. xi. Cf. *Matsya* 154. 506–12, *Kumārasambhava* 5. 14.
108. Ruben (1944), p. 159; Meyer (1937), i, 186 ff.
109. Meyer (1937), i, 206.
110. *Kārttika Māhātmya* 4. 33.
111. Carpenter, p. 232 n., citing *Epigraphica Indica* v, 13; Meyer (1937), i, 132, citing Crooke, p. 74; cf. Marriott, p. 210.
112. Crooke (1896), ii, 319–20.
113. Balys, motifs D 1886, E 42, and E 66.1.
114. *Śatapatha Brāhmaṇa* 6. 8. 2. 1–2 and 6; cf. 6. 2. 1. 15 and 2. 2. 4. 8.
115. *Brahmāṇḍa* 2. 27. 112–13; *Liṅga* 1. 34. 7–8 and 1–3; cf. *Haṭhayogapradīpikā* 3. 98; *Śatapatha Brāhmaṇa* 6. 8. 2. 1–6; *Padma* 4. 103–26; *Śiva*, Jñānasaṃhitā 48. 86–9.
116. *Bṛhaddharma* 2. 53. 45; *Kālikā* 45. 107, 115; 44. 125; *Mahābhāgavata* 24. 1–8; cf. *Brahmavaivarta* 4. 43. 27, 4. 45. 20; *Śiva* 2. 3. 19. 27, 2. 5. 23. 51; *Matsya* 154. 259; *Kumārasambhava* 4. 34, 4. 27.
117. *Kālikā* 45. 117–18.
118. *Brahmavaivarta* 4. 43. 27, 4. 38. 12; cf. *Śiva* 2. 5. 23. 51.
119. *Kumārasambhava* 4. 27 and 4. 34; *Matsya* 154. 259; *Śiva* 2. 3. 19. 27.
120. *Brahmavaivarta* 4. 45. 20.
121. *Brahmāṇḍa* 4. 11. 30–1 and 4. 16–29 *passim.*
122. *Bṛhaddharma* 2. 53. 44.
123. *Brahma* 38. 10; *Liṅga* 1. 101. 43; cf. Tulasī Dās, p. 45.
124. *Śiva* 2. 1. 2. 20–1.
125. *Manmathonmathana*, after 4. 30.
126. *Pārvatīpariṇaya* 4. 34 and 5. 32. 3.
127. *Mattavilāsaprahasana* 10, translated by L. D. Barnett.
128. *Bhaviṣya* 3. 4. 14. 80; *Śiva* 2. 3. 19. 37–48.
129. *Bṛhatkathāmañjarī* 3. 348.
130. *Kālikā* 52. 111; *Naiṣadhacarita* 17. 17.
131. *Saura* 40. 10–74.
132. *Kumārasambhava* 7. 92–3.
133. *Kathāsaritsāgara* 3. 6. 60–73; *Bṛhatkathāmañjarī* 3. 342–56.
134. *Brahmāṇḍa* 4. 30. 58–61 and 71–84.
135. *Skanda* 7. 1. 200. 9–30.
136. *Bṛhatkathāmañjarī* 3. 346.
137. *Śiva* 2. 1. 2. 8, 2. 2. 21. 28; *Kumārasambhava* 4. 8 and 6. 3.
138. *Brahmāṇḍa* 4. 30. 71–2; *Skanda* 5. 1. 34. 49.
139. *Śiva* 2. 2. 21. 28–41.
140. *Mārkaṇḍeya* 1. 44.
141. *Skanda* 2. 4. 17. 10; cf. *Padma* 6. 11. 6.
142. *Matsya* 154. 473; *Kumārasambhava* 7. 67; cf. *Vāmana* 27. 23–32; *Liṅga* 1. 29. 11; *Bhikṣāṭanakāvya* 8. 6.
143. *Śiva* 2. 3. 25. 45, 2. 3. 23. 5; *Skanda* 1. 1. 21. 150, 1. 2. 25. 67; *Matsya* 154. 327–8.
144. *Matsya* 154. 327–8.
145. *Śiva* 2. 3. 23. 12; *Skanda* 1. 1. 21. 155.
146. *Pārvatīpariṇaya* 4. 3–4.

147. *Kumarāsambhava* 5. 54.
148. *Subhāṣitaratnakoṣa*, No. 65, Ingalls's translation.
149. *Bhaviṣya* 3. 4. 14. 45.
150. *Brahma* 38. 1–13.
151. *Kathāsaritsāgara* 56. 170–2; cf. Murray Emeneau, *Kota Texts*; Balys, D 2061.2.1.1.
152. *Skanda* 5. 2. 14. 2–30.
153. *Skanda* 3. 3. 13. 33–44, 3. 3. 14. 16 ff.: 6. 245. 32–51, 6. 246. 1–18 ff.
154. MhB XIII. 83. 53.
155. *Kumārasambhava* 10. 1–25.
156. *Matsya* 154. 250–5.
157. *Subhāṣitaratnakoṣa*, No. 171, Ingalls's translation.
158. *Harṣacarita* 1. 17 (Kane ed.). Cowell and Thomas, p. 3.
159. *Bhaviṣya* 3. 4. 14. 53; *Śiva* 2. 3. 19. 10.
160. *Skanda* 3. 3. 26. 4.
161. *Kālikā* 44. 121–2; *Skanda* 1. 1. 21. 96.
162. Dessigane (1964), No. 48, pp. 61–2.
163. MhB XIII. 17. 68 (alternate verse); Nīlakaṇṭha on XIII. 17. 70.
164. *Kāmakalāvilāsa*, No. 7.
165. *Matsya* 7. 28–9.
166. *Yāgīśvaramāhātmya* 25b. 1 and 26a. 2; *Śiva*, Dharmasaṃhitā 10. 111; *Bhikṣāṭanakāvya* 8. 4–5; *Śiva* 5. 44. 96.
167. *Skanda* 5. 3. 38. 17; *Padma* 5. 53. 6.
168. *Śiva* 2. 3. 50. 38; *Brahmāṇḍa* 4. 14. 18–21.
169. *Śiva* 2. 2. 4. 6.
170. *Brahmavaivarta* 4. 46. 9–11, 21–30.
171. *Śiva* 5. 4. 16–39.
172. *Brahmavaivarta* 4. 35. 39.
173. P. Thomas (1959), p. 114.
174. Stacton, p. 40.
175. *Śiva* 7. 1. 24. 43–5.

CHAPTER VI

1. *Bhikṣāṭanakāvya* 9. 1.
2. *Yāgīśvaramāhātmya* 26a and 27.
3. *Liṅga* 1. 29. 25–36.
4. MhB XIII, Appendix 1, No. 4, 66–77.
5. *Daśakumāracarita* II, p. 85.
6. *Śiva*, Dharmasaṃhitā 10. 187 and 10. 78–80.
7. *Skanda* 6. 258. 18; *Padma* 5. 17. 62.
8. *Bhikṣāṭanakāvya* 9. 13.
9. MhB XIII. 17. 39; Nīlakaṇṭha on XIII. 17. 42.
10. *Devī* 8. 19, p. 29, lines 29 ff.; cf. Sonnerat, p. 176.
11. *Skanda* 1. 1. 34. 116–30.
12. *Skanda* 6. 258. 1–10, 6. 259. 75; 3. 3. 26. 3 and 11.
13. *Skanda* 7. 3. 39. 5–12; *Kālikā* 18. 1–111; Stacton, p. 108.
14. P. Thomas (1959), p. 114.
15. Stacton, p. 118.
16. *Padma* 5. 5. 3. 2.
17. *Yāgīśvaramāhātmya* 24–34.
18. *Skanda* 7. 3. 39. 5–12.

19. Versions of the myth: Herrenschmidt, pp. 110 and 327; Elwin (1947), pp. 175, 230, 240–8; Hislop, ii, 164–397, and iii, 29 ff.; Chenevix-Trench, p. 101 ff.; von Fürer-Haimendorf (1948), pp. 140–2, 162–5. Interpretations: Herrenschmidt, pp. 283, 321, 334, 336; Elwin (1947), pp. 68, 236–9, 252; Chenevix-Trench, ii, 111; von Fürer-Haimendorf (1948), p. 326; von Fürer-Haimendorf (1967), p. 326. Another part of this cycle is discussed above, pp. 100–1.
20. Elwin (1947), pp. 240–3.
21. von Fürer-Haimendorf (1943), p. 220, and Elwin (1939), p. 328.
22. *Padma* 6. 104. 28.
23. *Śiva* 2. 5. 22. 50–1.
24. Elmore, pp. 81–2.
25. Ibid., pp. 91–2.
26. *Padma* 5. 17. 269–71.
27. *Padma* 6. 282. 20–36; *Skanda* 6. 1. 55.
28. Elwin (1949), p. 392.
29. *Yāgīśvaramāhātmya* 24b.
30. *Saura* 69. 37–40.
31. *Bhaviṣya* 3. 4. 17. 67.
32. Sonnerat, pp. 176–9.
33. Dessigane (1967), pp. 191 ff. (6. 13. 43).
34. *Bṛhadāraṇyaka Upaniṣad* 6. 4. 3.
35. Manu 11. 121–2.
36. *Brahma* 35. 31–60.
37. MhB IX. 51. 1–23.
38. *Śiva* 2. 5. 23. 48–9; 2. 5. 24. 52; *Padma* 6. 106. 13–14.
39. Dessigane (1964), 43. 23.
40. Ingalls (1962), pp. 283–4.
41. Auboyer (1960), p. 62.
42. *Pāśupata Sūtra* 3. 6–19; Ingalls (1962), pp. 287–91.
43. Ingalls (1962), pp. 295 and 291.
44. *Śiva*, Jñānasaṃhitā 42. 23–4; *Śiva* 4. 12. 26–7.
45. Manu 3. 100.
46. *Kūrma* 2. 39. 56–62; cf. 1. 16. 117, and *Vāmana* 6. 87.
47. Dessigane (1967), pp. 192 ff. (6. 13. 43–85).
48. Alberuni, ii, 103.
49. Wilford (1795), p. 397.
50. *Pāśupata Sūtra* III. 16–17.
51. *Kūrma* 2. 38. 32.
52. Balys, motif K 1311.
53. *Śiva* 2. 5. 22. 3–43; *Padma* 6. 104. 20. Cf. *Liṅga* 1. 97.
54. *Padma* 6. 4. 50.
55. *Vāyu* 69. 144–5; *Padma* 6. 16. 46–7.
56. *Padma* 6. 27. 1–17.
57. *Śiva* 2. 5. 40. 1–43; 2. 5. 41. 1–34; *Brahmavaivarta* 2. 16. 1–208; 2. 17. 1–90; 2. 21. 1–104.
58. *Śiva*, Dharmasaṃhitā 4. 68–9; *Śiva* 2. 5. 59. 1–32; 7. 1. 24. 26–7, 47.
59. Balys, motif D 40.2.1.
60. Cited by Martin, p. 166, and MacMunn, p. 41.
61. *Śiva* 4. 10. 18–24; MhB I. 173. 1–24; *Bhāgavata* 9. 9. 25–49.
62. MhB I. 109. 5–31.
63. Elwin (1949), pp. 360–1.

64. *Śiva*, Dharmasaṃhitā 10. 5–6; *Skanda* 1. 2. 29. 78–9.
65. Tawney and Penzer, ii, Appendix 3, 'The Poison Damsel', pp. 275–313.
66. *Manasāmaṅgal* of Ketaka-Dasa, edited by Jatindramohan Bhattacarya (Calcutta, University of Calcutta, 1949); translated by Dimock (1963), pp. 250–5.
67. *Matsya* 155. 1–34, 156. 1–40. 157. 1–24, 158. 1–27; *Padma* 5. 41. 1–118; *Skanda* 1. 2. 27. 58–84; 1. 2. 28. 1–14; 1. 2. 29. 1–81.
68. *Matsya* 156. 37; *Skanda* 1. 2. 29. 30–1; *Padma* 5. 41. 72; cf. *Matsya* (1876), 155. 26.
69. *Śiva*, Dharmasaṃhitā 10. 49–55.
70. Daniélou (1964), p. 110; Sāyaṇa on Ṛg Veda 1. 114. 6.
71. *Śatapatha Brāhmaṇa* 4. 4. 2. 11–15.
72. *Skanda* 6. 258. 19.
73. *Padma* 6. 18. 82–90.
74. MhB XII. 278. 1–38; *Vāmana* 43. 25–44.
75. *Vāmana* 9–10, 33, 37, 40–4; *Kūrma* 1. 16. 123–240; *Liṅga* 1. 93. 1–25; *Matsya* 179. 1–86; *Padma* 5. 43. 1–95; *Saura* 29. 11–50; *Śiva*, Dharmasaṃhitā 4. 4–208; *Śiva* 2. 5. 42. 1–2, 2. 5. 49. 40; *Skanda* 7. 2. 9. 151–63; *Varāha* 27. 1–39; *Viṣṇudharmottara* 1. 226. 1–82.
76. *Brahmāṇḍa* 2. 27; *Skanda* 6. 1. 13.
77. *Haracarita* 10. 27–188; *Vāmana* S.22. 85.
78. *Yāgīśvaramāhātmya* 27b. 10.
79. *Skanda* 6. 258. 25–6.
80. *Śiva*, Dharmasaṃhitā 10. 79–215; *Haracarita* 10. 3–188; *Liṅga* 1. 29, 1. 31.
81. *Śiva* 2. 3. 12. 27.
82. *Śiva* 2. 2. 3. 43.
83. *Vāmana* S.22, 49–50.
84. *Haracarita* 10. 26–30.
85. *Haracarita* 10. 63; cf. *Darpadalana* 7. 25–54.
86. Agrawala (1964), p. 86.
87. Giteau, pp. 133–4.
88. Crooke (1906), p. 144.
89. *Liṅga* 2. 5. 52–154.
90. *Śiva* 2. 1. 2. 1–55; 3. 1–59; 4. 1–76; 5. 1–20.
91. *Śiva*, Jñānasaṃhitā 42. 1–51; *Liṅga* 1. 29. 5; Dessigane (1960), No. 32, 1–3.
92. MhB XIII. 2. 36–85; cf. *Śiva* 2. 3. 35. 10 and 34.
93. *Liṅga* 1. 29. 44–63.
94. *Brahmavaivarta* 4. 86. 81; cf. Dubois, pp. 534–5.
95. *Śiva* 3. 28. 1–31.
96. *Śiva* 3. 27. 1–69.
97. *Ayyar*, pp. 153–4; cf. Jesudasan, p. 153.
98. *Yāgīśvaramāhātmya* 25a; *Skanda* 5. 3. 38. 6–67.
99. *Skanda* 5. 3. 38. 1–15.
100. *Vāmana* S.22. 47–52; *Haracarita* 10. 3–188; *Darpadalana* 7. 17–71; *Saura* 69.
101. *Śiva*, Dharmasaṃhitā 10. 199.
102. Ibid. 10. 213–14.
103. *Vāmana* S.22. 84.
104. Agrawala (1964), p. 87.
105. *Kūrma* 2. 39. 39–40; *Haracarita* 10. 7–8; *Skanda* 7. 3. 39. 8; *Vāmana* S.22–3.
106. *Darpadalana* 7. 68; *Vāmana* S.22. 49–50.

107. *Skanda* 1. 1. 10. 71–4.
108. *Skanda* 5. 2. 11. 1–26.
109. *Brahmāṇḍa* 2. 27; cf. *Vāmana* S.22. 75–86; *Darpadalana* 7; *Kūrma* 2. 39. 40–55; *Liṅga* 1. 29 and 1. 31.
110. *Yāgīśvaramāhātmya*; *Śiva*, Dharmasaṃhitā 10; Jñānasaṃhitā 42; *Liṅga* 1. 29 and 1. 31; *Skanda* 5. 3. 11, 6. 1. 6, 7. 1. 187, 7. 3. 39; *Brahmāṇḍa* 2. 27.
111. *Yāgīśvaramāhātmya* 27b.
112. *Haracarita* 10. 31.
113. *Liṅga* 1. 29. 1–83; 1. 31. 21–45.
114. Rao, ii, 1, 302.
115. *Kūrma* 2. 38. 4–5 and 2. 39. 45–6.
116. *Kūrma* 2. 38. 25–32 (*Bib. Ind.* reading).
117. *Kūrma* 2. 38. 60–2, 2. 39. 2–6.
118. *Yāgīśvaramāhātmya* 27b; *Kūrma* 2. 39. 2–5, 2. 38. 60; (*Bib. Ind.* 2. 38, p. 734).
119. *Varāha* 33. 21.
120. *Śiva* 4. 12. 11; *Brahmāṇḍa* 2. 27. 2; *Yāgīśvaramāhātmya* 26b. 3; *Darpadalana* 7. 70–1.
121. Nīlakaṇṭha on MhB XIII. 17. 202 (XIII. 17. 99 in critical edition).
122. *Kathāsaritsāgara* 3. 6. 131–3.
123. *Saura* 29. 11–50; *Kūrma* 1. 16. 123–240; *Skanda* 7. 2. 9. 158; *Vāmana* 33. 35–8; *Śiva*, Dharmasaṃhitā 11. 1; *Rāmāyaṇa* 1. 47. 17; *Brahmavaivarta* 4. 47. 19–44; *Mārkaṇḍeya* 58. 34–78, 59. 1–31 (*Bib. Ind.* 61. 34–78, 62. 1–31); *Harivaṃśa* 2. 117. 1–25; *Śiva* 2. 5. 51. 44–62.
124. *Brahma* 81. 1–6.
125. Tulsī Dās, p. 31 (C. 52–3).
126. *Skanda* 1. 1. 35. 1–60.
127. *Kālikā* 52. 105. 122.
128. *Kālikā* 49. 1–92, 50. 1–64, 51. 1–60, 52. 1–55, 53. 1–217.
129. *Liṅga* 2. 5. 52–154; *Śiva* 2. 1. 2–5.
130. *Matsya* 157. 1–2, 158. 8–9; *Padma* 5. 41. 1–118; *Skanda* 1. 2. 29. 33–7; *Bhaviṣya* 3. 4. 17. 78; cf. *Kathāsaritsāgara* 114. 56–75.
131. *Brahmavaivarta* 4. 28. 17.
132. *Prabodhacandrodaya* III, 16; John Taylor's translation, p. 51.
133. Eliade (1958), p. 259.
134. Singer, p. 133.
135. MhB XIII, Appendix 1, No. 5, 69.
136. *Bhāgavata* 10. 8. 35–44.
137. Cf. *Bhagavad Gītā* 11. 5–31.
138. *Kālikā* 52. 150–1.

CHAPTER VII

1. *Vāyu* 2. 30. 38 (Bombay); cf. ASS 92. 31–2 and *Bib. Ind.* 2. 30. 31–2.
2. *Skanda* 4. 2. 87. 29–35.
3. *Brahmāṇḍa* 2. 27. 28–9.
4. *Matsya* 154. 330–9; *Padma* 5. 40. 322–33; *Haracarita* 9. 96–100.
5. *Bhāgavata* 6. 17. 1 ff.
6. *Śiva* 2. 2. 16. 41, 44, 2. 3. 36. 12, 2. 3. 27. 32; *Skanda* 1. 1. 35. 27–34, 1. 1. 22. 67–81, 2. 25. 59–66.
7. *Śiva* 2. 2. 16. 39, 44.
8. *Śiva* 2. 3. 26. 12.

9. *Skanda* 1. 1. 35. 27–34.
10. *Bhaviṣya* 3. 4. 14. 40–3.
11. *Bṛhaddharma* 2. 60. 7–31; cf. *Haracarita* 9. 175–84.
12. Elwin (1949), p. 431.
13. *Skanda* 1. 1. 22. 67–8; 1. 2. 25. 59–66; *Śiva* 2. 3. 27. 32; Narayan (1964), p. 94; Thomas (1958), p. 32.
14. *Śiva* 2. 3. 25. 45–51; Tulsī Dās, p. 41 (C. 79).
15. *Skanda* 1. 3. 2. 19. 10; *Śiva*, Dharmasaṃhitā 4. 97–102; *Śiva* 2. 5. 44. 50–5, 45. 47–8.
16. *Śiva*, Dharmasaṃhitā 4. 4–208; *Vāmana* 41. 49.
17. *Padma* 6. 11. 4–8.
18. *Padma* 6. 11. 45–7, 49; 6. 11. 25–6, 6. 101. 19–20; *Skanda* 2. 4. 17. 18–19; *Śiva* 2. 5. 19. 8–9.
19. *Vāmana* 27. 44.
20. *Skanda* 7. 2. 9. 24; *Bhāgavata* 4. 2. 11–16.
21. *Padma* 1. 5. 39–44.
22. Stacton, pp. 82 and 97.
23. *Nāradasmṛti* 12. 8–19, 12. 97; Manu 9. 78–9.
24. *Skanda* 1. 2. 23. 1–59; *Śiva* 2. 3. 8. 8–11; cf. *Matsya* 154. 145–6, 175–94.
25. *Haracarita* 9. 39, 9. 43.
26. *Skanda* 1. 1. 23. 6–9.
27. Manu 9. 88, 9. 79; *Agni* 154. 51; Vaśiṣṭha, cited in *Saṃskāraprakāśa*, p. 759; Parāśara, cited ibid., p. 757; Kātyāyana, cited in *Kṛtyakalpataru*, p. 32; *Gṛhastharatnākara*, p. 30; *Matsya* 154. 415–16.
28. *Manmathonmathana* II, 1–19.
29. *Śiva* 2. 3. 31. 1–52, 2. 3. 32. 1–65.
30. Cf. O'Flaherty (1971-A), pp. 304–5.
31. MhB XII. 329. 49. 1–5.
32. *Śiva* 2. 3. 44. 1–102.
33. *Śiva* 2. 3. 9. 5.
34. *Śiva* 2. 3. 30. 25–54; cf. *Brahmavaivarta* 4. 40. 71–111.
35. *Śiva* 2. 3. 43. 1–65; *Śiva*, Jñānasaṃhitā 16. 34–79, 17. 1–73, 18. 1–31.
36. Tulsī Dās, pp. 47–50 (C. 92–9).
37. Dessigane (1960), No. 23; William Taylor, p. 72.
38. *Śiva* 2. 3. 22. 20–3.
39. MhB XIII, Appendix I, No. 15, 358–60.
40. *Brahma* 38. 23–40.
41. *Śiva* 3. 27. 36.
42. *Skanda* 2. 2. 12. 22–43.
43. *Vāyu* 2. 30. 29–58 (Bombay); cf. ASS 92. 29–58; *Harivaṃśa* 1. 29. 37; *Brahmāṇḍa* 3. 67. 32–6.
44. *Vāmana* 1. 11–30; *Śiva* 2. 2. 22. 1–54; *Kālikā* 15. 1–53.
45. Stacton, pp. 78, 83, 84.
46. Edward J. Thompson and Arthur Marshman Spencer, xcii (anonymous), c (Ramprasad Sen), xcvi (Rajanikanta Sen), xciii (Ramprasad Sen), xcvii (Vaikuntha of Maliara).
47. Stacton, p. 100; and J. L. Shastri's translation of *Śiva* 2. 3. 25. 51.
48. *Kālikā* 46. 1–5.
49. *Pārvatīpariṇaya* 4. 17–18.
50. *Padma* 5. 40. 132–8.
51. *Padma* 4. 110. 248–69.
52. D. C. Sen, p. 248.

53. *Subhāṣitaratnakoṣa*, Nos. 34 and 59, Ingalls's translation.
54. *Kumārasambhava* 8. 49–51.
55. Shakti M. Gupta, p. 84, citing K. Basu, *Common Medicinal Plants of Darjeeling and Sikkim*, Government of West Bengal Press, 1956, p. 3.
56. *Skanda* 1. 1. 32. 70–112.
57. *Skanda* 1. 3. 1. 3. 45–52.
58. Nivedita, p. 300; cf. Dessigane (1960), No. 57; William Taylor, p. 103.
59. Tulsī Dās, pp. 31 and 33 (C. 51–2, 56–7).
60. Nanimadhab Chaudhuri, p. 183.
61. Elwin (1949), p. 481; (1954), pp. 177–8; cf. Sen, pp. 241–3; Maity, p. 189; P. Thomas (1959), p. 118; Wilkins, p. 273.
62. *Saura* 54. 4; *Mahābhāgavata* 23. 5–7; *Śiva* 7. 24. 33–5.
63. *Brahmavaivarta* 3. 2. 19–24.
64. *Matsya* 155. 5–9; *Padma* 5. 41. 5–9; *Skanda* 1. 2. 27. 63–8.
65. *Subhāṣitaratnakoṣa*, No. 35, Ingalls's translation.
66. Briggs, p. 57.
67. *Skanda* 1. 1. 22. 52; *Matsya* 155. 31, 156. 5.
68. *Śiva*, Dharmasaṃhitā 10. 32–4.
69. *Kālikā* 52. 105–22; *Manasāmaṅgal* of Jagajjīban, cited by Maity, p. 115; Briggs, p. 183.
70. *Bhaviṣya* 3. 4. 17. 67–78.
71. Balys, motif K 1813 and 1813.1.1.
72. *Kālikā* 52. 83.
73. *Kālikā* 47. 114–19.
74. *Manasābijay* of Bipradas, pp. 1–235, cited by Maity, p. 79.
75. Balys, motif K 1814 and 1814.4.
76. *Manasāmaṅgal* of Visnu Pala, cited on p. x of the introduction to the Manasabijay of Bipradas; also cited by Dimock (1966-A), p. 58.
77. *Brahmāṇḍa* 4. 10. 41–77.
78. *Bhāgavata* 8. 12. 12–35; *Agni* 3. 17–20.
79. Dessigane (1964), No. 59, 76–7.
80. *Śiva* 3. 20. 3–7.
81. Oppert, p. 508. Cf. *Bhāgavata* 10. 88. 14–36.
82. Baldaeus, pp. 17–18; Churchill, p. 737; Rhode, p. 236.
83. Dumont (1957-B), pp. 401–2; cf. Dumont (1959), pp. 80–1.
84. Dessigane (1967), pp. 84–5 (2. 32. 6–47).
85. *Mahābhāgavata* 12. 18–21; *Bṛhaddharma* 2. 41. 106–8.
86. *Rāmāyaṇa* 1. 34. 12–20; 1. 36. 7–9.
87. *Vāmana* 25. 1–20; 31. 5–18.
88. *Śiva* 5. 38. 48–57; *Liṅga* 1. 66. 15–20; *Vāyu* 88. 143–69; *Brahmāṇḍa* 3. 46–53; *Viṣṇu* 4. 4. 1–33; *Bhāgavata* 9. 8. 1–31, 9. 9. 1–15; *Rāmāyaṇa* 1. 37–43, MhB III. 104–8.
89. *Brahma* 74. 8–22, 75. 31–50.
90. Rao, ii, 1, 316.
91. Dessigane (1967), p. 190 (6. 13. 2–4).
92. Frontispiece of *Liṅga* (Bombay, 1858).
93. *Kāñchīmāhātmya* 25. 1–22, 26. 1 ff.; cf. *Skanda* 1. 3. 1. 4. 1–31.
94. *Padma* 5. 53. 1–17; *Kathāsaritsāgara* 114. 56–75.
95. *Bṛhaddharma* 2. 41. 106–8, 2. 42. 1–19, 2. 43. 9–12, 2. 53. 18–50.
96. *Manasāmaṅgal* of Jagajjīban, cited by Maity, p. 115.
97. *Manasākāvya* of Manakar, ed. by B. D. Barua and S. N. Sharma (Gauhati, 1951), cited by Maity, p. 120.

98. *Skanda* 1. 3. 2. 18. 2–16.
99. *Śiva*, Dharmasaṃhitā 10. 33–5; *Kathāsaritsāgara* 1. 43.
100. *Subhāṣitaratnakoṣa*, part 22, vv. 700–51; *Kāmasūtra* 2. 4–5; Dimock (1966), p. 212.
101. *Subhāṣitaratnakoṣa*, part 22, vv. 700–51.
102. *Kāmasūtra*, 2. 4–5; *Kumārasambhava* 8. 9, 18, 87.
103. *Matsya* 154. 58–70; *Padma* 5. 40. 58–73.
104. Eliade (1965), p. 117.
105. *Skanda* 5. 2. 18. 31–4.
106. Wilford (1792), p. 402.
107. Beswick, pp. 106–7; P. Thomas (1958), pp. 104–5.
108. *Skanda* 6. 253. 1–37; 6. 254. 1–104.
109. *Skanda* 1. 1. 21. 132; *Mahābhāgavata* 21. 56.
110. *Brahmavaivarta* 4. 41. 20–6.
111. *Kālikā* 45. 71–5; *Brahmavaivarta* 4. 40. 50.
112. *Brahma* 35. 14–19.
113. Thompson and Spencer, No. xcviii.
114. O. Ghosh, p. 111.
115. *Vāmana* 25. 66.
116. Stacton, pp. 126–7.
117. *Śiva* 2. 3. 8. 13.
118. Huxley, p. 172.
119. Zaehner, p. 43.
120. *Kālikā* 52. 19, 57–8.
121. Rao, ii, 1, 304–5.
122. Stacton, p. 108.
123. *Subhāṣitaratnakoṣa*, No. 56, Ingalls's translation.
124. *Kumārasambhava* 8. 1; *Śiva* 2. 2. 21. 19.
125. *Subhāṣitaratnakoṣa*, No. 75, Ingalls's translation.
126. *Harṣacarita* 1. 2, Cowell and Thomas's translation (Kane ed., p. 1).
127. This song appeared in the programme of a performance by Balasarasvati at the New Empire theatre in Calcutta on 5 February 1964; the Tamil text is included in the programme, but I have not been able to trace its source.
128. MhB III. 95. 1–24, 96. 15–25.
129. *Kumārasambhava* 5. 66–73; *Śiva*, Jñānasaṃhitā 14. 19–31.
130. *Skanda* 1. 1. 22. 50; *Śiva* 2. 3. 27. 13.
131. *Matsya* 155. 23–4.
132. *Śiva* 2. 3. 27. 36; *Skanda* 1. 1. 23. 60; *Matsya* 154. 435–6, 442.
133. *Bṛhannāradīya Purāṇa* 2. 73. 49; Agrawala (1966), p. 48.
134. *Kumārasambhava* 9–11.
135. Mathur, *Vaiṣṇava Padalaharī*, edited by Durgadas Lahiri (Calcutta, 1905), p. 85; translation by Edward C. Dimock. Cf. *Gītagovinda* 3. 11.
136. *Mahābhāgavata* 9. 46–7.
137. *Kālikā* 46. 44–8; *Śiva* 2. 2. 18. 23; *Śiva*, Jñānasaṃhitā 16. 4.
138. *Kumārasambhava* 7. 30–5.
139. Dessigane (1967), p. 13 (1. 9. 25–8).
140. *Śiva* 2. 3. 43–6; *Śiva*, Jñānasaṃhitā 18. 17–31.
141. *Mahābhāgavata* 27. 19–27.
142. *Brahmāṇḍa* 4. 15. 1–12.
143. *Kālikā* 45. 113–16.
144. *Śiva* 2. 3. 25. 66; 2. 3. 8. 13.

145. *Śiva* 2. 3. 30. 32–5.
146. *Śiva*, Jñānasaṃhitā 16. 3–8; *Śiva* 2. 3. 39. 36–42.
147. *Vāmana* 27. 6–7.
148. *Śiva* 2. 2. 18. 23.
149. *Śiva* 2. 2. 17. 4–5; *Skanda* 1. 2. 26. 17.
150. *Kumārasambhava* 7. 30–9.
151. Gupta, p. 39, citing a story told by Mrs. Roda Chinnoy.
152. Elwin (1949), p. 159.
153. Elwin (1954), pp. 422–3.
154. *Skanda* 1. 1. 23. 60 ff., 1. 1. 25. 21–4, 1. 1. 25. 8–9.
155. *Skanda* 1. 2. 26. 2–3, 11–19.
156. *Padma* 5. 40. 429–38; *Matsya* 154. 435–44.
157. *Brahmavaivarta* 4. 38. 55–7, 4. 39. 1–12.
158. *Haracarita* 10. 3–188.
159. *Kumārasambhava* 5. 78.
160. *Matsya* 155. 22.
161. *Matsya* 154. 584.
162. Rivett-Carnac, p. 18.
163. *Matsya* 154. 331.
164. *Śiva* 2. 3. 27. 31.
165. *Matsya* 155. 23.
166. *Skanda* 1. 1. 34. 128–31.
167. *Liṅga* 1. 34. 13–15; *Brahmāṇḍa* 2. 27. 18–19; cf. *Skanda* 1. 2. 25. 71.
168. Dubois, p. 519.
169. MhB XIII, Appendix 1, No. 4, 66–7, and XIII. 14. 101–2.
170. MhB XIII. 17. 39 and 42, with Nīlakaṇṭha; XIII. 17. 101, 14. 233.
171. Agrawala (1966), p. 40; Atharva Veda XX. 136. 11.
172. *Vāmana* S.22. 60–1.
173. *Subhāṣitaratnakoṣa*, No. 69, Ingalls's translation.
174. O'Flaherty (1971-C).
175. *Matsya* 155. 22; *Subhāṣitaratnakoṣa*, No. 35; *Skanda* 1. 1. 22. 53; *Śiva* 2. 3. 27. 27; MhB II. 71. 5 and 16.
176. MhB XIII. 17. 92; Nīlakaṇṭha on XIII. 17. 95.
177. MhB III. 81. 98–118; IX. 37. 34–50; *Skanda* 5. 2. 2. 2–37; cf. *Kathāsaritsāgara* 1. 5. 32–9; *Padma* 1. 27. 1–15; 5. 18. 132; *Vāmana* S.17. 1–22.
178. Agrawala (1964), p. 72.
179. Meyer (1937), i, 208; *Haṭhayogapradīpikā* 3. 82–96.
180. *Padma* 4. 101. 174–9.
181. MhB XIII. 17. 92; Nīlakaṇṭha on XIII. 17. 95.
182. Parasuram Caturvedi, *Mīrāṃbāi kī Padāvalī*, pada 46; cited by Pandey, p. 199.
183. *Subhāṣitaratnakoṣa*, Nos. 80 and 72, Ingalls's translation.
184. MhB XII. 47. 52.
185. *Skanda* 1. 1. 34. 130–9.
186. *Kāñchīmāhātmya* 23. 1–35, 24. 1 ff.
187. Elwin (1944), pp. 197–202; Steel, pp. 98–110.
188. *Śiva* 2. 3. 27. 25; *Skanda* 1. 1. 22. 66, 1. 2. 25, 67.
189. *Darpadalana* 7. 35.
190. *Śiva* 2. 3. 39. 38; *Śiva*, Jñānasaṃhitā 16. 5.
191. *Kumārasambhava* 7. 33; cf. *Śiva*, Jñānasaṃhitā 16. 5.
192. *Kumārasambhava* 8. 7 and 8. 19.
193. MhB 1. 203. 26, XIII. 128. 1–5.

194. *Skanda* 6. 153. 2–27.
195. MhB XIII, Appendix I, No. 15, 280–305.
196. MhB XIII. 127. 26–38.
197. MhB XII. 329. 14. 4; cf. *Vāmana* 5. 25.
198. *Skanda* I. 3. I. 3. 23–42.
199. *Śiva* 2. 5. 42. 14–22; *Śiva*, Dharmasaṃhitā 4. 4–10; cf. *Vāmana* 37. 8–9.
200. Dessigane (1967), p. 199 (6. 13. 364–72).
201. *Śiva* 2. 3. 20. 1–23; *Kālikā* 44. 124–36; *Mahābhāgavata* 22. 108–11; 23. 1–4; cf. *Śiva* 2. 5. 13. 1–50, 2. 5. 14. 1–4; *Padma* 6. 98. 5–19.
202. *Śiva* 2. 3. 51. 14.
203. MhB XIII, Appendix I, No. 15, 242; cf. XIII. 127. 26–38.
204. *Skanda* 5. 3. 150. 18.
205. Ghurye, p. 31; D. C. Sen, p. 67; Elwin (1954), p. 638.
206. Agrawala (1964), p. 99.
207. *Śiva* 2. 2. 1. 19.
208. *Śiva* 3. 13–15.
209. *Mahābhāgavata* 12. 17.
210. *Kālikā* 10. 26–8; *Vāmana* 28. 1–6.
211. *Matsya* 154. 554–60; *Skanda* 2. 7. 9. 94.
212. *Skanda* I. I. 27. 81–3.
213. *Skanda* I. I. 27. 107–8; *Subhāṣitaratnakoṣa*, No. 95.
214. *Subhāṣitaratnakoṣa*, No. 92, Ingalls's translation.
215. Ibid., No. 91. Cf. MhB III. 215. 23.
216. *Śiva* 2. 2. 1. 3–5.
217. *Brahmavaivarta* I. 6. 1–40.
218. *Kūrma* 2. 38. 25–32 (*Bib. Ind.* 2. 38, pp. 726–9).
219. *Śiva* 2. 2. 15. 61; cf. MhB XIII. 17. 56; Nīlakaṇṭha on XIII. 17. 58.
220. MhB XIII. 17. 56 and 58 with Nīlakaṇṭha. Cf *Śatapatha* 5. 4. 1. 2.
221. *Matsya* 47. 139; cf. MhB XIII, Appendix I, No. 15, 532–675.
222. *Kumārasambhava* 8. 81, with Mallinātha's commentary.
223. *Skanda* I. I. 27. 31; cf. *Skanda* 5. 1. 18. 16.
224. *Rāmāyaṇa* I. 35. 6.

CHAPTER VIII

1. *Liṅga* I. 86. 23.
2. Bharati (1965), pp. 296–7.
3. Watts, p. 96.
4. *Kālīvilāsa Tantra* 10. 20–1; Kane, V, 2, 1093.
5. *Bhikṣāṭanakāvya* 9. 15.
6. Nīlakaṇṭha on MhB XIII. 17. 51.
7. *Matsya* 70. 40–60; cf. MhB III. 2. 23.
8. *Brahmāṇḍa* 4. 30. 84.
9. *Mahābhāgavata* 24. 33.
10. *Padma* 5. 17. 162 ff.
11. *Śiva* 4. 12. 17–52; cf. MhB XIII. 14. 233; Nīlakaṇṭha on XIII. 14. 228–31; Sonnerat, p. 179; Baldaeus, pp. 17–18.
12. *Śiva* 2. 2. 23. 7–8.
13. Stacton, p. 13.
14. *Manmathonmathana* I, between 18 and 19.
15. Watts, pp. 204–5.
16. *Subhāṣitaratnakoṣa*, No. 82, Ingalls's translation.
17. Henry, plates IV, VIII, X, XI, XIX, XXI, XXII, XXIV, and XXVI.

18. Bharati (1961), p. 245.
19. *Kūlārṇava Tantra* 2. 23; cf. Dumont (1960), p. 53.
20. *Kūlārṇava Tantra* 2. 24; cf. *Haṭhayogapradīpikā* 3. 94.
21. *Kaularahāsya*, cited by Kane, v, 2, 1077, and by P. Thomas (1959), p. 122; also *Rudrayāmala Tantra*, cited by P. Thomas ibid., cf. *Haṭhayogapradīpikā* 3. 94.
22. Gonda (1963), ii, 39.
23. Woodroffe (1959), p. 577; Pott, p. 25.
24. Woodroffe (1959), p. 566.
25. Ibid., pp. 575 and 613.
26. Anand, p. 40, citing a Tantric text translated by Woodroffe.
27. *Karpūramañjarī*, I. 22–4; Lanman's translation, p. 235.
28. *Mattavilāsaprahasana* 7, translation by Barnett.
29. *Śiva* 2. 2. 10. 25.
30. *Bhāgavata* 8. 12. 33 and 43; *Agni* 3. 17–23.
31. *Gopāla Uttara Tāpinī Upaniṣad*, 15; in *Vaiṣṇava Upaniṣads*.
32. *Śiva* 2. 3. 18. 45.
33. *Kālikā* 43. 35–40; *Kumārasambhava* 1. 56.
34. *Śiva* 2. 3. 13. 21.
35. Tendulkar, p. 324.
36. *Narottamavilāsa* of Narahari-Dasa, edited by Ramanarayana Vidyaratna (Murshidabad, Berhampur; Radharaman Press, 1918), pp. 200–1; cited by Dimock (1966), p. 156.
37. Apte, p. 70, *asidhārāvrata*.
38. Dimock (1966), p. 156.
39. Ibid., pp. 53, 155, 16, and 157.
40. Pott (1966), p. 8; *Bṛhadāraṇyaka Upaniṣad* 6. 4. 5; *Yü-fang chih-yao* Ib, translated by Henri Maspéro (1937), p. 385.
41. Dimock (1966), p. 157.
42. *Majjhima Nikāya* I, p. 145, No. 24, *Rathavinītasutta*.
43. Eliade (1958), pp. 267–8.
44. *Śiva* 7. 1. 24. 43–5.
45. *Dyānabindu Upaniṣad* 84–6; *Bṛhadāraṇyaka Upaniṣad* 6. 4. 10; *Gorakṣa Śataka* 70–1, cited by Briggs, pp. 298, 333–4; *Haṭhayogapradīpikā* 3. 82–96; Sinha, pp. 194–5.
46. *Aitareya Brāhmaṇa* 13. 9; *Bṛhaddevatā* 5. 97; MhB XIII, Appendix 1, No. 5, 48–50; *Haracarita* 9. 196; *Kathāsaritsāgara* 3. 6. 81; *Kumārasambhava* 1. 51, 10. 54; *Vāmana* 28. 50; *Śiva*, Dharmasaṃhitā 10. 132–50; Elwin (1949), p. 293.
47. MhB XIII. 83. 45–7; *Rāmāyaṇa* 1. 35. 6–13; *Kumārasambhava* 8. 8; *Brahmavaivarta* 3. 1. 22, 40; *Kālikā* 48. 46–7; *Śiva* 2. 4. 1. 24, 2. 4. 2. 1, 2. 5. 22. 41–2.
48. *Śiva* 2. 4. 1. 24; *Brahmavaivarta* 3. 1. 22.
49. *Kumārasambhava* 8. 8; cf. *Śiva* 2. 4. 2. 1; *Brahmavaivarta* 3. 1. 40.
50. *Kālikā* 48. 43–53.
51. *Kālikā* 48. 77–83.
52. *Śiva*, Jñānasaṃhitā 19. 7–8; *Śiva* 2. 4. 1. 19–20.
53. *Skanda* 2. 7. 9. 55–94.
54. *Vāmana* 28. 61–3.
55. *Skanda* 6. 70. 24–68; 71. 1–20.
56. *Skanda* 6. 70. 46–9.
57. *Kālikā* 16. 39–68.

58. Daniélou (1962), p. 53.
59. Crooke (1913), vi, 701; cf. Monier-Williams (1885), i, 68, and Isherwood (1965), p. 48.
60. *Durlabhasāra* of Locana-dasa, in *Vaiṣṇava-Granthāvalī*, ed. by Satyendranath Basu (Calcutta; Basumati sahitya mandir, 1936), p. 137; cited by Dimock (1966), p. 213.
61. Eliade (1965), pp. 42–3.
62. Agrawala (1966), p. vi; Bharati (1965), p. 296; Watts, p. 96.
63. *Mahābhāgavata* 30. 10.
64. *Kālikā* 44. 37; *Kathāsaritsāgara* 3. 6. 81; cf. Agrawala (1963), p. 237.
65. Elwin (1949), p. 293.
66. Manu 9. 35.
67. Elwin (1949), pp. 275, 49, and 431.
68. *Mahābhāgavata* 29. 26–8; *Saura* 61. 62 and 61. 78.
69. MhB XIII. 83. 45, 47–8; cf. *Rāmāyaṇa* I. 35. 6–15.
70. *Saura* 60. 1–27.
71. *Bṛhaddharma* 2. 53. 48–53.
72. Dessigane (1964), No. 25. 35.
73. *Śatapatha Brāhmaṇa* 6. 1. 3. 6; *Taittirīya Saṃhitā* 3. 2. 1. 25–8.
74. *Vāmana* 28. 30–6; *Brahmāṇḍa* 3. 10. 23–4.
75. *Kālikā* 48. 12–24. Cf. MhB III. 215. 13–23, III. 216. 1–15.
76. *Brahmavaivarta* 3. 1. 12–43, 3. 2. 1–31, 3. 8. 9–89, 3. 9. 1–36, 3. 14. 1–33.
77. *Skanda* 1. 1. 20. 17; Dumont (1957-B), p. 402, (1960), p. 39 n.; *Bṛhaddharma* 2. 60. 7–51.
78. Dessigane (1960), No. 11; William Taylor, p. 62.
79. *Padma* 6. 11. 25.
80. MhB III. 220. 10.
81. *Brahmāṇḍa* 4. 30. 98–101; *Vāyu* (1860) 72. 23.
82. *Matsya* 158. 34–5.
83. *Devībhāgavata* 7. 40. 38–40; *Skanda* 1. 3. 2. 17. 23.
84. *Kathāsaritsāgara* 3. 6. 60–88.
85. Baldaeus, p. 27.
86. *Caturvargacintāmaṇi* 2. 2. 359; *Vāmana* 28. 71–2.
87. *Śiva* 2. 4. 13. 20.
88. *Caturvargacintāmaṇi* 2. 2. 366; Dessigane (1967), p. 17 (1. 12. 1–10).
89. *Vāmana* 28. 71–2.
90. Personal communication from Mircea Eliade.
91. *Vāmana* 2. 46–9; Baldaeus, pp. 17–18; *Kūrma* 2. 31. 84–7.
92. *Vāmana* 44. 30–8; *Kūrma* 1. 16. 123–240; *Matsya* 179. 1–86; *Padma* 5. 43. 1–95; *Varāha* 27. 26–39; *Viṣṇudharmottara* 1. 226. 1–82.
93. *Śiva* 5. 23. 55.
94. Blair, p. 63 and *passim*.
95. Hauer (1922), p. 17.
96. *Śiva* 2. 3. 10. 14.
97. MhB XII. 274. 45.
98. *Kālikā* 2. 45–7; *Śiva* 2. 2. 3. 48; 2. 2. 3. 51.
99. *Matsya* 252. 5–6; *Vāmana* 44. 41–3, 28. 57, 64–5.
100. *Śiva* 2. 5. 42. 14–22; *Śiva*, Dharmasaṃhitā 4. 4–10; *Vāmana* 37. 8–9; Dessigane (1967), p. 199 (6. 13. 364–72).
101. *Padma Purān* of Narayan Deb, ed. T. C. Dasgupta (2nd ed., Calcutta, University of Calcutta, 1947), cited by Maity, p. 108.
102. Elwin (1949), p. 7.

103. *Śatapatha Brahmāṇa* 9. 1. 1. 6–7.
104. *Kūrma* 1. 10. 22–7.
105. *Taittirīya Saṃhitā* 1. 5. 1. 1.
106. *Matsya* 23. 1–10; *Padma* 5. 12. 1–13.
107. *Śatapatha Brāhmaṇa* 10. 5. 2. 11–12; Pott, p. 8.
108. Elwin (1949), p. 251.
109. *Vāmana* 28. 50.
110. *Brahmavaivarta* 3. 8. 19–33, 83–8, 3. 9. 1–26.
111. *Śiva* 2. 4. 2. 46.
112. Manu 4. 222; cf. MhB vii. 51. 35a.
113. *Kāma Sūtra* 2. 9.
114. *Vaśiṣṭhadharmaśāstra* 12. 23.
115. *Skanda* 1. 1. 27. 42; *Padma* 5. 17. 165; *Kumārasambhava* 9. 16.
116. *Matsya* 158. 33–50.
117. *Haracarita* 9. 217.
118. Dessigane (1967), p. 19 (1. 13. 31–4).
119. *Śūnya Purāṇ* of Rāmāi Paṇḍit, 1, 95–187; cited by B. K. Sarkar, pp. 198–9.
120. Sukumar Sen, *Bangla Sahityer Itihas*, 1, 502; cited by Maity, pp. 198–9.
121. *Śūnya Purāṇ* of Rāmāi Paṇḍit, ed. by N. N. Vasu, 1–22; cited by Maity, pp. 198–9.
122. *Vāmana* 46. 16.
123. *Manasākāvya* of Manakar, MS. cited by Maity, p. 120.
124. MhB. 1. 57. 35–52.
125. *Manasābijay* of Bipradās, ed. by Sukumar Sen (Calcutta, Asiatic Society of Bengal, 1953), pp. 1–235. Cited by Maity, pp. 79–80.
126. Hartland, i, 12.
127. *Mārkaṇḍeya* 103–5 (*Bib. Ind.* 106. 11, 36; 108. 8–10); *Śiva*, Dharmasaṃhitā 11. 53–66. Cf. *Bṛhaddevatā* 6. 162–3, 7. 1–6.
128. MhB iii. 110. 12–15; *Śiva*, Dharmasaṃhitā 12. 42–5.
129. *Brahmavaivarta* 1. 20. 12–45.
130. MhB iii. 126. 5–29.
131. *Saura* 62. 5–12.
132. Getty, pp. 6–7; Jacobi, p. 807.
133. Elwin (1949), p. 349.
134. Hartland, i. 23.
135. *Kumārasambhava* 10. 54; *Skanda* 1. 2. 29. 117–18.
136. *Skanda* 5. 1. 34. 62–6.
137. Pott, p. 8.
138. *Kārttika Māhātmya* 4. 9–10.
139. Lommel, p. 21.
140. *Brahma* 128. 3–46; *Haracarita* 9. 196–221; *Matsya* 158. 32; *Kathāsaritsāgara* 3. 6. 60–88; *Vāmana* 28. 41; *Saura* 60. 1–66, 61. 2–89, 62. 1–33; *Śiva*, Jñānasaṃhitā 19. 7–15; *Skanda* 1. 2. 29: *Brahma* 38. 3.
141. *Śūnya Purān* of Rāmāi Paṇḍit, pp. 1–22; cited by Maity, p. 198.
142. Ṛg Veda 1. 80. 2, iv. 26. 6, ix. 68. 6, ix. 77. 2, x. 11. 4, x. 99. 8, x. 144. 4; *Śatapatha Brāhmaṇa* 3. 9. 4. 10.
143. Ṛg Veda 1. 65. 9, 1. 164. 52, vi. 3. 7, vii. 15. 4; Kuhn, pp. 130 ff., 144 ff., 172 ff.
144. *Śatapatha Brāhmaṇa* 3. 9. 4. 10; Ṛg Veda x. 99. 8; *Kāṭhaka* 37. 14.
145. *Ṣatcakranirūpaṇa*, verse 10; cited and translated by Arthur Avalon (1931). Śaṅkara's commentary.
146. *Bṛhaddevatā* 5. 97.

147. *Aitareya Brāhmaṇa* 13. 9; *Vāyu* 65. 31–9; *Brahmāṇḍa* 3. 1. 30–40; MhB XIII. 85. 1–12.
148. MhB XIII. 85. 1–12.
149. *Kumārasambhava* 1. 51.
149. MhB XIII, Appendix 1, No. 5, 48–50.
150. *Aitareya Brāhmaṇa* 1. 6. 1–6.
151. *Śiva*, Dharmasaṃhitā 10. 132–50.
152. *Chāndogya Upaniṣad* 5. 8; *Bṛhadāraṇyaka Upaniṣad* 6. 2. 13, 6. 43; *Śatapatha Brāhmaṇa* 1. 7. 2. 14, 11. 6. 2. 10.
153. *Śakti Sodhana* of the *Devīrāhasya*, a section of the *Rudrayāmala* text cited by Wilson (1864), i, 260.
154. *Śatapatha Brāhmaṇa* 9. 5. 1. 7–10.
155. *Saura* 61. 64–70.
156. *Kumārasambhava* 10. 55.
157. MhB I. 15. 1–4 and I. 16. 1 ff.; *Matsya* 249. 1–3, 250. 1 ff.; *Vāyu* 1. 54. 47–82; *Brahmāṇḍa* 4. 6. 31–47; *Bhāgavata* 8. 7. 8–11; *Viṣṇu* 1. 9. 1–75; *Agni* 3; *Padma* 5. 14. 1–27 ff.; *Skanda* 1. 1. 8–9 ff.
158. *Skanda* 5. 2. 14. 2–30.
159. *Skanda* 1. 1. 9. 90–2.
160. Ṛg Veda x. 136. 1–7; *Gorakṣa Śataka* 61, cited by Briggs, p. 336.
161. Anand, p. 40, citing a Tantric text translated by Avalon.
162. O'Flaherty (1971-A), p. 291; Leach (1970), p. 80; Lévi-Strauss (1969), *passim.*
163. Sinha, pp. 194–6.
164. *Chāndogya Upaniṣad* 5. 10. 3–6.
165. MhB XII. 278. 1–38.
166. *Padma* 5. 26. 91–125; cf. *Liṅga* 1. 106. 1–27; *Matsya* 252. 5–19, 179. 7–186; *Kūrma* 1. 16. 141–222.
167. *Varāha* 96. 1–44.
168. *Śatapatha Brāhmaṇa* 9. 1. 1. 1; 2. 2. 4. 1.
169. Elwin (1949), p. 261.
170. *Rāmāyaṇa* v. 22. 8–9.
171. *Agrawala* (1966), pp. 1–2.
172. *Śiva* 2. 5. 19. 30–50; cf. *Padma* 6. 11. 36–43.
173. *Vāmana* 43; *Viṣṇudharmottara* 1. 226. 1–82.
174. *Brahma* 113. 1–22.
175. *Padma* 5. 14. 92–115.
176. *Liṅga* 1. 95. 29–62, 1. 96. 1–98.
177. *Śiva* 3. 10. 34–7.
178. Anand, pl. XXXVI, entitled, 'A Yogic posture of the Kaula cult'; Bosch (1960), p. 91.
179. *Kālikā* 36. 1–11.
180. MhB XII. 273. 26–54. Cf. MhB v. 9–10; *Bṛhaddevatā* 6. 149–53.
181. MhB v. 13. 17; *Skanda* 5. 3. 118. 27; *Bhāgavata* 6. 9. 6–9; *Skanda* 1. 1. 16. 20–41. Cf. MhB XII. 273. 58.
182. MhB III. 124. 19–24; III. 125. 1 ff.; cf. *Rāmāyaṇa* VII. 86. 1–17.
183. O'Flaherty (1971-A), p. 296; cf. *Vāmana* 50. 1–26.
184. *Rāmāyaṇa* VII. 30. 20–45.
185. MhB XII. 274. 36–59; *Brahma* 40. 112–19; *Vāyu* 1. 30. 298–305; *Matsya* 72. 11–16; *Padma* 5. 24. 26–32.
186. Ṛg Veda x. 51–3; *Śatapatha Brāhmaṇa* 6. 3. 1. 31; Ṛg Veda x. 32. 6.
187. MhB IX. 46. 12–20. Cf. *Bṛhaddevatā* 7. 62.

188. MhB v. 15. 27–32.
189. MhB xiii. 84. 20–43; cf. *Kathāsaritsāgara* 3. 6. 60–88.
190. *Padma* 5. 4. 55; *Skanda* 1. 1. 27. 69.
191. MhB iii. 220. 10–11.
192. *Taittirīya Brāhmaṇa* 1. 1. 6. 1.
193. *Matsya* 154. 250–5; *Skanda* 1. 2. 24. 42–3; cf. *Haracarita* 9. 59.
194. *Vāmana* 6. 45–55.
195. *Śiva*, Dharmasaṃhitā 49. 76–8.
196. *Śatapatha Brāhmaṇa* 1. 7. 4. 1–7.
197. *Śiva* 2. 2. 20. 21–5.
198. *Skanda* 7. 3. 39. 30–4.
199. *Saura* 61. 60.
200. Atharva Veda vii. 87. 1.
201. *Śatapatha Brāhmaṇa* 6. 1. 1. 1–2, 8; 6. 1. 3. 1–4, 8–10.
202. MhB xiii. 146. 4. Cf. iii. 213. 28–33, xiii. 84. 80.
203. *Brahmāṇḍa* 2. 27. 106.
204. *Brahmāṇḍa* 2. 27. 112.
205. *Subhāṣitaratnakoṣa*, No. 70, Ingalls's translation.
206. *Śiva* 7. 28. 3–19.
207. MhB xii. 207. 13; cf. *Mṛcchakaṭika* iv. 4.
208. *Kālikā* 45. 117.
209. *Skanda* 6. 258. 1–4; 3. 3. 26. 1–5; *Vāmana* 6. 30–1.
210. *Vāmana* 3. 7–8, 34. 18–23, 36. 33–4, and *Varāha* 97. 15–16.
211. *Brahmāṇḍa* 4. 30. 65–89.
212. *Śiva* 2. 3. 25. 69, 2. 3. 26. 21–2.
213. *Skanda* 6. 259. 5; 3. 3. 27. 5, 75; Leach (1970), p. 81.
214. Elwin (1942), p. 119.
215. *Śiva*, Jñānasaṃhitā 42. 27–32.
216. Crooke (1896), i, 76.
217. Dubois, p. 553.
218. *Kumārasambhava* 8. 91. Cf. Song of Solomon, 8. 7: 'Many waters cannot quench love.'
219. O'Flaherty (1971-B), *passim*.
220. Böhtlingk, i, 25, No. 130.
221. *Śiva* 2. 3. 20. 1–23; *Kālikā* 44. 124–36; *Mahābhāgavata* 22. 108–11, 23. 1–4.
222. *Śiva* 2. 5. 131–50; 2. 5. 14. 1–4; *Padma* 6. 98. 5–19, cf. 6. 3. 38–41. Cf. Dessigane (1967), pp. 195–6 (6. 13. 198–270).
223. H. de Wilman-Grabowska, 'Brahmanic Mythology', in Hackin, p. 129.
224. Dessigane (1967), pp. 15–16 (1. 11. 1–91).
225. Rao, ii, 1, 188.
226. *Padma* 6. 5. 19–20; *Saura* 37. 22.
227. Elwin (1942), p. 99.
228. MhB xiii. 17. 54; Nīlakaṇṭha on xiii. 17. 56. P. C. Roy's translation, x, 88 (part i, Anuśāsana Parvan). Cf. *Varāha* 33. 22 and *Matsya* 2. 4.
229. Rao, ii, 1, 173, citing *Uttarakāraṇāgama*.
230. *Abhijñānaśākuntala* iii. 2 (alternative verse).
231. Ṛg Veda 1. 56. 1.
232. *Harivaṃśa* 2. 74. 23.
233. *Taittirīya Brāhmaṇa* 1. 115. 8–9.
234. *Kumārasambhava* 8. 91.

CHAPTER IX

1. Keith (1917), p. 110; MhB XIII. 128. 5–6; I. 203. 26; Rao, ii, 1, 145.
2. *Skanda* 3. 3. 27. 3–8.
3. Wilford (1792), p. 402.
4. Wilford (1795), p. 363.
5. Dessigane (1967), p. 7 (1. 3. 13–29) and p. 15 (1. 10. 96).
6. Stacton, p. 108.
7. Personal communication from Chancal Deb Roy, based on an unpublished Apabhraṃśa manuscript in Poona.
8. Wilford (1795), p. 367.
9. Ibid., pp. 368–70.
10. *Vāmana* 22. 9–10; Agrawala (1966), p. 12.
11. *Kālikā* 4. 7, 9. 30, 5. 68; *Śiva* 2. 2. 11. 21–7, 2. 2. 16. 8–19.
12. *Śiva* 7. 1. 24. 46.
13. *Kārttika Māhātmya* 4. 9.
14. MhB XIII. 146. 5–6; VII. 173. 94–7.
15. *Vāmana* 34. 2–3.
16. *Śiva*, Dharmasaṃhitā 4. 127–30; cf. *Śiva* 2. 5. 45. 12–14.
17. Agrawala (1964), p. 123; Gonda (1963), i, 258.
18. *Skanda* 5. 3. 67. 3–97.
19. Elwin (1949), p. 348.
20. *Kālikā* 5. 21–3, 49; MhB I. 57. 53–69; Appendix 1, No. 100, 107–8, 114; *Śiva* 5. 44. 10.
21. *Padma* 5. 53. 1–17; 1. 58. 1–12.
22. *Kāñchīmāhātmya* 25. 1–22, 26. 1 ff.; cf. *Skanda* 1. 3. 1. 4. 1–31; von Fürer-Haimendorf (1943), p. 227; *Kathāsaritsāgara* 114. 56–75.
23. *Bṛhaddharma* 2. 40. 18–54; cf. *Devībhāgavata* 7. 30. 44–50; *Mahābhāgavata* 11. 32–118.
24. Wilford (1795), p. 367.
25. *Kālikā* 18. 1–117.
26. Stacton, p. 107.
27. *Skanda* 1. 1. 27. 32.
28. *Śiva* 2. 4. 1. 44–6; *Mahābhāgavata* 29. 11–16; *Kathāsaritsāgara* 3. 6. 73; cf. *Vāmana* 28. 31–3.
29. From a tale current in the Punjab. Personal communication from Chanchal Deb Roy.
30. *Śiva* 2. 2. 22. 68, 2. 4. 1. 24; *Matsya* 158. 29; *Skanda* 6. 245. 50–1, 6. 246. 1; *Kumārasambhava* 9. 8.
31. Personal communication from Chanchal Deb Roy.
32. *Kārttika Māhātmya* 4. 3–38; cf. *Padma* 6. 117. 26–30.
33. *Padma* 5. 17. 141–67.
34. *Kālikā* 52. 105–22.
35. *Liṅga* 1. 71. 119–41.
36. *Padma* 6. 11. 7.
37. Cf. *Śiva* 4. 10. 18–24; MhB I. 173. 1–24; *Bhāgavata* 9. 9. 25–49.
38. MhB III, Appendix 1, No. 15, 16–20.
39. Biardeau (1970), p. 289.
40. *Brahma* 128. 10–12; *Saura* 60. 46–53.
41. *Saura* 60. 57–8.
42. *Śiva* 2. 4. 1. 28–39.
43. *Brahmāṇḍa* 3. 41. 43–51.

44. Cf. MhB XIII. 84. 20–43.
45. *Kumārasambhava* 9. 16; *Brahmavaivarta* 3. 1–2; *Kālikā* 48. 12–96; *Rāmāyaṇa* I. 35. 20–2; *Saura* 60–2; *Śiva* 2. 4. 2. 14–18; *Vāmana* 28. 54–5; *Viṣṇudharmottara* I. 228.
46. Ṛg Veda X. 95. 18; cf. MhB I. 75. 18–19; *Liṅga* 1. 65. 19 ff.; *Matsya* 11. 40 ff.; *Padma* 5. 8. 75 ff.; *Viṣṇu* 4. 1. 8 ff.; *Vāyu* 85. 25–8; *Brahma* 7. 3 ff.; *Harivaṃśa* 1. 10. 3 ff.; *Mārkaṇḍeya* 111. 6–18; *Bhāgavata* 9. 1. 3 ff.; *Rāmāyaṇa* VII. 87 ff.; Tawney ii, 305. Cf. the tale of Teiresias and the coupling snakes, Apollodorus III. 6. 7, and Ovid, *Metamorphoses*, III. 320.
47. *Bṛhaddharma* 2. 53. 50–5. Cf. MhB, verse inserted before III. 215. 1.
48. *Bhāgavata* 9. 1. 25–36; *Devībhāgavata* 1. 12. 1–35.
49. *Brahmāṇḍa* 3. 60. 23–7.
50. *Vāyu* 85. 25–8.
51. *Brahma* 108. 26–30.
52. *Liṅga* 1. 65. 19–23; *Matsya* 11. 44–8; *Padma* 5. 8. 75; *Rāmāyaṇa* VII. 87. 8–30; *Viṣṇu* 4. 1. 10–15; *Devībhāgavata* 1. 12. 35; *Padma* 1. 8. 82–116.
53. *Bhaviṣya* 3. 4. 17. 23–7.
54. *Rāmāyaṇa* VII. 87. 10–29 and VII. 90. 15–20.
55. *Padma* 6. 282. 20–36; cf. *Bhaviṣya* 3. 4. 17. 23–7.
56. Roger, pp. 247–8.
57. Dubois, pp. 626–30.
58. Newby, p. 39.
59. Thomas (1959), p. 114.
60. *Padma* 4. 101. 1–24.
61. Rao, ii, 1, 322–3.
62. *Kūrma* 2. 31. 64–109; Rao, ii, 1, 296; von Stietencron, p. 867; cf. Baldaeus, pp. 17–18; Churchill, p. 737; Rhode, p. 236; *Vāmana* 2. 46–9.
63. Stacton, p. 43.
64. *Śiva* 3. 21. 1–8; *Kālikā* 49. 1–92, 50. 1–64, 51. 1–60, 52. 1–155, 53. 1–217.
65. *Śiva*, Dharmasaṃhitā 10. 28–77; *Matsya* 155–8; *Padma* 5. 41. 1–117; *Saura* 53. 56–63.
66. Dessigane (1967), p. 6 (1. 3. 8–10) and p. 8 (1. 4. 77).
67. *Skanda* 5. 2. 20. 1–25.
68. *Rāmāyaṇa* VII. 16. 1–10.
69. Bharata Sena's commentary on the *Raghuvaṃśa*, at the end; cf. Hariprasad Shastri (1925), re *Kumārasambhava*.
70. *Bṛhatkathāmañjarī* 1. 1. 52–61.
71. *Bhaviṣya* 3. 4. 14. 45.
72. *Skanda* 1. 1. 34–5.
73. Leach (1962-B), p. 82.
74. *Kūrma* 1. 10. 39 (*Bib. Ind.* 1. 10, p. 92).
75. *Śiva* 2. 2. 16. 31 and 35, 2. 2. 23. 7.
76. *Saddharmapuṇḍarīka* XV. 21.
77. *Liṅga* 1. 29. 1–83; 1. 31. 21–45; *Kūrma* 2. 38. 2–6 and 129–31; cf. Rao, ii, 1, 302.
78. *Kālikā* 9. 47; *Śiva* 2. 2. 16. 30–5.
79. Eliot, p. lxxxi.
80. *Tantra Rahāsya*, cited by Woodroffe (1959), p. 150.
81. MhB VII, Appendix 1, No. 8, 99–116.

82. *Śiva* 3. 8. 14; MhB xiii. 17. 32.
83. Heimann (1964), pp. 97–8.

CHAPTER X

1. *Brahmavaivarta* 4. 47. 150–60; cf. Zimmer (1946), pp. 3–11.
2. *Bhāgavata* 10. 1. 8. 32–45; cf. 10. 1. 7. 34–7.
3. Goethe, *Faust* (Hamburg, 1959), Zweiter Teil, v, line 11582.

APPENDIX F

INDEX OF MOTIFS

8cd. transfer *tejas*: 20, 25, 70, 94, 96–7, 99, 105–6, 115–16, 157–9, 161–2, 168–9, 182–3, 270, 276, 280, 283–6, 288, 290, 298.
8d. destructive *tapas*: 10, 25, 30, 32, 36, 43–5, 47, 52, 54, 58–9, 62, 69, 71–2, 74–5, 81, 88, 90, 92–3, 97, 109–12, 120, 125, 129–30, 136, 139, 149, 151–3, 180–1, 188, 195, 200–1, 203, 206, 215–16, 228, 234, 279, 289, 297.
9c. fiery seed in water: Plate 11. 25, 29, 95–6, 107–11, 115, 161, 168, 180, 250, 275–6, 284–5, 287–8, 291, 294, 299.
9cd. liquid gold: 24–5, 88, 94–7, 99, 105–8, 117, 152, 190, 228, 240, 248, 274.
9d. poison: 8, 25, 29, 32, 40, 142–4, 157, 165, 167, 187, 191, 216, 222, 225, 230, 238–9, 242–3, 275, 279, 281–2, 285, 287, 290.
10c. oblation in fire: Plate 9. 7, 25, 29–31, 64–5, 94, 97, 99, 108, 110–11, 115–17, 122, 128, 139, 149, 161, 168, 229, 249, 255, 262, 264, 274, 277–81, 287, 291.
10cd. death and sex: Plate 4: 25, 29–31, 71–2, 83, 91, 93–4, 97, 110, 113, 121–2, 137, 139, 142, 155, 161, 174–5, 179–81, 186–90, 230, 235–7, 242, 275, 297–9, 306.
10d. *tapas* in water: 25, 41, 58–62, 77, 129–31, 134–5, 151, 154, 288.
11c. sweat: 24–5, 31, 41, 116, 118–19, 121, 136–7, 157, 237, 249–50, 271–2, 275, 284.
11cd. tears: 25, 31, 84, 107, 147, 239, 272–3, 299–300.
11d. water destroys fire: 107, 176, 273, 281, 284, 288.
12c. ashes in water: 161, 230, 281, 287.
12cd. fire/water balance: Plate 3. 42, 82, 161, 246, 250, 287, 289–90.
12d. fire destroys water: 31, 41, 125, 143, 231, 264, 279, 282, 285, 288–91.
13c. passion submerged: 25, 31, 41, 47, 80, 93–4, 111, 155, 158, 161, 174, 176, 181, 246, 256–8, 281, 286–9, 294–5, 297, 308.
13cd[1]. submarine mare: Plate 3. 25, 29, 31, 40, 62, 110, 115, 230, 250, 261, 276, 279, 284–5, 289–92, 305, 307.
13cd[2]. taming: Plate 3. 40, 49–50, 100, 279, 289, 292, 305.
13cd[3]. fire in mouth: 29, 31, 47, 90, 93, 100, 108, 129–30, 274, 279–80, 289, 305, 307.
13d. anger quenched: 25, 31, 42, 44, 47, 58–9, 89, 116, 122, 132, 137, 150–1, 164, 181, 222, 240, 249, 272, 282, 284, 289–90, 299.
14c[1]. cosmic waters: Plate 11. 86, 107, 123, 197, 229–31, 277, 283, 285, 287–8.
14c[2]. Soma: 25, 32, 53, 77, 109, 137, 139, 157–9, 161, 189, 207, 229, 237, 246, 250–1, 273, 275, 277–9, 281, 283, 287–9, 292.
14c[3]. moon: 25, 50, 93, 117, 157–8, 169, 223, 228, 238–9, 241–3, 252, 270, 273, 277, 286–8, 291, 296, 300.
14cd. ocean: 31, 40, 42, 93, 101, 127, 206, 230, 250, 279, 289–91, 299.
14d. doomsday flood: 31, 41, 45, 75, 123, 220, 231–2, 250, 286, 289–91.
15c. rain as seed: 31, 41–6, 49, 103, 109, 123, 159, 220, 268, 280, 286, 288, 295, 299.
15cd. blood: 32, 99–100, 137, 187, 229, 237, 245–6, 264, 268, 271, 276, 280–1, 283, 285.
15d. drought: 43–5, 47, 103, 288.
16c. drink seed: Plate 9. 25, 29, 32, 43–4, 47, 68, 90, 96, 99, 101, 106, 108–9, 116, 180, 206, 262, 264–5, 273–9, 288–9.
16cd. food and sex: 25, 42, 87, 103, 112–13, 131, 137, 176, 187, 190, 198, 201, 206, 214, 218, 221, 224, 229, 235, 244, 272–3, 279–82, 300.
16d. drugs/liquor: 25, 44–6, 57, 67, 85, 107, 113, 127, 133, 175, 177, 221, 224, 234–5, 259, 283, 289, 306.
17c. woman bathing: 20, 25, 29, 32, 46–7, 53, 59, 61–3, 81, 90, 97, 99–100, 106, 109, 137, 206, 226–7, 271, 276–7.

24a. ascetic reviled: 25, 58–60, 63, 68, 74, 86, 92, 98, 102, 115, 120, 126, 132, 154, 156, 162, 175, 181–4, 191, 194–5, 202–3, 205, 210, 214–16, 219, 231, 234–5, 238, 247–9, 272, 290, 300, 306–7.

25e. sex destroys *tapas*: 26, 31, 40, 43, 45–9, 51, 53–4, 56–7, 63, 68, 73, 80–1, 109, 117, 132, 141, 144, 149–51, 179, 181–2, 185–7, 190–1, 199–201, 204, 206, 245–6, 253, 271, 296, 298, 301–2.

25ea[1]. *tapas* for *kāma*: Plate 5. 11, 26, 31, 51, 64–6, 151, 156–7, 162–3, 188, 205, 233, 248, 253, 264.

25ea[2]. *tapas* for spouse: 7, 11, 26, 30, 39, 61, 64–5, 69–70, 72–3, 87, 120, 126, 152–4, 156–7, 163, 165, 204–5, 213, 216–17, 219, 224–5, 232–3, 235, 240, 248, 264.

25ea[3]. *tapas* for child: 26, 48, 52, 81, 84, 89, 96, 109–10, 136, 139, 163, 206, 234, 264, 268–9.

25a. *tapas* restores/expiates sex. 26, 31, 42–3, 48, 50, 53–4, 56–8, 61, 64–5, 68, 80, 114, 122, 133–5, 171, 191, 197, 199, 205–6, 232, 246, 256, 296, 298, 308.

26e[1]. bamboo reed: Plate 16. 26, 32, 52, 61, 88, 92, 94, 97, 99, 101, 105, 108, 118, 137, 149, 264–5, 274, 277, 280, 284, 289, 294, 297, 301, 310.

26e[2]. tree of Kāma: 26, 32, 62, 85, 94, 106, 108–9, 149–50, 157–60, 169, 179, 215, 220, 222–4, 234, 237, 239, 245, 252, 275–6, 280, 283–6, 289, 294, 301, 305, 310.

26ea. ithyphallic ascetic: Plates 1 and 4. 5–6, 8–11, 26, 32, 50, 52, 56, 58, 133, 135, 143, 164, 173, 176, 184, 226, 244, 247, 255, 265, 267, 311.

26a. Sthāṇu (ascetic pillar): Plate 2. 10, 26, 31, 72, 131, 135, 137–9, 160, 226, 268, 312.

27e. incest: 26, 30, 32, 51, 57, 62, 81, 110, 113, 115, 133, 190–1, 204, 211, 251, 267, 272, 275, 284, 309.

27ea. erotic *yoginī*: 7, 26, 36, 43–4, 49, 52, 54–6, 58, 60–1, 70–2, 80–1, 88, 105, 109, 153, 166, 174, 193, 197, 211, 223, 226, 233–5, 244, 256, 264, 268–9, 278, 294.

27a. regard woman as mother: 26, 32, 51, 60–1, 63, 81, 102, 113, 118, 190, 201, 204, 211, 275.

28e. erotic clothes: 11, 31, 39, 44, 54, 60, 63, 147, 174, 215–19, 222–3, 227, 238–48, 271, 307.

28ea. nakedness: 6–7, 31–2, 40, 56, 100, 102, 143, 151, 173–4, 176, 181, 183–4, 200, 202–4, 212–14, 217, 219, 221, 225, 229, 239, 244–5, 247–8, 255, 264, 272, 290, 304–5, 307–9, 312.

28a. ascetic clothes: 7, 31, 40, 44, 54, 60, 161, 174, 206–7, 213, 215, 217–18, 222–3, 238–40, 242, 259.

29e. eroticism/fertility: 26, 51, 53, 68, 113, 163, 225, 262–8, 270–1.

29ea. erotic/horrible: Plates 4 and 10. 7, 26, 112–13, 154–5, 187–8, 191, 206, 220, 233, 235–7, 242.

29a. barrenness: 26, 30, 32, 68, 104–5, 122, 139, 160, 178–9, 225, 230, 239, 263, 265–6, 268–70, 276, 290, 294–5, 301, 303.

30e. birds: Plate 15. 13, 26, 30, 32, 69, 88, 94–7, 100, 106, 108, 137, 149, 158, 167–9, 177, 220, 224, 237, 245, 252, 275–7, 279, 283–6, 298, 309.

30ea. wind: 26, 31–2, 40, 75, 83–4, 93, 107–8, 115–16, 155, 168, 220, 242, 265, 290, 310.

30a. snakes: Plates 8, 10, 13, and 14. 26, 30–2, 59, 112, 124–5, 142, 181, 187–8, 212–13, 215–16, 220, 222, 225, 237–45, 252, 277, 284, 290, 298.

31e. erotic dance/motion: Plate 7. 8–9, 26, 31–2, 51, 82, 84, 146, 166, 173, 176–7, 214, 216, 235, 241, 243, 245, 249, 257, 262, 268–9, 295, 297–8, 300–2, 307, 312.

APPENDIX G

INDEX OF CHARACTERS

Āḍi, a demon: 31, 33, 186–91, 205, 304, 309.
Ādyā, an epithet of Durgā: 275.
Agastya, a sage: 42, 52–5, 64, 66, 68, 103, 238.
Agni, the god of fire: Plates 9 and 15. Motifs 44 and 7c.
Agnisur Dano, a demon: 90.
Ahalyā, wife of the sage Gautama: 60, 85–6, 89, 133–4, 179, 246, 283, 301.
Aiyanar, a son of Śiva: 228–9, 311.
Alambusā, an *apsaras*: 43.
Anaraṇya, a king: 62–3.
Anasūyā (= Sukanyā, q.v.), wife of the sage Atri: 60–1, 102–3, 181, 226–7.
Andhaka, a demon: Plate 6. 31, 89, 188, 190–2, 200, 204, 247, 249, 272, 281, 296, 308. *See also* Bhṛṅgin.
Annapūrṇā ('Full of Food'), a form of Devī: 235.
Arjuna, a hero of the *Mahābhārata*: 132, 153, 303.
Arundhatī (Cassiopeia), wife of Vasiṣṭha, one of the Kṛttikās: 60, 65, 72, 87, 94–5, 99–103, 119, 151, 200.
Āsaṅga, a sage: 58.
Aśvins, the Dioscuroi, sons of Saṃjñā: 42, 58–60, 62, 283.
Atri (= Cyavana, q.v.), a sage: 60–1, 102, 181, 226, 272–3, 283.

Basaṃkara (= Bhasmāsura, q.v.): 297.
Bhaga, a solar god: 116, 129, 225.
Bhagīratha, a king, great-grandson of Sagara: 230.
Bhagwan, a name of god: 194–5.
Bhairava, a fierce form of Śiva or a son of Śiva: 69–70, 106, 124, 207, 308–9.
Bhasmāsura, a demon: 228, 297.
Bhimsen, a Gond deity: 112.
Bhola ('The Fool'), a name of Śiva: 235.
Bhṛgu, one of the Seven Sages: 58–9, 115, 216, 284, 303, 305–6.
Bhṛṅgin, a skeleton demon, a form of Andhaka: Plates 4 and 8. 307–8.
Brahmā, god of creation: Motifs 37–41.
Bṛhaspati, preceptor of the gods: 152, 182, 284, 290.
Buddha, founder of Buddhism: 82, 150, 312, 315, 318.

Cāmuṇḍā, a fierce form of Durgā: 242.
Cāṇḍālī, an Untouchable, outcaste woman: 231, 298.
Candraśekhara ('Moon-diadem'), an epithet of Śiva and the name of an avatar of Śiva: 205–9, 227, 309.
Cakravartī, Viśvanātha, a Bengali saint: 261.
Chaṇḍī (sometimes Caṇḍī), a fierce form of Durgā: 114, 227.
Citrāṅgadā, a princess, sister of Tārāvatī: 206, 208.
Cyavana (sometimes Cyavāna, = Atri, q.v.): 57–61, 102, 171, 283.

Dakṣa (sometimes Daksha), a primeval creator, father of Satī: Motif 38. 11–12, 30, 54, 61, 70–8, 85, 92, 94–6, 102–3, 112, 119, 126, 128–31, 134, 136, 146,